Europe
TravelBook

The Guide to Premier Destinations

Thirteenth Edition

Written by Des Hannigan, Sally Roy, Nia Williams
Thirteenth edition verified by Chris Bagshaw, Mark Baker, Big World Productions Ltd,
Anne Braathen, Antonia Cunningham, Adele Evans, Mary-Ann Gallagher,
Mike Gerrard, Louise McGrath, Christopher and Melanie Rice, Emma Rowley-Ruas,
Regine Smith-Thyme.
Series Editor: Sheila Hawkins
Project Editor: Bookwork Creative Ltd

Published by AAA Publishing, 1000 AAA Drive, Heathrow, Florida 32746.
The *AAA Europe TravelBook* was created and produced for AAA Publishing by AA
Media Limited, Fanum House, Basing View, Basingstoke, Hampshire, RG21 4EA, UK.

London's Millennium Bridge spans the River Thames near St. Paul's Cathedral, England

Foreword

Every traveler has a favorite destination in Europe. Its capitals have enraptured visitors for centuries: Paris, with its exceptional museums, superb food and broad 18th-century boulevards; London, where tradition and royal pageantry coexist with a robust arts scene; Prague, with its medieval grandeur; Rome, cradle of one of the world's great civilizations; and Vienna, with its heritage of world-renowned music.

The smaller cities hold their own enchantments. Odense, in Denmark, welcomes visitors to famed storyteller Hans Christian Andersen's birthplace, now a charming museum. In England the old center of York, webbed with ancient cobbled streets lined by leaning half-timbered shops and pubs, envelops guests in atmosphere. And Santiago de Compostela, in Spain, continues its centuries-old tradition of receiving Christian pilgrims journeying from the far corners of Europe to its monumental cathedral built around the reputed grave of St. James; today they are still drawn by the myth and beauty of this holy place.

To make your travels in Europe memorable and enjoyable, we've selected places that have special appeal, particularly for a first- or second-time visitor. This book will enable you, whether a seasoned or novice traveler, to get the most out of your trip. Its wealth of practical information includes tips about what to bring and about getting around, maps to help you find your way, detailed descriptions of things to see, and suggestions of where to stay and eat. Our insider advice is sure to increase your enjoyment of the fascinating cultures that make up Europe.

4

Contents

Key to symbols

🚻 map page number and coordinates
✉ address or location
☎ telephone number
◷ opening times
Ⓠ nearest subway/overground train station
▣ nearest bus/trolley bus/ tram/funicular route
⛴ ferry
🍴 restaurant
▨ admission charge
ℹ Information

For conversion charts, see the inside back cover

ICELAND

Norwegian Sea

0   200   400   600   800 km
0   100   200   300   400   500 miles

NORWAY

OSLO

SWEDEN

•Edinburgh

North Sea

DENMARK
COPENHAGEN
Odense

NORTHERN IRELAND

REPUBLIC OF IRELAND
DUBLIN

York

BRITAIN

Atlantic Ocean

Oxford
LONDON

NETHERLANDS
AMSTERDAM
The Hague

BERLIN

Bruges
Ghent BRUSSELS
BELGIUM
Cologne

GERMANY

LUXEMBOURG

PRAGUE
CZECH REPUBLIC

PARIS

Strasbourg

Munich

VIENNA
AUSTRIA

FRANCE

BERN
Geneva SWITZERLAND
Lyon

Zurich
Salzburg
Innsbruck

SLOVENIA

Venice

CROATIA

Santiago

Porto

PORTUGAL

SPAIN

ANDORRA

Nice

Florence

ITALY

LISBON

MADRID

Barcelona

Corsica

ROME

Naples

Seville

Balearic Islands

Sardinia

Mediterranean Sea

Sicily

ALGERIA

MOROCCO

TUNISIA

CONTENTS

Before You Go

Passports and Visas

The most important document you'll need to arrange before you travel is a passport. Passport application forms can be obtained at any AAA office. They also are available from many federal, state and probate courts, post offices, some public libraries and a number of county and municipal offices authorized to accept passport applications.

If you need a passport urgently (in less than two weeks) contact a passport agency located in major cities (check the *Yellow Pages* for the one nearest you). You also can request an application form from the National Passport Information Center (NPIC) at 1-877-487-2778. Automated information is available daily 24 hours; operators are available Mon.–Fri. 7 a.m.–midnight (Eastern Time), excluding federal holidays.

Passport information and downloadable application forms are available on the website for Passport Information at www.travel.state.gov. Travel warnings, consular information sheets, public announcements, publications information and information about individual countries also can be accessed.

Passport and consular/emergency services for Canadian citizens traveling abroad can be accessed at the Department of Foreign Affairs and International Trade Internet site at www.voyage.gc.ca.

Each person traveling must have a valid passport; apply early, since processing can take several months from the time of application until it arrives. Expedited service is available for an extra charge. Before departure, make sure your passport is valid for at least six months prior to the expiration date; some European countries require this.

Keep your passport in a safe place, since you'll need it whenever you board an international flight, train or ferry. In some countries, you will be required to leave your passport with the hotel when you check in; this is to satisfy regulations requiring the hotel to register all foreign visitors with local police authorities. In addition, you may be required to show your passport whenever you cash a traveler's check.

Passports also need to be shown whenever national borders are crossed, although in practice border controls have been relaxed between many European Union (E.U.) member countries. In Geneva, the city transportation system crosses national borders and the airport also straddles the border, so you'll need a passport simply to get around.

Make two photocopies of the identification page; leave one copy with a friend in case of emergency and carry one with you in case your passport is lost or stolen while traveling. If this occurs, inform local police immediately and contact the nearest U.S. embassy or consulate. The U.S. Department of State has a 24-hour travelers' hotline; phone (202) 647-5225.

In addition to a passport, some countries require a visa. Travel visas are not necessary when visiting any of the countries covered in this book, but if you'll be traveling to other nations, check their entry requirements before you leave home. AAA offices have visa information.

AAA and CAA members will want to visit www.AAA.com before setting out on their international travels. Check for merchants who will accept your AAA or CAA membership card

U.S. CITIZENS

The information in this guide has been compiled for U.S. citizens who are traveling as tourists.

Travelers who are not U.S. citizens, or who are traveling on business, should check with their embassies and tourist offices for information on the countries they wish to visit.

Entry requirements can be subject to change on short notice, and travelers are therefore advised to check the current situation before they travel.

Show your Card!

in order to obtain member savings at more than 150,000 locations throughout the world. Members visiting their club's www.AAA.com website should look under the "Savings Benefits" link for the "Show Your Card & Save ® discounts."

Travel and Health Insurance

Before leaving, make sure you are covered by insurance that will reimburse travel expenses if you need to cancel or cut short your trip due to unforeseen circumstances. You'll also need coverage for property loss or theft, emergency medical and dental treatment, and emergency evacuation if necessary. Before taking out additional insurance, check to see whether your current homeowner's or medical coverage already covers you for travel abroad.

If you make a claim, your insurance company will need proof of the incident or expenditure. Keep copies of any police report and related documents, or doctor or hospital bills or statements, to submit with your insurance claim.

Weather and When To Go

The European continent occupies a far more northerly location than its overall moderate climate would suggest. Different factors affect the weather at any given destination. The warming influence of the Gulf Stream affects all countries with an Atlantic coastline, from Spain and Portugal north through the British Isles into Scandinavia. The North and Baltic seas also affect temperatures and precipitation of the coastal areas they border, causing unpredictable weather.

Another definer is altitude, and Europe's great mountain ranges affect local temperatures and rainfall as well. The Pyrenees divide the Iberian Peninsula and France, while the Alps form an immense natural barrier across Austria, Switzerland and northern Italy south into France, where they descend to the Mediterranean Sea at Monaco. This entire region is popular with winter skiers, while summer visitors can expect clouds, mist and cool temperatures. The Apennines cut down the boot of Italy, also creating somewhat changeable conditions.

Destinations bordering the Mediterranean are ideal for summer vacations, with mostly sunny skies, warm temperatures and little rain. The flip side can be the heat – especially in southern Spain and Greece – so protect yourself from overexposure to the sun and carry drinking water for extended outdoor excursions. Winters in the Mediterranean region are cool and rainy, but temperatures are not usually severe and snow is rare in coastal areas.

Summer also is the main vacation season in central Europe, which has warm, mainly dry summers and cold winters with snow at higher elevations. The weather in spring is generally more unpredictable than in the fall.

The British Isles can have weeks of dry conditions in summer, although it's best to come prepared for rain; a collapsible umbrella should be an essential traveling companion. British winters are rainy, although temperatures are rarely extremely cold. Snow is uncommon except in the higher regions of northern England and Scotland.

Scandinavia has varying weather and overall lower temperatures. Daytime highs in the summer months rarely exceed 75 degrees Fahrenheit, and the coastal locations of Copenhagen, Oslo, Stockholm and Helsinki increase the probability of unsettled conditions. Winters are uniformly severe, with significant snowfall the rule.

European school vacations are a factor in planning when to travel. Schools in most countries are in session from September until early July, making May and June good months to visit.

What To Pack

Electrical appliances will require an adapter that changes the arrangement of the plug prongs, as well as an electrical voltage converter that will allow a normal 110-volt American appliance to take 220- to 240-volt European current. Two-in-one adapter/converters are available at some hardware stores and also at many AAA Travel Stores.

Bring a first-aid kit with bandages, sunblock, insect repellent and some over-the-counter remedies for minor ailments. Include written prescriptions for prescription medicines in case you need more or need to show the prescription to customs officials. Tissues will come in handy, as local restrooms in some areas will likely be below U.S. standards. European hotel rooms provide towels but often no washcloth, so pack one in case.

Check with your airline carrier prior to your flight to determine specific carry-on restrictions.

While You Are There

Emergencies
See the Essential Information section, pages 493–569, for information about a specific country.

Health
Take sensible precautions during hot weather. Wear a hat, sunglasses and sunblock, especially if you are on or near the water. Drink plenty of fluids, and remember that alcoholic beverages and the caffeine in coffee, tea and some sodas has a dehydrating effect.

The tap water in northern Europe is generally safe to drink, although its high mineral content can cause minor upsets if you're not used to it. Bottled water, still or carbonated, is inexpensive and widely available. In an area where the tap water is unsafe, avoid ice cubes and salads with ingredients that are likely to have been washed in water.

Pharmacists are a good first source for dealing with minor health problems; a pharmacist will be able to direct you to a doctor if necessary. For advice pertaining to specific topics, see the "Health" subheading under individual countries in Essential Information.

Language
Traveling is always more enjoyable if you can converse a bit in the local language. "Yes," "no," "please" and "thank you," accompanied by a pleasant smile and polite manner, will go far toward oiling

social wheels. Refer to the "Useful Words and Phrases" subheading under individual countries in Essential Information for a helpful list.

English is most likely to be spoken in Scandinavia, The Netherlands, Belgium, Luxembourg, Germany, Austria and Switzerland. In Britain and Ireland you may encounter strong regional accents, as well as unfamiliar words and expressions.

To some Europeans – particularly the French and the British – good manners are a social necessity. "Please" and "thank you" should be part of every request in Britain; in France, anyone you don't know personally (including the staff in stores and restaurants) should be addressed as "monsieur" ("sir"), "madame" ("madam") or "mademoiselle" ("miss").

If you're really stuck with communications, remember that hotel receptionists very often speak English, and are invariably helpful and friendly; you can ask them to phone for taxis and arrange for cleaning and similar personal services on your behalf.

Media
Room televisions in the larger hotels have satellite or cable connections and broadcast BBC channels, the British Sky network or CNN. On the radio you may be able to pick up Voice of America, Radio Canada or BBC broadcasts.

In larger cities, American newspapers (usually previous-day editions) and magazines are widely available; the most common are *USA Today*, the international edition of the *International Herald Tribune* and *Time* magazine. They can be purchased at airports and central train stations, as well as at newsstands, tobacconists and "stationers," shops that also sell books and stationery.

Money and Valuables
Having some of your funds in local currency is a necessity, but only carry what you'll need for a day or two. If it's lost or stolen you almost certainly won't get it back, and if you have to convert a large amount back to dollars or to another foreign currency, you may have to pay again for exchange charges. Customs

restrictions may apply if you need to carry large amounts of currency.

The euro (€) is the common currency of 17 European Union countries (Austria, Belgium, Cyprus, Estonia, Finland, France, Germany, Greece, Ireland, Italy, Luxembourg, Malta, The Netherlands, Portugal, Slovakia, Slovenia and Spain). For additional information see the "Money" subheading under individual countries in Essential Information.

Currency exchange facilities are widely available in Europe. There are exchange offices at airports and central train and bus stations, in the central business districts in cities, and at seaports and other international border crossing points. They are often open extended hours in summer and during vacations. Most hotel reception desks also will exchange currency. Exchange rates are normally displayed; local newspapers and the international editions of U.S. newspapers also provide the current rate of exchange. A commission may or may not be charged for each transaction. Although any commission is likely to be a little higher at hotels, it may be worth paying extra for the convenience.

Traveler's checks are reliable and safe. Keep a record of the check numbers you redeem, and carry numbers and receipts in a separate place in case you need to produce them in the event of loss. Be prepared to show your passport each time you cash in a check or offer one in payment. If you're going to be spending time in just one or two countries you may want to obtain traveler's checks in the local currency; traveler's checks in euros are recommended if traveling in the euro zone extensively. You can use them for purchases in stores, although you'll still need to show your passport.

Credit cards are an easy and trouble-free method of payment when traveling abroad. American Express, MasterCard and VISA are the most widely accepted (Diners Club is accepted less often). Check with your credit card company before departure if you have any doubt about its validity abroad. Keep a record of your card number in a separate place, and note the international phone number to report card loss in case yours is misplaced or stolen. You also can get cash advances with your credit card from an ATM, usually at favorable exchange rates.

Leave valuable jewelry at home; ostentatious displays mark you as a prospective target for theft. Make sure your luggage is lockable and labeled both outside and inside. Never leave your bags unattended. Train stations and main bus stations normally provide lockers or check desks where you can leave a heavy bag while sightseeing. If you're traveling by car, keep your doors locked in slow-moving traffic or when driving through busy urban areas, and put everything in the trunk while the car is parked.

If you do have any belongings stolen, report the incident to the police immediately and get a written police report or statement to provide to your insurance company as evidence for your claim.

Personal Safety

Most of the rules for personal safety constitute common sense. Keep valuables (passport, money, checks, credit cards) hidden when you're on the move; a money belt or neck purse worn inside clothing is the safest option. Put money in different places so that if one bag is lost you have another source of funds. Fanny packs and pockets are not safe places to carry valuables. Any bag you'll be carrying with you during the day should have a secure fastener, with a sturdy strap that goes over your neck and crosses your body – not simply over the shoulder. This helps ensure that bulkier items (cameras, binoculars, etc.) will be safe from pickpockets and petty thieves in crowded urban areas or on buses or trains.

The big tourist attractions are prime territory for pickpockets, as are buses, trains, subways, markets and airports. Be on guard for people who "accidentally" bump into you, or watch while you use an ATM. In large cities, be on the lookout for gangs of youngsters who create a commotion and then steal bags from tourists while their attention is distracted.

Street beggars can be quite persistent; walk quickly away without responding or making eye contact. Contact a police officer if anyone becomes particularly aggressive or threatening.

In general, avoid walking alone after dark. In southern European city centers during the summer, however, you'll almost certainly encounter throngs of locals out walking and shopping late into the evening.

Phone Service

You can make international calls from most European telephones; for specific information see "Telephones" under individual countries in the Essential Information section (see pages 493–569). To place a call to another country, first dial the international code, then the country code, then the area code (minus any initial zero) and the local number. Sometimes you'll need to wait for another dial tone after dialing the international code. In some countries the telecommunications infrastructure is fragile, and it may take a few tries to get through.

The easiest and least expensive way to make an international call is to use a calling card. Dialing the appropriate access number (numbers differ according to country) will connect you with an English-speaking operator who can place a collect call or a call credited to your card. To obtain a card and a list of country access numbers, contact your telephone service provider. Credit cards (American Express, Diners Card, MasterCard and VISA) are accepted in many public phones. If you use a pay phone, you may need to insert coins in the local currency (a minimum fee applies) to get an outside line to make the call.

The convenience of making a phone call from your hotel room will be offset by the hefty surcharges tacked onto the bill. It's always less expensive to use the pay phone in the lobby or even cheaper to use the phone on the street; ask the hotel staff for assistance if you can't figure out how the phone works.

Some cell phones may be adaptable for use in Europe, but the operating frequencies are different; check with your service provider. You can rent cell phones for use during your trip. Check with your AAA office for information. Fax machines are available in the central business centers of cities and at some hotels. If you can't do without e-mail, there are cybercafés in major cities throughout Europe – handy places to stop for coffee and a bite to eat, as well as using the computers to send e-mails and check your favorite websites.

If you're staying in one country for a few days, it may be worthwhile to obtain a local prepaid telephone card, which can be used with phones that accept them. They can normally be purchased at small stores called "tobacconists" that also sell cigarettes, candy, snacks, magazines and sometimes postage stamps.

Travelers with Disabilities

Facilities for disabled visitors in northern and central European countries are generally very good, but old castles, palaces, cathedrals and historic houses may not be adapted for special access. The Mediterranean countries, Czech Republic and Hungary are improving, but if you need help it is advisable to check in advance with local tourist offices. The old central cores of European cities are often difficult to change or adapt to make them suitable for those with special needs. Expect steps and stairways in city centers (some stairways have no handrails), in addition to cobbled and uneven street and sidewalk surfaces.

Almost all of the old buildings that you come across in Europe – including those that house hotels, restaurants and such attractions as museums and castles – are likely to contain stairways, narrow halls and doorways, and other access irregularities. Make certain that accessibility standards meet your requirements when reserving your accommodations.

In many instances hotels will be able to provide a room with adequate access if they know your needs in advance. Telephone ahead to museums, attractions and restaurants as well to ascertain the nature of their facilities and accessibility. There are usually motorized carts at airports that will whisk you to and from arrival and departure gates.

Getting Around

City Transportation

A good first stop when you arrive at your destination is either a central public transportation information center or the tourist information office (see the Essential Information boxes in the introduction to each featured city). Spend time here and obtain information on how to get around the city, including transportation maps and detailed city maps. You also may be able to purchase tickets for public transportation, including those valid for multiple rides or for one or more days; they will save you money and the inconvenience of having to buy a new ticket for every trip. The information office may be able to provide public transportation schedules also.

AAA has partnered with Gray Line to provide members with sightseeing tours in more than 150 destinations worldwide. Discounts are offered on tours lasting one day or less. Tours are available in Amsterdam, Dublin, Florence, Lisbon, Munich, Nice, Paris, Rome and Zurich, among other EU locations. In addition, there are a variety of public transportation options in Europe:

■ Subways (metros) are underground trains that travel beneath city centers, emerging to ground level in suburban areas, or to cross rivers.
■ Private bus companies operate along designated routes in city centers; double-decked buses are common for carrying larger numbers of passengers.
■ Long-distance buses are commonly known as "coaches" in Britain and Ireland.
■ Trams are vehicles that travel on rails set into the street surface. They are often powered by overhead electric cables that run along the route; be especially careful of trams since they have the right of way.
■ Trolley buses run on tires, but are powered by overhead electric cables running above the route, like trams. They have right of way and run quietly.
■ Funiculars are passenger cars that ascend and descend steep hills or cliffs on a track set into the ground, where there are steep inclines.

■ Cable cars are suspended from cables attached to the top of the cars. They are common at ski resorts, and in some cities.
■ Rack railways are a feature in Switzerland, where trains that climb steep mountains connect with a cog system between the rails and give extra power to get up the steep slopes.

In many continental European countries, you buy a travel ticket at a ticket office, booth or ticket machine and validate it by pushing it into a special machine, either at the stop or on the vehicle, which will give the ticket a date and time stamp for the appropriate trip or time period. If you buy a tourist ticket valid for a number of days, you will usually need to validate it only once before you first use it.

Between Cities

Trains Most countries in Europe have a national train system, with trains operating across national borders. Service is generally efficient, although local routes with frequent stops can be slow. If your entire trip is going to be by train it may be worth obtaining a Eurail pass from your AAA travel agent in the United States before you go. It is important to note that they are not on sale in Europe and must be purchased before you travel. Passes are valid for periods from a few days to three months. In addition, many national rail systems have their own passes for travel within a country; these also are available from travel agents in the United States and Canada, and also in Europe. Some trains require reservations.

Tickets for most trains are available either in advance or just before travel. For special trains (some express trains – for instance, in Spain; overnight sleeper trains; the Orient Express; or the Eurostar trains between Britain, France and Belgium that travel through the tunnel beneath the English Channel) you may need to buy tickets a few days in advance to be sure of getting a seat. This is especially the case during busy vacation times.

Information about main city train stations is in the Essential Information box for each city.

Airlines Most countries have a national airline, as well as independent operators that operate internationally, based on hub cities within the country. Additionally, smaller airlines serve smaller destinations, usually functioning within the country. Schedules, fares and availability are subject to frequent change.

If you have a specific itinerary in mind, your travel agent is the best place to start for flight information.

For the best choice of flights and prices, reserve your tickets well in advance. Big airports in major cities – Paris, London and Rome, for example – will have the largest choice of flights, but also are the busiest. For this reason it can be a good idea to begin your trip at a smaller, less busy destination.

Ferries Services transport individual passengers as well as cars, and in some cases trains (the cars of the train actually travel on the boat). Ferry companies offering longer-distance trips of two or three days have comfortable ships, and they promote these services as "mini-cruises" as a change to city sightseeing.

Ferries operate regularly in the Scandinavian archipelago and along the Norwegian fjords; among the Scottish islands; between Britain and Ireland, Scandinavia, Germany, The Netherlands, Belgium, France and Spain; and throughout the islands and coastal ports of Mediterranean countries and islands.

Generally speaking, transfers from ports to city centers are less straightforward than from airports and train stations. If you intend to carry a lot of luggage, it may be advisable to ask tourist information offices about this when planning your trip.

European Customs and Immigration

Each country has its own customs import regulations; see the Essential Information section beginning on page 493. For the purposes of customs and duty-free allowances, the countries of the European Union are considered as one customs area, and there are no limits on goods for personal use when traveling between any of the member countries. However,

customs restrictions do apply when traveling between E.U. countries and non-E.U. countries.

The E.U. member countries include all the countries in this book, with the exception of Norway and Switzerland.

At the immigration barrier in E.U. countries, travelers are separated into two lanes – one for E.U. citizens and one for non-E.U. citizens. Border controls between E.U. countries are gradually being relaxed. You will probably pass through an immigration desk when arriving in a new country by plane, train or ferry, but road barrier checkpoints within the E.U. have largely disappeared in recent years. There are still border controls in place between the E.U. and the rest of Europe, however.

Driving in Europe

European Automobile Clubs

For the benefit of members traveling abroad, AAA maintains reciprocal agreements with motoring clubs in Europe. Presentation of your valid AAA membership card at participating motoring clubs allows you to receive services they provide to their own members. Operating philosophies and facilities differ from country to country, however, so service may not be the same as back home. AAA members will need to visit their local club to obtain information

AAA TRAVEL AGENCIES
AAA Travel Agencies offer various member services to help simplify the logistics of international travel planning, especially for the first-time visitor. They can make airline reservations, book accommodations, set up escorted tours and independent travel packages, offer passport and visa assistance, arrange for car rentals and an official International Driving Permit, and provide fee-free VISA traveler's checks.

AAA members also are eligible for discounts on selected hotels and motels and receive exclusive savings on cruising vacations.

about services that can be expected from a specific European motoring club.

Refer to the Essential Information pages for each country for motoring club contact details, as well as documentation requirements and driving regulations.

Car Rental

If you intend to drive across national borders tell the rental company. This will affect both the rate and the type of insurance documentation required. Some rental agencies may require several days' notice to supply a car available for travel to continental Europe. Most car rental companies in Europe will not rent to an individual under 21.

To rent a car you will need a valid U.S. driver's license and preferably an International Driving Permit. You will probably be asked to show your passport. Some rental companies may require you to produce an additional credit card or further proof of identity for renting premium or luxury cars.

European cars are generally small and tend to have manual transmissions. Most rental companies offer vehicles equipped with air conditioning. Rates vary, but a AAA travel agent should be able to give you an accurate estimate. Reciprocal arrangements with European motoring clubs may not apply if you are driving a rental car (see the Driving section under Essential Information for each country). Be sure to inquire about local taxes; in France, for example, taxes increase rental rates by up to one-third. Find out exactly what insurance coverage is included, and check whether you need a collision damage waiver (CDW) – you might already be covered through your personal car insurance policy or credit card company. A CDW may not cover certain types of damage; for example, in Greece damage to the underside of a car caused by a rough road may not be covered.

AAA Travel Agencies can make rental car reservations, provide prepayment arrangements, or reserve a car for you for specified dates and destinations. Rates are generally lower if reservations are made in the United States prior to your departure. They also are guaranteed in

U.S. dollars if you prepay; it is recommended that you reserve well in advance. If you plan to travel through several countries, make certain that the rental company has been informed, and that you have the necessary documents.

Hertz Europe offers discounts in 31 European countries (including all those listed in this guide). Benefits include low, competitive rates; free unlimited mileage; a 24-hour toll-free telephone information line; 24-hour emergency roadside assistance; enhanced computerized driving directions; and English-speaking personnnel at every location. Hertz operates a fleet of more than 80,000 vehicles in more than 2,000 convenient locations in more than 31 European countries. There are free drop-offs between many major cities within the country of rental. For reservations contact a AAA Travel Agency or Hertz at 1-800-654-3001 (toll free) in the United States or 1-800-263-0600 (toll free) in Canada, www.hertz.com or www.AAA.com.

Green Card

If you drive a car in Europe you will need a Green Card (sometimes called an International Insurance Certificate) to prove that you have liability insurance. Most car rental agencies will provide this with the vehicle; most companies include it in the rental price.

A Green Card also is advised for motorists taking their own vehicle overseas; for additional information contact your automobile insurer.

International Driving Permit (IDP)

An International Driving Permit is a document containing your photograph and confirming that you hold a valid driver's license in your own country. It has a standard translation in several languages and is a useful document to carry if you plan to drive in Europe, even if it is not specifically required by the country. The permit is available from AAA Travel Agencies.

Driving Regulations

Driving in busy European cities can be challenging. If you are renting a car, get as much information about the country's driving conditions from the rental company as possible, including a chart of common road signs and an area road map. If you visit a city by car, park outside the city center, preferably close to a public transportation link, and travel to the center by public transportation.

Check parking signs where you leave your car: Ensure that there are no restrictions, that you pay for and display a parking sticker if necessary, and check closing times if you use a multistory parking garage or a gated street parking area. Parking regulations are strictly enforced in city centers throughout Europe and penalties, including the immobilization or the removal of your vehicle, can be the consequence of leaving your car in an unauthorized place. Some European cities offer free evening and weekend parking, but it is advisable to check before leaving your vehicle.

If you enter central London by car during the week you will incur a daily congestion charge of £10. Vehicles entering the charging zone (visit www.tfl.gov.uk to see the Congestion Charging zone map) must be registered; an area license permits drivers to enter and leave the zone an unlimited number of times within a particular day. The charging zone is clearly defined by signs and road markings at entrance and exit points. The daily charge must be paid by midnight on the day of travel if not already prepaid; between midnight on the day of travel and midnight on the next charging day, the fee goes up to £12. Payment can be made at pay stations, selected gas stations, retailers displaying the PayPoint logo and online. The zone charge is in effect Mon.–Fri. 7–6 (excluding public holidays and Dec. 25–Jan. 1). For more information phone 0845 900 1234 (Sun.–Fri. 6 a.m.–12:30 a.m., Sat. to 10 p.m.) or go online to www.tfl.gov.uk.

Specific driving regulations for each country are provided in the Essential Information section (see pages 493–569). In some European countries, police can levy on-the-spot fines for serious offenses – including speeding and drunk-driving.

Returning to the United States

Confirming Return Travel

If you are flying, contact the airport the day before your departure to check flight details. Some carriers require you to reconfirm flights after an extended stop-over of more than a few days; check the information that was supplied with your ticket.

Allow plenty of time for check-in and clearing security.

Tax-free Shopping

Some major stores offer "tax-free shopping" to tourists. Although specific procedures differ slightly between countries, this enables you to make purchases and have them either sent to the airport of your departing flight, or directly to your home address. Such shopping saves the (often substantial) sales tax, but these items are still subject to any applicable U.S. import duty, plus postage and handling charges.

U.S. Customs

During your flight or voyage returning to the United States, you will be required to complete a customs declaration form. Returning to the United States you are allowed $800 worth of personal goods and gifts (including items purchased in duty-free shops); keep sales slips and have them ready for inspection. The duty-free exemption can include 100 cigars and 200 cigarettes, as well as one liter of wine, beer or liquor if you are 21 or over. (Tobacco products of Cuban origin are prohibited unless they were acquired in Cuba.) Any purchases in excess of the $800 exemption will be subject to duty.

There is no restriction on the importing or exporting of currency.

For more information contact U.S. Customs and Border Protection, 1300 Pennsylvania Ave., N.W. Washington, D.C. 20229 visit www.cbp.gov where you can download a copy of the brochure *Know Before You Go*, which has details on customs requirements.

Premier Destinations

Austria

Opposite: Detail of cherubs on the Mozart memorial at the Hofburg Palace in Vienna

Austria

Small yet beautiful, Austria has unrivaled Alpine scenery, some of Europe's finest baroque architecture, and a long musical and cultural tradition. The Austrian people also are known for their warmth and hospitality toward visitors. Straddling the center of Europe, the country has exerted a critical influence on the history of the European region through the centuries, becoming a major player in world politics.

Today, despite loss of territory and power after two world wars, Austria retains its status as the crossroads of modern Europe. The grandeur of the mountains draws visitors from all over the world, while the combination of efficiency and charm makes Austria one of Europe's most beguiling tourist destinations.

The Land

Austria is the most mountainous country in Europe, with more than 70 percent of the land occupied by the Alps and Alpine valleys. This section of the eastern Alps is characterized by massive mountain chains with sheer rock faces and jagged ridges broken by deep valleys. The Tyrol region, bordering the Swiss and Italian Alps in western Austria, is renowned for its stunning scenery and is an extremely popular

skiing and hiking area. Below the tree line the mountains are heavily forested, giving way to lush Alpine meadows, grazed in summer by gentle-faced cattle and carpeted with vivid wildflowers.

Picturesque villages sit amid the pastures and along the valley bottoms, each with distinctive churches, clusters of traditional shuttered houses and wooden farm buildings. The Danube (Donau) river dominates northeastern Austria, and most of the country's people inhabit the rolling terrain around the river. The flat fields of the Vienna basin are intensely cultivated, producing grain, fruit and vines.

The Habsburg Legacy

Throughout six centuries of Habsburg rule, Austria dominated the politics of much of Europe. The Habsburg Empire spread from Spain to Hungary, with sons

More Top Destinations in Austria

- Baden E2
- Bad Ischl C2
- Eisenstadt E2
- Eisriesenwelt C2
- Graz D1
- Grossglockner Hochalpenstrasse C2
- Hallstatt C2
- Kitzbühel B2
- Maria Saal D1
- Melk D3
- Mondsee C2
- Ötztal B2
- Riegersburg E1
- St. Anton A2
- Salzkammergut C2
- Stein D3
- Wachau D3
- Zillertal B2

and daughters of the ruling families marrying into other European ruling houses, thus furthering its influence. Vienna, with its grandiose architecture, splendidly illustrates Austrian prestige, and the entire country is rich in buildings from the days of the empire.

The Viennese Court sent administrators and army officials into the provinces; they brought along Viennese customs, attitudes and manners, as did the nobility who spent time both in the capital and on their country estates. The high-handed approach of these outsiders throughout the provinces has left a legacy of mistrust of the Viennese still discernible today. Historically, too, because of the terrain, the different areas of Austria were immensely varied, each valley having its own dialect, dress, habits and way of life.

Crossroads of Europe

At the end of World War II, Austria was divided into four zones of occupation, with the Allied powers occupying most of the western half. With economic aid provided by the Marshall Plan after the war, this area was able to industrialize more efficiently than the Soviet-occupied zone, and the east–west divide continued even after the Second Republic was founded in 1945 and the country became independent 10 years later, in 1955.

Present-day Austria shares boundaries with eight other European countries: Germany, Italy, the Czech Republic, Hungary, Slovakia, Slovenia, Switzerland and Lichtenstein. Its 8 million inhabitants are spread across nine provinces, each one with its own very distinctive characteristics, but all with attractions for the visitor.

A view over the rooftops of Salzburg

manifests itself in an easy friendliness to everyone, and it's one of the first things visitors notice. Every region sees itself as the best, and people proudly wear regional dress and enjoy traditional music and festivals. So when you encounter people wearing *lederhosen* (leather pants) and *dirndls* (bodiced dresses), it's for their benefit, not yours.

There's an elegance and ease to much Austrian life; cafés buzz with the chatter of people, *bierkeller* (taverns) are packed with young and old, and streets are full of strolling crowds. Manners are conservative, even old-fashioned; this is a country where children open doors and give up seats for adults, and outside of the cities nearly every stranger is greeted with an amicable *"Grüss Gott."*

Environmental Issues

It's not only the magnificent tree-clad mountain slopes and verdant valleys that make Austria green; this is one of the most environmentally aware countries in Europe. Austria banned all nuclear power use in the 1970s, and since then its green policy has made giant strides.

Heavy investment in public transportation has considerably lessened the use of cars. This is a huge benefit to visitors, making travel in Austria, with its seamless connections between different forms of public transportation, very easy. Despite the Alpine terrain, Austrians cycle a lot, and every town has bike routes and parks.

Recycling is a way of life in Austria; there are many different types of garbage cans, each clearly labeled for the appropriate trash.

Sauerkraut and Strudel

Austrians take food seriously, and waiters are genuinely interested to know whether you've enjoyed a meal and alarmingly downcast if you can't cope with the vast portions served. Mealtimes are closer to American schedules than elsewhere, with lunch around noon and dinner any time after 6 p.m.

More than half the working population is employed in the service sector: education, tourism, administration and health. Traditional agriculture only continues thanks to large subsidies, and now employs less than 10 percent of the workforce.

The vast majority of Austrians speak German or a German dialect. Austria was only slightly affected by the Protestant Reformation and is still a Catholic country. Its fine baroque churches are packed for Sunday Mass.

Proud Traditions

Despite sharing a common language, Austrians are very different from their German neighbors – more lighthearted, and generally more relaxed in their approach to life. They see themselves, correctly, as hospitable and cordial, thus defining the term *Gemütlichkeit*. This

Each region has its own specialties, but the emphasis everywhere is on heavy soups, plenty of meat, *Knödel* (dumplings) and noodles, and cream, cream, cream. The latter appears in sauces, soups, coffee and whipped mounds decorating just about every dessert. Sauerkraut (pickled cabbage) frequently accompanies main courses, along with piles of potatoes. Salads are drenched in creamy dressings.

Austrians indulge their passion for coffee and cakes between meals, and you should certainly sample *apfelstrudel* (apple strudel), the delicious fruit dessert that is the hallmark of the country's pastry-making, and *sachertorte,* a wickedly rich chocolate cake oozing apricot jam.

There are many different types of beer, and some excellent wines. Austria has been cultivating vines for thousands of years, particularly in Styria, Lower Austria and The Burgenland. *Veltliner,* made from the Grüner Veltliner grape, is the country's best-known white wine. You should also try *Schnapps,* a strong fruit- or herb-based liqueur, drunk as a digestive aid.

Coffee is the national drink, with cafés sometimes serving as many as 20 or more different variations; hot chocolate is good, too. And on the healthy side, there are outstanding fruit and vegetable juices.

Summer and Winter

Austria offers visitors as much in the winter as in the summer. For Europeans, the Austrian Alps have been a favorite skiing destination for many years, with impeccably organized facilities, trails ranging from gentle slopes to world-class black runs, and wonderful après-ski dining and nightlife.

Summer sees the Alpine pastures at their best, and the whole country is crisscrossed with hiking trails through glorious mountain scenery. It's in summer, too, that the cities come alive, with strolling crowds, colorful flowers and a plethora of music and folk festivals. Spring starts late, so it's best to plan a visit in May or later.

In early spring and again in fall, you may experience the dreaded *Föhn* wind in western Austria; this is a fierce, warm, dry wind from the south that is notorious for making people generally tired and grumpy, so be prepared.

A quiet spot in Vienna's Schönbrunn Castle

Timeline

15 BC to AD 50	Romans establish frontier provinces along the Danube and found legionary fortress of Carnuntum.
500–700	After final withdrawal of Romans, Alamanni and Bavarian tribes settle lower Alpine regions.
966	Austmark, established as a bulwark against attacks from the east, is first referred to as Ostarrichi.
1278	Founding of Habsburg Dynasty, beginning 640 years of power.
1493–1519	Foundations of the Habsburg world empire laid by marriage contracts of Maximilian I.
1699	Conquest of Hungary; Habsburgs gain hereditary right to the Hungarian throne in the male line.
1805–1806	Napoleon defeats the Austrians at Battle of Austerlitz; end of Holy Roman Empire.
1814–15	Congress of Vienna restructures the political map of Europe.
1914	Assassination of heir to Austrian throne at Sarajevo leads to outbreak of World War I; Austria fights on losing side.
1919	Dissolution of Austro-Hungarian monarchy; loss of territories.
1938	Hitler incorporates Austria into the German Reich.
1939–45	World War II; Austrians fight in German army; following defeat, Austria is divided into four zones of occupation.
1955	Full sovereignty and neutrality of Second Republic; Austria is admitted to the United Nations.
1986	Kurt Waldheim is elected president.
1995	Austria joins European Union.
1999	Austria enters European Monetary Union.
2010–11	Concerts and events celebrate the life and works of composer Gustav Mahler (1860–1911).

The Last of the Knights

Maximilian I ruled from 1493 until 1519; these years saw the establishment of his family, the Habsburgs, as hereditary emperors of the Holy Roman Empire and rulers of Austria and far beyond, a dynasty that continued until 1918. Maximilian, through two strategic marriages, gained control over Burgundy (a region in northern France) and the Low Countries. He married his son into the Spanish royal family, giving the Habsburgs rights over Spain, Naples and Spanish America and thus laying the foundations for the vast empire that was to come. Maximilian reformed the governmental administration, patronized the arts, loved hunting and jousting, and was known as "the last of the knights" who led Austria from the Middle Ages to the bright light of the Renaissance and the empire.

Café tables on Franziskanerplatz in Vienna, where patrons can enjoy a meal or a coffee and a snack

Survival Guide

- Always return greetings; hospitality is Austria's most important national characteristic, and people expect a reply to their welcoming *"Grüss Gott,"* meaning "God's greeting."
- For the opera, men should wear a jacket and tie; women, a dress, suit or fashionable pants.
- When going into churches, remember that it's disrespectful to show bare shoulders or upper arms.
- Take an umbrella; it can rain heavily, anywhere, at any time of year.
- For a day in the mountains, remember that the temperature drops as you gain altitude. Take warm clothes so you can layer, and if you're hiking, wear suitable footwear, and bring water and food.
- Austrians are very litter-conscious and streets are immaculately clean; do your part to leave them that way.
- It's considered polite to stand in line when waiting for a bus or at an attraction, and to defer to the older members of society.
- Bedding in Austria generally consists of a large, puffy feather quilt in a cotton cover. This will be folded on your bed, waiting to be opened up.
- Austrians eat and drink with gusto, and spirits as well as the noise level will rise during the evening. Drunkenness, however, is always considered uncouth.
- All cafés, bars and restaurants have coat hooks and umbrella stands, and it's considered more respectful to leave coats and umbrellas there rather than on your chair.
- It's acceptable to spend up to an hour lingering over one or two drinks in a café.
- Public restrooms are free, numerous and spotless; you'll find them in virtually all public buildings, and you can also use bathrooms in cafés and restaurants.
- Always cross the street at official crossings and wait for the green man signal. It's illegal, though seldom prosecuted, to cross anywhere else.

Vienna

For much of the 20th century, Vienna (Wien) had an air of fading grandeur, a city whose days of imperial glory had passed. But in the 1980s Vienna began to redefine itself, and continues to do so. In the last two decades the population has increased for the first time since 1919; a vibrant youth culture has emerged; and the imperial architecture of the 18th and 19th centuries has been joined by exciting modern designs, such as the huge museum quarter built on the site of the emperor's former stables. Now, in the 21st century, Vienna seems to be shaking off its torpor and styling itself, once again, as a vibrant, dynamic European cultural center.

Finding Your Way

Between 1857 and 1865 Emperor Franz Josef I had the bastions surrounding Vienna's Old Town (Innere Stadt) demolished, and laid out a vast boulevard known as the Ring. Within the Old Town and the Ring are Vienna's most important sights, including St. Stephen's Cathedral (Stephansdom, see page 32) and the Imperial Palace (Hofburg, see pages 29–30).

It's possible to take in the main sights on foot, but the "Hop on, Hop off" buses are a flexible alternative, allowing you to hop on or off anywhere along their route. There are also trams and underground (U-Bahn) trains running through and around the area. A more

expensive option is a horse-drawn carriage (Fiaker) at Stephansplatz, Heldenplatz or Albertinaplatz. Be sure to agree on the price and length of trip before you begin your journey.

An outer ring road, the Gürtel (belt), links the city with major freeways. East of Vienna, the Danube river and the Danube canal cut through some 23 Austrian districts, and on the southern

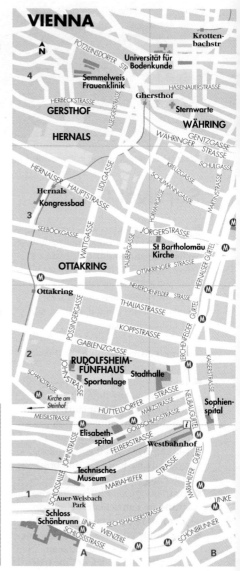

The Third Man

One of Vienna's favorite parks is the Prater, situated on the former imperial hunting grounds. It was opened to the public in 1766, and its attractions now include racing tracks, a fairground and a Ferris wheel built in 1897. This is where Joseph Cotten and Orson Welles had their confrontation high over the city in the 1949 film *Der dritte Mann (The Third Man)*.

outskirts are the Vienna Woods (Wienerwald). Maps showing walking routes through the woods are available from the efficient and helpful information center at the corner of Albertinaplatz and Maysedergasse.

Architecture

Wandering Vienna's streets is a treat for lovers of architecture. Styles range from the Gothic pointed arches of St. Stephen's Cathedral and the neo-Gothic arcades of the New City Hall (Neues Rathaus) to the baroque of the 17th and 18th centuries.

Imperial 19th-century majesty is typified in buildings lining the Ring and also in the art nouveau edifices, known here as the "Secession" style because its practitioners seceded from the staid

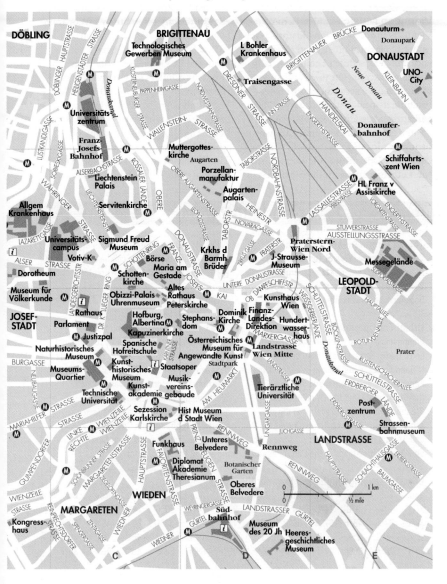

Association of Fine Artists in 1897. They later set up their own exhibitions in the Secession Building on Friedrichstrasse.

There also are modern styles, such as the shining glass curves of the 1990 Haas-Haus by Hans Hollein, opposite St. Stephen's; and a postmodern housing block by Friedensreich Hundertwasser, a Hansel-and-Gretel building of colored mosaics, in Kegelgasse.

Viennese Music

Vienna is proud of its long history as a center of classical music, and celebrates with a busy schedule of concerts, balls and café concerts. On the grand end of the scale is a series of annual balls, reaching its peak with February's Opera Ball at the State Opera (Staatsoper).

Some classical music venues are worth seeing just for their decoration: the State Opera (on Opernring); the Konzerthaus (on Lothringerstrasse); the Musikverein (at Karlsplatz); and the Royal Chapel (Burgkapelle) where the Vienna Boys' Choir sings at Sunday Mass.

Viennese Shopping

Expect high prices; you can get items of similar quality for up to a third less just over the border in Germany. Clothes are especially expensive – the best options are chain stores such as Humanic, in the SCS mall at Vösendorf on the southern edge of the city (go there by bus or tram from the Oper/Karlsplatz station).

Porcelain and glassware have been produced in Vienna for more than 200 years. Outlets on Kärntnerstrasse (near central Stephansplatz), include J & L Lobmeyr (No. 26), which has an exhibition of its early work on the top floor. The Old Town has plenty of window-shopping potential, and stores usually stay open until 7:30 one evening a week (either Thursday or Friday).

Essential Information

Tourist Information
Wien Tourismus (Vienna Tourist Board)
Albertinaplatz, corner of Maysedergasse (daily 9–7) ☎ 01 24 555 (information and hotel bookings); www.wien.info

Urban Transportation
Vienna has a network of subway (U-Bahn) lines, trams (Strassenbahn) and buses. U-Bahn lines 1, 2 and 4 meet at central Oper/Karlsplatz. Subways are marked with a U on the city map. A rapid transit railroad, the S-Bahn (Schnellbahn), travels into the city center from the suburbs. Hopper buses 1A, 2A and 3A stop near major Old Town sights. Pick up transportation maps at the Opern Passage/

Karlsplatz U-Bahn information counter (☎ 01 79 09 10-10). Taxis can be ordered: ☎ 01 31 30-0, 01 40 10-0 or 01 60 160.

Airport Information
Vienna International Airport (☎ 01 7007 22233; www.viennaairport.com) is a 20-minute bus ride from the City Air Terminal, in the city center. Shuttle buses run regularly between the two sites (☎ 01 93000 2300) plus from the airport to Südbahnhof and Westbahnhof railroad stations. There also are S-Bahn trains (line 7) and the faster nonstop city airport train CAT (☎ 01 25250; www.cityairporttrain.com) half-hourly from the airport to the city center.

Climate – average highs and lows for the month

Jan.	Feb.	Mar.	Apr.	May	Jun.	Jul.	Aug.	Sep.	Oct.	Nov.	Dec.
2°C	3°C	9°C	14°C	19°C	22°C	25°C	24°C	20°C	14°C	7°C	4°C
36°F	37°F	48°F	57°F	66°F	72°F	77°F	75°F	68°F	57°F	45°F	39°F
-3°C	-2°C	2°C	5°C	9°C	13°C	15°C	15°C	12°C	6°C	2°C	-1°C
27°F	28°F	36°F	41°F	48°F	55°F	59°F	59°F	54°F	43°F	36°F	30°F

Vienna Sights

Key to symbols

🚇 map coordinates refer to the Vienna map on pages 26–27 💵 admission charge: $$$ more than €5, $$ €2–€5, $ less than €2

See page 5 for complete key to symbols

Albertina

Housed within the beautiful Hofburg (Imperial Palace), the Albertina is named for its founder, Duke Albert von Sachsen-Teschen (1738–1822), who lived in the palace at the end of the 18th century. The Albertina's collection of more than a million drawings, prints and engravings dates from the 14th century and includes exquisite pieces by Raphael, Michelangelo, Goya and Cézanne and studies of children by Rubens. Also here is the world's most important collection of work by German-born artist Albrecht Dürer, which includes his masterpieces *Hare* and *Clasped Hands*. An ultramodern study and research center uses a state-of-the-art storage system to protect the museum's invaluable collection. There is also an architecture collection.

🚇 C2 ✉ Albertinaplatz 1 ☎ 01 534 83-0; www.albertina.at 🕐 Daily 10–6 (also Wed. 6–9 p.m.) 🚇 U-Bahn: Stephansplatz 🚊 Tram D 🍴 Restaurant 💵 $$$ 🎧 Guided tours (German only) Sat. and Sun. at 3:30 p.m; audio guide in English.

Hofburg

Blue and gold domes top the magnificent Hofburg (Imperial Palace), which took more than six centuries to build. The original fortress, built in 1275, made way for the Schweizerhof (Swiss Courtyard), whose Schweizertor (Swiss Gate) went up in the 16th century. Other sections were added during the 17th and 18th centuries, including the gorgeously decorated Hofbibliothek (Library) and the Hofreitschule (Riding School), where white Lipizzaner horses are put through their paces for visitors (see page 32). The Kaiserappartements (Imperial Apartments) were built in the 19th century, and new sections were added on as recently as 1913 to create today's enormous complex of 18 wings, 2,600 rooms and 19 courtyards. Many of the Habsburg trappings are on display, including the imperial crowns in the Schatzkammer (Treasuries). The first six rooms of the Kaiserappartements now house the Sisi Museum, dedicated to the life of Empress Sisi (1837–98).

Kaiserappartements 🚇 C2 ✉ Michaelerplatz (entrance: beneath Michaelerkuppel cupola) ☎ 01 533 7570; www.hofburg-wien.at 🕐 Daily 9–6, Jun.–Sep.; 9–5:30, Oct.–May 🚇 U-Bahn: Herrengasse, Stephansplatz or Volkstheater 🚌 2A, 3A, 48A; tram D, J, 1, 2, 46, 49 🍴 Augustinerkeller Restaurant, see page 463; café on site 💵 $$$ 🎧 Guided tours **Schatzkammer** ✉ Schweizerhof ☎ 01 525 240 🕐 Wed.–Mon. 10–6 🚇 U-Bahn: Herrengasse,

One of the six state rooms in the Kaiserappartements of the Hofburg that are dedicated to the Sisi Museum

A statue in the grounds of Schloss Schönbrunn

Stephansplatz or Volkstheater 🚇 2A, 3A, 48A; tram D, J, 1, 2, 46, 49 🍴 Augustinerkeller Restaurant, see page 463; café on site 💰 $$$

Kirche am Steinhof

Huge copper angels guard the portico of the eccentric, domed Kirche am Steinhof (Steinhof Church), built between 1904 and 1907 for people suffering from mental illness. Its white interior is full of light. Colored glass, and windows by Secessionist artist Kolo Moser brighten the vault and side altars. Short benches have plenty of space in between so that patients taken ill could be helped out. Running water was provided in the stoop (entranceway) to lessen the risk of infection. A ceiling under the cupola gives the effect of a starry sky.

➕ Off map at A2 ✉ Baumgartner Höhe 1, Penzing ☎ 01 91060 11007 🕐 Interior Sat. 4–5; guided tour (in German only) Sat. at 3 or by appointment 🚇 47A, 48A 💰 $$

Schloss Belvedere

The spectacularly baroque Schloss Belvedere (Belvedere Palace) was built for Austrian general and prince Eugene of Savoy, who led his army to many victories over the French. Begun in 1714, building was in two phases: the Unteres Belvedere (Lower Belvedere), where Eugene's military triumphs are celebrated in a ceiling fresco; and the Oberes Belvedere (Upper Belvedere), which housed his collection of paintings and later became the Imperial Picture Gallery. Archduke Franz Ferdinand, whose assassination sparked the events leading to World War I, lived here for 20 years until his death. The permanent collection in the Upper Belvedere displays Austrian art from the Middle Ages to the present. Among the highlights are Secessionist masterpieces of the late 19th and early 20th centuries, including *The Kiss* by Gustav Klimt and superb French Impressionist paintings by Manet, Renoir and Van Gogh. The Lower Belvedere and Orangery are used for special exhibitions.

➕ D1 ✉ Rennweg 6A (Unteres Belvedere); Prinz-Eugen-Strasse 27 (Oberes Belvedere) ☎ Palace: 01 79557-0; www.belvedere.at 🕐 Palace and gardens: daily 10–6 (gardens closed in bad weather) 🚇 Karlsplatz, Stadtpark 🚊 Tram 71 (Unteres Belvedere); bus 13A; tram D, O, 18 (Oberes Belvedere) 🍴 Café 💰 $$$ ℹ Tours by appointment ☎ 01 79577 135; audio guide

Schloss Schönbrunn

Empress Maria Theresa's (1717–1780) dreams of creating a Habsburg Versailles at Schloss Schönbrunn resulted in this magnificent baroque palace with more than 1,400 rooms. Nikolaus Pacassi designed this imperial summer residence between 1744 and 1749; the imposing facade looks out onto ornamental gardens, fountains and a park stretching into the distance. Here you will find the world's oldest zoo and the palm house. The main attractions are the state rooms and private apartments, inhabited by Maria Theresa and her 16 children, and later by Emperor Franz Joseph and his consort, the Empress Elizabeth ("Sisi"). The opulent surroundings form a vivid backdrop for the displays of Indian and

City of Composers

Many 17th- and 18th-century Habsburg rulers were music lovers and musicians: Leopold I was a composer; Charles VI was a violinist; and Maria Theresa played the double bass. Royal patronage drew some of the world's greatest composers to Vienna, including Beethoven and Brahms; Mozart gave his first concert in public at age six in Schönbrunn's Hall of Mirrors.

The waltz is inextricably linked to Vienna thanks to Johann Strauss, the "Waltz King," and every New Year's Day the Vienna Philharmonic Orchestra plays his waltzes to television viewers around the world. A statue of Strauss stands in City Park (Stadtpark).

In 1498 Emperor Maximilian I engaged 12 young male choristers to sing with the court orchestra. Over the centuries some of Austria's greatest composers served their apprenticeships with the choir, including Franz Schubert and Joseph Haydn. Schubert and Haydn would have been dressed in full imperial military uniforms, like the rest of the choir. The current naval-style dress wasn't implemented until 1919.

The elaborate and gilded Musikverein was built in the 19th century as a concert venue for the city's Society of the Friends of Music. (It's here that the Vienna Philharmonic performs its New Year concert.) In 1913 the hall was the scene of a brawl between conservatives and radicals of musical taste, at a concert performed by Arnold Schönberg.

Schönberg was responsible for changing the face of modern musical composition by abandoning the standard eight-tone scale familiar to the Western ear and devising a complex 12-tone system. Together with his former pupils Alban Berg and Anton von Webern, he formed the Second Viennese School of Music. Their contemporary, Gustav Mahler (1860–1911), studied at the Conseratory and became artistic director at the Vienna State Opera House (Staatsoper).

The unassuming entrance of the Beethoven Haus in a courtyard on Probusgasse in Vienna

Persian miniatures, Gobelin tapestries, 18th-century porcelain, furniture and delicately executed landscape paintings and frescoes.

🕀 A1 ✉ Schönbrunner Schlossstrasse 147 ☎ 01 81113 239 (palace); 01 52524-0 (coach collection); 01 877 9294-500 (zoo); 01 8775 087-406 (palm house); www.schoenbrunn.at; www.zoovienna.at ◉ Palace: daily 8:30–5, Apr.–Jun. and Sep.–Oct.; 8:30–6, Jul.–Aug.; 8:30–4:30, rest of year. Coach collection: daily 9–6, Apr.–Oct.; Tue.–Sun. 10–4, rest of year. Zoo: daily 9–6:30, Apr.–Sep.; 9–5:30, in Mar. and Oct.; 9–4:30, Nov.–Jan.; 9–5 in Feb. 🚇 U4 Schönbrunn 🚌 10A; tram 10, 58, 60 🍴 Tyrolean Restaurant in grounds of zoo; cafés 💷 $$$ (palace, zoo and palm house); $$ (coach collection) 🛈 Audio-guided tours. Concerts ☎ 01 812 50 04

Spanische Hofreitschule

In a glittering white arena of the Imperial Palace the white Lipizzaner horses of the Spanische Hofreitschule (Spanish Riding School) strut to the gavotte, quadrille and waltz and show off the leaping, rearing and trotting of the high school of dressage. Originally the horses were brought from Spain and bred at a 16th-century stud farm at Lipica, Slovenia (hence their name).

The nave of Stephansdom, looking to the high altar

Full performances, complete with music and uniformed riders, are booked well in advance, but same-day tickets for morning training sessions or a final rehearsal can be purchased at the visitor center, Michaelerplatz 1, Tue.–Sat. 9–4.

🕀 C2 ✉ Michaelerplatz 1 ☎ 01 533 9031; www.srs.at ◉ Performance: selected Fri. at 7 p.m., some Sat. and Sun. at 11 a.m., Feb.–Jun. and Sep.–Dec. Training: Tue.–Sun. 10–noon, early Feb.–late Jun., Sep.–Oct. and Dec. Final rehearsal: selected Fri. at 10 a.m. 🚇 U-Bahn: Herrengasse, Stephansplatz or Karlsplatz/Oper 🚊 Tram D, J, 1, 2, 62, 65 💷 $$$ ❓ Check well in advance as performance times vary

Stephansdom

Stephansdom (St. Stephen's Cathedral) is an unmistakable landmark, with its black-, yellow- and green-tiled roof and the 446-foot Gothic South Tower, known to locals as "Steffl," or "Little Steve." Relics of earlier churches are incorporated into the building, including the Giant's Door and the Tower of Heathens, supposedly the site of a pagan shrine. Inside, St. Stephen the Martyr is represented on a baroque 17th-century altar painting by Tobias Pock. The catacombs house an ossuary – a storage place for bones – where the remains of plague victims were kept.

🕀 D2 ✉ Stephansplatz 3 ☎ 01 515 52-3526; www.stephanskirche.at ◉ For tourists: Mon.–Sat. 6 a.m.–10 p.m., Sun. and public holidays 7 a.m.–10 p.m. 🚇 U-Bahn: Stephansplatz 🍴 Do & Co Im Haas-Haus, see page 463 🛈 Guided tours in English daily at 3:45, Apr.–Oct.

Uhrenmuseum

In 1917 Vienna's city councillors set up a museum devoted to timepieces across the ages in the Obizzi Palace, once home to Count Ernst Rüdiger von Starhemberg, who defended Vienna against the 1683 Turkish siege; it is in a side street by the Am Hof Church. The Uhrenmuseum (Clock Museum) displays over 3,000 fascinating items.

🕀 C2 ✉ Schulhof 2 ☎ 01 5332 265 ◉ Tue.–Sun. 10–6 🚇 U-Bahn: Herrengasse or Stephansplatz 💷 $$ (free on the first Sun. of the month)

Viennese Flavors

Coffeehouses and pastry shops (*konditoreien*) are two pretty good reasons for visiting Vienna. At the turn of the 20th century, artists, musicians and writers gathered in cafés to swap ideas, work, read or just sit, and some of their old haunts are still going strong. Stop by Bräunerhof (Stallburggasse 2, ☏ 01 512 38 93); Central (Herrengasse 14, ☏ 01 533 37 64-26); or the grand old Imperial (Kärtner Ring 16, ☏ 01 501 10-389), in the former city mansion of the Duke of Württemberg. Customers are generally left alone to linger in the grandiose surroundings, sipping one of the many coffee drinks.

On average, Austrians drink about 423 pints of coffee a year, and the menu usually offers many different varieties. *Mocca* is black coffee; a *kleiner* or *grosser brauner* has a little milk, a *melange* has more; a *fiaker* is mocca with rum or brandy; and an *einspänner* is a mocca with whipped cream. The *café-konditorei*, or pastry-shop-cum-café, is a showcase for Vienna's pastry makers. The most famous is Demel at Kohlmarkt 14, a must for visitors who love these light, fluffy edibles.

Wine made from the most recent grape harvest is known here as *Heuriger*, and this is also the name for the Viennese taverns that serve it. These *Heurigen* stand in their own vineyards in the Vienna Woods, and serve food – usually roast meat, cheese and salad – to complement and soak up the wine. A small music band is more than likely to be playing rousing folk music, and in summer there are often long tables and benches set outside. A bunch of fir twigs is traditionally hung outside the tavern door to show that it's open.

Viennese cooking is plain, simple and filling. It's collectively known as *Beisl* – a Yiddish word introduced by traditionally Jewish tavern owners. Dishes might include boiled beef (*Tafelspitz*), steak with crispy onions (*Zwiebelrostbraten*), chopped calves' heart and lungs in sauce (*Beuschel*) and – perhaps the best-known export – *Wiener Schnitzel*, a fried veal cutlet coated with egg and breadcrumbs. For dessert the popular choice is *Strudel*, fruit-filled baked dough with raisins and cinnamon (a perfect choice with a Viennese coffee).

The Demel coffee house has a view toward the St. Michael's Gate entrance to the Hofburg

Innsbruck

Strategically and beautifully situated on the Inn river, at the heart of the Alps, Innsbruck stands on a great European crossroads. The 19th-century construction of the east–west railroad through the Arlberg valley, in combination with the city's historic control of the north–south trade route through the Brenner Pass, placed it firmly on the trans-European map. Today, travelers from across Europe pass this way, and Innsbruck, with its excellent tourist and winter sports facilities, is well worth more than a brief stop en route.

Innsbruck Through Time

Innsbruck has had a checkered past. By the 12th century a fortified town was growing up beside the bridge over the Inn river, close to the site of an old Roman garrison.

By the 1360s, when the Habsburgs had acquired the Tyrol region, the settlement had outgrown its original fortifying walls.

Under Maximilian I, Emperor of the Germans from 1493 to 1519, Innsbruck was the administrative and cultural center of the Habsburg empire.

The next 200 years encompassed a golden age that continued through the reign of Empress Maria Theresa from 1717 to 1780. When Napoleon conquered the Tyrol in the 1790s Innsbruck became part of Bavaria, but was handed back to Austria in 1814.

After World War I Italy got the southern part of Tyrol (Bozen) and the Brenner Pass became the new frontier. The city suffered a great deal of damage during World War II, but since then it has prospered, and today it is a university city as well as a popular tourist destination.

Exploring Innsbruck

The center of Innsbruck is small, and it's likely your hotel will be within easy walking distance of the historic Old Town (Altstadt), a pedestrianized maze of picturesque streets.

Attractions outside the city are served both by regular local buses and special tourist shuttles that take you right to where the action is.

It's worth buying the Innsbruck Card, which gives you free entry to many museums and other attractions, plus free use of public transportation and four mountain cable-car systems, the latter otherwise very expensive. It's valid for 24, 48 or 72 hours and available at the tourist office (www.innsbruck.info).

A Rich Culture

Because of its long history, Innsbruck is richly endowed with some marvelous buildings, churches and museums.

The Old Town is a tiny area packed with handsome houses and narrow arcaded streets.

Outside this fascinating, ancient core you'll find splendid Renaissance, baroque and rococo architecture.

A street in the Old Town area of Innbruck where tables have been set out on the sidewalk for sunny summer dining

Many of these fine buildings house Innsbruck's museums, some devoted to history and the arts, others offering insights into such subjects as Tyrolean railroads, bells and hunting. The cathedral and churches are packed with artistic treasures.

Landmarks along the 17th- and 18th-century street, Maria-Theresien-Strasse, include a column topped by a statue of the Virgin (the Annasäule, built 1706), and a resplendent arch, the Triumphpforte, built in 1765.

Nowadays, six bridges span the Inn river – originally called the Innbrücke – from which the city gets its name, leading to the riverfront houses of the Mariahilf neighborhood. This area is also home to a botanic garden.

You can stroll beside the river, with mountains towering in the background, to the Hofgarten – a colorful and attractive garden which was first laid out in 1410 but later refined by Archduke Ferdinand II in the 16th century.

Located southeast of the city center, in a wonderful position overlooking the Inn valley, is Ferdinand's great palace, Schloss Ambras.

Mountain Scenery

Dramatic mountains encircle the city of Innsbruck, their lower slopes scattered with picturesque villages. The surrounding countryside offers year-round opportunities for fresh air and exercise amid some of Europe's loveliest upland scenery. The best way to experience this landscape is on foot, and the tourist office arranges good daily guided hikes outside the city in the summer; boots and a backpack can be rented. You can swim, ride, play golf, go rafting or summer skiing, or just enjoy the Alps from the comfort of a sightseeing airplane flight. Winter brings the skiing season, when sports fans flock to Innsbruck from all over the world and the city's architecture looks particularly beautiful under a fresh blanket of snow.

Tyrolean Tastes

Visitors can sample a wide range of Austrian and Tyrolean specialties at

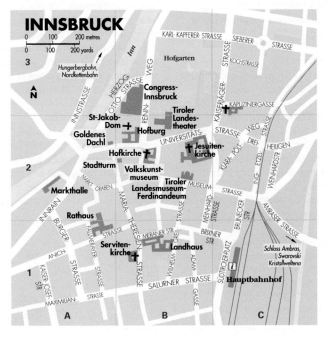

Innsbruck's restaurants, taverns and cafés (see page 464). The food is good and portions are generous, and you'll find the warm welcome that is so common all over the country.

In the summertime, follow your dinner with a cable-car ride up the Seegrube mountain where you can enjoy a drink while watching the sparkling lights of the city far below, or you can take a lantern-lit hike to a party held in a hillside hut.

Year round you can take in a Tyrolean folklore evening, which includes traditional dances, yodeling and a performance on brass instruments; during the summer, *Schuhplattler* dancers and brass bands perform in the center of town.

Innsbruck's casino offers a more sophisticated evening, and there's always a choice of classical music, and often opera.

Woodcarvings and *Christkindlmarkt*

Some of Innsbruck's most appealing stores are tucked away in the narrow, winding streets of the Old Town, where you'll find ethnic Austrian souvenirs, clothes, knitwear, antiques and interior design pieces. Woodcarvings make ideal presents, as do dried-flower garlands and baskets – especially charming decorations for Christmas and Easter – and intricately made national costumes.

Maria-Theresien-Strasse has a range of department, home furnishing and linen stores. Excellent bookstores offer English-language illustrated books about Austria, as well as beautiful calendars that make good gifts.

The atmospheric Christmas market (*Christkindlmarkt*) sets up in the Old Town, its stalls brimming with gifts, traditional decorations, cookies and a range of tempting sweetmeats.

Essential Information

Tourist Information
Innsbruck Tourismus (Innsbruck Tourist Board)
Burggraben 3 ☎ 0512 59850;
www.innsbruck.info
Accommodations reservation (same address)
☎ 0512 562000; fax 0512 562000-220

Urban Transportation
Many of Innsbruck's main sights are grouped together within walking distance in and around the Old Town (Altstadt); use the excellent tram and bus service for venturing farther afield. You can buy a day-use ticket, book of tickets or weekly transportation card from the tourist information office and also

from some tobacconists. Validate your ticket when boarding the bus or tram, and press the illuminated button near the door to open the doors when you want to get off. Local bus drivers are particularly helpful. There are taxi stands throughout the city center, or you can call a taxi (☎ 0512 1718, 0512 5311).

Airport Information
Innsbruck Airport (☎ 0512 22525-0; www.innsbruck-airport.com), with domestic and some European flights, is just 2 miles west of the city center. Bus F runs throughout the day to the central railroad station and the city center, or you can pick up a taxi outside the terminal.

Climate – average highs and lows for the month

Jan.	Feb.	Mar.	Apr.	May	Jun.	Jul.	Aug.	Sep.	Oct.	Nov.	Dec.
1°C	4°C	10°C	15°C	20°C	23°C	25°C	24°C	20°C	14°C	8°C	2°C
34°F	39°F	50°F	59°F	68°F	73°F	77°F	75°F	68°F	57°F	46°F	36°F
-7°C	-4°C	0°C	4°C	8°C	11°C	13°C	12°C	9°C	4°C	0°C	-4°C
19°F	25°F	32°F	39°F	46°F	52°F	55°F	54°F	48°F	39°F	32°F	25°F

Innsbruck Sights

The Golden Roof (a window) is superbly decorated

Goldenes Dachl

Innsbruck's Goldenes Dachl (Golden
Roof) is, in fact, an oriel (bay) window,
added onto the front of the previous
ducal palace to commemorate Emperor
Maximilian I's marriage to Bianca Maria
Sforza of Milan in 1493. Beautifully
decorated with reliefs of the Emperor, it
is roofed with more than 2,700 gilt
copper tiles – hence its name. It houses
the tomb (now empty) of Maximilian I,
among the finest existing works of
German Renaissance sculpture.
Twenty-eight larger-than-life-size bronze
statues surround the black marble
sarcophagus, decorated with 24 reliefs
showing scenes from the emperor's life.

These represent Maximilian's ancestors
and contemporaries, and were created
by the best artists of the time. Albrecht
Dürer was responsible for several,
including the figure of the legendary
King Arthur of England, considered the
finest statue anywhere of a Renaissance
knight. Elsewhere in the church you can
see bronze saints and busts of Roman
emperors, all figures destined for
Maximilian's unfinished sarcophagus.
➕ B2 ✉ Universitätsstrasse 2 ☎ 0512 59489-510
📷 Mon.–Sat. 9–5, Sun. 12:30–5 🚌 O, K, L, N; tram 1,
3, 6 💰 $$$

Hungerburgbahn and Nordkettenbahn

These connecting mountain
transportation systems take you from
Innsbruck city center up the Nordkette
to 6,250-foot Seegrube; from here you
can go to an even higher altitude, to the
7,657-foot Hafelekar.

The original Hungerburgbahn
transportation system was a steep
funicular, built around 1906 to link
lower and upper Innsbruck. The new
Hungerburgbahn/Nordkettenbahn lines
(designed by architect Zaha Hadid)
opened at the end of 2007. The cable
cars run up Hungerburg mountain over
precipitous slopes to the Seegrube
station, with ever-widening views over
Innsbruck, the valley and the high
Alpine peaks. A wonderful panorama of
mountains awaits you at the top.
➕ Off map B3 ✉ Hungerburgbahn: Rennweg 41;
Nordkettenbahn: Höhenstrasse 145
☎ Hungerburgbahn and Nordkettenbahn: 0512
293344; www.nordkette.com 📷 Sektion I Hungerburg
(Alpenzoo–Hungerburg): Mon.–Fri. 7 a.m.–7:15 p.m.;
Sat.–Sun. 8–7:15 (some seasonal variations); Sektion II
Seegrube (Hungerburg–Seegrube): daily 8:30–5:30
(also Fri. 6 p.m.–11:30 p.m.); Sektion III Hafelekar
(Seegrube–Hafelekar): daily 9–5 🚌 J, D, E, 4; tram 1
🍴 Cafés and restaurants at top and bottom of car
💰 Hungerburgbahn: $$; Nordkettenbahn: $$$ (reduced
Fri. after 9:30 p.m.)

Schloss Ambras

Schloss Ambras (Ambras Castle) lies
outside Innsbruck, a beautiful 16th-
century conversion of a medieval castle
standing in a landscaped garden above

the Inn valley. It was the home of Archduke Ferdinand from 1563 to 1595; an avid collector and patron of the arts, he built the superb Spanish Hall, with its colorful frescoes and beautiful ceiling, and amassed a collection of curiosities. They are displayed in the Wunderkammer (Wonder Room), a sort of early museum that offers great insight into the Renaissance mind.

The castle also contains a fine armory and a large portrait gallery dedicated to the imperial Habsburg family, although most visitors find Ferdinand's wife's bathroom far more interesting. It is a perfect and rare example of a 16th-century bathroom, complete with sunken copper bath.

🚹 Off map C1 ✉ Schlosstrasse 20 ☎ 01525 24-4802; www.khm.at/ambras ◉ Daily 10–5; 10–6 in Aug. 🚍 K; tram 3, 6, or special Sightseer from Maria-Theresien-Strasse (Altes Landhaus) 🍴 Castle restaurant and café 🖐 $$$

Stadtturm

For a bird's-eye view of Innsbruck, climb (there's no elevator) the 187-foot-high Stadtturm (Town Tower), built between 1442 and 1450 as a watchtower. The bulbous cupola was added in the 16th century.

🚹 A2 ✉ Herzog-Friedrich-Strasse 21 ☎ 0512 587113 ◉ Daily 10–8, Jun.–Sep.; 10–5, rest of year 🚍 O, L, K, N; tram 1, 3, 6 🖐 $$

Swarovski Kristallwelten

One of the Innsbruck area's most visited attractions, Swarovski Kristallwelten (Swarovski Crystal Worlds) in Wattens, 9 miles east of Innsbruck, has to be experienced to be believed. This multimedia theme park centers around the magic of crystal and features moving walls, sculptures and sparkling crystals in underground caverns. You enter through the Giant, a leafy face on the side of a hill with glowing eyes and a water-filled mouth, to experience strange sights and sounds.

🚹 Off map C1 ✉ Kristallweltenstrasse 1, Wattens ☎ 05224 51080; http://kristallwelten.swarovski.com ◉ Daily 9–6:30 (last admission 5:30) 🚍 Bus to Wattens every half hour from the Innsbruck railroad station 🍴 Restaurant and café 🖐 $$$

Tiroler Volkskunstmuseum

The appealing Tiroler Volkskunstmuseum (Museum of Tyrolean Folk Art) is housed in a 1553 abbey and is a great introduction to the traditional way of life in the Tyrol. There are displays on aspects of rural life, as well as complete Gothic and Renaissance house interiors. Don't miss the charming nativity scenes, where Jesus' birth is depicted in busy Alpine villages.

🚹 B2 ✉ Universitätsstrasse 2 ☎ 0512 59489-510; www.tiroler-volkskunstmuseum.at ◉ Daily 9–5 🚍 O, L, K, N; tram 1, 3, 6 🖐 $$; free to all Dec. 24

Ambras Castle stands in landscaped grounds

Winter Sports in Innsbruck

Innsbruck and its surrounding villages offer superb skiing amid beautiful Alpine landscapes. Winter-sports enthusiasts will find something for every taste, and some excellent all-inclusive deals can be arranged through the Innsbruck tourist office.

Skiing and Snowboarding

You can ski at spots throughout the Innsbruck area as well as at surrounding resorts such as Kitzbühel and Arlberg-St. Anton. There are some 322 miles of well-maintained downhill runs served by 210 lifts. Every skill level is accommodated, from gentle runs of hard-packed snow for families and beginners to extreme slopes and off-run skiing for experts. Special areas are designated for snowboarding and carving, and for the truly tough and experienced backcountry skier there are superb high-altitude itineraries.

Cross-country skiing on the downhill runs is very popular in Europe, and 12 different cross-country areas are accessible, offering 186 miles of tracks. Ski and snowboard schools operate daily, and ski guides can be hired on a daily basis. Several areas have snowmaking equipment to supplement early winter snow. Access to the slopes is by a combination of bus, funicular, cable car, chairlift and surface lift. Free buses take skiers from the city center to their chosen ski area and collect them at the end of the day; these buses also run to Kitzbühel and St. Anton. Innsbruck's season runs from mid-December to mid-April.

Winter Fun

There are plenty of other activities besides hitting the slopes. With its Olympic facilities, Innsbruck offers skating and curling, or you can take a piloted bobsled ride down the Olympic run. Dog- and horse-drawn sleigh rides give you a chance to appreciate the beauty of the mountains, and tobogganing and winter walking provide a gentler pace. Events take place throughout the season, culminating on New Year's Day with torchlit celebrations in the Old Town and on the mountains.

Snowboarding is increasingly popular in Austria and several schools run courses for novices

ℹ Information on ski packages is available from the tourist information office (✉ Innsbruck Tourismus, Burggraben 3, A-6021 Innsbruck, Austria ☎ 0512 59850; fax 0512 59850-107; www.innsbruck-pauschalen.com)

Salzburg

The beautiful little city of Salzburg, stretching along the Salzach river and tucked beneath the Mönchsberg hill, is a delightful combination of medieval, Renaissance and baroque architecture, the birthplace of Wolfgang Amadeus Mozart, its most famous son, and the gateway to some of Austria's most splendid landscapes. Add to this friendly people, a relaxed way of life and one of

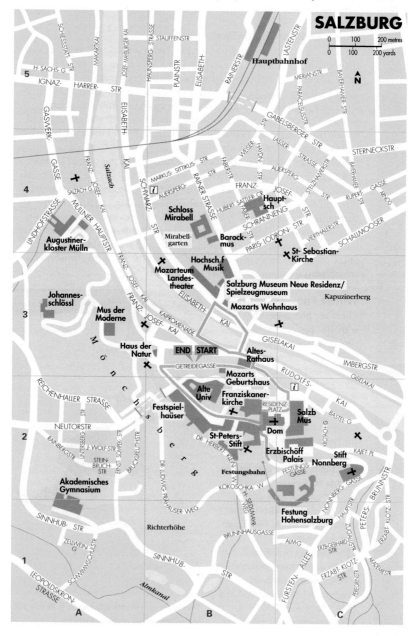

SALZBURG

Hauptbahnhof

Schloss Mirabell

Mirabellgarten

Barock-mus

St-Sebastian-Kirche

Augustiner-kloster Mülln

Hochsch f Musik

Mozarteum
Landes-theater

Salzburg Museum Neue Residenz/
Spielzeugmuseum

Kapuzinerberg

Johannes-schlössl

Mus der Moderne

Mozarts Wohnhaus

Haus der Natur

END START

Altes-Rathaus

Mozarts Geburtshaus

Alte Univ

Franziskaner-kirche

Festspiel-häuser

Salzb Mus

St-Peters-Stift

Dom

Erzbischöff Palais

Stift Nonnberg

Akademisches Gymnasium

Festungsbahn

Festung Hohensalzburg

Richterhöhe

Almkanal

the world's greatest music festivals, and it's easy to see why Salzburg is popular year-round with tourists.

For fans of the movie *The Sound of Music*, there's the added bonus that the city was home to the von Trapp family; you can find several of the movie's locations scattered around the city and various tour companies operate trips with English guides that take you to some of the sites associated with the popular film.

Mozart's Footsteps

For Mozart lovers, a visit to Salzburg is little short of a pilgrimage. You can see the composer's birthplace, the house the family rented when he was growing up, and the Residenz (see page 46) where he was literally kicked out by a steward for "getting above himself."

For classical music lovers, festivals are the other main draw (see pages 42 and 45); the city is packed during festival season and it's hard to find accommodations, so make reservations well in advance. Salzburg's charming cityscape, however, can be enjoyed any time of year. Late spring and autumn are good times to visit, but whenever you come it will probably rain: Salzburg has a reputation for being the country's wettest city.

Getting Your Bearings

Salzburg is an easy city to negotiate. The historic center on both banks of the Salzach river is pedestrianized. Although you can walk from end to end in roughly half an hour, you'll doubtless want to spend more time enjoying the medieval streets and spacious baroque squares. Most of what you'll want to see is on the left bank, with a few sights across the river.

Tourist offices sell the Salzburg Card, valid for 24, 48 or 72 hours, which offers free single admission to all museums and attractions and discounts on various services, and provides free access to public transportation.

Various companies will take you on city tours or farther afield to see the landscape of the Salzkammergut, one of the loveliest parts of Austria, with its shimmering lakes. There are fascinating walking tours around Salzburg, concentrating on different aspects of the city. If you just want to sit back and relax, you can take a trip in a horse-drawn carriage (*Fiaker*); pick one up on the Residenzplatz.

Cosmopolitan Cuisine

You'll eat extremely well in Salzburg, which has dozens of restaurants, inns, taverns and cafés where you can enjoy anything from local and regional specialties to Japanese sushi. Traditional cooking is hearty and filling: plates of meat with dumplings, soups and spicy *Gulasch* (meat stew). The local specialty is *Salzburger Nockerl* (an egg dessert), and a variety of drinks and open wines (available by the glass) also are offered.

Make a point of lingering an hour or so in one of Salzburg's traditional cafés, which specialize in coffee and cream cakes served in elegant surroundings. Many cafés and restaurants have summertime beer gardens, some in beautiful settings.

Austrian Cafés

There's no better way to get the feel of the country than by spending an hour or so in a café, a quintessential Austrian experience. Café decor ranges from chandelier-hung baroque splendor to wood-paneled coziness, but the basic elements are always similar: excellent service, a vast range of coffees, and a wide choice of feather-light cream cakes and pastries, all indulged in by well-dressed locals chatting or reading the newspapers. Reading materials are provided by the establishment and hung on wooden poles. Cafés often serve beer and wine, and some offer savory snacks. Many have summertime terraces, the perfect place to write your postcards and rest your feet.

Salzburg Souvenirs

Salzburg is filled with tempting stores, many of them lining the Getreidegasse (see page 44) and its surrounding streets, although there's a good cluster on the left bank of the river. Traditional women's clothes are appealing buys, but keep in mind that what looks lovely here might not look so good back home. Also look for wooden carvings, delicate porcelain and crystal, and bright china and linens, all with an Austrian theme, as well as big European designer names. Don't forget Austria's well-organized tax-free shopping service.

Music and Marionettes

Although classical music is the heart of the entertainment scene, it's not the only attraction. Folk, blues and jazz concerts take place year-round across the city or you can enjoy a traditional dinner in the largest preserved fortress in central Europe, the Festung Hohensalzburg (Hohensalzburg Fortress, see page 43), followed by a Mozart serenade by musicians in period dress. The main festival season runs from late July through August, but something happens most months. Tyrolean entertainments include an autumn jazz festival and fairs in September and the weeks before Christmas.

To keep the whole family happy, adults can visit the city's casino, while children will enjoy watching one of the famous puppet performances at the Marionette Theater.

Essential Information

Tourist Information

Tourismus Salzburg (Informationsstellen)
Mozartplatz 5 ☎ 0662 889 87-330; daily 9–7, May–Sep.; 9–6, Oct.–Apr.
Hauptbahnhof (Railroad Station): Bahnhofsvorplatz ☎ 0662 889 87-340; www.salzburg.info

Urban Transportation

Salzburg's small central core makes it possible to walk to everything you'll want to see. There are, however, good bus and trolley bus services covering the whole city. Buy your ticket before boarding, either at the machines at the main bus stops or from any tobacconist, and remember to validate it as soon as you board the bus. Validation machines are marked "Entwerter." There is no need to punch them again if you change buses. To open the doors from either outside or inside the bus you must press the illuminated button beside the door. For service information call ☎ 0662 4480 1500. There are several taxi stands outside the historic center, or you can call Taxi "2220" (☎ 0662 22 20) or Salzburger Funktaxi (☎ 0662 81 11). If you are driving to Salzburg, do not try to bring your car into the city center, where parking is an enormous problem. There are IRGE supervised parking lots outside the city where cars can safely be left, then take a shuttle bus to the city center.

Airport Information

Salzburg's W. A. Mozart Airport (☎ 0662 85 80-251; www.salzburg-airport.com), with domestic and some European flights, is about 4 miles west of the city center. Bus No. 2 runs every 10 minutes throughout the day to the railroad station, and there is a taxi stand outside the terminal.

Climate – average highs and lows for the month

Jan.	Feb.	Mar.	Apr.	May	Jun.	Jul.	Aug.	Sep.	Oct.	Nov.	Dec.
2°C	4°C	10°C	14°C	19°C	22°C	24°C	24°C	20°C	14°C	7°C	2°C
36°F	39°F	50°F	57°F	66°F	72°F	75°F	75°F	68°F	57°F	45°F	36°F
-5°C	-4°C	-2°C	2°C	8°C	12°C	13°C	13°C	9°C	4°C	-2°C	-3°C
23°F	25°F	28°F	36°F	46°F	54°F	55°F	55°F	48°F	39°F	28°F	27°F

Salzburg Sights

Dom

The ornate facade of the Dom (Cathedral), the first truly Italian-style church to be built north of the Alps, dominates the Domplatz, its four huge marble statues indicating the interior splendors. There's been a cathedral here since the eighth century; today's structure is the third on the site. It was constructed between 1614 and 1628, damaged during World War II, and restored by 1959.

The huge interior, accommodating 10,000 people, is a riot of stucco, marble and gilding, the simple 14th-century font providing a serene contrast. In the crypt see the medieval foundations and remains of the original Roman church. The museum has superb treasures such as an eighth-century cross.

➕ B2 ✉ Domplatz ☎ Museum: 0662 8047 7950 ◉ Cathedral: Mon.–Sat. 8–5 and Sun. 1–5, Jan.–Feb. and Nov.; Mon.–Sat. 8–6 and Sun. 1–6, Mar.–Apr., Oct. and Dec.; Mon.–Sat. 8–7 and Sun. 1–7, May–Jul. and Sep.; Mon.–Sat. 8–8 and Sun. 1–8, Aug. 🚌 5, 6, 51, 55 📖 Cathedral free; Museum $$ ❓ Guided tours Jul. and Aug. Mon.–Fri. at 2 p.m. or on request

Festspielhäuser

Even if you're not musically inclined, the Festspielhäuser (Festival Theaters) are well worth visiting. They stand on the site of the old court stables, the winter riding school that was converted to form the Kleines Festspielhaus (Little Theater). The Grosses Festspielhaus (Large Theater), built in 1960, runs right into Mönchsberg hill; vast amounts of rock were removed during its construction. To see the theaters, unless you attend a performance, take a guided tour; this will allow you to experience the acoustics of the 2,000-seat Large Theater, among the best in the world.

➕ B2 ✉ Hofstallgasse 1 ☎ 0662 80450 ◉ Guided tours daily at 3:30, Jun.–Sep.; 2 p.m., rest of year 🚌 1, 5, 6, 51, 55 📖 $$ ❗ Entry is only with a guided tour; tour times are subject to change if rehearsals are in progress. Check before you visit

Festung Hohensalzburg

The massive Festung Hohensalzburg (Hohensalzburg Fortress) dominates Salzburg from Mönchsberg hill. This fortress was built, altered and extended between 1077 and 1681. Walk up or take the funicular to admire the views before joining one of the guided tours, the only way to visit the interior. You'll see winding passages and ornate state rooms, including the Golden Room with its gilded tracery, and the Golden Hall, with a superb gold-and-blue coffered ceiling. The Rainer Museum displays weapons and coats of arms.

➕ C1 ✉ Mönchsberg 34 ☎ 0662 842 430-11 ◉ Grounds: daily 9–7, May–Sep.; 9:30–5, Jan.–Apr. and Oct.–Dec. Interior: closes 30 minutes earlier. Rainer Museum: daily same hours as interior, May 1 to mid-Oct. only 🚠 Festungsbahn funicular daily 9–5, Jan.–Apr. and Oct.–Dec.; 9–8 May–Jun. and Sep.; 9–10, Jul.–Aug. 🍴 Café and restaurant (see page 465) in fortress 📖 Combination ticket $$$

The rooftops of the Dom (Cathedral)

Franziskanerkirche

A short distance from the cathedral stands the Franziskanerkirche (Franciscan Church), a peaceful and lofty building dedicated to the Virgin that was Salzburg's parish church until 1635. The nave, with its Romanesque details, is the oldest part, its dimness set off by the airy Gothic choir, built in the 15th century. Be sure to go behind the altar to admire the ring of baroque chapels that encircle it.

➕ B2 ✉ Franziskanergasse 5 ☎ 0662 843 629; www.franziskaner.at ⏰ Daily 6:30 a.m.–7:30 p.m. 🚋 5, 6, 51, 55

Getreidegasse

The medieval street known as the Getreidegasse runs through the center of old Salzburg and is lined with stores, each with a distinctive wrought-iron sign hanging above.

Most of the houses date from the 15th through the 18th centuries and were built by prosperous burghers for their businesses and to house their families. Passages run through the buildings to connect with picturesque courtyards and squares; these are called *Durchhäuser*, meaning "through the houses."

Crowds throng the street and its continuation, the Judengasse, and there's no better place to come to soak up Salzburg's unique atmosphere.

➕ B3 ✉ Getreidegasse 🚋 5, 6, 51, 55

Haus der Natur

A few hours in Salzburg's Haus der Natur (Natural History Museum) provides a splendid antidote to an excess of fine architecture and Mozart.

Popular with families, the museum's more than 90 rooms house a wide range of scientific and nature displays, including a reptile zoo, European animal exhibits and an excellent aquarium complete with great white sharks. Children of all ages will enjoy the Space Research Hall, with its dioramas, models and mock-up of a future space city.

➕ B3 ✉ Museumsplatz 5 ☎ 0662 842 653; www.hausdernatur.at ⏰ Daily 9–5 🚋 10, 49, 60, 80, 95 🍴 Café in museum 🍽 $$

Mirabellgarten

The beautiful Mirabellgarten (Mirabell Garden) spreads around the Schloss Mirabell (Mirabell Castle), built in 1606 by Archbishop Wolf Dietrich as a home for his mistress, Salome Alt. The terraces, gardens, lawns and flower beds around the house are a splendid example of baroque garden design, where trees, shrubs and flowers contrast with statues and fountains to create a truly civilized landscape. Concerts are held in the Marble Hall, one of the loveliest places to hear Mozart's music.

➕ B4 ✉ Mirabellplatz ☎ 0662 8072-0 ⏰ Daily 6:30 a.m.–dusk 🚋 1, 5, 6, 51, 55

Mozarts Geburtshaus

Wolfgang Amadeus Mozart was born in a modest middle-class apartment in the heart of Salzburg on January 27, 1756. These rooms are among Salzburg's most visited sights, a place of pilgrimage for music lovers from all over the world.

Climb the stairs to enter the Mozarts Geburtshaus (Mozart's Birthplace), today a simple museum containing family portraits and mementos of the composer, including his first violin. The next-door flat has been filled with period furniture to give an idea of the appearance of 18th-century living quarters, where each room opens from its adjoining room and communal wooden balconies overlook a courtyard.

One floor down, you can study stage sets and costumes from festival productions of Mozart's works while listening to his sublime music.

➕ B3 ✉ Getreidegasse 9 ☎ 0662 844 313; www.mozarteum.at/museen ⏰ Daily 9–8, Jul.–Aug.; 9–5:30, rest of year 🚋 5, 6, 51, 55 🍴 Café on ground floor of museum 🍽 $$$ ℹ Last admission 30 minutes before closing

Mozart-Wohnhaus

In 1773 the Mozart family left their modest appartment in Getreidegasse and

Mozart and the Salzburg Festival

The facade of the Mozarts Geburtshaus in Salzburg where Mozart was born in 1756

Although Mozart spent much of his adult life in Vienna, his name is inextricably linked with his birthplace, Salzburg. Considered by many to be the world's greatest composer, Mozart's spiritual legacy to his native city is one of the world's greatest music festivals, the Salzburg Festival, a year-round program of musical events.

Mozart

Wolfgang Amadeus Mozart was born in Salzburg in 1756, the son of a respected court musician, himself a fine violinist whose treatise on violin technique is still respected. The boy soon showed signs of genius, playing a variety of instruments by sight and ear and starting to compose at an early age. Mozart's father touted his talented son all around the European courts, keeping a stern eye on his behavior, spending and morals, and thus storing up trouble for the pair's future relationship.

Eventually the small-town atmosphere of Salzburg, with its reliance on the bishops for employment, proved too stifling, and Mozart moved to Vienna, where he married Constanze Weber. He composed prodigiously and was capable of writing scores as if by divine dictation, while chatting to his friends. Unfortunately, Mozart's genius did not extend to managing his finances; weighed down by money worries and stress, he died in 1791 and was buried in a pauper's grave.

The Salzburg Festival

The Salzburg Festival is held annually during the last week of July and most of August. F. Gehmacher and H. Damisch founded the *Saltzburger Festspielhausgemeinde* in 1917, a predeccessor to the Salzburg Festival, which was established by Hugo von Hofmannsthal, Max Reinhardt, Richard Strauss and others. The music festival attracts audiences and renowned performers from all over the world. Its main venues are the Festival Theaters complex (see page 43), but performances are held in buildings all over the city. The program always includes Mozart operas and orchestral works, but many other composers are featured, as well as plays – in particular *Everyman*, which is traditionally performed outside in the Domplatz.

If you want to attend the festival it is essential to book far ahead; reservations start in December, when you should also reserve your accommodations.

Salzburg Ticket Service ✉ Salzburg Information, Mozartplatz 5, A-5020 Salzburg, Austria

☎ 0662 88 987-0; fax 0662 88 987-435; www.salzburgticket.com or www.salzburgerfestspiele.at

moved across the river to Makartplatz to occupy a far more spacious and elegant place, now the Mozart-Wohnhaus (Mozart's House). The building was badly damaged in World War II and was finally renovated and reopened for the 240th anniversary of Mozart's birth in 1996. The result is a superb state-of-the-art museum with evocative displays of Mozart memorabilia.

A true picture of the composer emerges – a man who loved games and jokes, who had an earthy sense of humor and a difficult relationship with his father. Here are scribbled letters, musical manuscripts, instruments and books, all brought to life through an English-language commentary. Two rooms are devoted to audiovisual programs about Mozart's early life and his travels through Europe, which, given 18th-century roads, were impressive.

🔲 B3 ✉ Makartplatz 8 ☎ 0662 874 227-40; www.mozarteum.at/museen ⓞ Daily 9–8, Jul.–Aug.; 9–5:30, rest of year 🚌 15, 27, 51 💷 $$$ ℹ️ Audio guide; last admission 90 minutes before closing

Residenzplatz

The Residenzplatz is the triumphant architectural landmark of the inner city, splendidly adorned with an ebullient baroque fountain (the largest in central Europe) complete with horses and dolphins and topped by a conch-blowing triton.

Opposite rises the Residenz (Archbishop's Palace), built between 1595 and 1619 around three courtyards. See the impressive baroque interiors on an audio-guided tour that leads through rooms of ornate decoration with stucco, gilding, marble and astonishing painted ceilings, to get a better sense of the scale of grandeur and luxury enjoyed by Salzburg's prince bishops.

The palace also contains an art gallery. Concerts are held in the state rooms.

🔲 B2 ✉ Residenzplatz 1 ☎ Palace: 0662 8042-2800; www.residenzgalerie.at. Art Gallery: 0662 840 4510 ⓞ Palace: Tue.–Sun.10–5 (hours vary around Easter and for events). Art Gallery: Tue.–Sun. 10–5, also occasional Mon.; closed most of Nov. and Dec. 24 🚌 5, 6, 49, 51, 55 💷 Palace $$$; Art Gallery $$$; reduced combination ticket $$$ ℹ️ Guided tours of Palace daily at 10 (German only) and audio guide

Salzburg Museum Neue Residenz/Spielzeugmuseum

Salzburg's primary museum has collections housed in two buildings. The Neue Residenz covers antiquities and art and the Spielzeugmuseum und Musikinstrumente (Toy Museum and Musical Instruments) has a charming collection of toys, dolls and musical instruments.

You can trace Salzburg's history from Roman times and admire some lovely 17th-century paneled rooms. Among the highlights is a beautiful Celtic ewer. The toys and dolls, some 250 years old, include train sets and puppet theaters.

🔲 B3 ✉ Neue Residenz, Mozartplatz. Toy Museum: Bürgerspitalgasse 2 ☎ Neue Residenz: 0662 620 808-700. Toy Museum: 0662 620 808-300; www.salzburgmuseum.at ⓞ Main Building: Tue.–Sun. 9–5. Toy Museum: reopening late 2011; please check website 🚌 10, 49, 60, 80, 95 💷 $$ (each museum) ℹ️ Combination ticket available for both buildings

Stiftskirche St. Peter

The lovely Stiftskirche St. Peter (St. Peter's Church) was built between 1131 and 1147 but later altered to its present rococo appearance in the 18th century. A simple Romanesque west door leads into a sumptuous interior, with 16 marble altars in its side chapels and decorated with green and pink molding and golden cherubs.

Make time to see the monument to Mozart's beloved sister Nannerl before leaving to explore the charming old Friedhof (cemetery), with its flower-bedecked graves.

🔲 B2 ✉ St. Peter-Bezirk 1 ☎ 0662 844 576; www.stift-stpeter.at ⓞ Church: daily 6:30 a.m.–9 p.m. Catacombs: Tue.–Sun. 10:30–5, May–Sep.; Wed.–Thu. 10:30–3:30, Fri.–Sun. 10:30–4, rest of year 🚌 1, 5, 6, 51, 55 🍴 Stiftskeller St. Peter, see page 465 💷 Catacombs $

A Day in Salzburg

Although several companies offer a variety of tours in and around Salzburg, the city is small enough to find your way around easily, so it makes sense to plan your own day's sightseeing.

A view across Salzburg from Festung Hohensalzburg

A Mozart Morning

After a hearty Austrian breakfast, spend the morning concentrating on Wolfgang Amadeus Mozart, Salzburg's most famous son. His father, employed as a musician in the city, lived in a house on Getreidegasse, where Mozart was born in 1756. After visiting the house and its museum you may be ready for a cup of coffee and a break; head for the atmospheric Café Tomaselli in the Alter Markt. It was here that Mozart's widow came with her second husband to write the composer's biography in 1820.

Next, cross the Staatsbrücke and walk along the river to Mozart's House (Mozart-Wohnhaus) on Makartplatz, a far grander house where Mozart lived between 1773 and 1780 in a spacious apartment. Nearby you'll find the Mozarteum, the music university that holds the Mozart archives. The hut on the grounds is the Little Magic Flute House (Zauberflötenhäuschen) which once stood in Vienna. Here, Mozart composed the opera in less than five months.

An Afternoon in the Altstadt

Back across the river, have lunch in one of the cafés and restaurants and then spend the afternoon exploring the Old Town (Altstadt). Most sights are clustered around the trio of lovely squares known as the Residenzplatz, the Domplatz and the Mozartplatz. Behind the cathedral (Dom, see page 43), take the funicular up to the fortress of Hohensalzburg (see page 43).

After this, visit the fine Salzburg Museum Neue Residenz (see page 46). En route, stop at the Pferdeschwemme (literally "horse-swim"), a frescoed fountain-cum-pool where horses were once led down sloping ramps in order to be washed. Leave time to enjoy the stores along Getreidegasse and in the alleys leading off it, where you'll find every imaginable Austrian souvenir.

A Salzburg Evening

No Salzburg visit would be complete without some music; many visitors enjoy special Mozart evenings, with dinner followed by a performance of the composer's works played by costumed musicians. Then wander back through the atmospheric streets to your hotel with music ringing in your ears. For details of the walk route, see the city map on page 40.

Belgium

Opposite: A flower market is held in Grand' Place in Brussels

Belgium

Belgium is a young country in terms of "old" Europe. Its name derives from a prehistoric tribe, the Belgae, but there is no racial or cultural link with such a distant past. The country has been in the melting pot of European history for centuries and only achieved true national identity in 1830 after the Belgian Revoution. Yet nowhere else on the Continent will you be so close to such a powerful sense of European history.

Influential Neighbors

The Belgium of today is a nation born out of a divided Europe, surviving in spite of differences in politics, territory and language that remain within its own borders. Too often it is seen as the administrative focus of the European Union, a country preoccupied with international politics and commerce. Geographically, it is tiny (about the size of Maryland) relative to the size of Europe's larger nations. The Netherlands lies to the north; Germany to the east; France to the south; and Luxembourg, an independent Grand Duchy linked historically to Belgium, to the southeast.

The northwestern coastline of Belgium faces Britain across the narrow English Channel. The influences and interests of all of these European countries have had an impact on Belgium and, in the case of France and the Netherlands, have radically shaped the country's north–south linguistic and cultural divide.

Landscape of History

Apart from the canals in the north, Belgium has no outstanding landscape features that define it in the way that Norway is defined by its fjords, Greece by its islands or Switzerland by its Alps. Yet Belgium has a powerful identity expressed through historic cities and a peerless artistic legacy. You will be seduced by medieval Bruges and old Brussels; feel a sense of history in Ghent,

Antwerp and regional cities such as Leuven and Mechelen; and be enchanted by the castles in the Ardennes region. The dazzling works of art of early Flemish Masters and medieval painters will fascinate you: prepare yourself for Jan van Eyck, Hans Memling and Peter Paul Rubens, as well as the Brueghels, Anthony van Dyck and Jacob Jordaens.

Belgium is about the landscape of history rather than of scenery. Yet outside the cities and towns lies a quietly charming countryside of fruitful

More Top Destinations in Belgium

- Antwerpen C4
- Damme B4
- Kasteel Alden Biesen D3
- Kasteel van Ooidonk B3
- Knokke-Heist B4
- Kortrijk B3
- Leuven C3
- Mechelen C3
- Oudenaarde B3
- La Roche-en-Ardenne D2
- Villers-la-Ville C3
- Ypres A3

farms, serene waterways and flower-filled meadows. On the immediate outskirts of Brussels to the south is the Forêt de Soignes, a superb beech forest that is an oasis of peace. In the Haspengouw region to the west of Brussels are several historic castles, such as the stately Gaasbeek with its formal gardens and the 13th-century, moated Alden Biesen. A more somber yet compelling aspect of Belgium is enshrined in the poem *In Flanders Fields* by Canadian poet John McCrae (1872–1918), who was a medical officer in World War I. Throughout Europe's turbulent history this northwestern corner of the Continent has seen conflict, none so bitter as World War I. Towns such as Mons and Ypres still resonate with memories, and you will find many memorials and graves in the now-healed landscape.

Beaches, Woodlands and Parks

Along Belgium's relatively short 42-mile coastline there are attractive sand dunes,

The Atomium is in northern Brussels

beaches and resorts, lively towns such as Oostende, quaint resorts like De Haan and stylish hangouts like Knokke Le Zoute, all connected by a tram line. There may be no dramatic mountains, but the hilly country of the Ardennes in southern Belgium offers a varied landscape of woods, rivers and soft moorland where you can walk or bicycle around Dinant and Rochefort.

Brussels has plenty of green spaces, such as the popular Bois de la Cambre, and the vast beech woodland of the Forêt de Soignes. For more gardens and floral displays, check out the Royal Greenhouses at Laeken or the National Botanic Garden in Meise, about 7 miles north of Brussels.

If theme parks appeal to you, Belgium has a variety of venues to excite children and adults alike. At Wavre, near Brussels, is Walibi Belgium, a huge theme park with thrilling roller-coaster rides such as "Buzzsaw" and "Cobra," as well as a fabulous water park, Aqualibi, adjacent; at Boudewijn

Seapark, just outside Bruges, is Europe's largest dolphinarium.

Exploring Belgium

Public transportation in Belgium is universally efficient, but the railroad network is by far the best way to travel. It is well integrated with systems in neighboring countries, and trains are frequent. Inter-city trains are fast and comfortable; local trains tend to be slower, and you may feel that some of the older equipment seems a little spartan and drab. Overall, however, the high standards that distinguish rail travel throughout northern Europe prevail.

City transportation systems are also well run. Trams are a northern European institution, and the larger cities in Belgium have good tram and bus services. Brussels and Antwerp have well organized subway systems that visitors will find useful.

Renting a car will give you independence, but driving in Belgium can be a challenge due mainly to the small size of the country and, in part, to its congested urban nature. The road system is excellent, but because distances between built-up areas can be short, you are frequently faced with busy intersections. Traffic in Brussels and in many of the larger cities is hectic, and navigation can be complicated for visitors because road signs are in French and Flemish. Out on the road, along the east–west dividing line between French-speaking and Flemish-speaking Belgium, destination names on road signs change suddenly and confusingly between French and Flemish.

Diverse Foods

Food in Belgium is often characterized as being French in quality and German in quantity. The reality is more subtle. Wallonian cuisine shares the French penchant for wine-based sauces, but traditional Belgian cuisine focuses particularly on beef and pork, and

A plaque commemorates the Battle of Waterloo in 1815, scene of Napoleon Bonaparte's defeat

specializes in seafood on the coast and game in the Ardennes.

In most good hotels you will find the generous buffet breakfasts that are an international staple, consisting of a variety of cereals, cheeses and hams, along with fish and smoked meats. For lunch and dinner, be adventurous. Try *maatjes*, marinated raw herring swallowed whole, but not quite the raw experience it seems. Or settle for *mosselen/moules*, Belgian mussels in a variety of tangy sauces. For a truly filling meal, try *waterzooi*, the traditional Flemish stew of fresh vegetables with rabbit, chicken or fish, originating in Ghent, or *anguilles au vert/paling in 't groen*, freshwater eels in a green herb sauce, or *carbonnades*, beef stewed in beer. And do not miss Ardennes *pâté*, the region's excellent *jambon d'Ardennes* (smoked ham) or some of the many delicious local cheeses, little known outside Belgium.

In spring look for an asparagus dish with a butter-based sauce, as well as chopped boiled egg and chopped ham. This goes nicely with one of Belgium's many excellent beers, which tend to be rich, mellow and smooth. In the Flemish and the Liège regions of Belgium the specialty is *jenever (genièvre)*, a grain

spirit like gin, flavored with juniper berries and other herbs and spices.

For those with a sweet tooth, Belgium's famous *chocolatiers* will be irresistible. The specialties are individually made pralines with liqueur or cream fillings, and truffles with the utterly indulgent ingredients of butter, cream and sugar. The shopfront displays are an art form in themselves and are guaranteed to tempt you inside. *Gaufres wafels*, tasty waffles, are a Belgian treat that you can buy from street vendors.

Traditional Courtesy

Throughout Belgium, visitors will find the local people unfailingly helpful. This is a conservative country with a strongly Roman Catholic religious tradition, factors that make people courteous yet reserved. The language divide (see page 54) lends a certain rivalry to relations between Flemings and Walloons, yet such cultural diversity seems to make most Belgians amenable to and interested in visitors. The people may seem busy and preoccupied, but they will respond politely if you ask for advice or information about their country, which is, after all, a distillation of the most significant aspects of old and new Europe.

Timeline

57 BC	Romans in northern Europe conquer Iron Age Belgae tribe territory, part of land now occupied by present-day Belgium.
AD 751	Carolingian Dynasty is formed; during reign of Charlemagne, Holy Roman Emperor, the Low Countries prosper.
993	King Baudouin I dies, and his brother, Albert II, becomes king.
1419	Central government established at Bruges; the city becomes a center of the cloth trade and a focus of early Flemish painters.
1519	Charles V of Spain is crowned Holy Roman Emperor; the Netherlands comes under Spanish control.
1581	The Netherlands divides into United Provinces of the Netherlands and Spanish Netherlands (Belgium).
1713	War of Spanish Succession ends; Austria controls Belgium.
1815	Congress of Vienna; Belgium and the United Provinces of the Netherlands form the Kingdom of the Netherlands, ruled from the Hague by the Dutch William of Orange.
1839	Belgian independence recognized by the (Dutch) Netherlands.
1914–18	Most of Belgium is occupied by Germany.
1940–44	Belgium again occupied by Germany.
1957	European Economic Community (now the European Union) establishes its headquarters in Brussels.
1967	NATO sets up headquarters in Brussels.
2006–present	Belgian politics is characterized by deep rifts based on Flemish/French language and cultural differences.
2011	No new government has been formed in Belgium since the general election of June 2010. Negotiations between the Flemish/French political parties continue.

Language Divide

There is a dramatic linguistic divide between north and south Belgium, a legacy of the country's formation from a southern French-influenced area and a northern Flemish-influenced area. In northern Belgium the dominant language is Flemish, a Germanic language similar to Dutch. In southern Belgium, in the area known as Wallonia, the prevailing language is a French dialect. Brussels lies within the Flemish half of Belgium and is officially bilingual, but within the city French is the dominant language. Be careful in associating Flemish too closely with Dutch. Brugeans (residents of Bruges) will tell you that theirs is a far subtler language, with more lyrical twists and turns. And Antwerpenaars (residents of Antwerp) will tell you that they speak better Flemish than Brugeans; if you visit more remote rural districts you will find even more regional differences.

Survival Guide

- Flemish and French are both spoken in Brussels, where even street signs are in both languages. You can try out your French in Brussels and Wallonia and your Flemish in Ghent, Bruges and in the north, but to use either language in the wrong area may elicit a frosty reaction. However, many Belgians speak English, and this is often the wisest option, particularly in the city of Brussels, where it is now lingua franca.

- You will usually find that the Flemish and French proper names have similarities; for example, Bruges is Bruges (French) and Brugge (Flemish), Louvain is Louvain (French) and Leuven (Flemish). But there are problematic differences. For example, Ghent is Gand (French) but Gent (Flemish), and Mechelen is Malines (French) but Mechelen (Flemish). If in doubt, especially when checking train or bus destinations, confirm the destination with an English-speaking official.

- There are a few public restrooms in Belgian cities, but they are often not very clean. Railroad and bus stations, restaurants and the bigger cafés tend to have public bathrooms with attendants, where you are expected to pay about 20 to 50 cents per person.

- In restaurants, the *menu* usually signifies the dish of the day. If you want to choose from a selection of dishes, ask for the *kaart* (Flemish) or *la carte* (French).

- In the rue des Bouchers area of Brussels, you may find that prominently displayed menus at reasonable prices become suddenly replaced as soon as you are seated. You may be repeatedly offered house specialties at inflated prices. If this is not what you want, move on to another restaurant.

King's House Café in Brussels' Grand' Place

- For a quick snack, there are numerous fast-food outlets, stalls and, in large shopping malls, café counter service. Apart from the universal hamburgers and french fries, there is usually a big selection of *broodjes*, rolls crammed with mouthwatering fillings. Belgians' favorite snack, whether it be day or night, is a packet of *frietjes/frites* (fries) from their local *frietkot* or fries to-go outlet. *Gaufres wafels*, tasty, vanilla-flavored waffles, are another favored treat, bought fresh from street stalls and spread with chocolate sauce and/or fresh cream.

- Beer brewing is a Belgian specialty, and there are hundreds of different Belgian brews to choose from. Have a beer at lunchtime or try a *bière/bier* with your meal at a restaurant. It is perfectly in keeping with the local cuisine, which incorporates beer in many dishes. Some of the best Belgian beers can be as distinctive as wine but some have a high alcohol content.

Brussels

Brussels (Brussel or Bruxelles) takes most people by surprise. The city's name is so closely associated with the modern trappings of the European Union (E.U.) that for many it is synonymous with modern high-rise buildings and the world of suited bureaucrats.

The real Brussels has a far more colorful and resonant life. It is an exciting, modern city, yet rich in beautiful medieval and art nouveau buildings, outstanding museums and galleries, and a cultural life vibrantly international in character.

Life in the City

You may feel intimidated at first by the hectic pace of the busy streets, but Brussels is genuine "old Europe" at heart – open, friendly and welcoming. Life between the busy boulevards is engagingly relaxed. There is a wonderful variety about Brussels, a sense of its being several urban "villages" within a whole. The heart of the city lies within a barrier of encircling main roads known

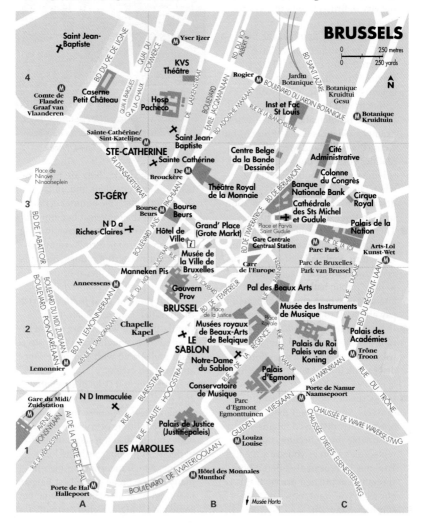

as the *Petit Ring/Kleine Ring*. You should be able to reach the inner city's finest features easily, and you should have no difficulty finding your way around; another option is to join one of the many guided tours.

For areas outside the *Petit Ring/Kleine Ring*, use the city's subway system, one of the easiest ways of getting around greater Brussels.

Medieval Townscape

Historic Brussels is celebrated by the breathtaking Grand' Place (Grote Markt, see pages 59 and 61), the best-preserved medieval townscape in Europe. North of here you will find the rue des Bouchers area, where narrow cobbled streets are lined with competing restaurants more reminiscent of Mediterranean cities. Nearby are the elegant, glass-roofed shopping malls of the 19th-century Galeries St.-Hubert.

A short distance west of Grand' Place, along rue au Beurre, is the massive neoclassical Bourse, the city's stock exchange, its front facing busy boulevard Anspach. Nearby is rue Neuve, a lively shopping street.

Head west from boulevard Anspach and discover Brussels' very old heartland of place St.-Géry, with its covered market, and place Ste-Cathérine and place du Béguinage, old cobbled squares with slightly worn but still splendid baroque churches. Between St.-Géry and Ste.-Cathérine lies rue Antoine Dansaert, a street featuring Belgian fashion stores.

Sightseeing and Shopping

Outside the Grand' Place area there are other atmospheric and stylish areas.

Le Sablon, near the southern edge of the *Petit Ring/Kleine Ring*, is convenient to the Royal Fine Arts Museums of Belgium (Musées Royaux des Beaux-Arts de Belgique, see page 60). The leafy place de Grand Sablon is the center of Brussels' antiques trade, and it has some fine restaurants and antiques shops. Just south of Le Sablon is the busy and fashionable shopping street of avenue Louise, at the heart of the upscale area of Ixelles/Elsene. This is where many of the trendy shops and restaurants are.

There is so much to see in Brussels that you'll need to use your time efficiently to visit as many of the superb attractions as possible.

Branch out beyond the *Petit Ring/Kleine Ring* to places like Heysel, 4 miles north of Grand' Place. Here stands the striking Atomium, by architect André Waterkeyn, a vast model of a metal crystal, its steel spheres gleaming in the sun. At its foot the popular Mini-Europe presents scaled-down versions of Europe's most famous buildings.

Visit the Parc du Cinquantenaire, Leopold II's 1880 celebration of the Golden Jubilee of the Belgian State. The park has a central avenue, named after John F. Kennedy, that leads to a triumphal arch linking monumental halls. Several major museums are located here.

Petit Julien

South of Grand' Place on rue du Chène (reached via rue Charles-Buls and Stoofstraat) stands the famous *Manneken-Pis* (right), a bronze fountain statuette of a naked little boy happily urinating. *Petit Julien*, as he is properly called, dates from 1619 and has long been an irreverent and endearing symbol of "carefree" Brussels.

Cuisine and Culture

Make sure you sample classic Brussels cuisine at gourmet restaurants such as Comme Chez Soi (see page 465); or try a less pricey local *geuze* or *kriek* beer in any of the café bars in and around Grand' Place and St.-Géry. Try mussels, of course, but also enjoy *paling in 't groen/anguilles au vert*, freshwater eels in sauce, or *waterzooi*, fish or chicken stew with vegetables and creamy sauce, and spoil yourself with Belgian chocolate.

Enjoy great music in the superb national opera house, Théâtre de la Monnaie, or in one of the lively rock and jazz venues. There also are colorful street theaters, annual festivals and puppet theater events for kids.

Essential Information

Tourist Information Brussels
Brussels Tourist Information Office
Hôtel de Ville, Grande' Place (Grote Markt)
Brussels Info Place, 2 rue Royale
☎ 02 5513 8940; www.visitbrussels.be
Flanders Region & Brussels Tourist Office
Marché des Herbes/Grasmarkt 61 ☎ 02 504 0390; www.toerismevlaanderen.be
Arrivals Hall Brussels International Airport
Arrivals Hall TGV/Thalys/Eurostar, Gare du Midi/Zuidstation

Urban Transportation
Brussels has three main railroad stations: the Gare du Nord/Noordstation (Brussels North), Gare Centrale/Centraal Station (Brussels Central) and Gare du Midi/Zuidstation (Brussels South). Eurostar service from London's St. Pancras International station (1 hour 51 minutes) arrives at Brussels Midi station, as does the TGV/Thalys train (1 hour 25 minutes) from Paris. For international rail information call ☎ 070 79 79 79 (Mon.–Fri. 8–8, Sat.–Sun. and public holidays 9–4:30); domestic services ☎ 02 528 2828 (daily 7 a.m.–9:30 p.m.); www.b-rail.be. There are metro (subway) stops at all three stations. Subway stations are marked on the map as "M" and are identified at entrances by a white letter "M" on a blue background. Brussels has subways, buses and an underground tram system (same ticket for all), and taxis. The subway lines have stations near major attractions. For general information about city transportation call ☎ 070 23 2000; Mon.–Fri. 8–7, Sat. 8–5 (Mon.–Fri. 8–6, Sat. 8–5, during school holidays); www.stib.be. Licensed, metered taxis can be hailed in the street or from a taxi stand at Grand' Place and at Gare Centrale; rates double when traveling outside the city. Call Taxis Bleus ☎ 02 268 0000; www.taxisbleus.be

Airport Information
Brussels International Airport is located at Zaventem, 8 miles northeast of the city. There is an Airport City Express train that runs to/from all of Brussels' main stations at 15-minute intervals (journey time 20 minutes), daily 5:30 a.m.–midnight from the airport and 5:40 a.m.–11:10 p.m. from the city. There is a Brussels International Tourism Office in the arrivals hall (daily 8 a.m.–9 p.m.). Accommodations can be reserved here, and you can obtain information about Brussels and northern Belgium. For flight information call ☎ 0900 70000 (daily 7 a.m.–10 p.m.; toll call); ☎ 32 2 753 7753 outside Belgium; www.brusselsairport.be

Climate – average highs and lows for the month

Jan.	Feb.	Mar.	Apr.	May	Jun.	Jul.	Aug.	Sep.	Oct.	Nov.	Dec.
4°C	6°C	10°C	13°C	18°C	22°C	22°C	22°C	20°C	15°C	9°C	5°C
39°F	43°F	50°F	55°F	64°F	72°F	72°F	72°F	68°F	59°F	48°F	41°F
-1°C	0°C	2°C	5°C	8°C	11°C	12°C	12°C	10°C	7°C	3°C	0°C
30°F	32°F	36°F	41°F	46°F	52°F	54°F	54°F	50°F	45°F	37°F	32°F

Brussels Sights

Cathédrale des Sts.-Michel et Gudule

Work began on the Cathédrale des Sts.-Michel et Gudule (Cathedral of St. Michael and St. Gudula) in the 13th century. Architecturally, the building shows the various forms of Brabantine Gothic that evolved over the 300 years it took to complete the work.

Inside, baroque style is lavishly celebrated by giant figures of the Apostles, while Renaissance influence shines from the fine stained glass of the 16th-century west window.

The Romanesque remains of an 11th-century church can be seen down in the crypt.

☩ C3 ✉ place Ste.-Gudule ☎ 02 217 8345; www.cathedralestmichel.be ⏰ Cathedral: Mon.–Fri. 7–6, Sat. 8:30–3:30, Sun. 2–6 (for visits); Mon.–Fri. 7–6, Sat.–Sun. 8:30–6 (for worship). Treasure Museum: Mon.–Fri. 10–12:30 and 2–5, Sat. 10–12:30 and 2–3, Sun. 2–5. Crypt: by appointment only 🚇 Gare Centrale 💰 Cathedral free; Museum $; Crypt $

Centre Belge de la Bande Dessinée

The Centre Belge de la Bande Dessinée (Belgian Center for Comic Strip Art)

encompasses a dazzling celebration of the strip cartoon, the *bande dessinée*. The strip cartoon is closely associated with Belgium, not least in the shape of Hergé's (Georges Rémi's) famous character Tin Tin, created in 1929. The labeling is in Dutch and French, but a good English-language guide is available at the bookshop. The museum building is an added delight, designed as a department store in 1906 by the architect Victor Horta (see below).

☩ B3 ✉ rue des Sables 20 ☎ 02 219 1980; www.cbbd.be ⏰ Tue.–Sun. 10–6 (library: Tue.–Thu. noon–5, Fri. and Sun. noon–6, Sat. 10–6) 🚇 Gare Centrale De Brouckère, Botanique or Rogier 🚋 Tram 92, 93, 94 🍴 Museum restaurant 💰 $$$ (includes reading room) ℹ Library: visitors over age 16 only Tue.–Sat.

Grand' Place

Brussels' Grand' Place (also see page 61), a UNESCO World Heritage Site, is an extravaganza of medieval architecture, as displayed in the numerous guild houses that complement the Place's awesome Hôtel de Ville (Town Hall, see page 61). Opposite stands the splendid La Maison du Roi (The King's House), which contains the City of Brussels Museum. At No. 10 La Maison de l'Arbre d'Or (the Golden Tree) is the Museum of Belgian Beer Brewers. At No. 13 is the Cocoa and Chocolate Museum.

☩ B3 ✉ Grand' Place ☎ 02 548 0442 (Town Hall for guided tours); www.brucity.be 🚇 Bourse, Gare Centrale 🍴 Taverne du Passage (see page 465) and t'Kelolerke on the Grand' Place ℹ Guided tours ($$) of the Town Hall in English: Tue.–Wed. at 3:15, Sun. at 10:45 and 12:15, Apr.–Sep.; Tue.–Wed. at 3:15, rest of year. Summer concerts; biennial (even years). Carpet of Flowers in mid-Aug.; medieval festival, the Ommegang, in early Jul.; Planting of the May tree procession on Aug. 9

Musée Horta

This is the house that Belgium's famed art nouveau architect, Victor Horta, built for himself. The art nouveau style,

The decorative Guild House on Grand' Place

popular in Europe and especially in Brussels between 1893 and 1918, typically used industrial materials like steel and iron in the visible parts of houses. Art nouveau originated in England with the Arts and Crafts movement, and it became known as Jugendstil in Germany and Modernismo in Spain. The movement was inspired by nature, and was a reaction against growing industrialism.

From outside, Horta's house and studio look much like the neighboring terraced houses, but the interior is light and sensuous. The beautiful stained-glass ceiling floods the superb wrought-iron stairwell with light, and gives the house a wonderfully airy feel. At the top floor is a glass-roofed conservatory with a winter garden.

➕ Off map at B1 ✉ rue Américaine 23–25 ☎ 02 543 0490; www.hortamuseum.be 🕐 Tue.–Sun. 2–5:30 🚌 54; tram 81, 91, 92, 97 ✋ $$$

Musée des Instruments de Musique

The excellent Musée des Instruments de Musique (Museum of Musical Instruments) is housed in a former department store, one of Brussels' most striking art nouveau buildings. The Old England store was built in 1899 by architect Paul Saintenoy in glass and steel. The airy and well-adapted space holds one of the largest and most varied collections of musical instruments in the world. The collection includes more than 7,000 items, dating from antiquity to the 20th century. Visitors are given infrared headphones that allow them to hear the sound of the musical instruments on display.

On the top floor is a pleasant tearoom-restaurant with a terrace offering views over the place Royale and Brussels.

➕ B2 ✉ rue Montagne de la Cour 2 ☎ 02 545 0130; www.mim.fgov.be 🕐 Tue.–Fri. 9:30–5, Sat.–Sun. 10–5. Last admission 45 minutes before closing 🚇 Gare Centrale, Porte de Namur 🚌 27, 38, 71, 95; tram 92, 94, 95 🍴 Rooftop restaurant ✋ $$; free to all first Wed. of the month after 1 p.m.

Musée de la Ville de Bruxelles

The Musée de la Ville de Bruxelles (City of Brussels Museum) is a local celebration of Brussels and has very little information in English. It merits a visit for its porcelain, pottery and tapestry collections as well as its paintings, including Brueghel the Elder's splendid piece *The Marriage Procession*.

The museum is on Grand' Place in the handsome building known as La Maison du Roi (The King's House). On the top floor there is an entertaining display of some of the more than 800 costumes comprising the "wardrobe" of the *Manneken-Pis* (see box page 57), which have been donated by heads of state and others since 1698.

➕ B3 ✉ rue du Poivre 1 (entrance from Grand' Place) ☎ 02 279 4350; www.brucity.be 🕐 Tue.–Sun. 10–5 🚇 Bourse, Gare Centrale ✋ $$

Musées royaux des Beaux-Arts de Belgique

The Musées royaux des Beaux-Arts de Belgique (Royal Fine Arts Museums of Belgium) are housed within the former court of Charles Lorraine. The entrance fee includes both the Musée d'Art Ancien (Museum of Ancient Art) and the Musée d'Art Moderne (Museum of Modern Art), linked by an underground passage. The complex contains one of the most comprehensive collections of paintings in Europe. The large Musée d'Art Ancien features Belgian and Western art from the 14th to the 19th centuries, with the Flemish Primitives including Hans Memling, the Pieter Brueghel and the Rubens collections as highlights. You'll enjoy it even more with the excellent audio guide. The vast Musée d'Art Moderne covers the 19th and 20th centuries.

➕ B2 ✉ rue de la Régence 3 ☎ 02 508 3211; www.fine-arts-museum.be 🕐 Closed for renovations and expected to reopen in 2012. Tue.–Sun. 10–5 🚇 Gare Centrale 🚌 27, 29, 38, 71, 95; tram 92, 94 🍴 Museum café ✋ $$ (includes both museums, free after 1 p.m. first Wed. of each month) ➕ English audio guide ($) is available

Grand' Place

The late medieval Grand' Place, or Grote Markt in Flemish, is one of the most glorious sights of urban Europe. A first glimpse of Grand' Place, whether by day or floodlit at night, should stop even the most jaded in their tracks. These are buildings that seem wrought from nature, yet their symmetry and elegance is ravishing. Any debate about the competing merits of traditional or Modernist architecture melts away in the face of such adventurous style. Even the bars packed full of revelers on the ground-floor premises pale into insignificance.

What you see in Grand' Place today are some of the finest examples of Flemish Renaissance and Gothic architecture, most of which are 17th-century replacements of older wooden-framed guild houses. The originals were destroyed in 1695 during a devastating bombardment of Brussels by the troops of a spiteful Louis XIV. The citizens rebuilt the heart of their city in a bold act of defiance.

The late Gothic-style Town Hall (Hôtel de Ville), dating from the 15th century, is the focus of Grand' Place (guided tours only, call 02 548 0442). Its soaring tower dominates the Brussels skyline; its facade is crammed with statues of dukes, duchesses, monks, saints and sinners.

The guild houses, which make up the remaining sides of the square, are named and represented by a collection of gilded statues, bas-reliefs, motifs and classical orders. They are a riot of exquisite forms and interesting symbols. Look for No. 7, Le Renard (The Fox), the Haberdasher's guild house; and No. 6, Le Cornet (the Horn), the guild house of the Boatmen, whose gable suggests the stern of a 17th-century sailing ship.

Opposite the Town Hall is La Maison du Roi (The King's House), known also as the Broodhuis (Bread House) and home to the City of Brussels Museum (Musée de la Ville de Bruxelles, see page 60).

On the east side of Grand' Place is the restored facade of the house of the Dukes of Brabant, six individual houses united by the cool elegance of a single Renaissance facade.

Finally, in the southeast corner to the left of the Town Hall, is No. 10, L'Arbre d'Or (The Golden Tree). This is the headquarters of the Brewers' Guild, the Knights of the Mash Staff, and also houses a Brewery Museum. Next door is Le Cygne (The Swan), complete with a graceful swan motif that rounds off the magnificent Grand' Place with a flourish.

Every two years a "carpet" of begonias is laid out in Grand' Place. The next event is in 2012

Belgium

Bruges

In Bruges (Brugge), the survival of exquisite medieval buildings provides a vivid architectural record of 16th-century Europe. Yet that survival is the result of a commercial decline that lasted for nearly 400 years. By the early 16th century, the Zwin river, which linked Bruges and its elegant canals to the North Sea, could not be navigated because of silting; the successful cloth trade had declined, and local and foreign traders moved their businesses to the flourishing port of Antwerp. There was no wealth with which to modernize the venerable townscape. We can thank the rough handling of history for a city that delights with the completeness of its medieval street plan and its ornate buildings, now a UNESCO World Heritage Site.

Finding Your Way

If you arrive at Bruges railroad station you will find a small tourist information office on Stationsplein, outside the station to the right. It is only a short bus ride from Stationsplein to Bruges' grand central square, the Markt (see pages

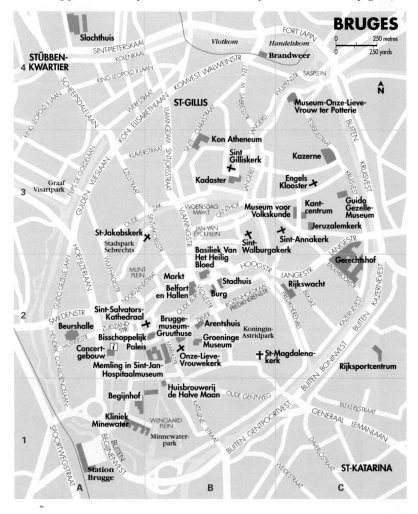

BRUGES

Sightseeing boats glide along a canal to pass under Groene Lei bridge

66–67), a good place to start sightseeing. A short walk along Breydelstraat, the street that begins at the southeast corner of the Markt, is the Burg (see pages 68–69), the historic heart of Bruges.

You can enjoy Bruges through guided tours, on foot, by bicycle, by bus or by canal boat (daily Mar.–Nov.). Trips on the famous horse-drawn carriages and trams of Bruges are enjoyable but more expensive. The city is easy to explore on your own, however.

A City of Canals

A few steps south of the Burg, along the narrow alley known as Blinde Ezelstraat (Blind Donkey Street), will bring you to the colonnaded Vismarkt (fish market), a lively scene Tuesday to Saturday mornings. From here proceed right to Huidenvettersplein, and then along Rozenhoedkaai (Rosary Quay) to the Dijver, a pretty, tree-lined walkway running alongside the canal. There is a splendid complex of museum buildings here, including the Groeningemuseum (see page 66), with a wonderful collection of paintings by the Flemish

Primitives, the Gruuthuse Museum (see page 66), which displays decorative arts, and the Church of Our Lady (Onze-Lieve-Vrouwekerk; see page 67). All are centered around Bonifaciusburg (St. Boniface Bridge), itself a reminder of medieval Bruges.

Across the road from the church is the Hans Memling Museum, which occupies the medieval St. John's Hospital (see page 67). Also nearby is the old Begijnhof (Beguinage; see page 65), and from there you can explore the city's ancient walls and gates. The many canals lend Bruges the nickname "the Venice of the north."

Lace

Bruges has long been famous for its lace. Since the 16th century, lace makers here specialized in bobbin lace, a method that used weaving and plaiting with thread-loaded bobbins, with the threads pinned to the pattern. In Italy, they made needlepoint lace, a method of embroidery with buttonhole and other stitches.

Belgium

Cosmopolitan Tastes

Amid this historical splendor, modern Bruges has its own delights. The city's social life is centered on the Market Square and 't Zand, both lined with sidewalk cafés and bars.

There is a Wednesday market on the first square and a larger Saturday Market on the latter. Between 't Zand and the Markt lie Bruges' busiest streets, Noordzandstraat and Zuidzandstraat, the latter leading into the shopping area of Steenstraat, with connecting squares and narrow streets harboring cafés and several bistros.

Eating out in Bruges is a diner's delight. You will find every type of international restaurant, but make sure you try Belgian specialties such as *kalfsblanket*, veal ragout, or *lapin à la gueuze*, which is rabbit cooked in *gueuze* beer. A warming winter specialty is *hutsepot*, a delicious hotpot made with vegetables (usually potatoes, carrots and onions) and lamb.

Lace, Chocolate and Music

If you like lace, make sure you do not miss the Gruuthuse lace shop on the Dijver for intricate, authentic work, or the many lace shops on Wollestraat, which is the street running south from the Markt.

For antiques and craft stores, Mariastraat running south from Simon Stevinplein on Steenstraat is the place to browse; and for mouthwatering chocolates, which make a good souvenir, try the locals' favorite store, Spegelaere at Ezelstraat 92, where all the chocolates and marzipan are made on the premises.

At night, Bruges spectacularly lights up; the buildings in the Markt and elsewhere are illuminated and there is plenty to keep you entertained. Find out what's happening at Cultuurcentrum (www.cultuurcentrumbrugge.be) in St. Jakobsstraat, or catch one of the summer concerts performed each year on the open-air stage on the Burg.

Essential Information

Tourist Information

Toerisme Brugge (Bruges Tourism)
Concertgebouw (Concert Hall), 't-Zand 34
☎ 050 44 4646; www.brugge.be ◉ Daily 10–6
Stationsplein, Bruges railroad station (contact details same as above)

Urban Transportation

Bruges railroad station lies a mile southwest of the Markt. The station is small, well kept and has standard facilities. There is also an efficient bus service that caters to the city and its environs (call ☎ Information line 059 56

5353). If you'd prefer to take a taxi, cab stands are at the Markt (☎ 050 33 4444) and at Stationsplein (☎ 050 38 4660).

Airport Information

Bruges does not have an airport; the nearest one is Brussels International Airport at Zaventem (see page 58). For flight information call ☎ 0900 70000; 32 2 753 7753 (outside Belgium, daily 7 a.m.–10 p.m., toll call); www.brusselsairport.be. Train connections for Bruges are made at Brussels' Nord/Noord (North), Centrale/Centraal (Central) and Midi/Zuid (South) stations.

Climate – average highs and lows for the month

Jan.	Feb.	Mar.	Apr.	May	Jun.	Jul.	Aug.	Sep.	Oct.	Nov.	Dec.
5°C	6°C	8°C	11°C	15°C	18°C	19°C	20°C	18°C	15°C	10°C	6°C
41°F	43°F	46°F	52°F	59°F	64°F	66°F	68°F	64°F	59°F	50°F	43°F
1°C	2°C	3°C	5°C	9°C	11°C	12°C	12°C	11°C	8°C	4°C	2°C
34°F	36°F	37°F	41°F	48°F	52°F	54°F	54°F	52°F	46°F	39°F	36°F

Bruges Sights

Basiliek van het Heilig Bloed

The Basiliek van het Heilig Bloed (Basilica of the Holy Blood, see also pages 68–69) has been a place of pilgrimage for centuries. The basilica consists of two chapels; the lower St. Basil's Chapel, which displays a Romanesque style, and the upper 15th-century Gothic-style chapel with the famous Relic of the Holy Blood. In the Middle Ages, this vial, containing two drops of Holy Blood, brought to Bruges in 1150 after the Second Crusade, was considered one of the holiest relics in Europe.

Veneration takes place after the Mass on Friday but the relic is on display within the reliquary at the following other times: Mon., Tue., Thu. 2–3 p.m.; Fri.–Sun. 2–4 p.m., Sun. after 11 a.m. Mass.

➕ B2 ✉ Burg 10 ☎ 050 336 792; www.holyblood. com ◷ Basilica: Thu.–Tue. 9.30–noon and 2–6, Wed. 9:30–noon, Apr.–Sep.; daily 10–noon and 2–4, rest of year. Museum: Thu.–Tue. 9:30–noon and 2–6, Wed. 9:30–noon, Apr.–Sep.; Thu.–Tue. 10–noon and 2–4, Wed. 10–noon, rest of year 🚌 All buses to station and market ▓ Chapels free; museum $

Begijnhof

The Begijnhof (Beguinage) complex, a wonderful testimony to a more sedate, spiritual age, has retained its tranquil atmosphere. It was founded in 1245 to accommodate pious single women, many of them lace makers, who lived reclusive lives. These inhabitants, known as Beguines, abandoned the complex in the 1920s, but Benedictine nuns later settled in the Beguinage and still live here today. The 17th-century little whitewashed cottages surround a peaceful square.

You can visit the Begijnhuisje (Beguine's House), a museum house that has old-style furnishings and a delightful little cloister. The Begijnhof Church of St. Elizabeth has a simple grace.

➕ B1 ✉ Wyngaardstraat ☎ 050 44 87 23 (museum reservation number) or 050 33 00 11 (monastery) ◷ Beguinage: daily sunrise–6:30 p.m. Beguine's House: Mon.–Sat. 10–noon and 1:45–5, Sun. 10:45–noon and 1:45–5. Church: daily 7–12:15 and 3–6 🚌 All buses to station and market ▓ Beguinage and church free; Beguine's House $

Belfort

Bruges' famous medieval Belfort (Belfry) dominates the Markt. You can reach the

After climbing the Belfort (Belfry) you can look down on the café-restaurants on the Markt

Allegorical Figure of the Christian Church by Master of the Legend of St. Ursula, in the Groeningemuseum

top of the 289-foot tower by climbing the 366 steps. You may marvel at the vast number of bricks and the tons of mortar holding everything together, including the 27 tons that the 47-bell carillon weighs. Below the belfry is the chamber containing the clock mechanism and copper carillon drum. The bells ring each quarter hour. You have time to watch the ingenious system whir and click into life, like a great mechanical beast, before the short climb to the belfry to enjoy the surprisingly muted peals and the view.

➕ B2 ✉ Markt ☎ 050 448 743 ⏰ Daily 9:30–5 🚌 All buses to station and market 💵 $$$ ℹ Check with the tourist office for carillon recitals

Bruggemuseum-Gruuthuse

The 15th-century city palace of the Gruuthuse family houses a collection of fine Flemish decorative arts, including a stunning display of 16th- and 17th-century tapestries. It features an interesting oratory overlooking the altar of the church next door. There is also

a fine collection of paintings by the innovative and popular Bruges-born British artist Frank Brangwyn. As well as the grand objects, the vast kitchen is a revelation, with an extensive range of crockery, cutlery and pottery.

➕ B2 ✉ Burg 12 ☎ 050 448 743 ⏰ Tue.–Sun. 9:30–5 🍴 Den Dijver, see page 466 💵 $$$ combined ticket with Onze-Lieve-Vrouwekerk Museum (includes audio guide)

Groeningemuseum

The Groeningemuseum is housed in a former Augustinian monastery on the Dijver and contains Bruges' superb civic collection of 15th- to 20th-century Flemish, Dutch and Belgian paintings. There are exceptional works here, including Jan van Eyck's *The Madonna with Canon Joris van der Paele*, the works of Pieter Pourbus and Hans Memling, and the nightmarish *The Last Judgment* by Hieronymus Bosch.

➕ B2 ✉ Dijver 12 ☎ 050 448 743 ⏰ Tue.–Sun. 9:30–5 🚌 1, 11 🍴 Den Dijver, see page 466 💵 $$$ (includes audio guide)

Huisbrouwerij de Halve Maan "straffe Hendrik"

Step into the Huisbrouwerij de Halve Maan "Straffe Hendrik" (The Half Moon "Strong Henry" Brewery), where the local Strong Henry beer has been brewed since 1546 (the present building dates from 1856). The air of the brewery is so aromatic that it might make your head spin, although a visit to the roof will clear it. To complete your visit there is a guided tour of the museum and a complimentary drink of beer at the bar.

➕ B1 ✉ Walplein 26 ☎ 050 444 222; www.halvemaan.be ⏰ Guided tours Mon.–Fri. and Sun. 11–4, Sat. 11–5, Apr.–Oct.; Mon.–Fri. 11 and 3, Sat. 11–5, Sun. 11–4, rest of year. Tours begin on the hour 🚌 1 💵 $$$

Markt

The Markt (Market Square) is a superbly atmospheric square, the heart of Bruges. The Gothic buildings of the Provinciaal Hof, seat of the government of West

Flanders, and the adjoining Central Post Office dominate the east side of the impressive square.

The Belfort (Belfry; see pages 65–66) stands on the south side. The crow-stepped gables of a row of guild houses are painted in bright colors. They stand behind a statue of Jan Breydel and Pieter de Coninck, heroes who led a 1302 uprising against French overlordship.

The west side of the Markt has a collection of handsome buildings, including the 15th-century Maison Bouchoute and the Craenenburg House (now the Café Craenenburg) flanking the entrance to Sint Amandstraat.

✚ B2 ☒ Markt 🚌 Most buses 🛈 Horse-drawn carriage trips ($$$) and mini-bus tours ($$$) start from the Markt

Memling in Sint-Jan – Hospitaalmuseum

St. John's Hospital, founded in the 12th century, was one of Europe's oldest surviving medieval hospitals, but it has been renovated into a spectacular background for Hans Memling's work.

A German painter, Memling settled in Bruges in 1465 and soon was in great demand. The chapel, which contains magnificent 15th-century Memling decorative panels and the St. Ursula Shrine, is the highlight of the complex, but the fascinating old hospital pharmacy is also worth a visit. Look for masterpieces such as the *Madonna with Child* and the *Lamentation of Christ*.

✚ B2 ☒ Mariastraat 38 ☎ 050 448 743 🕐 Tue.–Sun. 9:30–5 (pharmacy closed 11:45–2) 🚌 1 🏷 $$$ (includes audio guide)

Onze-Lieve-Vrouwekerk

The Gothic gloom of the Onze-Lieve-Vrouwekerk (Church of Our Lady) is emphasized by the continuously playing mournful piped music. Notices exhorting *stilte* (silence) will keep you hushed. Even Michelangelo's masterful sculpture the *Madonna and Child* seems constrained within the cold prison of its marble altar. Yet the church's powerful

sense of sanctity and its outstanding works of sacred art overpower the initial feeling of gloominess. The pulpit, designed by Bruges artist Jan Antoon Garemijn, is a marvelous rococo extravaganza that will cheer you on your way to the choir and the magnificent, gilded Renaissance mausoleums of Mary of Burgundy and Charles the Bold.

✚ B2 ☒ Mariastraat 🕐 Church: Mon.–Fri. and Sun. 9:30–5, Sat. 9:30–4:45. Museum: Tue.–Fri. 9:30–5, Sat. 9:30–4:20, Sun. 1:30–5. Last admission 30 minutes before closing 🚌 1 🍴 Den Dijver, see page 466 🏷 Church free; Museum $. Combined ticket with the Gruuthuse Museum $$$

Sint-Salvatorskathedraal

Bruges' churches reflect a sober Flemish style, but Sint-Salvatorskathedraal (St. Saviour's Cathedral) has many features to counteract its Gothic vastness. The high altar and the 15th-century choir stalls add a richly decorative note; the rood loft, beneath the organ case, contains a superb baroque sculpture of God the Father in white marble by Arthur Quellin the Younger. Visit the Cathedral Museum; among its treasures is the vivid realism of Dirk Bouts' 15th-century triptych *The Martyrdom of St. Hippolytus*.

✚ B2 ☒ Steenstraat ☎ 050 336 841 🕐 Cathedral: Mon. 2–6, Tue.–Fri. 8:30–noon and 2–6, Sat. 8:30–noon and 2–3:30, Sun. 9–10:15 and 2–5. Museum: Sun.–Fri. 2–5 🚌 1–5, 13, 89 and all buses that go to the market 🍴 Kardinaalshof, see page 466 🏷 Cathedral free; Museum $ 🛈 Major concerts held in cathedral

Stadhuis

The Stadhuis (Town Hall) stands in the medieval Burg (see pages 68–69) and dates from the 14th century. It has undergone renovation work over the years and has a superb carved Gothic facade. Inside this important building is the splendid former council chamber, the Gotische Zaal (Gothic Hall), where local policies were once decided.

✚ B2 ☒ Burg 12 ☎ 050 448 743 🕐 Daily 9:30–5 🚌 All buses to the Markt 🏷 Gothic Hall $ (combined ticket with Paleis van de Brugse Vrije, see page 68)

The Holy Blood Procession takes place in the town center on Ascension Day each year

A Medieval Experience:
The Burg

The Burg is medieval Bruges at its most tangible. Once it was a jealously guarded enclave, walled and with locked gates. The northern side of this outstanding architectural complex contained the 10th-century Romanesque Church of St. Donation, demolished in 1799 during the French occupation of the region. A scale model of the church under the trees on the square, the Burgplein, is a reminder of a lost final flourish to the Burg. Also on the northern side, on Breydelstraat, is the handsome baroque facade of the Provost's House of St. Donation.

On the east side of the Burg is the Paleis van de Brugse Vrije (Palace of the Liberty of Bruges). This was once the ruling seat of the Bruges Vrije, a territorial precinct of Flanders. One wing harbors a magnificent Renaissance chimneypiece created in honor of Charles V, Count of Flanders and Holy Roman Emperor. The lower section is in black marble with an alabaster frieze depicting the biblical story of Suzanna and the Elders. The main section is in exquisitely carved wood and depicts the Emperor and fellow members of the Habsburg family, the male contingent endowed with startling, embellished, Habsburgian codpieces.

To the right of the palace across narrow Blinde Ezelstraat (Blind Donkey Street) is the Stadhuis (Town Hall of Bruges; see page 67). This exquisite building dates from the 14th century but has been rebuilt and renovated over the centuries. The turreted, Gothic sandstone facade is a lyrical evocation of the mason's craft. Inside is the council chamber, the Gotische Zaal (Gothic Hall), with 19th-century romantic wall paintings that illustrate important events in the history of Bruges, and a handsome chimneypiece. Its glorious vaulted ceiling is all gilded wooden arches with slender ribs and hanging keystones. Fortunate couples are married here.

To the right of the Town Hall in the southwest corner of the Burg is the most medieval building of all, Basiliek van het Heilig Bloed (the Basilica of the Holy Blood; see page 65). In the building is a sacred vial believed to contain drops of Christ's blood, brought to Bruges in 1150 from the Holy Land by Diederik von den Elzas, count of Flanders. The Holy Blood is still

Outdoor café tables in Eiermarkt in the heart of the old city

deeply venerated every Friday. Each Ascension Day in May or June, the relic is the focus of one of the most important events in West Flanders, the Heilig-Bloedprocessie (Holy Blood Procession), a colorful and theatrical costume pageant depicting religious events, where the relic is taken around the center of town.

There is something strangely compelling about the Basilica of the Holy Blood. It has a medieval authenticity that is irresistible, even to the ungodly. The building contains an upper and lower chapel. You enter the lower chapel through a modest doorway and it is as if you are stepping straight into the Middle Ages.

The basilica dates from the 12th century and was built to house the relics of St. Basil. It has been partly restored, but is still one of the finest surviving examples of Romanesque architecture in Flanders. Squat pillars support the vaulted roof of the nave. Wall carvings are simple, almost primitive. The air is dense and exterior sounds are muffled and resonant.

Gothic Mood

You re-emerge into the daylight, pass through an enchanting Gothic doorway in the ornate facade of the main chapel and then mount a wide staircase beneath shallow vaults. The upper chapel is a breathtaking contrast to the somber Romanesque below the stairs. It is lavishly decorated in a late Gothic style that overlays original Romanesque themes. A rococo white marble altar, barrel roof, luminous stained glass, carved wood, and gold and silver artifacts all create a mood that is reminiscent of the heavy decoration of Orthodox churches.

There is a delightful spherical oak pulpit with disk canopy but with no visible access. The secret is a small door to the side of the Holy Blood altar, which opens onto hidden stairs. The Holy Blood is contained within a crystal sheath with a gold crown stopper and is supported by gilded copper and silver angels. Adjoining the upper church is a small museum with the gold and silver reliquary for the Holy Blood.

Return to the 21st century by visiting the pavilion under the trees, designed by famed Japanese architect Toyo Ito and built in 2002. This is a positive reminder that Bruges acknowledges the innovative talent of the present as well as the well-loved ornate architecture of the past.

Belgium

Ghent

At first glance Ghent (Gent or Gand), the fourth-largest city in Belgium, may seem slightly rough around the edges, a city lacking the sparkle of Luxembourg or the carefully preserved splendor of Bruges.

Ghent has been an industrial and commercial center throughout its long history, and the fabric of the city has suffered because of this. But apart from the urban realities, this is Belgium's "City of Flowers," containing some of the finest historical and cultural artifacts in Europe, along with architecture that encompasses soaring towers and exquisitely decorative domestic buildings.

Its citizens, the friendly Gentenaars, are shrewd, down to earth and personable. Many speak some English and are always ready to oblige the visitor with guidance and advice.

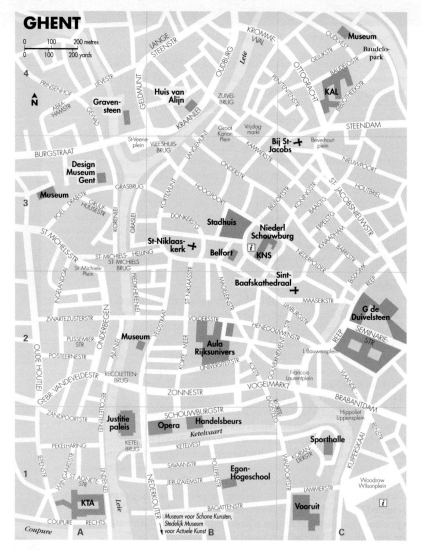

A magical scene in Ghent as nighttime descends and lights appear on buildings lining the River Leie

First Impressions

Ghent's main railroad station, Sint-Pietersstation (St. Peter's Station), is just over a mile south of the city center. The station can be a sobering experience for the first-time visitor. It is a busy place and has reasonable facilities, but there is not much information for new arrivals. Head to the heart of the city and the helpful tourist information center in the crypt of the Belfort (Belfry) in Botermarkt, Sint-Baafsplein.

Buses, trolley buses and trams leave regularly for Korenmarkt from a covered terminal on the east side of Sint-Pietersstation. Ghent's trams run along extremely narrow streets – a mildly alarming experience at first – but they do so with great efficiency. Do not be surprised to see the driver stop the vehicle, get out and adjust the sideview mirror of a parked car so that the tram may squeeze past.

The great central squares are the best places to get a handle on Ghent. Here are the powerful Gothic churches of Sint-Baafskathedraal (see page 74) and Sint-Niklaaskerk. Civic buildings between them include the Belfort (Belfry), the Lakenhalle (Cloth Hall) and the Stadhuis (Town Hall), with their distinctive mix of architectural styles. Take the glass elevator to the top of the Belfort for superb views of this remarkable city of towers and steeples.

Old Ghent

For a taste of old Ghent, go west from Sint-Niklaaskerk, past the neo-Gothic, neo-Renaissance flamboyance of the 1910 former post office, to the bridge of Sint-Michielsbrug that spans the Leie river. Look back from the bridge for a breathtaking view of the skyline. North of the bridge is Tussen Bruggen, once a busy harbor and still lined by the gabled buildings of Graslei, a popular place for taking photographs, and Korenlei.

North of Graslei is Groentenmarkt, a tree-shaded square flanked by the sturdy 15th-century Groot Vleeshuis (Great Butchers' Hall), though meat is no longer sold there. Today the Groentenmarkt is the scene of a bio produce market on Friday mornings between April and September; and an open-air art forum between 10 and 6 on Saturdays and Sundays.

A few steps farther is the Sint-Veerleplein, with a monumental baroque archway to the old fish market and handsome gabled houses. These houses are all overshadowed by the brooding mass of Het Gravensteen, the 12th-century Castle of the Counts (see page 73).

Across the street, to the east of Het Gravensteen, is the narrow, waterfront street of Kraanlei, an attractive row of late medieval buildings lining a stretch of the Leie river. This is one of Ghent's finest streetscapes. From Kraanlei's far end, the Zuivelbrug (Zuivel Bridge) crosses the canal into the square of Vrijdagmarkt, where there is a popular and large market on Fridays.

Shopping in Ghent

Ghent's main commercial and shopping area lies to the south of Korenmarkt and Botermarkt. The busy Veldstraat has stores of all types, but if you walk through the network of little streets just east of here, including Mageleinstraat, Sint-Niklaasstraat, Kortedagsteeg and Koestraat, you'll find numerous specialty shops. These include chic fashion boutiques, delicatessens, *chocolateries*, antiques and crafts shops, and Bloch, a patisserie and coffee shop that is second to none. At the heart of the area is the Kouter flower market, at its colorful best on Sundays, a vivid indication of Ghent's fame as the "City of Flowers."

Night Lights

Eating out in Ghent is an essential experience. Try such local specialties as *Gentse hazenpeper* (jugged hare) or *Gentse waterzooi van riviervis* (freshwater fish stew). There are many intimate restaurants in the Patershol area to the north of Kraanlei.

Enjoy Ghent by night, when the buildings are lit up and the streets hum with life. Spend an evening at the trendy and busy Handelsbeurs at Kouter 29 (www.handelsbeurs.be); at De Vlaamse Opera on Schouwburgstraat; or at the classical music venue Stedelijke Concertzaal De Bijloke (www.debijloke. be) on Josef Kluyskensstraat.

Essential Information

Tourist Information
Toerisme Stad Gent (Ghent Tourism)
Raadskelder, Belfort (Belfry), Botermarkt 17A
☎ 09 266 5660; www.visitgent.be

Mon.–Fri. 7–7, Sat.–Sun. 10–6;
www.delijn.be. There are taxis at the Korenmarkt and outside Sint-Pietersstation or call ☎ 0477 888 808; www.taxigent.be

Urban Transportation
Ghent railroad station (Sint-Pietersstation) is one mile south of the city center. For international rail information call ☎ 070 79 79 79 (Mon.–Fri. 8–8, Sat.–Sun. and public holidays 9–4:30), domestic services ☎ 02 528 2828 (daily 7 a.m.–9:30 p.m.); www.b-rail.be. Ghent's main bus and tram stations adjoin the railroad station. Most buses, trolley buses and trams run from the Korenmarkt. For information, call Delijn ☎ 070 220 200 (toll);

Airport Information
The nearest airport is Brussels International Airport at Zaventem (see page 58). For flight information, call ☎ 0900 70000; 32 2 753 7753 (outside Belgium, daily 7 a.m.–10 p.m., toll call). Train connections to Ghent can be made at Brussels' Nord/Noord (North), Centrale/Centraal (Central) and Midi/Zuid (South) stations. The trip from Brussels airport to Ghent takes about 30 minutes

Climate – average highs and lows for the month

Jan.	Feb.	Mar.	Apr.	May	Jun.	Jul.	Aug.	Sep.	Oct.	Nov.	Dec.
5°C	6°C	9°C	11°C	17°C	21°C	22°C	22°C	20°C	15°C	9°C	5°C
41°F	43°F	48°F	52°F	63°F	70°F	72°F	72°F	68°F	59°F	48°F	41°F
0°C	1°C	2°C	5°C	8°C	11°C	12°C	12°C	11°C	7°C	4°C	2°C
32°F	34°F	36°F	41°F	46°F	52°F	54°F	54°F	52°F	45°F	39°F	36°F

Ghent Sights

Het Huis van Alijn museum occupies several houses

Design Museum Gent

The Design Museum Gent is a Ghent experience not to be missed. Housed in the handsome old Hotel de Coninck, and with a stunning contemporary extension, the museum exhibits Belgian decorative and applied art, crafts and design from the Renaissance to 20th-century art nouveau, art deco and contemporary work.

The older part of the museum displays superb period interiors and has lucid explanations of baroque, rococo and classical styles. Look for the "banana skin" armchair.

➕ A3 ✉ Jan Breydelstraat 5 ☎ 09 267 9999; design.museum.gent.be 🕐 Tue.–Sun. 10–6 🚊 Tram 1, 3 💷 $$

Graslei en Korenlei

Graslei and Korenlei are the wharves flanking the medieval harbor Tussen Bruggen ("between the bridges") that lies to the north of the bridge of Sint-Michielsbrug. Their names relate to their role in the grain trade; their buildings were the trade and guild houses of the medieval period, carefully restored for the World Exhibition of 1913. The facades of these magnificent buildings offer an impression of Ghent in the days when the wharves were alive with the bustle of medieval trade.

➕ A3 ✉ Graslei en Korenlei 🚌 16, 18, 38 🍴 Belgaqueen, see page 467

Het Gravensteen

Magnificent Gravensteen (Castle of the Counts) has all the authentic menace of 12th-century feudalism. A visit to this well-restored building is irresistible, and merely passing through the shadowy

entrance feels like a commitment. The main castle is a series of intriguing rooms linked by staircases.

In the upper rooms there are historical exhibitions, including the Wapenmuseum (Weapons Museum) with historical weapons, and the Gerechtsmuseum (Museum of Instruments of Torture), which displays tools of torture and execution.

➕ A4 ✉ Sint-Veerleplein ☎ 09 243 9730 🕐 Daily 9–6, Apr.–Sep.; 9–5, rest of year 🚊 Tram 1, 10, 11, 12, 40, 42 🍴 De Blauwe Zalm, see page 467 💷 $$$ (includes museums) ℹ Last admission 1 hour before closing

Het Huis van Alijn

The intriguing Het Huis van Alijn (Alijn House) owes much of its charm to its location among the old buildings of the 14th-century Kinderen Alijns Hospitaal (Hospital of the Alijns Children), on the canalside street of Kraanlei. Children will be thrilled with the museum's marionette theater company, 't Spelleke van de Folklore, and other delights. The collections are spread throughout some quaint little houses surrounding a central square. The domestic and commercial life of Ghent through the ages is exhaustively represented in excellent set-piece tableaux and displays.

➕ B4 ✉ Kraanlei 65 ☎ 09 269 2350; www.huisvanalijn.be; puppet theater: 09 269 2367 🕐 Tue.–Sat. 11–5, Sun. 10–5 🚊 Tram 1, 10, 12 🍴 Museum tavern 💷 $$ ℹ Puppet shows Sat. at 2:30 (also Wed. during school holidays) ($$)

A tram on Korenmarkt in the historic center

Kraanlei

Kraanlei is one of Ghent's finest canal-side streets. Its name derives from a wooden crane that unloaded cargoes. The baroque facades of Kraanlei's buildings, with touches of Gothic, are survivors of an exuberant age of prosperity and Flemish culture. The houses have stepped gables and pediments. Look for Ghent's version of Brussels' *Manneken-Pis* (see page 57), perched above a restaurant door at the beginning of the street. Halfway along is the Het Huis van Alijn (Alijn House; see page 73). Three of the finest facades are at the far end of Kraanlei and include the exquisite 17th-century house known as "The Flying Deer."

A few steps north of Kraanlei, Patershol is a warren of cobbled streets lined with tall buildings. The area is being rejuvenated, with art galleries and trendy restaurants.

✚ A4 ✉ Kraanlei 🚊 Tram 1, 10, 11, 13
🍴 Restaurants nearby

Museum voor Schone Kunsten

The Museum voor Schone Kunsten (Museum of Fine Arts) is one of Belgium's oldest art galleries. It offers an overview of local Flemish art from the Middle Ages to the first half of the 20th century. Exhibits also offer insight into the tastes of the local bourgeoisie who were strongly connected with France but interested in the rest of Europe. The collection includes works by Flemish

and other European masters from the 14th to mid-20th centuries. Of special note are works by Hieronymus Bosch. Other superb works include Pieter Brueghel the Younger's *Wedding Feast* and Jef Lambeaux's monumental relief panel, *Human Passions*.

✚ Off map at B1 ✉ Fernand Scribedreef 1, Citadelpark ☎ 09 240 0700; www.mskgent.be
⏰ Tue.–Sun. 10–6 🚌 5, 34–36, 55, 57, 58, 70–74, 76–78; tram 1, 10 🍴 Museum café 💵 $$

Sint-Baafskathedraal

The tall four-stage tower of Sint-Baafskathedraal (St. Bavo's Cathedral) dominates the east end of Botermarkt. Externally, the cathedral is a mix of Gothic styles beneath a patina of city grime. Inside is one of the great art treasures of the world, the multipaneled *Het Lam Gods (The Mystic Lamb)*, known as the Ghent Altar (see page 75). Other treasures include the rococo pulpit in Carrara marble and Danish oak, with its carved staircases like twisted tree roots. The 12th-century Romanesque crypt of St. Baafs is full of religious artifacts and works of art.

✚ C2 ✉ Sint-Baafsplein ☎ 09 269 2045
⏰ Cathedral and crypt: Mon.–Sat. 8:30–6, Sun. 1–6, Apr.–Oct.; Mon.–Sat. 8:30–5, Sun. 1–5, rest of year. *The Mystic Lamb*: Mon.–Sat. 9:30–5, Sun. 1–5, Apr.–Oct.; Mon.–Sat. 10:30–4, Sun. 1–4, rest of year
🚌 16, 17, 18, 19, 38; tram 12, 41 💵 Cathedral and altar free; *The Mystic Lamb* $$ (includes audio guide)

Stedelijk Museum voor Actuele Kunst (S.M.A.K.)

Opposite the Museum of Fine Arts (see left) is the Stedelijk Museum voor Actuele Kunst (Municipal Museum of Contemporary Art), or S.M.A.K. Belgium's finest post-1945 art collection. It includes works by Andy Warhol, Francis Bacon, Joseph Beuys, David Hockney, Christo and Belgian artist Marcel Broodthaers, and often has outstanding temporary exhibitions.

✚ Off map at B1 ✉ Citadelpark ☎ 09 240 7601; www.smak.be ⏰ Tue.–Sun. 10–6 🚌 5, 34–36, 50, 55, 57, 58, 70–74, 76, 90 🍴 Museum café 💵 $$$

De aanbidding van Het Lam Gods – The Adoration of the Mystic Lamb

The famous Ghent Altar, *Het Lam Gods (The Mystic Lamb)*, lives up to your highest expectations. A visit to Sint-Baafskathedraal (St. Bavo's Cathedral) and a view of the altar should not be missed. This luminous work unveiled in 1432 has an impact that can change lives and attitudes.

The Ghent Altar is a polyptych, a painting made up of many panels. It is allegedly the work of two 15th-century Flemish painters, brothers Hubert and Jan van Eyck. There are doubts over whether or not Hubert van Eyck even existed, although Jan van Eyck was unquestionably the most famous painter of his generation. He was a technical master who is credited with developing oil painting to such an extent that the paint he used has retained its vivid colors, with help from restoration and refurbishment.

Two rows of paintings, one above the other, make up the altar. The centerpiece in the upper row is of Christ the King, who is flanked by the Virgin Mary, St. John the Baptist, singing angels, a musician and nude portraits of Adam and a pregnant Eve within the wing panels. The focus of the lower row is the Adoration of the Lamb of God. The flanking panels depict processions of the faithful, judges, knights, hermits and pilgrims. The painted wing panels fold over to enclose the central panels. All of this is presented in breathtaking color and luminosity against detailed Flanders landscapes.

The altar has survived the meddling of history. Iconoclasts sought to destroy it. In the 1780s, Emperor Joseph II prudishly replaced the sensual nude figures of Adam and Eve with clothed versions. During World War II, German soldiers stole the work and hid it in a mine, from which it was liberated by American troops. Two panels were stolen in 1934; the thief demanded a ransom, but was refused. The panel depicting John the Baptist was found wrapped in a blanket in Brussels Central railroad station. The panel of the Righteous Judges has never been traced and was replaced by a copy, painted by a Belgian artist, who incorporated his own likeness into one of the figures.

Lord in Majesty between the Virgin Mary and St. John the Baptist by Hubert and Jan van Eyck

Britain

Opposite: The Tudor Pond Garden at Hampton Court

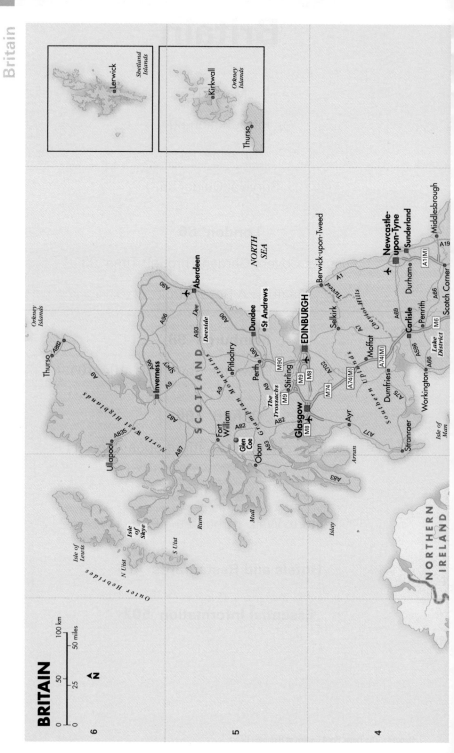

BRITAIN

100 km

50 miles

N

Shetland Islands
●Lerwick

Orkney Islands
●Kirkwall

Thurso

NORTH SEA

Orkney Islands

Thurso A882

Ullapool

Isle of Lewis

Outer Hebrides

N Uist

S Uist

Isle of Skye

Rum

Mull

Islay

North West Highlands

Inverness

A9

A82

A835

A87

A830

A96

A9

SCOTLAND

Grampian Mountains

Fort William

Oban

Glen Coe

A82

A85

A82

A83

Aberdeen

A90

A96

A93 Dee Deeside

A90

A9

Pitlochry

Perth

A90

Dundee ●St Andrews

The Trossachs

Stirling M90

M9

M9

Glasgow M8

EDINBURGH M8

M73

Ayr

Arran

A77

A71

A74(M)

A702

Southern Uplands

Cheviot Hills

Berwick-upon-Tweed

A1

Tweed

Selkirk

A7

Moffat

A74(M)

Dumfries

A75

Workington

Stranraer

Isle of Man

NORTHERN IRELAND

A7

A68

A69 Carlisle

A596

A66 Penrith

Lake District

M6

A19

Newcastle-upon-Tyne Sunderland

A1(M)

Durham

A66 Scotch Corner

Middlesbrough

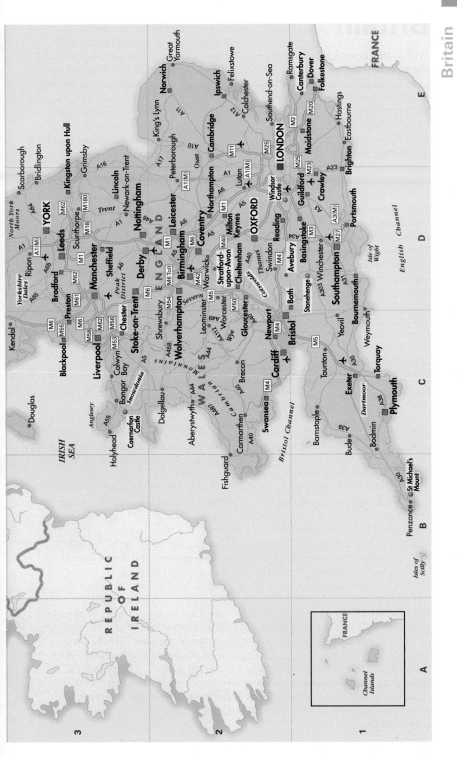

Great Yarmouth
Norwich
Felixstowe
Ipswich
King's Lynn
Colchester
Ramsgate
Canterbury
Dover
Folkestone
Southend-on-Sea
Cambridge
Peterborough
Northampton
LONDON
Maidstone
M2
Hastings
M20
Eastbourne
Brighton
Scarborough
Bridlington
Kingston upon Hull
Grimsby
Lincoln
Newark-on-Trent
Luton
Windsor Castle
Guildford
Crawley
Ripon
YORK
Leeds
Nottingham
Leicester
Coventry
Milton Keynes
OXFORD
Reading
Basingstoke
Winchester
Portsmouth
Isle of Wight
English Channel
North York Moors
Yorkshire Dales
Bradford
Manchester
Sheffield
Derby
Birmingham
Stratford-upon-Avon
Cheltenham
Swindon
Avebury
Stonehenge
Bath
Southampton
Bournemouth
Kendal
Preston
Peak District
Stoke-on-Trent
Shrewsbury
Wolverhampton
Leominster
Worcester
Gloucester
Newport
Bristol
Yeovil
Weymouth
Blackpool
Liverpool
Chester
Colwyn Bay
Bangor
Cardiff
Taunton
Exeter
Torquay
Plymouth
Douglas
Holyhead
Caernarfon Castle
Dolgellau
Aberystwyth
Carmarhen
Swansea
Brecon
Barnstaple
Bude
Bodmin
IRISH SEA
Anglesey
Snowdonia
WALES
Cambrian Mountains
Fishguard
Dartmoor
Bristol Channel
Penzance
St Michael's Mount
Isles of Scilly
ENGLAND
FRANCE
English Channel
Severn
Thames
Cotswolds
Wye
Trent
Ouse
REPUBLIC OF IRELAND
FRANCE
Channel Islands

A
B
C
D
E
1
2
3

Britain

Within this remarkable nation, an island barely 700 miles from north to south and less than 350 miles at its widest point, live just over 60 million people. From this small island, a large percentage of the world's population inherited many of the linguistic and cultural influences that shaped their lives.

A Diverse Unity

England, Scotland and Wales – collectively known as Britain – each retain individual cultural characteristics. To complicate matters further for the visitor, there are distinct regions within regions, all reflecting the resilient and determined individuality that is typically British. If you spend any time traveling through Britain, you will find that the landscape and the customs of the people change dramatically, sometimes within only a few miles.

People have been arriving at all points around Britain's corrugated coastline for centuries, but London is now the focus of the country as a whole. Here history, politics and culture meet in one of the most invigorating and exciting cities in the world.

Beyond London lies provincial and rural England. You'll find a landscape of meadows, hedgerows and woods, its earth relentlessly farmed for centuries. But much of the countryside has retained, in between the maze of roads and highways, a semblance of Old England, and in treasured corners the beauty of the past is preserved.

At Canterbury, in Kent, is the great cathedral that drew tens of thousands of medieval pilgrims to the relics of the revered Thomas Becket, the great English churchman who was murdered here in 1170. These pilgrims inspired the country's first great poet, Geoffrey Chaucer, to write his *Canterbury Tales*, as vivid a picture of the medieval world as you will find.

Yet before Chaucer and before Canterbury, the earliest Britons had raised their own pagan equivalents to the Christian cathedrals. At Stonehenge, and perhaps more hauntingly at Avebury in Wiltshire, in the heart of southern England, are the standing stones and burial chambers of Britons who commanded England centuries before Romans, Danes, Anglo Saxons and Normans ever did.

Village Greens and Seaside

Throughout scores of picturesque villages in southern and western England, you will find the essence of the country where people still play cricket on village greens, dance around maypoles on May Day and sell jars of local honey at village festivals – weather permitting, of course.

Yet England also boasts great cities and historic towns that bustle with life. The great seaport of Bristol is one. The Georgian city of Bath, where warm

---

Britain Explained

The name "Britain" (or "Great Britain") refers to the countries of England, Scotland and Wales located on the main island of Britain. To include Northern Ireland, the correct name is the "United Kingdom." The United Kingdom is the official unified entity, governed by the central parliament in London and (nominally) by Queen Elizabeth II. However, political boundaries are becoming increasingly blurred by the European Union (E.U.). Member countries are subject to E.U. rules and regulations, and regions are now being encouraged in their efforts at self-determination, with the result that Scotland and Wales – historically uneasy with what they saw as an English parliament (and Queen) in London – now have their own national assemblies and a degree of autonomy. But the legacy of London remains, and when the British talk about "this country" they usually mean Britain.

Stonehenge stone circle, on Salisbury Plain in Wiltshire, was built around 5,000 years ago

Cotswold stone and the classical elegance of 18th-century fashion conspired to create one of the world's most astounding cityscapes, seems consumed with golden light in the summer sun.

Miles of coastline fringe the English Channel. On the southern coast are the cliffs of Beachy Head, and famous resorts like Brighton and Bournemouth, as well as long stretches of undulating green and peaceful coast that run westward past Dorset's limestone cliffs and the rich red cliffs of Devon to the golden beaches of Cornwall.

From Oxford to the Lakes

North and west of London, in the counties of Oxfordshire and Warwickshire, are such cities as Oxford, university town par excellence, matched only by its rival Cambridge in the fen country of eastern England. Here, too, you will find the Cotswolds, with its beautiful honey-colored limestone villages and the historic town of Stratford-upon-Avon, home of the Bard.

Progress through the cultural heart of England is not an idyllic rural journey

by any means. Yet the cities of Manchester, Leeds, Birmingham and Liverpool are vibrant and exciting places, while historic cities such as Chester, on the Welsh Border, and York in the east have managed to preserve their medieval townscapes.

Beyond this great sprawl an unspoiled England survives. Derbyshire's Peak District, the Yorkshire Dales, the exquisite Lake District of Cumbria and

More Top Destinations in Britain

- Avebury D2
- Bath D1
- Caernarfon Castle C3
- Canterbury E1
- Chester C3
- Cotswolds D2
- Dartmoor C1
- Deeside C5
- Glen Coe C5
- Isle of Skye B6
- Lake District C4
- St. Andrews C5
- St. Michael's Mount B1
- Snowdonia C3
- Stonehenge D1
- Stratford-upon Avon D2
- The Trossachs C5
- Windsor Castle D2
- Yorkshire Dales D3

Urquhart Castle perches on the banks of the famous Loch Ness, near Inverness, in Scotland

the lonely heights of Northumberland appear like magic in the landscape.

Wild Wales

Wales is renowned as a land of poetry and song and as a part of Britain that seems older than time. In these green borderlands, the ruined castles of Norman Britain survive, relics of a time when England failed to entirely subdue the "wild Welsh." Strongholds of the Anglo-Norman conquerors, such as Caernarfon Castle, are reminders of a later age of determined feudalism. But in the beautiful countryside of central Wales, on the rugged west coast and in the great mountains of Snowdonia, the spirit of the ancient Welsh lives on, the powerful identity of modern Wales a token of that endurance.

North to the Highlands

North of Northumberland and Cumbria, the Southern Uplands guard Scotland's borderland, once infamous for its violent robber clans. It was this raw border country that gave courage to heroic Scottish patriots like Robert Bruce and William Wallace as they pitted themselves against England's might. And across these hills in 1745 marched Charles Edward Stuart – Bonnie Prince Charlie, the last of a moribund royal line – supported by the cream of the Highland clans in a doomed final gesture of defiance by Scotland against English domination.

North of the Southern Uplands are the Central Lowlands of Scotland, with the capital city of Edinburgh to the east and Glasgow, the great powerhouse of old industrial Scotland, to the west. Edinburgh is the historic distillation of all things Scottish, the political and cultural focus of the nation from a time when poet Robert Burns and novelist Walter Scott graced fashionable 18th-century salons, to the vigorous and progressive Edinburgh International Festival of today.

Across the Forth river (Firth of Forth) from Edinburgh lies the region of Fife, often referred to as the "Kingdom of Fife," home to the university town and golfing mecca of St. Andrews. To the north and west are the Scottish Highlands, Britain's most dramatic landscape, and some of the last great wilderness areas of Europe.

At the edge of the Highlands are the Trossachs, Scotland's equivalent to England's Lake District, steeped in the history of real-life characters like Rob Roy Macgregor, inspiration for the classic novels of Sir Walter Scott. Farther north are the mountains of Aberdeenshire. Here, on Royal Deeside, sits Balmoral Castle, traditional retreat of the Queen and her family.

Scotland's most spectacular mountain country lies to the far west and north, at the Pass of Glen Coe, and then for more than 100 miles northward along the west coast to Kintail and Wester Ross. Out to sea is the Isle of Skye and the misty Hebrides, romantic islands at Britain's far western edge.

Seeing the Country

Britain's essence lies in its diversity and in the hidden corners between the most popular places. Traveling independently by train or bus is one way to explore off the beaten track, but you will need to plan carefully. Britain's long-distance bus network is generally good, but away from major cities and main roads service can vary greatly. Organized bus tours, on the other hand, will whisk you efficiently to all the major tourist sights. Traveling by car is another option; Britain is so diverse that you can drive for a few hours on a main highway and then veer off onto quieter byways.

London is a year-round destination, but outside the main summer season and major vacation periods, Britain's hidden corners are quiet. May and June are good months to visit – the freshness of early June is invigorating in England's upland areas, northern Wales and the Scottish Highlands. Winter is another story, but even in December and January Britain's larger cities are vibrant; London, Manchester, Liverpool, Cardiff, Edinburgh and Glasgow all pulse with British fashion and style.

Great classical music can be savored year-round in London, Manchester and Edinburgh. Attend world-class theater in Cardiff and Glasgow. Outstanding choirs fill England's cathedrals with truly heavenly music, and the open-air performances by Welsh and Cornish choirs are enchanting. Join the singing customers or listen to folk music at a neighborhood pub, or discover a colorful local festival or time-honored custom in a Devonshire hamlet or Yorkshire town.

The Taste of Britain

The same variety applies to shopping. The British were dismissed by Napoleon as a "nation of shopkeepers," but the intended slight is actually a compliment. The British engaged in trade the world over, and today that spirit of enterprise, curiosity, good business sense and eclectic style is maintained. Fashion salons rival those in France and Italy. Britain has some of the finest antiques shops, art galleries and auction houses in Europe. Traditional and modern styles are blended to produce some colorful and out-of-the-ordinary clothing and craft items, and it is often in the provinces that the best examples are found.

Not so long ago, British food was seen as uninspired and overcooked. These days British modern cuisine is exciting yet still essentially British, the ingredients fresh and flavorful. British beer has rediscovered great traditions, too; every English county has a lively range of local ales to back up the standard brews. In Scotland, sample the best from the country's range of whiskies and superb single malts.

Timeline

8000 BC	Mesolithic hunter-gatherers journey into southern Britain.
4000 BC	Neolithic people settle in southern Britain in the latter part of the Stone Age.
circa 500 BC	Iron Age culture develops in Britain.
55–54 BC	Julius Caesar makes expeditions to Britain.
AD 43	Roman conquest of Britain begins; first settlement of London by Romans.
circa 400	Roman army and administration withdraws from Britain.
1066	Battle of Hastings; Norman Conquest of Britain.
1314	Battle of Bannockburn, in which England suffers disastrous defeat at the hands of Scotland's Robert Bruce.
1534	Henry VIII appoints himself head of the Church in England; beginning of English Reformation.
1649	King Charles I executed; Commonwealth established.
1707	Scotland and England unite by Act of Union.
1776	American colonies declare independence from Britain.
1815	Battle of Waterloo; Napoleon defeated by combined European force led by Duke of Wellington.
1914–18	Britain plays major part in World War I.
1939–44	World War II begins; Winston Churchill becomes Prime Minister of Britain; D-Day, Allied forces invade Normandy.
1945	War ends; Churchill loses in national elections.
1967	The Beatles album *Sgt. Pepper's Lonely Hearts Club Band* recorded at Abbey Road studios, London.
1973	Britain joins European Economic Community, now known as the European Union.
2003	Britain joins coalition invading Iraq.
2008	Global banking crisis leads to recession in Britain.
2011	Prince William, second in line to the British throne, marries Catherine Middleton. They take the titles of Duke and Duchess of Cambridge.
2012	Britain hosts the Olympic Games.

Protected by Sea

Britain's island location has protected it from invasion over the centuries. The country has experienced two definitive "invasions," by the Romans in the first century and by the Normans in 1066. Others tried their best. The Danes, or Vikings, steadily occupied eastern England during the ninth century but were later repulsed. The Anglo Saxons did not invade in the sense of armed occupation, but rather by a slow and steady immigration and integration after Roman withdrawal left chaos and uncertainty within the country. In later centuries Britain developed a powerful military and naval force, and although almost constantly at war with various European powers during the medieval period was itself never invaded. In more recent times both Napoleon and Hitler tried and failed to conquer. The English Channel and the surrounding seas have been Britain's greatest strategic blessing.

Watch the ceremony of the Changing of the Guard outside Buckingham Palace in London

Survival Guide

■ If visiting London, try to see one of the city's pageants, such as Trooping the Colour on Queen Elizabeth II's "official" birthday in June, or the Lord Mayor's Show in November. For something far more informal, join the fun at the fantastic Notting Hill Carnival during the last weekend (Saturday to Monday) of August.

■ In York and Bath, be careful where pedestrian zones end and traffic begins. As in all cities, watch out for pickpockets on crowded streets.

■ Try Britain's various regional foods. The national dish – fish and chips – can be found almost anywhere. In London, seek out genuine East End whelks (chewy marine molluscs). In Cornwall, look for Cornish pasties (savory pastry), a true hand-held meal. In Wales, sample Caerphilly cheese; in Yorkshire, try beef and Yorkshire pudding; and don't miss steak-and-kidney pie in any English country pub. In Scotland, tackle haggis, tatties (potatoes) and neeps (turnips), or kippers (smoked herring) – all accompanied by a thick and creamy regional beer or a good strong cup of tea with milk.

■ Be prepared for dramatic changes in the weather. They say that Britain has no climate, it just has weather. The truth is that the country is caught between the extremes of northern and southern Europe, while its island nature allows vast amounts of condensed Atlantic seawater to be deposited as wind-blown rain at regular intervals. Expect rain, and if it comes, enjoy it and carry on with your plans.

■ Make sure you always know what county of England you are in, and try not to confuse counties, especially not Yorkshire and Lancashire. Never refer to Welsh or Scottish people as English.

■ In southwest England especially, enjoy a cream tea. This grand traditional indulgence consists of a pot of tea and fresh, fluffy scones (cakes) spread with jam and delicious, thick clotted cream. The cream is either slathered on top of the jam or jam is dolloped on top of the cream.

■ The strength of the summer sun can deceive, often because there are passing clouds. Guard against sunburn even if there is a breeze.

London

London is one of the world's great experiences, a city that is always exhilarating, sometimes bewildering, sometimes exhausting, but never disappointing. This political, financial and commercial center is a year-round tourist city. The excitement is palpable.

There is a feeling that something is always happening, that you are in one of a handful of truly great cities.

London needs to be taken very much on its terms; if you do so, you will enjoy it. It is an expensive and sometimes stressful place; admission prices to major attractions are steep and the crowds of fellow visitors can be huge.

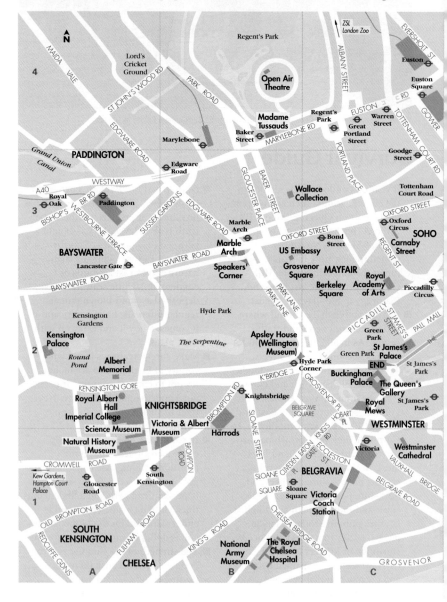

There are excellent guided tours, and bus tours are an easy way to sample all London (and beyond) has to offer. Exploring independently can be hugely rewarding, however, provided you plan well. Many attractions are some distance apart, and if you set out blindly determined to see everything you may end up frustrated and exhausted. Orient yourself by establishing two or three familiar focal points from which you can connect to other parts of the city.

Trafalgar Square to Big Ben

Trafalgar Square should be one of these focal points. It is the symbolic center of London; the towering pillar of Lord Nelson's column rises 169 feet into the

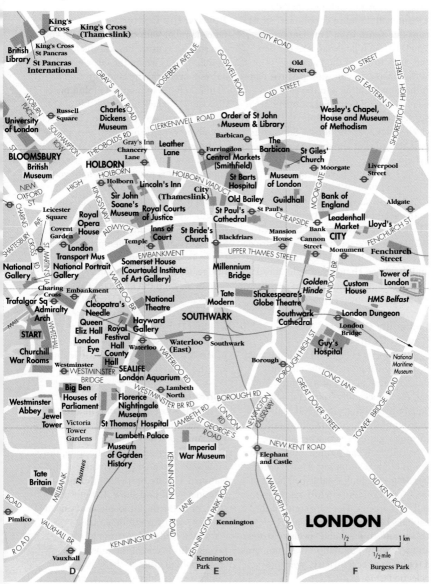

London sky. At the base of the column are fountains and monumental guardian lions. All around the central square a constant throng of people is besieged by fluttering pigeons. Trafalgar Square is overlooked from the north by the National Gallery. At the southwest corner of the square is Admiralty Arch, through which you reach The Mall and progress toward Buckingham Palace.

Whitehall, London's "political" street, runs due south from Trafalgar Square. You'll see such landmarks as Big Ben, the clock tower of the Palace of Westminster, as you walk past the Old Admiralty Building and the Horse Guards, where helmeted troopers in scarlet or blue sit immobile on their sleek, black, patient horses. Soon you pass the gates of Downing Street, where Britain's Prime Minister and Chancellor of the Exchequer have their homes. In the middle of Whitehall is The Cenotaph, a stark and simple memorial to the dead of two world wars. Beyond The Cenotaph, Whitehall merges with Parliament Street and then meets Bridge Street. To the left is Westminster Bridge and the River Thames; straight ahead are the Houses of Parliament and to the right is Westminster Abbey.

Piccadilly Circus to Covent Garden

Another focus of central London is busy Piccadilly Circus, with the elegantly poised statue of *Eros* at its center. You can reach Piccadilly from Trafalgar Square by walking along Pall Mall from in front of the National Gallery and then turning right up Haymarket. From Piccadilly you can plunge into London's world of great shopping. To the north lies Soho, the long-established heart of late-night London, slightly risqué but full of character. Here are some of the capital's best theaters, cafés and restaurants, offbeat and specialty stores, and a resident population that maintains a tradition of eccentricity, style and eclectic fashion.

Soho spills eastward through the small Chinatown area around Gerrard Street to reach Leicester Square, lined with movie theaters and restaurants. To the east, along Cranbourne and Garrick streets, is Covent Garden, a lively and entertaining venue, featuring stores, cafés, restaurants and a nonstop show of colorful street entertainers.

Beyond the Center

Once familiar with central London, you can start to venture beyond the focal points. This is where the city's excellent subway network, the Underground or "Tube," comes in handy. London buses also supply excellent service, but if you master the subway system you can reach just about everything worth seeing. Use of the subway does mean you lose some grip of how London lies above ground; sometimes it is more rewarding if you walk to your destination, if it isn't far.

Head northeast from Trafalgar Square, by subway or on foot, along the Strand, Fleet Street and Ludgate Hill, to St. Paul's Cathedral. Then proceed east to the Tower of London and Tower Bridge. Or go west from Trafalgar Square, beyond Buckingham Palace, to the great green space of Hyde Park and fashionable Knightsbridge, where you will find Harrods department store and three great museums: the Victoria and Albert Museum, the Science Museum and the Natural History Museum.

Something for Everyone

To get the most out of London during a short stay, pick and choose carefully. Visit museums in which you have a particular interest. Tackle shopping the same way. Attend a performance at the National Theatre on the South Bank, or take in a West End show. Eat out in style, or enjoy the atmosphere at one of London's many traditional pubs.

You will find a fascinating mix of people; this is one of the most cosmopolitan cities in the world. There can be a sharp edge to Londoners, but you will never be short of direction. When in doubt, remember that London police officers are perhaps the most helpful and courteous citizens of all.

Essential Information

Tourist Information

Britain and London Visitor Centre
1 Lower Regent Street, Piccadilly Circus, SW1 (personal callers only) ☎ 08701 566366 (within U.K. only); www.visitlondon.com

Urban Transportation

The London Underground or "Tube" (subway) trains operate Mon.–Sat. 4:30 a.m.–12:40 a.m., Sun. 7 a.m.–1 a.m.; Docklands Light Railway (DLR), connecting the Docklands (southeast London) with the Underground, runs Mon.–Sat. 5:10 a.m.–1 a.m., Sun. 6:30 a.m.–midnight. Services are every few minutes. The 12 Tube lines plus the DLR are named and color-coded and are divided into nine zones (Zone 1 is the central zone) on a map which posted in all subway stations. Buy tickets from attended booths in station entrance halls or from machines. For more than two trips, it is cheaper to buy a Travelcard or an Oyster card (an electronic smartcard) – both are also valid on suburban rail services and buses. The subway symbol is a red circle crossed by a horizontal line. London's red buses cover central London and suburbs and run from 5 a.m.–12:30 a.m.; many major routes operate 24 hours. Most routes in central London require that you buy tickets before you board from machines by bus stops. For information on London's public transportation call Transport for London (TFL) ☎ 0843 222 1234 (24 hours daily); www.tfl.gov.uk. London's cabs (various colors) are metered and can be expensive if traveling alone or after 8 p.m. They can be flagged in the street or at designated taxi ranks.

Airport Information

London is served by two major airports; Heathrow (☎ 0844 335 1801; www.heathrowairport.com), 15 miles west of the city, and Gatwick (☎ 0844 335 1802; www.gatwickairport.com), 30 miles south. Services below (except the subway) operate during the day, daily 5 a.m.–midnight; at night services will be less frequent. From Heathrow, the Heathrow Express (☎ 08456 001515; www.heathrowexpress.com) nonstop train goes to Paddington Station every 15 minutes; journey time is 15–20 minutes. The Heathrow Connect (www.heathrowconnect.com) makes the same journey every 30 minutes; journey time 25 minutes. The subway's Piccadilly line to central London departs every 4–5 minutes, Mon.–Sat. 5 a.m.–11:45 p.m., Sun. 5:45 a.m.–11:25 p.m.; journey time is around an hour. National Express buses (☎ 08717 81 81 78; www.nationalexpress.com) go to Victoria Coach Station, up to two buses an hour, with a travel time from 40 minutes. Taxis (expensive) are available 24 hours; travel time to central London is about an hour. From Gatwick, the Gatwick Express (☎ 08458 501530; www.gatwickexpress.com) and Southern Railway trains (☎ 08451 272920; www.southernrailway.com) go to Victoria Station every 15–20 minutes; travel time 30–40 minutes. First Capital Connect trains (☎ 08450 264700; www.firstcapitalconnect.co.uk) go to five central London stations up to every 15 minutes; travel time is 30–40 minutes. National Express buses go to Victoria Coach Station hourly; travel time takes from 2 hours 10 minutes.

Climate – average highs and lows for the month

Jan.	Feb.	Mar.	Apr.	May	Jun.	Jul.	Aug.	Sep.	Oct.	Nov.	Dec.
6°C	6°C	10°C	13°C	16°C	20°C	21°C	21°C	18°C	14°C	10°C	7°C
43°F	43°F	50°F	55°F	61°F	68°F	70°F	70°F	64°F	57°F	50°F	45°F
2°C	2°C	3°C	5°C	8°C	11°C	13°C	13°C	11°C	7°C	5°C	3°C
36°F	36°F	37°F	41°F	46°F	52°F	55°F	55°F	52°F	45°F	41°F	37°F

Britain

London Sights

British Museum

The British Museum, founded in 1753, is a treasure house of global artifacts, many of them the riches of Britain's imperial past.

There are 8 million exhibits here, including the Elgin Marbles, magnificent fifth-century BC relief sculptures taken from the Parthenon in 1801 by Thomas Bruce, the Earl of Elgin, and still the subject of Greek demands for their return.

Other highlights are the Rosetta Stone, the key to the understanding of Egyptian hieroglyphics; the 2,000-year-old Lindow Man, whose preserved body was found in an English peat bog; the Mildenhall Treasure, a collection of Roman silver; and Anglo Saxon artifacts from a ship burial discovered at Sutton Hoo on England's eastern coast during the outbreak of World War II.

Don't miss the Egyptian Galleries, the finest collection outside Egypt itself.

The Queen Elizabeth II Great Court opened in 2000. Enclosed by a massive glass roof, it is the largest covered public square in Europe. The area houses galleries, an education center, cafés and information desks and, at its heart, the Reading Room, resplendent in blue and gold. This is where Karl Marx wrote *Das Kapital*; today visitors can sit at the leather-covered desks and take in the atmosphere.

➕ D3 ✉ Great Russell Street ☎ 020 7323 8299; www.britishmuseum.org 🕐 Galleries: daily 10–5:30 (also selected galleries Fri. 5:30–8:30). Great Court: Sat.–Wed. 9–6, Thu.–Fri. 9–8:30 🚇 Holborn, Russell Square, Tottenham Court Road or Goodge Street 🚌 1, 7, 8, 10, 14, 19, 24, 25, 29, 38, 55, 59, 68, X68, 73, 91, 98, 134, 168, 188, 242, 390 🍴 Restaurant and cafés 🏛 Free; charge for special exhibitions

Houses of Parliament

The Houses of Parliament, also known as the Palace of Westminster, are mainly to be admired from the outside. The present building replaced an older palace dating from the 11th century. Most of this earlier building burned down in 1834. The structure's linear form is doubly enhanced by the vertical thrust of Victoria Tower and the clock tower known as Big Ben.

Inside access is limited because it is the workplace of British government. You can attend debates in the House of Lords

The Houses of Parliament seen across the River Thames from the South Bank

and House of Commons on a first-come-first-served basis; join the line for the "Strangers' Galleries" (public galleries) outside Cromwell Green Entrance. On Saturdays and during the summer recess (Aug.–Sep.) tours of the Houses of Parliament are available to overseas visitors. Tickets are available on the day of visit, but advance reservations are recommended (☎ 0844 847 1672).

➕ D2 ✉ St. Margaret Street ☎ 020 7219 4272; www.parliament.uk 🕐 Mon.–Thu. and some Fri. (times vary; phone for details), Oct. 3–end Jul. Closed 3 weeks at Christmas, 1 week in mid-Feb., 2 weeks at Easter and 1 week in late May; tours Sat. and during summer recess only 🚌 3, 11, 12, 24, 53, 87, 88, 148, 159, 211, 453 🚢 Westminster Millennium Pier 🍴 Café in Westminster Hall 🚇 Westminster 💷 Free; tours $$$

Imperial War Museum
Two vast guns stand in front of the handsome Ionic portico of the Imperial War Museum, where the story of modern conflict is documented. The museum was formerly the Bethlehem Royal Hospital, the notorious asylum for the insane known as "Bedlam." There are more than 50 historic aircraft, tanks and other field weapons on display, but the most fascinating exhibits involve the re-creations of World War I trench warfare and the London Blitz. The cruel lessons of conflict are not shirked, especially in the permanent exhibition on the Holocaust.

➕ E1 ✉ Lambeth Road ☎ 0207 416 5320; www.iwm.org.uk 🕐 Daily 10–6 🚇 Elephant and Castle, Lambeth North, Southwark or Waterloo 🚌 1, 3, 12, 45, 53, 59, 63, 68, 100, 159, 168, 171, 172, 176, 188, 344, 360, 453, C10 🍴 Café 💷 Free; charge for special exhibitions ℹ️ Audio tours $$

Kew Gardens
A World Heritage Site, the Royal Botanic Gardens at Kew date from 1759 and represent one of the finest collections of plants in the world, all contained within a 300-acre site. The vast Temperate House contains plants from every continent, and the architectural wonders are just as fascinating. Highlights include the Palm House, a billowing pavilion in glass and wrought iron that is a classic expression of creative 19th-century design. Scattered throughout the gardens are such interesting buildings as a 10-story, 18th-century pagoda (closed to the public) and Kew Palace. The latter was built in 1631 by a Dutch merchant and was used as a country retreat by George III. Also here is Queen Charlotte's Cottage, given by George III to his wife Charlotte and a superb example of "cottage ornée" style.

➕ Off map at A1 ✉ Kew Road, Kew ☎ 020 8332 5655 (24-hour recorded information); www.kew.org 🕐 Open daily at 9:30 a.m.; closes between 4:15 and 7:30 depending on season; times subject to change 🚇 Kew Gardens 🚌 65, 237, 267, 391 🚢 Kew Pier (Apr.–Oct.) 🍴 Restaurants and cafés 💷 $$$ (Kew Palace additional $$) ℹ️ Kew Explorer land train tour ($$), guided and self-guiding walking tours

London Eye
Built as part of the city's millennial celebrations, the London Eye is a superb feat of construction. A huge Ferris wheel-like structure, it slowly rotates (once every 30 minutes), giving visitors a bird's-eye view across London and up to 25 miles toward the horizon from within 32 glassed capsules. At 443 feet high, it is Europe's tallest cantilevered observation wheel.

➕ D2 ✉ Jubilee Gardens, South Bank ☎ 0871 781 3000; www.londoneye.com 🕐 Daily 10–9:30, Jul.–Aug.; 10–9, Apr.–Jun.; 10–8:30, rest of year. Closed for 10 days in mid-Jan. 🚇 Waterloo 🚌 77, 211, 381, RV1 🚢 Waterloo Millennium Pier 🍴 Cafés 💷 $$$

Madame Tussauds
A visit to Madame Tussauds' wax model museum could be described as blatant people-watching. It is expensive, but where else can you make faces at the rich and famous? Just about everyone is here: royalty, presidents, politicians, celebrities, stars, heroes and villains. The collections change all the time –

latest additions include *Twilight* star Robert Pattinson. The Chamber of Horrors, including SCREAM, has hideous charm, although perhaps not for the very young; the murderous are still menacing, even in effigy. In Chamber Live, actors unerringly bring to life bloodthirsty serial killers. Other attractions include Spirit of London, a quick trip through 400 years of London's history as glimpsed from a miniature city taxicab.

✚ B4 ✉ Marylebone Road ☎ 0871 894 3000; www.madame-tussauds.co.uk ⊚ Mon.–Fri. 9:30–5:30, Sat.–Sun. 9–7 (daily, 9–6 during school holidays) ⊚ Baker Street ▣ 13, 18, 27, 30, 74, 82, 113, 139, 189, 205, 274, 453 🍴 Café 💵 $$$; Chamber Live $$ extra ℹ Reserve ahead by credit card (or online for a discount) to avoid the sometimes hour-long line

Museum of London

This rewarding and enjoyable museum tells the story of London's fascinating history from prehistoric times to the present through set-piece galleries focusing on important periods.

The Roman section is superb; its reconstructed rooms, one with a fabulous mosaic floor, and its sculptures are particularly special highlights. Another highlight is the Lord Mayor's State Coach from the 1750s, a glittering golden extravaganza that is still used during the Lord Mayor's Show each November and for the coronation of a new sovereign.

The Museum in Docklands (☎ 020 7001 9844; www.museumindocklands. org.uk), affiliated with the Museum of London, brings to life dockland activity through the ages.

✚ E3 ✉ 150 London Wall ☎ 020 7001 9844; www.museumoflondon.org.uk ⊚ Daily 10–6; last admission at 5:40 ⊚ Barbican, Moorgate or St. Paul's ▣ 4, 8, 25, 56, 100, 172, 242, 521 🍴 Café 💵 Free; charge for special exhibitions

National Gallery

London's National Gallery contains one of the finest collections of Western European art in the world. You may find most of the world here on a busy day, but "the National" seems able to absorb the crowds. The collection is displayed chronologically from 1250 to 1900. You will need a floor plan to navigate. Portable audio guides are available ($$), with random-access commentaries about more than 1,000 paintings. They can also be used to follow a range of thematic tours.

Among the highlights not to miss are: Leonardo da Vinci's *Virgin of the Rocks*; Sandro Botticelli's *Venus and Mars*; Titian's vivid and agile *Bacchus and Ariadne*; Jan van Eyck's *The Arnolfini Portrait*; Diego Velázquez's sensual *The Rokeby Venus*; Rembrandt's haunting *Self Portrait at the Age of 34*; Paul Cézanne's *Bathers*; and Vincent van Gogh's *Sunflowers*.

Head to Room 34, the Sackler Room, where you are surrounded by British paintings from the late 18th century to the early 19th century – the works of English masters such as Thomas Gainsborough, Sir Joshua Reynolds, George Stubbs and J. M. W. Turner.

✚ D3 ✉ Trafalgar Square ☎ 020 7747 2885; www.nationalgallery.org.uk ⊚ Daily 10–6 (Fri. 6–9 p.m.) ⊚ Charing Cross, Embankment or Leicester Square ▣ 3, 6, 9, 11, 12, 13, 15, 23, 24, 29, 53, 77A, 88, 91, 139, 159, 176, 453 🍴 Restaurant and cafés 💵 Free. The National Gallery stages temporary exhibitions of major artists, for which there is usually an admission charge ℹ Free guided tours at 11:30 and 2:30

National Maritime Museum

A visit to the world's largest maritime museum offers insight into Britain's past maritime expertise. The Nelson and the Royal Navy gallery celebrates the great admiral, with his bullet-pierced coat from the Battle of Trafalgar adding drama. In the glass-roofed Neptune Court is the gilded state barge created for Frederick, Prince of Wales in 1732. Themed galleries tell of early explorers, the age of ocean liners, naval costumes and the British Empire. Children can try their hands at things nautical in the All

Covent Garden Through Time

London is an ever-changing city and, over the years, has evolved from surprising origins. A classic example of London's fascinating development is Covent Garden, today a lively and fashionable focus of entertainment, dining and shopping. The area gets its name from being the medieval-era "Garden of the Convent," when vegetables were grown here for the kitchens at Westminster Abbey.

During the 17th century it was laid out as the first and finest square in London, complete with the Church of St. Paul and arcaded houses. The architect was Inigo Jones, who planned it in Italianate style, with the square known as The Piazza. Then the owner of Covent Garden, the Earl of Bedford, decided to hold a market in the square. Commerce overcame culture; buildings were erected – first the older fruit and vegetable market and then the floral market. The Opera House building was added later.

In 1974 the market moved to new premises in south London and the piazza market halls were renovated and filled with new stores, cafés and restaurants that have transformed the old "Garden of the Convent" into a major leisure area.

From Covent Garden subway station, turn right and walk southeast, past Crabtree & Evelyn (renowned for bath oils and soaps) on your right, into the heart of Covent Garden. This is an excellent place to browse and wander at your leisure. There are fashion boutiques for all tastes. These line the cobbled piazza, tastefully blending in with the Italianate architecture and elegant columns. Under the glass-and-iron roof of the renovated market building set in the middle of the square, you'll find stalls selling crafts, jewelry, clothing and accessories. On the western side of the market, in front of St. Paul's Church, also known as the Actors'

Church because of its long association with the acting profession, street performers often entertain the crowds with comedy or magic tricks. You're likely to see clowns, fire-eaters, musicians and acrobats. It all adds to the exciting bustle of this area.

If you walk back toward the Covent Garden subway and head two blocks north, you will find yourself in the maze of small streets that intersect with Neal Street. Neal's Yard has a bohemian air, and there are some good places to buy vegetarian food or eat a light meal (eat in or take out). Neal's Yard Dairy sells some of the best cheese in the country – it's all British or Irish made.

Covent Garden market spreads across two levels with performers entertaining the crowds

The Millennium Bridge near St. Paul's Cathedral

Hands and Bridge galleries, while the Making Waves exhibit introduces complex oceanic processes.

🚩 Off map at F2 ✉ Romney Road, Greenwich ☎ 020 8858 4422 or 020 8312 6565 (24-hour recorded information); www.nmm.ac.uk 🕐 Daily 10–5; last admission 30 minutes before closing 🚇 Docklands Light Railway: Cutty Sark 🚌 53, 54, 177, 180, 188, 199, 202, 286, 380, 386 ⛴ Greenwich Pier 🍴 Cafés ✋ Free; charge for special exhibitions

Natural History Museum

The Natural History Museum shouldn't be missed and is a great favorite with children. The exhibitions display some fascinating specimens from the museum's incredible collection of more than 70 million items (not all on display), from the tiniest of preserved insects to a reconstructed blue whale. The museum is divided into four zones (Blue, Green, Red and Orange). The Blue and Green Zones cover life on Earth, the highlight of which is a huge, animatronic Tyrannosaurus rex, complete with smelly breath. The main exhibits tell the dinosaur story using a mix of science and entertainment to great effect. The Red Zone deals with the world beneath our feet and is every bit as fascinating; the Orange Zone contains a wildlife garden. In fall 2009 the Darwin Centre opened, where visitors can share the experience of exploring the natural world.

🚩 A1 ✉ Cromwell Road (Blue, Green and Orange zones entrance), Exhibition Road (Red Zone entrance) ☎ 020 7942 5000; www.nhm.ac.uk 🕐 Daily 10–5:50; last admission at 5:30 🚇 South Kensington 🚌 14, 49, 70, 74, 345, 360, 414, C1 🍴 Restaurant and cafés ✋ Free; charge for special exhibitions

St. Paul's Cathedral

St. Paul's Cathedral is one of Sir Christopher Wren's greatest achievements, and is easily reached from the Tate Modern on the South Bank by a walk over the Millennium Bridge. The twin towers and baroque elements of its facade and the crowning glory of its dome are still breathtaking. The airy, bright interior is full of stately monuments, memorials and statues. You can descend to the crypt, where you will find the tomb of Sir Christopher Wren among others, or ascend heavenward up 530 steps, first to the famous Whispering Gallery, where you can whisper your thoughts for everyone else to hear, on to the Stone Gallery and then to the Golden Gallery for superb views over London.

🚩 E3 ✉ St. Paul's Churchyard ☎ 020 7236 4128; www.stpauls.co.uk 🕐 Mon.–Sat. 8:30–4; closed during some services 🚇 St. Paul's 🚌 4, 11, 15, 23, 25, 26, 242 🍴 Restaurant and café ✋ $$$ ℹ Guided tours ($$) at 10:45, 11:15, 1:30 and 2; audio tours $$

Science Museum

Every aspect of science and technology is covered in this vast collection, and you will find everything from atoms to the *Apollo 10* command module. The museum's official guidebook will help you find your way around the seven floors. On display are George Stephenson's early locomotive, the *Rocket*, and Charles Babbage's enormous prototype computer. The huge Flight gallery contains ranks of aircraft, and in the Energy Hall great steam engines from the Industrial Revolution hiss and revolve. Many of the exhibits have a hands-on element. Check for any special events or demonstrations on the day you visit. The Wellcome Wing is a groundbreaking complex of up-to-the-minute exhibits that give visitors the chance to interact with and explore current scientific issues.

🚇 A1 ✉ Exhibition Road ☎ 08708 704868; www.sciencemuseum.org.uk 🕐 Daily 10–6 🚇 South Kensington 🚌 9, 10, 14, 49, 52, 70, 74, 345, 360, 414, 430, 452, C1 🍴 Restaurant and café 💲 Free; IMAX 3D cinema $$$; simulators $$; charge for some special exhibitions

Tate Britain

Tate Britain exhibits the world's greatest collection of British art, from 1500 to the present, in a mixture of historical and thematic displays. Works by major artists as diverse as Barbara Hepworth, William Hogarth and David Hockney are on display.

The Turner Collection in the Clore Gallery includes oil paintings, sketches and watercolors by J. M. W. Turner.

🚇 D1 ✉ Millbank ☎ 020 7887 8888 or 020 7887 8008 (24-hour recorded information); www.tate.org.uk/britain 🕐 Daily 10–6 (also 6–10 p.m. first Fri. of the month), last admission at 5:15 p.m. 🚇 Pimlico

🚌 2, 36, 87, 88, 185, 436, C10 ⛴ Tate Boat to Millbank Pier (from Tate Modern and London Eye) 🍴 Restaurant and café 💲 Free; special exhibitions $$$ ℹ Guided tours (free), events, talks and films

Tate Modern

Housed in the former Bankside Power Station, on the south bank of the River Thames, the Tate Modern opened in 2000. Britain's national museum of modern and contemporary art features an international collection from 1900 to the present. It includes works by major figures such as Salvador Dalí, Pablo Picasso, Henri Matisse, Edvard Munch, Piet Mondrian, Jackson Pollock, Andy Warhol and Roy Lichtenstein, as well as such contemporary artists as Damien Hirst. In a break with tradition, the collection is presented in themed groups rather than chronologically or by school. Adventurous and often controversial conceptual works and installations also are a feature.

You can approach the Tate Modern from north of the Thames across the pedestrian-only Millennium Bridge. The Tate Modern Project will extend the gallery by another 54,000 square feet by 2012.

🚇 E2 ✉ Bankside ☎ 020 7887 8888 or 020 7887 8008 (24-hour recorded information); www.tate.org.uk/modern 🕐 Daily 10–6 (also Fri.–Sat. 6–10 p.m.); last admission 45 minutes before closing 🚇 Blackfriars, Southwark, Mansion House or St. Paul's 🚌 45, 63, 100, 344, 381, RV1 ⛴ Tate Boat to Bankside Pier (from Tate Britain) 🍴 Restaurant and cafés 💲 Free; special exhibitions $$$ ℹ Guided tours (free), events and talks

Tower of London

There are crowds of visitors at London's foremost historical sight most of the year, and you may find yourself being hurried through some of the sections. Many of the nation's most daring personalities ended up here, as prisoners or as reluctant "guests," or, like Henry VIII's wives Anne Boleyn and Catherine Howard, on a final trip to the

The Tower of London was built in the 11th century

executioner's block. Tours conducted by the Yeoman Warders, or "Beefeaters," give an excellent introduction, after which you can wander at your own pace to see the Medieval Palace, White Tower, Bloody Tower, Traitors' Gate, the Crown Jewels, the Tower Ravens and the execution site at Tower Green.

✚ F3 ✉ Tower Hill ☎ 0844 482 7777; www.hrp.org. uk/toweroflondon 🕐 Tue.–Sat. 9–5:30, Sun. and Mon. 10–5:30, Mar.–Oct.; Tue.–Sat. 9–4:30, Sun. and Mon. 10–4:30, Nov.–Feb. Last admission 30 minutes before closing 🚇 Tower Hill 🚌 15, 42, 78, 100, RV1 🚢 Tower Millennium Pier 🍴 Restaurant and café 💷 $$$ (discount for online purchase) ℹ Guided tours, every half hour, included in price of ticket

Victoria and Albert Museum

The "V&A," as it is affectionately known, is recognized as being the world's greatest repository of applied and decorative art, containing ravishing collections of jewelry, silverware, ironwork, glass, ceramics, textiles, dress, furniture, sculpture, paintings, books, prints and photographs from all over the world.

The British Galleries, a chronological survey of British art and design from 1500 to 1900, are an attraction in themselves. The Medieval and Renaissance galleries (opened November 2009) alone are a day's work. The Asia, Ceramics, Glass, Sculpture and the Fashion and Jewellery galleries, along with the superb art collection, are all worth seeing. The highlight of the Metalwork collection is the national collection of English silver.

✚ A1 ✉ Cromwell Road ☎ 020 7942 2000; www.vam.ac.uk 🕐 Daily 10–5:45 (selected galleries also Fri. 5:45–10 p.m.) 🚇 South Kensington 🚌 14, 74, 414, C1 🍴 Cafés (one in garden, summer only) 💷 Free; charge for some exhibitions and events

Westminster Abbey

Westminster Abbey has been the ceremonial site of almost every British coronation, from William the Conqueror in 1066 to Queen Elizabeth II in 1953. Monarchs buried here include Henry

VII, Elizabeth I and Mary, Queen of Scots. The abbey is full of monuments and memorials to famous people from Britain's history. A tour of the many Coronation treasures offers insight into the grandeur of the occasion. The present abbey dates, in part, from the 13th century and is a powerful expression of English Gothic style.

Henry VII's chapel has a style of airy elegance that represents Gothic at its finest. Tiered sculptures line the walls, and the roof is hung with exquisite fan vaulting. The Tomb of the Unknown Warrior is to the hundreds of thousands of British servicemen killed in World War I. In the south transept is Poets' Corner, the resting place of Geoffrey Chaucer, Alfred Tennyson and others.

✚ D2 ✉ Broad Sanctuary ☎ 020 7222 5152; www.westminster-abbey.org 🕐 Mon.–Fri. 9:30–4:30 (Wed. until 7), Sat. 9:30–2:30; last admission 1 hour before closing. Cloisters: daily 8–6. Chapter House, Pyx Chamber and Abbey Museum: daily 10:30–4. College Garden: Tue.–Thu. 10–6, Apr.–Sep.; 10–4, Oct.–Mar. 🚇 Westminster or St. James's Park 🚌 3, 11, 12, 24, 53, 87, 88, 148, 159, 211, 453 💷 Abbey $$$. Cloisters, Pyx Chamber and Abbey Museum, and College Garden free ℹ Abbey tours $$; audio tour $$

ZSL London Zoo

London Zoo is irresistible for children but a treat for all, with more than 12,000 animals. The zoo has a strong conservation ethic and is working hard toward transforming the captive-animal emphasis of old-fashioned zoos.

Walk-through enclosures allow you to get even closer to animals. Into Africa brings you eye-to-eye with African animals like giraffes, zebras and okapis. Animal Adventure is a children's zoo that is great for kids.

✚ Off map at C4 ✉ Outer Circle, Regent's Park ☎ 020 7722 3333; www.zsl.org/zsl-london-zoo 🕐 Daily 10–5:30, early Mar.–late Oct.; 10–6, Jul.–Sep., Easter and public holidays in Apr.–May; 10–4, rest of year. Closes at 4:30 one week in late Oct. and in mid-Feb. 🚇 Camden Town, Regent's Park 🚌 274, C2 🚢 Waterbus from Camden Lock or Little Venice (☎ 020 7482 2550) 🍴 Cafés 💷 $$$

A Royal Stroll

Royal London begins at Admiralty Arch, at the southwest corner of Trafalgar Square. The arch dates from 1911 and was erected as part of a general celebration of Queen Victoria's life and reign. Beyond the arch is The Mall, a broad open avenue that runs southwest, directly toward Buckingham Palace. It was first laid out by Charles II in the 1660s as part of St. James's Park. It is open to traffic, but as soon as you pass beneath Admiralty Arch the city's character becomes less frantic.

Keep to the sidewalk on the left of the avenue and you'll soon pass a statue of the seafarer Captain James Cook. St. James's Park spreads out to the left – a great sweep of open lawns, trees and gardens with a lake at its heart. The right (north) side of The Mall is lined with stately buildings. First is Carlton House Terrace, broken halfway by the Duke of York's Steps that lead up to the Duke of York's Column. At St. James's Palace, sentries guard the Tudor Tower. Next to the palace is Clarence House, the official London residence of the Prince of Wales and the Duchess of Cornwall. Five of the rooms are open to the public for guided tours daily 10–4 from early August to late September (tickets must be reserved in advance; ☎ 020 7766 7303).

On your way to the large open area in front of Buckingham Palace is Lancaster House (a building now used by the government). In front of the palace is the spectacular bronze and marble Victoria Monument, erected in 1911 and constructed with more than 2,300 tons of marble. The exuberant bronze winged Victory crowns the monument.

Beyond the monument and behind a barricade of railings and gates stands Buckingham Palace. The "royal standard" (the Queen's flag) flies when the Queen is in residence. Changing the Guard takes place daily at 11:30 a.m. from May through July and on alternate days the rest of the year (weather permitting). The ceremony takes around 30 minutes to complete.

Nineteen of Buckingham Palace's state rooms are open from late July through early October (daily 9:45 a.m.–6:30 p.m.) when the royal family is not in residence. Buy a ticket on the day of your visit or in advance online at www.royalcollection.org.uk, or by calling ☎ 020 7766 7300.

The Royal Mews are worth a visit for their state carriages and splendid horses. For the walking route, see the city map on pages 86–87.

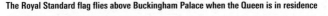

The Royal Standard flag flies above Buckingham Palace when the Queen is in residence

Edinburgh

Edinburgh is Scotland in microcosm. In this lively capital city, buildings do not overpower the spectacular landscape of hills and crags that march across the southeastern horizon. Yet Edinburgh's buildings – from the old houses of the Royal Mile to the elegant Georgian terraces and crescents of the New Town – are outstanding complements to the city's natural setting. Few other capitals seem to reflect the history and culture of their country so potently.

Edinburgh's famous castle sits high on a craggy promontory, Castle Rock, made inaccessible on three sides by steep cliffs and with a long descending ridge on its fourth side. The city's layout is linear, a pattern set by Castle Rock and Castle Ridge, down which the magnificent Royal Mile descends to the Palace of Holyroodhouse.

North of the Royal Mile lies a shallow valley once covered by swampy Nor' Loch, and now occupied by the lovely Princes Street Gardens, with Waverley Station, the city's main railroad station, at their eastern end. Above the gardens and to the north is Edinburgh's main thoroughfare, Princes Street, its south

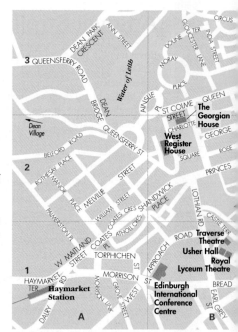

side uncluttered by buildings and thus serving as a splendid place from which to view the castle and Old Edinburgh.

First Impressions

Many visitors arrive by train at Waverley Station. Perfectly located between the old town and modern Edinburgh, Waverley Station first opened in 1846, but then was rebuilt at the end of the 19th century. Some detail of the original structure can still be seen on the domed ceiling, which is adorned with cherubs amid the fine ironwork trusses.

From the station you emerge onto Waverley Bridge and get an immediate first impression of the city's visual drama. The castle and the dark soaring back walls of the buildings that enclose the Royal Mile rise to the south, like extensions of the cliffs of Castle Rock.

From the northern exit of the station, a stairway takes you to Princes Street. Here, the Scott Monument, a towering Gothic steeple, dominates one view while the bulk of The Balmoral Hotel, itself castle-like, dominates the other.

Greyfriars Bobby

This Skye terrier's devotion to his dead master is enshrined in Edinburgh folklore. The famous Greyfriars Bobby was a trained police dog who worked with his master, Constable John Gray, guarding livestock at Edinburgh's city market, the Grassmarket, during the 1850s. When Gray died at age 45 he was buried in Greyfriars churchyard, and his devoted terrier took up what began a 14-year vigil by his grave. Bobby was cared for and beloved by everyone in the neighborhood. A statue of Greyfriars Bobby stands at the intersection of Candlemaker Row and the George IV Bridge, near the church gate and opposite a pub named after the faithful dog.

These two buildings are spectacularly illuminated at night.

From Waverley Bridge you can take an instant Edinburgh open-top bus tour that will introduce you to the city. Details about city transportation are available from Lothian Buses City Centre Travelshops at Hanover Street, Shandwick Place and Waverley Bridge. You can also find out about other guided tours from the Edinburgh and Scotland Information Centre on Princes Street, only a minute or so from Waverley Station. They include historical walking tours that take you through the Old Town's maze of historic lanes and courtyards and the highly entertaining Cadies and Witchery Tours (ghost tours and murder and mystery tours).

Two Edinburghs

Exploring the city on your own is straightforward. Old Edinburgh is the southern part, encompassed by the castle and the Royal Mile; beyond them are the areas of Southside, the Grassmarket and Canongate. To the south of the Royal Mile you will find the National Museum of Scotland (see pages 102–103) and the Edinburgh Festival Theatre, a venue presenting fine drama, ballet and opera. Edinburgh Castle (see page 101) and the Royal Mile, (see pages 104–105) are Old Edinburgh's main attractions.

You can easily spend an entire day here, and amid the souvenir shops and tourist spots there is a potent sense of history embodied by the splendid clutter of tall old sandstone buildings.

Also take time for a walk in Holyrood Park (see page 102), a lovely green world of spectacular craggy hills, lochs and glens that is a genuine slice of Highland Scotland.

North of Waverley Bridge is Edinburgh's New Town, where Old Edinburgh expanded during the 18th century as part of a typically Georgian exercise in town planning. Above Princes Street is George Street, center of Scotland's financial district, with Charlotte Square and St. Andrew Square at either end. The elegance and unity of

Georgian architecture – an exhilarating contrast to the equally splendid Royal Mile – can be appreciated at such locations as Queen Street Gardens, the Royal Circus (a circular residential street), Great King Street and Drummond Place – all north of George Street – as well as around Moray Place, west of Queen Street Gardens.

Life in Edinburgh

George Street and Princes Street, and the short connecting streets between them, are Edinburgh's main shopping streets. On Princes Street you will find an Edinburgh institution, Jenners, a labyrinthine department store that sells luxury items and has a wonderful food hall. This street also has branches of House of Fraser, Debenhams and Marks and Spencer as well as big-name brands like Gap. If you are tired of shopping, visit Rose Street, which has more pubs than any other street in Scotland.

Edinburgh is crowded during the summer, but the cultural feast of the Edinburgh International Festival, in the second half of August and early September, is well worth taking in. There also are good alternatives outside the festival season – modern Scottish drama at the Traverse Theatre, or musical performances at Usher Hall.

Stylish Edinburgh restaurants offer distinctive Scottish dishes such as wild salmon, Aberdeen Angus beef or game, such as grouse.

Local residents are friendly and always willing to help visitors. Traditional Scottish reticence is replaced here by a style that reflects sophistication without pretension, and by pride in the city's internationalism. And with a historic return to the Royal Mile by Scotland's governing body, The Scottish Parliament, Edinburgh entered the new millennium with renewed stature and optimism.

Essential Information

Tourist Information

Edinburgh and Scotland Information Centre
3 Princes Street ☎ 08452 255121 (U.K. only); 001 44 131 625 8663 (from the U.S.); www. edinburgh.org and www.visitscotland.com
Edinburgh International Airport
International arrivals area

Urban Transportation

The main railroad station is Waverley Station on Princes Street (☎ 0131 550 2031). There are good bus network services in Edinburgh. For bus information contact Lothian Buses City Centre Travelshops at Hanover Street, Shandwick Place or Waverley Bridge (☎ 0131 555 6363). Taxis can be hailed on the street or at Waverley Station and Waverley Bridge stands, or call Central Radio Taxis (☎ 0131 229 2468) or City Cabs (☎ 0131 228 1211).

Airport Information

Edinburgh Airport (☎ 0844 481 8989; www.edinburghairport.com) is 8 miles west of the city center. Airlink 100 buses go to Waverley Station every 10 minutes (20 minutes early morning), daily 4:30 a.m.– 12:22 a.m.; travel time 25 minutes. Night Bus N22, departing every 30 minutes, operates daily 12:47 a.m.–4:15 a.m.

Climate – average highs and lows for the month

Jan.	Feb.	Mar.	Apr.	May	Jun.	Jul.	Aug.	Sep.	Oct.	Nov.	Dec.
5°C	6°C	7°C	10°C	13°C	16°C	18°C	17°C	15°C	12°C	9°C	6°C
41°F	43°F	45°F	50°F	55°F	61°F	64°F	63°F	59°F	54°F	48°F	43°F
1°C	1°C	2°C	4°C	6°C	9°C	11°C	11°C	9°C	6°C	4°C	2°C
34°F	34°F	36°F	39°F	43°F	48°F	52°F	52°F	48°F	43°F	39°F	36°F

Edinburgh Sights

Key to symbols
➕ map coordinates refer to the Edinburgh map
on pages 98–99 🎟 admission charge: $$$ more
than £6, $$ £2–£6, $ less than £2
See page 5 for complete key to symbols

Calton Hill

Calton Hill, at the east end of Princes
Street, is crowned with neoclassical
buildings that have earned Edinburgh
the nickname "The Athens of the
North," though their dark stonework is
very different from the bare, bright
brilliance of the Parthenon or the
Temple of the Winds. There are great
views of Princes Street, Edinburgh
Castle and Arthur's Seat from this
hilltop, as well as Holyrood Park and
the Salisbury Crag. You can also climb
the 143 steps of the tall monument to
Admiral Horatio Nelson for an even
better view from its top. This site should
be avoided at dusk and after dark.

Calton Hill ➕ D3
Nelson Monument ✉ Calton Hill
☎ www.edinburghmuseums.gov.uk 🕐 Mon. 1–6,
Tue.–Sat. 10–6, Apr.–Sep.; Mon.–Sat. 10–3, rest of year
🚍 1, 3, 5, 7, 8, 14, 22, 25, 39, 30, 31, 33, 34, 37, 37A,
47, X47, 48, 49 🎟 $$

Edinburgh Castle

You can tackle Scotland's most visited
attraction in several ways. There are
official guided tours (included in
admission), which are entertaining
and informative.

A self-guiding audio tour ($$) is a
good option that helps focus the mind
amid inevitable crowds. you will need
to brace yourself for the One O'Clock
Gun, a 25-pounder that blasts off a
single blank charge from the Half
Moon Battery at 1 p.m. on Monday
to Saturday.

Highlights are the tiny, 12th-century
St. Margaret's Chapel (dedicated to
Margaret, mother of David I); the Stone
of Destiny; the Prisons of War exhibition
in the Vaults; the mighty medieval siege
gun, Mons Meg, which stands in grim
splendor like some huge black beast;
and the 16th-century Great Hall with its
glorious hammerbeam roof and masses
of weaponry.

The Honours of Scotland exhibition
is a journey through history that
culminates with a display of Scotland's
Crown Jewels.

➕ B2 ✉ Castlehill ☎ 0131 225 9846;
www.edinburghcastle.gov.uk 🕐 Daily 9:30–6,
Apr.–Sep.; 9:30–5, rest of year 🚍 2, 23, 27, 35, 41, 42,
45, 67 🍴 Cafés 🎟 $$$

Ramsay Garden, a range of private apartment buildings, seen from the Scott Monument

The Dugald Stewart Monument on Calton Hill has a clear view to Edinburgh Castle

The Georgian House

The Georgian House is the showplace of New Town's Charlotte Square and one of the most prestigious addresses in Scotland. Designed in 1791 by Robert Adam, this masterpiece of urban design was once home to the chief of the Lamont clan. Three floors are open, all full of delectable furnishings and beautiful paintings. The basement houses the wine cellar and kitchen.

⊞ B2 ✉ 7 Charlotte Square ☎ 0844 493 2118; www.nts.org.uk ⊙ Daily 10–6, Jul.–Aug.; 10–5, Apr.–Jun. and Sep.–Oct.; 11–4 in Mar.; 11–3 in Nov. Last admission 30 minutes before closing ▣ 3, 10, 19, 33, 41, X48 ▮ $$

Holyrood Park

Few cities are blessed with such a marvelous open space as Holyrood Park, or Queen's Park as it is also known. The park is dominated by the Salisbury Crags and by Arthur's Seat, a high, rounded hill. You can enter the park from the bottom of the Royal Mile (see pages 104–105), just beyond the Palace of Holyroodhouse (see page 103). The high ground is encircled by a public road, the Queen's Drive, but the area is better enjoyed on foot. A slanting path slices up the slopes below Salisbury Crags. It takes you high above the city, and the views are outstanding. Arthur's Seat can be climbed, but it is challenging; hiking boots are recommended. However, you can keep to the low ground of the park and still enjoy the splendid sights.

⊞ E1 ✉ Queen's Drive ☎ 0131 652 8150; www.historic-scotland.gov.uk ▣ 35, 36 ▮ Free

National Gallery of Scotland

The National Gallery is a large, 19th-century neoclassical building with a good selection of works from the early Renaissance to the end of the 19th century, including *The Trinity Altarpiece*, by Hugo van der Goes, and the seductive *Venus Anadyomene*, by Titian. Most of the major names in 17th-century European art are represented; there are some fine landscapes by Claude Lorrain, and Nicholas Poussin's *Seven Sacraments* are on display. There is a powerful work by Frederick Edwin Church, *Niagara Falls, from the American Side*. Scottish painting is well represented by Gavin Hamilton and Allan Ramsay. Sir Henry Raeburn's *The Reverend Robert Walker Skating on Duddingston Loch* and Sir George Harvey's *The Curlers* are wonderfully lively and very typical Scottish narrative works.

⊞ C2 ✉ The Mound ☎ 0131 624 6200 or 0131 624 6336 (24-hour recorded information); www.nationalgalleries.org ⊙ Daily 10–5 (also Thu. until 7), Sep.–Jul.; daily 10–6 in Aug. ▣ 1, 3, 4, 10, 11, 12, 15, 16, 17, 22, 23, 25, 26, 27, 29, 30, 31, 33, 34, 36, 37, 37A, 41, 42, 44, 45, 47, X47, 48 ▮ Restaurant and café ▮ Free; charge for special exhibitions

National Museum of Scotland

The National Museum of Scotland incorporates what used to be known as the Royal Museum in a bold space completed in 2011. The older part of the museum has retained its impressive Victorian ironwork grand gallery, though this now houses an grand floor-to-ceiling display of artifacts.

Along with the dramatic modern buildings, in golden stone, the museum tells the story of Scotland from its geological beginnings to the 21st century. There are new sections particularly aimed at children and highlighting the relationship between Scotland and the wider world. The core of the complex contains several levels, each displaying a particular era of Scotland's history. Make sure you pick up a copy of the floor plan from the information desk in the entrance hall, where you can get advice on finding your way around. You can also check the plasma screens for help.

🔲 D1 ✉ Chambers Street ☎ 0131 225 7534; www.nms.ac.uk ⏱ Daily 10–5 🚌 23, 27, 35, 41, 42, 45 🍴 Restaurant and cafés 🎫 Free; charge for special exhibitions ℹ Free guided tours

Palace of Holyroodhouse

Her Majesty Queen Elizabeth II's official residence in Scotland, Holyroodhouse was part of the Abbey of Holyrood, but much of the present palace was built during the reign of King Charles II. The severe neoclassicism of the courtyard block reflects the distinctly English fashion of the time; nevertheless it exudes Scottish history. The State Apartments are luxurious and grand, with artifacts and paintings elegantly displayed beneath superb stucco ceilings. Deep in the historic apartments is the bedchamber of Mary, Queen of Scots and the adjoining closet where, in 1566, her secretary and confidante, David Rizzio, was stabbed to death by associates of the Queen's delinquent husband, Lord Darnley. The Queen's Gallery, in an adjacent building, has exhibitions of art from the Royal collections. Behind the palace is Holyrood Park (see page 102), a wide open space dominated by Arthur's Seat, a great volcanic plug.

🔲 E2 ✉ Canongate ☎ 0131 556 5100; www.royalcollection.org.uk ⏱ Daily 9:30–6, Apr.–Oct.; 9:30–4:30, rest of year. Last admission 1 hour before closing 🚌 35, 36 🍴 Café

🎫 $$$ (includes audio tour) ℹ Closed for state functions. See the website for details

Royal Botanic Garden Edinburgh

The Royal Botanic Garden Edinburgh is just a mile north of the New Town. Rhododendrons are the highlight of Scotland's premier garden, at their colorful best from late April to early June. Other attractions are the glasshouses, where orchids, palms and other exotics flourish in defiance of Scotland's less than tropical climate; the Chinese Hillside; a decidedly Scottish heather garden; and the outdoor café with great views of the city.

🔲 Off map at C3 ✉ Inverleith Row ☎ 0131 552 7171; www.rbge.org.uk ⏱ Daily 10–6, Feb.–Oct.; 10–4, rest of year. Glasshouses 10–5:30, Feb.–Oct.; 10–3:30, rest of year. Last admission 30 minutes before closing 🚌 8, 17, 23, 27 🍴 Resturant and café 🎫 Free; glasshouses $$ ℹ Guided tours Apr.–Sep. at 11 ($$)

St. Giles' Cathedral

St. Giles' Cathedral (or the High Kirk of Edinburgh) is the mother church of Scottish Presbyterianism and a powerful feature of the Royal Mile (see pages 104–105). The Kirk is a mix of medieval Gothic and Georgian Gothic, the latter grafted on in the early 19th century; the interior reflects an enthusiastic Victorian restoration. There are some superb external features, including the 19th-century west door and the late medieval tower and spire, a dramatic sight on the skyline. Inside, the cathedral has many fine features and memorials. The Thistle Chapel was built in 1911 as a private chapel for the Knights of the Most Ancient and Most Noble Order of the Thistle. Richly carved stonework enlivens the interior of the chapel. Look near the entrance door for the tiny bagpipe-playing angel.

🔲 D2 ✉ Royal Mile ☎ 0131 225 9442; www.stgilescathedral.org.uk ⏱ Mon.–Fri. 9–7, Sat. 9–5, Sun. 1–5, May–Sep.; Mon.–Sat. 9–5, Sun. 1–5, rest of year 🚌 23, 27, 28, 35, 41, 42 🍴 Café 🎫 $$ (donations) ℹ Guided tours for groups only (free)

Many visitors buy a tartan garment; those with Scottish ancestors can choose a clan tartan

Stroll Down the Royal Mile

Edinburgh's Royal Mile is the epitome of Old Edinburgh. Made up of four linked streets – Castlehill, Lawnmarket, High Street and Canongate – it descends the sloping back of a long, steep-sided ridge from Edinburgh Castle (see page 101) at the west end to the Palace of Holyroodhouse (see page 103) at the east end. On either side of the Royal Mile are tall buildings, riddled with courtyards and passageways known as "closes" and separated by narrow streets known as "wynds," all of it a delight to explore. All the way down the Royal Mile historic buildings punctuate the streetscape, and there are numerous stores, cafés, restaurants and pubs.

You can begin a relaxed descent of the Royal Mile from the entrance to the Castle Esplanade, starting with Castlehill. Attractions beckon from both sides. On the left is the Tartan Weaving Mill and Exhibition, with its masses of tartan cloth and working mill. On the right is the Scotch Whisky Experience, which offers a fun barrel-ride tour and tasting. Next on the left and well worth a visit is the fascinating Camera Obscura and World of Illusions, where moving images of the surrounding area are projected onto a white viewing table. The street is narrow here but opens up just past the powerful Highland Tolbooth, a handsome Gothic building with the tallest spire in Edinburgh. It is now The Hub, home of the Edinburgh International Festival and a focus of the city's cultural life. At this point, the Royal Mile becomes the much wider Lawnmarket, once the city's linen market.

Keep to the left side of the street, where steps rise from street level to the sidewalk. There are several stores here selling woolen and tartan goods. Soon you come to Gladstone's Land, a 17th-century merchant's house now restored by the National Trust for Scotland. The house's Painted Chamber is stunning. Just a bit farther is the entrance to Lady Stair's Close. A narrow alleyway leads to an open square and to Lady Stair's House, now The Writers' Museum, a quiet little corner housing memorabilia associated with Scotland's finest writers, including Robert Burns, Robert Louis Stevenson and Sir Walter Scott. The spiral stairs have an uneven step halfway up, a common trick in medieval houses aimed at tripping an intruder in the dark.

The Lawnmarket reaches an intersection with Bank Street and the street called George IV Bridge, where the Royal Mile becomes High Street. Here

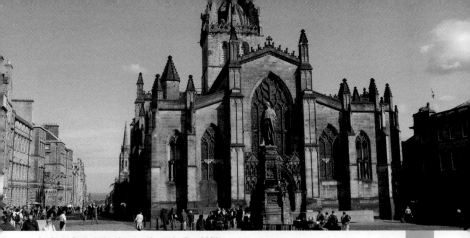

St. Giles' Cathedral and a view down the Royal Mile

you will find a remarkable concentration of historic buildings. On the east corner with Bank Street is the High Court, with a bronze statue of Scottish philosopher David Hume in front of it. Next to the High Court is Edinburgh City Chambers, with an arcaded entrance screen. Opposite is St. Giles' Cathedral (see page 103). Behind the cathedral is Parliament Square and the old Parliament House, seat of the Scottish Parliament until the union with England in 1707. Directly opposite St. Giles', in Warriston's Close, is the intriguing The Real Mary King's Close, a historically accurate interpretation of life in Edinburgh from the 16th to the 19th centuries.

High Street then descends gently to a junction with North and South Bridge Street. Stay on the north side of High Street, past the entrances to various alleys, and look for Chalmer's Close.

Go through the entrance and down the steps to the preserved apse of the 15th-century Trinity College Church, home to the Brass Rubbing Centre.

On the other side of High Street opposite Chalmer's Close is the entertaining Museum of Childhood. Farther down High Street, just before the intersection with Jeffrey Street and St. Mary's Street, is the John Knox House, a celebration of the 16th-century religious reformer who brought the Protestant Reformation to Scotland with more than a whiff of fire and brimstone. Beyond Jeffrey Street the Royal Mile becomes Canongate and narrows once more.

Halfway down Canongate is the old Tolbooth, with its wonderful clock and conical-roofed towers. Canongate Tolbooth was once a courtroom and jail and is now The People's Story, an exhibition of Edinburgh life. Just opposite is The Museum of Edinburgh, a beautifully restored late 16th-century building containing an excellent collection of artifacts of Edinburgh life.

Diagonally opposite The Museum of Edinburgh is the 17th-century Canongate Kirk and Kirkyard, which has a wonderfully bright interior. The church has close royal connections; the royal family worship here when they are in residence at nearby Holyroodhouse, and the royal coat of arms can be seen decorating one of the church benches, or pews. A short distance past the church the Royal Mile passes The Scottish Parliament building to the right, and continues as Abbey Street to end its progress through Scottish history at the gates of the Palace of Holyroodhouse (see page 103). For the walking route, see the city map on pages 98–99.

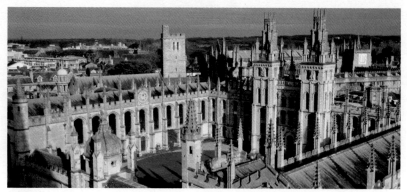

Looking down onto the soaring spires of All Souls College from the Church of St. Mary the Virgin

Oxford

Oxford, 56 miles northwest of London, is a typical English market town at heart. It is located within a hollow amid low hills at the gentle confluence of the River Thames and River Cherwell.

What makes Oxford exceptional is its university, the oldest in the English-speaking world, an institution that consists of not one single campus but 39 independent colleges that are scattered throughout the city. They represent elegant seats of learning, but they are also blessed with beautiful, historic buildings.

The history of Oxford is said to have begun with the founding of a priory by the Saxon St. Frideswide, near where the River Thames and River Cherwell meet. Christ Church Cathedral supplanted the priory, and in time wealth from the medieval wool trade led to the founding of other religious houses, where learning was revered. Scholars were drawn to Oxford, and from these beginnings the university evolved.

Unless you're a student, Oxford is more of a journey through history and great architecture than through academia. For the visitor, the experience may seem faintly voyeuristic. You visit the colleges, picking your way through elegant quadrangles, chapels, arched passageways, gardens and libraries, and at times you may feel you are intruding on a select world of academic privilege and of cultural paradigms. Yet the physical integration of Oxford's colleges with the realities of Oxford as a city dispel any sense of intrusion. This is a living, working city that retains its own identity and commercial life.

Take a ride on an open-top bus to see the principal sights, leaving the bus where and when you like, or take a

The Original Alice

The children's books *Alice in Wonderland* and *Alice Through The Looking Glass* were inspired by Oxford life. Charles Lutwidge Dodgson, a writer, mathematician and ordained deacon at Christ Church, wrote the books during the latter part of the 19th century. Dodgson was the oldest of 11 children born to his clergyman father and from an early age he loved to entertain his siblings with stories and poems. He formed an intense friendship with Alice Liddell, the young daughter of the Dean of Christ Church, and enjoyed entertaining her and her two sisters with his stories of Wonderland. Dodgson later published his stories under the pseudonym Lewis Carroll. Alice's Shop is where the real-life Alice bought her candy. It also sells Alice memorabilia (✚ A1 ✉ 83 St. Aldates ☎ 01865 723793; www.aliceinwonderlandshop.co.uk 🕐 Daily 9:30–6:30, Jul.–Aug.; 10:30–5, rest of year).

guided walking tour of historic Oxford or of the colleges. Stroll by the Thames or take a river cruise.

Oxford's Colleges

You can walk around central Oxford in less than an hour, but it is the density and complexity of colleges and great buildings that is so absorbing. The heart of the university lies between High Street and Broad Street and is enclosed by the colleges of Brasenose, All Souls, Hertford and Exeter. The University Church of St. Mary the Virgin (see page 110) is on High Street. Behind St. Mary's is Radcliffe Square, which has the elegant 18th-century Renaissance rotunda of the Radcliffe Camera (chamber) at its heart. On the east side of the square is All Souls College. On the west side is Brasenose College, named after a traditional brass "mask" door

knocker and a treasured college possession; a replica can be seen on the great oak doors.

From Radcliffe Square you can walk into the Schools Quadrangle of the Bodleian Library, with its superb Jacobean entrance tower and decorative inner walls. Through the arch on the north side of the quadrangle is the Sheldonian Theatre, where the *Encaenia* (the ceremony to confer honorary degrees each June) and the degree ceremony for Oxford graduates are held.

The Radcliffe Square area is the heart of the university, but try to visit some of the colleges when their grounds are open to the public (get the free leaflet *Visiting the University of Oxford* from the Tourist Information Centre). Include Christ Church (see page 109), the largest and most famous of the colleges, and do not miss nearby Merton College,

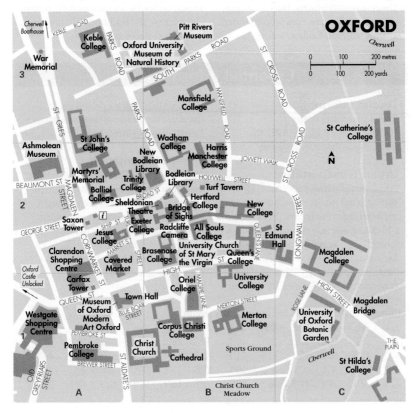

reputedly the oldest of them all and certainly one of the finest, with its delightful gardens, ancient quadrangle, medieval library and chapel. Adjoining Merton Street, cobbled and quiet, is one of the finest parts of the city. Merton counts among its alumni 14th-century religious reformer John Wycliffe, poet T. S. Eliot and actor-singer Kris Kristofferson. Then head east toward Magdalen (pronounced "Maudlin") and its superb tower, Cloister Quad, gardens and riverside walks. Magdalen alumni include playwright Oscar Wilde and actor Dudley Moore.

The Market Town

Oxford itself is famous for automobile manufacturing, and is the home of the Morris Oxford and the T-series MG sports car. They were produced at Oxford's Cowley factories, built up by William Richard Morris, later Viscount Nuffield, a self-made man who founded Oxford's Nuffield College among his numerous charitable acts. Visit the Museum of Oxford (see page 109) and discover the history of the city, and take in the Pitt Rivers Museum and the Oxford University Museum of Natural History (see page 110). Climb to the top of Carfax Tower for great views.

The streets radiating from Carfax constitute Oxford's main shopping area. Cornmarket has a range of well-known stores. Off Cornmarket's east side is Golden Cross, where Shakespeare's plays are said to have been performed. Just beyond is the celebrated covered market, with more than 50 shops and outlets under one roof.

Oxford's university population and townspeople exhibit a fascinating contrast of lifestyles. In medieval times this duality led to occasional bloody battles, but although today's students are noted for their boisterous post-exam antics, Oxford is an eminently civilized place where the traditions of "town and gown" rest easily side by side.

Essential Information

Tourist Information

Tourist Information Centre
15–16 Broad Street ☎ 01865 252200;
www.visitoxfordandoxfordshire.com

Urban Transportation

Oxford railroad station, Botley Road (☎ 08457 484950); offers regular train connections to and from London Paddington. Central Oxford is a 10-minute walk from the station. Local bus services in and around the city are frequent. Two companies provide all local services: The Oxford Bus Company (☎ 01865 785400) and Stagecoach Oxford (☎ 01865 772250). Taxi stands are located at the railroad station, Carfax and the Gloucester Green bus station. Call 001 Taxis (☎ 01865 240000).

Airport Information

The Airline buses (☎ 01865 785400) depart every 20 or 30 minutes for London Heathrow Airport (every two hours through the night) and every hour for London Gatwick Airport (every two hours through the night). Birmingham Airport has daily rail (☎ 08457 484950) and bus (☎ 08717 818181) connections to and from Oxford.

Climate – average highs and lows for the month

Jan.	Feb.	Mar.	Apr.	May	Jun.	Jul.	Aug.	Sep.	Oct.	Nov.	Dec.
7°C	7°C	10°C	13°C	16°C	16°C	21°C	18°C	18°C	14°C	10°C	8°C
45°F	45°F	50°F	55°F	61°F	61°F	70°F	64°F	64°F	57°F	50°F	46°F
3°C	3°C	4°C	5°C	8°C	10°C	13°C	13°C	11°C	8°C	6°C	4°C
37°F	37°F	39°F	41°F	46°F	50°F	55°F	55°F	52°F	46°F	43°F	39°F

Oxford Sights

Ashmolean Museum

The Ashmolean is a fascinating
museum of grand oddities and elegant
art, housed in a neoclassical building
dating from the 1840s. It is the oldest
museum in Britain, founded in 1683,
and its extensive collection includes
much medieval material; Greek,
Roman and Egyptian artifacts; and
fine Asian porcelain.

The museum reopened in November
2009 following a major redevelopment
that doubled its gallery space and added
an innovative approach to the way the
collection is displayed. The Egyptian
collection received a modern makeover
in 2011.

🔲 A2 🖂 Beaumont Street ☎ 01865 278 002;
www.ashmolean.org 🕐 Tue.–Sun. and public
holidays 10–6 🚌 All city center buses 🍴 Café
🔳 Free

Christ Church

Oxford's largest college, Christ Church,
is the most visited of all the university's
colleges. Visitors enter through a
turnstile by the War Memorial Gardens
in the street known as St. Aldates, where
college "bulldogs," immaculately dressed
custodians in bowler hats, cheerfully
order you around.

The present cathedral dates from the
12th century. Among its fine features are
exquisite stained-glass windows. Tom
Quad is Christ Church's glorious central
quadrangle; Mercury Pond, with
Mercury Fountain at its center, adds an
elegant accent. The figure of Mercury
often sprouts neckties and other
"outfits" donated by students. The
entrance to Tom Quad and to Christ
Church is the mighty gate tower, Tom

Tower, that holds a massive seven-ton
bell, Great Tom. Visit Christ Church's
vaulted Great Hall, the Picture Gallery of
Old Master works of art, and Canterbury
and Peckwater quadrangles.

🔲 A1–B1 🖂 College and cathedral: St. Aldates.
Picture Gallery: Oriel Square ☎ College and cathedral:
01865 276492; www.chch.ox.ac.uk. Picture Gallery:
01865 276172; www.chch.ox.ac.uk/gallery 🕐 College
and cathedral: Mon.–Sat. 9–5, Sun. 2–5. Picture
Gallery: Mon.–Sat. 10:30–5, Sun. 2–5, May–Sep.;
Mon.–Sat. 10:30–1 and 2–4:30, Sun. 2–4:30, rest of
year 🚌 All city center buses 🔳 College and cathedral
$$; Picture Gallery $$ 🔳 May close at short notice.
Check with the tourist office

Museum of Oxford

The Museum of Oxford, housed in the
Town Hall, has well-arranged displays
and gives an excellent account of
Oxford's history. Everyone who played
a part in the making of Oxford is here,
from prehistory through the Roman,
Saxon and Norman periods to the
present day. The realities of town life
from both sides of the tracks are
depicted through 19th-century house
interiors from middle- and working-
class districts. There is a program of
changing exhibitions covering subjects
from Roman times to space travel.

🔲 A1 🖂 Town Hall, St. Aldates ☎ 01865 252761;
www.museumofoxford.org.uk 🕐 Tue.–Thu. and Sat.
10–5 🚌 All city center buses 🍴 Café 🔳 Free
(donations) 🔳 Audio tours ($$)

Oxford Castle Unlocked

Eleventh-century Oxford Castle, a place
of incarceration from 1071 to 1996 and
once as notorious as Colditz, unlocked
its doors to the public for the first time
in 2007. Visitors can experience
something of the austere confines of
prison life over the centuries as people
and events from the site's turbulent past
are brought to life. Those with the
energy to climb the 101 steps of the
Saxon St. George's Tower are rewarded
with panoramic views of Oxford. The
19th-century wing of the prison has
been converted into a luxurious hotel.

➕ Off map at A1 ✉ 44–46 Oxford Castle ☎ 01865
260666; www.oxfordcastleunlocked.co.uk 🕐 Daily
10–5 (last tour 4:20) 🚌 4, 5, 13, X3 🍴 Restaurant
💲 $$$

Oxford University Museum of Natural History

This museum is housed in an Italianate-Gothic-style 19th-century building. The interior is a single open space, surrounded by an ambulatory and forested with slender iron columns that support a wrought-iron vault and glass roof. Exhibits range from dinosaur skeletons to minerals and fossils.

You can access the Pitt Rivers Museum from the rear of the building.

➕ B3 ✉ Parks Road ☎ 01865 272950; www.oum.
ox.ac.uk 🕐 Daily 10–5 🚌 2, 7A, 27 💲 Free

Fascinating Pitt Rivers Museum has been revamped

Pitt Rivers Museum

Founded in 1884, this fascinating museum is a marvelous example of 19th-century museum culture. It houses more than a million objects from many cultures around the world, including jewelry, pots, masks, boats, armor and weaponry, textiles, toys and medical and musical instruments. The museum includes also the often wildly eccentric collection of Lieutenant General Augustus Henry Lane Fox Pitt Rivers, who served throughout the British Empire and gathered many artifacts along the way.

After several months of closure, the museum opened its doors in May 2009 to reveal a vastly improved facility.

➕ B3 ✉ South Parks Road (enter through the Oxford
University Museum of Natural History) ☎ 01865
270927; www.prm.ox.ac.uk 🕐 Mon. noon–4:30,
Tue.–Sun. 10–4:30 🚌 2, 7A, 27 💲 Free

University Church of St. Mary the Virgin

St. Mary the Virgin is both the parish church of Oxford and the university's church. It forms the southern side of Radcliffe Square. The early 14th-century tower rises above Oxford's dreaming spires, domes and cupolas. The south porch, facing High Street, is a 17th-century addition that trumpeted Italian influence with its twisted columns and heavily decorated segmented arch.

You can climb up the tower's 124 steps as far as the base of the spire, and though the up and down flow of people can cause traffic jams, there is a resting place in the bell room halfway up.

➕ B2 ✉ High Street ☎ 01865 279111;
www.university-church.ox.ac.uk 🕐 Daily 9–6,
Jul.–Aug.; 9–5, rest of year (tower not open until 11:45
on Sun.) 🚌 All city center buses 🍴 Café 💲 Church
free; tower $$

University of Oxford Botanic Garden

The University of Oxford Botanic Garden was founded as a "physic garden" in 1621 and is Britain's oldest botanic garden. This delightful enclave has a collection of around 7,000 plant species. The River Cherwell and Magdalen College's tower enhance the setting, and the original layout survives today. There also are splendid greenhouses with 100-year-old cacti.

➕ C1 ✉ Rose Lane ☎ 01865 286690;
www.botanic-garden.ox.ac.uk 🕐 Daily 9–6 (last
admission at 5:15), May–Aug.; 9–5 (last admission at
4:15), Mar.–Apr. and Sep.–Oct.; 9–4:30, rest of year
🚌 5, 7A, 8, 9, 10, 13, 15, 16, U1, U5, X13 💲 $$

Shakespeare's Stratford-upon-Avon

Stratford-upon-Avon was the birthplace of William Shakespeare and today the town is something of a shrine to the poet-playwright, its numerous Tudor and Jacobean half-timbered houses enhancing the Shakespearean theme. Shakespeare's Birthplace on Henley Street has been restored with late 16th-century furnishings and is full of fascinating memorabilia. Another fine old building in the town is the Elizabethan Harvard House, which, although having no connection to Shakespeare, is interesting as the birthplace of John Harvard, who founded Harvard University in Massachusetts.

After an intriguing life, Shakespeare died in 1616 at the early age of 52 in a house called New Place in Stratford. The original house no longer exists as it was demolished by the owner in 1759 because he found visitors a nuisance. The foundations remain and are adjoined by the Elizabethan-style Knott Garden and Nash's House, the superbly restored 17th-century home of Thomas Nash, husband of Shakespeare's granddaughter, Elizabeth Hall.

Another famous Stratford building is the 13th-century Holy Trinity Church, where Shakespeare was baptized in 1564, located on the banks of the River Avon. Here you will see the remarkable alabaster bust of Shakespeare, modeled on a wax impression of the playwright's face at his death. Nearby is Shakespeare's tomb and those of his wife, Anne Hathaway, and their daughter, Suzanna. On the banks of the River Avon to the north of the church is the Royal Shakespeare Theatre, where the Royal Shakespeare Company performs the Bard's plays.

Arrange day trips to Stratford at the Oxford Tourist Information Centre or through Cotswold Roaming.

Oxford Tourist Information Centre ✉ 15–16 Broad Street, Oxford OX1 3AS ☎ 01865 252200; www.visitoxfordandoxfordshire.com

Cotswold Roaming ✉ 11 St. Andrew's Lane, Headington, Oxford OX3 9DP ☎ 01865 308300; www.cotswold-roaming.co.uk

Anne Hathaway's Cottage, just west of Stratford, was the childhood home of Shakespeare's wife

York

Two thousand years of English history are written across the face of York. Within the old city's walls, and within sight and sound of the magnificent York Minster cathedral, narrow, cobbled streets, ancient remains, medieval buildings, historic churches and award-winning museums sit happily alongside modern stores, restaurants and hotels.

York, although a city, is a small town at heart. It began life as a riverside encampment established by an ancient British tribe, the Brigantes. In turn, the Brigantes were usurped in AD 71 by Roman invaders who made York their empire's northern European capital. Anglo Saxons, who established York as a center of early Christianity, followed the Romans. In AD 867, the settlement was captured by the Danes – the plundering Vikings of romantic history.

In subsequent centuries York fell under the control of the Normans, who laid the first substantial foundations of the present minster and built the original city walls. During the 16th and 17th centuries, religious and dynastic struggles kept the city in the national forefront, at a time when poverty, plague and famine often made ordinary life harsh and terrible. As a major religious center, York suffered significantly as the monasteries were suppressed and church-owned houses in the city were seized and sold on to rich merchants under orders from the reigning monarch – King Henry VIII.

The more enterprising world of the 18th and 19th centuries and the emergence of York as the railroad capital of northern England made the city a fashionable commercial center, one that was only lightly touched by the more brutal aspects of the Industrial Revolution. Today visitors walk on hallowed ground that has supported more than 2,000 years of human achievement, as well as misery.

Sightseeing in York

Many parts of central York are pedestrian-only, and though crowds may throng the narrow streets, people have precedence over vehicles. In the nicest areas of old York there is no stream of roaring traffic pinning you to the sidewalk. You go with the flow, but there is no rush-hour element even during the busiest times of day.

The exterior of York Minster, northern Europe's largest Gothic cathedral

York

York's flavor can be captured via a York City Sightseeing open-top double-decker bus or in a horse-drawn carriage. The inner city can be explored on one of numerous city tours, led by local experts. Or you can take an evening "ghost walk," complete with an entertaining guide and actors making impromptu, phantom appearances in dark alleys. Leisurely daytime guided walks take in the city walls and navigate ancient streets.

You could also explore on your own. Central York is not large, and you're never far from the next fascinating building, museum or attraction. Few houses in York rise above two or three stories, and the sun finds its way into hidden corners, lighting the upper parts of old buildings. Take time as you stroll to appreciate the colorful facades and architectural features, like Stonegate's little red devil above the corner with Coffee Yard Lane.

The many different people who colonized York left an engaging but confusing legacy of local words. The word "bar" means gate and refers to the magnificent stone gateways, such as Bootham Bar and Monk Bar, that punctuate the city walls. On the other hand, the Viking word "gate," as in Stonegate and Petergate, means street.

Walk part of the city walls for a superb overview of York. Try the section from Monk Bar (location of the fascinating Richard III Museum), at the north end of Goodramgate, to Bootham Bar at the west end of High Petergate. The views of York Minster along this stretch of the

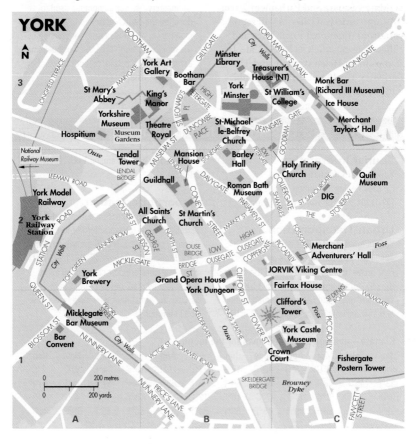

city walls are outstanding. Visit such main attractions as York Minster and JORVIK Viking Centre, but do not neglect other sights – like the hands-on archeological DIG in St. Saviour's Church and The York Dungeon on Clifford Street, both great fun for children. Enjoy the talented street entertainers and the many festivals and events staged here each year.

Shopping in Old York

Shopping in York is fun. Streets such as Stonegate and The Shambles are overflowing with specialty stores, including antiques shops, art and craft galleries, bookstores, jewelers, tea blenders and boutiques. Every major chain store is represented in the main shopping areas of Coney Street, St. Mary's Square and Parliament Street.

A huge variety of eateries will tempt you, from traditional English tea and coffee houses – such as Bettys Café Tea Rooms in St. Helen's Square and The Earl Grey Tea Rooms in The Shambles – to numerous restaurants, offering a choice of dining experiences. Authentic English pubs include Stonegate's Ye Old Starre Inne and the 15th-century Black Swan, on Peasholme Green.

York is essentially English at heart, but its northern regional identity makes it very different from London and southern England. Expect friendliness and helpfulness from locals, but be prepared for that matter-of-fact approach for which Yorkshire people are famous. You will be given facts rather than fiction and guidance rather than gossip to help you get the best out of the heartland of historic England.

Minster

The Old English word "Minster" was used in medieval England as a variant of the word "monastery." It was sometimes used to describe the church attached to a monastery, which was used for worship by the monks. Through time the word became associated with certain cathedral churches, like York Minster.

Essential Information

Tourist Information
York Visitor Information Centre
De Grey Rooms, Exhibition Square
☎ 01904 550099; www.visityork.org

Urban Transportation
York railroad station, Station Road (☎ 08457 484950). The center of York is pedestrian-only. First buses operate in and around the center of the city; for information ☎ 01904 551400. There are taxi stands at York railroad station and at Duncombe Place, near York Minster.

To hire a taxi call Streamline Taxis (☎ 01904 638833).

Airport Information
Leeds Bradford International Airport (☎ 0871 288 2288; www.leedsbradfordairport.co.uk), 31 miles southwest, is a 45-minute drive from York. Manchester airport (☎ 0871 271 0711; www.manchesteraiport.co.uk) is 56 miles southwest by road, but has direct train services to York; either way it's a travel time of 90 minutes.

Climate – average highs and lows for the month

Jan.	Feb.	Mar.	Apr.	May	Jun.	Jul.	Aug.	Sep.	Oct.	Nov.	Dec.
6°C	7°C	9°C	13°C	16°C	19°C	21°C	20°C	18°C	14°C	9°C	7°C
43°F	45°F	48°F	55°F	61°F	66°F	70°F	68°F	64°F	57°F	48°F	45°F
0°C	1°C	2°C	4°C	7°C	10°C	12°C	11°C	10°C	7°C	4°C	2°C
32°F	34°F	36°F	39°F	45°F	50°F	54°F	52°F	50°F	45°F	39°F	36°F

York Sights

Inside the paneled Merchant Adventurers' Hall

Fairfax House

This elegant house was lavishly decorated by Viscount Fairfax in 1759, but was neglected in later years. It was bought in 1980 by the York Civic Trust, which carried out an extensive and inspired restoration. Today, Fairfax House is one of the finest examples of an 18th-century town house in Britain. Enjoy the sumptuous plasterwork ceilings, damask hangings, marble fireplaces and magnificent furnishings. ✚ B2 ✉ Castlegate ☎ 01904 655543; www.fairfaxhouse.co.uk ⏰ Tue.–Sat. 10–5, Sun. 12:30–4., Mon. guided tours only at 11 and 2. Closed Christmas and Jan.–early Feb. 🚌 4 🖐 $$

JORVIK Viking Centre

This very popular attraction reveals the archeological remains of Viking York, or Jorvik, unearthed here from 1976 to 1981. Deep underground, you're shuttled back in time 1,000 years to a reconstructed Viking street complete with thatched houses, lifelike figures and the evocative sounds and smells of everyday life.

Traveling in a "time capsule" back to the year AD 975, you "fly" across the city, over streets and backyards, to discover how a Viking settlement of 10,000 people functioned on this very site. ✚ B2 ✉ Coppergate ☎ 01904 543400; www.jorvik-viking-centre.co.uk ⏰ Daily 10–5, Apr.–Oct.; 10–4, rest of year. Last admission 1 hour before closing 🚌 6, 10, 11, 12, 13 🍽 Café 🖐 $$$

Merchant Adventurers' Hall

This medieval guildhall is the finest of its kind to survive in Europe. Its brick and timber-framed exterior, the vast, open timberwork of the Great Hall and the interior paneling effortlessly transport visitors from the present into a convincing medieval environment. The hall was built from 1357 to 1361 by a religious fraternity that evolved into a merchants' guild, which survives today as a charitable organization and guardian of this outstanding building. ✚ C2 ✉ Fossgate ☎ 01904 654818; www.theyorkcompany.co.uk ⏰ Mon.–Thu. 9–5, Fri.–Sat. 9–3:30, Sun. noon–4, Apr.–Sep.; Mon.–Fri. 9–4, Sat. 9–3:30, rest of year 🚌 10 🖐 $$; audio tour included in admission

National Railway Museum

For travel enthusiasts young and old, this atmospheric museum – the world's largest – offers vivid insight into 200 years of transportation history. There are displays of more than 100 steam, diesel and electric locomotives, including a working replica of George Stephenson's famous 1829 *Rocket*; the wonderful *Mallard*, still the fastest steam engine in the world; the *Flying Scotsman* (undergoing restoration so not always on display), one of the world's most famous steam locomotives; and the only Shinkansen (Bullet Train) outside Japan. ✚ Off map at A1 ✉ Leeman Road ☎ 0844 815 3139; www.nrm.org.uk ⏰ Daily 10–6 🚌 Park & Ride 2; "Road Train" from Duncombe Place (next to York Minster) every 30 minutes, daily 11:15–4:15, Apr.–Oct.; Sat.–Sun. 11:5–4:15 in Mar. 🍽 Restaurant and café 🖐 Free; charge for special events

York Art Gallery

The excellent collection in this small, friendly gallery provides an overview of

600 years of Western European art from the Italian Renaissance to the present day. There are a number of paintings by York artist William Etty, who liked exuberant nudes, and a collection by 20th-century potters such as Bernard Leach and Shoji Hamada.

➕ B3 ✉ Exhibition Square ☎ 01904 687687; www.yorkartgallery.org.uk 🕐 Daily 10–5 🚌 1, 5, 6 🍴 Café 💷 Free

York Castle Museum

This museum is housed in two former prisons. Behind the building's handsome neoclassical facade is an outstanding collection of exhibits illustrating the social history of York, and of Britain, over the past 400 years. Walkways lead past vivid reconstructions of complete Victorian and Edwardian streets, lined with old stores full of authentic contents. Allow several hours to get the most out of the experience, which also includes a visit to the cell that once held highwayman Dick Turpin.

➕ C1 ✉ Eye of York ☎ 01904 687687; www.yorkcastlemuseum.org.uk 🕐 Daily 9:30–5 🚌 4 🍴 Café 💷 $$$ (valid for one year). Children free with paying adult

York Minster

York cathedral's present foundations were laid by the Normans in the 12th century and this is northern Europe's largest Gothic cathedral. A visit to the Minster is a historical as well as a religious experience; the walls are crowded with dramatic monuments and the architectural features are superb.

Past the broad introductory nave is the central crossing, where north and south transepts, nave and choir all meet below the soaring vaulted roof of the central tower, 200 feet above. The choir is full of intricate design and ornamentation. At the east end of the church you will find the Lady Chapel and the great East Window – as big as a tennis court and the largest medieval stained-glass window in the world. Also visit the intriguing Crypt, where the pillars are

York Minster seen from the medieval city walls

from the original Norman church. In the Chapter House, look for the wickedly irreverent figures of priests and prelates among the carvings above the encircling stalls. You can climb the 275 spiral steps of the great 234-foot tower, but only if you're fit.

➕ B3 ✉ Minster Yard ☎ 0844 939 0011; information Sat. and Sun. ☎ 0844 939 0016; www.yorkminster.org 🕐 Minster: Mon.–Sat. 9–5:30, Sun. noon–3:45, Apr.–Oct.; 9:30–4:30, Sun. noon–3:45, Nov.–Mar. Tower: Mon.–Sat. 9:45–4:45, Sun. 12:45–4:45 (open later during peak times), Apr.–Oct.; Mon.–Sat. 10:15 to 30 minutes before dusk, Sun. 12:30 to 30 minutes before dusk, rest of year. Undercroft, Treasury and Crypt: Mon.–Sat. 9:30–5, Sun. 12:30–5. Hours may change according to church services

🚌 1, 5, 6 🍴 Restaurant 💷 $$$ (separate charges to Minster, Tower and Undercroft, Treasury and Crypt) ℹ Free guided tours (Mon.–Sat.)

Yorkshire Museum and Gardens

This eclectic treasure house includes some of the finest Roman, Viking, Anglo Saxon and medieval artifacts in Europe. The 10-acre grounds feature fine gardens that contain York's oldest ruin, the Multangular Tower, part of fourth-century Roman fortifications.

The luminous Middleham Jewel, a 15th-century sapphire set within a gold pendant, engraved back and front, is a major exhibit. Also of interest is a collection of sea dragons from the Jurassic period. The museum building incorporates part of the ruins of medieval St. Mary's Abbey. This section, with its haunting reconstructions and medieval music, is a delight.

➕ A3–B3 ✉ Museum Gardens ☎ 01904 687687; www.yorkshiremuseum.org.uk 🕐 Museum: daily 10–5. Gardens: daily 7:30–6 (open later from late Mar.–late Oct.) 🚌 1, 5, 6 💷 $$$ (valid for one year); gardens free

Walk Through the Past

York's appeal stems largely from the survival of its central core of streets in their original form. While many cities and towns had their centers remodeled over the years, central York was spared wholesale change. Plans to demolish the city walls during the Victorian period were resisted, and within the precise boundaries of those restored walls the narrow streets and interlocking alleys and courtyards make up one of the best-preserved late medieval cities in Europe.

Many of York's old houses are not the original buildings; they have been rebuilt or restored over time. But their styles are medieval, and so venerable is the layout of central York that when you walk down Stonegate you follow the exact line of the Roman approach road to the imperial encampment of AD 71.

The most famous of York's ancient thoroughfares is The Shambles, a narrow street overhung by timber-framed houses. Its name derives from the butchers' shops and slaughterhouses once located here. The Shambles today is a delight. It typifies York's medieval character, but in times past this would have been a filthy, raucous, rough-and-ready place that would horrify modern sensibilities. Today it can be enjoyed for its quaintness, free of medieval realities. Don't miss bustling Newgate Market, with more than 100 stalls (open daily), between Parliament Street and The Shambles, where – within the rules of modern hygiene and legality – some of the liveliness of medieval times still survives.

To get the most out of old York, explore the interlocking alleys that connect the center. Wander at will with a city map, which will show you the main landmarks, but investigate the twists and turns of the numerous passages leading off Stonegate, Petergate, Davygate and Church Street. They'll land you unexpectedly in the bustle of St. Helen's Square, with its handsome Mansion House and Guildhall, or in King's Square, where old gravestones make up part of the paving. Brimming with charming little shops, cafés and restaurants, old York exudes unforgettable character.

The overhanging houses, so typical of The Shambles, are atmospheric at night

Czech Republic

Opposite: The Astronomical Clock in Prague was installed in the 15th century

Czech Republic

Since November 1989, the people of this landlocked country have been embracing change and finding their footing as a new republic. In that year, the Velvet Revolution saw Czechoslovakia throw out 40 years of Communist rule without firing a shot. In 1993, Czechs and Slovaks amicably split into the Czech Republic and Slovakia. More than 20 years later, the Czech Republic is a sucessful, prosperous member of the European Union.

Bohemia and Moravia

Most visitors head straight for Prague, but there is plenty to enjoy in the country's diverse landscapes. Locked between Poland, Germany, Slovakia and Austria, the republic takes in two regions: Bohemia, surrounded by mountains, and the easterly highlands of Moravia. Both have suffered from the effects of heavy industrialization – acid rain and deforestation among them – but both also have areas of real beauty.

In southern Bohemia, such medieval towns as České Budějovice (home of Budějovický Budvar or Budweiser beer) and Český Krumlov, with its 13th-century castle (one of Europe's largest), recall a time when kings and nobles were eager to build in one of Europe's richest regions. To the west are spa towns, best known by their German names: Franzenbad (Františkovy Lázně), Karlsbad (Karlovy Vary) and Marienbad (Mariánské Lázně).

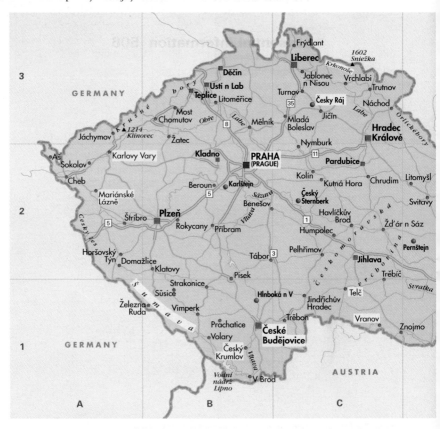

In Moravia, wedged between the western uplands and the eastern White Carpathian mountains, the city of Brno gives access to the Punkevní jeskyně (Punkva Caves).

Czech Culture

Despite the hijacking of the term "bohemian" by the West to mean "unconventional," the Czechs are generally rather reserved. Beyond this, though, is a friendliness and genuine interest in other cultures. Young Czechs often speak English, and are tuned in to Anglo-American pop culture. Love of arts and literature is also widespread. Václav Havel, the first post-Communist president, was better known among Czechs as a playwright.

Music has a special place in Czech life, too – from oompah-style brass bands to

A lovely way to explore Old Town Square in Prague

the classical tradition that produced such composers as Antonín Dvořák and Bedřich Smetana.

Generally speaking, most people who travel around the Czech Republic will be struck by the diversity of this small nation. As the republic embraces tourism, facilities for visitors continue to improve.

CZECH REPUBLIC

0   20   40   60   80 km
0 10 20 30 40 50 miles

N

POLAND

Jeseník
Hrubý
1491
Praděd
Jeseník
Krnov
Opava
Šumperk
Ostrava
Karviná
Morava
Odra
Šternberk
35
Olomouc
Frýdek-Místek
Nový Jičín
Prostějov
Přerov
Valašské Meziříčí
Punkevní jeskyně
Vsetín
Vyškov
Kroměříž
Zlín
Brno
Uherské Hradiště
Slavkov u Brna
2
Morava
Bílé Karpaty
Hodonín
Mikulov
Břeclav
SLOVAK REPUBLIC

D   E

More Top Destinations in the Czech Republic

- České Budějovice B1
- Český Krumlov B1
- Český ráj C3
- Karlovy Vary A2
- Krkonoše C3
- Mariánské Lázně A2
- Olomouc D2
- Punkevní jeskyně D2
- Šumava A1–B1
- Telč C1
- Vranov C1

Timeline

AD **872**	The Přemysl Dynasty begins its 421-year rule of Bohemia.
929	"Good" King Wenceslas is assassinated by his brother, Boleslav, and made the country's patron saint.
1346	Devout Charles IV, Holy Roman Emperor, is crowned king of Bohemia and ushers in its Golden Age.
1415	Religious reformer Jan Hus is burned at the stake in Constance; four years later, in Prague, his supporters throw Catholic councillors from town hall windows and start the Hussite Wars.
1583	The Habsburg court moves to Prague.
1620	Battle of White Mountain. Bohemia's Protestants are defeated and the Czech lands are occupied by the Austrian Habsburgs.
1848	The Habsburgs suppress an uprising of Czech nationalism.
1914	Czechs are forced to fight for the Austrian Habsburgs in World War I, but thousands desert to the Russians.
1918	With the defeat of Austria-Hungary, the new state of Czechoslovakia is proclaimed.
1938	Czechoslovakia is forced to hand over Sudetenland to Hitler. The country is occupied by Germany the following year.
1945	Slovakia and the Czech lands are liberated by the Red Army and the United States; the Communist Party seizes power in 1948.
1968	The First Secretary, Alexander Dubček, introduces "socialism with a human face" in the reforms of the "Prague Spring"; in August, Soviet troops invade Czechoslovakia.
1989	"Velvet Revolution"; Václav Havel elected president of Czechoslovakia.
1993	Czechoslovakia splits into the Czech and Slovak republics.
1999	Czech Republic becomes a NATO member.
2004	Czech Republic joins the European Union.

The Velvet Revolution

On November 17, 1989, a week after the fall of the Berlin Wall, there was an officially sanctioned demonstration in Prague to mark the 50th anniversary of the Nazi suppression of Czech universities. It soon turned into a protest march against the authorities, and was forcefully put down by riot police. A rumor began that the police had killed one demonstrator. In fact, it wasn't true, but the story was enough to fuel public anger. People poured into the streets night after night, watched by television viewers across the world. Alexander Dubček was brought back from obscurity in Bratislava to address the crowds. Human rights activist and writer, Václav Havel headed a newly established Civic Forum, and on December 10 a new government was formed, with the Communists reduced to a minority. Less than three weeks later, Havel was installed as president.

Trams on Malostranská náměstí in the Malá Strana district of Prague

Survival Guide

■ Czech pronunciation is difficult, but worth mastering if only for place names. Any attempt to speak Czech will be heartily appreciated, although many Czechs – particularly young city dwellers – may speak excellent English. The key is to stress the first syllable of a word. A grasp of German is also useful.

■ The cuisine is heavily meat-based – dumplings with pork and duck are popular dishes – and can be quite flavorful. Czechs claim to have the world's best beer, and the products of České Budějovice (Budweis) and Plzeň (Pilsen) are the most famous among a multitude of local varieties.

■ It's worth looking through bookstores, as the illustrated books are a treat. For souvenirs, take home Bohemian crystal, porcelain, lacework, wooden toys and puppets, garnets and prints.

■ Easter is as important a holiday as Christmas, and is marked by the bizarre fertility ritual of boys whipping girls' legs with birch twigs.

■ On St. Nicholas' Eve (December 5), trios in costume can be seen – St. Nicholas, an angel and a devil – walking the streets giving candy to good children and lumps of coal to "bad" ones. Christmas dinner is traditionally carp – sold live at street stalls to be eaten on Christmas Eve, fried, baked or cooked in a soup.

■ Prague is even busier than usual from mid-May to early June, when it hosts the Prague Spring International Music Festival (☎ 257 310 414; www.festival.cz): Reserve accommodations several weeks in advance for this period.

■ Public transportation is a good way of seeing the republic. Almost every town has a railroad station (*nádraží*), and side trips are cheap. The fast trains (*rychlík*) stop at major cities; local trains (*osobní vlak*) are slow, stop everywhere and usually have only second-class carriages.

■ Outside of Prague, the Czech Republic still suffers from a shortage of quality hotels and hostels, although this is fast changing. Many historic hotels have been overhauled, and there's been a surge of new accommodations in converted buildings. A sign saying *Zimmer frei* ("room available" in German) indicates a bed-and-breakfast in a private home.

Prague

Nothing will prepare you for the beauty of Prague. Its title of "Golden Prague" barely conveys the color and elegance of its historic center: painted medieval, baroque and Renaissance facades glinting pink and green and silver in the sun; a jumble of rust-red rooftops; mellow stone, turquoise domes, steel-gray Gothic spires. Prague's buildings and streets span 1,000 years. Wandering the cobbled passageways and alleys becomes the highlight of any visit.

Compass Bearings

Central Prague is made up of four towns, joined together in 1784. On the west bank of the Vltava river are Hradčany and the Lesser Quarter (Malá Strana); on the east bank are the Old Town (Staré Město) and New Town (Nové Město). In the 19th century the Jewish ghetto, Josefov, was also incorporated into the Old Town. Beyond this core is a circle of suburbs, but the main historic sights are within the substantially traffic-free center.

Charles Bridge and Prague Castle

The two banks of the Vltava are connected by a series of 15 bridges, the oldest of which, the Charles Bridge (Karlův most; see page 129), is a magnet

for tourists, performers and vendors. On the west bank, Hradčany, the area around Prague Castle and its hill, is the major attraction. It includes (along with the castle) Golden Lane (Zlatá ulička), with tiny 16th-century houses originally occupied by gatekeepers; the Gothic Mihulka Powder Tower (Prašná věž Mihulka), where alchemists tried to

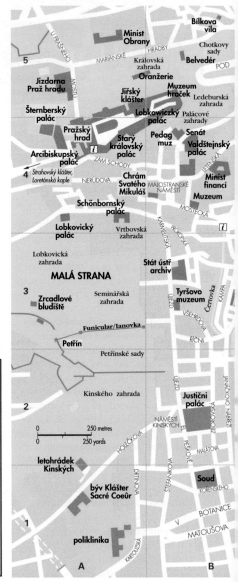

Nerudova

A steep street climbs from Malostranske Square, in the Lesser Quarter, all the way up to Prague Castle. This street, Nerudova, was named after journalist and writer Jan Neruda. He wrote stories about daily life in 19th-century Prague, and was born at No. 47, near the top. Eighteenth-century houses line the street, identified by intricately crafted signs; numbers weren't introduced until the 1770s. Look for The Three Fiddles (No. 12), The Golden Cup (No. 16), The Green Lobster (No. 43) and Neruda's home, The Two Suns (No. 47).

create gold; and the palaces surrounding Hradčany Square (Hradčanské náměstí).

Old and New Prague

Here, across the river, in the Old Town is the Old Town Square (Staroměstské náměstí), with the sprawling Old Town Hall (Staroměstská radnice, see page 130), the white Church of St. Nicholas (Chrám svatého Mikuláše; see page 127) and the dark towers of Týn Church (Týnsky chrám). This is a popular place for a variety of street artists to perform. The real hub of the New Town (Nové Město) is Wenceslas Square (Václavské náměstí), a thriving boulevard renowned as the focus of many protests during the Velvet Revolution of 1989.

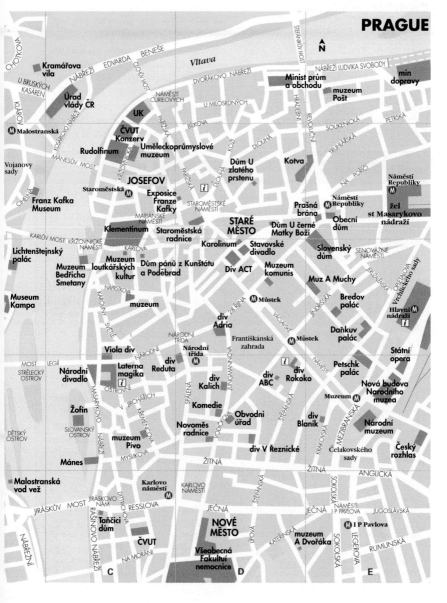

Czech Republic

Locals love their music – as Mozart found out, when he triumphed here after only moderate success in Vienna. Classical music seems to be everywhere in Prague, advertised in listings guides and on posters across the city. Tickets are reasonably priced and the performances can be superb.

Pražský hrad (castle) and the Malá Strana district

Czech Beer and Puppets

Restaurants and cafés fill up quickly in Prague, so it's a good idea to make reservations. You'll find a wide range of options as well as local cuisine, from American and Italian to Lebanese and Japanese. Don't leave the city without tasting at least one Czech beer. Some of Prague's own brews include Staropramen and U Fleků.

The best shopping is along elegant Pařížská Street in the Old Town, along the pedestrian-only street Na Příkopě and also along Celetná. There are some interesting souvenir shops on Karlova, near the Charles Bridge. If you're looking for souvenirs, puppets make ideal gifts – they're works of art, not just playthings. For a huge selection of books, try Palác knih Luxor (Palace of Books) at Václavské náměstí 41.

Essential Information

Tourist Information

Pražská informační služba (Prague Information Service)
Staroměstská radnice (Old Town Hall), Staroměstské náměstí 1
Rytířská 31
Hlavní nádraží (main railroad station)
Malostranská mostecká věž (Lesser Town Bridge Tower), Karlův most (Charles Bridge): Apr.–Oct. only.
For all ☎ 124 44 or 221 714 444; www.prague-info.cz

Urban Transportation

Prague has three subway lines: A (green), B (yellow) and C (red). Stations are indicated by the letter "M" (marked in a red circle on the city map). Trains run frequently every day between 5 a.m. and midnight. Trams and buses are frequent (4:30 a.m. to midnight, with some night services). Buses run outside the city center. One ticket can be used for the subway, buses and trams. For information call ☎ 296 191 817 (daily 7 a.m.–9 p.m.; www.dpp.cz). Make sure a taxi has a meter registering the fare, or else agree on a price before you get into the cab. Avoid taking taxis at a stand, especially one near a tourist spot or a nightclub. To hire a taxi call AAA Radio taxi (☎ 140 14).

Airport Information

Letiště Praha (☎ 220 113 314; or 220 113 321; www.prg.aero), 12.5 miles northwest of the city, is a bus ride from the center. Bus Nos. 100, 119, 179, 225, 254 and (at night) 510 operate between the airport and central Prague. The Airport Express (AE) bus provides direct service to Hlavní nádraží (main train station).

Climate – average highs and lows for the month

Jan.	Feb.	Mar.	Apr.	May	Jun.	Jul.	Aug.	Sep.	Oct.	Nov.	Dec.
2°C	2°C	8°C	12°C	18°C	20°C	22°C	23°C	18°C	12°C	5°C	2°C
36°F	36°F	46°F	54°F	64°F	68°F	72°F	73°F	64°F	54°F	41°F	36°F
-4°C	-4°C	0°C	2°C	7°C	10°C	13°C	12°C	9°C	4°C	0°C	-2°C
25°F	25°F	32°F	36°F	45°F	50°F	55°F	54°F	48°F	39°F	32°F	28°F

Prague Sights

Key to symbols

➕ map coordinates refer to the Prague map on pages 124–125 💶 admission charge: $$$ more than 110Kč, $$ 70Kč–110Kč, $ less than 70Kč
See page 5 for complete key to symbols

Chrám svatého Mikuláše

Mozart played the 2,500-pipe organ here in 1787; he couldn't have chosen a more grandiose setting than the Chrám svatého Mikuláše (St. Nicholas' Church). It was constructed in the 18th century to celebrate Catholic counter-Reformation doctrine. The church is a frenzy of decoration: pink-and-green mock-marble pillars; a 16,146-square-foot fresco; a copper statue of St. Nicholas; and huge sculptures of the four church fathers, including St. Cyril killing the devil.

➕ B4 ✉ Malostranské náměstí ☎ Church: 257 534 215; www.psalterium.cz 🕐 Daily 9–5, Mar.–Oct.; 9–4, rest of year. Tower: daily 10–6, Apr.–Oct. Ⓜ Malostranská 🚊 Tram 12, 20, 22 💶 Church $$; tower $

Josefov

Walls went up around Prague's Jewish community in 1254, in keeping with a church law that Christians and Jews should live apart. But the walls did nothing to protect the inhabitants of the ghetto from centuries of persecution. In 1389, 3,000 were killed in a pogrom, and at regular intervals, kings passed laws forcing Jews to wear particular clothes or colors to identify them.

Even in the face of such vicious discrimination, the ghetto developed as a center of learning, and some members were able to buy occasional privileges for the community from the imperial court. In 1784 Joseph II abolished residence restrictions (the area was later named after him).

The ghetto survived until the end the 19th century, when the area was cleared for residential housing, though many of the most important buildings were left standing. In the Starý židovský hřbitov (Old Jewish Cemetery), some 12,000 tombstones are crammed into the small but powerfully moving space, now part of the Jewish Museum. Other museum holdings are scattered throughout the quarter. An exhibition in the Pinkasova synagoga (Pinkas synagogue) remembers the 80,000 Czech and Moravian Jews who died in concentration camps in World War II.

The oldest building is the 13th-century Staronová synagoga (Old-New Synagogue), where legend has it the clay man, or Golem, created by Rabbi Löw in 1580 to serve and guard the ghetto, is still kept in the attic. The Rabbi had to return his creation to clay after it ran rampant through the streets. This and other synagogues around the cemetery survived World War II because of Hitler's perverse plan to create a museum dedicated to a vanished race. The synagogues (apart from the Old-New Synagogue) collectively form the Židovské muzeum (Jewish Museum) and can all be visited on one ticket.

➕ C4 ✉ Jewish Museum: U Staré školy 1; Old-New Synagogue: Červená 2; www.jewishmuseum.cz 🕐 Jewish Museum sites: Sun.–Fri. 9–6, Apr.–Oct.; 9–4:30, rest of year. Old-New Synagogue: Sun.–Fri.

A detail of the interior of St. Nicholas' Church

Kafka

Franz Kafka wrote two of the 20th century's most significant novels – *The Trial* and *The Castle* – but he died practically unknown, having made his friend, Max Brod, promise to destroy all his writings. It's only because Brod broke his promise that Kafka is read throughout the world today.

His tales of helpless individuals caught in the workings of massive bureaucracy were inspired by the overgrown Habsburg administration. They came to represent the menace and detachment of authority in general, and the term "Kafkaesque" was coined to describe a seemingly ordinary but surreal and dangerous world of systems with their own life and logic.

Kafka was born in Prague, and moved with his family from house to house around Old Town Square, where his father was a haberdasher. He studied law and worked as an insurance clerk, writing his stories by night. The city appears throughout his writings. *The Castle* was inspired by Prague Castle; his story *The Great Wall of China* was based on the "Hunger Wall" on Petřín Hill, built as part of a 14th-century job creation scheme and funded by money expropriated from Jews. Kafka rented a house between 1916 and 1917 on Golden Lane (Zlatá ulička) at No. 22, but his health was poor and he died of tuberculosis at the age of 41. His grave can be seen at the New Jewish Cemetery (Židovské hřbitovy) in the Vinohrady district. He left behind a third, unfinished novel, *Amerika,* and many short stories.

The most famous, *Metamorphosis,* related the story of Gregor Samsa, who awakens to find himself transformed into a giant insect and to his family becomes an object first of horror, then of pity and finally of contempt. The theme of a bewildered victim of inexplicable events is characteristic of Kafka's style.

The author also recorded his wanderings around Prague, his relationship with his father and with Felice Bauer (to whom he was twice engaged), and his tortured nights of writing in his diaries, which also were posthumously published.

The Communist regime subsequently suppressed Kafka's work, but he is now acknowledged and honored in the city he once described as "a little old mother with sharp claws: she won't let go."

Cobbled Golden Lane is built into the castle; Franz Kafka stayed here between 1916 and 1917

end – the Old Town Bridge Tower (daily 10–10, May–Sep.; 10–7 in Apr. and Oct.; 10–6 in Mar.; 10–5, rest of year) and the Lesser Town Bridge Tower (daily 10–6, Apr.–Oct.).

🚩 B4 ✉ Staré Město/Malá Strana Ⓜ Staroměstská 🚊 Tram 12, 17, 18, 20, 22

Loretánská kaple

As part of its campaign to win worshipers back to Catholicism after the Reformation, the Church made much of the cult of the Virgin Mary, and the ornate Loretánská kaple (Loreto Chapel) is one result. It was built in 1626 around a replica of Mary's house, supposedly flown by angels from Nazareth to Loreto in Italy, and it soon became a site of pilgrimage. Don't miss the painting of St. Starosta, who grew a beard to repel a suitor and was crucified by her father.

🚩 Off map at A4 ✉ Loretánské náměstí 7 ☎ 220 516 740; www.loreta.cz 🕐 Tue.–Sun. 9–12:15 and 1–4:30 🚊 Tram 22 💶 $$

Petřín

Woods and orchards cover this hill on the city's western bank, and a funicular railway (*lanová dráha na Petřín*), takes passengers up and down. The carriages were installed in 1891, the year that the Petřínská rozhledna (Petřín Lookout Tower) was built at the top. Steps (299 of them) lead to the viewing platform.

🚩 A3 ✉ Petřín Lookout Tower: Petřínské sady. Funicular railway: Újezd ☎ 257 320 112 🕐 Lookout Tower: daily 10–10, May–Aug.; daily 10–8 in Sep.; daily 10–7 in Apr.; daily 10–6 in Oct.; Sat.–Sun. 10–5, rest of year. Funicular: daily 9 a.m.–11:30 p.m., Apr.–Oct. (to 11:20 p.m., rest of year) 🚊 Tram 6, 9, 12, 20, 22 (then take funicular) 💶 Tower $$; Funicular $

Pražský hrad

Looming over the city and the river, Pražský hrad (Prague Castle) has been a symbol of Czech authority since the first fortress was built on this high, rocky site in the ninth century. The name refers to a complex of palaces, courtyards, churches and streets, all spread across the hill known as Hradčany. A long

Visitors in the vaulted Loreto Chapel

9:30–6, Apr.–Oct.; Sun.–Thu. 9:30–5, Fri. 9:30–2, rest of year. Closed Jewish holidays Ⓜ Staroměstská 🚊 Tram 17, 18 🍴 Restaurant ✡ Jewish Museum $$$; Old-New Synagogue $$$

Karlův most

Karlův most (Charles Bridge) is more than just a river crossing. A walk across the 1,700-foot span takes you past 30 sculptures, plus courting couples and musicians, and offers breathtaking views of the river and of the city's domes and looming spires. It was the work of Petr Parléř, who also created much of St. Vitus' Cathedral, and was built in 1357 to link the Old Town with the Lesser Quarter. Known until 1870 as the Stone or Prague Bridge, it has 16 sandstone arches but was originally relatively plain. The first ornament, a bronze crucifix, was added in 1657. Over the following 60 years more statues were erected, evenly spaced along the parapets; they include St. John of Nepomuk (with the spangled halo), who was thrown from the bridge in 1393 after taking the side of the church in a dispute with the king. You can visit the fortified towers at each

Cafés in the square under the Astronomical Clock

flight of broad steps (usually lined with souvenir sellers) climbs to the castle, a mixture of styles spanning 450 years of restoration and guarded by a series of courtyards. At the entrance to the outer courtyard, two soldiers stand at attention under some rather grotesque and threatening statues of the Titans. The guard is changed every hour on the hour (🕐 daily 5 a.m.–midnight, Apr.–Oct.; 6 a.m.–11 p.m., rest of year). In the second courtyard are the castle's art gallery and information center.

Finally, you reach the third courtyard and Katedrála sv Víta (St. Vitus' Cathedral), which took 600 years to complete – it was only finished in 1929. Starý Královský palác (Old Royal Palace), to the right, is a maze of rooms centered around the 15th-century Vladislav Hall, where mounted knights would trot down the Riders' Staircase to take part in indoor jousting matches.

➕ A4 ✉ Hradčany ☎ 224 373 368; www.hrad.cz
🕐 Castle precincts: daily 5 a.m.–midnight, Apr.–Oct.; 6 a.m.–11 p.m., rest of year. Castle sights: daily 9–6, Apr.–Oct.; 9–4, rest of year. Castle gardens: daily 10–9, Jun.–Jul.; 10–8 in Aug.; 10–7 in May and Sep.; 10–6 in Apr. and Oct. 🚇 Hradčanská or Malostranská
🚊 Tram 12, 18, 20, 22 🍴 Lví dvůr, see page 471
💷 Individual sights $$–$$$; gardens free ℹ Tours in English $$$

Staroměstská radnice

Since a merchant's house was earmarked for the city council in 1338, the Staroměstská radnice (Old Town Hall) has gradually expanded and taken over a row of houses.

A tower and chapel were added to the original buildings; features range from the original carved facade to the 19th-century house known as "At the Cock." Its main attraction is the 15th-century Astronomical Clock high on one wall, which gives the month, season, zodiac signs, course of the sun and Christian holidays. On the hour (9–9) a skeleton appears and chimes the bell, followed by a parade of the Twelve Apostles.

➕ D4 ✉ Staroměstské náměstí 1 ☎ 724 508 584
🕐 Mon. 11–6, Tue.–Sun. 9–6 🚇 Staroměstská
🚊 Tram 17, 18 💷 $$

Šternberský palác

In an alley off Hradčany Square Šternberský palác (Sternberg Palace), a town house built for Count Sternberg in 1698, has a fine collection of Old Masters. Highlights include *The Feast of the Rosary,* by German Renaissance painter and engraver Albrecht Dürer, and *Adam and Eve,* by artist and woodcut-designer Lucas Cranach the Elder, both housed on the first floor.

➕ A4 ✉ Hradčanské náměstí 15 ☎ 233 090 570; www.ngprague.cz 🕐 Tue.–Sun. 10–6 (also 6–8 p.m. first Wed. of the month) 🚇 Hradčanská 🚊 Tram 22
🍴 Café 💷 $$$ (free 3–8 p.m. first Wed. of the month)

Strahovský klášter

The baroque spires of Strahovský klášter (Strahov Monastery) dominate the hilltop west of Hradčany: the name means "to watch over" – it has guarded this site since the 12th century. Library halls store more than 130,000 books and manuscripts.

➕ Off map at A1 ✉ Strahovské nádvoří 1 ☎ 233 107 711; www.strahovskyklaster.cz 🕐 Daily 9–noon and 1–5 🚇 Malostranská 🚊 Tram 22 🍴 Peklo ("Hell") restaurant in the cellars below the monastery gardens 💷 $$

Excursion to Kutná Hora

The Italian Court was a royal palace

When silver and copper ore deposits were found on this hill 40 miles southeast of Prague, a town shot up virtually overnight, taking the appropriate name of Kutná Hora, which suggests "miners' mountain." That was in the late 13th century, and soon a royal mint was set up, hammering out the silver coin known as *pražské groše* in its workshops. Also constructed was a royal palace known as the Italian Court, a reference to the Florentine advisers of King Wenceslas II (1283–1305). The town flourished on its mining proceeds and by the 14th century was the country's most important center after Prague, and Kutná Hora even managed to recover after being taken over by one force after another during the Hussite Wars. But by the end of the 16th century the mountain was all mined out and the town fell into decay, suffering the final blow with a disastrous fire in 1770.

The handsome Cathedral of St. Barbara was paid for by miners and dedicated to their patron saint. For its design they turned to the prestigious architect of Prague's St. Vitus' Cathedral, Petr Parléř, who rose to the occasion with distinctive tent-like spires and flying buttresses.

Sculptures line Barborská ulice, a street leading to an impressive 15th-century house built for a profiteer who ran an illegal private mining operation. It's now the Mining Museum, and behind it is the medieval mine itself, consisting of 820 feet of tunnels; a horse-drawn winch at the entrance drew out the bags of ore. The royal mint is gone (although it is still possible to make out its outline); parts of the Italian Court – including the chapel, adorned with art nouveau frescoes – can be visited also. Kutná Hora is a UNESCO World Heritage Site. Some 2 miles north of town in Sedlec is the spooky *kostnice*, a chapel decorated with human bones, that was originally owned by Cistercian monks. During the 19th century its 40,000 human bones were put to artistic use by František Rint, who made them into bells and other items.

Contact the Prague Information Service (see page 126) for details of public transportation to Kutná Hora and Sedlec or, for an organized tour of Kutná Hora, contact:

Martin Tour ✉ Štěpánská 61, 110 00 Praha 1 ☎ 224 212 473; www.martintour.cz

For more information contact: **Informační centrum Kutná Hora** ✉ Palackého náměstí 377, Kutná Hora ☎ 327 512 378; www.kutnahora.cz

Denmark

Opposite: Copenhagen's famous *The Little Mermaid (Den Lille Havefrue)* statue in the harbor area

Denmark

Denmark was the cradle of ancient Scandinavia. When you talk of the first Vikings you talk of Danes. It was from this fragmented mosaic of peninsulas and islands between mainland Europe and the Swedish-Norwegian landmass that those consummate seamen first struck out in search of plunder and new territory to conquer. Denmark is the smallest of the four Scandinavian nations, and yet the Danes have made their country one of the most advanced and progressive in the world.

Danish Archipelago

The Kingdom of Denmark is just over 200 miles long, and the Jutland (Jylland) peninsula (the primary landmass) is only 75 miles wide. Nowhere in Denmark is much higher than 100 feet above sea level, and the country's highest point, Yding Skovhøj in central Jutland, only rises to 567 feet. Jutland's narrow southern border is with

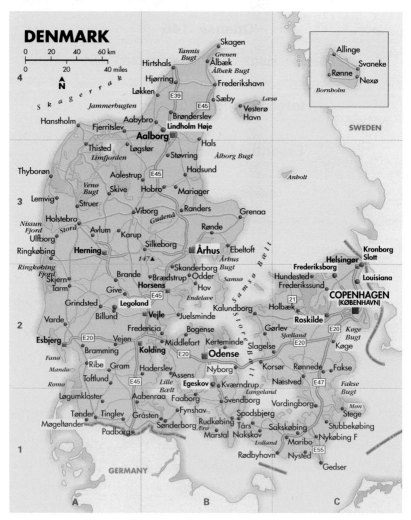

Germany, Denmark's only land frontier; its west coast adjoins the North Sea.

East of Jutland, and with barely a sliver of water in between, is Denmark's second-largest island, Funen (Fyn). East of Funen is Zealand (Sjælland), the largest island. Its northeastern tip is about 40 miles from the Swedish coast and home to the capital, Copenhagen (København), itself only a short drive or train journey across the Øresund bridge (see page 136) to Sweden. Zealand and Funen lie like natural fortresses across the Kattegat, the sea separating Denmark from Sweden. This position across the entrance to the Baltic Sea, to the south, has always placed the country at the maritime heart of northern Europe.

Houses on Bornholm, an island east of the mainland

The Jutland Peninsula

Copenhagen is the magnet for visitors, but the rest of this disparate and fascinating country has much to offer. Far western Jutland has an invigorating coastal landscape of long, sandy beaches backed by broad dunes and moorland. This landscape is repeated in north Jutland beyond the dividing waters of the Limfjord and all the way to the Skagen peninsula, the birdlike beak of land that thrusts into the sea at Denmark's northern tip. In north Jutland, outside the city of Aalborg, are evocative traces of Scandinavia's Viking culture at the archeological site of Lindholm Høje, a remarkable Viking burial ground of nearly 700 excavated graves, many marked by stones in the shape of long ships.

The heathland of the west coast of central Jutland gives way in the east to a fertile, undulating countryside of small farms and woodland, interspersed with country towns and pretty villages. On the east coast is Århus, a sophisticated and historic university city and Denmark's second largest. Here you will find the mighty Århus Cathedral and the intriguing Den Gamle By, the Old Town and its dozens of restored, timber-framed buildings. South of Århus is a

great stretch of woodland where you can enjoy peace and quiet along walking, bicycling and horseback riding trails. Southwest of Århus is the town of Billund, overshadowed by Denmark's famous Legoland Billund, the country's most visited attraction outside of Copenhagen. Beyond all the plastic bricks is the farming country of south Jutland, which claims to be Denmark's oldest region with such fascinating towns and villages as Ribe, the oldest town in Denmark, established in the eighth century AD, with its handsome cathedral, cobbled streets and gabled houses. The little village of Møgeltønder, in the far southwest of the country, has

More Top Destinations in Denmark

- Århus B3
- Bornholm C4
- Egeskov B2
- Frederiksborg C2
- Køge C2
- Kronborg Slot, Helsingbørg C3
- Legoland Billund A2
- Lindholm Høje B4
- Louisiana C2
- Møgeltønder A1
- Møn C1
- Nyborg B2
- Ribe A2
- Roskilde C2
- Skagen B4

a superb frescoed church and charming thatched houses.

Country of Islands

More than 400 islands are scattered around Denmark's coasts and out across the Kattegat and the Baltic Sea. About 100 islands are inhabited. Funen (Fyn) is hailed as the "Garden of Denmark," a term probably first used by author Hans Christian Andersen (see page 151) because of its rich alluvial soils, a legacy of the glacial debris left by retreating ice sheets. The capital of Funen is Odense, birthplace of Hans Christian Andersen.

Funen has a gentle rural nature, its lush farmland complemented by a pleasant southern coastline and by good beaches on the peaceful island of Langeland, off the southeast coast. Funen is connected to Denmark's largest island, Zealand, by a typically Danish feat of remarkable civil engineering. The 11-mile-long Storebælt (Great Belt) rail and road fixed-link bridge island hops, via Sprogø island, across the Storebælt channel. The project took nine years to complete and the first rail passengers crossed the rail bridge in 1997, followed in 1998 by cars on the road link.

The ferry connection, used by visitors prior to 1998, was more romantic, but Scandinavian efficiency triumphed with a tunnel and bridge combination. A similar joint Danish-Swedish project, linking Copenhagen to Malmö across an artificial island built in the middle of the Øresund, was completed in 2000, laying the foundations for a new cultural and economic region.

Historic Zealand

Copenhagen may dominate Zealand, but the whole island is a treasure house of Danish history. North Zealand has much to offer in terms of historic buildings: the lakeside setting of Frederiksborg Castle (Frederiksborg Slot) Denmark's magnificent Renaissance castle; and Elsinore Castle (Kronborg Slot) at Helsingør, thought to be the setting for Shakespeare's *Hamlet*, overlooking the Øresund and the Swedish coast.

Just west of Copenhagen is Roskilde, Denmark's medieval capital, with a splendid cathedral housing the decorated crypts of 38 Danish kings and queens. In southern Zealand is the city of Køge, whose medieval center survives; at Trelleborg, near Slagelse on the west coast where the new rail bridge slices across the Great Belt, are the remains of the finest Viking ring fort in Denmark. There are six circular forts in

Little villages nestle amid lush greenery on the coastline of Denmark

Traditional painted houses in Odense, birthplace of Hans Christian Andersen, on the island of Funen

Denmark and Sweden called Treleborgs – all named for this one, which was excavated first, in 1936–41.

Finally, just off the south coast of Zealand are the islands of Møn, Falster and Lolland, Denmark's third-largest island, after Zealand and Funen, all linked to the main islands by bridges. Of these, Møn is the most interesting because of its green hills and chalk cliffs, a landscape in startling contrast to Denmark's almost uniform flatness.

Exploring Denmark

Denmark is one of the most accessible European countries. Its compact size and the smooth transition from island to island that modern engineering has accomplished makes exploring various regions by car an easy option once you are clear of Copenhagen's urban center.

This compactness makes traveling by public transportation almost as convenient. Fast, comfortable trains can whisk you from Zealand to Funen, and then on to Jutland, in a few hours. The efficient and extensive rail network offers stiff competition to long-distance bus services in Denmark, although buses are less expensive than trains.

Denmark's climate is typical of a maritime environment, and the low elevation means there are no great extremes of temperature. Summers are pleasantly mild, but there can be wet spells; in winter snow is likely at times, but much less so than in the other Scandinavian countries.

In matters of food and drink Denmark remains engagingly Scandinavian. Danes relish the same hearty sandwich feast, here called the *smørrebrød*, that you find in Norway and Sweden, complete with its garnished mixes of delicious meat and seafood. Beer is a Danish specialty, and the famous Danish breweries of Carlsberg and Tuborg produce some of the most popular brews in the world.

You will find that Danes are generally helpful, friendly and speak good English. In rural areas and in provincial cities such as Odense, people are unfailingly polite, but in Copenhagen there may be a sharper edge to people's attitudes. At times you may detect an apparent reserve on the part of Danish people. It is not a negative sentiment; the Danes are supremely accomplished, and beneath the reserve is a fierce national pride in their country.

Timeline

4000 BC	Neolithic settlers begin developing a farming economy.
500 BC to AD 500	Iron Age people trade from Jutland and Funen.
AD 793	Danish Vikings raid England's east coast, plundering the monastery of Lindisfarne, and penetrate deep into mainland Europe along the northern rivers.
circa 925	Gorm the Old becomes first king of a united Denmark.
1167	The founding of Copenhagen by Absalon, Bishop of Roskilde.
1588	Christian IV becomes king of Denmark and promotes the construction of great Renaissance buildings, particularly in the city of Copenhagen.
1611–60	Periodic wars with Sweden.
1814	Union with Norway ends after 278 years.
1849	New constitution abolishes absolute monarchy, establishing a two-chamber parliament.
1914–18	Denmark is neutral during World War I.
1940	Denmark is invaded by the German army in spite of its declared neutrality; the Danish Resistance carries out a vigorous campaign against Germany.
1945	Denmark is liberated. A postwar reconstruction program begins.
1949	Denmark joins NATO.
1973	Denmark joins the European Economic Community.
1998	Opening of the fixed-link rail and road bridge across the Storebælt (Great Belt).
2000	Road and rail link opens to Malmö in Sweden.
2004	Prince Frederik marries Australian Mary Donaldson.
2009	Copenhagen hosts the United Nations summit on climate change. No legally binding treaty was agreed.
2011	Go-ahead given to underwater tunnel between Lolland Island and the German island of Fehmarn.

A Talented Royal Lady

Denmark's current queen, Margrethe II, was born in 1940. She was the eldest daughter of King Frederik IX, who had no sons. After a favorable 1953 referendum, the Danish constitution, which allowed only for a male heir to the throne, was amended to enable female succession. Margrethe became queen at the age of 32, after Frederik's death in 1972. She is Denmark's first female monarch since the 15th century. Queen Margrethe qualified as an archeologist after studying at Copenhagen, Århus, Cambridge and Paris. She is a talented artist, illustrating an edition of J. R. R. Tolkien's fantasy *The Lord of the Rings* and designing stamps for the Danish postal service. The queen has also designed theatrical costumes and stage settings for the Danish Royal Theatre. An accomplished linguist, Queen Margrethe has translated the work of the French novelist Simone de Beauvoir, a task in which she worked with her husband and consort, French-born Prince Henrik.

Survival Guide

- If you drive or cycle through Denmark, ask the tourist office for details about the "Marguerite Route," which is a series of linked routes (2,170 miles long) along quieter roads that wind through the most scenic parts of the country. Distinctive signs display a daisy (marguerite) motif on a brown background. A map, available from VisitDenmark (see page 510), indicates the route.

- The cOPENhagen card, valid for 24 or 72 hours, costs 229/459DKr. It entiles you to free travel by train, bus or metro, entry into more than 60 museums and other attractions and shopping and car rental discounts in Copenhagen.

- Danes celebrate Midsummer's Eve (*Sankt Hans*) on June 23. Bonfires are lit throughout the country on the longest day of the year.

- In Denmark *morgenmad* is the word for breakfast, and *frokost* is lunch. *Smørrebrød*, the tasty Scandinavian open-faced sandwich with a choice of toppings, including cheese, salami, smoked salmon and egg, remains a lunchtime favorite; but try *frikadeller*, delicious fried meat or fish patties with salad and potatoes; or dip into the heftier *koldt bord*, a buffet-style selection. For main meals, enjoy *kogt torsk*, poached cod in mustard sauce, or old-fashioned *Skipperlabskovs*, Danish stew.

- Danish pastries are called *wienerbrød* and come in a variety of shapes and mouthwatering flavors.

- Amber is a Danish specialty, the "Danish gold." The Amber Specialist (28 Frederiksberggade, Copenhagen, ☎ 33 11 88 03) is the place to look in Copenhagen, but you will find distinctive amber jewelry, such as earrings and necklaces, in stores throughout the country. If you're looking for Danish glass, porcelain

A soldier outside Amalienborg Palace, Copenhagen

and silverware, there are several shops on and leading off Strøget and also the Royal Copenhagen flagship store (Amagertorv 6, Copenhagen, ☎ 33 13 71 81).

- Denmark, like Sweden, is noted for its distinctive furnishing designs. The style known as "Danish Modern" is a classic merging of the functional with the aesthetic. Visit Illums Bolighus (Amagertorv 10, Copenhagen, ☎ 33 14 19 41) for some of the finest examples.

- Unlike some of the northern Scandinavian countries, Denmark has a far more relaxed approach to the sale of liquor. You can buy wines, spirits and beers in grocery stores.

- Traditionally formal, Danes have become more relaxed about what to wear when eating out. Nowadays, stylish, casual clothes, especially during the warm summer months, are acceptable for dining at most Danish restaurants.

Copenhagen

Copenhagen (København) is where the European experience becomes Scandinavian. This is a magnificent, vibrant city, far more a "Wonderful Wonderful Copenhagen" than even the

Danny Kaye song implies. It is a city of towers and steeples that are elegant and sculptural, as well as monumental. It is a city that draws you in along pedestrian-only streets that lead in and out of delightful squares. It is a city with fine museums and attractions, restaurants,

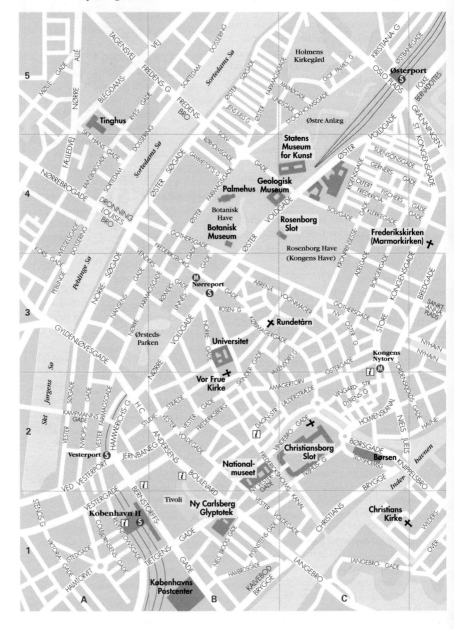

cafés and entertainment that place it among the finest of European capitals.

Copenhagen originated, like so many other Scandinavian towns and cities, as a small fishing village, its occupants taking advantage of the sheltered waters around Slotsholmen Island, the island that is now home to the Danish National Parliament (Folketing), and the Christiansborg Palace (Christiansborg Slot). By the 12th century Slotsholmen had been fortified in keeping with the settlement's growing commercial status, a status signified by its name, Kømandshavn, "port of the merchants," later amended to København. By the middle of the 15th century, Copenhagen was the recognized capital of Denmark.

The city's status was enhanced by the construction of many fine buildings during the reign of Christian IV of Denmark in the 17th century, and by the 19th century Copenhagen had emerged as a major European capital. Development continued during the 20th and 21st centuries, and today Copenhagen stands as a mature and hugely successful city.

First Impressions

The initial impression visitors have of Copenhagen is of a city overpowered by traffic. To reach the central City Hall Square (Rådhuspladsen) from Copenhagen's central railroad station (Hovedbanegården), visitors pass Tivoli and then negotiate busy downtown streets. Hans Christian Andersen Boulevard, a broad thoroughfare, is as far removed from Andersen's fairy-tale world as can be imagined. Keep your eyes open for cyclists as well as cars. The broad expanse of City Hall Square, a relaxed, traffic-free environment, leads to a refreshing world of lively streets, colorful squares and hidden corners, where pedestrians are the priority.

There is a lot to see in Copenhagen. Most attractions, including Rosenborg Castle (Slot; see page 145) and the National Museum (Nationalmuseet; see page 144), are based around the Old Town. The furthest sight, perhaps, is *Den Lille Havfrue (The Little Mermaid)*, a long walk along the waterfront from the central parts of the city.

Getting around is easy, however, if you take advantage of the various guided

COPENHAGEN

walking tours that are available, or pick up a map from the tourist office. Other sightseeing tours go by bus and by harbor or canal boats. The city's bus service is extremely efficient and comprehensive, complemented by a system of electric S-trains and a subway (metro). Because the city center is pedestrian-only, however, exploring on your own here, on foot or by bicycle (free rental in summer), is a pleasure.

Strøget and Beyond

Start at City Hall Square. Look up at the Nordea building, where you will see a bronze weathervane featuring a girl who appears on her bicycle in fine weather and with an umbrella when it rains.

The sequence of streets known collectively as Strøget (the Promenade) begins at Rådhuspladsen (City Hall Square), at narrow Frederiksberggade. Amid the many stores and restaurants, side streets lead to quaint antiques shops and specialty outlets; vistas suddenly reveal the city's impressively grand architecture and fashionable people.

City on the Water's Edge

At the far end of Strøget, cross the large, bustling square of Kongens Nytorv (New Royal Market) to reach Nyhavn (New Harbor), the old harbor inlet, now a picturesque area with trendy restaurants. Visit Amalienborg Plads (Amalienborg Square; see page 143), then head east to waterside Larsens Plads; from this square a pleasant walk north takes you to the city's symbol, *Den Lille Havfrue* (*The Little Mermaid*). Opposite is the Operaen (Opera House).

Nearby is the Frihedsmuseet (Museum of Danish Resistance), a celebration of resistance against the Nazis. These attractions all spotlight Copenhagen's lure for visitors: its astonishing variety.

Essential Information

Tourist Information

Copenhagen Right Now
Vesterbrogade 4A ☎ 70 22 24 42;
www.visitcopenhagen.dk

Urban Transportation

Copenhagen's main railroad station is København H/Central Station on Bernstorffsgade, a few minutes from the city center. For information call ☎ 70 13 14 15 (free service phones at all stations); www.dsb.dk. The train system consists mainly of S-trains (about 10 lines; trains every 20 minutes). Copenhagen also has a very good network of bus routes. Buses leave from Rådhuspladsen. For information call ☎ 36 13 14 15. There is

also a 24-hour driverless metro (light rail) system with two lines (M1 and M2). For information call ☎ 70 15 16 15. Taxis have fixed rates. Call Taxa 4X35 ☎ 35 35 35 35.

Airport Information

Copenhagen Airport (☎ 32 31 32 31, 24 hours; www.cph.dk) is at Kastrup, 6 miles south of the city center. Trains run to and from København H/Central Station daily every 10 minutes during the day (travel time 12 minutes). Metro Line M2 trains run every four to six minutes from 5 a.m. to midnight, and every 20 minutes from midnight to 5 a.m., Thursday to Sunday (travel time 15 minutes). Buses serve the airport; the 250S is best.

Climate – average highs and lows for the month

Jan.	Feb.	Mar.	Apr.	May	Jun.	Jul.	Aug.	Sep.	Oct.	Nov.	Dec.
3°C	3°C	5°C	10°C	15°C	19°C	20°C	20°C	16°C	11°C	7°C	4°C
37°F	37°F	41°F	50°F	59°F	66°F	68°F	68°F	61°F	52°F	45°F	39°F
-2°C	-2°C	0°C	2°C	7°C	11°C	13°C	12°C	10°C	7°C	3°C	0°C
28°F	28°F	32°F	36°F	45°F	52°F	55°F	54°F	50°F	45°F	37°F	32°F

Copenhagen Sights

Amalienborg Plads

The royal heart of Copenhagen is the octagonal Amalienborg Plads (Amalienborg Square), with a statue of King Frederick V at its center, rococo palaces on four sides, and broad avenues leading off the other four.

The Danish royal family spends most of the fall and winter in the palaces. Their very private presence gives the square a rather detached, lifeless atmosphere except during the changing of the guard, daily at noon when the Queen is in residence.

On the northwest corner of the square is Christian VIII's Palace, containing the Amalienborgmuseet (Amalienborg Museum), with royal memorabilia and a sequence of reconstructed private rooms that illustrate what life was like for the royal Glücksburg family between the 1860s and the 1970s.

🔢 D3 ✉ Amalienborg Plads ☎ Museum: 33 12 21 86 🕐 Museum: daily 10–4, May–Oct.; Tue.–Sun. 11–4, rest of year. Christian VIII's Palace: tours in English Sat.–Sun. 1 p.m. and 2 p.m., Jul.–Sep. 🚇 Kongens Nytorv 🚌 1A, 15, 19, 26, 29, 901, 902, 650S 🖐 Museum $$$

Christiansborg Slot

The monumental complex that makes up Christiansborg Slot (Christiansborg Palace) dominates the whole island of Slotsholmen. It presents a rather stern face to the city approaching across the encircling canal from Strøget and Højbro Plads. A visit to this complex may take you a whole day. The vast west wing houses the Danish Parliament

(Folketing), the Supreme Court and the Prime Minister's Office, built between 1907 and 1928 to replace a more stylish building that burned down in 1884.

Also here are the lavishly decorated Kongelige Repræsentationslokaler (Royal Reception Rooms).

Below the palace are the preserved Ruinerne (Ruins) of Bishop Absalon's Castle, dating from 1167, and its successor, Copenhagen Castle. Museums around the royal riding grounds include Museet Kongelige Stalde og Kareter (Royal Stable and Carriages Museum), the Teatermuseet (Theater Museum) and the Tøjhusmuseet (Royal Danish Arsenal Museum).

The Christiansborg Slotskirke (Christiansborg Palace Chapel), dating from 1826 but damaged by fire in 1992, reopened in 1997. It is used on royal and state occasions.

Christiansborg Slot 🔢 C2 ✉ Christiansborg Slotsplads ☎ 33 92 64 92; www.ses.dk 🖐 Combined ticket for Royal Reception Rooms, Ruins and Stables $$$ 🚇 Kongens Nytorv or Nørrebro 🚌 1A, 2A, 6A, 15, 26, 29, 40, 65E, 66, 350S
Kongelige Repræsentationslokaler ☎ 33 92 64 92 🕐 Guided tours in English daily at 3 🖐 $$$
Ruinerne ☎ 33 92 64 92 🕐 Daily 10–5, May–Sep.; Tue.–Sun. 10–5, rest of year 🖐 $$
Museet Kongelige Stalde og Kareter ☎ 33 40 26 76 🕐 Fri.–Sun. 2–4, May–Sep.; Sat.–Sun. 2–4, rest of year 🖐 $$

Den Lille Havfrue

Most visitors don't leave Copenhagen without seeing *Den Lille Havfrue (The Little Mermaid)*, the most popular expression of Hans Christian Andersen's fairy-tale world. Some may find the experience a little disappointing. Designed in 1913, she languishes in rather stark isolation at the northern end of the city's waterfront. Sadly, vandals have damaged *The Little Mermaid* by sawing off her arm and her head on separate occasions. The original molds survive, however, making this iconic statue – in one sense – forever renewable.

Teatermuseet ☎ 33 11 51 76 🕐 Tue. and Thu. 11–3, Wed. 11–5, Sat.–Sun. 1–4 📱 $$

Tøjhusmuseet ✉ Tøjhusgade 3 ☎ 33 11 60 37 🕐 Daily 10–4, Apr. 16–25 and Jul.; Tue.–Sun. noon–4, rest of year 📱 $$ (free on Wed.)

Christiansborg Slotskirke ☎ 33 92 64 51 🕐 Daily noon–4, Jul. and Oct. 15–23 ; Sun. noon–4, rest of year 📱 Free

Marmorkirken

Frederiks Kirke (Frederick's Church), known universally as Marmorkirken (Marble Church), seems out of place in a Copenhagen of slender, convoluted steeples and towers. The church was begun in 1749 as a final flourish to the nearby Amalienborg Palace, but was not completed until 1894. Modeled on St. Peter's in Rome, its dome measures almost 100 feet in diameter.

The nave is circular and is surrounded by a circular walkway, above which there is a whispering gallery with superb acoustics. Currently, major repairs are under way and tower tours will not resume until 2012–13. The paneled frescoes on the inside of the dome are glowingly painted and gilded.

Inside Marmorkirken, or the Marble Church

🔲 D4 ✉ Frederiksgade 4 ☎ 33 15 37 63; www.marmorkirken.dk 🕐 Church: Mon.–Thu. and Sat. 10–5 (also Wed. 5–6), Fri. and Sun. noon–5 🚇 Kongens Nytorv 🚌 A1, 15 📱 Church free; Dome $$

Nationalmuseet

Copenhagen's Nationalmuseet (National Museum) is one of the finest of its kind in Europe, with outstanding exhibits on Danish history.

The burial possessions of two Bronze Age bog people are a particular draw. There is a collection of *lur* (horn instruments used for ceremony and communication), and other major collections cover the Middle Ages and the Renaissance, Egyptian and classical antiquities, and human cultures. There is a children's museum and a theater. You can also visit the Victorian Home at nearby Frederiksholms kanal.

🔲 B2 ✉ Ny Vestergade 10 ☎ 33 13 44 11; www.natmus.dk 🕐 Museum: Tue.–Sun. 10–5. Victorian Home: Sat. 2 p.m., Jun.–Sep. 🚇 S-train København H 🚌 1A, 2A, 11A, 14, 15, 26, 19, 40 🍴 Restaurant and café 📱 Free ℹ Guided tours (free) in English, Tue., Thu. and Sun. at 11, Jun.–Aug.

Ny Carlsberg Glyptotek

A winter garden with huge palm trees is the unexpected focal point of the Ny (New) Carlsberg Glyptotek, one of the country's finest art museums. Carl Jacobson, owner of the Carlsberg breweries founded the museum more than 100 years ago. He was mostly interested in ancient art from the Mediterranean, and Danish and French art from the 19th century. Highlights are the Etruscan collection, one of the largest outside Italy, and French sculpture (including a Rodin collection) and paintings. The French collection, housed in a specially designed structure, includes works by the Impressionists and 40 works by Paul Gauguin.

🔲 B1 ✉ Dantes Plads 7 ☎ 33 41 81 41; www.glyptoteket.dk 🕐 Tue.–Sun. 11–5 🚇 København H 🚌 1A, 2A, 14, 15, 26, 33, 65E, 250S 🍴 Museum café 📱 $$$ (free on Sun.)

Rosenborg Slot

The early 17th-century Rosenborg Slot (Rosenborg Castle) is an outstanding example of Renaissance architecture and style; it stands at the edge of the lovely Kongens Have (King's Gardens).

The lavishly decorated rooms reflect the regal styles of Danish monarchs from Christian IV to Frederick IV. There are superb marbled ceilings, late 17th-century Dutch tapestries, gilded mirrors, silver lions, gold and enamelware, and beautiful ceiling paintings.

The Royal Treasury is in the castle basement; here the Danish Crown Jewels and other royal treasures glow in the delicate light.

➕ C4 ✉ Øster Voldgade 4A ☎ 33 15 32 86; www.rosenborgslot.dk 🕐 Daily 10–5, Jun.–Aug.; daily 10–4 in May and Sep.–Oct.; Tue.–Sun. 11–2 (Royal Treasury also daily 2–4, Jan.–Apr. and Nov.–Dec. 🚇 Nørreport 🚌 6A, 25, 150S, 173E, 184, 185 🍴 Restaurant 💲 $$$

Rundetårn

The Rundetårn (Round Tower) is on Købmagergade, one of the city's liveliest streets. A visit is a must for anyone fit enough to trek up the covered, cobbled ramp that winds its way for 685 feet and through seven and a half turns to the top of the 114-foot landmark. Peter the Great of Russia is said to have ridden his horse up the ramp while the Czarina followed in a horse-drawn carriage. Today, everybody walks; keep to the outside for the easiest angle. From the top there are marvelous views of Copenhagen's red-tiled roofs and far-flung outskirts. The Round Tower dates from 1642 and was built by Christian IV as an observatory. It still functions as such and at certain times (see below) the public has access to the astronomical telescope.

➕ B3 ✉ Købmagergade 52A ☎ 33 73 03 73; www.rundetaarn.dk 🕐 Tower: daily 10–8, late May–late Sep.; 10–5, rest of year (open later some evenings). Observatory: Tue.–Wed. 7–10 p.m., mid-Oct. to mid-Mar. 🚇 Nørreport 🚌 5A, 6A, 14, 42, 43, 150S, 173E, 184, 185, 350S 💲 $$

Statens Museum for Kunst

A huge number of works are on display at the Statens Museum for Kunst (National Gallery). International and Danish art from the 13th century to 1900, shown in the new building, includes superb 17th-century Dutch paintings by Pieter Brueghel, Rembrandt, Jacob Jordaens and Jacob van Ruisdael; 19th-century Danish painting is represented by Golden Age artists such as Christoffer Eckersberg and Christen Købke, and by the Skagen painters, Theodor Philipsen and the Funen Painters.

Twentieth-century art, displayed in the old building, includes works by Henri Matisse (*Odalisque*), Max Ernst, the CoBrA Group (*Springtime* by Asger Jorn), Georges Braque and Pablo Picasso, as well as other modern works.

➕ C4 ✉ Sølvgade 48–50 ☎ 33 74 84 94; www.smk.dk 🕐 Tue.–Sun. 10–5 (also Wed. 5–8) 🚇 Nørreport, Østerport or Kongens Nytorv 🚌 6A, 14, 26, 40, 42, 43, 184, 185, 150S, 173E 🍴 Café 💟 Free (special exhibitions $$$)

Tivoli

Copenhagen's famous Tivoli is unmissable, except during the winter months when the gardens are closed (though they are open for a week in October for Hallowe'en and from mid-November through December 30 for the Christmas holidays). At the heart of the city, the 21-acre park is given over to entertainment: flower gardens, lakes, theater, concert hall, carnival rides including a roller coaster, amusements, and, above all, people-watching.

There is an entrance fee, and separate charges for carnival rides and indoor attractions (you can buy a pass). Tivoli is never dull; it is lit brilliantly at night and there are shows, concerts and occasional fireworks during the summer.

➕ B1 ✉ Vesterbrogade 3 ☎ 33 15 10 01; www.tivoli.dk 🕐 Daily 11 a.m.–10 p.m. or midnight, Apr. 14–Sep. 25, Oct. 14–Oct. 23 and Nov. 11–Dec. 30 (closed Dec. 24 and 25) 🚇 S-train København H 🚌 2A, 5A, 6A, 250 🍴 32 restaurants 💲 $$$

Odense

Odense seems to radiate the persuasive charm of a story by its most famous son, Hans Christian Andersen. Even factory chimneys on the outskirts of the city are gaily painted, and the surviving medieval buildings of the Old Town are enchanting. Above all, this popular city makes a refreshing change from the urban bustle of Copenhagen. Odense's wealth of museums and attractions are worthy of a city several times its size. This important regional capital and university town retains its provincial charm, and is celebrated as the birthplace of Hans Christian Andersen and the great composer Carl Nielsen.

The Modern City

You will relax when you arrive at Odense's railroad station, on Østre Stationsvej. Street life is busy here and the traffic is just as heavy as in any city, but directly across the road is Kongens Have, the old Royal Park. The park provides a peaceful introduction to Odense and takes you along tree-shaded paths past the Odense Theater and the Funen Art Museum (Fyns Kunstmuseum) into the heart of the city.

The center of Odense is at Flakhaven, a pedestrian-only area in front of the red-brick Town Hall (Rådhus), in a mixture of architectural styles, the interior of which can be seen on a guided tour. The friendly and helpful VisitOdense (Odense tourist office) is to the left of the Town Hall.

All buses leave from stops near the Town Hall, but you will have little need of public transportation unless you travel outside the city. Most attractions are just a short walk from the center, and it is easy to find your way around. From Flakhaven, turn left along the

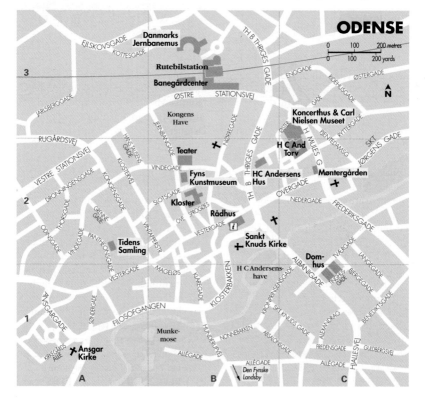

street Vestergade, which takes you into the pleasant, pedestrian-only heart of modern Odense. Here you will find a variety of stores, including top fashion boutiques. Visit Inspiration Zinck (Vestergade 82–84, ☎ 66 12 96 93) for the best in Danish design and handicrafts. Step down the adjoining street of Jernbanegade to Målet bar and restaurant for a *smørrebrød*, Denmark's delicious lunchtime snack, the ubiquitous open sandwich consisting of a piece of rye bread with sliced meat or fish and loaded with different garnishes.

The Old Town

Going east from the Town Hall takes you across the traffic-laden street Thomas B. Thriges Gade and into Odense's Old Town. Here in Hans Jensens Stræde is the Hans Christian Andersen House (entrance on Bangs Boder), amid a little complex of cobbled streets and doll-like houses that was once the poor quarter of the city. Nearby is the Carl Nielsen Museum (see page 148), which adjoins the Odense Koncerthus (Odense Concert Hall; Claus Bergs Gade 9, ☎ 63 75 00 55). Charming as this area is, the best of Old Odense is a couple of streets away, where the medieval thoroughfares of Overgade and Nedergade retain many of their detailed, interesting old buildings.

Pause at the entrance to Nedergade and look down the side street leading down to the river. This is Paaskestræde, location of the Old Poor House, with its rippled red-tile roof and scalloped cornice above the first floor. Hans Christian Andersen went to school here, and the wording on the wall is his touching comment: "Here I went with my wooden shoes to the poor school."

The combination of old and new is what makes Odense such a delight. The city's human scale, its sense of healthy provincialism and its vigorous regional culture are all enhanced by the international cachet of Hans Christian Andersen and Carl Nielsen. What you will find refreshing is that the locals have retained a friendly, unaffected nature in the face of all this.

Essential Information

Tourist Information

VisitOdense
Rådhuset, Vestergade 2 ☎ 63 75 75 20;
www.visitodense.com

Urban Transportation

Odense's railroad station (Odense Banegård Center) on Østre Stationsvej (☎ 70 13 14 15; for English press 3) has modern facilities and is about a 10-minute walk from the city center. Odense's main attractions are within a small area of the city center, but if you need bus information, call ☎ 63 11 22 33. For taxi service, call Odense Taxa ☎ 66 15 44 15.

Airport Information

Odense Airport only operates domestic flights. The nearest international airport is Billund Airport, on Jutland ☎ 76 50 50 50; www.billund-airport.com; Mon.–Fri. 8–5. There are no bus connections between Billund Airport and Odense so you will have to use a combination of train and bus. Call the airport for information or visit www.rejseplanen.dk.

Climate – average highs and lows for the month

Jan.	Feb.	Mar.	Apr.	May	Jun.	Jul.	Aug.	Sep.	Oct.	Nov.	Dec.
2°C	3°C	9°C	14°C	19°C	22°C	25°C	24°C	20°C	14°C	7°C	4°C
36°F	37°F	48°F	57°F	66°F	72°F	77°F	75°F	68°F	57°F	45°F	39°F
-3°C	-2°C	2°C	5°C	9°C	13°C	15°C	15°C	12°C	6°C	2°C	-1°C
27°F	28°F	36°F	41°F	48°F	55°F	59°F	59°F	54°F	43°F	36°F	30°F

Denmark

Odense Sights

Carl Nielsen Museet

Already blessed with Hans Christian
Andersen, Odense also has Denmark's
most famous composer, Carl August
Nielsen, as another native son. Nielsen
was born in 1865 at nearby Nørre
Lyndelse and began his musical career
as a trumpeter in a local band. His most
famous works are his six symphonies,
his opera *Saul and David* and choral
works such as *Spring of Funen*.

The Carl Nielsen Museum is a restful
place housed in an extension of the
Odense Koncerthus (Concert Hall).
It tells the story of his life through
displays of artifacts. Stop at key points,
don earphones and drift away listening
to Nielsen's music. His wife, Anne
Marie Broderson, was a sculptor, and
there are displays of her work here
to admire.

➕ C3 ✉ Claus Bergs Gade 11 ☎ 65 51 46 01;
www.museum.odense.dk ⏰ Wed.–Fri. 3–7,
Sat.–Sun. 11–3, Jan.–May; Wed.–Sun. 11–3,
Jun.–Aug.; Wed.–Fri. 3–7, Sat.–Sun. 11–3, Sep.–Dec.
Also 4–9:30 p.m. during performances by Odense
Symphony Orchestra 🖐 Free

Danmarks Jernbanemuseum

Danmarks Jernbanemuseum (Denmark's
Railway Museum) is ideally located
next to Odense railroad station and is
the biggest museum of its kind in
Scandinavia. It features a reconstructed
early 19th-century station and
locomotives, including luxurious royal
carriages. Add to this a model train
collection, trips on a mini train and a
section dedicated to ferries and you
might not even get out of the station.
Small boys will be in heaven here.

➕ B3 ✉ Dannebrogsgade 24 ☎ 66 13 66 30;
www.jernbanemuseum.dk ⏰ Daily 10–4 🍴 Café
🖐 $$$ ℹ Steam-train trips during school holidays

Den Fynske Landsby is an open-air model village, complete with a windmill

Den Fynske Landsby

The open-air museum of Den Fynske Landsby (The Funen Village) gives an interesting insight into ordinary rural life on the island of Funen during the 18th and 19th centuries. Around 30 thatched, timber-framed buildings are arranged like a farming village complete with picturesque duck pond, smithy, water mill and windmill.

Farming continues during the summer months, and visitors can watch the harvesting, beer brewing and craftwork that are conducted as part of village life.

There are some particularly imaginative tableaux detailing the contrasting lives of a poor and a well-off 19th-century villager.

🔒 Off map at B1 ✉ Sejerskovvej 20 ☎ 65 51 46 01; www.museum.odense.dk ◉ Daily 10–6, late Jun. to mid-Aug.; Tue.–Sun. 10–5, Apr.–late Jun. and mid-Aug. to mid-Oct.; Sun. 11–3, Jan.–Mar.; closed mid-Oct. to Dec. 🍴 Restaurant 💷 $$$ (free Jan.–Mar.)
🔷 Living history events in summer

Fyns Kunstmuseum

The Fyns Kunstmuseum (Funen Art Museum) is located in an elegant, classical building and contains a superb collection of art. The museum has a distinctive atmosphere of serenity that is missing from some major galleries.

Most of the works are by Danish artists from the 17th century to the present day. Highlights include Jens Juel's vivid self portrait and P. S. Krøyer's *Italian Field Workers*, with its interesting preponderance of left-handed men – a little art puzzle. H. A. Brendekild's big painting *Outworn*, with its prostrate worker in a vast, flat field, portrays the hard life of peasant workers in old Funen. By contrast, a real charmer is Gustava Emilie Grüner's *Group Portrait of the Family Leunbach*, with its cheerful, inviting faces. The museum also has some fine sculptures and a small collection of contemporary abstract art.

🔒 B2 ✉ Jernbanegade 13 ☎ 65 51 46 01; www.museum.odense.dk ◉ Tue.–Sun. 10–4
💷 $$–$$$

H.C. Andersens Hus

The.H.C. Andersens Hus (Hans Christian Andersen Museum) brings to life the story and brilliant works of Odense's most famous son. The museum describes Andersen's extraordinary life and the intensity of character that shaped his work. You are taken on a historical journey of one man, and introduced to his world and influences, tracing the great storyteller's development from humble beginnings as a cobbler's son to worldwide fame as a best-selling author.

Exhibitions throughout the museum show other aspects of the man, including his artistic qualities. The writer's original home and alleged birthplace is located at the heart of a charming complex of old single-story houses, which was once considered the "poor quarter" of Odense.

🔒 B2 ✉ Bangs Boder 29 ☎ 65 51 46 01; www.museum.odense.dk ◉ Daily 9–5, late Jun.–Aug.; Tue.–Sun. 10–4, rest of year 💷 $$$

Møntergården

Housed in a marvelous old building, with red-brick, red-timber framing and a red-tiled roof, Møntergården tells the story of Odense's past through a number of clever and interesting exhibits on local cultural history. Periods of history covered include the Stone Age and the Viking era. Behind the main building is a lovely yard with a huge tree in the center. On one side of the yard is a series of preserved domestic interiors from the 17th and 18th centuries right up to the 1950s. In keeping with Odense's charm, the museum has a wonderful air of quiet authenticity, which is often absent in big-city institutions.

🔒 C2 ✉ Overgade 48 ☎ 65 51 46 01; www.museum.odense.dk ◉ Tue.–Sun. 10–4 💷 $$$

Sankt Knuds Kirke

The elegant Gothic style of Sankt Knuds Kirke (St. Canute's Cathedral), Funen's cathedral, reflects the importance of early medieval Odense and the homage paid to King Knud (Canute). Knud, with his brother Benedikt (Benedict) and 17 retainers, was slaughtered here on July 10, 1086 – having taken refuge in the church – by Jutland farmers in a rather drastic protest against royal taxes (see below). The church has some powerful artifacts, not the least of which is its splendid rococo pulpit and its altarpiece, a dazzling wood triptych with exquisite carvings and gold leaf that is one of the finest pieces of religious art in northern Europe. Down the stairs, in the atmospheric and chilly crypt, are two reliquaries containing the reputed skeletons of Knud and Benedikt, macabre but endearing somehow in their gaunt way.

✚ B2 ✉ Klosterbakken 2 ☎ 66 12 03 92; www.odense-domkirke.dk ◷ Daily 10–5, Apr.–Oct.; 10–4, rest of year ✋ Free

Tidens Samling

For a museum with a difference, Tidens Samling (Time Collection) is hard to beat. The museum is on the third floor (there is an elevator). The Time Collection is a series of six set-piece interiors from various periods from 1900 to the 1980s, each one crammed full with authentic artifacts and stylish furnishings. The result is delightful – a unique look at changing domestic style and fashions in dress. One of the many charming aspects of the Time Collection is that you are able to step into the displays, relax in the chairs, have a good poke through the drawers, or if it takes your fancy, do a bit of sock-mending. There is even a period-style coffee bar. Occasional fashion shows are done with flair. There also are often exhibitions that have a cultural theme.

✚ A2 ✉ Farvegården 7, 3 sal ☎ 65 91 19 42; www.tidenssamling.dk ◷ Mon.–Fri. 10–4, first Sun. of month 11–3 🍴 Café ✋ $$

Sankt Knuds Kirke is a Gothic cathedral

The Martyred King

The violent death of the 11th-century Danish King Knud (Canute), a descendant of Canute, one-time king of England, did Odense a favor. The king and his brother, Benedikt, were slaughtered in Odense's old Church of St. Alban's on July 10, 1086, by Jutland peasant farmers angered by excessive taxes the king levied to finance war with England. Fourteen years later Pope Paschalis II canonized the king as St. Knud the Holy. In an ironic twist, Benedictine monks from England settled in Odense and successfully promoted the town as a place of pilgrimage to the murdered ruler.

The reputed skeletons of Knud and Benedikt can still be seen in Sankt Knuds Kirke (see page 149).

Hans Christian Andersen

Odense's most famous son left his native city at an early age. Yet Odense is still associated with Hans Christian Andersen. From humble beginnings – his mother was a washerwoman, his father a shoemaker – Andersen's astonishingly fertile imagination and creativity led him on extensive travels throughout Europe and established him as Denmark's major literary figure. He was born in 1805 in Odense, but it is not certain in which location. By the age of seven Andersen was inspired after visiting the theater in Odense; by 14 he was in Copenhagen, where he tried unsuccessfully to join the Royal Theater Company.

Andersen was a man of complex sensitivities whose relationships were profound and often difficult, although he was never short of friends and benefactors. He was essentially a poet and dramatist, and his early works reflect this. He had the urge to travel, and his first, self-published book was about a journey he made on foot through Denmark. In 1835 he published *Fairy Tales, Told for Children*. Plays, novels and travel accounts followed, along with a continuing output of the fairy tales that were to make his name.

Andersen's fairy tales were far more profound than mere fantasy, however charming. He was a powerful moralist, an intensely humane man who understood the human condition and injected into his stories remarkable life lessons. Famous and popular tales such as *The Emperor's New Clothes, The Little Mermaid, The Ugly Duckling, The Tinder Box* and *The Nightingale* have entered the consciousness of generations of readers worldwide, for their literary elegance as much as their theatricality.

Andersen remained an intense and sometimes troubled man throughout his life. He was a friend and associate of kings and of the famous. He never married, though he was deeply in love at times, not least with the Swedish opera soprano Jenny Lind. He died at 70 in 1875, in a friend's house near Copenhagen. In the Denmark of his day Andersen was criticized and diminished for what was seen as his absorption with the wider European world. As always with genius, however, his work transcended time. In Odense the spirit of this remarkable man is vividly present, at the Hans Christian Andersen Museum (see page 149) and also in quieter corners of the Old Town.

Hans Christian Andersen reads his story *The Angel* to a sick child

Finland

Opposite: A sauna house at the edge of a forested lake near Jyvaskyla

Finland

Finland, one of the world's great survivors, is a small nation that has had to contend with harsh nature and belligerent neighbors in an often hostile northern European world. For centuries Finland was trapped between the aggressive ambitions of Sweden and Russia, and then in the 20th century between the Eastern and Western protagonists of the Cold War.

The country's emergence as a self-confident, modern nation, with its historic identity intact, is a celebration of steady nerve, political shrewdness and tenacity.

A tall-masted vessel moored in Helsinki harbor

Land of Forests and Lakes

Finland is bordered on the east by Russia, on the northwest by Sweden and on the north by Norway. Most of Finland is less than 600 feet high, and over 70 percent of the country supports coniferous spruce and pine. The northern areas are covered with peat bog, and there are almost 188,000 lakes and nearly 180,000 islands. All of Finland is a seemingly endless blanket of trees, water and wide skies.

The main "lake district" of Saimaa in the east is a paradise of woodland and navigable rivers and lakes, punctuated by rugged cliffs and a glittering mosaic of islands and lakeside towns and villages. Apart from the special nature of the Finnish landscape, the main cities and towns – Helsinki, Turku (Åbo), Tampere, Porvoo, Savonlinna, Oulu and Rovaniemi – have much to offer the visitor. They are as modern as any other European urban center, yet retain a deep-seated Finnish identity.

The Islands and Lapland

The mirror image of the inland water world is Finland's coastal region. Off Finland's southwestern coast is the Saaristomeri archipelago, with its thousands of islands and little rock

islets known as "skerries." Farther out lie the Åland Islands, stepping stones to Sweden. You can explore the archipelago by ferry or steamship, or stay on shore at the beaches of Yyteri, near Pori, on the coast to the north.

In northern Finland, in the great wilderness of Lapland, you can learn about the life and culture of the Sami (Lapp) people in Rovaniemi's Arctic Center (Arktikum). The adventurous can go white-water rafting on the Tornionjoki river, follow one of the numerous hiking routes or head into the mountains of the northwest, where Finland's highest peak, Haltitunturi, reaches 4,300 feet. Up here in this wilderness, the Sami tend their reindeer herds and pursue the ever-hopeful prospect for gold.

Traveling in Finland

Traveling around the country by car is a good way to see rural Finland. There are excellent road systems around Helsinki and between the main towns, but in rural areas some roads may be poor or even just dirt tracks.

Finland's state railroad, Valtion Rautatiet, serves the whole country (except the extreme north), with the most frequent service in the south. There is an excellent bus service

The view from the summit of Koli hill toward scattered small islands on Lake Pielinen

throughout the country, and the east–west network in central and southern Finland is especially efficient.

The Finnish climate is far more amiable than you might expect. In spite of being in the same latitude as Alaska and Siberia, Finland and the whole Scandinavian peninsula enjoy a much milder climate owing to the influence of the Gulf Stream. There can be warm dry spells in summer; the southeast area of Finland has the highest summer temperatures throughout the Scandinavian region.

The Finnish people have a well-developed sense of irony, which may emerge in the form of jovial self-disparagement, especially among the young. The Finns know when to keep quiet and may appear to be unwilling to talk very much. But throughout the country you will be welcomed, and helped, with courtesy and kindness.

More Top Destinations in Finland

- Åland A1
- Helvetinjärven Kansallispuisto A1
- Lapland A3
- Loviisa B1
- Porvoo B1
- Rauma A1
- Rovaniemi A2
- Saimaa B1
- Savonlinna B1
- Tampere A1
- Turku A1
- Vaasa A1

Timeline

4000 BC	Sami peoples move into northern Finland from the east.
1600 BC	Development of Iron Age culture and emergence of the Finno-Ugric language.
1100	Finland is occupied by four tribal elements: the Sami in the north, Karelians in the east, Tavastians in the central lakes and Finns in the southwest.
1249	Swedish regent Birger Jarl establishes colonies in the southwest of Finland.
1290s	Invasions by Russia lead to Swedish–Russian conflicts.
1555	Finland is made a Swedish duchy.
1807	Czar Alexander I of Russia occupies Finland.
1917	Finland becomes an independent republic.
1939–44	Finland declares neutrality but Russia invades; Finland declares itself a "co-belligerent" with Germany in resisting Russian attacks.
1992	The 1948 Treaty of Friendship, Cooperation and Mutual Assistance between Finland and Russia is dissolved.
1995	Finland becomes a member of the European Union.
2000	Tarja Halonen becomes the first female president of Finland.
2002	Finland adopts the euro as its national currency.
2008	Former Finnish President Martti Ahtisaari awarded Nobel Peace Prize.
2009	Helsinki designated World Design Capital 2012.
2010	Finland becomes the first country in the world to give its residents a legal right to broadband Internet access.

A Bridge between East and West

Finland's 20th-century relationship with Russia has very often been misunderstood. The term "Finlandization" was used disparagingly by some to describe the country's carefully orchestrated policy toward its giant neighbor, but Finland's sensitive geographic position dictated this policy. For centuries, Russia competed with Sweden for domination over Finland. After 1807, Russian influence prevailed. Finland's declaration of independence in 1917 led to an uneasy relationship between the two countries, and resulted in bitter conflict during World War II. After the war, Finland was forced to tread a careful path between the Cold War policies of East and West. The Finnish politician who did the most to maintain national identity under these circumstances was Urho K. Kekkonen, who was the country's president from 1956 to 1981. Kekkonen's pragmatism and his careful balancing act between East and West earned him much criticism from Western politicians. But Finland remained essentially a Scandinavian country while maintaining "friendly coexistence" with Russia. Finland's rapid emergence, post-Cold War, as a democratic, pluralist and modern society is a testament to the wisdom of Kekkonen's strategy. It is said that he frequently conducted discussions with visiting Russian politicians in the relaxation of a traditional sauna, where everyone feels happily equal.

Survival Guide

- For Finnish and international fashion in Helsinki, try Marimekko, with locations at Pohjoisesplanadi 2 and 33, the Itäkeskus shopping mall and the Kamppi mall complex. For exclusive silkwear look for Marja Kurki's scarfs in Stockmann department store, Aleksanterinkatu 52. For traditional jewelry and Finnish national clothing, you cannot beat Kalevala Koru, Unioninkatu 25.
- Driving with dimmed headlights in the daytime is compulsory in Finland. When driving in rural Finland you will need to watch out for elk and reindeer on the roads.
- You will find that consumer goods are generally more expensive in Finland than in the rest of Europe, although prices are gradually starting to come down. Accommodations and restaurants also are more expensive.
- Many hotels have saunas, but most are electrically heated. The traditional Finnish "smoke" sauna is heated by a wood-burning stove and is said to be the real experience, an important cultural institution. For information on traditional saunas, contact the Finnish Sauna Society, Vaskiniementie 10, FIN-00200 Helsinki ☎ 10 439 5600; www.sauna.fi.
- In Helsinki you will find numerous "grill kiosks," little huts selling fast food in the form of hamburgers, french fries, meat-filled pies and grilled sausages (*grillimakkara*). The kiosks are good for daytime snacks, but late at night they often attract loud, drunken revelers.
- On the weekend that falls between June 20 and 26 there are midsummer celebrations throughout the country. After the long, dark nights of winter, Finns celebrate Midsummer's Day with gusto.
- Helsinki Card (www.helsinkicard.fi) entitles you to free entry to museums

An elk comes face-to-face with a camera

and major sights, unlimited travel on local public transportation, a free city sightseeing tour and a range of discounts. They are available for periods of 24 hours (€35), 48 hours (€45) and 72 hours (€55).

- There is a state monopoly on the sale of alcohol, apart from medium-strength beers, which can be bought in some grocery stores. Wine and spirits can be bought only in state-controlled outlets known as *Alko* (stores not open on Sunday). Restaurants usually serve alcohol.
- All public restrooms in Finland are generally clean and modern. Signs are *Naiset* for ladies and *Michet* for men.

Helsinki

Helsinki (sometimes referred to in Swedish as Helsingfors) will take your breath away. It does so quite literally in the frozen winter, but even then it can have days of glorious weather. In summer, the city will delight you even more with its stunning architecture and its blue Baltic waters.

City of the Sea

As with Oslo, the best way to approach Helsinki is by sea. The Lutheran Cathedral (Tuomiokirkko) and the Uspenski Cathedral (Uspenskin Katedraali) stand out against the skyline behind the handsome row of waterfront buildings that include the 19th-century City Hall (Kaupunki aula) and Presidential Palace (Presidentin linna). In front of them is Market Square, crammed with vendors selling just about everything, from fish to handicrafts.

You miss this introduction to the city if you arrive by plane, bus or train, but the early 20th-century railroad station is a striking example of Helsinki's remarkable architecture. Bus and railroad stations are close to the heart of things and only a few streets from Senate Square (Senaatintori) and the bustle of Mannerheimintie, the city's main street.

Helsinki is easy to explore independently. Trams and buses serve all parts of the city, but the subway system is of little help to visitors.

The heart of summertime Helsinki is the tree-lined Esplanade (Eteläesplanadi)

that runs west from Market Square (Kauppatori) and South Harbor (Eteläsatama) to Mannerheimintie. There is a bandstand next to the Kappeli restaurant (see page 473), where you can sample Finnish specialties such as salmon soup (*lohikeitto*).

The streets bordering the Esplanade have many stylish boutiques, as well as colorful cafés and restaurants. Stop for

Uspenski Cathedral in Northern Harbor, Helsinki

Finlandssvenska

The form of Swedish spoken in Finland is *Finlandssvenska*, "Finland's Swedish." Today about six percent of Finnish residents speak Swedish exclusively. Most of Finland's signs and street names are in Finnish and Swedish. Unless you are fluent in either language, you are best sticking to English, which is Finland's "second language."

coffee and pastries in the Swedish Theater (Svenska Teatern) at the west end of the Esplanade.

Quiet Corners

For green spaces and seashore walks go south from the Esplanade, past the University Observatory and the austere Russian Embassy, to reach Kaivopuisto Park. Beyond lies the seashore road of Ehrenströmintie, where moored yachts enhance the views of numerous islands. Alternatively, go north from the square in front of the railroad station to Kaisaniemi Park and the University Botanical Gardens, and on to the tree-fringed sea inlets beyond. Walk up Mannerheimintie to see the monumental Parliament House (Eduskuntatalo) and Finlandia Hall

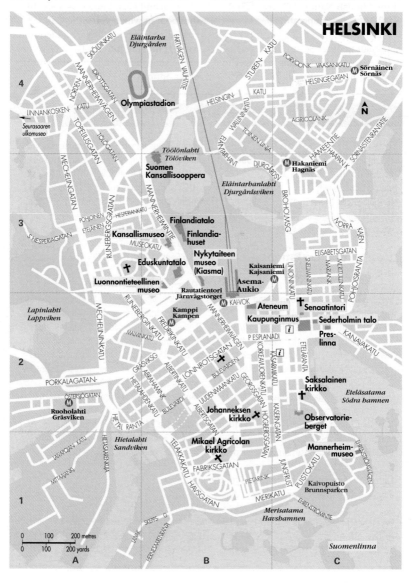

Finland

(Finlandiatalo); then go west to Temppeliaukio Church (Temppeliaukion Kirkko), a copper-domed church carved out of rock.

Despite Helsinki's reputation for long, dark winters, there is much to reward the visitor all year. Enjoy restaurants, listen to the music of Jean Sibelius in Finlandia Hall (☎ 09 402 41; www.finlandiatalo.fi) or attend a performance at the Finnish National Opera (☎ 09 4030 2211; www.operafin.fi).

You will find fewer English speakers here than in other Scandinavian countries, but Helsinkians are eager to help visitors enjoy this cultured city.

"Smoke" Sauna

Sauna is a way of life for Finns. Apart from being healthy and relaxing, it's a social, cultural – and, some say – almost religious practice.

A sauna is an insulated room that is traditionally heated by a wood-burning stove. In a "smoke" sauna, steam is generated by throwing water on the hot stones of the stove, and the correct mix of steam and heat, known as *löyly*, fills the room in which you sit naked. Sometimes pine needles are added to the water. Plunging into icy lakes or rolling in the snow between bouts of *löyly* are other options.

Essential Information

Tourist Information

Helsinki City Tourist & Convention Bureau
Pohjoisesplanadi 19 ☎ 09 3101 3300;
www.visithelsinki.fi
Helsinki Expert (Hotel Booking Center),
Helsinki railroad station ☎ 09 2288 1400;
www.helsinkiexpert.fi

Urban Transportation

Helsinki's railroad station is located on Kaivokatu. It is the terminus for main train services throughout the country and to Russia. For information ☎ 0600 41 902 (358 9 2319 2902 from outside Finland). Helsinki's bus, tram and subway network is operated by Helsingin Kaupungin Liikennelaitos (HKL). The city bus terminal is in the center of Simonleatu 3, with connections to the rest of Finland as well as citywide. Main tram stops are on Kaivokatu. For city bus, tram, subway and local train information call ☎ 0100 111 (from within Helsinki only; Mon.–Fri. 7–7, Sat.–Sun. 9–5). Long-distance buses arrive and depart

from the bus terminal, though some services may operate from surrounding streets. For information call Matkahuolto ☎ 0200 4000. Helsinki has a small subway system serving mainly suburban areas. Stations have a sign marked "M." Taxis have a yellow dome light and are available when it is lit. There is a taxi stand at the railroad station. Call the Helsinki Taxi Center at ☎ 0100 0700.

Airport Information

Helsinki-Vantaa Airport is 12 miles north of the city. The airport is a modern, well-appointed complex with every facility. Finnair buses run to and from the airport to Helsinki railroad station. The service is every 20 minutes, daily 5 a.m.–1:10 a.m., and the trip takes about 35 minutes. Slower, but less expensive, regular bus services (Nos. 615, 451 and 415) also run between the airport and the city center. For 24-hour information on flight arrivals and departures call ☎ 0200 14636; www.helsinki-vantaa.fi

Climate – average highs and lows for the month

Jan.	Feb.	Mar.	Apr.	May	Jun.	Jul.	Aug.	Sep.	Oct.	Nov.	Dec.
-3°C	-3°C	1°C	7°C	14°C	18°C	21°C	19°C	13°C	7°C	2°C	-1°C
27°F	27°F	34°F	45°F	57°F	64°F	70°F	66°F	55°F	45°F	36°F	30°F
-9°C	-9°C	-5°C	0°C	5°C	9°C	12°C	10°C	6°C	2°C	-2°C	-7°C
16°F	16°F	23°F	32°F	41°F	48°F	54°F	50°F	43°F	36°F	28°F	19°F

Helsinki Sights

Key to symbols

➕ map coordinates refer to the Helsinki map on pages 158–159 🎟 admission charge: $$$ more than €4, $$ €1.5–€4, $ less than €1.5

See page 5 for complete key to symbols

Ateneumin taidemuseo

The Ateneumin taidemuseo (Ateneum Art Museum) is housed in a handsome 19th-century building. Vincent van Gogh, Amedeo Modigliani and Paul Cézanne are represented, among many other international figures from the 19th century to the 1960s; but it is the significant collection of Finnish art, from the 18th century to the mid-1960s, that enhances the museum.

There are some powerful works by realist painters Fanny Churberg and Albert Edelfelt, such as Edelfelt's gossiping group, *Women of Ruokalahti on the Church Hill*. Finland's master Akseli Gallen-Kallela dominates with works such as the seductive *Aino-Taru*, the *Aino Myth* and the earthy and very Finnish *A New House*. Gallen-Kallela pupil Hugo Simberg's mildly disturbing and surrealistic *The Wounded Angel* is another highlight.

Guided tours in English can be reserved in advance.

➕ B2 ✉ Kaivokatu 2 ☎ 09 173 361 or 09 1733 6401 (information); www.ateneum.fi 🕐 Tue. and Fri. 10–6, Wed.–Thu. 10–8, Sat.–Sun. 11–5 🚌 All buses to Rautatientori Square bus terminus; tram 3B, 3T, 6, 9 🍴 Museum café 🎟 $$$

Helsingin kaupunginmuseo

The Helsingin kaupunginmuseo (Helsinki City Museum) is located in the "Street Museum" of Sofiankatu. The City Museum has branches throughout the city, including the nearby Sederholm House (see right). The main museum has an exhibition on Helsinki's history.

The open-air "Street Museum" portrays changing styles of street architecture and accessories. Begin at the harbor end and walk on cobbled surfaces past old street lamps and artifacts. You start in the late 18th century and finish in the 1930s.

➕ C2 ✉ Sofiankatu 4 ☎ 09 3103 6630; www.hel.fi 🕐 Helsinki City Museum: Mon.–Wed. and Fri. 9–5, Thu. 9–7, Sat.–Sun. 11–5; "Street Museum": daily 24 hours 🚌 Tram 1, 3B, 3T 🍴 Nuevo, see page 473 🎟 Free

Luonnontieteellinen museo

The venerable Luonnontieteellinen museo (Natural History Museum) is guarded by a very handsome bronze elk, just one of the animals in the museum's vast collection of mammals, birds, insects and minerals. The mammal collection is one of the best of its kind in Europe, showing exotic beasts and Finnish wildlife in their native habitats.

➕ B3 ✉ Pohjoinen Rautatiekatu 13 ☎ 09 1911 or 09 1912 8800; www.fmnh.helsinki.fi 🕐 Tue.–Wed. and Fri. 9–4, Thu. 9–6, Sat.–Sun. 10–4, Sep.–May; Tue.–Fri. 10–6, Sat.–Sun. 10–5, rest of year 🚇 Kampi 🚌 16, 13, 21v 🍴 Museum café 🎟 $$$ (free Thu. 4–6)

Nykytaiteen museo Kiasma

The Nykytaiteen museo Kiasma (Museum of Contemporary Art Kiasma) is housed in a custom-designed building. Its bold postmodern style, by American architect Steven Holl, aroused some controversy when it opened in 1998. The exhibitions of conceptual art and often radical installations are at the forefront of European contemporary art and emphasize the sophistication of Finnish culture.

➕ B3 ✉ Mannerheiminaukio 2 ☎ 09 1733 6501; www.kiasma.fi 🕐 Tue. 10–5, Wed.–Thu. 10–8:30, Fri. 10–10, Sat.–Sun. 10–6 🚌 All buses to Rautatientori Square bus terminus; tram 4, 10 🍴 Museum café 🎟 $$$ (free first Wed. of the month 5–8)

Sederholmin talo

The Sederholmin talo (Sederholm House), standing on the corner of Senate Square, is a rare survivor of old Helsinki and is said to be the city's oldest stone house (built in 1757). What distinguishes this rather unassuming building is the story it tells of its one-time owner, Johan Sederholm, an 18th-century Finnish businessman who rose from poverty to great wealth and distinction through hard work and skill.

✚ C2 ✉ Aleksanterinkatu 16–18 ☎ 09 3103 6529; www.hel.fi ◷ Wed. and Fri.–Sun. 11–5, Thu. 11–7 (hours may vary) 🚊 Tram 1, 3B, 3T, 4 💳 Free

Senaatintori

Senaatintori (Senate Square) is the focus of the Russian Imperial style. This form of architecture was encouraged by Tsar Alexander I in his bid to make Helsinki a stylistically eastern capital after it was annexed by Russia in 1809.

The square and its major buildings were designed by C. L. Engel. Helsinki's Lutheran Cathedral (Tuomiokirkko) dominates Senate Square and the city skyline. The cathedral, also by Engel and completed in 1852, is essentially classical but has Byzantine elements. Its domes are copper-sheathed and gilded, the only accents in an otherwise blinding whiteness. The buildings that flank the square and cathedral include the Senate House, University Building and University Library.

✚ C2 ✉ Senaatintori ☎ Lutheran Cathedral: 09 2340 6120 ◷ Lutheran Cathedral: daily 9–6 (also 6 p.m.–midnight, Jun.–Aug.) 🚊 Tram 1, 2, 3B, 3T, 7 🍴 Cafe Krypta, daily 11–5, Jun.–Sep. ℹ Summer festivals and events; organ recitals Wed. and Fri. at noon, Jun.–Aug.

Seurasaaren ulkomuseo

The Seurasaaren ulkomuseo (Seurasaari Open-Air Museum) is a collection of Finnish regional buildings from the 17th century. Located on Seurasaari Island, it is easily reached from central Helsinki. Most of the 87 buildings on the site date from the 18th and 19th centuries and buildings include a manor house, traditional farmhouses and a church.

✚ Off map at A4 ✉ Seurasaari ☎ 09 4050 9660; www.nba.fi/en/museums ◷ Buildings: daily 11–5, Jun.–Aug.; Mon.–Fri. 9–3, Sat.–Sun. 11–5, mid-May to May 31 and in early Sep. Park: daily, all year 🚊 24,

then a 10-minute walk 🍴 Museum café 💳 $$$ (park free) ℹ Guided tours in English daily at 3 p.m., Jun.–Aug.

Suomen kansallismuseo

The Suomen kansallismuseo (National Museum of Finland), designed by architects Herman Geselius, Amas Lindgren and Eliel Saarinen, dates from the early 20th century and is an excellent example of the art nouveau, or Jugend style of architecture. The building is easily recognized by its tower and the entrance is "guarded" by a statue of a bear by artist Emil Wilkstrom.

Spread over four floors, there are exhibits on Finnish history and many artifacts, including a Stone Age sculpture of an elk's head from around 3000 BC. The throne of Alexander I is on display, from which he proclaimed Finnish "incorporation" with Russia in 1809.

✚ B3 ✉ Mannerheimintie 34 ☎ 0 40 50 9544 (National Board of Antiquities exchange ticket office); www.nba.fi/en/nmf ◷ Tue. 11–8, Wed.–Sun. 11–6 🚊 Tram 4, 7A, 7B, 10 🍴 Museum restaurant 💳 $$$ (free Tue. 5:30–8 p.m.)

Suomenlinna

The historic sea fortress of Suomenlinna, a UNESCO World Heritage Site, is built on six interconnecting islands and was once dubbed the "Gibraltar of the North." First used by Sweden in 1748 under the name Sveaborg ("Sweden's Fortress"), the island was surrendered to Russia in 1808. It remained in Russian control until 1918, when newly independent Finland named it Suomenlinna ("Finland's Fortress").

The museums here include the Suomenlinna Museum, the Military Museum and the Customs Museum, as well as a Doll and Toy Museum.

✚ C1 ✉ Suomenlinna ◷ Visitor Center: 09 684 1880; www.suomenlinna.fi ◷ Visitor Center: daily 10–6, May–Sep.; 10:30–4:30, rest of year 🚢 Ferries leave regularly from Kauppatori 🍴 Choice of restaurants and cafés 💳 Site free; Visitor Center $$$; other museums $$$ ℹ Guided tours $$$ in English daily at 11 and 2, Jun.–Aug.; Sat.–Sun. 1:30, Sep.–May

Imperial City: The Buildings of Helsinki

Helsinki has some of the finest buildings in northern Europe, with the architectural heart of the city being Senate Square. Here, in the early 19th century, Berlin-born Carl Ludvig Engel was commissioned to create a new Helsinki in neoclassic Russian Imperial style. On its high podium, the gleaming white Lutheran Cathedral (Tuomiokirkko) is the focus of the square. Leave the square at its northeastern corner and take a stroll up Snellmaninkatu a short distance to where the Bank of Finland (Suomen Pankki) faces the regal-looking House of Estates (Säätytalo), built in the classical style with beautiful gilded Corinthian capitals.

Another great architectural theme in Helsinki is art nouveau, or Jugend as it is known in Finland. This style drew its motifs from Finnish culture and tradition; its materials are the timber and rough-faced granite of the country used in naturalistic ways. Jugend architecture is best seen in residential areas such as Eira, on the southern peninsula of the city, and on the little island to the east of the harbor, Katajanokka. The island is guarded by the magnificent Uspenski Cathedral (Uspenskin katedraali), the most impressive expression of orthodoxy you are likely to find in northern Europe.

Jugend architecture is characterized by turrets, castellated features and carved motifs. Yet the buildings remain elegant and restrained. Take a walk down Eira's streets of Huvilakatu and Laivurinkatu. On Laivurinkatu, look for No. 25, the Villa Johanna. Walk down Luotsikatu and Kauppiaankatu, a short distance east of the cathedral, where there are numerous examples of Jugend to compare with Senate Square's classicism and with the city's more modern buildings. Finlandia Hall and the Museum of Contemporary Art Kiasma maintain Helsinki's international reputation for architectural excellence.

The white Helsinki Cathedral (Tuomiokirkko) is the focal point on Senate Square

France

Opposite: The view across the water to Le Mont St.-Michel

France

France is the largest country in western Europe, geographically one of the most diverse, and among the most beautiful. Its cities contain some of the greatest treasures in Europe; its countryside is prosperous and well tended. The French combine practicality with romance; they lead a stylish life, eat delicious food and bask in a pleasant climate.

Historically, France has developed the notion of equality for all and, while retaining its sense of tradition, remains a forward-looking country. Over the past half-century, for instance, the French have forged ahead in modern technology. France is a country of contrasts, making it a delight to explore.

France Today

France was among the first European countries to dispense with its monarchy. Apart from a couple of brief periods, it has been a republic almost as long as the United States. The French Revolution gave a tremendous sense of patriotism to all French men and women, which continues to the present day.

Despite the apparently never-ending political ups and downs, French people have a strong sense of national pride and

unity; they are essentially one people and one country. Every town and village

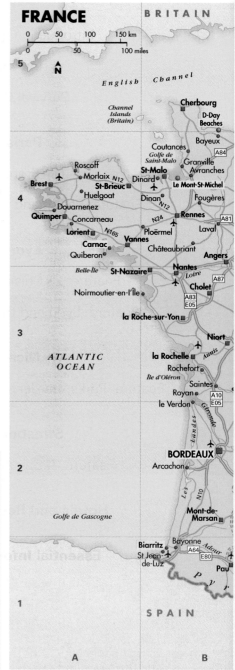

More Top Destinations in France

- Avignon D2
- Beaune D3
- Biarritz B1
- Bordeaux B2
- Carcassonne C1
- Carnac A4
- Château de Versailles C4
- Cirque de Gavarnie B1
- D-Day Beaches B5
- Grasse E2
- Grotte de Lascaux C2
- Honfleur B5
- Le Mont-St.-Michel B4
- Pont du Gard D2
- Rocamadour C2
- Sarlat C2
- Toulouse C1

in France flies the flag (*tricolore*) with pride, and displays a bust of Marianne in its town hall, the beautiful woman who epitomizes the spirit of the country.

France

The Château d'Azay-le-Rideau is built on an island on the Indre river

The French despair of their politicians, grumble at their government and taxation, and are quite capable of unruly demonstrations against the most surprising things, but *au fond*, at heart, they remain proud and devoted admirers of their country.

La belle France

La belle France – beautiful France – is indeed truly beautiful. Hexagonal in shape, each of its six sides acts as a natural boundary. The English Channel and the rolling Atlantic guard the west coast, the Pyrenees and Alps, the southwest and southeast borders, the Mediterranean laps along the southern coast and the mighty Rhine river forms a barrier against Germany in the northeast. Within this area lies a huge variety of landscape, with plains, arable flatlands, forested hills, vine- and olive-growing terraces, lush river valleys, inhospitable mountain massifs and a combined coastline stretching for almost 2,000 miles.

As you travel around France you'll notice how sparsely populated the land is compared to most other European countries. Miles go past without a sign of a town or village, yet the land is mostly cultivated, forested or tended in some way. France has always been an agricultural country, and today is the largest agricultural producer and exporter in the European Union.

Cities, Towns and Villages

In a country as geographically varied as France there is bound to be a diverse range of architecture, as styles evolved to suit the environment. In southern rural areas, the population lived in easily defensible communities and worked the fields daily, leaving a legacy of picturesque hilltop villages, with narrow streets for shelter against the fierce sun. In the mountains the design was dictated by the climate, and cozy wooden chalets evolved, with steep or flat roofs depending on the region.

The whole country in general enjoyed great prosperity during the 17th and 18th centuries, and in most of the major cities there are architectural reminders of this time, in the shape of churches, fine civic buildings, spacious squares and well-planned streets.

Before the French Revolution, the aristocracy spent several months a year on their estates and built fine fortified houses and beautiful châteaux in which they lived.

This wonderful mixture of styles still exists, and the French have been far more successful than some other European nations at preserving the historic centers of their towns. The second half of the 20th century saw some truly imaginative and innovative civic building projects in major cities, which you'll certainly notice.

The French Character

Other Europeans have a peculiar relationship with the French people, in which there may be more than a touch of envy. The French have much to boast about, and are rightly proud of their culture. As a result, they have gained a reputation with their neighbors for being arrogant. They are often accused of seeing themselves as decidedly superior to every other nation.

For years the French have been criticized and stereotyped for their attitude. But the minute a foreigner steps on French soil he or she is once more seduced: by the country, the overwhelming charm of the people, the way of life.

Lifestyle

The French strike a happy balance between the work-driven culture of northern Europeans and the wonderfully alluring, but overly relaxed, southern European approach to life. This is a prosperous country with a high standard of living, where both men and women hold down prestigious and influential jobs in every sector. It is also a highly efficient country with an excellent infrastructure, making things very easy for visitors.

Public transportation is first-rate, with Europe's best and fastest train system. If you're driving, you'll find the roads fast and in good condition; the country's speeding and drunk-driving laws are strictly enforced.

Hotels are comfortable, restaurants provide good value, and tourism is a well-organized, thriving industry.

All this is augmented by the innate French sense of style, which is obvious the minute you arrive. This is evident in everything from the way produce is artfully stacked in market stalls to the sensible layout of an airport.

You'll find the French have a relaxed approach to most problems, but note that the wheels of daily life are oiled with a high level of politeness. Even if you don't speak the language, bear in mind that courtesy is extremely important in everyday dealings.

People work hard in France, but indulge in relaxation as well. In the evenings they enjoy themselves over a lengthy meal or sit for hours in cafés. French citizens have always backed their country's achievements in culture and

The Vieille Ville (Old Town) area of Nice in Provence

France

The national game of *boules* is taken very seriously by its devotees, and is fun to watch

the arts, so there's a lively arts scene everywhere. You'll also find that almost everyone has strong views on a wide range of artistic, political and economic events, which they're eager to share.

Religion

France is nominally a Catholic country, with the church separated from the state in 1905.

More than 80 percent of its 64 million inhabitants have been baptized into the Catholic church, although only a small percentage regularly attends services.

There are approximately one million Protestants, who for historical reasons tend to be more active churchgoers. Immigrants from France's former colonies make up a large proportion of the considerable number of Muslims, while the Jewish population in France never recovered its numbers after World War II.

Every large town has one or more churches with Sunday services.

Pastimes

The French take relaxation seriously. They enjoy sports, both as spectators and participants, with soccer the national favorite, closely followed by rugby. Cycling is popular with the Tour de France rolling through the streets around the country in July, watched by millions. Tennis and golf are other popular sports, both with good facilities for tourists, and you'll find challenging golf courses all over France. Resort areas offer a huge range of pastimes, from tennis to sailing to organized hiking.

With the Alps on their doorstep, many people ski, especially during early February when children are out of school and families head for the slopes. As well as the Alps, the Pyrenees and the Massif Central at Le Mont-Dore are also destinations for French skiers.

You may often see *boules* being played. This is a game where players attempt to surround a small target ball on the ground by throwing larger, heavier balls

Les Aiguilles (literally "The Needles") is a mountain range in Chamonix, a popular skiing area

from a specified distance. A game local to the Basque area is *pelota*, where two teams hit a ball against a wall.

Pleasures

Food and drink are among the national pleasures of France, and much time is spent shopping for and preparing food. Although modern life has taken its toll, fast food, frozen meals and "grazing" items are not considered mealtime options. If the French can't be bothered to cook, they can pick up fresh dishes from a *traiteur*, a type of delicatessen. Desserts are rarely homemade, bought instead from a *pâtisserie* (cake shop), ensuring the highest quality.

Every region has its own food specialties and these are taken so seriously that some foodstuffs have an *appellation controlée* label, similar to the labeling used for wine, meaning that the product must be from the area for which it is known. Well-known regional dishes include *pot au feu de la mer* (seafood stew) from Brittany, *salade Niçoise* (Niçoise salad, made with fresh tuna, anchovies and eggs) from Provence and quiche Lorraine from the north.

French wines need no introduction, and visitors can enjoy winery visits and tastings in all the wine-producing areas. Champagne is kept for special occasions, while alongside wine, everyday drinks include many varieties of beer and the *pastis* family – an aniseed-flavored spirit diluted with water so it turns milky.

Material pleasures are important in France, where shopping is an art form. This is the country that produces cognac, internationally famous scents, and some of the world's most desirable clothes and accessories. Prices won't differ hugely from those back home, but the satisfaction is great from buying luxuries in their native land.

Expect a wealth of experience and pleasure in France: natural beauty, historic cities and good value despite the relatively high cost of living.

Timeline

15,000 BC	Lascaux cave paintings; first works by tribal group in area now covered by modern France.
3000 BC	Carnac stones erected.
58 BC	Julius Caesar invades Gaul.
AD 500	Frankish King Clovis unites tribes to form France.
800	Charlemagne crowned first Holy Roman Emperor.
1431	Joan of Arc burned at the stake; resulting patriotism gives France national identity.
1763	France loses North American possessions to England at end of Seven Years War.
1789	Start of French Revolution; monarchy overthrown and republic established.
1804	Napoleon proclaimed emperor; Napoleon defeated at Waterloo in 1815.
1889	Eiffel Tower built for Paris Exhibition; beginning of *belle époque* era.
1914–18	France allies with Britain, Russia and United States against Germany and Austro-Hungary to fight World War I.
1939–45	France swiftly defeated by Germans in World War II; Charles de Gaulle leads Free French Army from England.
1957	France becomes a founder member of European Community.
1968	Student and Trade Union unrest almost bring down the government of President de Gaulle.
2003	The French government votes against military intervention in Iraq and takes no part in the coalition action.
2007	Nicolas Sarkozy is elected as French president for a five-year term.
2010	The left's success in mid-term regional elections in May shows a slide in President Sarkozy's popularity.

Impressionism

By the 1870s a group of Parisian artists had become increasingly bored with the traditional style of paintings. They were obsessed with light and its effects; painting outside, they worked on several canvases at a time. Among these artists were Monet, Manet, Pissarro, Renoir, Dégas and Sisley. In 1874 they held their first public exhibition, where their work was ridiculed. One critic was scathing about Monet's painting *Impression of a Sunrise*, and so the name of the movement was born. Literary figures such as Zola and Flaubert supported Impressionism, feeling they could do with words what artists were doing with paint, and public opinion was gradually won over.

A sunny day can be spent in rowboats on the lake in the Bois de Boulogne, Paris

Survival Guide

■ Many French people speak some English and young people in particular are keen to practice their language skills. It's polite to master the phrase "*parlez-vous anglais?*" to use before asking a question.

■ Politeness is highly regarded in France, so preface requests with "*bonjour*" (hello) and always say "*merci*" (thank you).

■ French people can be among the world's best dressed, with a casual style that's difficult to emulate. Make an effort to be well groomed, as an attractive appearance will usually ensure better service everywhere.

■ Smoking is banned in all public buildings. This includes all cafés, bars and restaurants. However, smoking is still allowed on terraces attached to restaurants and bars, and smoking is still a popular habit with French people.

■ It's a good idea to count your change in shops and markets, and make sure taxi meters are set at zero when starting a trip.

■ You'll probably find a bidet in your bathroom, an appliance that looks like a toilet with faucets, designed for washing intimate body areas. It's handy for washing socks, as well!

■ Restrooms in most places are generally modern, but in some rural areas the toilet may consist of two floor-level porcelain plaques, on which the user squats. This often flushes automatically at high pressure causing splashes, so watch out for your shoes.

■ Parisians are notoriously inconsiderate drivers, giving little leeway to other road users, but elsewhere you'll encounter few problems. If you are driving long distances, use the toll (*péage*) highway system. It's faster and less crowded.

■ Sodas and soft drinks are very expensive in France; a beer (*bière*) often costs less than a Coke.

■ Ice water and ice in drinks is not served routinely in France. Ask for *des glaçons* if you want ice. Legally, restaurants are obliged to serve tap water if you ask for it.

■ French coffee is strong, so if you want a weaker cup ask for a *café américain*. Unless you ask for milk (*lait*) or cream (*crème*), it will always be served black (*noir*).

France

Paris

It's hard to be indifferent to historic, hectic, elegant Paris. With all its moods, this is a city that can exhilarate you, exasperate you and leave you speechless with wonder, but it won't leave you cold. Paris is beautiful no matter when you visit: the quality of light ranges from crystalline brilliance to mellow gold; distant sounds mingle with bustling main streets; and with each season a new scent blows in to announce its arrival.

Getting Your Bearings

It would take months to explore all of Paris, so resign yourself to the idea that you're not going to be able to see everything on just one trip to this great city. Some people prefer to familiarize themselves with the city by wandering the different neighborhoods; others will try to see as many attractions as possible. Consider which style best suits you and then plan ahead.

You will probably be surprised by the compressed scale of the city; the 2.2 million inhabitants of inner Paris all live within an area bounded by the 21-mile boulevard Périphérique that encircles the city. Even so, be prepared to walk considerable distances, even within the museums, some of which are on a grand scale.

Your first stop should be at one of the seven city tourist offices, the main office being at rue des Pyramides or Carousel du Louvre (open daily). Here you can get excellent maps, leaflets and information on excursions and events. Ask about tourist passes, which may reduce entry fees into the city's many museums and attractions and offer discounts on eating and shopping.

Tours and Excursions

Taking a city tour is an excellent way to get your bearings. Most tours cover the main sights on either side of the Seine river and take about two hours. An alternative is to take a bus run by Paris L'Open Tour (www.parislopentour. com), a choice of four routes that cover the city center, Bastille-Bercy, St.-Germain and Montmartre with stops along the way, allowing you to get on and off to do your own sightseeing. Tickets are valid for one or two days, and there's English commentary. You may want to take a tour outside Paris;

obvious choices are the fabulous Palace of Versailles built for Louis XIV, or the old royal hunting lodge of Fontainebleau and its surrounding forest, a favorite retreat of the kings of France. If you'll be spending your entire stay in Paris, consider taking a day trip to the châteaux of the Loire Valley, Chartres and its cathedral, or the magical island of Le Mont-St.-Michel in Normandy.

Parisian Neighborhoods

Most Parisians mentally split their city into two neat halves – Left Bank (Rive Gauche) and Right Bank (Rive Droite) – with the sinuous curve of the Seine dividing them. Traditionally, the Right Bank has stood for order and elegance, typified by the monumental architecture running from the Louvre up to the Arc de Triomphe; while the Left Bank is an

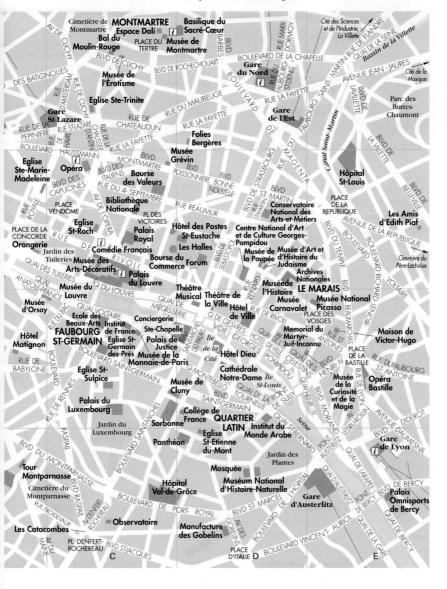

A sightseeing boat heads toward Pont Notre Dame, soon to pass the cathedral on the Île de la Cité

altogether more raffish place. This is too simplistic, however. Paris, in fact, is a series of extremely individual *quartiers*, districts, each with its own personality, style and charm.

Riverbanks and Bridges

More than 30 bridges crisscross the Seine, and the banks, known as *quais*, offer lovely views of the city. The best stretch of riverside for walking lies between the Pont de la Concorde (Concorde Bridge), leading to the place de la Concorde, and the Pont de Sully (Sully Bridge), at the eastern end of the Île St.-Louis. Browse in the *bouquinistes* (secondhand booksellers) stalls that line the riverbank, or simply revel in the subtly blended colors of sky, river, trees and stone. Several companies operate cruises on the Seine, an ideal way to enjoy the river.

Parisians

As inhabitants of a capital city, Parisians are surprisingly able to combine the inevitable pace of big-city life with the ability to switch off and spend hours strolling, window-shopping or endlessly chatting in a café. This is the quintessential image of the chic Parisian. To get a good taste of another side of life in the city, however, you should visit a neighborhood market: Food shopping is a serious business.

One characteristic you will notice is how much people seem to read: There are countless bookstores, and métro (subway) commuters seem to always have their noses in a book. Your overall impression may be that the pace of life here is hurried, and the people can seem brusque, but they can also be charming, particularly to those who love their city.

Shopping

The selection in the stores makes shopping irresistible for some. Haute couture stores cluster mainly around the Faubourg St.-Honoré and avenue Montaigne, with boutiques selling ready-to-wear (*prêt-à-porter*) designer outfits. Paris has a number of department stores; the best known are Galeries Lafayette and Printemps, on the monumental boulevard Haussmann. Both are architectural "tours de force" and purveyors of high-quality merchandise.

Visit some of the covered shopping arcades, built in the 18th and early 19th centuries; Galerie Colbert and Galerie Vivienne are among the most attractive. Food stores are a must. Head for the world-famous Fauchon, 26 place de la Madeleine; Androuët, 134 rue Mouffetard, the ultimate cheese shop; and Lionel Poilâne, 8 rue du Cherche-Midi, Paris' most famous baker.

Essential Information

Tourist Information
Office de Tourisme et des Congrès de Paris (Paris Convention and Visitors Bureau)
25 rue des Pyramides (daily)
Anvers (daily)
Gare du Nord (daily)
Paris Expo (during trade shows only)
Montmartre (daily)
Gare du Lyon (daily)
Gare de l'Est (daily)
For all tourist offices ☎ 08 92 68 30 00 (toll call); www.parisinfo.com

Urban Transportation
The easiest way to get around Paris is by the métro (subway), which runs Mon.–Fri. and Sun. 5:20 a.m.–1:20 a.m., Sat. 5:20 a.m.–2:20 a.m. The RER (Réseau Express Régional), a suburban express train, connects with the métro inside Paris. Tickets are available singly or in *carnets* (books) of 10; they are available at the stations and from tobacconists *(tabacs)* and must be validated before boarding. Keep your ticket, as there are heavy fines for travelers without tickets. The Paris Visite card, valid for 1, 2, 3 or 5 consecutive days, is interchangeable with the métro, bus and SNCF (main line) trains within the Île-de-France. Buses run daily 5:30 a.m.–8:30 p.m. (some routes until 5 a.m.); tickets are interchangeable with the subway. For transportation information in English, phone ☎ 32 46 (toll call) from within France or ☎ 33 8 92 69 32 46 from outside France;

www.ratp.info. A tourist bus, the Balabus, operates on Sundays and holidays noon–8 from mid-Apr. through Sep.; stops are marked "Balabus (Bb)." Taxis can be hailed on the street or from stands around the city. From early Feb. to early Jan. you can take the Batobus (☎ 0825 050 101; www.batobus. com); this boat runs between the Eiffel Tower and the Jardin des Plantes daily 10–9:30, Jun.–Aug.; Mon.–Fri. 10–7, Sat.–Sun. 10–9:30, May; daily 10–7, Apr. and Sep.–early Nov. (but 10–9:30, Easter); 10:30–4:30, early Nov.–early Feb. and mid-Feb.–Mar.

Airport Information
Paris has two international airports, Roissy-Charles-de-Gaulle and Orly (both aiports ☎ 3950 within France; 33 1 70 36 39 50 from outside France; www.aeroportsde paris.fr). Most U.S. visitors arrive at CDG. It is 14 miles north of Paris; taxis are available at both terminals (terminal 2 serves Air France only). Roissybus buses run every 15–20 minutes daily 6 a.m.–11 p.m. into central Paris, and RER trains every 12–15 minutes daily 4:56 a.m.–11:56 p.m. (travel time 45 minutes; buses will replace some trains until Jul. 2012). Orlybus buses (for Roissybus and Orlybus ☎ 32 46 within France; 33 8 92 69 32 46 from outside France) run from Orly, 8 miles south of Paris into the center, every 15 minutes Sun.– Thu. 6 a.m.–11:30 p.m., Fri.–Sat. 6 a.m.–12:30 a.m.; RER trains leave every 20 minutes daily 6 a.m.–11 p.m.

Climate – average highs and lows for the month

Jan.	Feb.	Mar.	Apr.	May	Jun.	Jul.	Aug.	Sep.	Oct.	Nov.	Dec.
2°C	3°C	9°C	14°C	19°C	22°C	25°C	24°C	20°C	14°C	7°C	4°C
36°F	37°F	48°F	57°F	66°F	72°F	77°F	75°F	68°F	57°F	45°F	39°F
-3°C	-2°C	2°C	5°C	9°C	13°C	15°C	15°C	12°C	6°C	2°C	-1°C
27°F	28°F	36°F	41°F	48°F	55°F	59°F	59°F	54°F	43°F	36°F	30°F

Paris Sights

Arc de Triomphe

At the western tip of the Champs-
Élysées, the Arc de Triomphe is a
splendid starting point for a day's
sightseeing. Commissioned by
Napoleon, the 164-foot-high Arc is now
dedicated to the Unknown Soldier of
World War I; the eternal flame burns
beneath. Twelve avenues radiate from it,
giving the surrounding square its
original name of place de l'Étoile (the
star); today it's called place Charles-
de-Gaulle, in memory of the famous
general. There are 284 steps to the top,
and no elevator.

➕ A3 ✉ place Charles-de-Gaulle ☎ 01 55 37 73 77;
www.monuments-nationaux.fr 🕐 Daily 10 a.m.–
11 p.m., Apr.–Sep.; 10 a.m.–10:30 p.m., rest of year.
Last admission 30 minutes before closing 🚇 Métro/
RER Charles de Gaulle-Étoile 🖐 $$

Cathédrale Notre-Dame

The great Gothic Cathédrale Notre-
Dame (Cathedral of Our Lady), built
between 1163 and 1345, stands on the
Île de la Cité, the oldest part of Paris.
The outside elevation is as impressive

as the lofty interior; admire the twin
towers, buttresses and the symmetry of
the facade.

Arrive early to climb one of the towers,
and to view the paintings and the rose
window at each end of the transept.

➕ D2 ✉ 6 place du Parvis de Notre-Dame
☎ Cathedral: 01 42 34 56 10; www.cathedraledeparis.
com 🕐 Mon.–Fri. 8–6:45, Sat.–Sun. 8–7:15 (no visits
during religious services). Towers: Mon.–Fri. 10–6:30,
Sat.–Sun. 10 a.m.–11 p.m., Jul.–Aug.; daily 10–6:30,
Apr.–Jun. and in Sep.; daily 10–5:30, rest of year. Last
admission 45 minutes before closing 🚇 Cité; RER
Châtelet or St.-Michel Notre-Dame 🖐 Cathedral free;
Tower $$ ℹ Organ recitals are held Sun. at 4:30

Centre National d'Art et de Culture Georges-Pompidou

This controversial modern art center,
opened in the 1970s, quickly earned the
nickname "the refinery in the center of
the city," due to its similarity to an oil
refinery. The architectural team of
Richard Rogers and Renzo Piano
designed it as the first postmodernist
public building to show its structural
elements on the outside.

It's home to a movie theater, library
and exhibition space, and the Musée
National d'Art Moderne (National
Modern Art Museum), which displays
art from 1905 to the present day,
including Salvador Dalí's *Six images
de Lénine*, Pablo Picasso's early
Cubist *Femme Assise*, and pop art by
Andy Warhol.

The Arc de Triomphe is a symbol of the city and those who climb to the top have far-reaching views

✚ D3 ✉ place Georges Pompidou ☎ 01 44 78 12 33; www.cnac-gp.fr ◷ Wed.–Mon. 11–10 (museum and exhibitions close at 9 p.m. except the Level 6 exhibition, which closes at 11 p.m. Thu.). Ticket counter closes an hour before galleries ⊜ Hôtel de Ville, Rambuteau; RER Châtelet-Les-Halles 🍴 Restaurant ♿ Center free; Musée $$ (free first Sun. of the month)

Champs-Élysées

The stately and much-loved Champs-Élysées (Heavenly Fields) runs from the place de la Concorde (see page 184) up to the Arc de Triomphe, and divides neatly into two sections, with the Rond-Point at the halfway mark. The lower section is bordered with grass and chestnut trees, behind which stand the Grand and Petit Palais, both devoted to the arts. Along the upper section from bustling Rond-Point are stores, offices, movie theaters and sidewalk cafés.

✚ B3 ✉ avenue des Champs-Élysées ⊜ Concorde, Champs-Élysées-Clémenceau, Franklin D. Roosevelt, George V or Charles de Gaulle-Étoile

Cité des Sciences et de l'Industrie

On the northeast edge of Paris stands a modern park, La Villette, scattered with sculptures and fountains, and devoted to science and music. Once home to the city's slaughterhouses, the site has been remodeled and converted to house the ultramodern Cité des Sciences et de l'Industrie (City of Sciences and Industry). You would need a day to do it justice, but if time is short, visit the main exhibition, Explora, focusing on life, natural resources and technological development. Go to the Géode, a movie theater with a hemispheric screen; the Cinaxe, a multisensory movie theater; or let the kids enjoy interactive games in the Cité des Enfants (Children's City). Nearby the Cité de la Musique complex is devoted to music; it houses the Musée de la Musique (Music Museum), with its permanent exhibition of instruments.

Cité des Sciences et de l'Industrie ✚ Off map at E4 ✉ 30 avenue Corentin Cariou ☎ 01 40 05 70 00; www.cite-sciences.fr ◷ Tue.–Sun. 10–6 (also Sun. 6–7 p.m.) ⊜ Porte de la Villette 🍴 Restaurant

The glowing interior of the church of Ste.-Chapelle

♿ $$ (combined ticket with Cité de la Musique $$$) **Cité de la Musique** ✉ 221 avenue Jean-Jaurès ☎ 01 44 84 44 84; www.cite-musique.fr ◷ Music Museum: Tue.–Sat. noon–6, Sun. 10–6 ⊜ Porte de Pantin 🍴 Restaurant ♿ Concert Hall free; Music Museum $$ (combined ticket with Cité des Sciences et de l'Industrie $$$)

Conciergerie et Ste.-Chapelle

The Conciergerie, so called because it was administered by a "concierge" or governor, gained a sinister reputation during the 1790s, when Marie Antoinette, queen of France, and the infamous revolutionary Robespierre were imprisoned here. It is the only remaining part of the royal complex on the Île de la Cité, a superb Gothic building with twin round entrance towers and a distinctive roofline. Inside, its huge vaulted hall is the highlight, along with reconstructed prison cells.

Nearby stands Ste.-Chapelle, commissioned by Louis IX in 1245 to house the Crown of Thorns and a fragment of the True Cross. Built as two chapels, the upper was reserved for the royal family. Slender pillars divide the 13th-century 50-foot-high stained-glass windows showing scenes from the Old and New Testaments.

Conciergerie ✚ C2 ✉ 2 boulevard de Palais ☎ 01 53 40 60 80; www.monuments-nationaux.fr ◷ Daily 9:30–6, Mar.–Oct.; 9–5, rest of year ⊜ Cité;

The Cathédrale Notre-Dame is one of the world's greatest churches with twin rose windows

RER St.-Michel Notre-Dame 🚇 $$. Last admission 30 minutes before closing 🛈 Guided tours in English; for reservations call ☎ 01 44 54 19 30

Ste.-Chapelle ✉ 4 boulevard du Palais ☎ 01 53 40 60 80; www.monuments-nationaux.fr 🕐 Mon.–Fri. 9:30–1 and 2–6, Sat.–Sun. 9:30–6, Mar.–Oct.; Mon.–Fri. 9–1 and 2–5, Sat.–Sun. 9–5, rest of year 🚇 Cité; RER St.-Michel Notre-Dame 🚇 $$ 🛈 Guided tours in English; without reservation 10:30 Wed. By reservation ☎ 01 44 54 19 33. Security is overseen by the *gendarmerie nationale* (National Police), who will confiscate any sharp metal objects

La Défense

It's worth the trip to Paris' prestigious modern business district, with its shopping center, IMAX movie theater and the Center of New Industry and Technology (CNIT). The area is divided into 12 sections; the tallest skyscraper rises to 614 feet. A pedestrian esplanade leads to the Grande Arche de la Défense, the city's triumphant architectural celebration of the French Revolution's bicentennial. Take the glass elevator 360 feet to the top of the Arche, a stark and elegant hollow white marble cube, and a great view unfolds across Paris to the Arc de Triomphe (see page 178) and the obelisk in the place de la Concorde (see page 184).

🚇 Off map at A4 ✉ La Défense ☎ Grande Arche: 01 49 07 27 27; www.grandarche.com 🕐 Grande Arche: daily 10–8, Apr.–Sep.; 10–7, rest of year

🍴 Restaurant 🚇 Métro/RER Grande Arche de la Défense 🚇 Grande Arche $$ 🛈 Last ascent 30 minutes before closing

Île de la Cité

One of the loveliest parts of Paris, the Île de la Cité is the ancient heart of the city; in medieval times it was the monarch's capital and a religious and intellectual center. Here you'll find famous monuments, including Notre-Dame (see page 178) and Ste.-Chapelle (see pages 179–180), impressive civic buildings such as the Palais de Justice, and pleasant streets and squares.

🚇 C2/D2 ✉ Île de la Cité 🚇 Cité

Île St.-Louis

Pont St.-Louis will lead you straight from the Île de la Cité on to the Île St.-Louis, ideal for a peaceful stroll, a light lunch and some expensive shopping. Once two islands, this largely residential area was developed in the 17th century, when most of its lovely streets and houses were built; since then little seems to have changed.

🚇 D2 ✉ Île St.-Louis 🚇 Pont Marie 🍴 Nos Ancêtres les Gaulois, see page 474

Jardin des Tuileries

The Jardin des Tuileries (Tuileries Gardens) is a good place to recharge your batteries after the rigors of a visit to

The French Revolution

All over Paris there are reminders of France's 1789 Revolution, when the monarchy was swept away and equal rights for all citizens were established under the law. America's own Revolutionary War served as the catalyst for events in France.

By the end of Europe's Seven Years War in 1763, France had lost all its North American possessions. Louis XVI of France, thirsting for revenge, was happy to offer arms and troops to help American colonists during their struggle against the English. These soldiers came home inspired by the American ideals of liberty and equality, taking what was, in France, an intellectually led and tiny movement to a larger grass-roots level.

France had enjoyed a Golden Age during the 17th and much of the 18th centuries; power became centralized in the hands of the monarchy, the country prospered and Paris became a center of art and sophistication. But this was at the expense of most of the population, whose standard of living dropped lower and lower. Meanwhile the nobility, deprived of any real political power, threw itself into a reckless and hedonistic lifestyle. The divide between the rich and the poor grew ever wider; time was ripe for republican ideas to bear fruit.

In 1789, the Third Estate, representing some 96 percent of France's commoners, declared itself a National Assembly and demanded social and constitutional reform. On July 14, a Parisian mob attacked Les Invalides to procure arms then stormed the Bastille prison, a hated symbol of royal power. Matters moved quickly, and within weeks France was in the grip of revolution as peasants across the country rose in revolt against the nobility and clergy.

In August, the Declaration of the Rights of Man was signed and the cry "*Liberté, égalité, fraternité*" (liberty, equality, brotherhood) was heard all over France. These high ideals soon degenerated into a bloodbath resulting in more than 40,000 people being executed. This period, aptly known as the "Terror," was halted only by Napoleon's rise to power.

The excesses of royalty who built Versailles while peasants starved led to the revolution

the Louvre. Designed by Le Nôtre, it's an excellent example of a 17th-century formal garden, its long central *allée* (alley) carrying the eye from the Louvre buildings and fountains to the expanse of the place de la Concorde.

⊞ C3 ✉ place de la Concorde ☎ 01 40 20 90 43 ◷ Daily 7:30 a.m.–7:30 p.m., Sep.–Mar.; 7 a.m.–9 p.m., Apr.–May; 7 a.m.–11 p.m., Jun.–Aug. Ⓜ Concorde or Tuileries Ⓦ Free

Le Marais et place des Vosges

For many people, le Marais is the loveliest part of Paris. Its charm lies in the combination of architecture, atmosphere, the crowds that wander its streets, and its restaurants and shops. In the early 17th century Henri IV launched development by building the place des Vosges, Paris' oldest square. Its brick-and-stone facades, arcades and central garden make it one of the world's most harmonious and beautiful examples of city planning. Surrounding it are fine mansions built along streets such as the rue des Francs-Bourgeois – forming an unspoiled enclave of superb domestic architecture. The area boasts excellent museums, among them the Carnavalet Museum; National Picasso Museum; and Victor Hugo's House.

Musée National Picasso ⊞ E2 ✉ 5 rue de Thorigny ☎ 01 42 71 25 21; www.musee-picasso.fr ◷ Closed for restoration until 2012 Ⓜ St. Paul; RER Châtelet-Les Halles ⊮ Restaurant Ⓦ $$ (free first Sun. of the month) ⓘ Guided tours in English

Maison de Victor Hugo ⊞ E2 ✉ 6 place des Vosges ☎ 01 42 72 10 16 ◷ Tue.–Sun. 10–6; last admission 5:30 Ⓜ Bastille or St.-Paul ⊮ Le Grizzli, see page 474 Ⓦ Free (charge for exhibitions)

Montmartre

Over-commercialized and crammed with tourists, Montmartre still draws thousands of visitors daily. The neighborhood, once famous for its 40 or more windmills, gained a Bohemian reputation in the late 19th century when artists and writers moved in, among them Pierre-Auguste Renoir, who portrayed the area in some of his liveliest and most popular paintings. Later came a new wave of talent, when Montmartre became home to Pablo Picasso and fellow Cubist painters. The place du Tertre is the hub of the quarter; nearby is the Basilique du Sacré-Cœur (Sacred Heart Basilica), an ornate 19th-century church built of brilliant white stone, whose domes are a familiar landmark on the skyline of the city.

⊞ C4 ✉ Montmartre ☎ Basilique du Sacré-Cœur: 01 53 41 89 09; www.sacre-coeur-montmartre.com ◷ Basilique du Sacré-Cœur: daily 6 a.m.–10:30 p.m. (last admission at 10:15); crypt and dome: daily 9–6; 9–7 in summer Ⓜ Anvers, Abbesses or Lamarck-Caulaincourt Ⓦ Basilique du Sacré-Cœur free (crypt and dome $$)

Musée Carnavalet

The Musée Carnavalet (Carnavalet Museum) combines a chance to see the

At the Musée du Louvre old and new are juxtaposed with the new Pyramide in the courtyard

interior of one of the finest houses in the Marais with a fascinating introduction to the history of Paris itself. Built in 1540 and remodeled in the 17th century, this beautiful Renaissance mansion was the home of Madame de Sévigné, a famous hostess and literary figure during the reign of Louis XIV. Parts of the museum still feel like her home, where the sumptuous furnishings give an idea of the luxury of upper-class life. Allow time to study the models showing Paris' development, as well as the reconstructed rooms, porcelain and objets d'art.

D2 ✉ 23 rue de Sévigné ☎ 01 44 59 58 58; www.carnavalet.paris.fr ⏰ Tue.–Sun. 10–6. Last admission 30 minutes before closing 🚇 St.-Paul or Chemin Vert 🍴 Restaurant 💰 Free; temporary exhibitions ($$)

Musée du Louvre

The Musée du Louvre (Louvre Museum) started life as a palace in the 1190s. Demolished, rebuilt and extended over the centuries, this vast royal residence on the Seine assumed its present form by the 18th century, when the court of Louis XIV moved to the palace at Versailles. The Revolutionary government of 1793 transformed it into a museum to house the royal collections, and subsequent donations and purchases have enabled it to be augmented.

By the 1980s the collections had outgrown their home and President François Mitterrand launched the "Grand Louvre" project to renovate and extend the existing museum space. Chinese-born U.S. architect I. M. Pei was commissioned to design a new entrance in the Cour Napoléon. Below his stunning glass Pyramide lies a vast new foyer giving access to the main museum areas, named Richelieu, Denon and Sully. The Louvre seems confusing on arrival, but signage is excellent. It is best to go early and study the plan before you begin your visit.

The museum is divided into eight departments, ranging from Egyptian, Greek, Etruscan, Roman and Oriental antiquities through a huge painting collection, to sculpture, objets d'art, prints and drawings. Most visitors head straight for the famous pieces, with Leonardo da Vinci's enigmatic and mysterious *Mona Lisa* topping the list (now in a prominent position in the refurbished Salle des Etats). Another great work of art to admire is the *Virgin of the Rocks*, also by da Vinci, a work in better shape and just as representative of his genius. The Louvre also has six wonderful paintings by Georges de la Tour, the 17th-century French painter of candlelit night scenes. Take time, too, for Jan Vermeer's light-infused *Lacemaker*; Veronese's *Marriage Feast at Cana*, the largest work in the Louvre and full of fascinating detail; and Raphael's *Beautiful Gardener*, one of the sweetest of all his paintings of the Virgin Mary.

Two classical sculptures draw the crowds: the *Winged Victory of Samothrace*, a second-century BC marble figure, full of movement and tension and standing at the top of a grand staircase; and the *Venus de Milo*, a Hellenistic figure of the goddess Aphrodite from the fourth century BC. Contrast these two with Michelangelo's *Slaves*, sculpted almost 2,000 years later but clearly inspired by classical work.

C3 ✉ rue de Rivoli (main entrance: Pyramide, Cour Napoléon) ☎ 01 40 20 53 17; www.louvre.fr ⏰ Main museum and collections: Mon., Thu. and Sat.–Sun. 9–6, Wed. and Fri. 9 a.m.–10 p.m. Napoleon Hall: Wed.–Mon. 9 a.m.–10 p.m. 🚇 Palais-Royal Musée du Louvre 🍴 Restaurants 💰 $$ (reduced 6–9:45 p.m.; free first Sun. of the month and Jul. 14); temporary exhibitions $$; combined tickets for permanent collection and temporary exhibitions: $$$ ℹ Self-guiding audio tours ($$) and guided tours ($$) in English are available. Sections are sometimes closed on a rotating basis, so call ahead to check

Musée d'Orsay

The architecturally controversial Musée d'Orsay (Orsay Museum) was opened in 1986 in the old railroad station, the Gare d'Orsay. Whatever your view, the art collection inside cannot fail to impress.

The whole field of visual arts – painting, sculpture, architecture and design – from 1848 to 1914 is represented.

The major draw is the Impressionist and Postimpressionist collection. Here hangs Edouard Manet's *Olympia*, a portrait of a naked prostitute that caused a sensation when it was painted in 1863. Also in the gallery is a series of garden scenes by Alfred Sisley and Camille Pissarro. You'll find world-famous paintings such as Manet's *Déjeuner sur l'Herbe*, and Claude Monet's radiant light-filled images of Rouen Cathedral and his water gardens at Giverny. Here, too, are James McNeill Whistler's portrait of his mother, glowing examples by Renoir, and Edgar Degas' pert little dancers.

The museum is undergoing renovation which is due to be finished in late 2011.
➕ B2 ✉ 1 rue de la Légion d'Honneur ☎ 01 40 49 48 14; www.musee-orsay.fr ⓞ Tue.–Wed. and Fri.–Sun. 9:30–6, Thu. 9:30 a.m.–9:45 p.m. ⓜ Solférino; RER Musée d'Orsay 🍴 Restaurant and snack bar 💷 $$ (reduced fee after 4:15 p.m. Tue.–Wed., Fri.–Sun. and after 6 p.m. Thu.; free first Sun. of the month); combined ticket with Musée Rodin ($$) ℹ Guided tours in English ($$); contact the museum for details. Audiotape ($$) available in English

Place de la Concorde
Nothing better epitomizes the self-confidence, wealth and flair of 18th-century France than the place de la Concorde, scene of Louis XVI's execution in 1793. From this elegant

---

What's On Where
Brochures published weekly and monthly help you track down evening entertainment in Paris. English-language publications include *Where Paris*, *Gogoparis* and *Time Out* (monthly) and the weekly *Pariscope*, which has an English section. These list an enormous selection of entertainment, including temporary events, shows and festivals. You can find them at tourist offices and many English-language bookstores.

---

square there are sweeping views up the Champs-Élysées (see page 179) and down to the Louvre (see page 183), and from the Madeleine to the Assemblée Nationale across the river. The octagonal square is decorated with statues, while in the center rises the slender 3,000-year-old Egyptian obelisk, flanked by two fountains.
➕ B3 ✉ place de la Concorde ⓜ Concorde

Le Quartier Latin and vicinity
The area around the Sorbonne, Paris' ancient university, has long been known as Le Quartier Latin (The Latin Quarter) because until the 1789 Revolution, Latin was the language spoken by students and today it's still thronged with young people. Cross the boulevard to admire the Jardin du Luxembourg (Luxembourg Garden), then move on to the Panthéon, where great Frenchmen, including Voltaire and Victor Hugo, are buried.
Jardin du Luxembourg ➕ C2 ✉ rue de Medicis/rue de Vaugirard ⓞ Daily, opens 8 a.m. and closes 4:45–9:30 p.m. ⓜ Odéon; RER Luxembourg
Panthéon ➕ D1 ✉ place du Panthéon ☎ 01 44 32 18 00; www.monuments-nationaux.fr ⓞ Daily 10–6:30, Apr.–Sep.; 10–6, rest of year. Last admission is 45 minutes before closing ⓜ Cardinal-Lemoine or Jussieu; RER Luxembourg 💷 $$

Tour Eiffel
When it was built by engineer Gustave Eiffel in 1889, the Tour Eiffel (Eiffel Tower) was, at almost 1,000 feet, the world's tallest man-made structure. Part of the World Exhibition, it became a familiar symbol of Paris. You can take an elevator to each of its three levels. Mail a letter from the first-floor post office and the postmark will be "Paris Tour Eiffel."
➕ A2 ✉ Champ de Mars ☎ 01 44 11 23 23; www.tour-eiffel.fr ⓞ Daily 9 a.m.–0:45 a.m., mid-Jun. to Aug. (final elevator to top floor at 11 p.m., steps close at midnight); 9:30 a.m.–11:45 p.m. (final elevator for top floor 10:30 p.m., steps close at 6:30), rest of year
ℹ Last admission 30 minutes before closing 🍴 Two restaurants in the Tower ⓜ Bir-Hakeim; RER Champ de Mars Tour Eiffel 💷 Elevator: 2nd floor $$; top floor $$$; Staircase: 2nd floor $

Eating and Drinking in Paris

Your hotel will probably provide you with breakfast (normally at an extra charge), consisting of fruit juice, freshly baked baguettes and a selection of croissants and *viennoiseries* (assorted pastries). However, a basic Continental breakfast can be purchased at most street cafés for a fraction of the price charged in many hotels, and usually with a genuine Parisian atmosphere.

Main Meals

Lunch is generally served from midday until 2:30, and dinner from 7:30 until after 10. If you want either earlier, head for a brasserie, where you'll get simple, freshly cooked meals, and drinks and snacks throughout the day. Bistros are more modest than restaurants, although not always cheaper. You'll get the best value anywhere by choosing from the menu (often called *la formule*), where there's a choice of three or four courses for a fixed price. Some noted restaurants also serve what they term a *menu gastronomique*, which will include small portions of many of the famous house specialties, an excellent way to sample a wide range of dishes. If you order water, you'll probably get bottled mineral water (still or carbonated), for which you'll be charged. Wine can be fairly expensive, but all restaurants serve their own house wine in bottles and carafes, which is often good value. A typical meal will include a starter, frequently some type of salad; a main course with vegetables; and cheese, followed by the dessert.

Snacks, Fast Food and Picnics

If you want a light lunch head for the cafés, which usually have tables outside when the weather's nice. They serve sandwiches and other snacks, and hot, cold and alcoholic drinks. A popular lunch place in Paris is the *bar à huîtres* (oyster bar), where other seafood also is available, or a cyber café where you can have a snack or a drink while you surf the net. There also are plenty of burger joints, as well as the *boulangerie* (bakery), where you can get a variety of savory pastries to take out. For those with a sweet tooth, a *pâtisserie* (cake shop) is the place for a mouthwatering range of cakes and pastries. Summer weather may tempt you to plan a picnic: you can put together a wonderful feast at any of the many food markets that are scattered throughout the city.

A chalked menu lists the dishes of the day at Le Petit Fer à Cheval restaurant in Le Marais

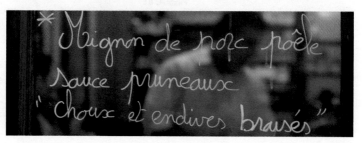

Lyon

France's second-largest city, once a hub on a vital trade route, has much to offer. It's a fascinating place where history and tradition, excellent civic facilities and architectural merit combine with commercial importance to give a real big-city feel on a very human level.

The City and the Presqu'Île

Lyon's sprawl may be daunting if this is your first visit, but the city's major tourist attractions are in a surprisingly compact area. Public transportation is excellent, so it should take little time for you to get your bearings.

Lyon's name is derived from the Latin *Lugdunum*, the capital of Roman Gaul, which was founded at the top of the hill called Fourvière in 43 BC, from where the settlement spread to above the confluence of two great rivers known today as the Rhône and the Saône. After Rome fell, the medieval town gradually established itself, spreading out slowly to occupy the narrow spit of land immediately above the rivers' junction. This became known as the Presqu'Île (the isthmus), and here the city grew in

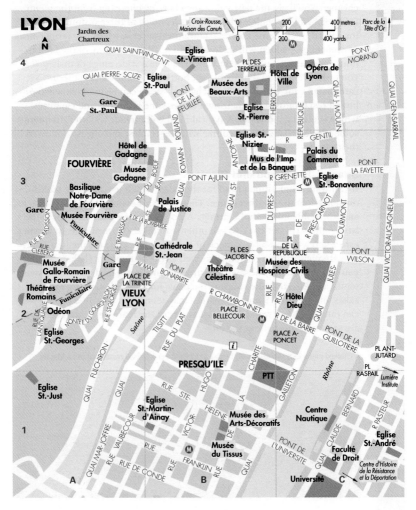

the 17th and 18th centuries; it was only later that it expanded farther to the north and east. For visitors, the main sights are almost all either along the west bank of the Saône river or on the Presqu'Île, the oldest parts of the city.

Exploring Lyon

Most visitors use the métro system, or subway, to travel around. Although it will get you from place to place effortlessly, you'll get a better sense of the city's layout if you set out on foot, and walking can actually be quicker. The hill of Fourvière (see pages 189–190) is a useful landmark; if it's on your left you're heading north, right and you're walking south. For orientation purposes remember that the Saône is the river immediately below Fourvière, while the Rhône lies on the other side of the Presqu'Île. Lyon is remarkably hilly, especially the climb up Fourvière and the slopes of the Croix-Rousse district (see pages 189 and 193), so a trip to these places probably merits the short métro or bus ride.

The tourist office offers an excellent one-, two- or three-day pass called the Lyon City Card. This moderately priced ticket gives you unlimited travel on the bus, trolley bus, tram and métro network, a river cruise (April through November), free admission to Lyon's best museums, a guided tour, a self-guiding audio tour of the Fourvière Basilica, access to the observatory, a performance at the Théâtre le Guignol and discount entrances to the aquarium and other sights, as well as a mass of literature to help you make the most of your stay.

The Lyonnais – with their reputation for common sense, wit and kindness – are helpful and friendly, and are usually happy to assist strangers.

Enjoying the Sights

Lyon, like so many historic cities, really needs to be explored at leisure. Get a flavor of the city by wandering through its picturesque neighborhoods, sit in cafés, pause in the lovely squares and linger on the bridges to admire the river scene. If pressed for time, consider taking a tour. The tourist office can provide details for both bus and walking tours, and cruises run during summer.

This prosperous city is well endowed with museums, some of which are remarkably esoteric. If you're an avid old-film fan, period automobile fanatic or if medical history or the discovery of electricity rivets you – you'll not be disappointed. Lyon also has many child-friendly attractions, including a museum of automation history, a puppet museum and a huge and well-presented natural history museum.

La Cuisine

Ask any French citizen what he or she thinks is Lyon's main attraction and the answer will probably be "la cuisine" (the food). This is a city where eating is taken very seriously indeed. There are hundreds of restaurants, ranging from very simple, family-run places to world-class establishments, and then there is the wine.

North of Lyon, miles of famous vineyards produce quality reds and

A view of Lyon from Notre-Dame de Fourvière

whites, with names to excite a wine lover – Mâcon, Pouilly, Fleurie and Beaujolais, to name but a few. Wine enthusiasts may consider an excursion to the wine country; the tourist office can help with this.

Souvenirs of Silk

Lyon has all the shopping you would expect from a city of its size and importance. The most fashionable stores lie in and around rue Président Edouard Herriot, and in the streets near place Bellecour and place des Terreaux, on the Presqu'Île. All the big international names are here, from jewelers, fashion designers and interior decorators to the best of shoe, leather, china and glass stores. The modern city center, around Part-Dieu railroad station, is home to downtown malls and chain stores, and there also are branches of France's top department stores, such as Galeries Lafayette. Lyon has its own specialties, with silk topping the list, and you'll find lovely silk goods to take home. Silk has been produced in Lyon for hundreds of years and the history and craft can be seen still in workshops in Passage Thiaffait as well as on the slopes of the Croix-Rousse (see pages 189 and 193).

On the Town

Lyon has plenty to offer in the way of evening entertainment. Opera, ballet, classical concerts, theater, jazz, rock and movies all thrive, with constantly changing programs; listings are available from the tourist office. There are dozens of bars playing live music; cabaret restaurants; nightclubs and floor shows; discos and karaoke bars; English, Irish and Australian pubs; a casino – the list goes on and on.

Essential Information

Tourist Information
Office du Tourisme et des Congrès du Grand Lyon (Lyon Convention and Visitors Bureau) place Bellecour ☎ 04 72 77 69 69; www.lyon-france.com

Urban Transportation
Central Lyon is well served by an extensive bus, trolley bus, tram and subway (métro) system. The subway runs daily 5 a.m.–midnight and is easy to use. You can pick up subway, bus and tram maps from station service booths and tourist offices. Subway stations are marked with an "M" on the city map. Tickets, available singly (valid for one or two hours' travel) or in *carnets* (books) of 10, are interchangeable between the métro, bus and tram systems. A one-day travel pass (Ticket Liberté Journée) gives unlimited access to the transportation system and is good value. For information ☎ 04 26 10 12 12 (toll call); www.tcl.fr. Remember to validate tickets before boarding. Taxis can be hailed or called. Try Arobase Lyon Taxi ☎ 04 72 27 15 15 or Allo Taxi ☎ 04 78 28 23 23.

Airport Information
Lyon-Saint Exupéry Airport (☎ 08 26 80 08 26, toll call; or 33 426 00 70 07 outside France; www.lyonaeroports.com) is 13 miles from the city. Rhonexpress runs a tram service between the airport and Part Dieu train station), 5 a.m.–midnight (travel time 30 minutes, ☎ 08 26 00 17 18; www.rhonexpress.fr.

Climate – average highs and lows for the month

Jan.	Feb.	Mar.	Apr.	May	Jun.	Jul.	Aug.	Sep.	Oct.	Nov.	Dec.
5°C	8°C	12°C	14°C	20°C	23°C	27°C	26°C	22°C	17°C	10°C	7°C
41°F	46°F	54°F	57°F	68°F	73°F	81°F	79°F	72°F	63°F	50°F	45°F
0°C	1°C	3°C	5°C	10°C	14°C	17°C	16°C	12°C	8°C	4°C	2°C
32°F	34°F	37°F	41°F	50°F	57°F	63°F	61°F	54°F	46°F	39°F	36°F

Lyon Sights

> **Key to symbols**
> ➕ map coordinates refer to the Lyon map on page 186 🖐 admission charge: $$$ more than €12, $$ €5–€12, $ less than €5
> See page 5 for complete key to symbols

Cathédrale St.-Jean

Post-Roman Lyon grew up around the site of the Cathédrale St.-Jean (St. John's Cathedral), a serene and lofty building with a flamboyant Gothic facade, flanked by a Romanesque 11th-century choir school.

Much of the interior dates from the 14th and 15th centuries. The rose windows in the transept are older; their glowing colors first illuminated the center of St. John's in the 1200s.

➕ A3 ✉ place St.-Jean ☎ Cathedral: 04 78 42 11 04; www.cathedrale-lyon.cef.fr 🕐 Cathedral: Mon.–Fri. 8:15–12:05 and 1:45–7:30, Sat.–Sun. 8:15–12:05 and 1:45–7 🚇 Vieux Lyon 🖐 Free

Centre d'Histoire de la Résistance et de la Déportation

World War II saw a highly organized, fearless and active resistance movement in Lyon, so it's fitting that the city should have created the fascinating Centre d'Histoire de la Résistance et de la Déportation (Center of the History of the Resistance and Deportation). Permanent and temporary displays, documents, audiovisual guides and videos commemorate the past as well as educate the young.

➕ Off map at B1 ✉ 14 avenue Berthelot ☎ 04 78 72 23 11; www.chrd-lyon.fr 🕐 Wed.–Fri. 9–5:30, Sat.–Sun. 9:30–6 🚇 Jean Macé 🚌 4, 11, 32, 60; tram T2 (Centre Berthelot) 🖐 $

Croix-Rousse

The slopes of the Croix-Rousse (Red Cross) area rise at the north end of the Presqu'Île, the neck of land between the Saône and Rhône rivers.

This fascinating area was mainly occupied by religious institutions before the French Revolution, but the institutions were dissolved in 1789, leaving the area open to redevelopment by the silk industry. Today it is a UNESCO World Heritage Site and one of the liveliest, earthiest areas of Lyon.

➕ Off map at B4 ✉ Croix-Rousse 🚇 Croix-Rousse
ℹ You can arrange a guided tour at the tourist office

Fourvière

One of your first impressions upon arriving in Lyon will be the hill of

The Cathédrale St.-Jean stands at the center of the old city of Lyon

Fourvière, the site of Roman Lugdunum, with its amphitheaters (France's oldest, begun in 15 BC), a second-century *odeum* (a small, roofed theater) and remains of a craft district.

The hill rises above the Saône river, topped by the ornate mass of the 19th-century Basilique Notre-Dame de Fourvière and what appears to be a scaled-down copy of the Eiffel Tower – actually the Tour Metallique (Metal Tower), built in 1894 and now a radio and television transmitter.

Take the funicular to the top and enjoy the fabulous views across the city.

✚ A3 ✉ Roman theaters: 6 rue de l'Antiquaille, Fourvière ☎ 04 72 38 49 30 (for information about the site) or 04 72 57 15 40 (for information about concerts); www.fourviere.org 🕐 Daily 9 a.m.–dusk 🚇 Vieux Lyon then Fourvière funicular 🍴 Restaurant de Fourvière 💶 Free

Maison des Canuts

The Maison des Canuts (Silk-weavers' House) is a museum-cum-workshop devoted to the history of silk and silk-weavers (*canuts*) in the heart of the Red Cross area.

Here you can enjoy an informative video, browse through old machinery displays and watch silk-weaving demonstrations on traditional looms. On a clear day you can enjoy wonderful views right across to the Alps.

✚ Off map at B4 ✉ 10–12 rue d'Ivry ☎ 04 78 28 62 04; www.maisondescanuts.com 🕐 Guided tours only Tue.–Sat. 11 and 3:30 🚇 Croix-Rousse 🚌 6, 13, 33, 45, 61 💶 $$

Musée des Beaux-Arts

The elegant building of the Musée des Beaux-Arts (Museum of Fine Arts) is the dominant feature on one side of the spacious place des Terreaux, with the impressive Hôtel de Ville (Town Hall) at right angles to it.

The building was formerly the Benedictine convent of St.-Pierre, rebuilt between 1659 and 1685, and it opened as a museum in 1803. The museum has interesting exhibits from Egypt and the ancient world, and collections of pottery, porcelain, glass and sculpture.

Track down the Lalique glass display and the charming animal figurines, including a cumbersome yet graceful polar bear by 19th-century sculptor François Pompon.

In the entrance foyer Pietro Perugino's *Ascension of Christ* is a fitting introduction to what's in store.

✚ B4 ✉ 20 place des Terreaux ☎ 04 72 10 17 40; www.mba-lyon.fr 🕐 Wed.–Thu. and Sat.–Mon. 10–6, Fri. 10:30–8 (some galleries close during lunch between 12:30 and 2) 🚇 Hôtel de Ville 🚌 1, 3, 6, 13, 18, 19, 44 🍴 Museum restaurant 💶 $$

Musée Gadagne

The Musée Gadagne (Gadagne Museum) consists of two museums, the Musée Historique de Lyon (Lyon Historical Museum) and the Musée International de la Marionnette (International Puppet Museum), both of which are housed in one of Old Lyon's stateliest Renaissance mansions, the 15th-century Hôtel de Gadagne. The building underwent a 10-year renovation program, opening again in 2009.

The history museum galleries display over 80,000 objects explaining Lyon's long and fascinating history.

✚ B3 ✉ 1 place du Petit Collège ☎ 04 78 42 03 61; www.gadagne.musees.lyon.fr 🕐 Wed.–Sun. 11–6:30 🚇 Vieux Lyon 🍴 Le Petit Glouton, see page 475 🚌 1, 3, 28, 30, 31, 40, 44, 91, 99 💶 $$

Musée Gallo-Romain de Fourvière

Housed in an innovative underground building designed by B. H. Zehrfuss, the 17-room Gallo-Roman de Fourvière displays fascinating objects found in Lyon.

Highlights include the "Claudius Tablet," part of a bronze tablet inscribed with a speech given by Emperor Claudius to the Senate in AD 48, and the Circus Mosaic, which vividly portrays a chariot race.

✚ A2 ✉ 17 rue Cléberg ☎ 04 72 38 49 30; www.musee-gallo-romain.com 🕐 Tue.–Sun. 10–6 🚇 Vieux Lyon then Fourvière funicular 💶 $$

Musée des Tissus et Musée des Arts Décoratifs

The Musée des Tissus (Fabric Museum) is appropriately located in Lyon – home of some of the most beautiful silk and innovative production methods the industry has seen. An 18th-century mansion houses the collection, which has fabrics from all over the world, dating from as early as the fifth century.

The Far Eastern silks and embroideries are exquisite, but the Lyon silk and costumes steal the show. These intricate pieces – including designs by Philippe de Lassalle – are still stunningly vivid. Also exhibited are articles of clothing, featuring Mariano Fortuny's Greek-influenced gowns, as wearable today as they were in the 1920s.

The Musée des Arts Décoratifs (Museum of Decorative Arts) is packed with furniture, china and glass.

✚ B1–B2 ✉ 30–34 rue de la Charité ☎ 04 78 38 42 00; www.musee-des-tissus.com ◉ Both museums: Tue.–Sun. 10–5:30 🚇 Ampère Victor Hugo 🎟 $$ (includes both museums) 🍴 Chabert et Fils, see page 475 ➕ Musée des Tissus: guided tours 3 p.m. Sun.

Parc de la Tête d'Or

Rose lovers should visit the superb 262-acre Parc de la Tête d'Or (Golden Head Park), home of Lyon's botanical gardens, which are beautifully landscaped around a lake.

The *roseraie* (rose garden) has more than 60,000 bushes and 350 varieties, all

An equestrian statue of Louis XIV in place Bellecour

thriving and filling the summer air with an overwhelming scent.

✚ Off map at C4 ✉ place Général-Leclerc ☎ 04 72 69 47 60 ◉ Daily 6:30 a.m.–8:30 p.m., mid-Oct. to mid-Apr.; 6:30 a.m.–10:30 p.m., mid-Apr. to mid-Oct. 🚇 C1; tram T2 🚇 Masséna 🎟 Free

Place Bellecour

The sweeping expanse of the place Bellecour – the old place Royale – is one of Europe's biggest squares.

In the center is a bronze equestrian statue of Louis XIV; within the park are gravel paths and shade trees, making this a splendid oasis of calm in the heart of the busy Presqu'Île.

✚ B2 ✉ place Bellecour 🚇 Place Bellecour 🍴 Chabert et Fils, see page 475

Vieux Lyon

Until the 1960s, Vieux Lyon (Old Lyon) was a run-down, derelict area. Happily, both the French government and the city of Lyon stepped in with the funds to save this historic quarter, the largest Renaissance-era urban area in France and a UNESCO World Heritage Site.

Here the medieval cathedral town grew and prospered as an international trade and banking center. Rich merchants and bankers built superb, ornately detailed houses along the narrow streets that included the St.-Paul, St.-Jean and St.-Georges neighborhoods. They still stand today, rescued and restored, with their spick-and-span mullioned windows, vaulted walkways, towers and galleries. Many streets are linked by the passages known as *traboules*, which wind through courtyards and under other buildings; the name is derived from the Latin words *trans ambulare*, meaning "to walk through."

Today Old Lyon hums with new life; there are studios, boutiques, bars and restaurants, thronged in summer with both locals and visitors.

✚ A2 ✉ Vieux Lyon 🚇 Vieux Lyon 🍴 Le Petit Glouton, see page 475 ➕ Guided walking tours available with audiocassette or English-speaking guides. Apply at the tourist office

France

La Cuisine Lyonnaise

Lyon is said to have more restaurants per capita than any other city in the world; no wonder that even other French people will admit, *"on mange bien à Lyon"* ("you eat well in Lyon").

Geography helps: the city stands at an agricultural crossroads, benefiting from prime beef from Charolles, excellent wines from Beaujolais and superb dairy products from the Dauphiné. The commercial fruit and vegetable gardens of France supply the freshest ingredients, and better *boulangers* (bakers) and *pâtissiers* (cake-makers) than the Lyonnais are hard to find. Here you can spend happy hours practicing the art of *lèche-vitrines*, literally "licking the windows," but in reality window-shopping for food. Have a look in the *boucheries* (butchers), *traiteurs* (delicatessens) like you've never seen before, and *épiceries* (grocer shops) piled high with olive oil, vinegar, honey and jam. Afterward, go to the morning markets (except Monday) on the quai St.-Antoine along the river and drool over the gleaming vegetables, glistening fish and mounds of fruit. Then you can find a restaurant and eat – *bon appetit!*

Lyon has a long tradition of professional kitchens being managed by women, a legacy from times when all restaurants were family-run and *Maman* (mother) did the cooking. Such restaurants, known as *bouchons*, still exist, and are usually small and friendly, with visible kitchens. You can count on authentic Lyonnaise dishes accompanied by straightforward wines, which are served in small jugs called *pots*, holding a standard amount. Some restaurants are renowned, and it's often necessary to book ahead to secure a table.

What should you eat? The cooking is classic French, with quality ingredients, subtle sauces, properly aged meat and perfectly ripe cheeses. *Boudin blanc*, a veal sausage, is a specialty, as are *quenelles*, lighter-than-air poached fish dumplings served with Lyon's classic crayfish-based *sauce Nantua*. Tripe, pigs' feet and brains may not be what you're used to, but don't rule them out. *Pommes Lyonnaises* (potatoes fried with onions) are eaten worldwide, but try *gratin dauphinois* (a satisfying dish of potatoes baked in butter, cream, garlic and mustard) as well.

Leave room for a dessert, such as a luscious fruit tart; *île flottante*, a dish with floating islands of meringue on a custard lake; sinful chocolate mousse; or the simplicity of *fromage blanc* – a fresh cream cheese eaten with sugar and cream, or simple *crêpes* with different flavorings.

People watching the world go by at a sidewalk café tables in Lyon

Lyon and the Silk Tradition

Nearly 5,000 years ago the Chinese discovered that the cocoon of an insignificant moth, *Bombyx mori*, could be gently unraveled in a continuous thread and woven to produce a light and luxurious fabric. This fabric is silk, still one of the softest and most desirable of all textiles.

Silk made its way overland from China to Europe by the 12th century, and by the 1600s Lyon had become the center for European silk production. (The silkworm also came to Europe and is now a domesticated insect with a ravenous appetite for mulberry leaves, which grow well in southern France and elsewhere.) The industry thrived, producing sophisticated weaves to supply France's rich and demanding upper classes. Sumptuous designs in dazzling colors were achieved on hand looms; silk damask, patterned silks and brocades, and figured silk velvets poured out of the workshops of Lyon.

In 1804, Joseph-Marie Jacquard invented the mechanical loom, which enabled patterns to be programed using a punch-card system. These very large looms were moved from the Old Town into special buildings in the Croix-Rousse (Red Cross) area (see page 189) that were designed to accommodate their size. The silkweavers (*canuts*), who also moved, were paid an abysmally low price for each pattern, with the middleman scooping the profits. Social unrest finally erupted in 1831, after a three-year struggle by the *canuts* to get better pay and conditions.

By 1870 the industry had recovered and Lyon silk was considered to be among the best fabrics in the world. The creation of artificial silk and other man-made fibers in the 20th century brought an end to large-scale silk production. Lyon's 30,000 weavers dwindled, and today there are only a handful of workshops where people still weave manually; hand-woven weaves are in high demand and are used to help restore the interiors of France's historic buildings.

If you're interested, follow the silk trail in Lyon, from the Old Town to the slopes of the Red Cross district, where you can visit silk workshops and working hand looms. Be sure not to miss the Fabric Museum (see page 191), keeping in mind that the most a skilled worker could hope to weave was three to four inches a day.

Ties, scarves and colorful fabrics make excellent souvenirs to take back home (see page 188).

Healthy silk worms and their cocoons are essential in the production of high-quality fabric

Nice

Nice, France's fifth-largest city and its biggest tourist resort, is perfectly situated on the sweeping Bay of Angels (Baie des Anges). With hills as its backdrop, it is blessed with gorgeous surroundings, a superb climate, a historic past and friendly people. Until 1860 Nice belonged to the County of Savoy, which became part of Italy in 1870, and to this day both the way of life and the inhabitants seem to combine Italian charm and flair tempered with a strong dash of Gallic sophistication.

The City

The Greeks built their settlement on the hills above the bay, and 300 years later the Romans settled here. The modern city stands on the same spot and has spread down to the flat land along the sea. Sheltered to the east and west by substantial promontories, and with the Maritime Alps to the north, Nice has its own microclimate, with mild winters and perfect summers. Over the centuries city planners have taken advantage of these conditions, resulting in one of the most graceful and flower-filled cities in Europe – the average Frenchperson's retirement-home fantasy. In recent years, Nice has marketed itself as a convention center and vacation hotspot, attested by the variety of hotels. It has more museums than any other French city outside of Paris, and plenty of festivals and events throughout the year.

Getting Around

Nice is a big city, with several districts – each of which you'll want to experience. The best way to orient yourself is to take a bus or taxi to an area, then explore on foot. Start with the atmospheric and picturesque Old Town (Vieille Ville, see page 198), which you'll probably want to visit more than once. The seafront stretches nearly 4 miles west of the Old Town, with the famous Promenade des Anglais running along much of it.

Behind the promenade and situated around the place Masséna is the commercial and business center, punctuated by peaceful gardens. The upscale residential suburb of Cimiez lies on the hill behind the old port and is home to excellent museums. As you explore, notice how the ambience varies, from the earthy gaiety in the streets of the Old Town to the haute couture you'll find along the Promenade des Anglais. You can see the different parts of Nice in style by hiring a *calèche* (horse-drawn carriage), or by taking the tourist train around the old quarter.

Flavors of the South

The French- and Italian-influenced cuisine of Nice is complemented by the sunny flavors of southern France. Look for fish and seafood. Vegetable dishes include *ratatouille* (Mediterranean vegetable stew), which was created here. Also try *mesclun*, a bitter selection of wild leaves. Stuffed vegetables and zucchini flowers fried in batter accompany grilled fish and meat. *Estocaficada* is a Niçois dish made from dried Norwegian cod and tomatoes. *Pissaladière*, an onion and anchovy tart, makes a good light lunch.

The area produces several wines, Château de Bellet (only 100,000 bottles each year) and Villars among them.

Local Wares and Souvenirs

Nice combines the temptations of big-city chain stores and designer outlets with local markets, antiques shops and souvenir stores. Department stores and big-name labels are found around place Masséna, while local products are sold in the Old Town. Traditional brightly printed cottons, scents from the hills around Grasse, food, oils and wines make lovely gifts, but the best souvenirs

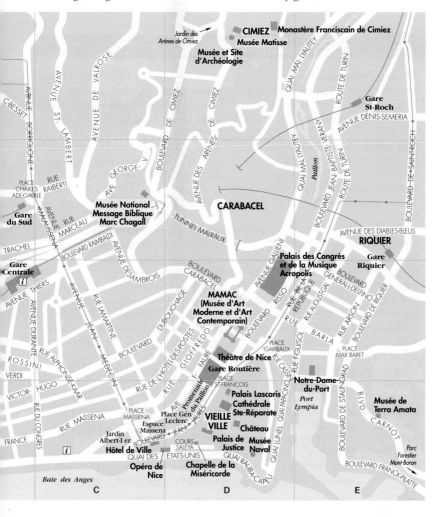

France

from Nice are traditional carved figurines, known as *santons*.

Carnaval

Nice has dynamic theaters, concert halls and an opera, as well as movie theaters, nightclubs, a casino and cabaret restaurants, live-music bars and discos. See what's going on in *La Semaine des Spectacles* published weekly with listings for the whole Côte d'Azur' (on sale at newsstands). Enjoy the local festivals, popular all year. The biggest and most colorful is the *Nice Carnaval et Bataille de Fleurs* (Nice Carnival and Battle of Flowers) in February.

Beaches

Nice has some public beaches but, to spend a day in the sun as the Niçois do, go to one of the city's 15 private beaches (open April through October). A fee is payable but included in the fee is an outdoor lounge chair and sun-shade umbrella, changing rooms, freshwater showers, a range of activities and access to a private bar/restaurant.

The beaches are covered in pebbles here, not sand, and topless sunbathing is the rule rather than the exception on the stylish French Riviera.

Essential Information

Tourist Information

Office de Tourisme et des Congrès de Nice (Nice Convention and Visitors Bureau)
5 Promenade des Anglais;
www.nicetourisme.com
SNCF railroad station, avenue Thiers,
fax 04 93 16 85 16
Terminal 1, Aéroport Nice Côte d'Azur,
fax 04 93 21 44 50
Tourist information line ☎ 08 92 70 74 07
(24 hours)

Urban Transportation

Ligne d'Azur operates all over the city; maps are available from 3 place Masséna (☎ 08 1006 1006; www.lignedazur.com ⊕ Mon.–Fri. 7:45–6:30, Sat. 8:30–6) or from tourist offices. Buy your ticket – Multi or Pass 1 Jour (valid for 1 day), Pass 7 Jours (valid for 7 days) or books of tickets valid for different numbers of days – at a kiosk before you board; don't forget to validate your ticket. Buses run until around 8 p.m. with limited night service. The

Nice tram system links the city center with the northern suburbs, with future plans to link to the airport and western suburbs. Ticket prices are the same as for the bus. Taxis can be found at city-center cab stands (Esplanade Masséna, Promenade des Anglais and place Garibaldi are convenient), or call Taxi Riviéra (☎ 04 93 13 78 78; www.taxis-riviera.fr).

Airport Information

Aéroport Nice-Cote d'Azur (☎ 08 20 42 33 33 for inquiries in English; www.nice.aeroport.fr) is west of the city. International flights leave from terminal 1; Paris and other French destinations are served by terminal 2. Shuttle bus services from terminals 1 and 2, linking the airport to the city center, are 98 (to main bus station and city center every 20 minutes 5:59 a.m.–11:37 p.m.) and 99 (to train station, every 30 minutes from 7:53 a.m. to 8:53 p.m.). Taxis are at airport exits, and take about 15 to 20 minutes to reach the city.

Climate – average highs and lows for the month

Jan.	Feb.	Mar.	Apr.	May	Jun.	Jul.	Aug.	Sep.	Oct.	Nov.	Dec.
13°C	13°C	14°C	17°C	20°C	24°C	25°C	27°C	24°C	20°C	17°C	13°C
55°F	55°F	57°F	63°F	68°F	75°F	77°F	81°F	75°F	68°F	63°F	55°F
5°C	6°C	8°C	9°C	13°C	17°C	19°C	20°C	17°C	13°C	9°C	6°C
41°F	43°F	46°F	48°F	55°F	63°F	66°F	68°F	63°F	55°F	48°F	43°F

Nice Sights

Cathédrale Orthodoxe Russe St.-Nicolas

The Cathédrale Orthodoxe Russe St.-Nicolas (St. Nicholas' Russian Orthodox Cathedral) is an exuberant pink-and-gray church with six green and gold onion-shaped cupolas and an ornate exterior.

Tzar Nicolas II built it from 1903 to 1912, and inside is a dazzling collection of treasures and memorabilia relating to the Russian nobility's presence in Nice, a city they favored as a temperate relief from the bitter climate of their homeland.

 B2 avenue Nicolas II 04 93 96 88 02; www.acor-nice.com Tours: Mon.–Sat. 9–noon and 2:30–6, Sun. 2:30–6, May–Sep.; Mon.–Sat. 9:15–noon and 2:30–5:30, Oct. and mid-Feb. to Apr.; Mon.–Sat. 9:30–noon and 2:30–5, Sun. 2:30–5, early Nov. to mid-Feb. Closed during religious services 4, 7, 23, 64, 71, 75 $ Religious services: Sat. 6 p.m. (5:30 p.m. Nov.–Feb.), Sun 10 a.m. (some Sun. also at 6 p.m.)

Cimiez

Cimiez is a residential area packed with attractions, including the Matisse Museum, a 16th-century Franciscan church and monastery, a small museum and cloister devoted to St. Francis, and the cemetery where artists Henri Matisse and Raoul Dufy are buried.

The Roman site has been excavated, revealing the remains of an amphitheater and public baths. The attached museum holds the treasures uncovered.

Franciscan Church, Monastery and Museum

 D4 place du Monastère 04 93 81 00 04 Church: Thu.–Mon. 9–6; Monastery and Museum: Mon.–Sat. 10–noon and 3–6 15, 17, 20, 22 Free Concerts in monastery cloisters in Aug.

This Genoese-style villa houses Musée Matisse

Musée d'Archéologique Nice–Cemenelum D4 160 avenue des Arènes de Cimiez 04 93 81 59 57; www.musee-archeologique-nice.org Wed.–Mon. 10–6 15, 17, 20, 22, 25 Free

Jardin des Arènes de Cimiez D4 avenue des Arènes Daily dawn–dusk 15, 17, 20, 22, 25 Free

Musée d'Art Moderne et d'Art Contemporain (MAMAC)

The Musée d'Art Moderne et d'Art Contemporain (Museum of Modern and Contemporary Art), or MAMAC, is an impressive museum constructed of four gray marble towers linked by glass walkways. The collection, founded by Nice artist Yves Klein, includes new realism, minimalism and pop art, with works by Roy Lichtenstein and Andy Warhol. Look for Klein's innovative *Mur du Feu* (*Wall of Fire*).

 D2 Promenade des Arts 04 97 13 42 01; www.mamac-nice.org Tue.–Sun. 10–6 3, 6, 4, 7, 9, 10, 16, 17; tram 1 (Garibaldi) Musem café Free

Musée Matisse

The whole range of artworks covering the working life of this remarkable artist forms the collection, along with personal possessions and photos. Bequeathed to the city by Henri Matisse (and then his heirs), it traces the artist's evolution through Impressionism and Fauvism. The artworks are housed in a

17th-century Genoese-style villa with a stunning modern extension.

➕ D4 ✉ 164 avenue des Arènes de Cimiez
☎ 04 93 81 08 08; www.musee-matisse-nice.org
🕓 Wed.–Mon. 10–6 🍴 Café/restaurant 🚍 15, 17, 20, 22, 25 🎟 Free 🔖 Guided tours in French Wed. at 3:30, in English by appointment only; send fax requests to 04 93 53 00 22

Musée National Message Biblique Marc Chagall

The Marc Chagall Bibilical Message Museum is a dramatic modern gallery, designed by A. Harmant, that houses Chagall's donations to the city and is the world's most important single collection of his work. The 17 canvases that make up the Biblical Message were painted between 1954 and 1967 and depict the artist's interpretation of the Bible's story. Other rooms display the 39 gouaches, 105 etchings and copper plates, and 200 sketches that Chagall used to help create the finished pieces.

➕ C3 ✉ avenue Dr. Ménard ☎ 04 93 53 87 20; www.musee-chagall.fr 🕓 Wed.–Mon. 10–6, Jul.–Sep.; 10–5, rest of year 🚍 15, 22 🎟 $$

Place Masséna and vicinity

The Niçois regard the elegant, arcaded place Masséna as the heart of their city. Around the square, with its sparkling fountain representing the planets, are broad boulevards and gardens. Take time to see the palms and roses at the Jardin Albert 1er (Albert I Garden), Nice's oldest gardens, and the Jardins Suspendus du Paillon (Hanging Gardens of Paillon), a stepped garden filled with azaleas, camellias and aromatic pines.

➕ C1 ✉ Promenade des Anglais 🕓 Gardens: daily dawn–dusk 🚍 8, 11, 52, 59, 60, 62, 94, 98, 217; tram Masséna 🎟 Gardens free

Promenade des Anglais

Early in the 19th century the English discovered that France's sheltered Mediterranean coast had mild winters, and soon they flocked here in large numbers. Afternoon strolls were fashionable, but the rocky, 6-foot-wide path along the shore was hardly suitable for gentle walks. In 1820 the Reverend Lewis Way organized the construction of a sweeping promenade, planted with palm trees and decked with flowers. The locals soon called it the Promenade des Anglais (the Englishmen's Walk). Today a busy highway cuts between the sea and the ornate exteriors of the *belle époque* luxury hotels. Even amid the sprawl of ugly concrete apartment blocks, the palms, flowers and strolling crowds and views remain unchanged.

➕ A1–B1 ✉ Promenade des Anglais 🚍 8, 11, 52, 59, 94 🔖 *Nice Carnaval et Bataille de Fleurs* (Feb.); *Fête Nationale* fireworks display (Jul. 14); *Nuits Estivales*, summer music evenings (Jul. and Aug.)

Lido Plage is near Promenade des Anglais

Vieille Ville

Until the 1970s Nice's Vieille Ville (Old Town) was a decaying slum, but today it's one of the liveliest neighborhoods in the city, with shops and bars mixed with fine old houses, baroque churches and 17th- and 18th-century civic buildings. The cours Saleya is the hub of the quarter, an elongated square that is the home of Nice's famous fresh produce and antiques markets.

➕ D1 🕓 Fruit and vegetable markets: Tue.–Sun. morning. Antiques market: Mon. Flower market: Tue.–Sat. all day, Sun. morning. All located on cours Saleya 🚍 Any bus for the Gare Routière; tram Opéra–Vieille Ville and Cathedral–Vieille Ville

Parks, Gardens, Trees and Flowers

Many Mediterranean cities have lovely *parcs* (parks) and *jardins* (gardens), but none more so than Nice. The green swath cutting through the city's heart is only one example, and every street is decked with tubs, planters and window boxes filled with colorful flowers.

Formal parks lie within the city center, forming a green oasis for locals and visitors; the Jardin Albert 1er, L'Esplanade du Paillon and the Espace Masséna are good examples. Also in the city center, the wooded Parc du Château features winding paths and cascading water. The wilder Jardin des Arènes de Cimiez is a beautifully tended olive grove, the wind rustling the silver-gray foliage on the shapely trees.

Lovely, aromatic Aleppo pine trees, planted in 1866, abound in the Parc Forestier du Mont-Boron; they line almost 7 miles of trails that are edged with wild carnations and tiny orchids. Views from this park are spectacular: to the east is St.-Jean Cap Ferrat, and to the west is Nice's own Bay of Angels.

Avid gardeners should head for Nice's Jardin Botanique (Botanic Garden) at the west side of Nice, with a comprehensive and classic collection of Mediterranean flora as well as some tropical plants. The Parc Floral Phoenix is another garden attraction focusing on tropical plants and fruit trees. A vast greenhouse, thought to be the largest in Europe, dominates the 17-acre site and is packed with numerous exotic and rare orchids among other delights. There is also an aviary and beautifully colored butterflies.

Most of Nice's trees and flowers are common to all Mediterranean countries, where this vegetation thrives in lime-rich, sandy or poor soil, can withstand months of summer heat and drought, and can endure an occasional wet or cold spell in winter. Olives, palms and pines are native; citrus trees, bougainvillea, mimosa, gerbera and many succulents have been introduced. Roses love Mediterranean conditions, which is why you'll see bigger and brighter ones here than anywhere else.

If you're in the countryside – nature's own glorious garden – in April, May or June, you'll find spreads of wildflowers to rival any city park.

Detail of a fountain in Nice's Jardin Albert 1er

France

Strasbourg

Strasbourg's tiny historic center, circled by arms of the Ill river, could easily lull a visitor into thinking that there was little more to the city than picturesque streets, a breathtakingly beautiful cathedral and a huge number of restaurants. But beyond its medieval core lie grandiose 19th-century civic buildings, an ancient university and the gleaming buildings housing European institutions, since Strasbourg is the seat of the European Parliament.

It's a prosperous, cosmopolitan city, a beguiling blend of ancient and modern, Teutonic and French.

A Visitor's Strasbourg

For tourists, modern everyday Strasbourg need not intrude upon enjoyment of the old city. Aim to stay within the old, mostly pedestrian quarter; it's a delightful place to walk around, with an impressive choice of hotels, bars and restaurants.

There's a large presence of European parliamentary officials, many of whom speak English, and the range of English-language tourist literature is excellent.

Strasbourg's appeal lies in its combination of history, architecture and culture. First impressions are of a very German city, the timbered houses and cobbled streets reminiscent of villages across the Rhine river, a little to the east. But the atmosphere is definitely French, with the style and way of life that it implies. Lying so near the German border, however, Strasbourg is a favorite destination for day and weekend visits, and you'll see and hear many Germans.

Exploring the City

Undoubtedly, it's best to explore Strasbourg on foot. Apart from visiting the wonderful cathedral, museums and fine churches, most visitors spend time simply strolling the streets. You'll find hidden corners and buildings waiting to be photographed around every turn, so take your time. Water plays a large part in the city's layout; the center is encircled by water, divided into different channels and crossed by graceful bridges. Old mills and fortifications along the river bear witness to the city's

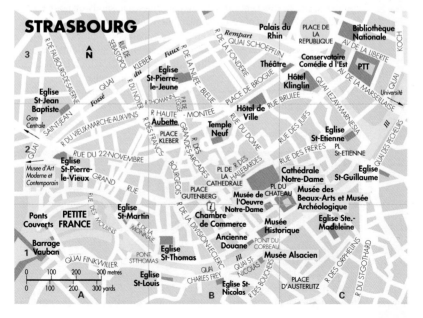

The medieval Ponts-Couverts in the heart of old Strasbourg leads to interesting old streets

historic importance, while the mighty Rhine, the German border, lies only a stone's throw away.

If you're interested in architecture, you could follow one of several marked routes through the heart of the old city center (see Petite France, page 204). The tram can be useful for saving your legs, and taxis are easily available. There's also the peaceful boat trip around the center (see page 205).

Eat, Drink and Enjoy

The Strasbourg and Alsace area is one of the few regions in Europe that produces both notable wines and beers, and it also is home to some of the finest cooking in France. There are strong German influences here, giving the cuisine a different character from typical French fare. History has played a part in this, and it's a pleasure to see the past so clearly reflected at the table – the

popular dish *choucroute*, for instance, is really the same thing as sauerkraut.

But don't be fooled. There's much more to the cuisine in Strasbourg than German cooking; you'll find Italian, Chinese, Lebanese, Tex-Mex, Moroccan and others. Don't overlook the opportunity to try some real Strasbourg specialties (see page 478). Stop in a *winstub*, a small family-run restaurant often housed in an historic building, where you'll be able to sample the best of local cooking and flavors in a cozy setting with a friendly atmosphere.

Alsace produces some notable wines, mainly whites, which are similar in character to the best of German wines. They are traditionally labeled with the name of the grape rather than the place of origin. Riesling, Gewürztraminer, Pinot Blanc and Muscat are all reliable varieties to look for. Beer also is big in Alsace, the home of Heineken and

Kronenbourg, two of Europe's biggest sellers. Other smaller local breweries produce excellent beer.

Evening Diversions

Strasbourg has a rich cultural life, with its own orchestra participating at the renowned International Music Festival in June; in late September through early October there's the annual *Musica*, a festival of contemporary music. Opera, theater, jazz and dance performances are held year-round and are widely advertised. In summer, most tourists are drawn to the nightly folklore displays of music and dance held in some of the old city's most picturesque squares.

Malls and Markets

Shopping in Strasbourg is a real pleasure, with an excellent choice of the designer names, jewelers, antiques shops and international bookstores clustered around the center of the old city. Across the river, Centre Halles is a fair-sized shopping mall housing France's familiar chain stores.

The weekly market takes place on Saturdays at place du Vieux Marché aux Poissons (7 a.m.–1 p.m.) – stalls of fresh produce, cheese and meat jostle with inexpensive and cheerful clothes and household goods. Souvenir shops sell Alsatian handicrafts; pottery, lace and carved wood are worth looking at. Strasbourg is famous for its colorful Christmas market, Christkindelsmärik, first held in 1570 in the cathedral (www. noel.strasbourg.eu). Each year, from late November to late December, the festive market attracts thousands of shoppers from across Europe (see page 203).

Essential Information

Tourist Information
Office de Tourisme de Strasbourg (Strasbourg Tourist Office)
17 place de la Cathédrale
☎ 03 88 52 28 28;
place de la Gare
☎ 03 88 32 51 49;
www.otstrasbourg.fr

Urban Transportation
Buy tickets for the trams from machines located at stops, and validate them before boarding. Outer Strasbourg is served by an efficient bus service, which you can use to visit the European Institutions (again, validate your ticket). Transportation maps are available at the railroad station and the tourist office (for information call Compagnie des Transports Strasbourgeois ☎ 33 88 77 70 70; www.cts-strasbourg.fr). Taxis are reasonably priced; find them at the station, place Kléber or place Gutenberg, or call Taxis 13 ☎ 03 88 36 13 13.

Airport Information
Strasbourg-Entzheim International Airport (☎ 03 88 64 67 67; www.strasbourg.aeroport. fr), with connections to most major European cities, is about 10 minutes south of the city by car A train service links the central train station to the airport running every 15 minutes Mon.–Fri. 5:20 a.m.–9:25 p.m.; every 30 minutes Sat. 6:30 a.m.–10:30 p.m.; Sun. 8:15 a.m.–9:55 p.m.

Climate – average highs and lows for the month

Jan.	Feb.	Mar.	Apr.	May	Jun.	Jul.	Aug.	Sep.	Oct.	Nov.	Dec.
4°C	5°C	10°C	15°C	19°C	22°C	24°C	24°C	20°C	14°C	8°C	4°C
39°F	41°F	50°F	59°F	66°F	72°F	75°F	75°F	68°F	57°F	46°F	39°F
-2°C	-2°C	1°C	5°C	9°C	12°C	14°C	13°C	10°C	6°C	2°C	0°C
28°F	28°F	34°F	41°F	48°F	54°F	57°F	55°F	50°F	43°F	36°F	32°F

Strasbourg Sights

> **Key to symbols**
> ✚ map coordinates refer to the Strasbourg map on page 200 💷 admission charge: $$$ more than €12, $$ €5–€12, $ less than €5
> See page 5 for complete key to symbols

The red sandstone facade of the cathedral

Cathédrale Notre-Dame

A superb example of Gothic architecture, the Cathédrale Notre-Dame (Cathedral of Our Lady) dominates old Strasbourg; its single steeple soaring to 466 feet.

Built between 1176 and 1439, th cathedral stands in a cobbled square on the site of an earlier basilica. A team of masons from Chartres worked on it in the 13th century, creating superb statuary and a harmonious interior, subtly lit by fine stained-glass windows. The main facade, a riot of sinuous, graceful biblical figures and saints, was completed half a century later. A platform constructed in the late 14th century to connect the two towers is reached by 329 stairs.

The astronomical clock in the south transept is a huge timepiece with a planetary dial constructed in the 1540s. Its automated figures perform daily at 12:30 (entrance at the south doorway noon–12:20), when the Apostles march before Christ, a cock crows and beats its wings, and the seven ages of man can be seen.

The cathedral's loveliest sculpture is the *Pilier des Anges* (*Pillar of the Angels*), a wondrously carved pillar entwined with the four evangelists and trumpeting angels, all heralding the Last Judgment.

✚ B2 ✉ place de la Cathédrale ☎ 03 88 21 43 34; www.cathedrale-strasbourg.fr ⏰ Cathedral: daily 7–11:20 and 12:35–7; Platform: daily 9–7:15, Apr.–Sep., 10–5:15, Oct.–Mar. Late opening on Fri.–Sat. until 9:45, Jul.–Aug.; until 8:45, early Aug. to mid-Aug., until 7:45, mid-Aug, to end Aug. Cathedral closed during Mass 🚋 14, 15a, 21, 24, 72; tram A, B, C, D, F 🍴 Au Bon Vivant, see page 476 💷 Cathedral free; platform $; clock $

Les Grandes Places

Strasbourg is scattered with *grandes places* (large squares). The main three – place Kléber, place Gutenberg and place de la Cathédrale – are all within a five-minute walk of each other. The cathedral square, with its cobblestones and timber-framed houses, is distinctly medieval; 18th-century Kléber square has an elegant spaciousness; and Renaissance-style place Gutenberg nicely bridges the architectural time gap. From late November through December, all three squares are the backdrop for Strasbourg's famous *Christkindelsmärik* (Market of the Child Jesus), a month-long street market dating from 1570.

✚ B2 ✉ place Kléber, place Gutenberg, place de la Cathédrale 🚋 14, 15a, 21, 24, 72; tram A, B, C, D, F ℹ Christkindelsmärik, last week in Nov. through Dec.

Musée Alsacien

If you have time to visit only one museum, it should be the Musée Alsacien (Alsatian Museum) – a charming regional venue housed in a disorderly canalside building. Not only does it offer a chance to see the interior courtyards and inside of a 15th-century house, but it's crammed with attractive displays, all illustrating traditional Alsatian life.

There are complete rooms and workshops, colorful pottery and glass, regional costumes and much more. Look for the votive pictures – naive religious paintings commissioned as prayer and

France

thanks to God, and illustrating farm animals, children and loved ones.

➕ B1 ✉ 23–25 quai St.-Nicolas ☎ 03 88 52 50 01 🕐 Mon. and Wed.–Fri. noon–6, Sat.–Sun. 10–6 🚃 10; tram A, D 🍴 Au Petit Tonnelier, see page 476 💰 $$, combination ticket with Musée des Beaux-Arts and Musée de l'Œuvre $$; free to all first Sun. of the month

Musée Archéologique

Strasbourg is proud of the Musée Archéologique (Archeological Museum), one of France's most important museums of its kind. Imaginatively laid out, it's housed in the basement of the Rohan Palace and takes visitors through Alsace from 600,000 BC to AD 800. There are interesting prehistoric sections, but more appealing are the reminders of everyday life in Roman Gaul.

➕ C2 ✉ 2 place du Château ☎ 03 88 52 50 00 🕐 Mon. and Wed.–Fri. noon–6, Sat.–Sun. 10–6 🚃 10, 14, 15a, 21, 24, 72; tram A, B, C, D, F 🍴 Aux Armes de Strasbourg, see page 476 💰 $$ (free first Sun. of the month)

Musée d'Art Moderne et Contemporain

The Musée d'Art Moderne et Contemporain (Modern and Contemporary Art Museum) is an airy building across the water from the Old Town. It covers painting and sculpture from 1870 to the present day. The room devoted to Gustave Doré gives a fine introduction to his many works of art.

➕ Off map at A2 ✉ 1 place Hans-Jean Arp ☎ 03 88 23 31 31 🕐 Tue.–Wed. and Fri. noon–7, Thu. noon–9, Sat.–Sun. 10–6 🚃 4, 10; tram B, F 🍴 Museum restaurant 💰 $$ (free first Sun. of the month)

Musée des Beaux-Arts

The elegant first-floor rooms of the Palais Rohan (Rohan Palace) house the Musée des Beaux-Arts (Fine Arts Museum), a comprehensive provincial collection covering European paintings from the Middle Ages to 1870. Memling's *Polyptych of Vanity* steals the show, although the museum is justly proud of *La belle Strasbourgeoise*, by

Nicolas de Largillière – a portrait of an enigmatic local lady. The ground floor of this same Renaissance building is home to the separate Musée des Arts Décoratifs (Decorative Arts Museum).

➕ C2 ✉ 2 place du Château ☎ 03 88 88 50 68 🕐 Mon. and Wed.–Fri. noon–6, Sat.–Sun. 10–6 🚃 10, 14, 15a, 21, 24, 72; tram A, B, C, D, F 🍴 Aux Armes de Strasbourg, see page 476 💰 $$, combination ticket with Musée Alsacien and Musée de l'Œuvre $$; free to all first Sun. of the month

Musée de l'Œuvre Notre-Dame

The Musée de l'Œuvre Notre-Dame (Museum of the Works of Our Lady) occupies a building used from the 14th to 16th centuries for cathedral maintenance. In addition to the rambling warren of fine rooms and staircases, there are courtyards, one of which is planted with medicinal herbs and plants similar to a 13th-century garden. Some of the cathedral's most precious sculptures are kept here, giving the public a chance to admire the elegance of 14th-century Gothic sculpture. The streamlined *Seven Wise Virgins* is a highlight, as is the nearby group of singularly unintimidating lions from the cathedral's main facade.

➕ B1 ✉ 3 place du Château ☎ 03 88 52 50 00 🕐 Tue.–Fri. noon–6, Sat.–Sun. 10–6 🚃 4, 10, 11, 14, 21, 24; tram B, F 💰 $$, combination ticket with Musée Alsacien and Musée des Beaux-Arts $$; free to all first Sun. of the month

Petite France

As you stroll around Strasbourg, sooner or later you'll reach the picturesque Petite France (Little France). On the banks of the Ill river, at the west end of the town's historic center, cobbled streets are lined with medieval and Renaissance timbered houses, dripping with colorful geraniums and shaded by ancient trees. Little France got its name in the 16th century, when sufferers of syphilis were isolated here, to keep them well away from "worthier" citizens.

➕ A1 ✉ place Benjamin-Zix 🚃 10; tram A, D 🍴 Le Baeckeoffe d'Alsace, see page 476

A Day in Strasbourg

You awake early in the morning, and your time in this wonderful old city is limited. Here's what to do: Spend an hour or so strolling around the historic center, visiting one of the daily produce markets and taking some photos in the morning light. Bakers and *pâtisserie* (cake) shops will be open, and you may be tempted to nibble on something as you go. Around mid-morning head for the Ill river, near the Palais Rohan, and buy your ticket for one of the 70-minute boat tours of Strasbourg. On the tour you can sit back and listen to the English commentary about the city's history and important monuments. The tour circles the central island, passing churches, fine buildings and flower-hung, timber-framed houses before heading upstream to give you a glimpse of the modernistic glass-and-steel palaces housing the buildings connected with the European Union.

Head next for the cathedral, timing your visit so that you'll be there at 12:30, when the marvelous astronomical clock (see page 203) swings into action. For lunch there is a wide choice of pretty outdoor eating places. Try a local specialty, such as *tarte flambée* (onion tart) or a beautifully presented *salade composée* (chef's salad).

If you enjoy museums, the afternoon's the time for checking out two of the best. At the top of the list is the Alsatian Museum (Musée Alsacien; see pages 203–204), closely followed by the Gothic treasures in the Museum of the Works of Our Lady (Musée de l'Œuvre Notre-Dame; see page 204). After this, you may be ready for a drink at a sidewalk café.

Evenings in Strasbourg feature a special dinner in one of the dozens of superb restaurants; be sure to eat a local dish, or follow the set menu, which is bound to be good. Afterward you can go to the movies (in English), a concert, enjoy a folklore display or simply stroll through the atmospheric old streets, and have a nightcap at a music bar. For night owls, there are discos and clubs that stay open into the early hours.

🛈 Boat tours leave from the landing stage near the Palais Rohan daily every half-hour 9:30 a.m.–10 p.m., May–Sep.; 9:30 a.m.–9 p.m., Apr. and Oct.; at 10:30, 1, 2:30 and 4, rest of year. Call Batorama (☎ 03 88 84 13 13; www.batorama.fr) for details 🚶 $$. Consult the tourist office about the 3-day inclusive "Strasbourg Pass" and for evening events

This half-timbered house is characteristic of the older houses in the center of the city

Germany

Opposite: Pleasure craft on the Mosel river at Cochem

Germany

Germany is not easily summed up. Before 1871 there was no single, unified German state: The area was made up of several territories, loosely knit together in alliance. Their local languages and loyalties still have first claim on many Germans' hearts.

After World War II, the country was split between two opposing powers: the West, whose territory was known as the Federal Republic of Germany; and the Soviets, who created the German Democratic Republic (G.D.R.). In 1989, faced with popular protests and a retreating Soviet authority, the G.D.R.'s government opened the Berlin Wall, which had divided the city's eastern and western zones since 1961.

A year later the country was reunited, and a new Germany was born. But within its unified political boundaries, this is still a nation of diversity, where the people and cultures vary as dramatically as the landscapes.

Traveling in Germany

Germany's 16 administrative states (*Bundesländer*) extend from the tail of Denmark south to the Swiss and Austrian Alps; the Netherlands, Belgium,

More Top Destinations in Germany

- Bamberg C2
- Berchtesgaden D1
- Bodensee
  (Lake Constance)
  B1
- Dresden D3
- Freiburg B1
- Goslar C3
- Hamburg C4
- Heidelberg B2
- Lübeck C5
- Mecklenburgische
  Seenplatte D4
- Regensburg C2
- Rheintal B3
- Sächsische
  Schweiz D3
- Trier A2
- Tübingen B1
- Ulm C1

DENMARK

Sylt
Nord-Friesische Inseln
Flensburg
A7
Schleswig
Kieler Bucht
Puttgarden
Rügen
Sassnitz
Heide
Bucht
Nord-Ostsee-Kanal
Kiel
Mecklenburger Bucht
Bad Doberan
Stralsund
Greifswald
Brunsbüttel
A23
Itzehoe
Neumünster
Rostock
A20
Cuxhaven
A7
Lübeck
Wismar
E55
Stade
E45
A1
E22
Schwerin
Güstrow
Bremerhaven
Hamburg
A24
E26
Parchim
Mecklenburgische Seenplatte
Waren
Neubrandenburg
A27
A1
Lüneburg
Ludwigslust
Neustrelitz
Bremen
E22
Müritz See
Prenzlau
A11
Soltau
A7
Elbe
Wittenberge
Neuruppin
E28
POLAND
Uelzen
Eberswalde
Nienburg
Aller
Salzwedel
Havel
A24
Oder
Celle
Stendal
BERLIN
Frankfurt (Oder)
Hannover
Wolfsburg
Brandenburg an der Havel
A10
Herford
E30
A2
A2
Braunschweig
A2
Potsdam
Hildesheim
Wolfenbüttel
Magdeburg
A9
A13
Bielefeld
Hameln
Salzgitter-Bad
Treuenbrietzen
Paderborn
Goslar
Halberstadt
Dessau
E15
Luckau
Lübben
Guben
Lippstadt
Scherfede
Northeim
Quedlinburg
Lutherstadt Wittenberg
Cottbus
A44
Göttingen
Unterharz
Saale
A14
A15
Kassel
A38
Nordhausen
Halle
A13
Lauchhammer
A7
Mühlhausen
Leipzig
Elbe
Neisse
Fulda
Naumburg
Mulde
Meissen
Görlitz
Marburg
A4
Gotha
Weimar
Colditz
Dresden
A4
Alsfeld
Eisenach
Jena
Gera
Freiberg
Bautzen
Zittau
Giessen
A5
Arnstadt
Erfurt
A71
A4
E40
Sächsische Schweiz
E45
Thüringer Wald
Saale
Zwickau
Chemnitz
Bad Nauheim
Fulda
Rhön
Bad Neustadt an der Saale
Plauen
Erzgebirge
A72
Frankfurt Am Main
Coburg
Offenbach
Hof
Aschaffenburg
Schweinfurt
A9
Darmstadt
Main
E51
Michelstadt
Würzburg
Bamberg
A70
Bayreuth
Odenwald
Bad Mergentheim
Erlangen
Weiden i d Opf
Rothenburg ob der Tauber
Ansbach
Fürth
Amberg
CZECH REPUBLIC
Heilbronn
Schwäbisch Hall
Nürnberg
A6
A3
Naab
A93
Stuttgart
A7
Dinkelsbühl
E56
Regensburg
Nördlingen
A9
Eichstätt
Fränkische Alb
A3
Tübingen
E43
Ingolstadt
A93
Hechingen
A8
Isar
Passau
Ulm
Lech
A92
Landshut
A7
Augsburg
Dachau
Donau
A96
MÜNCHEN (MUNICH)
Burghausen
Überlingen
Kempten
Chiemsee
Konstanz
Oberammergau
Rosenheim
AUSTRIA
Bodensee
Füssen
Lindau
2962
Zugspitze
Garmisch-Partenkirchen
Berchtesgaden
Mittenwald
2713
Watzmann

C   D   E

Luxembourg and France border on the west, Poland and the Czech Republic on the east. Each state has enough of interest for the visitor to occupy a whole vacation in its own right, and Germans are themselves often tourists in their own country, especially as westerners and easterners explore each other's previously unknown territories.

Traveling – by automobile or by public transportation – is not a problem, despite the country's size. The road network in western Germany is excellent, from the highways (*Autobahnen*) to minor roads. In the east, roads were in poorer condition for many years, but there have been recent improvements.

The biggest culture shock to drivers is likely to be the speed of traffic. There is no official upper limit on highways, and many drivers ignore, and drive in excess of, the recommended 130 k.p.h., the equivalent of which is 80 m.p.h. Driving etiquette is taken seriously, though: You can be stopped and fined for swearing or making rude gestures.

Taking the train is a convenient way to cover large areas. The quickest and most comfortable trains are the InterCityExpress (ICE), InterCity (IC) and EuroCity (EC) trains linking major centers – but the InterRegio (IR) trains connecting smaller towns are also fast.

The North and the Baltic

Northern Germany has a maritime character. Schleswig-Holstein, a province Germans and Danes have often fought over, is made up of two former dukedoms and shares the coastline with Lower Saxony. Together they take in a shore ranging from the fjords and hills of the Baltic coast to the wind-lashed North Sea beaches. Inland, the countryside is rolling farmland and peat bogs; offshore, the North Friesian islands are favorite summer destinations, with beaches and brisk sea air. The inhabitants of coastal Friesland have their own culture and language.

Northern Germany's cities were a force to be reckoned with in the Middle Ages. In the interests of trade and power, they banded together to form the Hanseatic League, a protected market that monopolized trade between the North and Baltic seas. The league's merchants made huge fortunes and had impressive houses and churches built in seaports such as Hamburg, Lübeck and Bremen.

Some of their legacies have survived – or at least have been rebuilt after the heavy bombing raids of World War II. The Gothic/Renaissance architecture of Bremen's Town Hall and Lübeck's Music Academy, both converted from merchant homes, still suggest the affluence and style of the region's medieval heyday.

Lower Saxony has many features that are quintessentially German. Its historic center, Hannover, is a thriving commercial city; towns such as Celle, Brunswick, Hildesheim and Wolfenbüttel, the latter with its painted, half-timbered facades, have been restored after wartime damage.

The winter-sports resort of Goslar, once a silver- and lead-mining town, has picture-book streets and squares lined with Gothic, Renaissance and baroque buildings, some inscribed with gold lettering, others featuring curving, sinuous slate roofs. To the east are the Harz Mountains, on the old East/West border, where witches are said to celebrate their Sabbath on *Walpurgisnacht*, the eve of May Day.

The Rhine

The great 820-mile Rhine flows from the Swiss Alps across the western regions of Germany, through the ancient city of Koblenz and the former seat of West German government, Bonn, and through the industrial country of Ruhr toward Rotterdam. Its valleys and those of its tributaries, the Mosel, Main, Nahe and Neckar, have been producing wines (mainly white) since Roman times. Castles with fairy-tale Gothic towers

Gilded statuary sits at the center of a pond in the grounds of Schloss Linderhof, built for Ludwig II

loom over the river, built for their powerful princes' protection and profit, which was gleaned from tolls on passing river traffic.

On the Lorelei rock, above the twisting Rhine gorge, the beautiful siren Lorelei is said to lure sailors to their death with her enchanting song. This is a romantic, myth-laden part of the country, and a river cruise is one of the most popular ways of seeing it.

The East

After years of restricted travel, border guards and obsessive document checking, eastern Germany is now completely open to visitors. When the Berlin Wall came down, East Germans poured into the West, eager to boost incomes, and some West Germans raised their voices against the sudden influx and resulting unemployment and uneasiness.

After the initial euphoria of reunification came the backlash of mutual resentment and offshoots of xenophobia. Integration has pressed on, nevertheless, and financial investment in the East (another grievance to some western taxpayers) has brought new business and better facilities, although there is still a marked difference compared to the affluent West. English is less likely to be spoken here.

One of eastern Germany's highlights is Dresden, which recreated itself after devastation by more than 2,000 Allied bombers in 1945. Fine 18th-century buildings surround its Brühlsche Terrace, an elevated section on the bank of the Elbe river, and the nearby baroque Zwinger pavilions house a marvelous collection of museums. Leipzig, the famous medieval university town, also is worth visiting, with its pedestrian-only center and attractive gardens and squares.

Weimar, once the home of the poet and dramatist Johann Wolfgang von Goethe, composer Franz Liszt and philosopher Friedrich Nietzsche, has a core of lovely historic buildings, parks and boulevards.

The gentle hills and red-roofed villages of the Thüringian Forest form a stretch of popular walking country, despite some parts suffering from industrial pollution; the region has a growing

The gilded clockface on the exterior of the Altes Rathaus (Old Town Hall) on the Marienplatz in Munich

industry of family-run lodgings and restaurants which is attracting visitors.

The Black Forest and Bavaria

Two states make up southern Germany: Baden-Württemberg in the southwest and Bavaria in the southeast. As the name suggests, Baden-Württemberg is itself made up of two distinct areas: mainly Catholic Baden, where the inhabitants are said to be amiable and easy-going, and traditionally Protestant Württemberg (Swabia), where the work ethic is strongly established and the Swabian dialect is spoken.

Lovers of the outdoors flock to the Black Forest (Schwarzwald), a swath of highlands reaching over 3,900 feet and encompassing attractive villages, lush valleys, orchards and meadows, as well as woods. Clock-making has been a successful industry here since the 1660s, and cuckoo clocks are on sale at every gift shop. The other notable local product is Black Forest cake – the authentic and superior original is called *Schwarzwälder Kirschtorte*.

East of the Black Forest is a range of limestone cliffs and hills known as the Swabian Jura, where castles peer down at the Danube (Donau) river as it begins its long journey to the sea. Pleasant resorts surround the "Swabian Ocean," Lake Constance (Bodensee), which straddles the German-Austrian-Swiss border. The Neckar river flows through Swabia's vineyards and past romantic Heidelberg, where students and tourists really do raise huge beer tankards over tavern tables, as they did in Sigmund Romberg's operetta *The Student Prince*.

Clichés also come true in southern Bavaria. Here the people are characterized by their detractors as loud and brash, and by their admirers as humorous, warm and fun-loving. They are often seen in traditional leather trousers (*Lederhosen*) or embroidered dresses, and are primarily Catholic and conservative: the standard daily greeting here is "*Grüss Gott,*" or "God's greeting."

Between the Bavarian capital, Munich (München), and the magnificent Alpine peaks lie the wooded hills, pretty villages, lakes and castles that attract so many visitors from all over the world to this part of the country. The spectacular Deutsche Alpenstrasse (German Alpine

Road) takes in the mountain scenery and passes the theatrical 19th-century castles of Linderhof, Herrenchiemsee and Neuschwanstein – all almost always packed to the brim with sightseers.

Northern Bavaria has its own character. In fact, not everyone here appreciates being labeled "Bavarian." This is the region known as Franconia (Franken), and its main city is Nuremberg (Nürnberg). Architecture and art come into their own here. During the late Middle Ages and early Renaissance, artists such as Lucas Cranach and Albrecht Dürer were prominent in Germany, and Nuremberg's wonderful German National Museum displays some of their best work. A more sinister aspect of the city's past is recalled in the giant stadium and Hall of Congress, built for Hitler's mass rallies, and preserved as chilling memorials to that era.

The hugely popular Romantische Strasse (Romantic Road), running from ancient Würzburg and the Franconian wine country all the way to the Alps, 217 miles south, links several unspoiled medieval towns. On the way, it passes Rothenburg ob der Tauber, one of the loveliest old towns in Germany – and as a result one of the most crowded.

Also along this route are the old walled, half-timbered town of Dinkelsbühl and the wonderful Renaissance city of Augsburg.

Spa Towns

Health and fitness are national preoccupations, apparent in the German love of soccer, skiing and tennis, and in the spa towns that thrive all over the country. At these spas Germans reap the benefits of the medicinal waters and enjoy the other facilities, which can include mud baths, saunas and steam treatments.

Germany's oldest casino is one of the features of Baden-Baden, a celebrated spa town with graceful 19th-century hotels. Other spas also are worth

investigating. Bad Ems, in the Rhineland's picturesque Lahn valley, was 19th-century ruler Kaiser Wilhelm's personal favorite. A steam train travels from Bad Doberan, near Rostock in eastern Germany, to the country's oldest seaside resort, Ostseebad Heiligendamm, founded in 1793. Bad Kissingen, Bavaria's most popular spa, is on the banks of the Saale river.

A view of Freiburg in the Black Forest region

Timeline

800–700 BC	Celtic tribes settle around the Rhineland.
AD 800	Franks overrun the territory; Charlemagne, the Frankish king, is crowned Holy Roman Emperor.
1273	Rudolf of Habsburg is elected king, founding the 600-year Habsburg dynasty.
1517	Martin Luther precipitates the Reformation.
1740	Frederick the Great is crowned king of Prussia.
1871	Franco-Prussian War ends with states united under the Prussian King and German Kaiser Wilhelm and chancellor, Otto von Bismarck.
1914–19	Habsburg claims to the Balkans lead to World War I; the Treaty of Versailles demands huge war reparations and surrender of territories from defeated Germany.
1930	The Nazis gain power in elections.
1933	Adolf Hitler is made chancellor; under Hitler's dictatorship, millions of Jews and minorities are persecuted and killed.
1939	Hitler invades Poland; Britain and France declare war on Germany.
1945	Allied forces enter Berlin; Hitler kills himself.
1949	Western occupying powers create the Federal Republic of Germany; Russia forms the German Democratic Republic.
1961	The Berlin Wall is built.
1990	A year after the demolition of the wall, East and West Germany reunite.
1999	Government moves to Berlin. Parliament meets in the newly refurbished, glass-domed Reichstag.
2006	Germany hosts the soccer World Cup championship.
2009	Twentieth anniversary of the fall of the Berlin Wall marked with celebrations and fireworks.

Mad King Ludwig

Ludwig II of Bavaria lost all interest in running his kingdom after it was drawn first into war and then into the German Empire by the Prussian Chancellor, Otto von Bismarck. The late 19th-century ruler was left with nothing to do but amuse himself, which he did by having three flamboyant castles built – Herrenchiemsee, Linderhof and Neuschwanstein – and watching them take shape through his telescope. Ludwig found other ways to spend his money, too, supporting Richard Wagner while he wrote his operas, but eventually he ran out of cash altogether. This and his eccentric manner made him an increasing liability to the Bavarian government. Its ministers plotted with Ludwig's uncle Luitpold to depose him and certify him insane. Only days later, Ludwig and his doctor drowned in the Starnberger See, a boating lake near Munich – whether by accident or design, no one knows.

everyone gears up for the three "Crazy Days" (*Tolle Tage*) – Thursday, Sunday and Monday.

There are costume balls at night, and more informal revelry on the streets and in the taverns. On Sunday there's a procession of floats, and on Monday a spectacular parade provides the lively and colorful climax.

For the rest of the year, there is a choice of calmer entertainment at the city's main cultural centers. Concerts are performed at the Philharmonie, beside the Wallraf-Richartz/Ludwig museums building which is located on Bischofsgartenstrasse.

Other concerts take place regularly in the city's churches and are usually free. Opera is staged at the Opernhaus. Cologne has a famous puppet theater – the Puppenspiele – but dialogue is in the local *Kölsch* dialect.

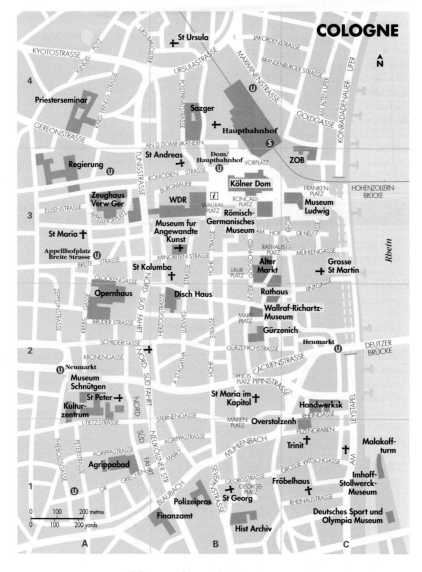

COLOGNE

Listings for movies, theater and concerts are published in the magazines *Kölner Illustrierte*, *StadtRevue* and *Köln-Magazin*.

Nightclubs and discos are concentrated on the streets around Gross St. Martin; in the St. Severin quarter, Südstadt; and in the university quarter – the Kwartier Lateng, in the southwest part of the city.

Eau de Cologne

Probably the most appropriate souvenir to take home from Cologne is a bottle of the world's most famous fragrance, *eau de cologne*, first distilled from flower blossoms by an Italian immigrant in the 18th century and intended as an aphrodisiac. Known here as *Kölnisch Wasser*, it's made by about 20 businesses, including one of the originals, Farina, which has been in operation since 1709. Stores all over the city sell it, but the Old Town is the best place to browse around for gifts.

An all-day market takes place each Friday in the Old Market Square. On spring weekends, during April and May, the same square is completely taken over by hundreds of flower stalls. Wine markets set up in New Market to sell their wares in May and late June. Just before Lent Cologne celebrates *Karneval* (Carnival), and all shops close during the "Crazy Days."

Crazy Days

On the first of the *Tolle Tage* (Crazy Days) of Carnival, a procession takes place based on the local legend of Jan and Griet. Jan von Werth worked for a farmer and was very much in love with Griet, who refused him, hoping to find a wealthy husband. In desperation, Jan went off to fight in the Thirty Years' War. However, he came back many years later as a highly honored hero who went on to become a general.

Essential Information

Tourist Information

Köln Tourismus (Cologne Tourist Office)
Kardinal-Höffner-Platz, in front of the cathedral ☎ 0221 2213 0400;
www.koelntourismus.de

Urban Transportation

Cologne has an integrated transportation system. Trams travel through the Old Town, some above ground (east–west lines), some underground (north–south lines); they also share some lines with freight trains. Subway stations are marked on the Cologne city map by the letter "U" in a red circle. Tickets are sold individually or for groups of up to five

people (valid 9 a.m.–3 a.m.); you can also buy a 7-day travel card. The bus and railroad stations are next to the Cathedral. For information call Cologne transportation information ☎ 0180 350 4030.

Airport Information

The Cologne/Bonn airport is approximatley 20 minutes by taxi from the city center. Suburban (S-Bahn) trains operate from the airport to the city center, and InterCity-Express (ICE) trains take passengers to destinations across Germany. For flight information, call
☎ 02203 400 (24 hours).

Climate – average highs and lows for the month

Jan.	Feb.	Mar.	Apr.	May	Jun.	Jul.	Aug.	Sep.	Oct.	Nov.	Dec.
3°C	4°C	10°C	14°C	19°C	22°C	24°C	24°C	20°C	14°C	8°C	3°C
37°F	39°F	50°F	57°F	66°F	72°F	75°F	75°F	68°F	57°F	46°F	37°F
-2°C	-2°C	0°C	4°C	8°C	12°C	14°C	13°C	10°C	6°C	3°C	0°C
28°F	28°F	32°F	39°F	46°F	54°F	57°F	55°F	50°F	43°F	37°F	32°F

Cologne Sights

Detail of reliquary busts in St. Ursula's church

Gross St. Martin

From its consecration in 1172 until the 19th century, the church of Gross St. Martin was the most distinctive feature of Cologne's skyline. Its tower, with four turrets at the corners, makes an interesting contrast to the lacy stonework of the spires.

Originally this was a monastery church, built for Benedictine monks from Ireland and Scotland.

➕ C3 ✉ An Gross St. Martin ☎ 0221 1642 5650 🕐 Tue.–Sat. 9–7:30, Sun. 12:45–7:15 🚇 Lines 5, 12, 16, 18 to Dom/Hbf 🚋 Tram 7, 9 to Heumarkt 🍴 Päffgenbraverei Max Päffgen (see page 477), nearby at Heumarkt 🅰 $

Kölner Dom

It took more than 600 years to complete the Kölner Dom (Cathedral), a Gothic masterpiece that incorporated the original architects' plans right to the end. The purpose of the project (begun in 1248) was to provide an appropriately grand setting for the relics of the Three Magi, which were snatched from Milan and kept here in a golden shrine. The final result is majestic, with intricately worked masonry serving to lighten the great mass of the facade and the two 515-foot spires – at the time they were built, the tallest structures in the world.

The golden shrine is the main focus of the interior, but there are many other treasures. In the south ambulatory chapel, the altarpiece of the *Adoration of the Magi* is a superb work by Stefan Lochner, one of the 15th-century artists of the Cologne School.

In the north chapel is the 11th-century Gero Crucifix. One of the church's most inspiring features is the stained glass, ranging from the 13th-century Bible Window in the ambulatory to the Bavarian windows in the nave, donated by King Ludwig I in the 19th century.

➕ B3 ✉ Am Hof ☎ Cathedral: 0221 9258 47-30; Treasure Chamber: 0221 179 40530 🕐 Cathedral: daily 6 a.m.–10 p.m., May–Oct.; 6 a.m.–7:30 p.m., Nov.–Apr. Treasure Chamber: daily 10–6. Tower: daily 9–6, May–Sep.; 9–5, Mar.–Apr. and Oct.; 9–4, rest of year 🚇 Lines 5, 12, 16, 18 to Dom/Hbf 🍴 Brauhaus Sion, see page 477 🅰 Cathedral free (guided tours $$$); Treasure Chamber $$; Tower $$

Museum für Angewandte Kunst

Founded in 1888, the Museum für Angewandte Kunst (Museum of Applied Art) has an exquisite collection of applied arts ranging from medieval to contemporary times.

One of the most interesting pieces is the Nikolaus Kanne, created around 1660 in Hamburg. There also is a fine collection of art nouveau works.

➕ B3 ✉ An der Rechtschule ☎ 0221 2212 3860 🕐 Tue.–Sun. 11–5 (also 6 p.m.–10 p.m. first Thu. of the month) 🚇 Lines 5, 12, 16, 18 to Dom/Hbf 🍴 Café 🅰 $$$

Museum Schnütgen

Some fine medieval religious art and furnishings can be seen at the Schnütgen Museum, which occupies the deconsecrated church of St. Cäcilien.

Among other treasures are original carvings from the cathedral altar and some ivory pieces. The carved memento mori (reminders of mortality) are

Germany

chilling depictions of human bodies in a state of decay.

✚ A2 ✉ Cäcilienstrasse 29 ☎ 0221 2212 3620 ⏰ Tue.–Fri. 10–5, Sat.–Sun. and public holidays 11–5 (also 6–10 p.m. first Thu. of the month) 🚇 Lines 3, 4, 12, 16, 18 to Neumarkt 🚊 Tram 1, 2, 7, 9 to Neumarkt 🍴 Brauhaus Sion, see page 477 💷 $$ ℹ Guided tours

Rathaus

The Rathaus (Town Hall) is a Cologne landmark at the heart of the Old Town. A flamboyant, octagonal, 15th-century tower tops off the 14th-century body of the building. The Renaissance loggia (porch) was added in the 1570s.

Under a glass pyramid in front of the hall is a 12th-century Jewish bathhouse, the *Mikwe*. There was once a ghetto here, where the city's Jewish community lived until they were expelled in 1424.

✚ B3 ✉ Rathausplatz ☎ 0221 2213 0100 ⏰ Mon.–Thu. 9–3, Fri. 8–noon 🚇 Lines 5, 12, 16, 18 to Dom/Hbf 🚊 Tram 1, 7, 9 to Neumarkt 🍴 Restaurant in Ratskeller ℹ Contact Tourist Office to book guided tours (see page 226)

Römisch-Germanisches Museum

For hundreds of years Cologne was under Roman rule; city status was granted in AD 50 by Emperor Claudius. The Römisch-Germanisches Museum (Roman-Germanic Museum) depicts daily life in the Roman Empire through locally excavated items.

The main exhibit is the astonishing 230-foot Dionysus Mosaic, once part of a third-century Roman villa: it shows Dionysus, god of wine, indulging in drunken revelry. An older exhibit is the 49-foot-high tomb of a legionnaire called Poblicius, who died about AD 40.

There's a display of third- and fourth-century glass designs from Cologne, as well as jewelry found at Frankish burial sites.

✚ B3 ✉ Roncalliplatz 4 ☎ 0221 2212 4438; www.museenkoeln.de ⏰ Tue.–Sun. 10–5 (Wed. also 5–8) 🚇 Lines 5, 12, 16, 18 to Dom/Hbf 💷 $$$ ℹ During special exhibitions, hours and admission may vary. Guided tours available

St. Ursula

North of the city center is the church of St. Ursula; it was named for the daughter of a fourth-century king of Britain, who was said to have been killed in the city by Huns, along with her 11,000 virgin companions. The popularity of the cult of St. Ursula contributed to the city's development as a center of pilgrimage, and she appears in the Cologne coat of arms. The church sacristan can provide visitor access to the baroque Goldene Kammer (Golden Chamber).

✚ B4 ✉ Ursulaplatz 24 ☎ 0221 9258 4730 ⏰ Mon.–Tue. and Thu.–Sat. 10–noon and 3–5, Wed. 10–noon and 3–4:30, Sun. 3–4:30 🚇 Lines 5, 12, 16, 18 to Dom/Hbf 🍴 Bosporus, see page 477 💷 $

Wallraf-Richartz-Museum-Fondation Corboud/ Museum Ludwig

Cologne's major collection of German and international art is here, with works through the 19th century shown in the Wallraf-Richartz-Museum, and 20th-century art shown in the Museum Ludwig, which occupies the rest of the building. At the Wallraf-Richartz you can study the work produced in Cologne in the 15th century, when the city was at the forefront of artistic development. In particular, look for the triptychs by the artist known as the Master of St. Bartholomew, one of the last of the Cologne School, whose brightly colored paintings resemble carvings.

Many 20th-century greats are represented in the Ludwig Museum, including Otto Dix and Max Ernst; the section on pop art has works by Andy Warhol and Roy Lichtenstein.

✚ B2–C3 ✉ Wallraf-Richartz-Museum: Martinstrasse 39. Museum Ludwig: Bischofsgartenstrasse 1 ☎ Wallraf-Richartz-Museum: 0221 2212 1119. Museum Ludwig: 0221 2212 6165 ⏰ Wallraf-Richartz Museum: Tue.–Fri. 10–6 (also Tue. 6–8), Sat.–Sun. 11–6; Museum Ludwig: Tue.–Sun. 10–6 (also 6–11 p.m. first Fri. of the month) 🚇 Lines 5, 12, 16, 18 to Dom/ Hbf 💷 $$$ (each museum) ℹ During special exhibitions, opening hours and admission charges may vary

An Excursion to Bergischer Dom

Bergischer Dom (Altenberger Dom), about 11 miles northeast of Cologne, is set on the Dhünn river in the woods of the hilly country called Bergisches Land. The original church of this former Cistercian monastery was built using stone from the manor of the Count of Berg, who left it to the monks after moving his headquarters elsewhere in 1133. It took a little more than 100 years to finish building the present monastery, which was begun in 1259 – only seven years after work had started on the cathedral in Cologne (which took more than six centuries to complete). In medieval times it was a stopping-off place for pilgrims on the way to Santiago de Compostela in Spain.

The end result is one of Germany's best examples of 13th-century Gothic style: no elaborate embellishments and no tower, but a marvelous sense of space and light, enhanced by the simple, silvery stained-glass windows in the chancel. The west window representing *Das Himmlische Jerusalem (Holy Jerusalem)* is the biggest stained-glass window in the country. You will find tombs of the past counts, princes and abbots of Berg in the north transept.

During the Napoleonic Wars in the late 18th and early 19th centuries, the church fell into disuse and disrepair. Luckily, King Frederick William IV took an interest in its restoration, and it was opened to worshipers on the condition – decreed by the king – that both Catholics and Protestants could attend. This holds true today, and on Sundays both Catholic and Protestant congregations attend services. The outbuildings house various restaurants; at any of these, you can ask for the key to the oldest standing part of the monastery, the 13th-century Markuskapelle (chapel). An exquisite feature of the complex is the choir surrounded by chapels, viewed most rewardingly from the slope east of the monastery.

It takes an hour to reach Bergischer Dom from Cologne's center: The underground trams (U-Bahn lines 4, 15, 16, 18, 19) take you to Wiener Platz for a connection with bus 434.

Guided excursions from Cologne can be arranged by the Cologne tourist information office (Köln Tourismus – see page 226) ⊙ Sat.–Thu. 7–6, Fri. noon–6 (or sunset if earlier). No visits during services and concerts ⓘ For information about free guided tours, call 02202 30008; www.altenbergerdom.de

Fine stonework dominates the light, airy interior of Bergischer Dom

Munich

The capital of Bavaria is one of Germany's most appealing and popular cities. Even though Munich (München) is the country's third-largest city, with a cosmopolitan society and culture, it has retained a village-like atmosphere with parks and a pedestrian-only center. It's just an hour from the Alps, and also has the easygoing feel of a Mediterranean town. Even on the briefest German tour, Munich is a city not to be missed.

Munich on Foot

Central Munich is compact and attractive and the easiest way to explore is on foot. Long pedestrian-only streets (Kaufingerstrasse and Neuhauser Strasse) run from the main railroad station and from Karlstor, one of the city gates, to Marienplatz, the square at the heart of the Old Town. Here you can watch the mechanical characters of the carillon (*Glockenspiel*) at the front of the New Town Hall (Neues Rathaus, see page 234) and visit the twin-towered cathedral. To the north of the square is the tree-lined Maximilianstrasse, which leads to the Bavarian Parliament building and the Residenz (palace). Great art collections – the Old and New Picture Galleries and the Modern Art Picture Gallery – are a short distance northwest of the city center; to the south are the history museum and, on an island in the Isar river, one of the world's foremost museums of science and technology, the German Museum (Deutsches Museum, see page 233).

Bavarian Eateries

There are innumerable restaurants and cafés in Munich, and its large foreign population ensures a wide range of cuisines. At specifically Bavarian cafés, the Munich *Weisswürste* (white veal sausage with parsley) is a staple, served in hot water to be peeled and covered in mustard before eating. This delicacy is usually eaten before noon. Meals are generally early in Munich, as people start work at 7 or 8 a.m. Lunch can begin at 11:30 but is often substantial, and the "lunch hour" can last until 2 p.m. Dinner is served between 6:30 and 11 p.m., but locals tend to stick to a light supper (*Abendbrot*). The Schwabing district, north of the city center, is a busy area of sidewalk cafés and taverns. Snack bars (*Lokal* or *Schnellimbiss*) and even butcher shops (*Metzgereien*) sell tasty meatloaf and sausages all day.

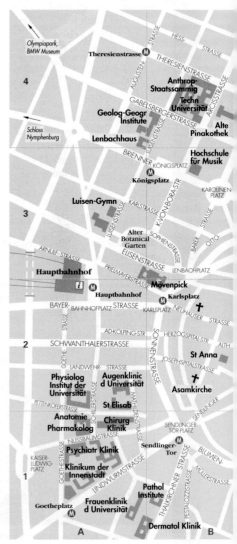

Music and Film

Munich is a major European cultural center, with thriving movie and publishing industries and a proud musical tradition. Three symphony orchestras are based here, and the Residenz provides an impressive venue – either in the concert hall or, in summer, in the courtyard. Opera and ballet are staged at the Bavarian State Opera, where the July Opera Festival is the highlight of the city's calendar. The main cultural center is the modern Gasteig, home of the Munich Philharmonic Orchestra; students from the Richard Strauss Conservatory give free lunchtime or early-evening recitals in the Small Concert Hall during the week. The annual International Film Festival takes place at the Gasteig in late June and early July – the high point of a series of festivals devoted to the movies.

Munich tends to shut down early, but Schwabing has many cabarets, theaters

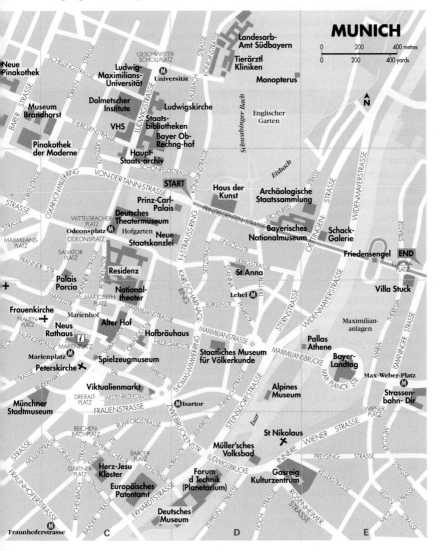

and live music venues ranging from rock to folk and jazz, including Jazzclub Unterfahrt at Einsteinstrasse 42.

Boutiques and Markets

There's good window-shopping all over the old center, especially along Neuhauser Strasse and Kaufingerstrasse. Maximilianstrasse is a browser's paradise, lined with designer boutiques, art galleries and jewelers. More stores abound in the arcades and lanes leading off Residenzstrasse. Antiques and secondhand stores are concentrated in the student area of Schwabing, and Bavarian crafts are sold in the streets that run off Max-Joseph-Platz.

Munich's open-air Viktualienmarkt, with its formidable vendors and fresh goods ranging from local cheese to Alpine flowers, sets up south of the Marienplatz every day except late Saturday afternoon and Sunday.

City of Monks

Munich's city emblem is the *Münchner Kindl*, or "little monk," recalling its origins as a monastic settlement. The first recorded mention of *Munichen*, or "the home of monks," was in AD 777. The city itself was founded nearly 400 years later by Henry the Lion, Duke of Saxony.

Essential Information

Tourist Information

Tourismusamt München (Munich Tourist Office)
Sendlinger Strasse 1
☎ 089 23 39 65 00;
www.muenchen-tourist.de
Hauptbahnhof, Bahnhofplatz 2
Neues Rathaus (New City Hall), Marienplatz

Urban Transportation

A U-Bahn (subway) and S-Bahn (suburban) train network covers the city center and beyond. The U-Bahn is marked on the city map by the letter "U" in a red circle, the S-Bahn by the letter "S" in a red circle. Trains run daily 5 a.m.–1 a.m. Buy tickets from machines at Münchner Verkehrs-und Tarifverbund (MVV) stations, MVV sales desks, newsstands and on buses and trams. Purchase tickets individually, in strips or for 1, 3 or 7 days: multiple tickets are valid for buses and trams, too. Validate your ticket in the machine as you

board, except for tickets bought from machines on trams (these will stamp automatically). One ticket is good for up to four bus/tram or two train stops; two tickets for additional stops. For MVV information ☎ 089 41 42 43 44; hotline: 01803 44 22 66 (Mon.–Fri. 8–8). Taxi stands can be found all over the city. Call Taxi-München ☎ 089 21610 or 089 19410, or IsarFunk Taxizentrale ☎ 089 45 05 40.

Airport Information

The international airport, Flughafen München Franz-Josef-Strauss, is 19 miles northeast of the city center. S-Bahn (lines 1 and 8) trains run 3:18 a.m.–12:38 a.m. to the main railroad station (Hauptbahnhof), a 40-minute trip; airport buses run to the station from the North Terminal daily 6:20 a.m.–9:40 p.m., a 45-minute trip. For flight information ☎ 089 97 52 13 13.

Climate – average highs and lows for the month

Jan.	Feb.	Mar.	Apr.	May	Jun.	Jul.	Aug.	Sep.	Oct.	Nov.	Dec.
2°C	3°C	9°C	14°C	19°C	22°C	25°C	24°C	20°C	14°C	7°C	4°C
36°F	37°F	48°F	57°F	66°F	72°F	77°F	75°F	68°F	57°F	45°F	39°F
-3°C	-2°C	2°C	5°C	9°C	13°C	15°C	15°C	12°C	6°C	2°C	-1°C
27°F	28°F	36°F	41°F	48°F	55°F	59°F	59°F	54°F	43°F	36°F	30°F

Munich Sights

See page 5 for complete key to symbols

Key to symbols

➕ map coordinates refer to the Munich map on
pages 230–231 🖐 admission charge: $$$ more
than €4, $$ €2–€4, $ less than €2
See page 5 for complete key to symbols

Alte Pinakothek

More than 850 pre-18th-century
paintings are being rehoused in the huge
Alte Pinakothek (Old Picture Gallery),
built in 1836 to store the expanding
royal art collection.

The museum has been extensively
restored over the last 50 years. Among
the treasures are works by Albrecht
Dürer and the world's best collection of
work by Peter Paul Rubens.

➕ B4–C4 ✉ Barer Strasse 27 ☎ 089 23 80 52 16
🕐 Tue.–Sun. 10–6 (also Tue. 6–8 p.m.) 🚇 U-Bahn to
Königsplatz 🚃 Tram 27 🖐 $$$ ($ on Sun.)

Asamkirche

The Asamkirche (Asam Church) is
a stunning example of baroque
architecture. Built as a private chapel
(1733–46) by architect and sculptor
Egid Quirin Asam and his brother
Cosmas Damian Asam, it was opened to
the public in 1746. One of Asam's works
is at the altar, showing the crucified
Christ in God's embrace – *The Throne
of Mercy*.

➕ B2 ✉ Sendlinger Strasse 62 🕐 Daily 8–5:30
🚇 U-Bahn to Sendlinger Tor; S-Bahn to Marienplatz
🚌 15, 18, 20, 25

BMW Museum

This stylishly revamped museum is
now five times bigger than before and
celebrates nine decades of BMW
technology and expertise. There are
plenty of vehicles to see, of course, along
with themed areas and displays relating
to automobile design, media design and
architecture. A central route leads
visitors along a historical time line.

➕ Off map at A4 ✉ Am Olympiapark 2 ☎ 089 38 22
33 07 🕐 Tue.–Sun. and public holidays 10–6
🚇 U-Bahn to Olympiazentrum or Petuelring
🚌 36, 43, 81, 136, 184 🖐 $$$

Deutsches Museum

One of the biggest science and
technology museums in the world,
the German Museum has more than
100,000 items on display, and deals
with everything from lightning
demonstrations to space travel to
hydraulics to the first German
submarine. Audiovisual displays and
different hands-on exhibits add to
the fun.

➕ C1–D1 ✉ Museumsinsel 1 ☎ 089 21 79-1
🕐 Daily 9–5; closed holy days 🚇 U Bahn to
Fraunhoferstrasse; S-Bahn to Isartor 🚌 17, 18
🍴 Café on site 🖐 $$$

Englischer Garten

Stretching along the bank of the Isar
river, the landscaped park Englischer
Garten (English Garden) was created
in 1789. Today it is busy with street
entertainers and people lunching,
boating and taking in the fresh air. Boats
can be rented at the Kleinhesseloher See
and there is a beer garden, the Seehaus,
near the lake. Enjoy good city views
from the circular "temple," the
monopteros; other popular attractions are
the Chinese Tower and beer garden. In
summer, surfers ride the waves on the
small Eisbach river that runs through
the park.

➕ D4 ✉ Kutscherei Hans Holzmann 🕐 Daily 24
hours 🚇 U-Bahn to Universität or Giselastrasse;
S-Bahn to Marienplatz 🚌 54, 154 to Chinesischer

Englischer Garten offers surprising sports options

Germany

Turm; tram 17 to Tivolistrasse ⑪ Beer gardens, cafés and restaurants in park

Frauenkirche
Munich's twin-towered cathedral (Church of Our Dear Lady), was built between 1468 and 1488, but was left without a roof. In 1524 its Italian Renaissance, green onion domes were "temporarily" added – and have been there ever since. Near the entrance is a footprint in the floor, said to be that of the devil, who stamped with glee thinking that the architect had forgotten to put in the windows. In fact, the windows can't be seen from where the devil was standing – but they are there. The south tower can be climbed.
➕ C2 ✉ Frauenplatz 1 ☎ 089 29 00 82-0
⊙ Church: Sat.–Thu. 7–7 (also Thu. 7–8:30 p.m.),
Fri. 7–6; south tower: Mon.–Sat. 10–5, Apr.–Oct.
🚇 U-Bahn/S-Bahn to Marienplatz, Karlsplatz 🚌 52;
tram 19 💲 Church free: south tower $$

Haus der Kunst
Opened by the Nazis in 1937 as "Haus der Deutschen Kunst" (House of German Art) the large white columned building was immediately mocked by its detractors as "Weisswirtsallee" (White Sausage Boulevard). The gallery was part of Hitler's campaign against modern so-called *entartete Künstler* (degenerate artists). Today the Haus der Kunst shows sophisticated thematic exhibitions and retrospectives.
➕ D3 ✉ Prinzregentenstrasse 1 ☎ 089 211 27-113
⊙ Daily 10–8 (also Thu. 8–10 p.m.) for exhibitions only; closing times are extended for special exhibitions
🚇 U-Bahn to Odeonsplatz or Lehel 🚌 100; tram 17
⑪ Café in gallery 💲 $$$; exhibition admission varies

Lenbachhaus
Built in 1887 as the home of aristocratic painter Franz von Lenbach, the Lenbachhaus is now an art gallery. It shows the progression of art in Munich from the 15th and 16th centuries to the 19th-century Romantics. Highlights of the collection are works by the Munich Expressionists, the so-called *Blaue Reiter*

(Blue Rider) group of the 20th century, with more than 90 abstract paintings and 900 other works by Wassily Kandinsky – the world's largest assemblage of his art.

Although the gallery is closed for restoration until 2012, the Kunstbau (Exhibition Hall) on Königsplatz remains open.
➕ A4 ✉ Luisenstrasse 33 ☎ 089 23 33 20 00
⊙ Tue.–Sun. 10–6 🚇 U-Bahn U2 to Königsplatz;
tram 27 to Karolinenplatz ⑪ Café 💲 $$$ ($ on Sun.)

Neue Pinakothek
Across the street from the Renaissance-style Alte Pinakothek (Old Picture Gallery, see page 233) is Neue Pinakothek (New Picture Gallery), a modern building featuring art from the late 18th to the 20th centuries.

It has examples of the French and German Impressionists, Romantic and rococo paintings, and the art nouveau style known in Germany as *Jugendstil*.
➕ B4 ✉ Luisenstrasse 33 ☎ 089 23 33 20 00
⊙ Tue.–Sun. 10–6 🚇 U-Bahn U2 to Königsplatz;
tram 27 to Karolinenplatz ⑪ Café 💲 $$$ ($ on Sun.)

Neues Rathaus
A forest of neo-Gothic turrets, towers, spurs and gargoyles, the 19th-century Neues Rathaus (New Town Hall) sprawls around six courtyards on the north side of Marienplatz.

On its central tower is a 43-bell clock (Glockenspiel), which comes to life every day at 11 a.m. (also at noon and 5 p.m., Mar.–Oct.) as life-size figures from Munich's history come dancing out to its four melodies. The *Schäfflertanz*, a dance which celebrates the end of the plague in 1517, is performed by dancers in the city streets every seven years (the next is due in 2012).
➕ C2 ✉ Marienplatz 8 ☎ 089 23 300
⊙ Tower: daily 10–7, May–Oct.; Mon.–Fri. 10–5, rest of year 🚇 U-Bahn/S-Bahn to Marienplatz 🚌 52
⑪ Ratskeller, see page 478 💲 Tower $$ ℹ For information about guided tours in English, see www.hausderkunst.de

Hofbräuhaus

Wilhelm V of Bavaria founded Munich's Hofbräu brewery in 1589 to brew a dark ale more to his liking than the local beer. At this time, beer was a drink restricted to the Bavarian upper classes: they had made it their own preserve after losing their vineyards in a series of severe winters. In 1828, the brewery became an inn, and the delights of its beer were made accessible to all townspeople.

The huge beer hall and its tree-shaded courtyard have been the scene of political upheaval and violence in recent history. The Nazi party held its early mass meetings here, and a fight broke out during one of Adolf Hitler's speeches that became known as the Battle of the Hofbräuhaus.

Nowadays, there is nothing sinister about the hall's fame: tourists flock to the long benches, listen to the Bavarian brass bands and drink beer served by traditionally dressed waitresses. They no longer practice the customary quality test for *Bock* beer, though, which is probably just as well. The test apparently consisted of drinkers sitting at one of the Hofbräuhaus' beer-soaked benches and consuming *Bock* beer for hours at a time, staying put even while nature took its course. If, at the end of the session, they stuck to the benches when they tried to get up, the beer was reckoned to be thick enough and ready to sell.

The Hofbräuhaus is the city's most popular beer hall and fills up very quickly, especially during the world-famous, 16-day *Oktoberfest*, a beer festival that ends on the first Sunday in October. Barbecues, processions and music all play their part in this annual jamboree, but beer is the main ingredient.

If the Hofbräuhaus is too crowded, there are other options all over town, plus numerous beer gardens where you are allowed to bring your own food. The *Oktoberfest* action takes place on the fairground at Theresienwiese, west of the city.

Whether you choose to drink at the Hofbräuhaus or elsewhere, make sure you don't sit at the regulars' table *(Stammtisch)*. You'll soon know you've made this mistake if the waitress refuses to take your order!

Musicians perform traditional Bavarian music in Munich's Hofbräuhaus (beer hall)

A detail of the ceiling in the fabulous Residenz

Odeonsplatz

This regal square was laid out for Ludwig I early in the 19th century and marks the beginning of Ludwigstrasse and Prinzregentenstrasse. The Feldherrnhalle (Military Commanders' Hall) was added as a tribute to the Bavarian army, and is guarded by two bronze lions. Overlooking Odeonsplatz is the lovely baroque, golden-stone Theatinerkirche, the church where Wittelsbach family members were laid to rest. The lovely gardens of Hofgarten are next to the square.

✚ C3　🚇 U-Bahn to Odeonsplatz　🚌 53　🍽 Halali, see page 478

Olympiapark

The park built for the 1972 Olympics has become a focus for strollers, joggers and swimmers. Its television tower, the Olympiaturm, is the highest reinforced concrete tower in Europe, and has a platform and revolving restaurant with Alpine views. The Rock Museum, on the platform, features memorabilia from famous rock groups. A tour train takes visitors around Olympic Lake; Olympic Hill, made of wartime debris; and the Olympic Village. You also can visit the Olympiastadion (Olympic stadium).

✚ Off map at A4　✉ Spiridon-Louis-Ring 21　☎ 089 30 67-0; www.olympiaparkmuenchen.de
🕐 Olympiapark: daily 9–6, Apr.–May 15 and Sep. 16–Nov. 6; 9–8, May 16–Sep. 15; 11–4, rest of year. Olympiaturm: daily 9 a.m.–midnight (last admission at 11:30 p.m.)　🚇 U-Bahn to Olympiazentrum　🚌 50, 51, 173, 174; tram 12, 20　🍽 Revolving restaurant, Olympiaturm　💳 Olympiapark free; Olympiastadion $$; Olympiaturm $$$

Pinakothek der Moderne

Opened in 2003, this is one of the most important art museums in Germany. The light, airy building, innovative in design and architecture, displays 20th- and 21st-century art.

✚ B4　✉ Barer Strasse 40　☎ 089 2 38 05 3-60
🕐 Tue.–Sun. 10–6 (also Thu. 6–8)　🚇 U-Bahn to Königsplatz　🚌 54; tram 27　💳 $$$

Residenz

The 112 rooms of the Wittelsbach dynasty's dazzling palace are a treasure trove of artworks, ornaments, furnishings and statues – too much to take in during just one visit. Highlights include the vaulted Antiquarium, built between 1568 and 1571; the rococo Cuvilliés Theater; the crown jewels in the Treasury; and the Ahnengalerie (Ancestral Portrait Gallery).

✚ C3　✉ Residenzstrasse 1/Max-Joseph-Platz 3
☎ 089 29 06 71　🕐 Daily 9–6, Apr. 1 to mid-Oct.; 10–5, rest of year　🚇 U-Bahn to Odeonsplatz; U-Bahn/S-Bahn to Marienplatz　🚌 100 to Odeonsplatz; tram 19 to Nationaltheater　🍽 Spatenhaus an der Oper, see page 478　💳 $$$

Schloss Nymphenburg

For centuries the mighty Wittelsbach family ruled Bavaria. Schloss Nymphenburg (Nymphenburg Palace) was built as their summer villa by Agostino Barelli between 1664 and 1674. Generations of Wittelsbachs added to his creation, and the palace now measures 1,640 feet in length. In the central section is the Schönheitsgalerie, or Gallery of Beauties – 36 paintings of beautiful women produced between 1827 and 1850 for Ludwig I. The former palace stables house the Marstallmuseum, a museum of porcelain and a collection of state carriages and sleighs, and in the 1734 Amalienburg hunting lodge there is a Hall of Mirrors.

✚ Off map at A4　☎ 089 17 90 8-0　🕐 Palace: daily 9–6, Apr. to mid-Oct.; 10–4, rest of year. Gardens: daily dawn– dusk　🚇 U-Bahn to Rotkreuzplatz　🚌 51; tram 17　🍽 Schlosscafé im Palmenhaus, see page 478　💳 $$$

A Walk Along Prinzregentenstrasse

This grand boulevard runs east from the 17th-century Court Garden (Hofgarten), with its beautiful fountains and Renaissance arcades. A startling modern addition, the steel-and-glass Neue Staatskanzlei, houses the Bavarian State Chancellery. Prinzregentenstrasse was laid out at the end of the 19th century and named for Prince Luitpold, who ruled as regent after his nephew, Ludwig II, had been declared mad and deposed.

Today it takes visitors through one of the city's main museum and gallery quarters. Running past the southern end of the English Garden (see page 233), the boulevard first reaches the Haus der Kunst (House of Art, see page 234), formerly a gallery of Nazi-approved art. It exhibits the kind of work the Nazis had condemned.

Next door is the Bavarian National Museum (Bayerisches Nationalmuseum), in a turn-of-the-20th-century building incorporating different architectural styles.

The next notable monument is the former Prussian embassy, now the Schack-Galerie (Prinzregentenstrasse 9), named for one of the 19th century's great patrons of the arts, Count Schack. His own collection of paintings is represented by such artists as Franz von Lenbach and Arnold Böcklin, who relied on the count for their livelihoods. The gallery is open Wed.–Sun. 10–6.

Prinzregentenstrasse continues across the Isar river and past the *Angel of Peace (Friedensengel)*, a golden monument to peace, erected to commemorate the end of the Franco-Prussian War. Nowadays citizens gather on New Year's Day to enjoy fireworks displays and the view of Munich. Farther along, past the Europaplatz, is the Villa Stuck (Prinzregentenstrasse 60), a 19th-century house built in a mix of styles by artist Franz von Stuck. Von Stuck was part of the 1890s *avant-garde* school known as the Munich Secession, and his own work is displayed inside. There also are exhibitions by such modern artists as Brian Jungen from Canada. For guided tours in English, phone ☎ 089 45 55 551–0. The boulevard continues east to the Prinzregententheater (☎ 089 21 28 99), which stages drama, concerts and musicals. It was designed in 1900–01 to emulate the neoclassic Wagner Festival Theater in Bayreuth and sits on Prinzregentenplatz 12, where there is a U-Bahn station; trains travel back to Odeonsplatz and the Hofgarten. For the walking route, see the city map on pages 230–231.

The Diana Temple stands at the heart of the Horgarten; musicians often entertain visitors there

Greece

Opposite: The narrow streets and old white-painted houses that are typical of the Plaka area in Athens

Greece

Subconsciously, we all feel we have a stake in Greece. The language, political systems, values and ethics of the Western world are inextricably connected to this lovely country's ancient civilization. Visitors often arrive with high expectations and romantic notions, snippets of myths, history and hearsay mingled in their minds. Those experiencing the country for the first time are likely to be captivated. Greece evokes strong feelings, and even months of travel would scarcely be enough to do this stunning country justice.

The Land

Greece's landscape is as dramatic as the people who inhabit it. There are about 200 inhabited islands in Greece, scattered on three sides of the mainland. Some are lush and studded with pine and eucalyptus, and others are arid or mountainous. Most are blessed with idyllic sand beaches and picturesque villages, and many have superb ancient sites, Frankish castles or Venetian fortifications.

You could spend years discovering them all, so spare at least a few days to visit one or two. Greek islands are a vital part of the country and have bedazzled travelers for centuries. There are regular ferry services to the main islands in summer, but services to more remote islands are less regular and can be challenging – though worth the effort – to organize. Check the website www.gtp.gr, which lists monthly ferry routes.

Much of mainland Greece is very mountainous. The slopes of Olympus and Parnassus are carpeted with wildflowers in spring, offering superb vistas and rewarding hiking, as do the eerie and stony landscapes of the Máni, a region of rugged mountains and isolated villages, and the steep-sided gorges and wild coastline of Crete.

Public transportation, especially by bus, is usually regular and reliable in mainland towns.

If you prefer to be more independent, car rental is simple to arrange. If you do rent a car, be prepared for some poorly surfaced roads, and avoid driving in cities and some of the larger rural towns if possible.

Traditional Culture

Greece has one of Europe's most vigorous cultures, perpetuated through architecture, crafts, music and dance. Traditional customs permeate everyday life, despite the growing impact of Western consumer values. If you can, see traditional dancing and listen to the music – the real thing is often easier to find in rural areas.

As in many other Mediterranean countries, much of life is lived in the full gaze of the public eye, hence the strolling crowds and packed cafés.

The worldwide recession sparked riots in Athens in 2010 and 2011.

The Greeks and You

Tourism is not a slick operation in Greece; everything works, things eventually happen, but not necessarily with streamlined efficiency. So relax, slow down and you'll get much more out of your trip.

The Greeks have been dealing with foreign incursions for centuries, so they took the late 20th-century tourist influx in their stride. The classical Greek tradition of hospitality to strangers is still strong, which makes for a relaxed attitude toward visitors, particularly when you go off the beaten track.

Greek is the official language, but English is widely spoken, though in remote areas it is likely that only Greek will be understood.

Hospitality often takes the form of innumerable personal questions, among which "How much do you earn?" is usually near the top of the list. Don't be offended, as this is considered an acceptable and friendly exchange. If someone offers you something – a drink, some fruit, a flower – accept it graciously, as the donor is acting out a tradition that goes back thousands of years.

Greeks have a strong code of honor, which makes Greece a safe country to visit. It's highly unlikely you'll be cheated in any way, and you can still safely walk most streets at night without worrying.

Society has changed beyond recognition in the last 40 years, and young Greeks are far more emancipated than their parents. Female virtue – especially in rural areas – is still held in high regard. As a consequence young Greek males may occasionally pester foreign girls in the often mistaken belief that they will respond more readily to their advances.

There's still a large rural class in Greece, and outside cities and tourist areas you'll see black-garbed figures laboring in tiny fields. This traditional way of farming has been going on for centuries, a lifestyle that is a million miles from that of city dwellers.

More Top Destinations in Greece

- Chaniá B1
- Delfoí B2
- Ídra B2
- Kefalloniá A2
- Léros C2
- Máni B1
- Metéora A2
- Monemvassía B1
- Mykínes B2
- Mikonos C2
- Náxos C2
- Óros Píndos A2
- Samothráki B3
- Skópelos B2
- Thíra/ Santorini C1

Greece

Timeline

776–700 BC	City-states established; first Olympic Games.
499–400 BC	Persian Wars; Golden Age of classical Greek culture; Peloponnesian Wars against Sparta.
336–323 BC	Alexander the Great conquers the known world.
146 BC	Greece becomes a Roman province.
AD **394**	Christianity established throughout the Roman Empire; the Olympic Games finish and the Delphic Oracle is closed.
476–1453	Greece ruled from Constantinople; fall of Constantinople in 1453; Greece ruled by Turks for next 400 years.
1821–29	Greek War of Independence; Greece becomes an independent modern state.
1917–18	Greece sides with Allies in World War I.
1920–23	Greece continues a misjudged war against Turkey, ending in defeat.
1940–44	Axis occupation during World War II.
1945–60	Many Greeks emigrate to the United States and Australia; others flood into Athens from the countryside.
1974	Conflict with Turkey over Cyprus; situation remains tense into the 21st century.
1975	Tourist boom begins with foreigners visiting classical sites, islands and coastal resorts.
1981	Greece joins European Community; community funding catapults much of the country into mainstream Europe.
1996	Macedonian claims by former Yugoslavs seen as implicit threat to northern Greek region of Macedonia.
2001	Greece adopts the euro as its new national currency.
2004	Athens hosts the 2004 Olympic Games.
2009	George Papandreou of the PASOK party is elected as prime minister.
2010–2011	Widespread protest marches take place against austerity measures to deal with the country's ongoing debt crisis.

The Golden Age of Classical Greece

The peace following the defeat of the Persians in the fifth century BC marked the start of a cultural, artistic and intellectual blossoming for Athens and the other city-states. Much of what truly epitomizes "the glory that was Greece" dates from this era. The great architectural triumphs, the start of drama and comedy, and the first steps in philosophical thought can all be traced to Athens at this time. The Acropolis took the form whose remains are seen today, decorated by Pheidas' sublime marbles, and subtly harmonious temples were built everywhere. The names Sophocles, Euripides, Aristophanes, Socrates and Plato are familiar worldwide; it's worth remembering that they lived and worked in this tiny state in the eastern Mediterranean more than 2,500 years ago.

Survival Guide

■ Athens is best avoided during the sweltering summer months, when temperatures can soar above 90°F, noise levels are high around the clock, and the ever-present pollution is at its worst.

■ Head for restaurants and tavernas where the locals eat; the food will be good. If you don't understand the menu in a *taverna* you may be invited into the kitchen for a look – choose what you want and point!

■ In some areas of Greece there is an enduring belief that hot food harms the stomach, and food may therefore be served lukewarm. However, the preference for hot food is normally accommodated.

■ Remember to *never* flush toilet tissue down the toilet – it goes in the basket provided. You'll flood the bathroom if you put paper down the narrow pipes. The only exceptions are modern, luxury hotels. Public restrooms are few and far between, and many of them leave much to be desired. Carry your own toilet paper as it is not always available.

■ Greeks prefer to be cool and comfortable rather than stylish, but usually don't wear shorts in the city. It's respectful to cover bare shoulders and upper arms when visiting churches or religious establishments. Topless and nude sunbathing are widely but discreetly practiced.

■ Taxis outside main cities are fairly inexpensive, but in Athens drivers may hike rates for foreign visitors. Ask what the destination fare is before getting into a taxi or compare fares before deciding which one you'll use. On arrival by ferry or plane, if you already have a hotel reserved, resist being talked into going to another hotel.

■ Don't rent a scooter; more tourists have accidents on them than by any other means.

Guarding the Tomb of the Unknown Warrior, Athens

■ At important sites you may be approached by guides wanting to be paid for their services; some are good, others barely speak English. If you want guide service, use an official one or take a tour.

■ There's a plethora of attractive, handmade items to buy in Greek stores and markets. Most prices are fixed, but you can try a little gentle haggling in markets.

■ Be careful after it rains, when marble-surfaced walkways in Athens become very slippery. Also look out for unmarked holes on sidewalks, especially in poorly lit areas at night.

Athens

Athens is one of the Mediterranean's great cities, boasting some of the world's most treasured relics; it's also noisy, crowded, traffic clogged and polluted, with sprawling, unattractive suburbs. Summertime heat and the lack of shady spots can be oppressive, but the city is exhilarating, fascinating and stimulating, as much for its past as its present. Enjoy it for the colorful place it is.

Tackling Athens

You'll probably spend most of your visit in Athens' tiny historical center. Base yourself near Syntagma Square or Pláka, which are only a 10- to 15-minute walk from most of the main tourist sights. Try to plan your day carefully, getting an early start, so you can lie low during the heat of the afternoon.

If you need information or advice, you will find that most people connected with tourism speak English, ranging from a few words to polished and idiomatic speech.

Moving around the historic center on foot is easy, but is occasionally challenging at busy street crossings. Be aware that where there are no traffic lights local drivers rarely take note of

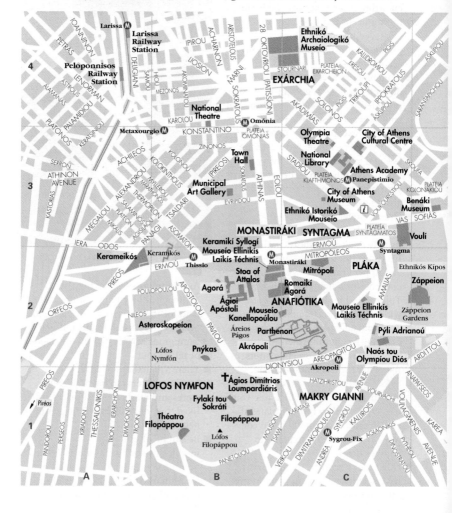

pedestrian crossings; wait for a clear gap in the traffic before crossing. In the last few years there has been an expanding pedestrianization program in the center.

City buses and trolley buses are often packed and may be delayed by traffic jams. Taxis are convenient for excursions out of the city, as is the greatly improved metro (subway) system. The main road systems into the city have also been improved.

Athenian Flavors
Sitting at a shady café table, lingering over a gargantuan lunch, munching sunflower seeds, melon, pistachios and pine nuts, or eating ice cream as you stroll on balmy evenings are true Athenian pleasures.

In a country where hospitality to strangers is one of the bedrock rules of society, it's not surprising that eating and drinking socially play an important role. Eating establishments are known as *estiatorio* (restaurants) or *tavernas* (less expensive, simpler and often family run). Greek food is delicious and healthy – fresh salads with feta cheese and olives, fantastic *mezédhes* (hors d'oeuvres), grilled meats, moussakas, and tasty stews and vegetables, perhaps washed down with one of the increasingly good selections of Greek wines. Dessert is normally fresh local fruit; if you want something sweeter, head for a *zaharoplastío*, a café serving the honey-soaked pastries much loved by the Greeks.

Festivals and Theater
Athens has theater, movies, dance, galleries and nightlife; everything changes rapidly, so pick up a free copy of one of the English-language newspapers to find out schedules.

In summer, the main tourist attraction is the Hellenic Festival (www.greekfestival.gr), which runs from June through September. The festival offers a wonderful program of excellent cultural events, although it's most famous for classical Greek theater, some taking place at the Odeon of Herodes Atticus on the slopes of the Acropolis.

ATHENS

| 0 | 100 | 200 metres |
| 0 | 100 | 200 yards |

Lykavitós Theatre
LYKAVITÓS
ZOGRAFOU
Lykavitós
†Ágios Georgios
Funicular Railway
Megaro Moussikis
KOLONÁKI
N
IOAKEIM
Alsos Syngrou
Evangelismos
VAS SOFIAS
Goulandris Museío Kykladikís Téchnis
Vyzantinó kai Christianikó Mouseío
EFFRONIOU
GEORGIOU
GEORGIOU
Proedrikó Mégaro
PAGKRATI
Panathinaikó Stádio
EFTICHIDOU
Próto Nekrotafío Athinón

D   E

The Greek Alphabet
At first it may be daunting to see Greek script everywhere, but it won't be a major inconvenience. All street signs are in both Greek and Roman letters, as are signs to museums and most restaurants and shops. Public transportation is usually displayed in Greek. But you'll get the hang of it and will feel a real sense of achievement when you do.

Greece

Ceramics and Honey

There's a wide range of shopping in Athens, from international labels to traditional Greek products. In Kolonáki and on and around Ermoú Street, the most fashionable retail areas of the city, you'll find familiar merchandise.

Ethnic buys are another matter, with much to hunt down around Pláka and its vicinity. Leather and woolen goods, ceramics and tapestries, felt slippers, olive oil, honey and pistachio nuts are all excellent buys. For something that bit more special, check out jewelry or religious stores; Greece has a long tradition of gold craftsmanship, and traditional icons are still made.

Keep a look out for Athens' *periptera* (kiosks) – much more than newsstands, they sell everything from snacks and

A view of Lykabettos Hill from the Acropolis, Athens
Opposite: A walkway in Athens' Olympic complex

drinks to bus tickets, simple medicines and telephone cards. In central Athens you will find that some *periptera* open 24 hours a day.

Essential Information

Tourist Information
Tsoha 24, Ambelokipi ☎ 210 870 7000; www.gnto.gr
Athens International Airport Arrivals Hall
☎ 210 353 0445

Urban Transportation
The metro (subway) system is being expanded, but it's a long-term project and for now the easiest way to get around Athens is to walk or take one of the numerous yellow taxis. Taxis are hailed on the street and often shared; you pay for your segment of the trip, so check the meter when you get in. Alternatively, your hotel can arrange a taxi for you. Buses, trolley buses and the metro operate daily 5:30 a.m. –midnight (Fri.–Sat. metro operates until 2 a.m.); tickets are available at kiosks and are interchangeable with subway tickets, which

can be bought at stations. Validate bus and trolley bus tickets on board, and subway tickets at entrances to platforms. The Athens Urban Transport Organization's (OASA) website, www.oasa.gr, is useful for finding bus, trolley bus and metro routes.

Airport Information
Athens International Airport (Eleftherios Venizelos) is at Spáta, 17 miles east of Athens (☎ 210 353 0000; www.aia.gr). The metro line 3 linking the airport to the city is the easiest way into Athens. There are four 24-hour express bus lines, connecting the airport with Athens and Piréas: the X93 to the Kifíssos Coach Station, X95 to Syntagma Square, X96 to Piréas and X97 to the Dafni metro station. Tickets cost €6 one way. For details see the airport's website: www.aia.gr

Climate – average highs and lows for the month

	Jan.	Feb.	Mar.	Apr.	May	Jun.	Jul.	Aug.	Sep.	Oct.	Nov.	Dec.
	13°C	13°C	15°C	19°C	24°C	30°C	31°C	32°C	28°C	23°C	17°C	14°C
	55°F	55°F	59°F	66°F	75°F	86°F	88°F	90°F	82°F	73°F	63°F	57°F
	6°C	6°C	7°C	11°C	15°C	20°C	22°C	22°C	19°C	15°C	11°C	8°C
	43°F	43°F	45°F	52°F	59°F	68°F	72°F	72°F	66°F	59°F	52°F	46°F

Athens Sights

Agorá

The stately civic center and marketplace of ancient Athens is at the foot of the Acropolis, to which it was once linked by the Panathenaic Way.

Today the site is a jumble of atmospheric, tree-shaded ruins, and you'll need to use your imagination to visualize its glorious heyday. Dominating one end is the virtually reconstructed, fifth-century BC Doric temple known as the Thieío.

Opposite, the two-story Stoá Attálou, a second-century BC arcade, has been restored by the American School of Archeology to give an idea of the glory of these ancient public buildings. It contains a museum with finds from the site.

➕ B2 ✉ Adrianou or Theorias ☎ 210 321 0185
🕐 Daily 8–7:30, Apr.–Oct.; 8–3, rest of year.
Museum closes Mon 8–11 🚇 Thiseío or Monastiráki
✋ $$

Akrópoli

The Akrópoli (Acropolis) should top your sightseeing list. This naturally defensible rock was the sacred focal point of ancient Athens. What you see today dates mainly from the fifth century BC, an era of peace and prosperity thought of as the true "Golden Age" of Greece.

You reach the summit through the Propylaia, a magnificent stepped gateway, with the graceful little temple of Athena Nike to your right. Ahead rises the great Doric temple of the Parthenón, one of the world's most beautiful buildings; built using no perpendicular lines, its columns actually taper, giving the whole structure a feeling of lightness. It was decorated by Athenian sculptors and dedicated to the goddess Athena Parthenos, whose statue by the sculptor Pheidias stood inside.

To the left of the Parthenón stands the Erechtheion, shrine to Athena and Poseidon, and said to be the place where the goddess created the first olive tree. The roof of the south portico is supported by six caryatids, stately maidens dressed in pleated tunics.

At the foot of the Acropolis you can see two Roman theaters, and visit the Acropolis Museum (see page 250).

Looking toward the Acropolis on its rocky setting, as the sun sets across the city

➕ B2 ✉ Akrópoli ☎ 210 321 0219; www.acropolisofathens.gr 🕐 Daily 8–8, Apr.–Oct.; 8:30–3, rest of year 🚇 Akrópoli 🎟 $$$

Ethnikó Archaiologikó Mouseío

For lovers of classical art the Ethnikó Archaiologikó Mouseío (National Archeological Museum) is one of the world's top sights. This vast and varied collection covers all the finest art from ancient Greece, with the added bonus of an exceptional Egyptian collection.

The best approach is to concentrate on only the prime examples. Head first for the treasures from the royal tombs at Mycenae, dating from 1500 BC; they include exquisite gold funerary masks, necklaces and filigree flowers. Next, take in the sixth-century BC *kouros*, vibrant statues of nude male athletes; Aristodikos' superbly tactile athlete is one of the finest ever carved. Move on to admire the huge statue of Poseidon and the little jockey urging on his horse, both found in the sea off Cape Artemision on the island of Evvoia in 1927. There's also a stunning bronze by the famous sculptor Praxiteles in room 28. Upstairs you'll find frescoes from Santorini (Thíra), buried 3,500 years ago during a volcanic eruption, showing charming riverside scenes. Rooms 49–56 house the fascinating pottery collections; look for the rare *lekythoi* (white-ground clayware), and the exquisite red and black Attic vases.

➕ C4 ✉ 44 Patission ☎ 210 821 7724 🕐 Tue.– Sun. 8–7:30, Mon. 1–7:30, mid-Apr. to mid-Oct.; Tue.–Sun. 8:30–3, Mon. 1:30–8, rest of year 🚇 Omonia 🚌 2, 3, 11, 13, 15, 022, 224, 226 🍴 Café in museum 🎟 $$$

Ethnikós Kípos

The green and somber Ethnikós Kípos (National Gardens) provide a wonderful oasis of cool off noisy Leóforos Amalias. Laid out in the 19th century by Queen Amalia, wife of King Otto, this is a true southern Mediterranean garden – no colorful flowerbeds, but deep shade and sylvan green. With plenty of cafés, the gardens are a good place for lunch. Within the grounds is a botanical museum with samples of all the gardens' plants, many of them rare.

➕ C2–D2 ✉ Amalias ☎ Museum: 210 721 1178 🕐 Daily dawn to 30 minutes before dusk (museum: Tue.–Sun. 9–3) 🚇 Syntagma 🚌 1, 2, 4, 11, 12, 022, 025, 026

Goulandris Mouseío Kykladikís Téchnis

The beautifully presented Goulandris Mouseío Kykladikís Téchnis (Museum of Cycladic Art), which houses a superb collection of prehistoric artifacts from the Aegean islands, was established in 1986. The collection, once the private property of the shipowning Goulandris family, dates from the Cycladic civilization, which flourished on the Greek islands from 3000 until 2000 BC. The figures, carved from local marble, could be taken for 20th-century work, elegant and minimalist, yet full of powerful feeling.

➕ D3 ✉ 4 Neophytou Douka ☎ 210 722 8321; www.cycladic.gr 🕐 Mon.–Wed., Fri.–Sat. 10–5, Thu. 10–8, Sun. 11–5 🚇 Syntagma, Evangelismos 🚌 3, 7, 13, 224, 235 🍴 Café in museum 🎟 $$$

Lykavitós and Kolonáki

From Kolonáki Square, the hub of one of Athens' most fashionable shopping areas, the slopes of Lykavitós (Lykabettus Hill) rise steeply to the 912-foot-high summit, one of the city's great vantage points. You can walk up or take the funicular for panoramic views over the city, from the Acropolis down to the sea at Piréas. Get there for sunset, and visit the whitewashed chapel of Agios Giorgios (St. George), which crowns the top of the hill.

➕ D3–D4 ✉ Kolonáki 🕐 Funicular: daily 9–midnight (times may vary) 🚌 022, 060 🍴 Terrace restaurant at top 🎟 $$ (funicular)

Monastiráki

This bustling area surrounds Monastiráki square, named for a former monastery on this site. Today the square's focal point is the 18th-century Tzistarakis Mosque, a relic of Turkish rule, which houses the Keramiki Silogi (Museum of Greek Ceramics). Most people head straight for Monastiráki's famous flea market, selling anything from clothes and kebabs to icons and CDs. Sunday is the big day here.

➕ B3 ✉ Monastiráki 🏛 Museum of Greek Ceramics: 210 324 2066 🕐 Market open daily, but largest on Sun. Museum: Wed.–Mon. 9–2:30 🚇 Monastiráki 🍴 $ (free to all some Sun. in winter)

Naós tou Olympiou Diós and Pýli Adrianoú

Along with the Tower of the Winds in the Roman Agora, Naós tou Olympiou Diós and Pýli Adrianoú (Temple of Olympian Zeus and Hadrian's Arch) are Athens' most impressive Roman legacy. Both of these structures were completed around AD 130 by the Emperor Hadrian; the temple as a shrine to this paramount Roman god, and the arch to mark the boundary between the old Greek city and Hadrian's new one. Fifteen massive columns remain of what was once the largest temple in Greece.

➕ C2 ✉ 2 Vasilissis Olgas ☎ 210 922 6330 🕐 Tue.–Sun. 8–7:30, Mon. 11–7:30, Apr.–Oct.; daily 8:30–3, rest of year 🚇 Akrópoli 🚌 1, 4, 11, 040, 057 🍴 $$

Piréas

Piréas is a town in its own right, although it's only five stops on the

subway from Athens' center. It's a noisy, bustling port, one of the biggest in the Mediterranean, and many of the interisland boats leave from its harbor. It boasts a magnificent cathedral, rebuilt after World War II; a fine archeological museum with some striking exhibits; and Greece's naval museum.

Sunday is a good day to browse in the flea market.

➕ Off map at A1 🚇 Piréas

Pláka

Visitors return time and again to the pretty Pláka neighborhood, at the foot of the Acropolis. The maze of colorful narrow streets, flower-bedecked squares and huge range of stores and *tavernas* may be touristy, but also radiate charm. Bustling Kidhathineon and Adrianoú, the main streets, teem with street life and are lined with mainly 19th-century, colorfully painted houses.

Don't miss the dazzling white alleys that make up Anafiotika, on the northern slopes of the Acropolis. This area was built in the 1840s by masons from the Cycladic islands, and it still retains a village atmosphere.

➕ C2 ✉ Pláka 🚇 Syntagma, Monastiráki 🚌 9, 11, 15, 025, 026

Platéia Syntagmatos

Noisy, crowded, Platéia Syntagmatos (Constitution Square) is at the heart of modern Athens, where you'll find a variety of hotels, offices, banks, restaurants and myriad jostling Athenians. The neoclassic edifice at the top is the Voulí (Parliament Building), which was once the royal palace. In front of it is the Tomb of the Unknown Soldier, patrolled around the clock by the Evzones, a guard of honor whose dress uniform features a short pleated kilt and pom-poms on their shoes.

The central area is pleasantly pedestrianized, with several cafés.

➕ C3 ✉ Syntagmatos 🚇 Syntagma 🚌 1, 2, 4, 5, 022, 025, 026 ℹ Changing of the guard at varied times Mon.–Fri., at 11 a.m. on Sun.

Acropolis Museum

The stunning museum, built at a cost of €130 million, finally opened in June 2009. The interior of the controversially modern building is phenomenal with its superbly designed galleries, subtle lighting and spectacular views of the Acropolis. The museum exhibits some 4,000 artifacts.

➕ B2–C2 ✉ Dionysiou Areopagitou 15 ☎ 210 900 0900; www.theacropolismuseum.gr 🕐 Tue.–Sun. 8–8 (last admission 7:30 p.m.). Closed public holidays 🚇 Akropoli 🍴 $$

An Excursion To Delphi

The sacred site of Delphi (Delfoí), 93 miles northwest of Athens, is the obvious choice for a day trip. The greatest shrine of the ancient Greek world, the center of their earth, lies in an unrivaled position below the great peaks of Mount Parnassós. Dedicated to the god Apollo, in ancient times Delphi was independent – belonging to no state – so enemies could worship there together. It was famed for its oracle, which gave enigmatic and prophetic advice through the medium of a priestess.

In return for this, petitioners brought gifts and erected treasure houses to hold them; ancient writers referred to the marble and precious stones of the sanctuary. For centuries, pilgrims trudged through the mountains to bathe in the sacred Castalian spring and worship here, but in the fourth century Christianity triumphed and the last oracle slipped away. Below the site, olive groves spread down to the sea, the ground is carpeted with flowers and the sky is full of birds.

The French excavated Delphi in the 1890s, and today it lies on a series of terraces below Parnassós. The paved Sacred Way leads past treasure houses – one has been sensitively reconstructed – to the remains of the Temple of Apollo. Six columns still stand, giving an idea of the ancient ruin's former size and grandeur.

Up the hill you'll find the 5,000-seat theater and the marvelously evocative and well-preserved athletic stadium, set amid pine trees. To visit the ruins of the Sanctuary of Athena, you will need to leave the main site and cross the modern road. Use the columns of the fourth-century BC Tholos, undoubtedly the most photographed of all Delphi's wonders, as your guide.

The adjacent museum contains the finds from Delphi, some of the finest in Greece. Sculptures from the Temple of Apollo, two superb examples of archaic *koroi* (statues), ivory, jewelry and pottery are all here. The highlight of the collection is the striking bronze sculpture of a charioteer, which dates from 478 BC and is an artistic and technical masterpiece.

➕ See page 240, B2 ✉ Delphi ☎ 226 508 2312 or 226 508 2346 🕐 Daily 8–8 (except museum closed Mon. 8–1:30), Apr.–Oct.; Tue.–Sun. 7:30–5, Mon. 11–5, rest of year 💲 $$$ ℹ️ A guided excursion is the easiest way to visit Delphi

Excursion Operators Chat Tours (✉ 9 Xenofontos Street, off Amalias Avenue ☎ 210 323 0827; www.chatours.gr) is an experienced tour operator in Athens

The Sacred Way leads past this well-reconstructed Treasury building at Delphi

Hungary

Opposite: Hősök tere (Heroes Square), Budapest, with statues of the tribal leaders who founded Hungary

Hungary

Hungary is situated at the heart of Europe. Surrounded by Austria, Slovakia, Ukraine, Romania, Serbia, Croatia and Slovenia, it has absorbed the cultures of such peoples and conquerors as the Romans, Magyars, Turks and Habsburgs. Its majestic capital, Budapest, sits on the broad Danube river, which has brought trade and settlers through the country on its course from Austria to Serbia.

For centuries Hungary has been a nation in flux, its territories expanding or diminishing through a series of invasions, occupations and liberations.

It is today undergoing yet further change after emerging from more than 40 years of life behind the Iron Curtain and joining the European Union in 2004.

Landscape of History

Northern, western and southern Hungary are different worlds. In the north, beyond the capital of Budapest and the industrial city of Miskolc, are the uplands and their wide, rolling, forested hills. The vineyards in this region produce the famous Tokay (Tokaj) and Bull's Blood (Egri Bikavér), the "wine of kings and king of wines."

In the west there continue to be strong links with Western European culture. The rich farmlands are punctuated with historic towns that have many examples of both fine Renaissance and ornate baroque buildings.

In the south the landscape changes completely. Vast, flat grasslands form the *puszta* of the Great Plain (Alföld), dotted with tiny farmsteads and presided over by the capital, Debrecen. In the far south, the medieval city of Pécs, provincial capital of the county of Baranya, preserves many relics of its 143 years under Turkish rule.

Making Contact

The Hungarian language, related to Finnish and Estonian, can be daunting for visitors. English may be spoken in the main tourist areas, but German is more frequently used. When you find a common language, however, you will discover that Hungarians are courteous, generous and formal.

Hungary is a multiracial nation, and despite its close proximity to the Balkan region, it considers itself to be West European.

Hungarian Heritage

Hungarians have strong folk traditions and customs, especially when it comes to music and dance. You can enjoy them at a dance house (*táncház*); there are

HUNGARY

several in Budapest. Bands usually include bagpipes, cimbalom (a stringed instrument) and a hurdy-gurdy, and the dancing is fast and furious.

In Kiskunság National Park, between the Danube and the Tisza rivers, a horse-drawn buggy takes visitors to see farmsteads, long-horned cattle and curly-horned Podokan sheep. There also are displays at Hortobágy National Park – Hungary's first national park – with its endless grasslands.

In the Cserhát hills of the north, the village of Hollókő sits at the foot of a 13th-century castle. The village is home to the Palóc people, who speak a distinct regional dialect and wear colorful embroidered costumes and elaborate headdresses. For another insight into

Hungary's heritage, visit the famous Király thermal baths in Budapest and enjoy the luxury of a Turkish-style bath or massage.

More Top Destinations in Hungary

- Balatonfüred B2
- Bugac-Puszta C2
- Eger D3
- Fertőd A2
- Gödöllő C2
- Hollókő C3
- Hortobágy Nemzeti Park D2
- Kecskemét C2
- Mátra C3
- Pécs B1
- Sopron A3
- Szabadtéri Néprajzi Múzeum B2
- Szentendre C2
- Tihany B2
- Tokaj D3
- Visegrád C3

Timeline

13 BC	The Roman province of Pannonia is established on the west bank of the Danube; nomadic tribes occupy the east.
AD 896	Seven Magyar tribes cross the Carpathian Mountains and invade the Hungarian plains.
1000	King Stephen is crowned and makes Hungary a centralized, Christian state.
1526	The Turkish army of Sultan Suleiman I defeats the Hungarians at Mohács.
1686	Habsburg troops recapture Buda, on the west bank of the Danube (later united with Pest, on the east).
1896	The Great Exposition celebrates the 1,000th anniversary of the Magyar Conquest.
1919	Hungary briefly becomes a Bolshevik republic.
1920	Under the Treaty of Trianon, Hungary loses two-thirds of its territory to Czechoslovakia, Yugoslavia and Romania, and comes under the rule of an Austro-Hungarian regent.
1939	Hungary enters World War II as a German ally.
1944	German occupation; most Jews are deported.
1948	Communists take power.
1956	Rebellion against Communist rule is crushed by Soviet troops.
1989	Hungary opens its borders to Austria and the Iron Curtain begins to lift.
1990	Free elections are won by a center-right coalition.
1999	Hungary officially joins NATO.
2004	Hungary joins the European Union.
2006	Danube floods to record levels.
2010	Pécs is the European Capital of Culture.
2011	Celebrations mark the 200th anniversary of the birth of composer Franz Liszt

The Good Old Days

Hungary enjoyed two "golden ages" – one in the 15th century and another in the 19th. Under 15th-century ruler King Matthias, the son of a Transylvanian general, the nation expanded its borders and established its court in Vienna. Matthias patronized some of Europe's most brilliant scholars, and employed the best Italian artists to work on his palace in Visegrád. Ruins were unearthed here in the 1930s. His reign became a byword for good government. When he died, say Hungarians, justice died with him. The man known as "the greatest Hungarian" ushered in a second age of achievement. In the 19th century Count István Széchenyi modernized the country, laying surfaced roads, introducing steamships and founding an academy of sciences. He also linked Buda and Pest with the Chain Bridge, and stopped the regular cycle of floods around the Tisza river by building dams that regulated its flow.

Survival Guide

- Hungary is not a place to visit if you are on a strict diet. Its best-known export, *gulyás* (goulash), is made with beef, onions, potatoes, paprika, tomatoes, garlic and caraway seeds. Salami is a familiar item, as is *lecso*, a mix of peppers, tomatoes, onions and bacon fried in pork fat. Tempting pastries also are specialties, sold in the *cukrászda* (pastry shop). Try *palacsinta*, thin pancakes filled with all manner of goodies, from poppy seeds to chocolate to curd cheese.

- Rural Hungarians produce and sell beautifully crafted items such as embroidered blouses and carved wood furniture. Buy these in city stores, at national parks and from street sellers like the costumed Transylvanian (Romanian) Hungarians.

- Wine is another good Hungarian buy, sold by dealers in the main vineyards, such as Eger. The vineyards on the slopes of Lake Balaton are delightful and many give tastings in their barrel-lined cellars.

- Go to street markets in the main towns and cities, such as the popular morning flea market on the southwest outskirts of Pécs. This is one of the biggest open-air markets in the country, selling antiques, crafts and food. On Sundays it also sells livestock, and the place is packed with country people.

- Some of the most fascinating ethnic communities have inevitably become big tourist magnets. Hollókő is filled with visitors for the August Palóc Festival and for Easter – an important celebration everywhere, marked with processions, egg-painting and a water-splashing ceremony.

- Summer festivals attract crowds to Pécs and Sopron in June, and on St. Stephen's Day on August 20. There are fireworks, fairs and processions all over Hungary.

- The state railroad, Hungarian Railways (operating passenger trains as MÁV-Start), travels all over the country, though the service is being reduced in rural areas. Special InterRail One Country tourist passes offer unlimited use of the network for 3 to 8 days: contact MÁV-Start (BH-1426 Budapest, P.O. Box 56 ☎ (06) 40 49 49 49; 1 444 4499 from outside Hungary; www.mav-start.hu).

- Accommodations are not limited to city hotels. The Danube bend, a spectacular deep gorge north of Budapest, is lined with attractive towns where many private homes offer rooms. The resorts around Lake Balaton are another option.

- For overnight stays on the Great Plain, try the Hortobágy Club Hotel in Hortobágy National Park (BH-4071 Hortobágy-Máta; www.hortobagy hotel.hu) or the Sarlóspuszta Club Hotel near Dabas (BH-2375 Tatárszentgyörgy-Sarlóspuszta ☎ 29 319 118; www.sarlospuszta.hu).

Detail of the entrance of National Széchényi Library

Hungary

Budapest

Until the 19th century, two communities faced each other across the Danube. Royal, medieval Buda, with its majestic architecture, stood on the hilly western bank; and modern Pest, a flat area of busy boulevards, was on the east bank. Then the Chain Bridge (Széchenyi lánchíd) was built and Budapest, "Queen of the Danube," was created, linking the western and eastern landscapes of Hungary: the green uplands behind Buda, and the flat fields of the Great Plain beyond Pest.

Crossing the Divide

The best place to get a feel for the capital's character and history is at Buda. Here you will find the oldest and

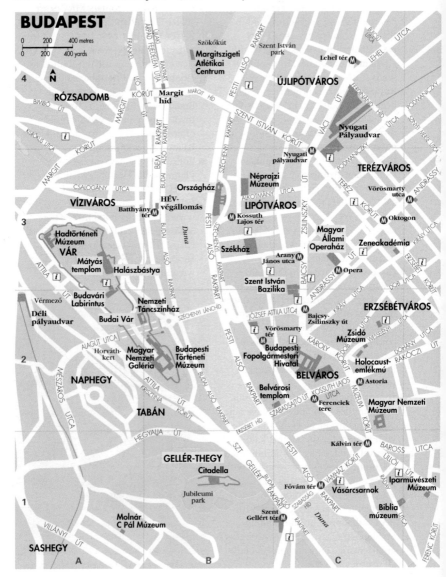

BUDAPEST

| 0 | 200 | 400 metres |
| 0 | 200 | 400 yards |

N

grandest architecture, museums and galleries, and cafés and bars. You can survey the whole city from Gellért Hill (Gellért-hegy), and visit Castle Hill (Várhegy), a renovated medieval quarter which is reached by funicular railroad from the Buda end of Chain Bridge (Budavári Sikló). This is where you'll find the Buda Castle (Budai Vár) and the Fisherman's Fortress (Halászbástya).

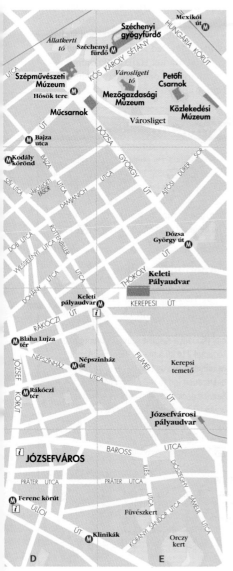

Pest has a much more contemporary feel; its main landmark is the parliament building (Országház), a neo-Gothic fantasy in stone dominating the riverbank. Also worth visiting are the Hungarian State Opera House (Magyar Állami Operaház) and the Museum of Fine Arts (Szépművészeti Múzeum). Between the riverbanks is tranquil Margaret Island (Margit-sziget), named after St. Margaret, a medieval nun of royal birth, providing a haven of gardens in the middle of the Danube.

Local Flavors

In the late 19th and early 20th centuries Budapest ranked with Vienna and Paris as part of European café society, drawing artists and intellectuals to argue, work and read newspapers in its great coffee-houses. At the end of World War II, few of these hubs of creative life remained. The Café Restaurant New York, at Erzsébet körút 9–11, manages to preserve the aura associated with those days. Now fully restored, it reopened in spring 2006.

Traditionally, Hungarian meals rely on the staples of spices, meat and cream and include intriguing specialties such as *túrós csusza* (pasta with cheese curd and sour cream). Since 1989 the range of international restaurant options has increased immeasurably.

Budapest at Night

The main home of opera and ballet is the Hungarian State Opera House (Magyar Állami Operaház, Andrássy út 22, ☎ 13 53 01 70; www.opera.hu), a massive neo-Renaissance confection. Classical concerts take place in the Academy of Music (Zeneakadémia, Liszt Ferenc tér 8, ☎ 1 342 017). There are many clubs, rock venues bars and discos. Since the mid-1990s Hungary has been in the mainstream of European pop and rock. There are several English-language websites with entertainment listings, and the monthly magazine *Budapest Panorama*.

Halászbástya (Fisherman's Bastion) in Budapest

Shopping

Pedestrian-only Váci utca, on the Pest side of the river, is the perfect place to begin shopping trips, and to look for antiques and art bargains. Other main boulevards in central Pest also are lined with stores. In Buda, there's an excellent browsing area around Móricz Zsigmond körtér.

A well-known flea market (Ecseri) sets up daily (mornings on Sunday) at Nagykőrösi út. It's also a pleasure to wander among the heaped food stalls of the renovated Nagy-vásárcsarnok (Central Market Hall) on Fővám tér. The market is open all day Monday to Friday and on Saturday until 2 p.m.

Essential Information

Tourist Information

BTH Budapesti Turisztikal Szolgáltató Kht. (Tourism Office of Budapest)
Sütő utca ☎ 1 438 8080
Liszt Ferenc tér 11 ☎ 1 322 4098
Budapest Airport: Terminals 1, 2a and 2b
Written inquiries to: H-1115 Budapest,
Bartók Béla út.105-113; www.budapestinfo.hu

Urban Transportation

Subway lines are color coded: yellow (M1), red (M2) and blue (M3). A fourth line is due to open in 2011. Buy tickets from the counter *(pénztár)* until 8 p.m., then from the section called *forgalmi ugyelét*. Trains run daily 4:30 a.m.–11 p.m. Buses with red or black numbers and no letter stop all over the city; avoid the express buses, which have a letter "E." Trams and trolley buses also have an extensive network and run daily 4:30 a.m.– 11 p.m. Tickets are available from transport terminals, subway stations, vending machines

or newsstands. For public transportation information ☎ (36) 1 258 4636; www.bkv.hu. Subway stations are marked with an "M" on the city map. Make sure that taxis display a sign, and be sure the meter is on and running. The biggest city company is Fötaxi (☎ 1 222 2222).

Airport Information

Ferihegy Airport (renamed Franz-Liszt airport in 2011) is 10 miles southeast of the city. The 200E Reptérbusz (Airport bus) service runs every 10 minutes at peak times between the city (Kőbánya-Kispest subway station) and terminal 2 (4:30 a.m.–11:45 p.m.). Airport Minibuses (run by LRI) travel to any requested destination (go to the Airport Minibus Service desk on arrival or book ahead at www.airportshuttle.hu). Bus 93 runs to Kőbánya-Kispest subway station. For flight details ☎ 1 296 7000; general inquiries ☎ 1 296 9696; www.bud.hu

Climate – average highs and lows for the month

Jan.	Feb.	Mar.	Apr.	May	Jun.	Jul.	Aug.	Sep.	Oct.	Nov.	Dec.
2°C	4°C	10°C	15°C	22°C	24°C	26°C	26°C	22°C	15°C	7°C	3°C
36°F	39°F	50°F	59°F	72°F	75°F	79°F	79°F	72°F	59°F	45°F	37°F
-4°C	-3°C	1°C	5°C	10°C	14°C	15°C	15°C	11°C	6°C	1°C	-3°C
25°F	27°F	34°F	41°F	50°F	57°F	59°F	59°F	52°F	43°F	34°F	27°F

Budapest Sights

Budai Vár

A UNESCO World Heritage Site, Budai Vár (Buda Castle) looks down over the Danube from the southern end of Várhegy (Castle Hill). Little is left of the earliest castle, built in the 13th century under Béla IV.

What remains is in the underground passages and cellars, now part of the Budapesti Történeti Múzeum (Budapest History Museum), in Wing E, which displays Roman, medieval and more recent finds, and has an excellent collection of historical paintings and prints. The castle was rebuilt in the second half of the 20th century with a neoclassical dome.

Matthias Fountain on the north wall of Buda Castle

The Magyar Nemzeti Galéria (Hungarian National Gallery) collection of Hungarian art is housed in the Central Wings B, C and D, under the dome. A walk from here through a peaceful garden square and past the lovely Matthias Well fountain takes you to the West Wing (F) and the Országos Széchényi Könyvtár (National Széchényi Library), which stores approximately 2 million books.

There are several statues outside the palace, including Prince Eugene of Savoy, who routed the Turkish armies; King Matthias, in the west courtyard; and a mythical bird called the Turul.

➕ A2 ☒ Várhegy 🚌 For all attractions: 5, 16, 78, Várbusz (Castle Bus) from Moszkva tér; tram 18; funicular from west end of Chain Bridge
Budapesti Történeti Múzeum ☒ Szent György tér 2 ☎ 1 487 8800; www.museum.hu 🕐 Tue.–Sun. 10–6, Mar.–Oct.; Tue.–Sun. 10–4, rest of year ▨ $$$
Magyar Nemzeti Galéria ☎ 20 4397 325; www.mng.hu 🕐 Tue.–Sun. 10–6 🍴 Gallery café ▨ $$ (free on public holidays) ℹ Guided tours (book in advance)
Országos Széchényi Könyvtár ☎ 1 224 3700; www.oszk.hu 🕐 General collection Tue.–Sat. 10–9 ▨ $

Budavári Labirintus

A maze of catacombs extends for 16 miles under Várhegy (Castle Hill), made up of a honeycomb of caverns linked by passageways originally built for use by the Turkish military. Only a tenth of the Budavári Labirintus (Buda Castle Labyrinth) complex can be visited by the public, but even this gives a vivid impression of a strange, enclosed, underground world. Reconstructions explore the history of Hungary from the misty past through the golden Renaissance age of King Matthias. During the siege of Budapest in World War II, thousands of people took shelter down here while above their heads the city was destroyed. Since March 2011 the catacombs are open throughout the day and night.

➕ A2 ☒ Uri utca 9 ☎ 1 212 0207; www.labirintus.com 🕐 Daily 24 hours 🚌 16, Várbusz (Castle Bus) ▨ $$$

The columned entrance to Magyar Nemzeti Múzeum

Gellért-hegy

Bishop Gellért failed to convert the pagan Magyars to Christianity; legend has it they stuck him in a barrel and threw him into the river from this 771-foot-high limestone cliff. His statue stands at the bottom of Gellért-hegy (Gellért Hill).

At the top is the Citadella (Citadel), a stronghold built after the 1848–49 War of Independence to watch over the restive citizens. Inside the fortifications are a war museum, an exhibition, hotel and restaurant. The Szabadság szobor (Freedom Monument), also at the top, was erected by the Russians in 1947. Before the fall of Communism, the monument featured a Soviet soldier as well as the now lone woman brandishing a palm leaf.

➕ B1 ✉ Between Erzsébet híd (Elizabeth Bridge) and Szabadság híd (Freedom Bridge) 🚌 7, 7a, 8, 27, 78, 86, 112; tram 18, 19, 47, 49 🍴 Panorama, see page 479

Halászbástya

Halászbástya (Fisherman's Bastion) is one of the city's greatest tourist draws: a fairy-tale, seven-towered rampart in pale stone wedged into the eastern rim of Castle Hill. The architect, Frigyes Schulek, designed the fortress as part of the city's millennial celebrations of Magyar nationhood in 1896.

This is the perfect place to enjoy some great river views, and the souvenir stalls and shops make for a pleasant afternoon's browsing.

➕ A3 ✉ Szentháromság tér, Várhegy 🕐 Daily 24 hours 🚌 16, Várbusz (Castle Bus) from Moszkva tér 🚻 $ 🍴 Alabárdos, see page 479

Hősök tere

At the end of the grand Andrássy út and at the entrance to Városliget (City Park) is magnificent Hősök tere (Heroes' Square), designed to mark the city's 1896 millennial celebrations. On either side are the Műcsarnok (Palace of Arts) and the Szépművészeti Múzeum (Museum of Fine Arts, see page 264); between them is a monument to Hungarian successes. Perched on a 118-foot-high column is the Archangel Gabriel; guarding the foot of the column are statues of the seven fierce and triumphant Magyar chiefs, with Árpád, their leader, in the center. They are flanked by colonnades bearing the figures of Fame, Knowledge, Peace and War; between the columns are more Hungarian icons, including King Stephen (who would later be sainted).

➕ D4 ✉ Andrássy út 🚇 Hősök tere 🚊 4; trolley bus 79

Magyar Állami Operaház

The Magyar Állami Operaház (Hungarian State Opera House) building has beautiful marble-work, gold leaf and frescoes. Opened in 1884, it celebrates the musical world with statues of Beethoven, Mozart, Verdi and Wagner on the stone cornice of the front terrace. Pride of place goes to Hungarians Franz Liszt and opera composer Ferenc Erkel, whose statues flank the entrance.

Inside the building an enormous bronze chandelier hangs over the auditorium, which is decorated with dazzling frescoes of the Greek gods by Károly Lotz.

➕ C3 ✉ Andrássy út 22; tours begin at Hajós utca entrance ☎ 1 353 0170 (box office) or 1 332 8197 (tours); www.opera.hu 🕐 Tours daily at 3 and 4 (duration 45 minutes) 🚇 Opera 🚊 4 🍴 Művész Kávéház, see page 479 🚻 Tour $$$

Spires and turrets characterize the Országház, the parliament building

Magyar Nemzeti Múzeum

Five collections form the Magyar Nemzeti Múzeum (Hungarian National Museum), Hungary's largest museum, covering an area of 861,111 square feet. They include Roman artifacts, medieval and modern displays, a numismatic collection and historical portraits. The prize among the exhibits is the mantle from St. Stephen's 11th-century crown. The crown jewels were recovered from Nazi sympathizers at the end of World War II and found their way to the United States. President Jimmy Carter ordered their return in 1978. The crown and other regalia are at the Hungarian Parliament Building (Országház, right). Other curiosities are the inscribed brick from a 13th-century monk's tomb and the tent of a Turkish commander taken at the siege of Vienna in 1683.

✚ C2 ✉ Múzeum körút 14–16 ☎ 1 317 7806 or 1 327 7773 (booked tours); www.hnm.hu 🕐 Tue.–Sun. 10–6 🚇 Astoria or Kálvin tér 🚌 7, 7a, 9, 15, 78; tram 47, 49 🍴 Café 🎟 $$$ 🛈 Tours (book in advance)

Mátyás-templom

Fifteenth-century King Matthias was married twice in the Mátyás-templom (Matthias Church), which had already been in existence for two centuries. It later served the Turks as a mosque, and was remodeled in the 19th century in striking neo-Gothic style. Medieval touches have been reproduced in the interior, along with dramatic features such as the soaring 262-foot spire. The tombs of 12th-century monarch Béla III and his wife, Anne of Châtillon, are in the Trinity Chapel near the main door.

✚ A3 ✉ Szentháromság tér 2 ☎ 1 489 0716 🕐 Religious visits: daily 6 a.m.–8 p.m.; tourists generally Mon.–Fri. 9–5, Sat. 9–1, Sun. 1–5 🚌 16, Várbusz (Castle Bus) from Moszkva tér 🎟 Religious visits free; tourists $$

Országház

Bristling with neo-Gothic spires and turrets, the Országház (Parliament) building sits on the eastern bank of the Danube, covering an area of nearly 200,000 square feet. Its red dome is 315 feet high and rises above a 16-sided hall between the upper and lower houses of parliament.

✚ B3 ✉ Kossuth Lajos tér 1–3 ☎ 1 441 4904, 1 441 4412, 1 441 4415 or 1 441 4138; www.parlament.hu 🕐 Guided tours in English daily at 10, noon and 2 (subject to parliamentary sessions) 🚇 Kossuth tér 🚌 15; tram 2; trolley bus 70, 78 🎟 $$$ 🛈 Long lines for tours in summer

Szent István Bazilika

Budapest's biggest church, Szent István Bazilika (St. Stephen's Basilica), took 55 years to finish, and its dazzling interior includes 90 pounds of 24-carat gold. Transylvanian and Hungarian heroes are represented by 88 statues, and the most cherished item – the mummified right hand of St. Stephen – displayed in a glass case. The 315-foot-high dome provides views of the city.

➕ C2 ✉ Svent István tér 33 ☎ 1 317 2859 🎫 Church: Mon.–Fri. 9–5, Sat. 9–1, Sun. 1–5. Chapel: Mon.–Sat. 9–5, Sun. 1–5, Apr.–Oct.; Mon.–Sat. 10–4, Sun. 1–5, Nov.–Mar. Dome: daily 10–5:30, Apr.–Oct. Tours in English Mon.–Fri. at 11, 2, 3:30, Sat. at 11 🚇 Bajcsy-Zsilinsky út or Deák tér, Arany János utca 🚌 15; trolley bus 70, 72, 78 💷 Free; dome $; tour $$$

Szépművészeti Múzeum

The Szépművészeti Múzeum (Museum of Fine Arts) is a neoclassic temple built to celebrate the millennial anniversary of the Magyar nation. The museum's permanent collections are wide-ranging and of high quality. They include Egyptian and classical art, old masters, Impressionist works by Monet, Cézanne and Gauguin, and some outstanding 20th-century paintings.

➕ D4 ✉ Dósza György út 41 ☎ 1 469 7100; www.szepmuveszeti.hu 🎫 Tue.–Sun. 10–5. Tours in English (free) Tue.–Fri. at 11 and 2, Sat. at 11 🚇 Hősök tere 🚌 4, 20, 30; trolley bus 75, 79 💷 $$$

Városliget

Beyond the boulevards of Pest is Városliget (City Park). It was laid out in the 18th century and has acquired several extras over the years. The oddest is Vajdahunyad vára (Vajdahunyad Castle), built for the 1896 World Exhibition. Based on a Transylvanian fortress, its popularity ensured permanent survival. Inside the walls is the Magyar Mezőgazdasági Múzeum (Hungarian Agricultural Museum). The Állatkert (zoo) is another favorite. There's also the Fővárosi Nagycirkusz (circus) and a slightly faded Vidámpark (amusement park).

In the southeast corner are the Közlekedési Múzeum (Museum of Transportation) and the Petőfi Csarnok youth center, hosting pop concerts in summer. The hall contains the Repüléstörténeti Múzeum (Aviation

Museum), with the space capsule flown by the first Hungarian cosmonaut.

Magyar Mezőgazdasági Múzeum ➕ E4
✉ Vajdahunyad vára ☎ 1 363 1117; www.mezogazdasagimuzeum.hu 🎫 Tue.–Sun. 10–5, Mar.–Oct.; Tue.–Sun. 10–4 (also Sat.–Sun. 4–5), rest of year 🚇 Széchenyi fürdő 🚌 4, 20, 30; trolley bus 70, 72, 75, 79 🍴 Gundel, see page 479 💷 $$

Állatkert ➕ D4 ✉ Állatkerti Körút 6–12 ☎ 1 273 4900; www.zoobudapest.com 🎫 Mon.–Thu. 9–6:30, Fri.–Sun. 9–7, May–Aug.; daily 9–4, Nov.–Feb.; Mon.–Thu. 9–5, Fri.–Sun. 9–5:30, in Mar. and Oct.; Mon.–Thu. 9–5:30, Fri.–Sun. 9–6, rest of year 🚇 Széchenyi fürdő 🚌 4; trolley bus 72 🍴 Gundel, see page 479 💷 $$$

Fővárosi Nagycirkusz ➕ E4 ✉ Állatkerti út 12 ☎ 1 343 8300; www.maciva.hu 🎫 Telephone or check website for details 🚇 Széchenyi fürdő 🚌 4; trolley bus 70, 72, 79 🍴 Gundel, see page 479 💷 $$$

Vidámpark ➕ E4 ✉ Állatkerti körút 14–16 ☎ 1 363 8310; www.vidampark.hu 🎫 Daily 10–8, Jul.–Aug.; varies, rest of year (check web for details) 🚇 Széchenyi fürdő 🚌 4; trolley bus 72 🍴 Gundel, see page 479 💷 Free entrance (rides $)

Közlekedési Múzeum ➕ E4 ✉ Városligeti körút 11 ☎ 1 273 3840 🎫 Tue.–Sun. 10–5 (also Sat.–Sun. 5–6), May–Sep.; Tue.–Sun. 10–4 (also Sat.–Sun. 4–5), rest of year 🚇 Széchenyi fürdő 🚌 Tram 1; trolley bus 70, 72, 74 🍴 Gundel, see page 479 💷 $$

le Petőfi Csarnok/Repüléstörténeti Múzeum ➕ E4 ✉ Zichy Mihály utca 14–16 ☎ 1 363 3730; Aviation Museum 1 363 0809 🎫 Tue.–Sun. 10–5 (also Sat.–Sun. 5–6), May–Sep. 🚇 Széchenyi fürdő 🚌 Tram 1; trolley bus 70, 72, 74 🍴 Gundel, see page 479 💷 $

The Danube Esplanade

Running alongside the river on the Pest bank, between Chain Bridge (Széchenyi lánchíd) and Elizabeth Bridge (Erzsébet híd), is the broad, tree-lined Danube Esplanade (Duna-korzó). In the 19th century, this was the most fashionable place to be seen. Café tables were set out in the evening, and gypsy bands played by lamplight under the stars. The elaborate Pesti Vigadó (Pest Concert Hall) is a legacy of that era, and still a venue for classical music concerts.

Excursion to Esztergom

Hungary's largest cathedral towers over the stunning scenery of the Danube Bend at Esztergom, former royal city and the birthplace of King Stephen I (975–1038). There has been a settlement here, guarding the western approach to the gorge, since Roman times. Medieval Esztergom was destroyed by the Turks in 1543, but the city rose again, and it now boasts a center full of ornate baroque buildings.

The cathedral (*bazilika*) is by far the most imposing: It is 328 feet from the floor to the top of its huge, glittering dome, which is visible for miles around. It includes one of the world's biggest paintings – an altarpiece based on the work of 16th-century Italian artist Titian. The white marble altar itself was designed in 1519 and made by expert craftsmen from Florence, Italy.

Among other treasures are the impressive Renaissance interior of the Bakócz Chapel, dedicated to Archbishop Tomás Bakócz, and a gold and enamel Gothic cross, studded with pearls and precious stones, known as the Calvary of Matthias Corvinus. The dome offers a spectacular view over Esztergom and its surroundings.

The present version of the cathedral was begun in the 1820s: Hungarian composer Franz Liszt celebrated its reconsecration in 1856 with a Mass. Long before this second lease of life, Esztergom was the seat of the Hungarian Primate – head of the nation's Catholic Church – and an important royal base. King Stephen was crowned in a church on the site in AD 1000, and the remains of a royal palace are housed in the Castle Museum (Vár Múzeum) next door.

Two other museums are worth a visit. The Museum of Christian Art (Keresztény Múzeum) has a superb collection of medieval religious paintings and works by Italian artists such as Duccio di Buoninsegna, Lorenzo di Credi and Giovanni di Paolo. The Danube Museum (Duna Múzeum) features displays that clearly illustrate (despite Hungarian-only captions) the role of the river and its effects on the life of the town.

Esztergom is 41 miles north of Budapest. To travel by bus, take metro M3 to Ujpest-Városkapu, then the Vólanbusz intercity bus direct to Esztergom.

In summer, boats leave from Vigadó tér landing stage (journey time 70 minutes). Contact Mahart ☎ 1 484 4013; www.mahartpassnave.hu.

There is a regular service from Nyugati (Western) railroad station.

Hungary's largest cathedral, begun in the 1820s, dominates Esztergom

Ireland

Opposite: Giant's Head in County Antrim, with Dunluce Castle in the background

Ireland

People long for Ireland in a way that they pine for few other countries. Call it romantic, call it sentimental, but there is something about this remarkable country that tugs at the heartstrings of even those who have no Irish blood.

The beauty of the country, its powerful Gaelic traditions and the irrepressibly romantic and creative nature of the Irish people underscore this potent appeal.

This is a country that is not without problems, however, and its political and religious divide has had far-reaching, universal impact.

Mists of Time

Ireland claims with pride that it was a "land of saints and scholars" when the rest of Europe was deep in the Dark Ages. It is often described as a Celtic country, with all the myth-making that goes along with that term.

The Celts are seen as being a distinctive lost race of Iron Age people who, in the face of first Roman and then Anglo-Saxon aggression, retreated into Scotland, Ireland, Wales and Cornwall in England, from which they passed down the cultural values of their time. They did not call themselves Celts, and the term may be only a convenient label, but what is certain is that the influence

of the earliest Bronze Age and Iron Age cultures survives on the peripheries of the British Isles. This is especially true in Ireland, where the Gaelic language, still heard today and experiencing a revival, is its greatest expression.

There are thousands of prehistoric sites in Ireland, including megalithic tombs, stone circles and cairns littering the countryside: on the remote western seaboard, on the Beara peninsula, in County Kerry, and at exceptional places such as the Brù na Bòinne burial complex, in County Meath, north of Dublin. Together with evidence of primitive dwellings such as *crannógs* (island settlements) and ring forts, Ireland's heritage is everywhere to be seen. Even where they are ruinous and vestigial, these ancient sites are hauntingly evocative.

You will find within the same landscape the music, song, wit and drama of Ireland that have been enshrined in hundreds of films, songs, dances and stories. A sense of the past is intense here; it has shaped Ireland in a seminal way, for better or for worse.

From Dublin to Kerry

Dublin is the boisterous heart of Ireland, the "family home." It should not be missed, of course, but Dublin will only whet your appetite for the rest of the country. Save time to explore other areas for the essential Irish experience. South of the capital lie the Wicklow Mountains, with the popular Glendalough at their heart – half religious site, wholly spectacular from a scenic point of view.

Farther south lies the fascinating Viking town of Wexford, from where the long, rambling southern coast of Ireland runs through endless great bays toward the distant west (and the most spectacular scenery).

The western coast stretches for nearly 180 miles from north to south, but measures much more if all the many sinuous indentations, bays, river

More Top Destinations in Ireland

- Aran Islands (Oileáin Árann) A2
- Beara peninsula A1
- Blarney Castle B1
- Brù na Bòinne (Newgrange) C3
- The Burren A2
- Clifden A3
- Dingle (An Daingean) A1
- Galway A2
- Giant's Causeway C4
- Glendalough C2
- Kilkenny B2
- Killarney A1

IRELAND

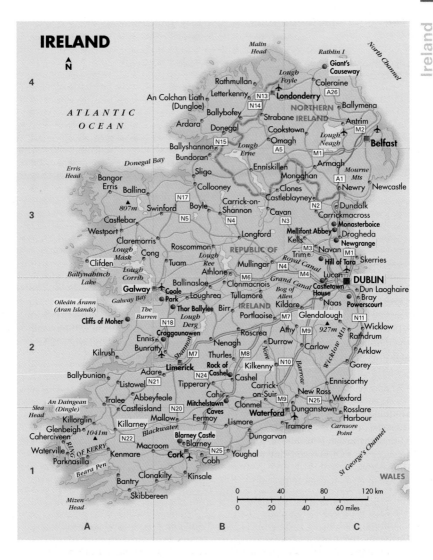

Malin Head
Rathlin I
Giant's Causeway
Lough Foyle
Coleraine
Rathmullan
Letterkenny [N13] **Londonderry** [A26]
An Colchan Liath [N14]
(Dungloe)
Ballybofey [N14]
NORTHERN Ballymena
Strabane **IRELAND** Antrim [M2]
Ardara Donegal Cookstown
Omagh *Lough Neagh* **Belfast**
Ballyshannon [N15] *Lough Erne* [A5] [M1]
Bundoran
Sligo Enniskillen Armagh **Mourne Mts**
Colooney Monaghan [A1] Newry Newcastle
Clones
Carrick-on-Shannon Castleblayney [N2] Dundalk
Swinford [N17] Boyle [N5] Cavan [N3] Carrickmacross
Castlebar Monasterboice
Westport [N4] Longford Mellifont Abbey Drogheda
Claremorris Kells Newgrange
Lough Mask Cong Roscommon **REPUBLIC OF** Navan [M1]
Clifden *Lough* Tuam *Lough Ree* Trim Hill of Tara Skerries
Ballynahinch Lake *Lough Corrib* Athlone [N4] Lucan **DUBLIN**
Galway Coole Ballinasloe Clonmacnois Castletown House Dun Laoghaire
Oileáin Árann (Aran Islands) *Galway Bay* Park Loughrea Tullamore Bray
The Burren Thor Ballylee Birr **IRELAND** Kildare Naas Powerscourt
Cliffs of Moher [N18] *Lough Derg* Portlaoise [M7] Glendalough [N11]
Craggaunowen Roscrea Athy [M9] Wicklow
Ennis Durrow Carlow Rathdrum
Kilrush Bunratty [M7] Nenagh Arklow
Adare Thurles [M8] Kilkenny [N10] Gorey
Ballybunion **Limerick** [N24] Rock of Cashel Enniscorthy
Listowel [N21] Tipperary Cashel Carrick-on-Suir New Ross Wexford
Tralee Abbeyfeale Cahir Clonmel [M9] Dungarstown Rosslare
An Daingean (Dingle) Castleisland [N20] Mitchelstown Caves **Waterford** Harbour
Killorglin Mallow Lismore Tramore
Glenbeigh Killarney Fermoy Dungarvan
Cahirciveen [N22] Blackwater Blarney Castle
Waterville Macroom Blarney [N25]
Parknasilla Kenmare **Cork** Youghal Cobh
Clonakilty Kinsale **WALES**
Bantry
Mizen Head Skibbereen

ATLANTIC OCEAN

Erris Head Bangor Erris Ballina

Kilrush Bunratty

Slea Head

Beara Pen

Ring OF KERRY

0   40   80   120 km
0   20   40   60 miles

---

mouths, peninsulas and islands are taken into account.

Try to visit the far southwest. Take in the charming historic city of Kilkenny on the way; and visit Cork, the Irish Republic's second largest city, where you can kiss the nearby Blarney Stone. Beyond Cork lies the Beara peninsula. The bigger Iveragh peninsula is part of County Kerry to the north, land of the mountains of Macgillycuddy's Reeks and the lakes, and town, of Killarney.

Islands and Lakes

North of County Kerry lies the beautiful and romantic Dingle peninsula (Corca Dhuibhne) and County Clare. County Clare's southern half is mundane, but becomes increasingly spectacular the farther north you go, past the huge, echoing Cliffs of Moher and into the limestone country of the Burren, with its karst landscape (natural limestone pavement), dramatic stone burial chambers and hill forts.

Fishing boats moored in the harbor at Dingle in County Kerry

In the pubs of Clare you will encounter the foot-tapping essence of Irish music and song, in an environment that preserves the best of the past with energy, vitality and lyricism.

Off Clare's northwestern coast are the stunning Aran Islands (Oileáin Árann), the magic names of Inishmore (Inis Móir), Inishmaan (Inis Meáin) and Inisheer (Inis Óirr) resonating with all things Irish.

Beyond Clare is Galway Bay and Galway City (known as "The City of the Tribes"), the latter a lively, unfailingly charming place on the threshold of the Gaeltacht, the major area of Gaelic-speaking Ireland. Here, the mountains of Connemara and the broad lakes Lough Corrib and Lough Mask match an astonishing coastline of raw, rocky wilderness that lies to either side of the romantic town of Clifden.

Inland, Ireland also has much to offer. The heart of the country is a green bowl of rich farmland, of lakes, rivers and isolated ranges of rounded hills.

Landlocked Ireland is outshone by the stupendous coastline of the far west, but it is a charming country full of character and tradition, where you will hear talk of horses and history and where lakes and rivers throng with fish.

Traveling North

Farther north is the remote county of Mayo, where you can follow the pilgrims' route up the Holy Mountain of Croagh Patrick, if you feel fit enough for the grueling four-hour clamber over rough rocks to the place where St. Patrick is said to have banished the snakes. Beyond Mayo are Sligo and Donegal, and golden beaches and tumbling Atlantic surf. Lakes and remote peninsulas enhance north Donegal, where the coast turns east toward the beautiful City of Derry (Londonderry), gateway to Northern Ireland, and Antrim, Armagh, Down, Londonderry, Fermanagh and Tyrone – the six (of a total of nine) counties of Ulster known as Northern Ireland.

This British-ruled area was riven for decades by sectarian violence, but the Good Friday Agreement of 1998 began the slow process of peace. Ulster's image has suffered much from "the Troubles" (the resumption of political

The unusual "organ-pipe" cliffs of the Giant's Causeway, County Antrim

violence since 1969), yet the beauty of its coast and countryside is of classic Irish quality.

The Giant's Causeway area, on County Antrim's north coast, is Northern Ireland's most famous landmark, an astonishing landscape of perfectly formed hexagonal rock sections. Farther east lies the seaside town of Ballycastle, beyond which are the towering cliffs of Fair Head and then the green and peaceful Glens of Antrim.

South of Antrim lies Belfast, Northern Ireland's capital, a city that in the past has shown a grim face but is now welcoming a new generation of tourists. Belfast has rediscovered its waterfront and invested in redevelopment. The old Gasworks site is internationally recognized as an area of excellent regeneration, as is the redeveloped Victoria Square, now a modern shopping center. All this new building has brought an exciting dynamic to the city.

The Gaelic Lifestyle

In Dublin you will find museums, stores, theaters and restaurants to match those anywhere else in Europe, all suffused by the richness of Irish culture and by a modern sophistication.

In parts of rural Ireland things are different. You may come across an easygoing attitude, a relaxed approach reflecting the fact that the Irish have been around for a long time and often see no reason to rush things. At the same time, you may find yourself swept off your feet in places like beautiful, bustling Galway City, where a vigorous student population adds a contemporary note to the Gaelic culture that most young people continue to embrace.

If you travel through Ireland, you will find the Irish a particularly hospitable and friendly people. Often, if you ask a local for the way to a nearby site or place in town, you will be taken there rather than given directions.

The Irish are fired by an all-consuming curiosity and have an almost total lack of pretension. They are a people whose history has often been terrible, bleak and unforgiving. Yet they have survived as the inheritors of a bewitching country that lies off the western edge of the Continent but is also an integral part of modern Europe.

Timeline

circa 3000 BC	Neolithic burial chambers constructed at Brù na Bòinne.
circa 500 BC	Celtic tribes arrive from Europe.
AD 430	St. Patrick brings Christianity to Ireland.
circa 795	Vikings found Dublin, Waterford, Wexford and Limerick.
1170	Powerful Anglo-Irish hegemony established in Ireland.
circa 1610	Large areas of Ulster are confiscated by the English Crown.
1845–51	The Great Famine; a million Irish people die and a million emigrate, chiefly to America.
1921	Anglo-Irish Treaty partitions Ireland into the Irish Free State and Northern Ireland, which remains under British rule.
1948	Irish Free State is declared a republic.
1969	Beginning of "the Troubles" in Northern Ireland.
1972	Republic of Ireland joins the European Community.
1985	The Anglo-Irish Agreement promises co-operation on Northern Ireland's future.
1994	Main paramilitary groups in Northern Ireland call a ceasefire.
1997–2007	Ireland undergoes a rapid period of economic growth known as the "Celtic Tiger."
1998	Good Friday Agreement paves the way for a Northern Ireland Assembly. Sporadic violence continues.
2007	Devolved government returns to Northern Ireland with an historic power-sharing agreement.
2008–10	The global financial crisis causes Ireland's booming property bubble to burst, resulting in a bailout by the EU/IMF in 2010.
2010	Devolved power completed with the transfer of Policing and Justice to the Northern Ireland Assembly.

Divided Ireland

Ireland has been a divided country for centuries. The reasons are complex and lie in historical developments over hundreds of years. The largest part of modern Ireland is the Republic of Ireland, Poblacht na h' Eireann – mainly Roman Catholic, with a small minority of Protestants and a strong Irish Gaelic culture and identity. After years of economic stagnation the nation enjoyed a period of great success and modernization. This ended in 2008 when the global economic crisis took effect. It will be a long time until the "Celtic Tiger" roars again. The northern part of Ireland is called Northern Ireland, and remains part of the United Kingdom. Its majority Protestant community is traditionally unionist and wishes to maintain the union between Great Britain and Northern Ireland. The smaller, but substantial, Catholic community is traditionally republican and wishes to break the union with Great Britain and establish an all-Ireland republic. The political differences and the lack of civil rights for Northern Ireland Catholics gave rise to some 30 years of violent conflict. Through the peace process, the 1998 Good Friday Agreement created a devolved legislative Assembly for Northern Ireland and a framework for multiparty power-sharing. Violence was largely eliminated, and following a temporary reversion to direct British rule, the Northern Ireland Assembly reconvened in 2007 and continues to strive for peace.

Survival Guide

- If you visit the city of Dublin in the early spring, try to be there on March 17, St. Patrick's Day, when the city celebrates with song and dance, culminating in a parade, all-night parties and fireworks displays.
- If you're interested in shopping for Celtic crafts, don't miss the Kilkenny Design Centre in Kilkenny. This is the city's finest showcase for stylish Irish housewares, glass, books, fashion and jewelry. The upstairs restaurant serves generous portions of delicious homestyle food.
- Ireland is rapidly modernizing its road system, but there are still some very poor public roads, especially in the rural parts of the country. Look for unexpected potholes on otherwise smooth surfaces.
- One of the best ways to learn a little about the complexities of Irish politics is to take a tour. Coiste Political Tours provides walking tours of Belfast's historical and political sites, led by ex-prisoners, and Blue Badge Guides take visitors on tours of Derry City and the Bogside. In Dublin, there are tours covering the Great Famine, the 1916 Easter Rising, the War of Independence and Partition.
- Be aware that there is a no-smoking policy throughout the Republic of Ireland in all public places.
- Visit the local pubs in rural Ireland, especially in County Clare, where in towns like Ennis you will find some of the greatest Irish music of all and the ubiquitous *craic* (good times, enjoyment and fun).
- Visit popular places such as Glendalough in County Wicklow, Killarney in County Kerry and the Cliffs of Moher in County Clare outside of peak season (July and August). Glendalough, especially, can become jammed with traffic.
- Enjoy the beautiful and often remote beaches of Ireland's west coast, but

A statue of James Joyce at Dublin's Merrion Hotel

take great care if you go swimming. The tides are very strong here and there can be unexpected sea currents.
- Irish road signs began to appear in both Gaelic and English in the Republic of Ireland shortly after partition and today they must appear in both languages by law, the Irish first in italics with the English underneath. In the Gaeltacht (Irish-speaking) areas only the Irish name is written.
- Ireland's Roman Catholic churches are extremely important places to the communities they serve, and you'll usually find someone praying if you visit. Be as discreet as possible when walking around church interiors, especially in front of the altar. Please refrain from taking photographs during Masses and services.

Dublin

All roads seem to lead to Dublin; it is a
homecoming city where the visitor will
feel as welcome as the Irish do. Dublin
is celebrated today as one of Europe's
most vibrant, colorful cities. It is a rich
distillation of all things Irish – music,
conversation and laughter amid the
city's lively streets, buzzing pubs and
magnificent Georgian buildings.

Finding Your Way

The Dublin tourist office is located
in the handsome old church of
St. Andrew's, just southwest of Trinity

College in the city center. Here you can
obtain information about guided
summer walking tours. Central Dublin
is a reasonably easy and rewarding place
to explore on foot. The main museums
and notable buildings are concentrated
in more fashionable south Dublin, but
there are not-to-be-missed attractions
across the River Liffey in north Dublin.
A good starting point is the famous
O'Connell Bridge, where Dublin begins
with a rush.

Take time to adjust to the breezy pace
of it all. To the north is O'Connell Street,
one of the broadest streets in Europe.
Lively shopping streets such as Abbey

Street Lower and Earl Street North lead off to either side. On Earl Street you will find a genial, roguish statue of James Joyce, Ireland's most famous writer and the masterful chronicler of Dublin life. Go down Earl Street and then turn left onto Marlborough Street to visit St. Mary's Pro-Cathedral, a magnificent neoclassic building.

Opposite Earl Street is the very busy and revitalized Henry Street, with the huge ILAC and Jarvis shopping centers and the adjoining fruit and vegetable market on Moore Street. This whole area leading down to Smithfield Village has been the subject of much renovation work. The men and women who work the stalls are famous for their lively Joycean banter.

On O'Connell Street, just before Henry Street, is the General Post Office. This is a landmark site of the 1916 Easter Rising against British Rule, when Irish nationalists mounted an uprising against British rule and occupied the building. Opposite is the dramatic Monument of Light, a stainless-steel needle unveiled in 2002.

At the north end of O'Connell Street, by the Parnell Monument, is Parnell Square; on the square's north side is the Dublin City Gallery: The Hugh Lane (see page 277–278) and the Dublin Writers Museum (see page 279).

The Heart of Dublin

South of O'Connell Bridge is the buzzing heart of Dublin. From the south side of the bridge, walk down Westmoreland Street to College Green, a frantic concentration of traffic that initially detracts from the stupendous buildings that surround it. Admire the neoclassic splendor of the Bank of Ireland and the elegant entrance to Trinity College, through which you can escape to the crowded but relaxing college campus.

Otherwise, carefully cross College Green to the south and then continue past the buxom statue of Molly Malone, heroine of the famous "Cockles and Mussels" refrain, wheeling her cart in the midst of Dublin shoppers. The statue has become cheerfully known, through irrepressible Dublin wit, as "The Tart with the Cart."

Ahead lies pedestrian-only Grafton Street, with interesting stores and delightful side streets; plus a variety of street performers. Stop at Bewley's Oriental Café, a Dublin institution. Head east and make for Leinster House, seat of Irish government, and to the National Museum and National Gallery.

Beyond these lie the 18th-century Georgian splendors of Merrion Square and Fitzwilliam Street. Alternatively, go west from Grafton Street along store-lined Wicklow Street, then on to Dublin Castle and Christ Church Cathedral; or head back north across Dame Street and into lively Temple Bar, the now rejuvenated old riverside district that is the buzzing and exciting focus of Dublin by night.

Vary your Dublin experiences. Enjoy Temple Bar's restaurants and lively lanes, visit St. Patrick's Cathedral on Patrick Street, or take a look at the rejuvenated Docklands district. Enjoy outstanding drama at Dublin's Abbey Theatre on Abbey Street, or classic Irish entertainment at the Olympia on Dame Street. Above all, visit Dublin's famous pubs (see page 281) for great music and chat. There is a quicker, sharper edge to the Irish here, as befits a busy, cosmopolitan city.

The Ha'penny Bridge

Dublin's Ha'penny Bridge, over the River Liffey, is best reached from Temple Bar by going down the narrow Merchant's Arch – look closely for the symbols of nearby stores carved into the street.

The bridge dates from 1816 and is made of cast iron; its elegant arches are lit up at night. It was officially named the Wellington Bridge after the British Duke of Wellington, but gained its popular name from the half-penny toll once charged for crossing it.

Ireland

A view along the sun-drenched River Liffey toward the Ha'penny Bridge and Batchelor's Walk area of Dublin

Essential Information

Tourist Information

Dublin Tourism Centre
Suffolk Street ☎ 01 850 230 330 and 00353 669 792 083 (outside Ireland)
www.visitdublin.com
Also at:
14 Upper O'Connell Street
Arrivals Hall, Dublin Airport
Dún Laoghaire Ferry Terminal

Urban Transportation

Dublin has two main railroad stations. Heuston Station, Kingsbridge, is where services from southern and western Ireland terminate. Connolly Station, on Amiens Street, is where ferry connections arrive and the termination point for trains from the southeast, north and northwest, including Belfast. The Dublin Area Rapid Transit (DART) railroad line runs north to Malahide and Howth, and south to Greystones. Connolly Station, Pearse Station and Tara Station are convenient city-center stops. The LUAS Green Line tram system (St. Stephen's Green to Sandyford) and Red Line (The Point to Tallgaht) bring passengers from the suburbs into the city center. For train

information call ☎ 01 836 6222. For DART call ☎ 01 703 3592. For LUAS call ☎ 1800 300604 within Ireland or 00353 1 461 4910 from outside Ireland. There is a good citywide bus service run by Dublin Bus (Bus Átha Cliath), 59 Upper O'Connell Street (☎ 01 873 4222); buses daily 7 a.m.–11:30 p.m. (some begin earlier). Nitelink service Fri.–Sat. midnight–4 a.m. Countrywide services leave from the main bus station, Busáras, on Amiens Street. Dublin taxis are expensive and difficult to hail on the street. Stands are at O'Connell Street, St. Stephen's Green, College Green and Dame Street, or phone City-Cabs (☎ 01 872 7272) or Budget Cabs (☎ 01 459 9333).

Airport Information

Dublin Airport (www.dublinairport.com) is 7 miles north of the city. A tourist office is in the arrivals hall. Aircoach runs a bus service to the city center every 15 minutes, 24 hours a day; the trip takes 30 minutes (☎ 01 844 7118). The Dublin Bus Airlink (No. 747) runs to/from Busáras. A slower, regular bus service (No. 41) runs to/from Eden Quay.

Climate – average highs and lows for the month

Jan.	Feb.	Mar.	Apr.	May	Jun.	Jul.	Aug.	Sep.	Oct.	Nov.	Dec.
8°C	8°C	9°C	11°C	14°C	17°C	19°C	18°C	16°C	13°C	10°C	8°C
46°F	46°F	48°F	52°F	57°F	63°F	66°F	64°F	61°F	55°F	50°F	46°F
3°C	3°C	4°C	5°C	7°C	10°C	12°C	12°C	10°C	8°C	5°C	4°C
37°F	37°F	39°F	41°F	45°F	50°F	54°F	54°F	50°F	46°F	41°F	39°F

Dublin Sights

Christ Church Cathedral

Dublin's great cathedral dates from the 12th century, but much of the surviving building is a 19th-century renovation in Gothic Revival style.

The most authentic parts of Christ Church are the late 13th-century transepts and the ancient crypt, one of the largest medieval crypts in Europe. It is 175 feet long. Thickets of rough stone pillars support the weight of the massive building above; the air is dense with age. Monuments and artifacts lie half hidden in niches and dark corners. They include battered statues of English kings and oddities such as a mummified cat and rat.

Linked to the cathedral by a covered stone bridge is Synod Hall, where the colorful interactive exhibition "Dvblinia and the Viking World" details Dublin's history during the medieval period.

Christ Church Cathedral ✚ A3 ✉ Christchurch Place ☎ 01 677 8099; www.cccdub.ie 🕐 Mon.–Sat. 9:30–7 (last entry 6:15), Sun. 12:30–2:30 and 4:30–6:15, Jun.–Aug.; daily, hours vary, rest of year 🚌 49X, 50X, 78A 🖐 $$

Dvblinia and the Viking World ✚ A3 ✉ St. Michael's Hill ☎ 01 679 4611; www.dublinia.ie 🕐 Daily 10–5 (closes 4:30 Oct.–Feb.) 🚌 49X, 50X, 78A 🍴 Tea rooms open Easter–Aug. 🖐 $$

Dublin Castle

Dublin Castle dates from the early 13th century but has been largely rebuilt and expanded. It is a powerful and at times brooding reminder of the past. Look for deep scars in the stonework of the Guardroom, at the main (north) entrance leading to the cobbled upper yard. They are the result of repeated bayonet sharpening, an eerie symbol

The State Drawing Room in Dublin Castle

of 950 years of British rule. The state apartments open to the public include St. Patrick's Hall, the Throne Room, the State Drawing Room and the Picture Gallery, all of which have sumptuous decorations and furnishings. A reconstruction during the 1980s uncovered original 10th-century Viking defenses, a reminder that the Vikings founded Dublin on this spot. The castle's Chapel Royal is a glorious neo-Gothic indulgence dating from 1814. Its exterior bristles with pointed Gothic motifs and 90 or so carved heads of historical figures. The interior has lavish plaster vaulting and superb carved oak galleries. You can also visit the Garda (Police) Museum, the Revenue Museum and the Chester Beatty Library.

✚ B3 ✉ Dame Street ☎ 01 645 8813; www.heritageireland.ie 🕐 Mon.–Fri.10–4:45, Sat.–Sun. 2–4:45 🚌 56A, 77, 77A, 123 🍴 The Vaults Bistro Restaurant 🖐 $$ ℹ Guided tours only; reservations recommended. State apartments may be closed at times for official functions

Dublin City Gallery: The Hugh Lane

The Hugh Lane Gallery is located in the delightful Charlemont House. The collection, bequeathed by Sir Hugh Lane to Dublin Corporation in 1908, features 19th- and 20th-century Irish and

James Joyce

Ireland's most controversial novelist, James Joyce, was one of world literature's most important figures. Joyce was an innovator of the highest order, a writer of dazzling intellect.

He was born in 1882 into a Dublin Catholic family of some gentility, although poverty overtook the family while Joyce was in his teens. He was educated at Ireland's leading Jesuit school and then at Catholic University College in Dublin.

Joyce rebelled early against the tenets of his class and religion and against Ireland's prevailing politics and culture, both of which he felt were too "nationalistic." He left Ireland in 1904 with Nora Barnacle, who became his lifelong partner. After a visit in 1912, Joyce never returned to Ireland and remained in Europe until his death in Zurich in 1941.

Joyce wrote several books of poetry and novels; his most famous novels were *Ulysses* and *Finnegans Wake*. *Ulysses* was a monumental work, an allegorical saga describing the daylong wandering of its central character, Leopold Bloom, through the streets of Dublin. The novel developed new literary forms in its exploration and use of language and in its epic structure. It was published in Paris in 1922 but was banned for obscenity in Britain and in the United States until 1936. *Finnegans Wake* was published in 1939 and carried the "stream of consciousness" style of writing to revolutionary limits.

Joyce is a national hero in Ireland, something that would have amused this complex and essentially solitary man. The James Joyce Centre is at No. 35 North Great George's Street in north Dublin. Each year on June 16, Dublin celebrates Bloomsday, during which there are guided walks, readings and numerous events based on Leopold Bloom's progress through the Dublin of *Ulysses*. Visits to famous Dublin pubs play a lively part in the festivities; participants dress in Edwardian clothes from the period featured in the novel and readings and other celebrations of *Ulysses* are staged.

Cafe Ulysses at the James Joyce Centre has a Parisian atmosphere

international painters, including Claude Monet, Edouard Manet and Edgar Degas. There are several outstanding works, including Renoir's *Les Parapluies*. Notable Irish artists include Jack B. Yeats, and there are contemporary Irish works and temporary exhibitions, often of daring conceptual art. The gallery also has a fine collection of stained glass. A new extension houses a collection of Sean Scully paintings donated by the artist. Francis Bacon's studio was gifted to the gallery in 1998. Painstakingly removed from its London home, the studio was reconstructed here and opened to the public in 2001.

➕ B4   ✉ Charlemont House, Parnell Square North
☎ 01 222 5550; www.hughlane.ie   🕐 Tue.–Thu. 10–6,
Fri.–Sat. 10–5, Sun. 11–5   🚇 DART Connolly Station
(10-minute walk)   🚌 3, 7, 10, 11, 13, 16, 19, 46A, 123
🍴 Gallery café   🎫 Free

Dublin Writers Museum

Literary Dublin in all its glory is represented by this engrossing museum's large collection of documents, artifacts, portraits and memorabilia of famous Irish writers, including Oscar Wilde and Samuel Beckett. The combined buildings that contain the museum date from the late 18th century and are an experience in themselves. There is magnificent stuccowork, especially in the ground-floor rooms. The colonnaded main salon, which is now the Gallery of Writers, has busts and some paintings of famous names, a decorative ceiling and various boisterous friezes.

➕ B4   ✉ 18 Parnell Square North   ☎ 01 872 2077;
www.writersmuseum.com   🕐 Mon.–Sat. 10–5,
Sun. 11–5. Last admission 4:15   🚇 DART Connolly
Station (15-minute walk)   🚌 10, 11, 11B, 13, 13A, 16,
16A, 19, 19A   🍴 Museum coffee shop; Chapter One
restaurant (see page 480) in basement (separate
entrance)   🎫 $$$ ℹ Self-guiding audio tour lasts
about 40 minutes

Guinness Storehouse

Dublin without Guinness is like the earth without air. You can sample Guinness in its creamy, lip-smacking

The interior of Kilmainham Gaol

originality in the city's multitude of pubs (see page 281), but to reach the heart of things visit the enlightening and entertaining Guinness Storehouse, located in an original hop store at the brewery. Admission includes a pint of the famous stout in the Gravity Bar.

➕ Off map at A2   ✉ St. James's Gate
☎ 01 408 4800; www.guinness-storehouse.com
🕐 Daily 9:30–7, Jul.–Aug.; 9:30–5, rest of year
🚊 LUAS James Street   🚌 51B, 78A, 123   🍴 Bars
and restaurant   🎫 $$$

Kilmainham Gaol

The notorious Kilmainham Gaol (prison) has been the scene of great misery. Kilmainham opened in 1796 and until 1924, when it closed, just about every famous name in the struggle for Irish independence and statehood was a "guest" at one time. They included Robert Emmet, Charles Stewart Parnell and Eamon DeValera. Fourteen leaders of the 1916 Easter Rising were executed in the prison yard. Explore the gloomy cells and chilly corridors. Guided tours give a graphic picture of Irish history.

➕ Off map at A2   ✉ Inchicore Road   ☎ 01 453 5984;
www.heritageireland.ie   🕐 Daily 9:30–6, Apr.–Sep.;
Mon.–Sat. 9:30–5:30, Sun. 10–6, rest of year. Last tour
begins 1 hour before closing   🚊 LUAS Suir Road
🚌 51B, 51C, 78A, 79, 79A   🍴 Tea room on site
🎫 $$ (includes guided tour)

National Gallery

Ireland's national art collection eschews quantity for quality, and this fine building holds works that represent all major schools of European art. The Shaw Room, dedicated to early benefactor George Bernard Shaw, is an elegant statement in its own right. Painters represented include Francisco de Goya and Caravaggio. Thomas Gainsborough and J. M. W. Turner are here as well, and there are strong collections of leading Irish artists such as Nathanial Hone, Jack B. Yeats and Sir John Lavery. The Millennium Wing specializes in 20th-century art and themed exhibitions.

➕ C2 ✉ Merrion Square West (entrance also on Clare Street) ☎ 01 661 5133; www.nationalgallery.ie ⊙ Mon.–Sat. 9:30–5:30 (also Thu. 5:30–8:30), Sun. noon–5:30; last admission 30 minutes before closing ⊟ DART Pearse Station (5-minute walk) 🚌 5, 7, 7A, 10, 13A, 44C, 48A 🍴 Restaurant and café 🎟 Free; charge for some exhibitions ℹ Self-guiding audio tours

National Museum of Archaeology and History

Part of the National Museum of Ireland, this museum fills buildings that date from the 1890s. Together with the National Library opposite, the complex forms the approach to Leinster House, the seat of the Irish Government. Exhibits dating from 7000 BC to the 20th century include examples of Celtic and medieval art and the finest collection of prehistoric gold artifacts in Europe. Highlights include the Tara Brooch, the Derrynaflan and the Ardagh Chalice.

➕ C2 ✉ Kildare Street ☎ 01 677 7444; www.museum.ie ⊙ Tue.–Sat. 10–5, Sun. 2–5 ⊟ DART Pearse Station 🚌 7, 7A, 8, 10, 11, 13 🍴 Museum café 🎟 Free; guided tours $

St. Stephen's Green

Delightful St. Stephen's Green has been a public park since 1664, when Dublin Corporation set aside 22 acres of open ground, albeit for use by its well-to-do citizens. Access was by payment only until 1880, when the park was made free to all. There are statues and busts of famous Irish men and women, including James Joyce, Robert Emmet, Constance Markiewicz and Sir Arthur Guinness.

The park is surrounded by some of the finest buildings in Dublin. They include the Shelbourne Hotel, the Royal College of Surgeons and the Roman Catholic University Church, with a neo-Byzantine interior.

➕ B2 ✉ St. Stephen's Green ⊙ Mon.–Sat. 7:30–dusk, Sun. 9:30–dusk ⊟ DART Pearse Station; LUAS St. Stephen's Green 🚌 10, 11, 11A, 15A, 25X, 32X, 46X, 84X

Trinity College

Dublin's Trinity College is an outstanding architectural and cultural oasis at the heart of a busy city. It was founded in 1592 on the site of an Augustinian monastery, but all of the present buildings date from after 1700. Enter the complex from College Green, between statues of poet Oliver Goldsmith and orator Edmund Burke, and then go through the Corinthian facade of the Palladian Regent House. This leads into cobbled Parliament Square, lined with grand buildings and dominated by a tall campanile.

Trinity's Old Library and its Long Room contain some outstanding artifacts, including the ninth-century *Book of Kells*, an illuminated manuscript of the four gospels of the New Testament. The "Turning Darkness into Light" exhibition in the Old Library leads you up to the *Book of Kells*. It offers a historical perspective on the manuscripts, allowing greater understanding of the work.

Campus ➕ B3 ✉ College Green ☎ 01 896 1000; www.tcd.ie ⊙ Daily 🚌 All cross-city buses 🎟 Free ℹ Walking tours lasting 30 minutes depart from inside the Front Gate daily beginning at 10:15 a.m. mid-May to late Sep. 🎟 $$
Old Library ✉ College Green ⊙ Mon.–Sat. 9:30–5, Sun. 9:30–4:30, May–Sep.; Mon.–Sat. 9:30–5, Sun. noon–4:30, rest of year. Closed 10 days from late Dec. to early Jan. 🚌 All cross-city buses 🎟 $$$

Dublin's Pubs

Irish pubs are fueled by good drink, but they are rooted in the gregarious nature of the Irish, and in lively gossip. Many pubs also are outstanding folk music venues, inevitable in a country so well suited to such spontaneous music.

A local favorite is the Brazen Head, at 20 Lower Bridge Street, hailed as the oldest pub in Dublin. Davy Byrnes, on Duke Street, just off busy Grafton Street, has an art deco lounge with lively murals that were painted by Irish playwright Brendan Behan's father-in-law. For Victorian authenticity try the Stag's Head, on Dame Court, with its stained-glass windows and wood paneling. Very popular with Dubliners in the 1890s, the pub was also a favorite of author James Joyce.

You can hear great Irish music with your Guinness in some of the busy Temple Bar pubs like Oliver St. John Gogarty's, on the corner of Fleet and Anglesea streets.

One of the best Dublin music pubs is O'Donoghue's, on Merrion Row, down from St. Stephen's Green. This was the favored haunt of the Dubliners folk group in its 1960s heyday, and the city's best folk musicians regularly raise the roof here.

Other good traditional pubs are Doheny & Nesbitt on Lower Baggott Street; McDaid's on Harry Street, just off Grafton Street; O'Neill's, on Suffolk Street, opposite the tourist information office; and old-fashioned Mulligan's on Poolbeg Street, a last outpost of Joycean Dublin amid the chilly lifelessness of modern office blocks. South of St. Stephen's Green at the corner of Camden Street Upper and Harcourt Road is The Bleeding Horse, formerly a blacksmith's shop and a church; it is a warren of little rooms called "snugs."

If you want Dublin sophistication try Café en Seine on Dawson Street, where a trendy, sophisticated crowd drinks in extravagant surroundings, or for a fusion of old and new, try the Chop House Gastro Pub on Lansdowne Road. For a down-to-earth atmosphere, visit the Foggy Dew on Fownes Street, with music memorabilia behind the bar, a laid-back, young crowd and regular live music.

Temple Bar is at the heart of Dublin's lively nightlife and has several notable pubs

Italy

Opposite: Santa Maria della Salute, Venice, illuminated at night

Italy

Italy

Few countries have as much to offer as Italy, with its warm and passionate people, varied and beautiful landscape, a rich artistic, historic and cultural heritage, some of the world's best food and wine, and a stylish and relaxed philosophy on life.

Italy has something for everyone, whether the visitor is seeking great cities, tiny villages, idyllic countryside or beautiful beaches.

Bell' Italia

Of all European countries, Italy is the one to which many travelers return time and again, their love affair blossoming with each trip. Whether your visit is a chance opportunity or the dream of a lifetime, Italy will fulfill and exceed your expectations, capture your heart and senses, and leave you longing to return.

From the Alps in the north, through the prosperous and fertile heartland to the stark beauty of the deep south, Italy is blessed with some of the world's most beguiling landscapes. The northern half features Tuscany's classic olive, vine and cypress-studded rolling countryside; the dramatic peaks of the Dolomites (Dolomiti); pine-clad white cliffs and turquoise seas; and the eerie loveliness of mist-laden mornings in the great river valleys. The south is equally lovely, with an arid and fierce beauty during the

More Top Destinations in Italy

- Agrigento C1
- Assisi C4
- Lago di Garda B5
- Molveno B5
- Paestum D2
- Piazza Armerina C1
- Portovénere B4
- Ravello C2
- Ravenna C4
- San Gimignano B4
- Siena B4
- Sovana B3
- Urbino C4
- Verona B5
- Vieste D3

AUSTRIA

HUNGARY

Sluderno
Merano/Meran
Bolzano/Bozen
Molveno A22
Trento
Belluno
A23
Cividale
del Friuli
Lago di
Garda
A27
Údine
A4
SLOVENIA
Asolo Treviso
Monfalcone
VERONA E70 Vicenza
TRIESTE
A22
PADOVA
Mantova
A13 Rovigo
VENÉZIA
(VENICE)
Réggio
nell'Emília Ferrara
Parco
Delta
del Po
CROATIA
Módena E76
BOLOGNA
Ravenna
A1 A14
SERBIA
E35 Faenza E45
Prato
Rímini
FIRENZE
(FLORENCE) Urbino
SAN MARINO
Pésaro
BOSNIA &
HERZEGOVINA
San Gimignano A14 Ancona
Cortona Gúbbio
Loreto
Siena Perúgia
E55
E35 Assisi
Orvieto Spoleto
Sovana Todi
Áscoli Piceno
Viterbo Terni
A24
MONTENEGRO
L'Aquila Pescara
Civitavécchia E45 Rieti Chieti
A25
A12 Tivoli Avezzano
Vasto
ROMA
(ROME) Subiaco
A14
Latina Frosinone
Vieste
Cassino
Campobasso San Severo
Terracina A1
Fóggia
ALBANIA
A45 Benevento E55 Barletta
Caserta
Molfetta
NÁPOLI
(NAPLES)
1281
Vesúvio
E842 Melfi
BARI
Isola d'Ischia
Pompei
Altamura A14 Ostuni
Sorrento
Salerno
Matera
Bríndisi
Isola di Capri Ravello
A3 Potenza
Paestum E45
TÁRANTO
Lecce
Metaponto
Gallipoli
Golfo di
Taranto
Marina di
Leuca
Castrovillari
Rossano
Cosenza
Crotone
A3
Catanzaro

Palmi
Érice PALERMO
Trápani Cefalù MESSINA
Segesta A20 E90
Réggio di Calabria
A29 3323
A19 Etna A18
Selinunte Enna Taormina
Caltanissetta CATÁNIA
Agrigento
Piazza
Armerina
Siracusa
Sicília Ragusa
Noto

0   100   200 km
0   50   100 miles

C   D   E

long hot summers, when the intense color of the sea offsets the bleached ocher of the mountains.

Most of Italy is mountainous, the long spine of the Apennines (Appennini) running almost from top to bottom and stretching virtually from coast to coast. Some hilly areas are immensely fertile, as in Tuscany and Umbria in central Italy, while in other places, such as Basilicata and Calabria in the south, the combination of altitude and extreme climate can make the land unproductive.

The largest area of flatland is the great plain of the Po river valley in the north, which extends down the eastern seaboard, an agriculturally rich and productive swath. Much of upland Italy is wooded, and there is a wide variety of indigenous plants.

Diverse Regions

Until 1870 Italy was a collection of separate and disparate states with a complex history, which does much to explain the diversity of people and attitudes. Camillo Cavour (statesman and first prime minister of a united Italy) remarked after unification in 1860, "We have made Italy, now we must make Italians." This aim still seems to await fruition, such is the gulf between the different regions. Italy has been a republic since 1946, the 20 regions (regioni) enjoying a large degree of self-government; some, such as Sicily and Sardinia, are semiautonomous.

Italians would be the first to agree that there is no such thing as "an Italian." Ask an Italian where he or she is from and the answer will be "from Tuscany, from Rome, from Naples, from Sicily," but rarely "from Italy." Primary loyalties are firmly local and regional. The Italian character, attitudes, outlook and prejudices have been formed by the native region, not by the country as a whole. So the fiery Sicilians are light years away from the Milanese and their urbane efficiency, the cool and rational Tuscans or the abrasive Romans.

Language has also played a part. Modern Italian, rich, elegant and musical, derives from Tuscan, a medieval dialect used by Dante and Petrarch and firmly based on Latin. But throughout Italy there are some 1,500 diverse dialects, which were in daily use until widespread literacy and access to television. There are still some elderly people who have difficulty speaking modern Italian, although mass media are rapidly weakening dialects.

The considerable geographic differences between the north and south have produced another element of regionalism – a very real economic and cultural divide between the halves of the country. The cooler, more fertile north is richer, more advanced and more successful than the arid and impoverished south.

The People

All Italians do seem to share the same attitude toward life, one that is instantly apparent to foreigners. Life is for living, for enjoying, for savoring. There's always time to pause to chat, time for kindness, time to laugh; passions run high but anger is quickly over and forgotten. Pause in any Italian piazza and listen to the voices; there are no strident tones or harsh and ugly notes. Watch the way Italians treat children or the elderly, without condescension but with respect for their age. Problems are solved with little fuss on a personal level, although the labyrinth of Italian bureaucracy might drive visitors crazy.

Despite having one of the world's lowest national birthrates, family ties are exceptionally close, with children often living with their parents into their 30s, and elderly people are still mainly cared for at home. The mother's role is pivotal; Italian men, it is said, spend their whole lives searching for a woman to live up to their mother.

If you want to attract the opposite sex, you have to do your best to look good. This helps explain the importance of the

bella figura, literally "beautiful form," but meaning infinitely more. Italians have an innate sense of style, and it matters greatly that their clothes, cars and other personal possessions are stylish and contemporary.

Bella figura dictates that these must all be admired, and what better way to display them than during that fine Italian tradition, the *passeggiata*? This nightly outdoor perambulation occurs in every village, town and city in the land, when citizens exit en masse from their homes, strolling through the streets, exchanging news and gossip, but above all admiring and hoping to be admired in return.

Landscapes and Townscapes

A rich historical and cultural past has shaped the townscape in Italy. Cities, towns and villages are crammed with fine buildings, churches and works of art, a legacy of pre-Unification days. But over the past century, and notably since World War II, there has been huge development and growth in urban areas, with unattractive spreads of industrial buildings and blocks of soulless

The evening stroll around Piazza Rotonda, Rome

apartments on the outskirts of countless towns. Every town still retains its central piazza, with civic buildings and a church grouped around or near it.

In many rural areas, people have traditionally lived in villages rather than on the land they work, traveling daily to the fields, so in some areas isolated country farmhouses are rare. There has sometimes been a huge gulf between the urban and rural populations, possibly due to the very early development of Italian towns.

The middle class was a late arrival in Italy and only really emerged during the great economic boom of the 1950s and 1960s. Even now there are still large numbers of agricultural workers and small shareholders, working the land as it has been worked for centuries, while their cousins may be employed in high-tech industries.

Exploring Italy

Prosperous Italy has one of Europe's highest standards of living, making traveling easy and pleasurable. Tourism is a major industry, so you'll find English widely spoken in city hotels and restaurants, although not away from the main tourist areas.

Italian engineering prowess has produced an excellent road network, with both toll roads and good highways. Minor roads are often unpaved. Italians drive fast and aggressively but mostly safely; once you're accustomed to the style of driving you should have no problems. All major cities have an airport, with frequent internal flights. Trains are cheap and punctual, although cross-country routes can be slow and complicated; it's safer to stick to the intercity services. Buses connect even the smallest villages.

Italian hotels are rated and inspected by regional authorities; regardless of the price range, they are spotlessly clean. Bathtubs are rare except in deluxe establishments, and showers frequently dribble when turned on; water is

Gondoliers in San Silvestro in the San Polo district of Venice

precious in many parts of the country. Air-conditioning is becoming more widespread but is by no means universal, and buildings can be stifling in summer. Laws govern the date when public places turn their heat on or off.

Culinary Traditions

Italian cooking is regional and simple, relying on the superb quality of the ingredients, and you'll find wonderful dishes wherever you go. In a country where frozen food is only now becoming widespread, menus are dictated by the seasons, with a rich variety of dishes punctuating the different months.

The various types of restaurant can be confusing. The terms *ristorante*, *osteria* and *trattoria* are fairly interchangeable; *tavola calda* and *pizzeria* imply something a bit more humble. Lunch has traditionally been the main meal, but there is a trend toward making dinner the extravaganza. The evening menu often consists of *antipasto* (hors d'oeuvre), the first course (*primo*) of pasta, soup or rice, the meat or fish second course (*secondo*) with its accompanying *contorni* (vegetables) or *insalata* (salad), followed by *formaggio*, *dolce* or *frutta* (cheese, dessert or fruit).

If a meal this size seems a bit daunting, choose just a couple of courses.

Many Italians automatically drink wine with their meals. *Denominazione d'Origine Controllata* (DOC) is a method of classification that guarantees the origin of the wine, and that it has been made following the guidelines for a particular area. However, it is no indication of quality.

Pastimes

The favorite Italian pastimes are probably eating, drinking and talking; preferably all together. Immensely sociable people, they tend to relax en masse, making group activities of every type very popular. Soccer is the national sport, and despite the national team's ignominious exit from the 2010 World Cup tournament, Italy remains Europe's most successful soccer nation, and second in the world. Almost every Italian male either attends or follows Sunday matches.

Deeply traditional, Italians prefer their pleasures to be family-oriented; a Sunday drive, a day at the beach or a gentle stroll, accompanied by a non-stop stream of chatter, constitute most people's idea of leisure.

Timeline

3000–1800 BC	First traces of migratory peoples in peninsula.
700–300 BC	Etruscan federation exists alongside Roman republic.
264–146 BC	Punic Wars against Carthage.
AD 200–400	Decline of Roman Empire.
550–770	Peninsula fragmented with different areas under Byzantine, Papal, Lombard and Frankish influence.
1300–1400	Emergence of the city-states in north; Renaissance era.
1500–1848	Fragmentation of peninsula under foreign domination.
1848–61	Struggle for unification, with brief republic established in 1848; kingdom of Italy proclaimed in 1861.
1870	Rome and the Papal States become part of a unified Italy.
1890	Emergence of Fasci Siciliani movement to help the poor and exploited – which was to evolve into the Mafia
1915–18	Italy sides with Allies during World War I.
1940	Italy enters World War II on Axis side.
1943	Fall of Mussolini and armistice with Allies; Mussolini reinstated by Germany as head of puppet republic; Rome liberated in 1944.
1946	Italian Republic established.
1957	Treaty of Rome; Italy becomes a founding member of European Community, now called the European Union.
1985–2000	Corruption is rife, but Italy flourishes as desire for political and institutional reform grows.
2005	Cardinal Joseph Ratzinger is elected the 265th pontiff, Pope Benedict XVI, following the death of Pope John Paul II.
2009	An earthquake decimates L'Aquila in the Abruzzo region.
2009	Prime Minister Berlusconi is attacked by a member of the public after giving a speech in Milan.
2010	Forbes rates Berlusconi Italy's third richest man with estimated assets of $9 billion.

The Etruscans

Travelers in central Italy will frequently come across signs of the Etruscans in monuments, tombs and museums. For centuries historians have questioned exactly who they were. This enigmatic race preceded the Romans and were at the height of their power from 800 to 400 BC. They formed a confederacy of 12 cities, built towns, passed laws, traded overseas and believed firmly in an afterlife. A lively and imaginative people, they also had highly developed cultural, political and social systems. The Romans, admirers of Etruscan culture, absorbed much of it as they rose to power. By the third century BC the Romans had virtually assimilated the entire nation, along with much of its language, customs and religious beliefs. Today only the monuments remain, particularly those to the Etruscan dead. Wonderful finds have been made in these tombs – jewelry, vases, sculpture and frescoes. They are preserved in museums all over ancient Etruria, the name given to the area they inhabited. You can visit Etruscan sites at Tarquinia and Cerveteri, both a short distance north of Rome, and see the finest Etruscan collection in the world at the Villa Giulia museum in Rome.

People viewing paintings displayed on a street stall in Rome

Survival Guide

- The fashion-conscious Italians spend much time and thought on looking good. Dressing appropriately means no shorts in cities. If you do show too much leg or arm, you won't be allowed to enter churches.
- Inevitably, Italy's star attractions in Rome, Venice, Florence and other major cities become packed during the hot summer. Get out early to avoid the main rush or, better still, visit in the late fall or winter when it's quieter and cooler.
- Nowadays, many of the stores and major sights in larger cities throughout the country stay open all day, but in rural towns everything closes from around 12:30 until 4:30 or 5, while in high summer most of the population eats a large lunch and has a siesta. Plan your day around this, remembering that most museums, churches, galleries and stores will all be closed for several hours too.
- Italians love their wine, which they drink with meals, but they disapprove of people who drink to excess.
- It is typical to go out to eat lunch from around 12:30 to about 2:30, and dinner at around 7:30 or 8.

- Vegetarians will find plenty of choices in most restaurants. As for children, Italians genuinely love them, and most restaurants – even upscale ones – welcome them. Italian coffee is extremely strong, so if you want it weaker just ask for a *caffè americano*.
- Bars are much more than the name suggests. They are open from dawn until midnight or later, and offer coffee, tea, soda, snacks and pastries, as well as alcohol. All bars have restrooms and a public telephone.
- Many Italians are enthusiastic smokers, but smoking is prohibited in all public places, including bars, cafés and restaurants. The law is generally well observed.
- One of the joys of Italy is shopping in local stores and at the colorful street markets. However, Italian shopping habits are slowly changing and out-of-town shopping centers are becoming more common. All shop and market prices are fixed.
- Facilities for visitors with disabilities are improving, but are not yet as good as those back home. If you need help it's best to check ahead with local tourist offices and with hotels and sights themselves.

Rome

There's almost too much to Rome (Roma); too much history, too much art, too much noise, confusion, traffic.

This is an overwhelming city in every way, with splendors and frustrations in equal measure. Nowhere else in the world will your senses be assaulted by such a glorious mélange of ancient,

medieval, Renaissance, baroque and modern sights.

Expectations run high, and every visitor comes with preconceptions of sun-filled days of *dolce vita* and romantic strolls through ancient streets. Put them aside, take it slow, accept Rome not as you think it should be, but as it is, and you'll discover a city that is virtually impossible to describe.

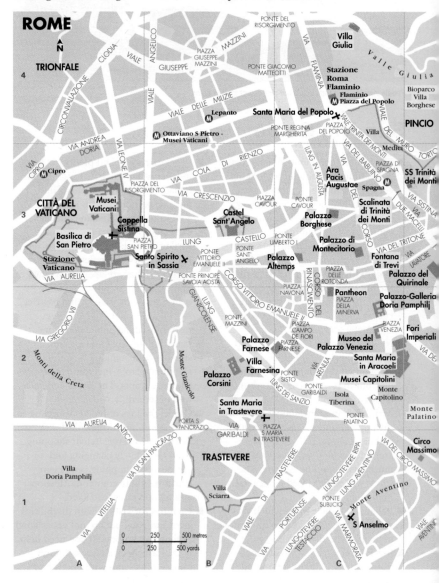

Mapping the City

It's a good idea to stay as centrally located as you can, but avoid the unwholesome area around the central railroad station, Stazione Termini, and keep in mind that few areas of the city offer peace and quiet.

You'll quickly realize that Rome has no discernible center, although Piazza Venezia, dominated by the vast, wedding cake-like monument of Victor Emmanuel II, is a good place to orient yourself. From here, the Via del Corso stretches north, and to the south lies the Forum (Foro Romano), the heart of classical Rome.

Between the Corso and the Tiber (Tevere) river lies the *centro storico*, or historic center, a maze of medieval streets and Renaissance squares and one of the city's most beguiling areas.

On the other side of the Corso are Rome's most elegant shopping streets, more sun-dappled piazzas, some lovely green spaces and the Via Vittorio Veneto, with its luxury hotels and galaxy of upscale cafés.

Across the river lies Trastevere, filled with charming streets and squares and noted for its excellent restaurants.

To the north is Vatican City (Città del Vaticano), home of the Pope and St. Peter's Basilica (Basilica di San Pietro).

Seeing the Sights

It would take months to see all of Rome, so before you arrive, it's a good idea to decide where your priorities lie. It's a mistake to rush out, exhausted from travel, and see the Vatican on your first day; instead wander around the back streets or linger over a cup of coffee before you plunge into serious sightseeing. If you're not a sightseer, enjoy the street life and the stylish stores and restaurants.

It's best to tackle the highlights early in the day, before the crowds and heat intensify and while you're still fresh. Make a point of resting during the early afternoon; most stores and attractions are closed then anyway, and you can venture out again refreshed and relaxed in the late afternoon.

If time is short and you want to see a lot, think about taking a tour; your hotel will be able to advise you.

Other options include walking tours with local experts to explore off-the-beaten-track areas, or a boat trip on the Tiber river.

Peace and Quiet

Tranquility is in short supply in Rome, but there are moments when it seems within reach. In addition to the Villa Borghese (see page 301), other green spaces exist around the city, where the roar of the traffic is at least muted.

One of the best is the Palatine Hill (Palatino) above the Forum, a good place to picnic after a morning's sightseeing, with scattered ruins, cypresses and wildflowers. The Botanical Garden (Giardino Botanico) in Trastevere provides cool shade amid the 7,000 species of plants, while the park Colle Oppio, with its strolling mothers and babies, is a good bet after a morning at the Colosseum.

Roman Cuisine

Romans enjoy dining out, and there are plenty of restaurant choices. Trastevere and the streets around Piazza Navona are packed with eateries; as always in Italy, look for places that are patronized by locals.

Roman specialties center heavily around the less attractive parts of animals, such as offal, brains and tripe, but staples like grilled meat and the delicious *saltimbocca alla Romana* (veal scaloppine cooked with prosciutto and sage) are easy to find. Pasta dishes include spicy *rigatoni all'amatriciana* (pasta with bacon, chili and tomato), and the delicious and familiar *spaghetti alla carbonara*, made with bacon, egg and fettuccine.

Artichokes are a great Roman specialty, eaten either deep fried or raw; look for asparagus in early summer. Desserts are simple, but Roman ice cream is mouthwatering, and it's worth forgoing restaurant desserts and opting instead for a *gelateria*. Pizzas are excellent.

Local wines come from the hills outside Rome, in an area known as the Castelli Romani; Frascati is the best known. You'll also find wines from all over Italy, as well as herbal aperitifs and liqueurs.

Boutiques and Markets

Shopping can be a pleasure in self-indulgent Rome, where there is a superb range of luxurious silk, linens, leather and accessories. Shoes, bags, handmade evening wear and exquisite china and porcelain are found in the very chic stores clustered around the Via Condotti and the Via Frattina, just off the Piazza di Spagna. You'll find moderately priced shops along the Via del Corso and the Via Nazionale; knitwear and sweaters are good buys.

Rome also has several department stores, including the upscale La Rinascente in Piazza Colonna; Upim and Standa are inexpensive and cheerful chain stores with plenty of surprisingly stylish buys.

If you enjoy markets, head for the popular daily food and vegetable market in the lovely Campo dei Fiori, or the many smaller street markets dotted around the city.

Nightlife

Romans consider having a meal in a restaurant the pinnacle of evening

Roman Fountains

Lovely fountains are scattered around Rome, and their beauty will stick in your mind when much else has faded. They provide cool places for a few minutes of rest, and the soothing sound of splashing water somehow manages to make itself heard over the noise of Rome's frenetic traffic. Be sure to pause at the Fontana delle Naiadi in Piazza della Repubblica, with its bronze nymphs; the dolphin-decorated Fontana del Tritone in Piazza Barberini; and the charming tortoise fountain, the Fontana delle Tartarughe, in Piazza Mattei.

The city's most famous fountain is the Fontana di Trevi in the small Piazza di Trevi (see page 297). This awesome baroque masterpiece of carved figures flanking the central figure of Neptune is the most photographed fountain in Rome.

entertainment, but there are many other options and events going on. Pick up a copy of *Roma c'è* or *Trovaroma* for up-to-date information on where to go and what to do in the city.

There are plenty of music bars and discos to satisfy music lovers. Opera is a good option, either at the Teatro dell'Opera or outdoors in summer at the Villa Borghese gardens.

Rome has a clutch of movie theaters showing films in their original language. Concerts and recitals are frequently held in the city's churches.

Essential Information

Tourist Information

Call Centre ☎ 06 0608 (for all offices)
Daily 9:30–7 (English speaking)
Via Leopardi 24 (main city tourist office)
Ostia Lido: Lungomare Paolo Toscanelli
Castel Sant'Angelo: Piazza Pia
Ciampino airport: arrivals hall
Minghetti: Via Marco Minghetti
Navona: Piazza delle Cinque Lune
Nazionale: Via Nazionale, near Palazzo delle Esposizioni
Santa Maggiore: Via dell'Olmata
Sonnino: Piazza Sidney Sonnino
Termini: Termini Railway Station
www.romaturismo.com or www.060608.it

Urban Transportation

Public transportation in Rome consists of red-gray, orange or green buses and trams and a two-line subway system. Subway stations are marked on the Rome city map by the letter "M" in a red circle. Bus tickets must be purchased from automatic machines before boarding, or from shops and newsstands displaying an ATAC or COTRAL sticker. They are valid for multiple bus trips plus one subway trip within a 75-minute period, and must be validated at the rear of the vehicle when boarding. The *Biglietto Integrato Giornaliero* (BIG) is valid for a day's unlimited travel on buses, trams, the subway and the suburban train service. A weekly pass, the *Carta Integrata Settimanale*, also is available. Taxis are white, and park next to the stands with a blue-and-white sign; they do not stop on the street. Call a taxi from Radio Taxi (☎ 06 3570); the meter will start running straight after your call. Be sure that the meter is set at zero if you begin your ride at the taxi stand. Do not get in a "private" taxi, especially at the airports.

Airport Information

Rome has two airports: Leonardo da Vinci, at Fiumicino (west of the city); and Ciampino, south of Rome, for charter flights. The easiest link from Leonardo da Vinci to the city center is by train to Stazione Termini (the central railroad station); trains leave every 30 minutes 6:37 a.m.–11:37 p.m. (precise times vary) at 7 and 37 minutes past the hour. Buses also run to Termini and Tiburtina stations (☎ 06 6595 8646; www.terravision.eu), including four night services between 1:15 a.m. and 5 a.m. Tickets cost €8 return. Travel time is 70 minutes, with four stops. Taxis cost a fixed €45 to central Rome. Only take official white or yellow taxis with meters, numbers and names. From Ciampino, take the COTRAL bus from the airport and then subway line A to Anagnina; both run daily 6:47 a.m.–00:15 a.m. Shuttle buses (€5 one-way) meet many low-cost flights and connect to Termini (☎ 06 7934 1722; www.terravision.eu).

Climate – average highs and lows for the month

Jan.	Feb.	Mar.	Apr.	May	Jun.	Jul.	Aug.	Sep.	Oct.	Nov.	Dec.
13°C	14°C	16°C	19°C	23°C	27°C	31°C	31°C	27°C	23°C	18°C	14°C
55°F	57°F	61°F	66°F	73°F	81°F	88°F	88°F	81°F	73°F	64°F	57°F
3°C	4°C	7°C	8°C	12°C	15°C	18°C	18°C	14°C	11°C	9°C	5°C
37°F	39°F	45°F	46°F	54°F	59°F	64°F	64°F	57°F	52°F	48°F	41°F

Italy

Rome Sights

Basilica di San Pietro

The spiritual heart of Catholicism, the
Basilica di San Pietro (St. Peter's
Basilica) stands on the site of the saint's
burial place.

This is architectural grandeur on a
triumphant scale, from the sweeping
colonnades branching from the
magnificent facade to the soaring dome
above the twisted columns of Giovanni
Bernini's High Altar *baldacchino*.

There's much that dates from 1506
to 1626, when Donato di Angelo
Bramante and Bernini were the principal
architects.

Near the end of his life, Michelangelo
designed the dome, from which there
are superb views; inside you can see the
sublime *Pietà*, one of his earliest works.
The right nave contains a bronze statue
of St. Peter, his right foot worn away by
pilgrims' caresses. Other artists that

worked on the decoration of this
exquisite basilica include Antonio
Canova and Pietro da Cortona.

⊞ A3 ✉ Piazza San Pietro, Città del Vaticano
☎ 06 6988 3731; www.vatican.va ◷ Daily 7–7,
Apr.–Sep.; 7–6:30, rest of year. Dome: daily 8–6,
Apr.–Sep.; 8–5, rest of year ◻ Ottaviano ▣ 62 to
Piazza San Pietro; 23, 32, 49, 81, 271, 590, 982, 990
to Piazza del Risorgimento ⚌ Admission free ($$ for
elevator to terrace and steps to dome)

Colosseo

The massive Colosseo (Colosseum)
dates from AD 72, and the design has
never been bettered. This is a functional
stadium that once seated 55,000; its
sophisticated "backstage" facilities
allowed the arena to be flooded for
mock sea battles. Most ancient
entertainment featured animals, slaves
and gladiators, but few Christians were
martyred here.

During the Middle Ages the Colosseum
was a source of building stone, which
explains the missing sections.

⊞ D2 ✉ Piazza del Colosseo, Via dei Fiori Imperiali
☎ 06 700 5469; 06 3996 7700 or www.pierreci.it for
advance reservation ◷ Daily 8:30 a.m. to 1 hour
before dusk ◻ Colosseo ▣ 3, 60, 81, 84, 85, 87, 117,
175, 186, 271, 571, 810 ⚌ $$$ (includes Palatino and
Foro Romano; valid 48 hours)

The arena and arcades in the Colosseum – the world's largest surviving structure from Roman antiquity

Fontana di Trevi

Among Rome's delightful fountains, none is more famous than the Fontana di Trevi (Trevi Fountain), a baroque creation tucked into a tiny piazza. There's been a fountain here since Roman times; the present example dates from 1732 and takes its name from the three roads – *tre vie* – that converged here. With your back to the fountain throw two coins over your shoulder into the water; legend claims that the first coin grants a wish, the second guarantees that you will return to this great city.

➕ D3 ✉ Piazza di Trevi 🚇 Spagna or Barbarini
🚌 52, 53, 61, 62, 63, 71, 80, 85, 160, 492, 850

Foro Romano e Monte Palatino

Heart of the Roman Empire, the Foro Romano (Roman Forum) contained all of the ancient city's most important political, religious and municipal buildings. Today it's a romantic jumble of tumbled columns and walls set amid cypresses and wildflowers. It's worth spending time here, tracking down the fine second-century Arch of Septimius Severus, the Temple of Antoninus and Faustina (AD 141), the stately columns of the fourth-century Portico of the Dei Consentes, and the House of the Vestal Virgins, home of the guardians of the sacred fire. On the Palatino (Palatine Hill), overlooking the Roman Forum, there are ruins of the homes of wealthy Romans, emperors and aristocrats.

➕ D2 ✉ Via dei Fori Imperiali, Largo Romolo e Remo 1 ☎ 06 3996 7700 🕐 Daily 8:30 a.m. to 1 hour before dusk 🚇 Colosseo 🚌 40, 60, 63, 70, 75, 81, 85, 87, 95, 117, 160, 170, 186, 175, 271, 571, 628, 716 ✋ Foro Romano free; Palatino $$$ (includes Colosseo and Palatino; valid 48 hours)

Musei Capitolini

The two *palazzi* housing the great classical collection of the Musei Capitolini (Capitoline Museums) are set on either side of a square designed by Michelangelo. Look for the *Dying Gaul* and the tautly muscled *Discobolus*

(Discus Thrower). Bronzes include the famous fifth-century BC *Capitoline Wolf Suckling Romulus* and *Remus* and, finest of all, the superb equestrian statue of *Marcus Aurelius*. Paintings include major works by Titian, Paolo Veronese, Van Dyck and Caravaggio.

➕ C2 ✉ Piazza del Campidoglio 1 ☎ 060608; www.museicapitolini.org 🕐 Tue.–Sun. 9–8
🚇 Colosseo 🚌 40, 63, 70 81, 87, 95, 160, 170, 271, 628, 630, 716 ✋ $$$

Musei Vaticani

The Musei Vaticani (Vatican Museums) make up the world's largest museum complex, with around a dozen self-contained museums in 1,400 rooms. It would take days to see it all, so it makes sense to follow either one of the color-coded routes or pick out the highlights that appeal to you. However, do not miss the Cappella Sistina (Sistine Chapel), with its frescoes by Michelangelo covering the ceiling and the altar wall, showing scenes from the Old Testament, and the powerful *Last Judgment*. The Stanze di Raffaello (Raphael Rooms), among the artist's masterpieces, were started in 1508. Classical sculpture, an Egyptian collection and modern religious art are among the other features at this venue.

➕ A3 ✉ Viale Vaticano 100, Città del Vaticano
☎ 06 6988 4676; www.vatican.va 🕐 Mon.–Sat. 9–6, (last ticket 4). Also last Sun. of month 9–2 (last ticket 12:30). Closed major religious holidays 🚇 Ottaviano, Cipro-Musei Vaticani 🚌 49 (to front of museums), 32, 81, 982 to Piazza del Risorgimento or 492, 990 to via Leone IV, both 5 minutes' walk ✋ $$$; free to all last Sun. of month

Museo e Galleria Borghese

The Museo e Galleria Borghese (Borghese Museum and Gallery), housed in the 17th-century summer palace of Cardinal Scipione Borghese, is a treasure-house of sculpture, mainly collected by the cardinal. He admired Giovanni Bernini, whose works dominate – the *David* is said to be a self-portrait.

Look for Antonio Canova's *Paolina Borghese*; this beautiful little minx, with her come-hither look, was Napoleon's sister, married off to a later Borghese. Stunning paintings include Caravaggio's famous *Boy with a Fruit Basket*.

➕ D4 ✉ Villa Borghese, Piazzale del Museo Borghese 5 ☎ 06 841 7645; www.galleriaborghese.it ⏰ Tue.–Sun. 8:30–7:30 🚇 Spagna 🚌 30, 40, 46, 62, 63, 64, 70, 81, 87, 116, 119, 130, 186, 190, 492, 571, 628, 810, 916 🍴 Museum/gallery restaurant 💵 $$$ (advance reservations necessary ☎ 06 328 101 Mon.–Fri. 9–6, Sat. 9–1, or online at www.ticketeria.it)

Pantheon

The superb Pantheon, erected between AD 118 and AD 128 and still in use today, gives a better idea of the splendor of ancient Rome than any other monument. Built as a temple, it became a Christian church in AD 609 and now houses Raphael's tomb and also those of two Italian kings. Its dome is the largest ever built before the introduction of reinforced concrete in the 20th century.

➕ C2 ✉ Piazza della Rotonda ☎ 06 6830 0230 ⏰ Mon.–Sat. 8:30–7:30, Sun. 9–6:30, holidays 9–1 🚇 Spagna 🚌 64, 70, 81, 86, 87, 90, 119, 170 and all services to Largo di Torre Argentina 💵 Free

Piazza di Spagna e Scalinata della Trinità dei Monti

The Scalinata della Trinità dei Monti (Spanish Steps), curving gracefully up from Piazza di Spagna to the church of Trinità dei Monti, attract myriad visitors; this is a favorite meeting place, situated at the heart of Rome's trendiest shopping area. The steps, built in 1723, get their name from the piazza, which once housed the Spanish embassy. The eccentric-looking "sunken boat" fountain dates from 1627, while on the right of the steps (at No. 26) you'll find the Museo Keats-Shelley, in the lodgings where poet John Keats died in 1821.

➕ C3 ✉ Piazza di Spagna 26 ☎ Museo Keats-Shelley: 06 678 4235; www.keats-shelley-house.org ⏰ Museum: Mon.–Fri. 10–1 and 2–6, Sat. 11–2 and 3–6 🚇 Spagna 🚌 116, 117, 119, 590 💵 Museum $$

The interior of the Pantheon, seen from the doorway

Piazza Navona

Piazza Navona owes its shape to the Roman racetrack that once stood here. Pope Innocent X, who commissioned Giovanni Bernini to design the focal point, the Fountain of the Four Rivers, rebuilt the piazza in 1644. The 17th-century church of Sant'Agnese is a good example of Francesco Borromini's work.

➕ C2 ✉ Piazza Navona 🚇 Spagna 🚌 30, 56, 60

San Clemente

No church in Rome gives a better idea of history than San Clemente, a multilayered structure whose newest part dates from the 12th century. In its dim interior, the apse mosaics glitter above the marble panels of the choir screen and pulpits. From here, descend to the fourth-century lower church, with its ghostly traces of eighth- to 11th-century frescoes, before plunging deeper to examine the fine altar of the Roman Mithraic temple (the Mithraic cult was most popular in Rome from 67 BC to the late second century).

➕ E2 ✉ Via Labicana 95 ☎ 06 7740 0201; www.basilicasanclemente.com ⏰ Mon.–Sat. 9–12:30 and 3–6, Sun. 10–12:30 and 3–6 🚌 3, 85, 87, 117, 186, 571, 810, 850 💵 Church free; Temple $

The Vatican

The Città del Vaticano is a focus of universal adoration, though it had has its detractors. Thomas Paine, the English-born American revolutionary, writer, pamphleteer and inventor, once said it "is a dagger through the heart of Italy". Even so, it remains perhaps the world's greatest monument to art and beauty. The Vatican, an area covering about 109 acres around the Basilica of St. Peter (Basilica di San Pietro), in the heart of Rome, is the world's smallest independent sovereign state. Until Italian unification in 1870, the Papacy had held territory covering a large part of central Italy, known as the Papal States. These became part of the new united Italy, and the Pope, Pius IX, retreated to the Vatican, a virtual prisoner, but in 1929 the Treaty of the Lateran brought the Vatican State into existence.

The Pope, as well as being head of the Catholic church, is also Europe's only absolute monarch, ruling over the 200-plus inhabitants of the Vatican. In April 2005, 78-year-old Cardinal Joseph Ratzinger of Germany was elected Pope following the death earlier in the month of Pope John Paul II, who had reigned for 26 years.

The present Pope, who has taken the name Pope Benedict XVI and is the 264th such spiritual successor to St. Peter, is known for his conservative views and dislike of liberal reform. Even so, he is a popular choice among the faithful and was greeted by the cheers of tens of thousands of followers when he stepped onto the balcony of St. Peter's Basilica to give his first blessing, proclaiming that he was but "a simple, humble worker."

The Pope has been defended by the Swiss Guard since 1506. Their distinctive, colorful striped red, yellow and blue dress uniform, said to have been designed by Michelangelo, is instantly recognizable. The 90 members are Swiss, young men recruited between the ages of 19 and 25, from Switzerland's four Catholic cantons. They are Swiss rather that Roman because it was unthinkable that the army of the Church of Rome should take up arms against Romans in defence of the Papacy.

The Pope gives a weekly general audience on Wednesdays at 11 a.m. in the Papal Audience Chamber, and occasionally in the Basilica of St. Peter or in the piazza. These occasions, for up to 7,000 people, are open to everyone and tickets are free. The Pope also gives a blessing from the windows of his rooms overlooking the piazza on Sundays at midday.

Audience tickets are available by writing to Prefettura della Casa Pontificia, 00120 Città del Vaticano, online on www.viator.com/papal-audience or by visiting the office through the bronze doors in the right-hand colonnade of Piazza San Pietro, open daily 9–1.

The Biblioteca Vaticano (Vatican Library) holds more that 1.5 million books

Excursion to Tivoli

Most visitors to Rome seize the chance to escape the city by taking an excursion to Tivoli, a small town in a lovely wooded location 19 miles northeast of Rome. Its main attractions are the gardens of the Villa d'Este, among the world's most beautiful, and the vast classical site of Villa Adriana (Hadrian's Villa), about 4 miles southwest of Tivoli.

It's easy to make an independent trip to Tivoli, either by train from the central railroad station, Stazione Termini, then local bus, or by bus from central Rome. There are guided excursions from the city, while an English-speaking guide tells you all you need to know.

Villa d'Este

The Villa d'Este is famous not so much for the villa itself, built by Cardinal Ippolito d'Este in 1550, but for the stunning gardens, terraces and fountains that belong to it. The main attractions are two Giovanni Bernini fountains, the elegant Fontana di Biccierone and the Fontana dei Draghi, and the breathtaking Avenue of a Hundred Fountains (Viale delle Cento Fontane), a wooded walkway. Nearby lies the lovely Villa Gregoriana, where a pair of waterfalls cascades into a deep-cut gorge.

Villa Adriana

Many prosperous Romans built retirement villas at Tivoli, and in AD 125 the Emperor Hadrian embarked on the construction of his own. The villa and its gardens grew and grew, eventually covering as much ground as Imperial Rome itself. The site is vast and romantic, and you'll need a map to make sense of it all and plenty of imagination to appreciate how the site once looked. Don't miss the Maritime Theater (Teatro Marittimo), a colonnaded palace on an island in the middle of a lake.

Villa d'Este 🚫 Off map 🖂 Piazza Trento 5 ☎ Toll-free in Italy 199 766166 or 0011 39 0445 230 310 from the U.S.; www.villadestetivoli.info 🕐 Tue.–Sun. 8:30 to 1 hour before dusk (last admission 1 hour before closing) 🚌 COTRAL bus from Via Tiburtina to Tivoli 🚆 Train to Tivoli 🍴 Refreshments available in gardens 💰 $$

Villa Gregoriana 🖂 Piazza Tempio di Vesta ☎ 0774 382733; www.villagregoriana.it 🕐 Tue.–Sun. 10–6:30, Apr. to mid-Oct.; Tue.–Sat. 10–2:30, Sun. 10–4 in Mar. and mid-Oct. to Nov.; by appointment rest of year 💰 $$

Villa Adriana 🖂 Via di Villa Adriana 204 ☎ 06 3996 7900 for reservations; www.pierreci.it 🕐 Daily 9 a.m. to 1 hour before dusk 🚌 COTRAL bus from Via Gaeta to Tivoli; then local bus Tivoli, Piazza Garibaldi, to Villa Adriana 🚆 Train to Tivoli 🍴 Refreshments at villa site 💰 $$

The Avenue of a Hundred Fountains in the gardens at Villa d'Este

Santa Maria in Aracoeli

Santa Maria in Aracoeli (Our Lady of the Altar of Heaven) was built around 1260 to replace an older church. Approached by 124 steep steps, built in 1348 to celebrate the end of a plague epidemic, the church's plain facade hides a superb interior. The nave columns were taken from Roman buildings, while the gilded ceiling dates from the 1570s.

➕ C2 ✉ Piazza d'Aracoeli ☎ 06 679 8155
🕐 Daily 9–12:30 and 3–6:30, May–Sep.; 9–12:30 and 2:30–5:20, rest of year 🚌 40, 63, 70, 81, 87
🖐 Free

Santa Maria Maggiore

Mass has been said daily in Santa Maria Maggiore (St. Mary the Major) since the fifth century, when it was built on a site marked by a summer snowfall, as predicted by the Virgin when she appeared before the reigning Pope. The mosaics in the nave date from the fifth century, those in the apse from the 13th century. The gilding on the ceiling reputedly comes from the first gold to arrive from the New World.

➕ E2 ✉ Piazza di Santa Maria Maggiore 42
☎ 06 481 4287 🕐 Daily 7–7, Apr.–Sep.; 7–6:30, rest of year 🚇 Cavour, Termini 🚌 5, 16, 75, 84, 105, 360, 590, 649 🖐 Free

Santa Maria in Trastevere

The facade of Santa Maria in Trastevere, with its lustrous 12th-century mosaics, overlooks an atmospheric fountained piazza. The charming portico, added in

The beautiful apse of Santa Maria in Trastevere

1702, leads to an interior with nave columns that once supported Roman buildings. The 12th-century, Byzantine-style mosaics of the apse represent the glorification of the Virgin.

➕ B2 ✉ Piazza Santa Maria in Trastevere
☎ 06 589 4802; www.santamariaintrastevere.org
🕐 Daily 7:30 a.m.–8 p.m (may close 12:30–3:30 in winter) 🚌 H, 23, 44, 75, 170, 181, 280, 630, 780

Via Appia Antica

A short bus ride from central Rome takes you to the Via Appia Antica (Old Appian Way), built in 4 BC to link Rome with Brindisi in southern Italy. Here, Spartacus and his men were executed, and St. Paul marched to prison. This cobbled way, shaded by pine trees, is lined with monuments and tombs; you can visit the catacombs, with their mementos of early Christian life.

➕ Off map at E1 ✉ Catacombe di San Sebastiano: Via Appia Antica 136 ☎ 06 785 0350 🕐 Catacombs: Mon.–Sat. 8:30–noon and 2:30–5 (5:30 in summer); closed Nov. 🚌 118, 714 🖐 $$

Villa Borghese

If you long for some cool green grass, head for the extensive grounds of the Villa Borghese gardens, central Rome's largest park, an oasis of verdant lawns, umbrella pines, lakes and fountains. The adjoining Pincio Gardens offer views across the rooftops to St. Peter's.

➕ D4 ✉ Porta Pinciana 🕐 Daily dawn–dusk
🚇 Flaminio, Spagna 🚌 52, 53, 88, 116, 120, 150, 490

Villa Giulia

Visit the Villa Giulia to learn more about the Etruscans (see page 290). The collection is housed in a late Renaissance villa; its architects included Michelangelo. Highlights are the Castellani exhibits and fine Greek vases. Be sure to see the Sarcofago degli Sposi, sixth-century BC figures of a reclining married couple, and the terracotta Hercules and Apollo.

➕ C4 ✉ Piazzale di Villa Giulia 9 ☎ 06 322 6571
🕐 Tue.–Sun. 8:30–7:30 🚇 Flaminio 🚌 3, 19, 30, 52, 926 🖐 $$; online booking at www.ticketeria.it

Italy

Florence

More than 6 million tourists visit
Florence (Firenze) annually, the capital
of Tuscany, whose resident population
is about 400,000. Visitors come with
high expectations of beauty, stunning
art and history. Sadly, they can be
overwhelmed by heat, crowds, noise and
cultural overload that the city fails to

live up to expectations. When touring
Florence, planning pays off.

Choose the time you visit carefully.
If art and architecture are the main
purpose of your trip, try to come
off-season, when Florence is quieter
and the heat in this largely non-air-
conditioned city won't wipe you out.
Be prepared for crowds, time gallery
visits for early and late in the day,

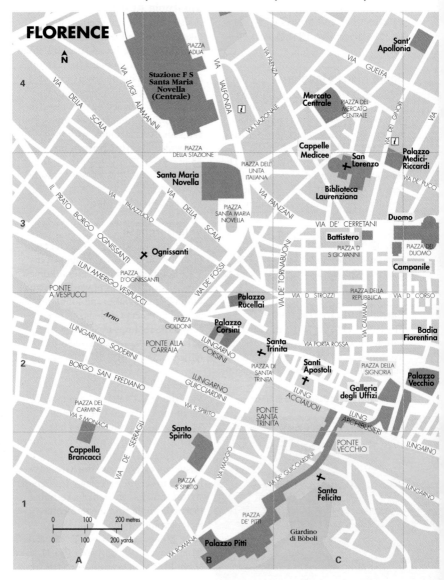

and check opening times for museums and churches before you visit to avoid disappointment. Reserve accommodations before you come, and don't plan to use Florence as a base for touring the rest of Tuscany.

Florence and Florentines

Florentines are Tuscans – generally restrained and rational, and less given to fiery displays. They also are more reserved. Accustomed to huge numbers of visitors, they do not go out of their way to befriend tourists but are courteous and professional in their everyday dealings.

Florence at first glance is not as instantly appealing as Rome or Venice – let it grow on you and experience it as a living city, not merely as a vast treasure-house of art. Get away from the major sights and their crowds of sightseers, and explore the quieter areas, with atmospheric streets and traditional activities. Vary the artistic glories with a bit of hedonism, and take time to relax.

The best way to see Florence is on foot. Most of the main attractions are clustered together in the largely pedestrian central core, making walking easier (but watch out for enthusiastic scooter riders).

Eating in Tuscany

There are all types of restaurants in Florence, from fast-food joints to world-class establishments. Many are specifically aimed at tourists and have prominently displayed fixed-price (but mediocre) menus. To ensure a memorable meal, eat where the Italians themselves eat and be prepared to pay somewhat high prices. For a simple lunch, try a slice of fresh-baked pizza to go or a quick snack in a *vinaio* or *fiaschetteria*, traditional wine bars.

Food markets are particularly tempting, where you can put together the makings of a picnic – bread, salami, cheese, fruit and a bottle of wine. Tuscan food is simple and excellent, centered around basic ingredients such as olive oil, fresh vegetables and meat, with plenty of soups, superb pork dishes, grilled meats and vegetables. Bean dishes are especially popular (Tuscans are fondly nicknamed *mangiafagioli*, or "bean-eaters"). The most famous wine is Chianti, a delicious red wine, but look also for Brunello di Montalcino, a superb red from Tuscany.

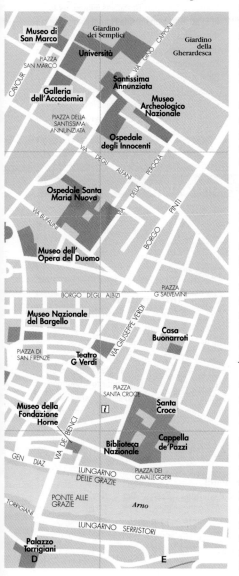

Pucci, Gucci and More

Intriguing stores, markets and boutiques are scattered throughout the center of Florence. Shoes and leather goods are famous, as are fine china, exquisite bed and table linen, and jewelry. Designer-label fans can visit Pucci and Gucci on their home ground; other tempting gifts include glazed majolica pottery, marbled paper, prints and antiques.

Via de'Tornabuoni and the surrounding streets house the most elegant stores; less expensive fashion is found around Piazza della Repubblica and Via dei Calzaiuoli, while jewelers line the Ponte Vecchio. There are many factory leather outlets near Santa Croce. Be sure to spend time browsing in a market; the huge Mercato San Lorenzo is probably the most enjoyable. Most stores will ship to the United States.

Festivals Galore

A summer visit is likely to coincide with one of the cultural festivals, the *Estate Fiesolana* or the *Maggio Musicale Fiorentino*, which run from May through August, with concerts, opera and ballet – often outdoors in an historic setting.

Excursions

Even if your time in Tuscany is limited, try to fit in an excursion outside Florence, viewing the timeless landscape en route to another of the region's superb historic towns. Possibilities include Pisa, Siena, San Gimignano and the wine country of Chianti, all easily reached by tour bus or public transportation. Nearer still lies Fiesole, a picturesque hill town just above Florence, the perfect escape from noise and heat.

Essential Information

Tourist Information

Via Cavour 1r ☎ 055 290 833
Piazza della Stazione 4 ☎ 055 212 245
Borgo Santa Croce 29r ☎ 055 234 0444;
www.firenzeturismo.it.

Urban Transportation

Buses, both regular and electric, run from Santa Maria Novella station all over town. Buy tickets (€1.20) before boarding: passes are available from machines and tobacconists and are valid for an unlimited number of trips within a period of 90 minutes; 24-hour (€5), 3-day (€12) and 7-day passes (€18), or an electronic Carta Agile (10 or 20 90-minute tickets), are also available. Maps and timetables can be found at the ATAF office (✉ Piazza della Stazione ☎ 800 424500

toll free; www.ataf.net). Stamp tickets, as you board, in the orange box on the bus. Hail taxis at central locations, or call Radio Taxi Cotafi (☎ 055 4390) or Radio Taxi Socata (☎ 055 4242).

Airport Information

Most visitors arrive and leave from Pisa's Galileo Galilei Airport (☎ 050 849 111; 050 849 300 for flight information; www. pisa-airport.com), connected to Florence's Santa Maria Novella railroad station by bus or train services; travel time 1 hour to 1 hour and 20 minutes. Some railroad services are direct, others require a connection at Pisa Centrale. Florence Airport (Amerigo Vespucci Airport) is at Peretola (☎ 055 306 1300; www.aeroporto. firenze.it), 4 miles outside the city.

Climate – average highs and lows for the month

Jan.	Feb.	Mar.	Apr.	May	Jun.	Jul.	Aug.	Sep.	Oct.	Nov.	Dec.
10°C	12°C	15°C	18°C	23°C	27°C	31°C	30°C	26°C	21°C	14°C	10°C
50°F	53°F	59°F	64°F	73°F	81°F	88°F	86°F	79°F	70°F	57°F	50°F
1°C	2°C	5°C	7°C	11°C	14°C	17°C	17°C	14°C	10°C	5°C	2°C
34°F	36°F	41°F	45°F	52°F	59°F	63°F	63°F	57°F	50°F	41°F	36°F

Florence Sights

Cappelle Medicee

The beautiful Cappelle Medicee (Medici Chapels) were built as the mausoleum for Florence's most powerful family.

The Sagrestia Nuova, built by Michelangelo between 1520 and 1534, contains some of his most powerful sculptures. Carvings of reclining figures representing *Night* and *Day* and *Dawn* and *Dusk* decorate the tombs of Lorenzo, duke of Urbino, and Guiliano, duke of Nemours. The fluid lines are a perfect foil for the austerity of the architecture.

➕ C3 ✉ Via Madonna degli Aldobrandini 6 ☎ 055 238 8602; www.firenzemusei.it ⓘ Daily 8:15–1:50. Closed second and fourth Sun., and first, third and fifth Mon. of the month 🚌 14, 22, 31, 23, 71, C1 🖐 $$

Duomo, Battistero e Campanile di Giotto

The Gothic Duomo (Cathedral) of Santa Maria del Fiore, the first domed structure erected in Europe since Roman times, was built between 1296 and 1436. Its austere interior, with a Paolo Uccello fresco, leads to the 463 steps to the top of Brunelleschi's Cupola (Dome).

The chief draw of the 11th-century marble Battistero (Baptistery) is the three sets of bronze doors, with their Old Testament scenes. Andrea Pisano cast the south pair in 1326, and they inspired Lorenzo Ghiberti to design those at the north and east in the 1400s.

The Campanile (Bell Tower), designed by Giotto, was built between 1334 and 1359. Its marble walls are decorated with superb relief sculptures. The 280-foot, 414-step climb offers lovely, if vertiginous, views over Florence.

➕ C3–D3 ✉ Piazza del Duomo ☎ Duomo and Campanile: 055 230 2885; www.duomofirenze.it ⓘ Duomo: Mon.–Wed. and Fri. 10–5, Thu. 10–3:30, Sat. 10–4:45 (last Sat. of the month 10–3:30), Sun.1:30–4:45. Cupola: Mon.–Fri. 8:30–7, Sat. 8:30–5:40. Battistero: Mon.–Sat. noon–7 (first Sat. of the month 8:30–2), Sun. 8:30–2. Campanile: daily 8:30–7:30 🚌 23, 71, C1, C2 🖐 Duomo free; Cupola and Campanile $$ each; Battistero $

Galleria dell'Accademia

Founded as an art school in 1784, the Galleria dell'Accademia (Academy Gallery) today houses the world's most important collection of Michelangelo sculptures, as well as works by other artists. The main attraction is his *David*, a huge and technically perfect nude male figure, possibly the most famous in the history of sculpture. More moving by far are the other sculptures by the artist, particularly the four *Prisoners*, the figures struggling to break free from their block of marble.

➕ D4 ✉ Via Ricasoli 58–60 ☎ 055 238 8609; advance booking (advisable) 055 294 883 or www.b-ticket.com ⓘ Tue.–Sun. 8:15–6:50 🚌 71 🖐 $$

The frescoes decorating the cupola of the Duomo were created by Giorgio Vasari and Federico Zuccari

Galleria degli Uffizi

Arguably the world's greatest collection of Renaissance paintings, the Galleria degli Uffizi (Gallery of the Offices) is housed in an elegant arcaded building designed by Vasari as administrative offices – hence the name.

Here, in chronological order, are paintings representing the greatest names in art, among them Giotto, Paolo Uccello, Botticelli, Piero della Francesca, Leonardo da Vinci, Michelangelo, Raphael and Caravaggio.

Come early or late to avoid waiting in the the longest lines, though the surprisingly small rooms are likely to be thronged with visitors.

🚹 C2 ✉ Loggiato degli Uffizi 6 ☎ 055 238 8651; 055 294 883 for reservations or book online at www.b-ticket.com; www.uffizi.firenze.it/english ◎ Tue.–Sun. 8:15–6:50 (occasionally stays open later in summer) 🚌 14, 23 🍴 Café in gallery 💷 $$

Museo di San Marco

Rebuilt in 1437, the convent attached to the church of San Marco, decorated by Fra Angelico, is one of Florence's loveliest treasures. It's a peaceful religious house, where each monk's cell is adorned with a tiny fresco to aid prayer. The pilgrim's hall contains many paintings by Fra Angelico and his school, and additional works are on display in the cloisters and on the stairs, notably the radiant *Annunciation*.

🚹 D4 ✉ Piazza San Marco 3 ☎ 055 238 8608; www.polomuseale.firenze.it ◎ Mon.–Fri. 8:15–1:50, Sat.–Sun 8:15–6:50 (closed first, third and fifth Sun., and second and fourth Mon. of each month). Closed Jan. 6, Easter, Apr. 25, Jun. 2, Aug. 15, Nov. 1 and Dec. 8 and 26 🚌 1, 6, 7, 10, 11, 14, 17, 23, 25, 33, C1 💷 $$

Museo Nazionale del Bargello

Surrounding a courtyard, in a building dating from 1255, the Museo Nazionale del Bargello (National Bargello Museum) houses Italy's finest collection of Renaissance sculpture. The first floor has works by Michelangelo, Benvenuto Cellini, the flamboyant Giambologna and other late Renaissance artists, but the vaulted second-floor hall contains the museum's masterpieces. Here are Donatello's bronze of a vulnerable *David,* his exquisite *St. George,* and the superb Baptistery door reliefs showing *The Sacrifice of Isaac* by Lorenzo Ghiberti and Brunelleschi, made for a competition in 1401.

Upstairs are bright enameled terracottas by the della Robbia family.

🚹 D2 ✉ Via del Proconsolo 4 ☎ 055 238 8606; www.polomuseale.firenze.it ◎ Tue.–Sun. 8:15–5, Apr.–Oct.; 8:15–1:50, rest of year. Closed first, third and fifth Sun., and second and fourth Mon. of the month 🚌 23, 71, C1, C2 🍴 Alle Murate, see page 481 💷 $$

Ponte Vecchio

If not the most beautiful Florentine bridge, then certainly the most photographed, the Ponte Vecchio (Old Bridge) was built in 1345 to replace an earlier one. It has been picturesquely lined with exclusive goldsmiths and jewelers' shops since 1593. Above it runs a corridor used by members of the Medici family to travel from the Pitti Palace to the Uffizi. The sole bridge across the Arno river in Florence not destroyed by the Germans in World War II, the Ponte Vecchio also survived the floods in 1966.

🚹 C1–C2 ✉ Ponte Vecchio 🚌 C3, D

Santa Croce

This huge Franciscan church was built in 1294, but was badly damaged by the 1966 floods. Today it contains superb early frescoes telling the story of the Santa Croce (Holy Cross). Michelangelo is buried here, along with Ghiberti, Machiavelli and Galileo Galilei.

In the serene cloisters is a museum featuring Cimabue's famous *Crucifix,* and the Cappella dei Pazzi (Pazzi Chapel) by Brunelleschi.

🚹 E1 ✉ Piazza Santa Croce 16 ☎ 055 246 6105; www.santacroceopera.it ◎ Mon.–Sat. 9:30–5:30, Sun. 1–5:30 🚌 14, 23, 71, C3 💷 $$ (includes entry to adjoining Museo dell'Opera di Santa Croce)

A Day in Florence

Many Florentines start working by 8 a.m., when food stores also open. Since many people live in centrally located apartments, visitors have the chance to see the neighborhoods waking up. Housewives go to market early, children walk to school and people pause for a quick bar breakfast on their way to work.

For the tourist in Florence an early start makes sense. Head straight for major sights such as the Galleria degli Uffizi, Galleria dell'Accademia, Duomo or Palazzo Pitti (Pitti Palace) while you're still fresh and before the big tour groups arrive. Most of the museums open at 8:30 a.m. and the churches earlier, so it's feasible to pop into a specially noted church first thing.

Pause mid-morning for a drink and a rest, but bear in mind that some attractions shut for several hours in the middle of the day, as do stores. It's a good idea to follow the siesta habit – a leisurely lunch and a quiet hour or so digesting all you've seen will leave you fresh for more touring in the late afternoon. Early evening is a popular time for Florentines to shop, and a good opportunity for you to track down that must-have leather bag, beautiful fabric, silk tie or marbled paper souvenir.

Florentines are back at work and out on the streets again some time after 4:30, looking rested, relaxed and ready for the rest of the day and evening. By 6:30 the town is thronged with well-dressed crowds, strolling, meeting friends and whole-heartedly enjoying the evening *passeggiata* through the streets of their beautiful city. Crowds thin out and shops close around 8:30, when people head home or to a restaurant for dinner, and there's a break before the evening's activities.

Florence has plenty of nightlife to choose from, with a wealth of cultural offerings such as theater, opera and classical music, movies, and numerous discos and bars with live music. The streets are busy well into the early hours – especially in the height of summer – with locals and foreigners alike enjoying the balmy night air.

Detail from *Madonna with Child and Angels*. c.1455, by Fra Filippo Lippi, in the Uffizi Gallery

Naples

Vibrant, noisy, crumbling Naples (Napoli), the capital of southern Italy and one of Europe's most beautifully located cities, is light years removed in atmosphere from the prosperous north. The city epitomizes southern Italy: confusing, passionate, dirty and charming, redolent with a rich and complicated history that has physically shaped it and emotionally shaped its residents. Naples can feel alien and intimidating, but also inspires fierce loyalty as visitors are quickly won over by its exuberance, way of life, attractions and, above all, its people.

Shops on the narrrow Via San Gregorio Armeno

The people of southern Italy are generally charming, warm and enthusiastic, and Neapolitans are no exception. They live at what appears to be a fever pitch of excitement and noise, which you'll notice on the street. You'll find people eager to help, and anxious for you to enjoy Naples. Authorities have encouraged citizens to welcome tourists, and have succeeded admirably.

Getting Around

Central Naples is best tackled on foot, as the traffic is so horrendous that any form of transportation can be excruciatingly slow. Much of what you'll want to see is walkable, and sights are grouped together in different areas, so take a bus or cable car to your general destination and then walk. Wandering around is an essential and fascinating part of the Naples experience, as the street life is lively and beguiling – but stick to well-frequented areas.

You'll want to travel down the coast to Pompeii and the Sorrento peninsula; both can be reached by train.

The best way to appreciate the beauty of Naples' spectacular setting on the bay is from the sea; you could combine a visit to the Sorrento peninsula with a boat trip to Sorrento or to the ravishing islands of Capri and Ischia.

Mediterranean Flavors

Neapolitan cooking ranks among the best in Italy, with a strong emphasis on the freshest fish and seafood, and local fruit and vegetables from the fertile volcanic soil of the hinterland. Flavors are intense, and the combination of ingredients unusual and interesting. There are pasta dishes with shellfish, grilled fish of all varieties, mozzarella cheese dripping with freshness, and numerous salamis, as well as some excellent local prosciutto.

Naples is the home of thin, tasty and crisp pizzas; they are always baked in wood-fired ovens, and can be eaten as a snack or light meal. Neapolitan cakes

Safety in Naples

The city authorities have done much to clean up Naples in every way, making it a much safer and more attractive city to visit. However, it is still wise to avoid the labyrinthine back streets, the docks and, at night, the railroad station. Avoid carrying a lot of cash, and be aware of pickpockets, particularly in crowded tourist areas.

Be careful when crossing the street: Neapolitan drivers often ignore pedestrian crossings, and unless you step off the sidewalk you could be stranded for what seems like hours. Scooters appear to come out of nowhere, and they frequently use the sidewalks or go against the direction of traffic.

and pastries are famous and best enjoyed from a *pasticceria* (a specialist pastry and cake shop). Try honeyed *stuffoli*, iced chocolate *mustaccioli*, *zeppola* (doughnuts) and *sfogliatelle* filled with ricotta cheese. Don't miss out on the fantastic ice cream. Local wines to try are Lacrima Christi and Greco di Tufo. Be sure to sample Limoncello, a lemon-flavored liqueur, or delicious *mirtillo* (bilberry) and *finocchietto* (fennel) liqueurs.

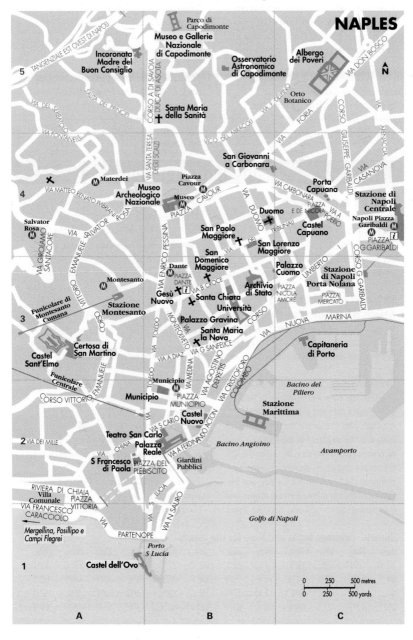

NAPLES

Shopping and Nightlife

Naples' upscale stores are clustered along the Via Toledo and the Via Chiaia, where you'll find outlets for Italy's top designers, as well as local stores selling fine leather goods, fashion and knitwear. Jewelers abound near Via San Biagio; the traditional best buys in Naples are coral necklaces, bracelets, earrings and cameo brooches. If you like antiques, head for Via Domenico Morelli, where stores specialize in 18th-century furniture and paintings.

Wonderful, traditional nativity figurines are still made in the historic area around San Biagio, along with fabulously decorated masks and elaborately dressed dolls. There are useful shopping centers located at Galleria Vanvitelli and Galleria Scartelli in the Vomero district, and you'll find a branch of the department store la Rinascente in downtown Naples.

If you like opera and classical music, a performance in the wonderful San Carlo opera house, the oldest working theater in Europe, should be high on your list. Traditional Neapolitan music is easy to find, and even the least tourist-oriented restaurants generally have musicians ambling through their premises serenading diners.

Essential Information

Tourist Information

Piazza del Gesù Nuovo 7 ☎ 081 551 2701
Via Santa Lucia 107 ☎ 081 245 7475 and
081 764 7064
Via San Carlo 9 ☎ 081 402 394;
www.inaples.it

Urban Transportation

Neapolitan traffic makes any form of transportation slow, so it's best to walk if it's feasible. Longer distances can be covered by subway, bus and *funiculari* (cable cars), all of which are slow. There are two types of *Giranapoli* tickets, valid for either 90 minutes or all day; they are interchangeable between buses, cable cars and the subway, and obtainable from tobacconists or newsstands. They must be validated in the special machines on board buses; before boarding cable cars; and at the entrance to subway platforms. To travel around the bay, use the Circumvesuviana railroad, which leaves from the railroad station on Corso Garibaldi every half-hour and takes an hour to reach Sorrento, its farthest point. You can also travel to Sorrento by ferry or hydrofoil from the Mergellina or Molo Beverello docks; the same companies also serve Capri, Ischia and the other islands (www.caremar.it, www.alilauro.it, www.snav.it). There are taxi stands throughout the city, or you can call Taxi Napoli (☎ 081 556 4444) or Consort Taxi (☎ 081 551 7070).

Airport Information

Naples' Capodichino Airport (☎ 081 786 6111, 24-hour flight information: 081 751 5471; www.gesac.it), with internal and European flights, is northwest of the city center. The airport "Alibus" (☎ 0800 639 525, toll-free within Italy; www.anm.it) buses run at 20-minute intervals to Piazza Municipio via Piazza Garibaldi, daily 6:30 a.m.–11:30 p.m. Tickets cost €3. ANM route 35 links the airport with the central station every 30 minutes (contact details the same as Alibus).

Climate – average highs and lows for the month

	Jan.	Feb.	Mar.	Apr.	May	Jun.	Jul.	Aug.	Sep.	Oct.	Nov.	Dec.
	12°C	13°C	15°C	18°C	22°C	26°C	29°C	29°C	26°C	22°C	17°C	13°C
	54°F	55°F	59°F	64°F	72°F	79°F	84°F	84°F	79°F	72°F	63°F	55°F
	4°C	5°C	7°C	9°C	13°C	17°C	19°C	19°C	17°C	13°C	8°C	5°C
	39°F	41°F	45°F	48°F	55°F	63°F	66°F	66°F	63°F	55°F	46°F	41°F

Naples Sights

Key to symbols

✚ map coordinates refer to the Naples map on page 309 🎟 admission charge: $$$ more than €7, $$ €4–€7, $ less than €4

See page 5 for complete key to symbols

Castel Nuovo

The five massive towers of the 15th-century Castel Nuovo (New Castle) dominate the Naples waterfront. A magnificent Renaissance gateway accesses the central courtyard, which is surrounded by buildings housing the Museo Civico (Civic Museum), the Gothic Sala dei Baroni (Barons' Hall) and the Cappella Palatina (Palatine Chapel), the only surviving part of a 13th-century building.

Nearby is the 17th-century Palazzo Reale (Royal Palace) and the San Carlo opera house.

✚ B2 ✉ Piazza Municipio ☎ 081 420 1241 🕐 Mon.–Sat. 9–7 🚇 R2, R3; tram 1, C55 🍴 Trattoria Medina, see pages 482–483 🎟 $$

Castel dell'Ovo

Encircled by the sea, the Castel dell'Ovo (Egg Castle), Naples' oldest castle, was built between the ninth and 16th centuries. Run down by the 1970s, it has been fully restored and is used for cultural events.

✚ A1 ✉ Borgo Marinaro ☎ 081 764 0590 🚇 R3; tram 1 🍴 La Cantinella, see page 482 🎟 Free

Certosa di San Martino

Visible from all over Naples is the hilltop complex of the Certosa di San Martino (St. Martin's Charterhouse), constructed mainly between the 16th and 18th centuries.

Highlights include the sumptuous baroque church, the arcaded Chiostro Grande (Main Cloister) and the lavishly decorated Quarto del Priore (Prior's Quarters).

Don't miss the exhibition of *presepi* (crib figures), a charming collection of figures and everyday objects fashioned for Christmas cribs in the 19th century, in the Museo Nazionale de San Martino (San Martino National Museum).

Pompeii

The 20,000 inhabitants of Roman Pompeii enjoyed a civilized lifestyle in their prosperous city, with fine civic amenities, temples, public baths, and housing suitable for every taste and pocket. The one drawback was Pompeii's location on the slopes of Vesuvius, an active volcano. In AD 79 its worst eruption occurred, engulfing the city and many of its inhabitants in a thick layer of pumice and volcanic ash. For nearly 1,700 years Pompeii remained buried, perfectly preserved beneath a hard layer of volcanic debris. About 1750 it was rediscovered, excavations started, and gradually the ruins emerged. It's a complete small city that can be explored like any other, wandering the streets and visiting the sites that appeal. It has the main features of every Roman city – the forum, two theaters, an amphitheater, a sports stadium and symmetrical streets laid out in a grid pattern.

Start at the forum and walk through the paved streets, looking into houses and shops. Track down the covered market, the bakery, the laundry and the numerous taverns, some advertising bargain prices on the outside walls. The House of the Vetii, with its lovely garden and frescoed dining room, is a highlight, as is the House of the Tragic Poet, whose owners had a portrait mosaic of their dog displayed by the front door with "cave canem" (beware of the dog) carefully inscribed at the entry.

✚ Page 284, C2 ✉ Pompeii ☎ 081 857 5347; www.pompeiiturismo.it 🕐 Daily 8:30–7:30, Apr.–Oct.; 8:30–5, rest of year 🚇 Circumvesuviana or Trenitalia train to Pompeii Scavi station 🚌 SITA Napoli–Salerno (stop at Piazza Esedra); CSTP No. 4 Salerno Trenitalia –Pompeii (stop at Villa dei Misteri) 🍴 Self-service restaurant and bar outside forum, many in modern Pompeii 🎟 $$$ ✚ Last admission 90 minutes before closing

The elegant glass-roofed Galleria Umberto I arcade has a range of shops and cafés

🚩 A3 ✉ Largo San Martino 5 ☎ 081 578 1769 or 081 229 4498 🕐 Thu.–Tue. 8:30–7:30 🚇 Montesanto 🚌 V1 💷 $$ (price varies according to temporary exhibitions)

Mergellina

This picturesque waterfront area, traditionally the fishermen's quarter, is a delightful place to stroll. Fishing boats and island ferries still leave from the harbor here.

🚩 Off map at A1 ✉ Mergellina 🚇 Mergellina 🚌 R3, C4, C16

Museo Archeologico Nazionale

The Museo Archeologico Nazionale (National Archeological Museum) houses one of the world's most important collections of classical sculpture, mosaics, gems, glass, silver and Egyptian antiquities.

Finds from Pompeii are here; don't miss the graceful fresco portrayal of Flora. The *Farnese Hercules* and *Farnese Bull* are equally impressive; the *Bull* is the largest classical sculptural group to have survived, dating from 200 BC.

Allow two or three hours for your visit to do the museum justice.

🚩 B4 ✉ Piazza Museo Nazionale 19 ☎ 081 292 823

🕐 Wed.–Mon. 9–7:30 🚌 1, 24, 42 🍴 AI 53, see page 482 💷 $$; $$$ during exhibitions

Museo e Gallerie Nazionali di Capodimonte

Built in the 18th century as a palace and museum, and surrounded by a wooded park, Capodimonte has been restored and rearranged. Be sure to see Masaccio's *Crucifixion*, which is the star of the Renaissance painting collection, and the majolica and porcelain exhibits, much of it made by the Capodimonte factory.

🚩 B5 ✉ Parco di Capodimonte, Via Miano 1 ☎ 848 800 288 🕐 Museum: Thu.–Tue. 8:30–7:30. Park: daily 8–1 hour before closing 🚌 C63; metro line 2 to Cavour and then bus M2, 178, 201 💷 Museum $$$; park free

Posillipo e Campi Flegrei

Posillipo and the Campi Flegrei (literally "Burning Fields," named because of the area's volcanic activity) lie east of Naples on a lovely stretch of coast. Classical ruins, fishing villages, beaches, inlets and grottos dot the area, which is well worth exploring.

🚩 Off map at A1 ✉ Posillipo 🚇 Mergellina or Campi Flegrei

Excursion to Capri

A favorite with the Roman emperors, Capri has been a tourist hot spot for more than 150 years. This tiny island, with its lovely scenery and crystal-clear waters, now welcomes more than 2 million visitors annually.

You can travel from Naples' Mergellina or Molo Beverello docks by ferry or hydrofoil, a trip that takes between 50 and 90 minutes. Spectacular views open up back to the city and across to Mount Vesuvius as you approach the hills of the Sorrento peninsula, with the island of Capri lying off its tip. Boats dock at Marina Grande, the island's main harbor.

The charm of Capri lies in the combination of lovely scenery, picturesque villages and a holiday atmosphere. The two main settlements are Anacapri and Capri; their whitewashed houses and narrow, winding streets are crammed with boutiques, outdoor cafés and lively fish restaurants, and many visitors do no more than enjoy these. Most, however, take a boat trip to Capri's most famous sight, the Grotta Azzurra (Blue Grotto), a spectacular sea cave filled with glorious refracted turquoise light. Another highlight is the beautiful Villa San Michele in Anacapri. Built in the late 19th century by Swedish physician Axel Munthe, this dreamlike villa is filled with classical statues. There also is a peaceful green garden, and from its shady pergola you can enjoy some of the island's loveliest views.

Walk to the ruins of Villa Jovis, Emperor Tiberius' clifftop villa, from which he allegedly threw his enemies into the sea. Or stroll to a lookout above the Faraglioni, a cluster of offshore rocks, for beautiful sea views.

Capri ✚ See page 284, C2 ☎ Tourist offices: Banchina del Porto, Marina Grande ☎ 081 837 0634; Piazza Umberto I, Capri ☎ 081 837 0686; Via G. Orlandi 59, Anacapri ☎ 081 837 1524; www.capritourism.com ▣ From Marina Grande to Marina Piccola, Capri and Anacapri ▣ Ferry operator: Caremar, from Molo Beverello, Naples (☎ 081 551 3882 or, within Italy only, 892 123, or, from the U.S., 0011 39 02 2630 2803; www.caremar.it). Hydrofoil operators: Caremar, from Molo Beverello (☎ 081 551 3882 or, within Italy only, 892 123; www.caremar.it); SNAV, from Mergellina (☎ 081 428 5555; www.snav.it). Alilauro (☎ 081 497 2238; www.alilauro.it) and Metro del Mare (☎ 199 600 700; www.metrodelmare.com) also operate ferries and hydrofoils to the islands and points in the Bay of Naples

Blue Grotto ☎ 081 837 0973; www.battelliericapresi.com ◷ Daily 9–1 hour before dusk ▣ From Marina Grande ✋ $$$

Villa San Michele, Anacapri ☎ 081 837 1401; www.villasanmichele.org ◷ Daily 9–6, May–Sep.; 9:30–5 in Apr. and Oct.; 9–4:30 in Mar.; 9–3:30, rest of year ▣ From Capri ✋ $$

Villa Jovis ☎ 081 837 4549 ◷ Daily 9–1 hour before sunset ▣ From Capri ✋ $

Large boats and sailing craft at Marina Grande, Capri, on the Bay of Naples

Venice

No matter how many pictures or films you've seen, nothing can prepare you for the impact of the real Venice (Venezia), one of the world's most captivating cities. Whether it's sparkling in late spring sunshine or shrouded in winter mist, it will enchant you in every way.

Tackling Venice

When you first arrive in Venice, don't head straight for the main sights (which will invariably be packed); take time to get a feel for the city, either from the vantage point of a ferry or by strolling the streets and squares.

As for accommodations, luxury hotels lining the Grand Canal (Canal Grande) are clearly the optimum choice, but

there are many with great charm elsewhere. The *sestieri* (city areas) of Dorsoduro, San Marco, Castello and San Polo are among the nicest parts of the city to stay. Avoid the area around the train station, which is noisy and less attractive and under no circumstances should you stay in Mestre, which is an industrial sprawl across the causeway on the mainland.

Accept that you will do a great deal of tiring walking around the city, and come prepared with comfortable shoes. Make a point of working out your daily itinerary; shortcuts across the city save valuable time. Main routes are clearly marked along the streets by yellow signs.

There are numerous tour options; if time is short these can be helpful, and you'll have the benefit of English-speaking guides.

Venetian Glass, Velvet Slippers

The city's main fashion and leather stores cluster along the Calle dei Fabbri, the Frezzeria and the so-called Mercerie, a district made up of the streets connecting Piazza San Marco with the Rialto area.

Glass is a true Venetian specialty, made for centuries on the island of Murano. Marbled paper, made here for centuries, is another good buy, and Venetian masks make wonderful souvenirs. Other typical products are velvet slippers in jewel-bright colors or a real gondolier's hat; you'll find one at Emilio Ceccato, near the Rialto.

Festivals

Carnival lasts for the 10 days before *martedì grasso* (Shrove Tuesday), the start of Lent, when thousands of people wearing costumes parade the city streets.

The summer sees several ancient festivals, most notably the feast of *La Sensa*, when the mayor and his entourage sail out into the lagoon in the state barge and enact a symbolic

VENICE

0   250   500 metres
0   250   500 yards

N

Canale della Fondamenta Nuove

Palazzo Donà

Palazzo Wildmann

Santa Maria dei Miracoli

Santi Giovanni e Paolo

CAMPO SAN ZANIPOLO

CASTELLO

CAMPO SANTA MARIA FORMOSA

Santa Maria Formosa

Palazzo Querini

Basilica di San Marco

San Zaccaria

Palazzo Prigioni

Palazzo Ducale

S Francesco della Vigna

Scuola di San Giórgio degli Schiavoni

San Giórgio dei Greci

CAMPO BANDIERA E MORO

San Giovanni in Bragora

S M della Visitazione

Museo Storico Navale

Canale di San Marco

San Giórgio Maggiore

Ísola di San Giórgio Maggiore

Teatro Verde

D   E

Gondolas

The shiny black gondola – symbol of Venice – is a shallow-draft vessel propelled by a single oarsman, the gondolier, who stands at the back of the boat. A ride in a gondola is a great Venetian experience for many visitors, but it is expensive and normally follows a set route. Be sure to ascertain what you're getting before you set out.

marriage to the waters. This is followed in July by the *Festa del Redentore*, a thanksgiving festival for deliverence from the plague.

During the *Regata* Storica in September, there are races of spectacular decorated craft, manned by crews in period dress down the Grand Canal.

Essential Information

Tourist Information

Call center ☎ 041 529 8711 (for all offices)
Palazzina dei Santi, Giardini ex Reale
San Marco 71f, Ascenzione
Aeroporto Marco Polo
Stazione Santa Lucia
Gran Viale 6f, Lido di Venezia
Piazzale Roma
www.turismovenezia.it

Urban Transportation

If you arrive by car, you must leave the vehicle in one of the parking lots on the outskirts of the city. The parking at Piazzale Roma is the nearest to the city center. Venice's public transportation system is operated by ACTV (office at Piazzale Roma, ☎ 041 2424; www.actv.it) and uses two types of boats – *vaporetti* (big and slow) and *motoscafi* (small and fast). All are numbered on the front of the boat and follow set routes. *Vaporetti* boats leave from *pontile* (floating docks), which are clearly marked with service numbers and a route map. As the same numbers head in two directions, check that you are going the right way before you board. Tickets (€6.50), valid for 1 hour, can be bought at the *pontile* or at shops showing the ACTV sticker. Save money by buying 12-, 24-, 36-, 48-, 72-hour and 7-day tickets (€16, €18, €23, €28, €33 and €50 respectively). All tickets must be validated before boarding. There is a limited night service on most routes. *Vaporetti* stops are marked on the Venice city map with a "V." *Taxi motoscafi* (water taxis) are fast and

expensive; they can be hailed on various canals, or call ☎ 041 240 6711; www.motoscafivenezia.it. Gondolas can penetrate even the narrowest canals, but are very expensive. As there are only three bridges over the Grand Canal, the seven *traghetti* (ferries) crossing at various points are useful. These ferries are old gondolas and are marked by yellow signs. Pay as you board and watch your balance, as it is customary to stand.

Airport Information

Venice's Marco Polo airport (☎ 041 260 9260; www.veniceairport.com) is 5 miles from the city center on the northern edge of the lagoon, and handles both domestic and international flights. For city connections take a bus (shuttle bus ATVO [☎ 0421 383672; www.atvo.it] or ACTV bus No. 5) from the terminal to the Piazzale Roma at the edge of the city, where the road ends, and then connect with your hotel by *vaporetto* (water bus). The transfer takes 20 minutes by ATVO bus and 25 minutes by ACTV bus; ACTV tickets (€3) must be purchased from the office inside the airport arrivals terminal before boarding; buy ATVO tickets (€3) on the bus. An *Alilaguna* (boat) leaves from the dock outside the terminal for San Marco and the Lido; transfer time is around 50 minutes (☎ 041 240 1701; www.alilaguna.it). The fastest way to reach the city is by water taxi; they leave from the dock outside the terminal and take 20 minutes to reach the center, but are expensive.

Climate – average highs and lows for the month

Jan.	Feb.	Mar.	Apr.	May	Jun.	Jul.	Aug.	Sep.	Oct.	Nov.	Dec.
5°C	8°C	12°C	17°C	21°C	24°C	27°C	26°C	23°C	18°C	12°C	8°C
41°F	46°F	54°F	63°F	70°F	75°F	81°F	79°F	73°F	64°F	54°F	46°F
0°C	2°C	5°C	9°C	13°C	17°C	19°C	18°C	16°C	12°C	7°C	3°C
32°F	36°F	41°F	48°F	55°F	63°F	66°F	64°F	61°F	54°F	45°F	37°F

Venice Sights

Basilica di San Marco

The Basilica di San Marco (St. Mark's Basilica) is a fusion of western and Byzantine styles and is connected to the Doge's Palace. Dating from 1094, it stands on the site of the ninth-century basilica built to house the body of St. Mark.

Pause before entering to admire the Romanesque carvings, then proceed inside to take in the ornate marble pavements; the gem-encrusted altar screen, the Pala d'Oro, a masterpiece of Gothic-Byzantine goldsmith art; and the third-century bronze horses, which once adorned the facade.

⊞ D2 ✉ Piazza San Marco 1 ☎ 041 270 8311; www.basilicasanmarco.it ◷ Mon.–Sat. 9:45–5, Sun. 2–5, Easter–Oct. 31; Mon.–Sat. 9:45–5, Sun. 2–4, rest of year 🚏 1, 2, 41, 42, 52, N ☝ Basilica free; Loggia $; Pala d'Oro $

Ca' d'Oro

The facade of the Ca' d'Oro (House of Gold), so called because it was once gilded, is a perfect example of the finest Venetian-Byzantine architecture.

Behind the facade is a beguiling small museum with an impressive *St. Sebastian* by Andrea Mantegna and a lovely *Madonna* by Giovanni Bellini, as well as sculptural fragments, bronzes and tapestries. All pieces are arranged in rooms around the *palazzo*'s central *portego*, or inner courtyard.

⊞ C4 ✉ Calle di Ca' d'Oro 3932, off Strada Nova ☎ 041 523 8790, reservations: 041 520 0345; www.cadoro.org ◷ Tue.–Sun. 8:15–7:15, Mon. 8:15–2 🚏 1 ☝ $$$

Campanile

The graceful Campanile, Venice's tallest building, is less than 100 years old. The original bell tower, reputedly built in AD 912, collapsed in 1902, killing no one and leaving St. Mark's unscathed. A cry of *"Dov'era e com'era"* ("where it was and how it was") went up, and 10 years later a replica was completed. Take the elevator up for superb views – on a clear day you can see as far as the Alps.

⊞ D2 ✉ Piazza San Marco ☎ 041 522 4064 ◷ Daily 9–9, Jul.–Sep.; 9–7, Apr.–Jun. and in Oct.; 9:30–3:45, rest of year. Closed 3 weeks in Jan. 🚏 1, 2, 41, 42, 51, 52, N ☝ $$$

Canal Grande

The allure of the Canal Grande (Grand Canal), Venice's magical highway, never

Poeple looking onto a canal from the shady loggia of the Ca' d'Oro

Italy

seems to fade. Almost 4 miles long, with an average depth of 16 feet, it divides Venice in two and is crossed by three bridges. The canal is lined with palaces and churches, built over the course of 500 years.

By day numerous boats chug up and down; at night it epitomizes romance, with reflected lights twinkling on the water. Take a No. 1 or No. 2 water bus from stops on the Grand Canal.

➕ B2, B4, C2, C3, C4 🚏 1, 2, N

Collezione Peggy Guggenheim

American Peggy Guggenheim's modern art collection (opened on public view since 1951) is installed in her 18th-century *palazzo* on the Grand Canal. Here you'll find works by Pablo Picasso and Salvador Dalí and fine examples of paintings by Jackson Pollock and Mark Rothko. The garden makes a wonderful background for some Henry Moore sculptures and Marino Marini's *Angel of the Citadel.*

➕ C2 ✉ Palazzo Venier dei Leoni, Dorsoduro 701 ☎ 041 240 5411; www.guggenheim-venice.it ⏰ Wed.–Mon. 10–6 🚏 1, 2 🏛 $$$

Gallerie dell'Accademia

Allow plenty of time to admire the masterpieces in the Gallerie dell'Accademia (Academy Galleries), the finest collection of Venetian painting in the world. Arranged chronologically, the gallery's 24 rooms contain masterpieces such as Giorgio Giorgione's enigmatic *Tempest*, Giovanni Bellini's luminous *Virgins*, and superb works by Mantegna. Don't miss the dramatic *Translation of the Body of St. Mark* by Jacopo Tintoretto and Paolo Veronese's sumptuous *Feast in the House of Levi.*

Among other highlights are the cycles of paintings in rooms 20 and 21; *The Miracle of the True Cross* had several contributors, while the *Life of St. Ursula* is wholly by Vittore Carpaccio.

➕ B2 ✉ Campo della Carità 1023 ☎ 041 522 2247, reservations: 041 520 0345; www.gallerieaccademia.org ⏰ Tue.–Sun. 8:15–7:15, Mon. 8:15–2; last entrance

45 minutes before closure 🚏 1, 2 🍽 Taverna San Trovaso, see page 483 🏛 $$

Museo Storico Navale

Venice's Museo Storico Navale (Maritime Museum) is fittingly housed near the Arsenale, the great shipyards that once manufactured the city's fleets. It tells the story of the city's sea power through superb displays of every type of maritime artifact; the highlight is the collection of gondolas and other historic boats, including a scale model of the Doge's ceremonial barge, the *Bucintoro*, which are housed in one of the Arsenale's old sheds.

➕ E2 ✉ Campo San Biagio 2148 ☎ 041 244 1399 ⏰ Mon.–Fri. 8:45–1:30, Sat. 8:45–1 🚏 1 🏛 $

Palazzo Ducale

The huge Gothic complex of the Palazzo Ducale (Ducal Palace) was the seat of Venice's government, where the Council of Ten met, ambassadors were received and the Doge (Duke) held councils of state. The present building dates from the 15th century, with later alterations following two fires in the 1500s.

The marked route leads through some sumptuous rooms to the vast Sala del Maggior Consiglio (Great Council Chamber), dominated by Jacopo Tintoretto's *Paradiso*, the world's largest oil painting.

The famous Ponte dei Sospiri (Bridge of Sighs) spans a canal to the right of the *palazzo's* waterfront facade.

➕ D2 ✉ Piazzetta San Marco ☎ 041 271 5911; www.museiciviciveneziani.it ⏰ Daily 9–7 (last admission at 6), Nov.–Mar.; 9–5 (last admission at 4), rest of year. Guided tours a.m. only 🚏 1, 2, 41, 42, 51, 52 🏛 $$$ (includes entry to Museo Correr and Museo Archeologico)

Piazza San Marco

The only piazza in Venice (all the others are officially *campi*) is thronged around the clock with strolling and chattering crowds. Go early or late to avoid the worst crush, and marvel at the harmony of this wonderful open space.

The Sala del Maggior Consiglio (Great Council Chamber) in Palazzo Ducale

Highlights here are the 15th-century Torre dell'Orologio (Clock Tower) and its zodiac clock, the graceful architecture of the Libreria Sansoviniana (Sansoviniana Library), and the two columns near the waterfront, topped by the lion of St. Mark and St.Theodore with his crocodile emblem.

➕ D2 ✉ Piazza San Marco 🚢 1, 2, 41, 42, 51, 52, N

Rialto

Throughout the Middle Ages the Rialto was Europe's financial and banking center; the name had the same connotations as does Wall Street now. Today, you can admire the bridge and browse in Venice's food markets, one of the city's great sights. Wander through the fruit and vegetable stalls, but leave time to enjoy the scents and sights of the fish market, full of the day's catch.

➕ C3 ✉ Rialto 🚢 1, 2

San Giorgio Maggiore

To visit the superb Palladian church of San Giorgio Maggiore (St. George the Great), whose serene bulk dominates the view of St. Mark's Basin, you must take a waterbus across the canal of St. Mark's to St. George's island. Built by Andrea Palladio in 1559, the church embodies order, grace and harmony. Take the elevator up the campanile (bell tower) to enjoy fine views across to the Doge's Palace and the Campanile of San Marco.

➕ D1 ✉ Campo San Giorgio, Isole San Giorgio ☎ 041 522 7827 🕐 Daily 9:30–12:20 and 2:30–6, May–Sep.; 9:30–12:30 and 2:30–4:30, rest of year. Mass: Mon.–Sat. 8 a.m., Sun. 11 a.m. 🚢 2 💷 Free; $ (elevator to campanile)

Santa Maria dei Miracoli

The jewel-like church of Santa Maria dei Miracoli (Our Lady of the Miracles) was built around 1480 to house an image of the Madonna credited with reviving a man who spent half-an-hour at the bottom of the Giudecca canal. Pietro Lombardo, who adorned the face of his church with colored marble and porphyry rock, created the harmonious interior as a frame for fine sculpture and beautiful carvings.

➕ D3 ✉ Campo dei Miracoli ☎ 041 275 0462 🕐 Mon.–Sat. 10–5 🚢 1, 2 💷 $ or $$$ "Chorus Pass" for entry to Venice's minor churches (www.chorusvenezia.org)

The church of Santi Giovanni e Paolo

Santa Maria della Salute

During the 1630 plague the Senate promised to build a church in honor of the Virgin if she would save the city. The pestilence passed, an architect was commissioned and the great dome of Santa Maria della Salute (Our Lady of Health and Salvation) rose at the entrance to the Grand Canal. An outstanding skyline feature, the interior has fine sculptures and paintings.

➕ C2 ✉ Campo della Salute 1 ☎ 041 241 1018; www.seminariovenezia.it ⏱ Daily 9–noon and 3–5:30 🚊 1 🍴 Taverna San Trovaso, see page 483

Santa Maria Gloriosa dei Frari

Santa Maria Gloriosa dei Frari (Glorious Virgin Mary of the Brothers), a lofty Franciscan church, is the resting place of Titian and the composer Claudio Monteverdi. Built as a preaching church about 1250, it contains Titian's great *Assumption*, hung over the high altar, and his *Madonna of Ca' Pesaro*. Best of all in the right transept of the church, is Giovanni Bellini's *Madonna and Child with Saints* tryptych, considered among the world's finest paintings.

➕ B3 ✉ Campo dei Frari ☎ 041 272 8611; www.basilicadeifrari.it (Italian only) ⏱ Mon.–Sat. 9–6, Sun. 1–6 🚊 1, 2 💵 $ (accepts multi-church "Chorus Pass" ticket $$$)

Santi Giovanni e Paolo

More than 20 of Venice's doges are buried in the Gothic church of Santi Giovanni e Paolo (St. John and St. Paul), rising majestically on one side of its *campo* (square). The square's focal point is the great equestrian statue of Bartolomeo Colleoni, a 15th-century Venetian army officer who left his wealth to the Republic in return for a monument. The 13th-century church contains many tombs, their monuments representing the best of Venetian medieval sculpture, and some lovely paintings, including Giovanni Bellini's *St. Vincent Ferrer*.

➕ D3 ✉ Campo SS Giovanni e Paolo ☎ 041 523 5913; www.basilicasantigiovanniepaolo.it ⏱ Mon.–Sat. 9–12:30, 3:30–7 and Sun. 3:30–6; closed during services 🚊 41, 42 💵 $

Scuola di San Giorgio degli Schiavoni

Carpaccio painted one of the city's most delightful picture cycles between 1502 and 1508 for the headquarters of Venice's Dalmatian, or Slavic, community – the Scuola di San Giorgio degli Schiavoni (School of St. George of the Slavs). He used Dalmatia's patron saints, St. George, St. Tryphon and St. Jerome, as his inspiration. Highlights are *St. George Slaying the Dragon* and *St. Augustine in his Study*, with his dog.

➕ E3 ✉ Calle dei Furlani 3259/a ☎ 041 522 8828 ⏱ Tue.–Sat. 9:15–1, Sun. 2:45–6, Apr.–Oct.; Tue.–Sat. 10–12:30, Sun. 3–6, rest of the year 🚊 1, 2, 52 🍴 Da Franz, see page 483 💵 $$

Scuola Grande di San Rocco

In 1564 the brotherhood of St. Roche ran a competition to choose an artist to decorate the walls of the Scuola Grande di San Rocco (Grand Meeting Halls of the Confraternity of St. Roche). Tintoretto (real name Jacopo Robusti) won, and spent 23 years working on a stupendous cycle of 54 paintings, including the wonderful *Crucifixion*. New Testament scenes line the walls of the ground floor's main hall. Works on the staircase are by other artists.

➕ B3 ✉ Campo San Rocco ☎ 041 523 4864; www.scuolagrandesanrocco.it ⏱ Daily 9–5:30 🚊 1, 2 💵 $$

The Lagoon Islands

You can spend a delightful day exploring some of the islands in the lagoon. Most visitors opt for Murano, famous for its glass; Burano, with its lace-making; or Torcello, a virtually uninhabited island with an ancient cathedral and church. Guided excursions run to all three, but a more flexible option is to take the LN (Laguna Nord) boat, which leaves from the Fondamenta Nuove and takes around 40 to 50 minutes to reach Burano and (with a shuttle boat) Torcello.

Murano: Venetian glass has been made here since 1291, when the furnaces were moved away from the city to avoid the constant danger of fire. A visit to the fascinating Museo del Vetro (Glass Museum) will give you an idea of glass-blowers' skills through the ages. Murano also has two exquisite churches: San Pietro Martire, which contains a glowing altarpiece by Giovanni Bellini; and Santi Maria e Donato, a beautiful 12th-century basilica with a colonnaded exterior apse and fine mosaics on its walls and floor.

Burano: Here, colorful canalside houses, narrow streets and sun-splashed squares are as picturesque as anything in Venice itself. This is still a fishing community, with a robust workaday atmosphere, and you'll see moored fishing boats and nets drying in the sun. Local women have always been skilled lace-makers, and you can admire the fragility of their exquisite work in the Lace Museum (Museo del Merletto).

Torcello: This is one of the most evocative and magical places in Venice. The sleepy island, with its overgrown canals and green fields, was the lagoon's first settled area, and once had fine buildings and palaces. A combination of the build up of silt and outbreaks of malaria caused its 12th-century decline. Today the only remaining signs of its past importance are the Cathedral of Santa Maria Assunta and the adjacent church, Santa Fosca. The cathedral's main glories are two 12th-century mosaics, which completely cover the apse and the opposite rear wall. High above the seventh-century altar stands a lovely *Byzantine Madonna and Child*, its poignant beauty highlighted by the simple gold background, while the graphic *Judgment* scenes make a telling contrast. The campanile (tower) is solid and square. The nearby church of Santa Fosca, with its arcaded porch full of nesting swifts, is lovely in its own way.

Modern glassware is still made on the island of Murano

Luxembourg

Opposite: Medieval tranquility on the Alzette river in the district of Grund, Luxembourg City

Luxembourg

Luxembourg lies at the heart of the European landmass. It is a minuscule country, measuring 51 miles from north to south and a mere 32 miles from east to west. Belgium lies to the north and west, France to the south and Germany to the east. Because of its attractive financial laws and constitutional stability, it has become a center of European politics and finance.

And despite a rather turbulent history, Luxembourg retains its independence and sovereignty; it is a true survivor of the Continent's stormy past.

Luxembourg Landscapes

Luxembourg is a Grand Duchy, the only one in the world, with the city of Luxembourg as its main focus, although its rural areas are remarkably varied for such a small country.

They include part of the delightful Ardennes region, the hilly area that lies across the northern third of Luxembourg

Château de Bourscheid

and extends into Belgium. The Ardennes have a distinctive landscape of forested plateaus sliced through by deep valleys that are drained by beautiful rivers. Fairy-tale castles crown wooded bluffs. At Vianden, a medieval castle, one of the Grand Duchy's finest historic sites, dominates the landscape. The equally magnificent Bourscheid Castle stands guard above the winding Sûre and Wark rivers. At Clervaux, the castle is matched in impact by the red-roofed Benedictine Clervaux Abbey, which stands amid the wooded heights above the beautiful town.

At the southern edge of the Ardennes, in the area where the hills meet the flatter, more fertile land known as Le Cour du Bon Pays, or "The Good Land," lies the picturesque little town of Diekirch. Only a short distance southwest is Ettelbrück, where there is a monument to General George S. Patton Jr. and the General Patton Memorial Museum containing many personal items from his life.

The most southerly part of Luxembourg is the country's economic powerhouse. Here in the "Good Land" are farms and orchards, forests and even more castles. In fact, the lovely valley of the Eisch river is known as the Vallée des Sept Châteaux (Valley of the Seven Castles).

Farther south from the city of Luxembourg is Les Terres Rouges, or

More Top Destinations in Luxembourg

- Abbaye Benédictine C3
- Abbaye St.-Maurice et St.-Maur B4
- Château Bourscheid B3
- Diekirch B3
- Esch-sur-Sûre A3
- Grevenmacher C2
- Mondorf-les-Bains B1
- Vallée du Müllerthal B2
- Vallée des Sept Châteaux A2
- Vianden B3

"The Land of the Red Rocks" around the towns of Dudelange and Pétange, home to much of the country's industry.

East of here is Mondorf-les-Bains, a fashionable spa town on the edge of the famous Moselle region. This area, running north to south along the border with Germany, is Luxembourg's wine-growing district, which has a heritage of more than 2,000 years.

Exploring the Country

You will find Luxembourgers are very cosmopolitan and friendly, and a large percentage of them speak English. The Grand Duchy has an excellent road system and distances are short between the many towns and villages, making independent travel a good option. There also are numerous day-trips organized from the city of Luxembourg.

Timeline

AD 963	Count Siegfried of the Ardennes builds a castle called the Lützelburg ("Little Castle") on the Bock promontory.
1354	Luxembourg becomes a duchy.
1447	The Duchy of Luxembourg comes under the rule of the Habsburgs through marriage.
1542	The city of Luxembourg is captured by the French.
1554	The Spanish capture the city of Luxembourg.
1713	Under the terms of the Treaty of Utrecht, Luxembourg is controlled by the Kingdom of the Netherlands.
1815	Congress of Vienna establishes the Grand Duchy of Luxembourg as a sovereign, neutral state.
1839	Under the terms of the Treaty of London, the western part of the Grand Duchy is ceded to Belgium.
1867	Luxembourg becomes an independent state.
1914	Germany occupies Luxembourg in World War I.
1940	Germany invades Luxembourg again in World War II.
1944	American troops liberate Luxembourg; Germany launches its "Ardennes Offensive."The Battle of the Bulge follows.
1945	Luxembourg becomes a member of the United Nations.
1948	Luxembourg joins Belgium and the Netherlands in forming BENELUX, a trading and economic union.
1949	Luxembourg abandons neutrality and joins NATO.
1958	Luxembourg becomes a founding member of the European Economic Community (now known as the European Union).
1992	Luxembourg ratifies the Maastricht Treaty.
1994	City of Luxembourg declared a World Heritage Site by UNESCO.
2009	The Cabinet announces a relaxation of banking secrecy laws to help cut global tax evasion.

Luxembourg: the Great Survivor

Luxembourg, with its long history at the heart of Europe, has secured a major part in the working of the European Union. The country today is a constitutional monarchy ruled by HRH Grand Duke Henri, who heads a Cabinet of 12 ministers appointed from an elected Chamber of Deputies. Consensus politics is used in Luxembourg's government, and coalitions of more than one party usually hold power. On the international front, Luxembourg is home to, among others, the General Secretariat of the European Parliament, the European Court of Justice, the Court of Auditors, the European Bank of Investment, the Plenary Hall of the European Parliament and several Directorates of the European Commision – all of which are based in the city of Luxembourg's Centre Européen (European Center).

Sidewalk cafés amid the downtown bustle of the city of Luxembourg

Survival Guide

■ The *Schueberfouer* (☎ 4796-4294; www.fouer.lu), one of Europe's largest city fairs, takes place for nearly three weeks from mid-August to early September.

■ Most shops in the city of Luxembourg are closed on Monday until noon and may close Tuesday through Friday between noon and 2 p.m., but often stay open until 8 p.m. on Thursdays.

■ There are numerous stores in the Gare district of the city of Luxembourg, especially on avenue de la Liberté.

■ Enjoy an evening in the Grund district. There are lovely areas, good bars and restaurants, and a different ambience from the city center, which is known as the Ville area.

■ Earthenware bird whistles (*peckvillerchers*) are a popular present given on Easter Monday, when their sound fills the air.

■ The city of Luxembourg has many designer shops, such as Hermès, Dolce & Gabbana, Armani, Louis Vuitton and Claudia Sträter along Grande-Rue and rue Philippe II. There also are tempting treats in Leonidas, the renowned Belgian chocolatiers.

■ Typical Luxembourg souvenirs include cast iron from the Mersch foundry, in the heart of the Grand Duchy. Designs incorporate castles and coats of arms. Authentic Luxembourg porcelain and earthenware are produced by Villeroy & Boch (330 rue du Rollingergrund, Luxembourg City ☎ 46 82 13 17; www.villeroy-boch.com; factory shop ◑ Mon.–Fri. 9:30–7, Sun. 9:30–6).

■ If you travel in the Moselle wine-producing region, enjoy some of Luxembourg's dry white and sparkling vintages, such as the subtle Rivaner; Pinot Blanc to go with fish dishes; or the strong Pinot Gris to complement a meal of *judd mat gaardebounen* (roast, smoked pork).

■ Children will love the Jardin des Papillons (exotic butterfly garden; route de Trèves, Grevenmacher ☎ 75 85 39; www.papillons.lu ◑ Daily 9:30–5, Apr. to mid-Oct. ⚑ $$$). They also will enjoy Parc Merveilleux (route de Mondorf, Bettembourg ☎ 51 10 48-1; www.parc-merveilleux.lu ◑ Daily 9:30–6, early Apr. to mid-Oct. ⚑ $$$), at the southern tip of Luxembourg, where there are attractions from fairy-tale tableaux and exotic birds and reptiles to children's animal enclosures and children's games of all types.

City of Luxembourg

The city of Luxembourg is known as the landlocked "Gibraltar of the North" because of its once-fortified location. It is set above the cliffs that flank the canyon-like valleys of the Alzette and Pétrusse rivers. Today, the city of Luxembourg is more fairy tale than fortress. The old city, especially, is a pleasing mix of the past and present. Its elegant towers, spires and turrets and its walls of golden sandstone helped win Luxembourg the UNESCO designation of World Heritage Site in 1994.

The steep-sided plateau on which Luxembourg stands explains its origins. The Romans first set up camp here. They had one eye on military control and the other on the advantages of a strategic trading position at the crossroads of northern Europe. In AD 963, Count Siegfried of the Ardennes built a castle on the narrow Bock promontory above the Alzette river.

Over the next 900 years, Luxembourg evolved into one of the mightiest fortifications in Europe. In 1867, the terms of the 1831 Treaty of London were applied, and Luxembourg became a neutral state. The military fortress was dismantled and the encircling walls were replaced by wide outer boulevards.

Ville and *Gare*

The main parts of the city of Luxembourg are the city center, known as *Ville*, perched on the high plateau above the Pétrusse and Alzette river valleys; and the more modern district, known as *Gare*, south of the river. The two are connected by bridges across the Pétrusse valley; the main ones are the pont Adolphe and the pont Viaduc, the latter known locally as *Passerelle*. Below the cliffs lies Grund, the main part of the city's valley settlements.

The area around the railroad station is emphatically modern and downtown. Buses leave regularly from outside the station and take you to place E.-Hamilius, on the western side of *Ville*. From here a short walk east along rue de la Poste leads to the large central square of place d'Armes.

At the east end of place d'Armes is the handsome City Hall (Palais Municipal, or Cercle). Nearby in place Guillaume II is the Luxembourg City Tourist Office. Ask here for details on guided tours and the LuxembourgCard, which is good for one, two or three days and costs €10, €17 and €24 respectively. Two- and three-day cards must be used within two weeks and give free entry to 56 museums and attractions plus reductions to 10 other sites and free use of public transportation in the Grand Duchy (www.ont.lu/card-en.html).

The maze-like streets of the Old Town (Vieille Ville, see page 332) and the complex of steps and terraces that connect plateau and valley floor make Luxembourg a very walkable place.

Conversation and Music

The place d'Armes is a public space shaded by lime trees. In summer it is filled with the chairs and tables of the surrounding restaurants and cafés, where you can enjoy the hum of relaxed conversation and the music of regular concerts on the nearby bandstand.

All around the place d'Armes are the city's pedestrian-only shopping streets. To the north is Grande-Rue, known locally as Groussgaass, the city's main shopping street. Here, and in the

A Lift in Luxembourg

You can reach the riverside Grund district in the Alzette valley by public elevator from place du St.-Esprit, near the intersection with boulevard F. D.-Roosevelt. Look for the glass-fronted elevator shelter in the corner of the place du St.-Esprit. The elevator takes you to a tunnel that emerges at montée du Grund.

adjoining streets of rue Phillipe II and rue des Capucins, are fashion boutiques, as well as good restaurants and cafés. Stop for coffee at Namur, on the corner of Grande-Rue and rue des Capucins. At the east end of Grande-Rue look for the fountain known as Hämmelsmarsch, "The March of the Sheep."

Exploring Historic Luxembourg

To reach historic Luxembourg, leave the southeast corner of place d'Armes, where a covered passage leads between bookshops and into the large place Guillaume II. A colorful flower and vegetable market is held here on Wednesdays and Saturdays.

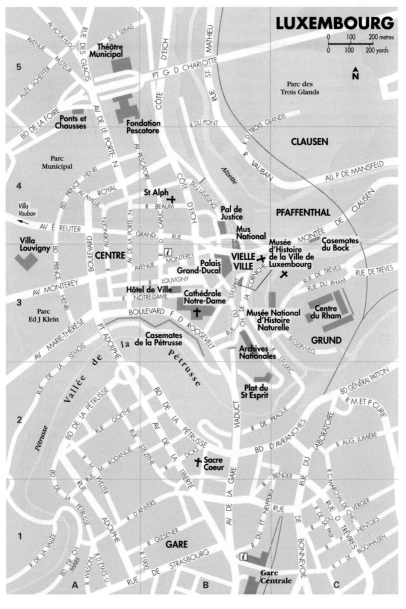

From here you can quickly reach the Grand-Ducal Palace on rue du Marché-aux-Herbes.

Behind the palace lies the Old Town (Vieille Ville). Look for rue de l'Eau, with its cluster of restaurants known as Îlot Gastronomique. Then head down rue Sigefroi to the stunning viewpoint of the Bock, above the Alzette valley.

From here you can see the famous pont Grande-Duchesse Charlotte, known as the Red Bridge because of its color. It connects the city center plateau with the Kirchberg plateau and the ultramodern European Center (Centre Européen), home of numerous European Union institutions (see page 326).

Visit the famous Bock Casemates, the maze of underground tunnels in the cliffs, and then walk the Chemin de la Corniche, the terrace that leads south above the Alzette valley.

Discover the valley district of Grund, a riverside haven of well-preserved old houses, restaurants and taverns. From here you can turn left and wander along the paths and terraced lanes of the Alzette to reach the 17th-century riverside church of St. John (Saint-Jean Baptiste), with its rich baroque altar and famous Black Madonna statue.

The city center (Ville) is more relaxed than other European cities, although city life is sophisticated in its restrained way. Fine music can be enjoyed at the city's Grand Théâtre de la Ville de Luxembourg, Philharmonie Luxembourg and Music Conservatory. The top fashion stores of Grande-Rue speak for themselves, and Ville restaurants are excellent.

Essential Information

Tourist Information
Luxembourg National Tourist Office
Gare Centrale (Central Station)
☎ 42 82 82 20; www.ont.lu or www.visitluxembourg.lu
Luxembourg City Tourist Office
30 place Guillaume II, Luxembourg City
☎ 22 28 09; www.lcto.lu

Urban Transportation
Buses are the only form of public transportation in the city of Luxembourg. Visitors will probably require the service only between the airport or the railroad station and the city terminus at place E.-Hamilius as the city is largely pedestrian-only and most places are within walking distance. A flat fare of €1.50 is valid for two hours or you can buy a pack of 10 tickets for €12. Buses run daily from 5 a.m.–midnight. For information ☎ 47 96 29 75; www.autobus.lu. Taxis are expensive, but can be hired by calling City Taxis Centrale ☎ 48 00 58; www.citytaxis.lu

Airport Information
Luxembourg's Findel Airport (☎ 24 56 50 50; www.luxairport.lu) is located 4 miles east of the city of Luxembourg. Public bus No. 16 runs every 10–15 minutes (30 minutes on Sundays) between the airport and the city center and railroad station (journey time is 25 minutes, fare €1.50, plus €1.50 for baggage, which can be refused during peak periods if too bulky). Taxis between the airport and city are expensive (around €25) ☎ 48 00 58; www.citytaxis.lu

Climate – average highs and lows for the month

Jan.	Feb.	Mar.	Apr.	May	Jun.	Jul.	Aug.	Sep.	Oct.	Nov.	Dec.
3°C	4°C	9°C	14°C	18°C	21°C	23°C	22°C	19°C	13°C	7°C	4°C
37°F	39°F	48°F	57°F	64°F	70°F	73°F	72°F	66°F	55°F	45°F	39°F
-2°C	0°C	2°C	4°C	8°C	11°C	13°C	12°C	10°C	6°C	3°C	0°C
28°F	32°F	36°F	39°F	46°F	52°F	55°F	54°F	50°F	43°F	37°F	32°F

City of Luxembourg Sights

Casemates

The great cliffs of the Pétrusse and Alzette valleys are honeycombed with tunnels, stairways and chambers called the Casemates, hollowed out of rock during the 17th and 18th centuries. Originally the network of Casemates measured over 14 miles and accommodated thousands of soldiers. There was room for the stabling of their horses, and for all the garrison supply services.

Today about 10 miles of the Casemates survive. Two sections, the Casemates du Bock (Bock Casemates) and the Casemates de la Pétrusse (Pétrusse Casemates), are open to the public in summer (see also Fortress Luxembourg, page 333).

Casemates du Bock ✚ C4 ✉ montée de Clausen ☎ 22 28 09 (4796-2709 for guided tours) 🕐 Daily 10–5, Mar.–Oct. 🚌 7, 9 💷 $

Casemates de la Pétrusse ✚ B3 ✉ place de la Constitution ☎ 22 28 09 (4796-2709 for guided tours) 🕐 Daily 11–4, Jul.–Sep. (also 11–4, Easter and Whitsunday) 🚌 All city center buses 💷 $

Cathédrale Notre-Dame

The steeples of the 17th-century Cathédrale Notre-Dame (Cathedral of Our Lady) form a striking part of the city's skyline. Inside, the high altar is a shrine to Our Lady, "Comforter of the Afflicted." Stone steps lead to the crypt; at the rear, two bronze lions guard the barred entrance to the burial chamber of the grand-ducal family. A sarcophagus lies in a dark blue marble setting.

The steeples of Cathédrale Notre-Dame

✚ B3 ✉ rue Notre-Dame ☎ 22 29 70–1; www.cathedrale.lu 🕐 Mon.–Sat. 10–noon and 2–5:30, Sun. 2–5:30, except during services 🚌 No buses in city center 💷 Free

Musée d'Histoire de la Ville de Luxembourg

A late 1990s restoration of the Musée d'Histoire de la Ville de Luxembourg (Luxembourg City History Museum) has created a superb must-see venue. Take care in some rooms where sunken channels containing hidden lighting run around the edges of the room. The museum is located in four old 17th-, 18th- and 19th-century, six-story town houses. This is a sophisticated, interactive museum; visitors are given a card to operate audiovisual displays and touch screens that explain the city's history from the 10th century to the present day. Follow the room numbers counterclockwise, and do not miss a trip in the glass elevator that rises through layers of history and architecture.

✚ B3 ✉ 14 rue du St.-Esprit ☎ 47 96 45 00; www.mhvl.lu 🕐 Tue.–Sun. 10–6 (also Thu. 6–8 p.m.) 🚌 No buses in city center 🍴 Café 💷 $$$

Musée National d'Histoire Naturelle

The Musée National d'Histoire Naturelle (National Museum of Natural History),

The magnificent Palace of the Grand Dukes is on a city street

or Natur Musée (Nature Museum), is tucked away in the Grund area, below the cliffs.

The museum is housed in the old Hospice of St. John, later a women's prison and the building's splendid entrance survives. It features interactive activities of a geological and geographical nature, plus information on local flora and fauna, and landscapes. ✚ C3 ✉ 25 rue Münster ☎ 46 22 33-1; www.mnhn.lu 🕐 Tue.–Sun. 10–6 🚌 6, 23 🍴 Café 💷 $$$

Palais Grand-Ducal

The Palais Grand-Ducal (Palace of the Grand Dukes), home to Grand Duke Jean of Luxembourg, is on rue du Marché-aux-Herbes. The building is a much-renovated and extended replacement of a medieval town hall, which was destroyed in a fire in 1554. The 16th-century Spanish rulers of Luxembourg rebuilt it 20 years after the fire, and you can see the architectural influences of southern Spain in its Renaissance facade.

The interiors are exquisite, especially the Main Hall, the King's Room and the Banqueting Hall. ✚ B3 ✉ 17 rue du Marché-aux-Herbes 🕐 Guided tours run Mon.–Fri. 2:30–5, Sat. 10–11, mid-Jul. to early Sep. English-language tours only Mon.–Fri. 4:30. Contact the Luxembourg City Tourist Office for details (☎ 22 28 09) 🚌 No buses in city center 💷 $$$

Vieille Ville

Luxembourg City's Vieille Ville (Old Town) lies between the rear of the Palais

Grand-Ducal and the Bock promontory. The area of the Old Town is small, lying within narrow streets and squares such as rue de l'Eau, rue de la Loge, rue du Rost and the Marché aux Poissons (Fish Market).

The feeling of medieval Luxembourg is palpable here, although today's fine streets and buildings hardly reflect the din and dirt of those days. The market was once the heart of the community outside the castle walls.

Down rue Sigefroi from the Marché aux Poissons is Église Saint-Michel (St. Michael's Church – open daily 10–5, except during religious functions; admission is free). It is the oldest church in the city and is built on the site of the 10th-century castle church, but its oldest surviving parts date from the 17th century. The church's baroque altar is superb, and there is a wonderfully vivid carved oak pietà. ✚ B3

Villa Vauban (Galerie d'Art de la Ville de Luxembourg)

The elegant Villa Vauban (Luxembourg City Art Gallery) stands in City Park, on the foundation of the former Vauban Fort. The gallery has an excellent permanent collection of the works of Dutch and Flemish masters and of later European painters, and hosts many temporary exhibitions. ✚ Off map at A4 ✉ 18 avenue Emile Reuter ☎ 47 96 45 65; www.villavauban.lu 🕐 Mon., Wed.–Thu., and Sat.–Sun. 10–6, Fri. 10–9. Closed Tue. 🚌 1, 2, 3, 7 💷 $$$

Fortress Luxembourg

The history of the city of Luxembourg as a medieval fortress is fascinating. Ringed by impregnable cliffs on every side but the west, it was easy to secure the western approach by building a defensive wall. The narrow and rocky Bock promontory offered the first natural fortification.

It was here on this narrow shelf, 300 feet above the Alzette valley, that prehistoric settlers may have established a camp. The Romans built their own fortifications on the Bock and called it Castellum Lucilinburhuc. Then, in AD 963, Count Siegfried of the Ardennes built his castle and linked it to the main plateau by a drawbridge. This Lützelburg, the "Little Castle," gave the city and the country its present name.

By 1050 a defensive western wall nearly 30 feet high, with numerous towers and gateways, protected the castle and the community that was growing around it to the west. Soldiers and knights were billeted within Siegfried's fort, while traders and artists began to settle outside of its walls. This then gave the first impression of an upper and a lower city area, until the 12th century when stone ramparts were built to define the whole city.

In 1554 a massive explosion of stored gunpowder destroyed much of the settlement. New fortifications were built during a period of Spanish rule. They included excavation of the Pétrusse Casemates (Casemates de la Pétrusse, see page 331); the Beck Bastion; and the ramparts known today as the Corniche and dubbed the "Balcony of Europe" because of the spectacular views.

In the late 17th century Vauban, the French military engineer, reshaped and extended the ramparts. In the 18th century the Austrians extended them once more and excavated the Bock Casemates (Casemates du Bock, see page 331). Such was the strategic importance of Luxembourg as a fortification that all buildings on the Bourbon Plateau, where *Gare* (the modern town) now stands, were built of wood so that they could be quickly destroyed before an attack on the fortress, thus robbing the enemy of any cover.

On May 11, 1867, Luxembourg became an independent state. As part of the agreement, and after nearly a thousand years, the city's fortifications were dismantled or destroyed. At that time, the fortress walls enclosed an area to the west that was larger than the city.

What remains today are the Casemates, the retaining walls of the cliffs and ruins concentrated on the cliff edges, all adding to the city's already spectacular position. City boulevards and parkland lie where great walls and towers once protected the western approach.

The Bock Casemates above the Alzette river and alongside St. John's Church in the Grund

The Netherlands

Opposite: This historic windmill in Zaanse Schans is part of a collection

The Netherlands

The Netherlands is a country where freedom has come with responsibility and hard work. It is a country where the word "land" means something special – a valuable resource won from the sea. For, in literal terms, when you walk on dry land in The Netherlands, your head is barely above sea level in some places, and well below it in others. Amsterdam itself is 10 feet below sea level.

Dutch Icons

To the outside world, the enduring image of The Netherlands is of a land unremittingly flat, crisscrossed by canals and dotted with windmills. Popular imagination conjures up pictures of clogs, cheese and swaths of brightly colored tulips. Then there is Amsterdam, the lively, lovely and evocative capital, seen by many as a slightly wicked city.

The Netherlands is, of course, a far more complex and fascinating entity than such assumptions imply. Although the country is often known as Holland, this name actually only relates to the country's heavily populated western

Buildings along Prinsengracht Canal, Amsterdam

provinces of Noord (North) and Zuid (South) Holland. These provinces contain the main cities, such as Amsterdam, Rotterdam and The Hague (Den Haag), known collectively as the Randstad, or "Ring Town."

Compared with this heavily urbanized area, The Netherlands' other provinces offer the visitor a remarkably diverse landscape and regional cultures that will correct any misconception that the country is homogeneous.

Land from the Sea

The Netherlands is a small country, just over 15,500 square miles in area. Its eastern neighbor, Germany, is nine times larger. To the south lies Belgium, once part of the United Provinces of The Netherlands (see page 50) but an independent nation since 1830. To the north and west of The Netherlands lies the North Sea, and it is with this near neighbor that the Dutch have their most pressing relationship. You will not be too aware of the sea in Amsterdam or The Hague. You will need to go north to Noord Holland and Friesland, or south to Zeeland, to fully appreciate the astonishing control over their watery environment that the Dutch have engineered.

For the definitive story of land reclamation, visit the fascinating Zuiderzeemuseum in Enkhuizen or travel across the Afsluitdijk, a 20-mile dam that seals the great inland lake of IJsselmeer and connects Noord Holland to Friesland.

You could go south to Zeeland, a glittering mosaic of water within a vast web of land. There you'll want to visit the Delta Expo at Neeltje Jans in Zeeland to learn about the Delta Plan, a massive engineering program. This system of huge dams and movable barriers was built after the storm-driven North Sea breached the existing dykes during a high spring tide in 1953, killed more than 1,800 people and devastated the countryside.

Exploring Inland

Beyond these water lands – and beyond the great dunes and beaches of the North Sea coast, and the red, white and neon-bright lights of downtown Amsterdam – lie the delights of the landlocked Netherlands.

In the south, Limburg is known as the Dutch "hill country." In the province of Noord Brabant, the De Kempen region's landscape of sandy heath and woodland is a very different image from that of the "flat" Holland most people envision. You can explore Gelderland

meadows and orchards; the serene villages and waterways of Overijssel;

More Top Destinations in The Netherlands

- Arnhem B2
- De Hoge Veluwe B2
- Delta Expo A2
- Edam B3
- Enkhuizen B3
- Haarlem B3
- Het Loo B3
- Heusden B2
- Keukenhof B3
- Maastricht B1
- Orvelte C3
- Scheveningen A2
- Utrecht B2
- Zwolle C3

De Magere Brug (The Skinny Bridge) over the Amstel opens to allow a barge pass through

and the moorlands and flower-filled bogs of Drenthe, so beloved by Vincent van Gogh. They all add to the variety of rural Netherlands. In the north country in Groningen, the quintessential Dutch images of windmills, clogs and flat green landscapes reassert themselves. In neighboring Friesland you will find another country altogether, a province with its own language and distinctive cultural heritage.

Reaching these fascinating districts is not difficult since public transportation in The Netherlands is efficient and generally inexpensive. Virtually every place is within a three-hour train ride of Amsterdam.

Excellent bus services run between cities, and there is an extensive bus network linking towns and villages in the provinces.

Driving in rural areas is convenient and reasonably straightforward, but in urban areas it can be stressful. Regular ferry services connect the mainland with the islands farther afield.

The Dutch

The Dutch people are self-confident and accomplished, qualities that have evolved from their history and surroundings. Although they could easily boast of the way in which their environment has been mastered, they are refreshingly modest and restrained. Once the ice is broken, however, people are enthusiastic and friendly, and show tolerance and mutual respect for others.

Pancakes and Beer

Contemporary Dutch cuisine, especially fish dishes, is fast reversing the view that Dutch food is dull. In larger cities – especially in Amsterdam – Holland's colonial past has left a fine tradition of Indonesian cooking. Most hotels have plentiful buffet breakfasts, including smoked meats, pickled herring and a variety of cheeses. For a traditional lunch try *erwtensoep*, a satisfying soup of peas and pork, accompanied by a hunk of crusty bread; or *uitsmijter*, an open sandwich of ham with cheese, topped

pannekoek, pancakes with *stroop* (molasses) or *poedersuiker* (powdered sugar). If you're on the move, street stalls also serve a smaller type of pancake, *poffertjes*.

As in Belgium, beer is the most popular drink. Dutch beers tend to be lighter, although you will know that you are drinking something substantial when you sample lager in a Dutch "brown café" – a traditional bar. An excellent and popular light beer is Grölsch, often drunk with meals as a replacement for wine. Heavier Belgian beers also are available, as is *jenever*, a grain spirit. *Oude jenever* is the sweetest; *jonge* is for the stronger palate. These and vintage gins and liqueurs can be enjoyed in a *proeflokaal*, or "tasting house."

Porcelain and Jewelry

Some stores in Holland are closed all day Sunday and on Monday morning, but many open every day, and stores in the larger cities usually stay open late one night a week. Cities such as Amsterdam and The Hague have a variety of international clothing stores, but the real shopping experience is in the antiques and craft districts, looking for such specialties as jewelry and porcelain. In the provinces, look around and you will find some excellent regional buys.

with a fried egg. For dinner have a *hutspot* stew of vegetables, smoked bacon and meat; or *stampott*, mashed potatoes and vegetables with smoked sausage or bacon. For more exotic experiences, eat Indonesian specialties, especially *rijsttafel* ("rice table"), or any of several dozen other spiced, sauced, tangy, exquisite dishes. For sweets try

Blue-and-white Delft ceramics are known throughout the world

Timeline

AD 50	Iron Age Frisian and Batavi tribes settle in present-day Netherlands.
751	Charlemagne, the Holy Roman Emperor, rules the Low Countries, the lands alongside the North Sea.
12th century	Herring fishermen settle at the mouth of the Amstel river, later site of Amsterdam.
1519	Charles V of Spain is crowned Holy Roman Emperor; the Low Countries come under Spanish rule.
1566–67	Repression by Spain leads to lengthy struggle against Spanish control.
1579	Formation of Republic of the United Provinces of The Netherlands.
1602	Formation of Dutch East India Company; "Golden Age" of Amsterdam as a world trading center lasts for most of the 17th century.
1815	Northern and southern Netherlands become a united kingdom after fall of Napoleon.
1831	Southern Netherlands becomes independent of Belgium.
1914–18	The Netherlands remains neutral during World War I.
1940	Germany invades The Netherlands; Amsterdam finally liberated in 1945.
1947	Formation of Benelux Trade Treaty between Belgium, The Netherlands and Luxembourg.
1957	The Netherlands signs up as a founding member of the European Community.
1980	Queen Beatrix is crowned.
2002	The Netherlands adopts the euro as its official currency.
2004	Queen Mother Juliana, who ruled for 32 years from 1948, dies at age 92.

Tulips

Tulips are a universal symbol of the country. They also are part of the Dutch flower trade, which accounts for 60 percent of the world market in exported flowers. In the 17th century the importation of tulip bulbs from Turkey led to "tulip mania;" during the 1630s, single bulbs sold for thousands of dollars. The tulip has been a major focus of Dutch flower growing since, although carnations, roses and chrysanthemums outsell tulips today. The great floral explosion is in late April, when the fields just inland from the east coast are vibrant with color. Visit the Keukenhof Gardens at Lisse, north of Leiden, for floral extravaganzas from about mid-March to late May.

Tulips at the Keukenhof Gardens; this 79-acre historic park is situated between The Hague and Amsterdam

Survival Guide

■ Large cities have regulated routes for pedestrians, cyclists, trams and automobiles. Next to the sidewalk there may be a bicycle lane. Always remember that bicycles approach silently, and always check to your left. Beyond the cycle lane you may find a second sidewalk, then a tram track, then the main thoroughfare for buses and automobiles. This sequence is the same on both sides of the road. Remember that trams also approach quietly from the left.

■ There are few public restrooms, and those that exist are not known for their cleanliness. Railroad and bus stations, restaurants and the bigger cafés have public bathrooms with attendants. You are expected to pay about 10 or 20 cents to use them.

■ Eating out in The Netherlands is considered a fashion event as much as an eating experience. The Dutch tend to dress their best when going out for a meal, although attitudes are gradually relaxing.

■ You may tip for good restaurant service. Always tell the waiter or waitress that you're tipping them, and the amount; don't leave a cash tip on the table when you leave.

■ You may be tempted to sample raw herring. Follow local custom: Dip the herring in a bowl of diced onions, hold it by its tail, tip your head back, and savor.

■ For tasty snacks, try the always-available *patat* (french fries) with mayonnaise or spicy sauce dips; *kroketten*, small rolls of meat filling covered in bread crumbs and fried; and pickled herring or smoked eel. *Broodjes* are baguettes filled with smoked sausage, spicy meat and delicious cheeses.

■ If you buy a present in a shop, especially chocolates, tell the assistant that it is a present and it will often be carefully wrapped in gift paper.

■ If you buy Delftware porcelain, make sure the trade name has a D, and buy from reputable outlets only.

Amsterdam

Amsterdam's past, canals and decorative buildings have all combined to make it one of the most exciting and seductive capitals in western Europe.

The city began life in the 12th century, when fishermen built a dam across the mouth of the Amstel river and settled nearby in wooden houses. Amsterdam developed on reclaimed land around a network of canals. By the end of the 17th century the city was the world's leading commercial port, its success was based on entrepreneurial skills.

For most of the 18th century Amsterdam prospered – until its ships lost command of the seas to England. The city became the capital of the Netherlands in 1813. During World

War II, Amsterdam was occupied by the Germans. Since then its history has been characterized by consolidation, urban maturity and social liberalism – influences that have produced the vigorous and tolerant city of today.

First Impressions

Most visitors arrive by train at Amsterdam's Centraal Station, a smoothly run modern complex within a handsome 1880s neoclassic building. A helpful tourist information office is on platform (*spoor*) 2b; the main tourist office (see page 344) is just outside the train station.

In front of the station is the busy Stationsplein, a mix of tramline, bus track, bicycle lane and pedestrian concourse, with added passenger traffic heading to the subway station (45 feet underground). Straight ahead lies the Damrak thoroughfare; watch out for traffic here, and always wait patiently for the green light at pedestrian crossings.

A Cultural and Liberal City

Amsterdam's liberal traditions are apparent in the notorious Red Light District (*Walletjes*), located mainly between Warmoesstraat and Oudezijds Achterburgwal. Be advised – do not take photographs of prostitutes' booths. Be on the lookout for pickpockets.

The city also is notorious for its "coffee shops," where hashish and marijuana sold for personal use is tolerated by the authorities, though there are currently proposals to ban sales to overseas visitors. *Eetcafes*, on the other hand, are conventional cafés where coffee is served. "Brown Cafés" (*Bruine Cafés*) are traditional bars where liquor is sold.

All this alternative culture is a minor aspect of the larger Amsterdam, a sophisticated city and a working community. There are peaceful canals and shaded, cobbled streets lined with narrow gabled houses. It's a flower-filled

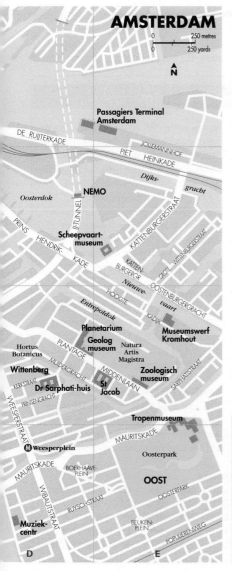

AMSTERDAM

0   250 metres
0   250 yards

N

Passagiers Terminal Amsterdam

DE RUIJTERKADE

JOLLEMANNHOF

PIET HEINKADE

Dijks- gracht

NEMO

Oosterdok

IJ-TUNNEL

PRINS HENDRIK- KADE

Scheepvaart- museum

KATTENBURGERSTRAAT

KATTEN- BURGERGR.

Nieuwe

GROTE WITTENBURGERSTRAAT

HOOGTE

OOSTENBURGERGRACHT

vaart

Entrepotdok

KADIJK

Planetarium

Geolog museum

Natura Artis Magistra

Museumswerf Kromhout

Hortus Botanicus

PLANTAGE

Wittenberg

MUIDERGRACHT

MIDDENLAAN

Zoologisch museum

SARPHATISTRAAT

KERKSTRAAT

Dr Sarphati-huis

PRINSENGRACHT

St Jacob

Tropenmuseum

WEESPERSTRAAT

MAURITSKADE

Weesperplein

Oosterpark

MAURITSKADE

BOER-HAAVE-PLEIN

OOST

OOSTERPARK

WIBAUTSTRAAT

RUYSCHSTRAAT

Muziek- centr

BEUKEN-PLEIN

POPULIERENWEG

D

E

Supporting the City

Amsterdam is built on hundreds of thousands of pilings that have been driven through the surface layers of soft peat to rest soundly on hard sand. The 17th-century Royal Palace (Koninklijk Paleis, see page 346) on the Dam rests on 13,659 wooden pilings. Concrete pilings sunk to 65 feet have replaced the original ones.

The Netherlands

city of exhilarating art museums, glorious civic buildings, medieval churches, quality stores, superb restaurants and entertaining street life.

Getting to Know Amsterdam

Purchase one of the "I amsterdam" cards (valid for one, two or three days) for free admission to more than 20 museums, the Holland Casino, use of the tram, bus and subway system and a canal tour, a guided tour of a diamond factory, a 25 percent reduction on city attractions and restaurants, plus other benefits. For a taste of the city's canal culture, take a trip on a Museum Line boat. Two routes stop near the major museums and you get up to a 50 percent discount on entry to the museums. Walking tours show you the city's architecture, history, art and special neighborhoods.

Amsterdam is a rewarding city to explore by foot. Enjoy street theater in Leidseplein, or walk in the footsteps of Rembrandt through the Jewish Quarter. The major shopping street of Kalverstraat leads to the busy open space of Spui, or try wandering down to the daily Bloemenmarkt (Flower Market) along the Singel canal.

Essential Information

Tourist Information

VVV Amsterdam Tourist Office
Stationsplein 10 (opposite Centraal Station entrance)
Ebbehout 31, Zaandam, northern outskirts of Amsterdam
Holland Tourist Information (HTI), Amsterdam Airport Schiphol (arrival hall 2)
Koestraat 6, Purmerend, 12 miles north of Amsterdam
For general tourist information telephone ☎ 0900 400 4040; www.holland.com, www.iamsterdam.com

Urban Transportation

Trains run from Centraal Station (central railroad station), Stationsplein. Gemeentevervoerbedrijf Amsterdam-Spoorwegen (GVB) is the public transportation authority. For information and tickets there is a GVB office opposite Centraal Station; open Mon.–Fri. 7 a.m.– 9 p.m., Sat.–Sun. 10 a.m.– 6 p.m. Amsterdam's subway (metro) mainly serves suburban areas. Subway stations are

marked with an "M" on the city map. There is a station and information desk at Centraal Station. For information on all public transportation within the Netherlands ☎ 0900 9292 (Mon.–Fri. 6 a.m.–midnight, Sat.–Sun. 7 a.m.–midnight); www.gvb.nl or www.9292ov.nl. Taxis are expensive, but can be picked up at the stands at Amsterdam Airport Schiphol, Centraal Station, Dam and Leidseplein. You also can call Taxicentrale (☎ 020 777 7777, 24-hour service).

Airport Information

Amsterdam Airport Schiphol (☎ 0900 0141, or 020 794 0800 from outside The Netherlands; www.schiphol.com) is 11 miles southwest of the city. Fast trains run from a station south of the airport complex to Amsterdam's Centraal Station; the trip takes 15 to 20 minutes. Trains depart every 15 minutes daily 4 a.m.–12:30 a.m., on the hour 1 a.m.–5:40 a.m. Buses run regularly to Amsterdam from Schiphol Plaza. Arrival hall 2 has post offices, banks, shops and a Holland Tourist Information office.

Climate – average highs and lows for the month

Jan.	Feb.	Mar.	Apr.	May	Jun.	Jul.	Aug.	Sep.	Oct.	Nov.	Dec.
5°C	5°C	9°C	11°C	15°C	18°C	20°C	21°C	18°C	13°C	9°C	7°C
41°F	41°F	48°F	52°F	59°F	64°F	68°F	70°F	64°F	55°F	48°F	45°F
1°C	0°C	3°C	5°C	8°C	11°C	13°C	13°C	10°C	8°C	4°C	2°C
34°F	32°F	37°F	41°F	46°F	52°F	55°F	55°F	50°F	46°F	39°F	36°F

Amsterdam Sights

Amsterdams Historisch Museum

Amsterdam's story is well told in the Amsterdams Historisch Museum (Amsterdam Historical Museum). Once a monastery, and then a city orphanage for four centuries, the museum is now an elegant complex of bright and airy rooms. Highlights include a model of a Dutch East India sailing ship and the silver drinking horn of the medieval Guild of St. George.

To the right of the entrance is the glass doorway into Schuttersgalerij. This was once an open street and is now the Civic Guards Gallery, with group portraits of 17th-century city militiamen.

⊞ B3 ✉ Entrances: Kalverstraat 92 or Nieuwezijds Voorburgwal 357 ☎ 020 523 1822; www.ahm.nl ◉ Mon.–Fri. 10–5, Sat.–Sun. 11–5 🚃 Tram 1, 2, 4, 5, 9, 14, 16, 24, 25 🍴 Museum café 🖐 $$$

Anne Frank Huis

No matter how often you have heard the Anne Frank story, a visit to Het Achterhuis, "The Secret Annex," is unforgettable. Here, in the Anne Frank Huis (Anne Frank House), the Frank family and their friends lived secretly in Nazi-occupied Amsterdam until their arrest just months before the Liberation. The only one to survive the concentration camps was Anne's father, Otto. The lively, passionate diary kept by Anne during her years in hiding was later published to worldwide acclaim. The museum has absorbing displays and multimedia installations, but the secret annex is the heart of it all. The stark emptiness intensifies the experience. From every corner Anne Frank bears

witness on behalf of millions of Nazi victims. After your visit, a quiet walk through the peaceful, reflective Jordaan district is recommended.

⊞ B3 ✉ Prinsengracht 267 ☎ 020 556 7105; www.annefrank.org ◉ Sun.–Fri. 9–9, Sat 9 a.m.–10 p.m., mid-Mar. to mid-Sep. (also 9–10 p.m., Jul.–Aug.); Sun.–Fri. 9–7, Sat. 9–9, rest of year. Closed Yom Kippur 🚌 21, 170, 171, 172; tram 13, 17 🚢 Museum Line stop 🍴 Museum café 🖐 $$$ ℹ Last admission 30 minutes before closing

Begijnhof

Amsterdam's secluded Begijnhof (Béguinage) is an outstanding example of a medieval almshouse community. It was built in the 14th century to accommodate Béguines, pious single women of the Catholic faith, who lived a religious and charitable life without the stricture of holy vows.

The Béguines were later ostracized because of their faith, and today the discreet facade of the Béguinage's once clandestine Catholic church masks a

Regent's Chamber, Amsterdams Historisch Museum

The tomb of Michiel de Ruyter, a renowned 17th-century admiral, in the Nieuwe Kerk

haunting little Italianate chapel. Opposite is the original church that was transferred to the city's Protestant community in the late 16th century.

In the south corner of the Begijnhof is the 15th-century Houten Huys, one of Amsterdam's oldest houses, wooden-fronted and steeply gabled. Today's Begijnhof still accommodates single women of modest means.

✚ B2 ✉ Access via a gateway at Gedempte Begijnensloot (9–5) and then via the gate at the Spui (after 5 p.m.) ☎ 020 622 1918 ⊙ Chapel: Tue.–Fri. 9–6:30, Sat.–Sun. 9–6, Mon. 1–6:30 🚊 Tram 1, 2, 5 💷 Free

Nieuwe Kerk

The 17th-century Nieuwe Kerk (New Church) was new only in its original form, as compared with the more venerable Oude Kerk (Old Church). The New Church is a fine counterpoint to Dam square's Koninklijk Paleis (Royal Palace), with its beautifully decorated rooms.

Today the church is used for major art exhibitions. There are a dozen or more side chapels and a magnificent vaulted roof. The fine organ and the pulpit are permanent features. Dutch monarchs

have been crowned here, including the present Queen Beatrix.

✚ C3 ✉ Dam 34–38 ☎ 020 638 6909; www.nieuwekerk.nl ⊙ Exhibitions: daily 10–5; opening hours may vary depending on the event 🚊 Tram 1, 2, 4, 5, 9, 16, 24, 25 🍽 Café 💷 $$$

Oude Kerk

The Oude Kerk (Old Church) is the oldest building in Amsterdam. The church stands on the banks of the Oudezijds Voorburgwal canal in the heart of the Red Light District. Its glorious stained-glass windows, featuring Lambert van Noorts' *Annunciation* and *The Visit of Mary to Elizabeth*, look down on prostitutes' booths in the narrow Enge Kerk Straat, much as they might have done in medieval times. A triple nave and high-vaulted roof give added spaciousness to the dramatically bare interior of the Old Church. A poignant feature is the gravestone of Rembrandt's wife Saskia van Uylenburgh, set below the choir organ.

✚ C3 ✉ Oudekerksplein 23 ☎ 020 625 8284; www.oudekerk.nl ⊙ Mon.–Sat. 11–5, Sun. 1–5 🚇 Centraal Station or Nieuwmarkt 🚊 Tram 4, 9, 14, 16, 20, 24, 25 💷 $$ (may be more expensive for concerts and exhibitions) 🔢 Art exhibitions and music recitals at various times

Rijksmuseum

The Rijksmuseum (National Museum) contains some of the world's greatest works of Dutch art. The building dates from 1885 and was designed by Pierre Cuypers. Its neo-Gothic facade is something of a mirror image to Cuypers' Centraal Station.

From December 2003 until 2013, the museum's main building will be undergoing extensive renovation. During that period its finest works will continue to be on display in the redesigned Philips Wing, under the title *The Masterpieces*. Featuring more than 400 17th-century Dutch paintings, it includes such highlights as Johannes Vermeer's *The Kitchenmaid*, a masterpiece of complementary colors, and Rembrandt's *The Nightwatch*. These are shown in conjunction with dazzling displays of sculpture, Delftware, silverware, furniture, dolls' houses and historical artifacts from the Dutch Golden Age.

➕ B1 ✉ Jan Luijkenstraat 1 ☎ 020 674 7000; www.rijksmuseum.nl 🕐 Daily 9–6 🚋 Tram 2, 5, 6, 7, 10 🚌 Museum Line stop 🍴 Café Cobra, Museumplein (discount for museum ticket-holders) ✋ $$$ 🔢 Audio tour available

Van Gogh Museum

To view the finest and largest collection of Vincent van Gogh's paintings, visit the Van Gogh Museum, where the artist's works (200 paintings and nearly 500 drawings) chart his intense and ultimately tragic life. The collection takes you through his early period, when he was a missionary in the Dutch coal fields; pieces include such dark social commentary as *The Potato Eaters*. His later Parisian work reflects the influence of the Impressionists, but it is the paintings inspired by his life at Arles, in sunny Provence (France), that exhilarate with their fiery yellows and oranges. The most famous works are the iconic *Sunflowers* series. Conversely, *The Garden of St. Paul's Hospital*, painted at St.-Rémy mental asylum the year before van Gogh's death, is a heartrending evocation of a dejected figure. But the sum of the Van Gogh Museum, the painter's legacy of outstanding work, is uplifting. There are other works by such contemporaries of van Gogh as Toulouse-Lautrec, Gauguin and Redon. The adjacent Stedelijk Museum (due to reopen on this site in September 2011) is one of the finest collections of modern art in the world.

➕ B1 ✉ Paulus Potterstraat 7 ☎ 020 570 5200; www.vangoghmuseum.nl 🕐 Daily 10–6 (also Fri. 6–10 p.m.) 🚋 Tram 2, 3, 5, 12 🚌 Museum Line stop 🍴 Museum restaurant ✋ $$$ (more for special exhibitions) 🔢 Audio tour ($)

Vondelpark

The Vondelpark, Amsterdam's principal park, is named after 17th-century playwright Joost van den Vondel. The park starts as a green avenue that leads southwest from a busy corner on Stadhouderskade, just south of Leidseplein. Soon it opens into a broad green space peppered with trees and interspersed with ornamental lakes and linked waterways. There are children's playgrounds, a sweetly scented rose garden, teahouses, a bandstand and (until it moves to new premises during 2012) the Nederlands Filmmuseum (Netherlands Film Museum).

➕ A1 ✉ Stadhouderskade 🕐 Daily dawn–dusk 🚋 Tram 1, 2, 3, 5, 6, 12 🚌 Museum Line stop 🍴 t'Blauwe Theehuis ("The Blue Teahouse"), by the lake 🔢 Open-air theater and concerts during summer

Wheatfield with Crows in the Van Gogh Museum

A tour in an open-topped pleasure craft along Amsterdam's canals

Amsterdam's Canals

So many northern European capitals claim the title "Venice of the North" that the sobriquet has become devalued. Some say there is no substitute for the real thing, but perhaps Amsterdam has the strongest claim to the title. While the city lacks Venice's romantic splendor, there is a restrained beauty about Amsterdam's canals (*grachten*) and their attendant buildings.

The finest canals are west of the city center, beyond the bustling main streets of Damrak and Nieuwezijds Voorburgwal, both of which once were canals. A stroll along side streets from Nieuwezijds Voorburgwal and across the Spuistraat brings you to the great waterways of Singel, Herengracht, Keizersgracht and Prinsengracht.

Herengracht

Herengracht is the finest canal of the *grachtengordel*, the ring or girdle of canals that were built in the early 17th century to defend the city. The name Herengracht translates into English as the "Gentlemen's Canal," a sign of contemporary male ascendancy. This was the district where the wealthiest Amsterdam merchant families built themselves handsome canalside mansions notable for their superb ornate gables. The houses were designed to be tall and narrow because of limited space.

Take a stroll down Herengracht to appreciate it all. You can start from the canal's northern end at its intersection with Brouwersgracht. The Brouwersgracht (Brewery Canal) is the short stretch of canal that links Herengracht to the Singel canal at the Haarlemmer Sluis, one of the 40 or so sluices that are opened each night to flush clean water through the canal system. Haarlemmer Sluis can be reached from Centraal Station by walking northwest along Prins Hendrikkade for about 300 yards and then turning left. Cross the wide sluice bridge. (There is a superb cheese shop, Kaasland de Roompof, on the opposite corner.) Go left, then turn right along Brouwersgracht to reach the tree-shaded bridges at the intersection with Herengracht.

Walk south, then east for a mile of scenic history to where the Herengracht meets the Amstel river. You can stroll down either side of

Blauwburgwal is a canal in Jordaan

the great canal and cross over bridges to get the best views of canalside houses. Herengracht 168, formerly the Theatermuseum, and the exquisite Bartolotti House next door are particularly impressive. The latter is a 17th-century Renaissance mansion built by the head of the Bartolotti Bank. Enjoy the *Gouden Bocht*, which translates as "Golden Bay" or "Bend," between Leidsestraat and Vijzelstraat – note the decorative double-fronted houses along the elegant curve of the canal.

The curve is an engaging motif amid Amsterdam's general flatness – in the decorativeness of house gables, the elegant bridges, the sweep of railings, even in the curved handlebars of the wonderful old upright bicycles still favored by Amsterdammers. There are said to be 700,000 bicycles in the city, and it seems that everybody cycles in Amsterdam. Elderly *dames* and *heren* (ladies and gentlemen) cruise past to the tinkling of bells like songbirds. Stylishly dressed young people skim along with their backs straight and a wary eye on the tourists' uncertain bid to run across the street in front of them.

Connections

Explore the Prinsengracht (Princes' Canal) and the Keizersgracht (Emperors' Canal), as well as the main canals, and don't neglect the connecting waterways. There's the Leidsegracht on the Golden Bend, or the peaceful, leafy Egelantiersgracht near the Anne Frank House (Anne Frank Huis, see page 345) that takes you into the quiet heart of the Jordaan district. Sidestep between Herengracht and the Singel canal into enchanting streets such as Gasthuismolensteeg or Oude Spiegelstraat, where craft and antiques shops and boutiques rub shoulders with delightful little cafés and restaurants. And try a nighttime walk along the great canals, when many of the finest houses are floodlit and the numerous bridges twinkle with lights.

In summer the canals become venues for concerts by the water, rowing regattas, Chinese dragon boat races and various other events. Amsterdam is many things to many people, but the city's fascinating network of canals will always be the enduring motif of this very special city. For the walking route, see the city map on pages 342–343.

The Hague

The Hague (Den Haag), third largest city in The Netherlands, is justly proud of its status as the political and royal capital of this beautiful country and as a focus of international affairs. Although it lacks the fast pace and excitement of Amsterdam, a sense of well-being and security underpins the rich cultural and political heritage.

The city's name derives from Gravenhage, which means "the Count's hedge." In the 13th century the Count of Holland built a hunting lodge among sand dunes – this is where The Hague's historic center, the Binnenhof (Inner

Court), now stands. The settlement that developed around the lodge was the Count's "hedge," sheltering him against the outside world.

In the 16th century the States General of the United Netherlands met at The Hague, and since then the city has been the seat of Dutch government. The Hague Convention of 1907, which formulated laws governing warfare worldwide, gave this city international status. The 1913 opening of the Peace Palace (Vredespaleis, see page 354) further enhanced The Hague's standing, and it is today considered a center of international diplomacy and business. The Permanent Court of Arbitration and

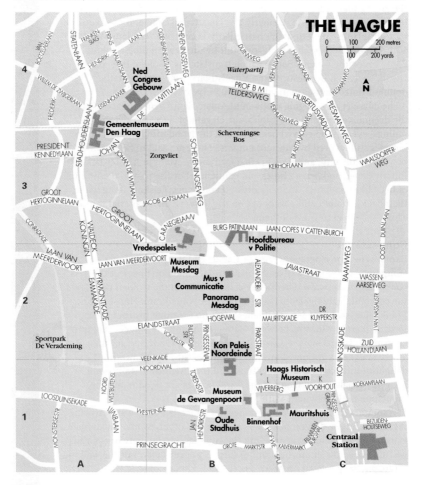

THE HAGUE

the International Court of Justice are located at the Peace Palace; numerous embassies, ministries and headquarters of international organizations also have their offices here.

In 1980, after the then Dutch queen, Juliana, abdicated in favor of her daughter Beatrix, the royal residency was relocated from Utrecht to The Hague, where there are three palaces.

Arrival

The Hague's main railroad station, Den Haag Centraal Station, is undergoing a major development. The Nieuw Centraal was completed by mid-2011. Look for local notices explaining current arrangements. A short walk southwest leads to the heart of The Hague, where the Binnenhof and several fine museums cluster around a graceful little lake, Hofvijver.

Guided bus, cycling and walking tours of the city are offered during summer, as well as self-guiding itineraries. Among these, available from the tourist information center near the Centraal Station, are a walk discovering the city's lost Jewish Quarter; an introduction to the "Royal Miles" in and around the city; and cycling routes that bring together the best of the coast and city center.

On Your Own

Exploring The Hague on your own on foot can be a very satisfying experience. The oldest section centers on the Hofvijver, the "Court Pond." On its south side the Hofvijver laps against the walls of the Binnenhof and the Mauritshuis (see pages 353–354), which houses The Hague's outstanding art collection. Its northern side is lined with trees and is backed by the elegant 18th-century street Lange Vijverberg.

From the Hofvijver you can stroll north beneath the lime trees on the wide avenue Lange Voorhout. A colorful arts and antiques market is held here on Thursdays and Sundays from early May to late September.

Continue past the grand facade of the Hotel des Indes to reach Denneweg, a charming street with a Parisian flavor and a host of interesting antiques and craft galleries, delicatessens, popular restaurants and cafés, and distinctive fashion boutiques.

Quickening Pace

West of the Hofvijver and the Binnenhof lies the bustling open area of the Buitenhof, where the pace quickens to that of a busy city.

Beyond the Buitenhof is The Hague's commercial and shopping district and the pedestrian-only streets that lead to the Kerk Plein (Church Square) and the hexagonal-towered Grote Kerk (Great

The Binnenhof (Dutch parliament) in The Hague

Church). The Wednesday market that used to be a feature here has been moved to nearby Hofweg.

North of the church is the Hofkwartier, one of the oldest areas of The Hague. There are quite a few specialty shops, restaurants and cafés here. Be sure to stroll along the Hoogstraat (Palace Promenade) and on into Noordeinde, one of The Hague's most attractive streets. Along here you will find a marvelous selection of art galleries, antiques shops and fashion boutiques, restaurants and the Paleis Noordeinde (Royal Palace).

Enjoy this fine city by filling your day with activities involving the arts and history and then seek out the numerous musical and cultural events that take place in the summer.

A short ride on tram 1, 9 or 11, or bus 14, 22 or 23 will take you to the coast and the popular resort of Scheveningen (proper pronunciation of the name Scheveningen is the sign of a true local; try "Shravin-eeng-e" and you might get by). You can break the journey halfway at the miniature "town" of Madurodam, a favorite with children.

In addition to Scheveningen's superb beach and promenade, the numerous attractions include the Holland Casino, the Muzee Scheveningen and a pier.

Hooigracht

Several ring canals were built around The Hague during the 17th century. Although many of them have been filled in, you can walk east from Denneweg to reach the serene little stretch of surviving canal, the Hooigracht, its leafy banks lined with elegant and attractive old buildings.

Essential Information

Tourist Information
Tourist information centers are known as VVV (Vereniging Voor Vreemdelingenverkeer)
VVV, Koningin Julianaplein 30, near the Centraal Station
☎ 070 363 5676
www.denhaag.com
VVV, Gevers Deynootweg 1134, Palace Promenade shopping center, Scheveningen
☎ 0900 340 3505
www.scheveningen.com

Urban Transportation
Den Haag has an excellent transportation system with tramlines serving The Hague, Scheveningen, Kijkduin and neighboring Voorburg, Rijswijk, Wassenaar, Wateringen, Leidschendam, Delft and Nootdorp. For information and tickets for buses and trams inquire at the tourist information centers, or call ☎ 0900 9292 or ☎ 070 384 8666; www.journeyplanner.9292.nl. Taxi stands are at the railroad stations and throughout the city. To call a taxi try HTMC ☎ 070 390 7722.

Airport Information
Amsterdam Airport Schiphol (see page 344) serves The Hague. Trains for The Hague leave the airport at regular intervals (travel time 30 minutes). Trains from the airport stop first at Station Hollands Spoor, south of the city center. If you are going to the city center, stay on the train until Centraal Station.

Climate – average highs and lows for the month

Jan.	Feb.	Mar.	Apr.	May	Jun.	Jul.	Aug.	Sep.	Oct.	Nov.	Dec.
5°C	5°C	9°C	11°C	15°C	18°C	20°C	21°C	18°C	14°C	9°C	7°C
41°F	41°F	48°F	52°F	59°F	64°F	68°F	70°F	64°F	57°F	48°F	45°F
1°C	0°C	3°C	5°C	8°C	12°C	14°C	13°C	11°C	9°C	4°C	3°C
34°F	32°F	37°F	41°F	46°F	54°F	57°F	55°F	52°F	48°F	39°F	37°F

The Hague Sights

Key to symbols

🔲 map coordinates refer to The Hague map on page 350 💲 admission charge: $$$ more than €6, $$ €3–€6, $ less than €3

See page 5 for complete key to symbols

Binnenhof

The Binnenhof (Inner Court) of the original lodge of the Counts of Holland is the oldest part of The Hague.

The turreted Ridderzaal (Knights' Hall), where medieval guests were received, stands at the heart of a central square; behind it is the parliament building.

The main room is the Knights' Hall, restored in 1900 to its medieval glory, with coats of arms, Dutch provincial flags, stained glass and artifacts. Ceremonies, including *Prinsjesdag*, the day of the Queen's speech to the Dutch parliament, are held here.

There are guided tours of the Knights' Hall and the two chambers of parliament when they are not in use. There also is an exhibition containing a scale model of the Binnenhof.

🔲 B1 ✉ Binnenhof 8a ☎ 070 364 6144 🕐 Mon.–Sat. 10–4; closed holidays (except Good Friday) and 2 days in mid-Sep. for the opening of parliament 🚌 4, 5, 22; tram 1, 16, 17 💲 $$$ (exhibition free) 🎫 Last tour at 3:45 (subject to demand). Reservations recommended. May be closed to the public on other occasions

Gemeentemuseum Den Haag

The Gemeentemuseum Den Haag (The Hague Municipal Museum) has collections of musical instruments and ceramics, including Delftware and The Hague silverware. The modern art collection includes works by Pablo Picasso and Claude Monet, and there is a large collection of paintings and drawings by the 20th-century Dutch painter Piet Mondrian. The fashion department features exhibitions of Dutch and international fashion, and there are also major visiting exhibitions.

🔲 A3 ✉ Stadhouderslaan 41 ☎ 070 338 1111; www.gemeentemuseum.nl 🕐 Tue.–Sun. 11–5 🚌 24; tram 17 🍴 Museum café 💲 $$$

Haags Historisch Museum

Haags Historisch Museum (The Hague Historical Museum) is very much a Dutch institution; there are no English translations to supplement the Dutch labeling of the paintings. But a visit is rewarding, especially to see such big paintings as Jan van Goyen's *View of The Hague*. In the attic there is a permanent exhibition illustrating the history of The Hague; look for the explanatory panels that are translated in English.

🔲 C1 ✉ Korte Vijverberg 7 ☎ 070 364 6940; www.haagshistorischmuseum.nl 🕐 Tue.–Fri. 10–5, Sat.–Sun. noon–5 🚌 4, 5, 22; tram 1, 16, 17 💲 $$

Mauritshuis

The original Mauritshuis (Maurits' House) was built as a private home in

---

The Binnenhof is the complex where The Hague had its beginnings

the 17th century by Johan Maurits van Nassau-Siegen and was reconstructed after a disastrous fire in 1704.

Today it contains the Royal Cabinet of Paintings, an outstanding collection of Dutch art. As well as temporary exhibitions, highlights include Johannes Vermeer's *Girl with a Pearl Earring* and the crowning glory, Rembrandt van Rijn's famous *The Anatomy Lesson of Doctor Nicolaes Tulp*.

✚ C1 ✉ Korte Vijverberg 8 ☎ 070 302 3456; www.mauritshuis.nl ◷ Mon.–Sat. 10–5, Sun. 11–5, Apr.–Aug.; Tue.–Sat. 10–5, Sun. and public holidays 11–5, rest of year 🚌 4, 5, 22; tram 1, 16, 17 🍴 Museum café 💰 $$$ ℹ Includes admission to Galerij Prins Willem V (Prince William V Gallery), 35 Buitenhof

Museum de Gevangenpoort

A guided tour of the Museum de Gevangenpoort (Prisoner's Gate Museum) is great fun, but is not for the fainthearted. The Prisoner's Gate Museum was The Hague's notorious prison for hundreds of years. Interrogation rooms, a debtors' chamber and a torture room give a gruesome picture of medieval justice. The Dutch treat the whole thing with a commendable black humor.

Maritshuis (left) and the Peace Palace

The tour commentary is mostly in Dutch, but information sheets in other languages are available and the guide will answer questions in English.

✚ B1 ✉ Buitenhof 33 ☎ 070 346 0861; www.gevangenpoort.nl ◷ Tue.–Fri. 10–5, Sat.–Sun. noon–5 🚌 4, 5, 22; tram 1, 16, 17 💰 $$ ℹ Tours Mon.–Fri. hourly from 10:45–4:45, Sat.–Sun. hourly from 12:45–4:45; extra tours Jul.–Aug.

Museum Mesdag

Hendrik Willem Mesdag was a leading figure in the art world of The Hague during the 19th century.

Famous for his *Panorama Mesdag* (a cylinder-shaped painting of coastal resort Scheveningen in 1881), Mesdag was himself a painter and an avid collector of other artists' works, especially of the Barbizon School of French painters, including Jean-François Millet, Jean Baptiste Camille Corot and Gustave Courbet. Their works – along with those of Mesdag's and other members of The Hague School – grace the museum, built as an annex to Mesdag's house.

The museum reopened in 2011 after a major renovation.

✚ B2 ✉ Laan van Meerdervoort 7f ☎ 070 362 1434 ◷ Wed.–Sun. noon–5 🚌 24; tram 1 💰 $$

Vredespaleis

The Vredespaleis (Peace Palace) is an awe-inspiring building symbolizing the power of statehood.

Scottish philanthropist Andrew Carnegie, who made his fortune in America, paid for its Gothic splendor in the early 20th century. Its exquisite furnishings and artifacts were donated by nations around the world.

A guided tour of the building includes a visit to the International Court of Justice. Due to security control, you must wait outside at the palace gates for the hourly tour to begin.

✚ B2 ✉ Carnegieplein 2 ☎ 070 302 4137; www.vredespaleis.nl ◷ Visit by guided tour only 🚌 24; tram 1 💰 $$ ℹ Tours require advance reservation and times are subject to change

Delft

Fine ceramics and architecture are the main features of Delft. The ceramics have been exported worldwide, but Delft's buildings remain much as they were when immortalized on canvas by Johannes Vermeer, a native of the city. The Vermeercentrum, 21 Voldersgracht, takes you into the painter's 17th-century world.

There are organized motorcoach trips to Delft from The Hague, and seats can be reserved through tourist information centers (see page 352). The town is only 20 minutes from The Hague via tram 1, and takes even less time by train. Tram and train both arrive at a two-lane highway, but a few steps along cobbled lanes transport you into a delightful medieval world enclosed by tranquil canals. Delft centers on an imposing main square, the Markt, where there are numerous stores, cafés and restaurants.

Delft is a popular tourist destination, and in summer the Markt can be especially crowded. Explore farther afield; follow the canalside street of Oosteinde from behind the New Church (Nieuwe Kerk) to reach the medieval city gate of Oostport. Visit the Old Church (Oude Kerk) west of the Markt, at the head of the lovely street of Oude Delft. The Old Church is a splendid Gothic building full of interest and charm. View it from the Peperstraat Bridge, three bridges to the south on Oude Delft, to fully appreciate its remarkable leaning tower. Close to the Old Church is the Prinsenhof Museum. Stop for coffee and crêpes at Stads Pannekoeckhuys, Oude Delft 113–115.

Many stores on the Markt sell Delft china. The Lambert van Meerten Museum at Oude Delft 199 (☎ 015 260 2358) has a superb collection of Delft earthenware and tiles from around the world. The Koninklijke Porceleyne Fles, a factory involved in producing Delftware since the 17th century, is just out of town at 196 Rotterdamsweg (☎ 015 251 2030) and has guided tours.

🛈 Hippolytusbuurt 4 ☎ 0900 5151 555 or 015 215 4051; www.delft.nl

Canals thread through the pretty streets of Delft just as they did in medieval times

Norway

Opposite: Majestic mountains at Hardangerfjord, the second-largest fjord in Norway

Norway

Norway forms the edge of Europe's most northerly landmass, with land borders to Finland, Sweden and Russia, and where sea and mountains have merged to produce one of the world's most breathtaking and dramatic landscapes.

This is a country whose ancient peoples, the Vikings, helped shape the history of northern Europe. The Vikings once controlled half of Britain, and sent mariners as far west as Newfoundland and as far south as the Strait of Gibraltar, as well as establishing some cities in the Republic of Ireland.

It is this vigorous and resourceful national character, reflected in Viking tradition, that still exemplifies modern Norway. This is a nation that has mastered an inhospitable landscape, though beautiful, without despoiling it, becoming a leading oil and gas producer in the hostile environment of the North Sea.

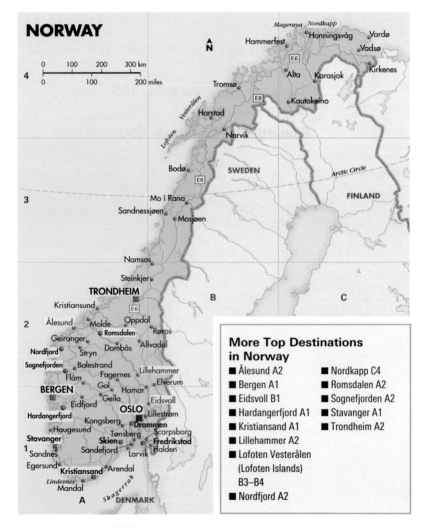

More Top Destinations in Norway

- Ålesund A2
- Bergen A1
- Eidsvoll B1
- Hardangerfjord A1
- Kristiansand A1
- Lillehammer A2
- Lofoten Vesterålen (Lofoten Islands) B3–B4
- Nordfjord A2
- Nordkapp C4
- Romsdalen A2
- Sognefjorden A2
- Stavanger A1
- Trondheim A2

Landscape

Norway's spectacular landscape is dominated by intervening seas – the Barents Sea to the north, the Norwegian Sea to the west, the North Sea to the southwest and the Skagerrak inlet farther south. The corrugated coastline measures nearly 13,600 miles, including fjords and the country's 150,000 offshore islands. This scattered mosaic of islands – the "Skerry Guard" – is Norway's natural sea defense. The islands break the onslaught of the ocean, creating the country's sheltered seaways to the north and south and protecting the gateways to the fjords.

Norway is shaped like a Viking club, narrowing in the north and with a broad base in the south. The country's mountain system runs from northeast to southwest and reaches its greatest height at Galdhøppigen, at 8,100 feet, in the Jotunheimen National Park.

The mountains separate the rugged western seaboard, known as the Vestlandet, from the gentler eastern region, the Øslandet.

The broad southwestern half of the country is known as Sørlandet, the South Country. Here, on the coastal fringe and around Oslo, is lowland Norway, where the sheltered coast is a favorite vacation destination for Norwegian families – a landscape of mellow woods and fields and tranquil blue waters. On the southern tip of Sørlandet is the sunny town of Kristiansand, with its flock of offshore islands. Southwest along the coast is Mandal, where attractive beaches catch the best of the summer sun; nearby is the promontory of Lindesnes, where a *fyr* (lighthouse) marks Norway's southernmost point.

Then the coast turns to the northwest, twisting through a rugged landscape of rocky headlands and deeply indented fjords, past the pleasant town of Egersund and finally through rich farming country to Stavanger and the open west.

Fjordland

Norway's famous Fjordland begins at Stavanger. Stretching for more than 375 miles is one of the most spectacular landscapes and seascapes in the world. In the Ryfylke area, northeast of Stavanger, lies the stunning Lysefjord, with its flat-topped and sheer-sided Pulpit Rock. Farther north is the mighty Hardangerfjord, with its massive cliffs, and the silver-white waterfalls of Skykkjedalsfoss and Vøringfoss, set off by snowcapped mountains.

Even farther north into Hordaland lies fascinating Bergen, against a setting of islands and mountains. Bergen is the starting point for boat journeys to the north along the coastal islands and into the 127-mile-long and 4,291-foot-deep Sognefjord, the deepest and longest fjord in Norway and second longest in the world. Its side fjords twist between towering cliffs and penetrate as far as Flåm and Gudvangen, at the head of Nærøyfjord (the narrowest fjord in Europe), and to Fjærland, below the southernmost edge of the great Jostedalsbreen glacier (the largest glacier in continental Europe, covering an area of 188 square miles).

Along Sognefjord are lovely villages such as Balestrand. Throughout the area, ancient pagoda-like stave churches survive at settlements such as Vik, Kaupanger and Urnes. Inland to the east lies the mountain range of Jotunheimen, known as the "Land of the Giants."

The Northern Fjords

Beyond the Sognefjord lies Nordfjord and then the county, or *fylke*, of Møre og Romsdal. The coastal town of Ålesund is renowned for its art nouveau architecture of turrets, towers and medieval motifs. Inland is the Geirangerfjord and its magnificent waterfalls. From Ålesund, spectacular roads lead over the mountains to the town of Åndalsnes and the Romsdalsfjord. Along the coast farther north is the Atlantic Road, a highway

A bronze statuary group alongside a pond in Oslo

linking a chain of islands. Northeast from here lies Trollheimen, the mountainous "Home of the Trolls," and then comes the great expanse of Trondheimsfjorden and Trondheim itself – once called Nidaros – the ancient capital of Norway.

Beyond Trondheim is the narrowing edge of Norway's northwestern seaboard, fertile coastal lands backed by barren mountains that reach into Nordland and to the Arctic Circle. At Narvik, you look out across the waters of Vestfjorden to the spectacular Lofoten Islands – including Austvågøy, Gimsøy, Vestvågøy and Flakstadøy – before continuing north to Tromsø, known as "The Paris of the North." You then go on through Finnmark, the land of the Sami people and of the midnight sun, to the Arctic island of Honningsvåg and Nordkapp (North Cape), the symbolic northern end of Europe.

Traveling in Norway

Norway is a pleasant country in which to travel, but to enjoy this magnificent land you should be selective about how and where to explore. Roads are well maintained throughout. Good driving skills are required, however, where roads are narrow and twisting and where they pass through long tunnels.

Norway's public transportation system is excellent. This is a country that copes with some of the most difficult winter conditions in Europe. Only in severe conditions are train services to the northwest likely to be curtailed. Buses serve more remote villages throughout the north and west.

Travel by boat is a way of life in Norway, especially on the western seaboard. There is no finer way of touring Fjordland than by boat.

Most of Norway has a comparatively mild, wet, maritime climate, as it is influenced by the Gulf Stream. The west coast and mountains have high rainfall even in midsummer. But there can be long spells of fair weather, when Fjordland is glorious. In eastern and southeastern Norway, summers can be warm and dry. Winter in the higher elevations is cold and extremely snowy, creating excellent skiing conditions at Norway's winter resorts. In the far north the weather conditions border on the subarctic. The Norwegians are philosophical about their weather, preferring to think of it as invigorating.

The Norwegians

Norway, as a constitutional monarchy, is extremely well run. The moderate Labor Party dominated government from the 1930s to 1981 when coalition governments began to be the norm, with its ministers being elected through a system of proportional representation. The Norwegians are a level-headed, open, courteous and generous people. Only in busy Oslo does an occasional impatience with visitors emerge.

The people share the Scandinavian tendency toward self-effacement, but they are understandably proud of their success at shaping a modern nation out of such a wild landscape.

Wooden houses on the small island of Omaholmen, amid Hardangerfjord's striking scenery

Timeline

2000–1000 BC	Early neolithic and Bronze Age people leave numerous rock carvings throughout Scandinavia.
AD 787	Viking expansion begins with increased expeditions to Britain and northern Europe.
870	Vikings settle in Iceland.
1000	Christianity is introduced to Norway; Lief Eriksson reaches the coast of Labrador.
1070	Bergen is founded on the southwest coast of Norway.
1262	Iceland finally accepts rule of Norwegian kingdom after long and bloody conflict.
circa 1300	Oslo becomes capital of Norway.
1350	The Black Death kills over half of Norway's population.
1397	Union of the Three Crowns of Denmark, Sweden and Norway signed at Kalmar.
1536	Norway is reduced to a "province" of Denmark and remains so for nearly 300 years.
1814	The country is forced into union with Sweden.
1905	Prince Carl of Denmark is invited to become king of an independent Norway.
1911	Norwegian Roald Amundsen reaches the South Pole.
1914–18	Norway remains neutral during World War I.
1925	City of Christiana reverts to its original name of Oslo.
1940	Invasion of Norway by Germany, in spite of Norway's declaration of neutrality.
1945	German troops surrender; Norway becomes one of the founders of the United Nations.
1949	Norway becomes a founding member of NATO.
1970s	Oil and gas extraction from Norwegian sector of North Sea boosts Norway's economy.
1994	In a referendum, Norwegians reject membership of the European Union.
2005	Norway celebrates 100 years of independence.
2008	Stavanger is European Capital of Culture 2008.

The Viking Settlers

History has painted the Vikings as aggressive, anarchic sea raiders, but this view has changed somewhat in recent times. The restless voyaging that took the Vikings around the coast of Britain and into the deep estuaries of northern France led to bloody conflict. There seems no question that the Vikings plundered and destroyed. But modern theory argues that a desire for new territory made them settlers in foreign lands more often than just violent raiders. In later, more stable times, the Vikings' commercial success was just as powerful as their military ferocity had been.

Norway

Sunset among the cliffs of Nordkapp (North Cape), Mageroya Island

Survival Guide

■ Mid-June to mid-August is the national vacation period, and many Norwegians escape the cities and towns and head for the fjords, mountains and countryside. This summer period can be a good time to visit Oslo.

■ During the peak summer vacation season, North Cape (Nordkapp), Europe's northernmost viewpoint, and its approaches are very busy with traffic and visitors.

■ When driving in Norway, dimmed headlights must be kept on at all times, even during daylight hours.

■ Because of Norway's strict control on the sale of alcohol, you will have difficulty buying wines and spirits outside of larger towns. You cannot buy alcohol (except beer) from supermarkets. Special state-controlled Vinmonopolet outlets are the only liquor stores, and they are very expensive. You must be at least 18 to buy wine and beer and 20 to buy spirits. Most restaurants are licensed; you may be able to buy beer in some grocery stores.

■ Norwegians are catching up with international fashion and trends, but there is more interest in good quality outdoor clothing. For something to wear that's thoroughly Norwegian try the Oslo Sweater Shop at the Radisson SAS Scandinavia Hotel (✉ Tullinsgate 5, ☎ 22 11 29 22; www.sweater.no) or the Clarion Royal Christiania Hotel (✉ Skippergaten/Biskop Gunnerus' gate 3, ☎ 22 42 42 25). Other souvenirs include ceramics, pewter, glass, wooden troll figures, enamel jewelry and woven wall hangings.

■ You can eat very well in Norway, especially in Oslo and the larger towns. Norwegians are experts at buffets, the ideal lunch experience, often with elaborate fish specialties. Smoked salmon and trout, and lamb dishes such as *fenalår* (smoked leg of lamb) are delicious, or try reindeer or elk for a taste of mountain Norway.

■ Overall, prices are higher here than elsewhere in Europe, with some things about 30 percent more expensive. Several passes and discount programs offer reduced prices at hotels (contact your local travel agent for information). If you're on a budget, watch for Lavpris (low-price) food stores.

Oslo

Oslo is a small, modern city of great character, but without the grandeur of many larger European capitals. Its spacious suburbs, forests and parks, all within sight and sound of the sea, give the city great vistas. It has outstanding art galleries and maritime museums, music venues, cafés, restaurants and fashionable boutiques. Yet there is always that inescapable feeling that wide-open spaces are not too far away.

Oslo Through History

Oslo was founded in 1000, but its progress to capital city was checkered. It was significant only as a fjord settlement during the Viking age. In the 11th century, the Norwegian King Harald Hardråde chose to make Oslo a rival to the northern capital of Trondheim. Oslo's fortunes rose and fell thereafter.

It was devastated by plague, and in the 17th century, following a disastrous fire and while under Danish rule, the settlement was rebuilt to the west of its original site and renamed Christiana, after the Danish King Christian IV.

Christiana became the capital of Norway in 1814. Throughout the 19th century the profitable timber trade and the economic advantages of union with Sweden increased its prosperity. By 1905, when Norway broke with the union, Christiana was a mature city economically and politically, and by 1925 the country was confident enough to reinstate the traditional name of Oslo.

The story of Oslo in the final decades of the 20th century was one of rapid modernization, as much on cultural as on social, political and economic terms. Wealth from the oil industry, the internationalization of Norwegian culture and a growing Norwegian self-confidence transformed the city into the vibrant capital that it is today.

The City's Stage

The most impressive way to arrive in Oslo is by sea. Viewed from the narrow neck of the Oslofjorden, the city's buildings are set against a backdrop of serene peninsulas and wooded hills. The hills are dotted with houses and accented by the great white viewing tower at the famous Holmenkollen ski jump.

Arrival by train, however, brings you to Jernbanetorget, the big open space in front of Oslo's central railroad station. This is not the most attractive part of the city, but a short walk along Karl

Holmenkollen ski jump in Oslo

Nobel Peace Prize

The Nobel Peace Prize has been awarded in Oslo Rådhuset (Oslo City Hall) since 1990. The award was founded at the end of the 19th century by Swedish inventor and industrialist Alfred Bernhard Nobel (1833–96). The Peace Prize winner is decided on criteria in Nobel's will citing "the person(s) who shall have done the most or the best work for brotherhood between nations,…." The prestigious ceremony takes place each year on December 10, the anniversary of Nobel's death. Some famous recipients of the award are Marie Curie (1911), Martin Luther King (1964), Amnesty International (1977), Mother Teresa (1979), Desmond Tutu (1984), Nelson Mandela (1993) Jimmy Carter (2002), Al Gore (2007), Barack Obama (2009) and Lin Xiaobo (2010).

Johans Gate (the city's main street) takes you quickly to Oslo Cathedral (Oslo Domkirke) and the busy open space of Stortorget, with its colorful flower market.

A few steps farther on is the Parliament (Stortinget). Before it lies the open space of Eidsvollsplass, the busy city center, alive with action and entertainment in summer. Its pond becomes a skating rink in winter.

To the northwest of Eidsvollsplass is the neoclassic Nationaltheatret (National Theater), where statues of Norwegian dramatists Bjørnstjerne Bjørnson and Henrik Ibsen stand guard. Farther northwest is tree-lined Slottsparken, which encompasses the unfenced and accessible Slottsparken (Royal Park) and the Kongelige Slott (Royal Palace) within its bounds.

To the south of the National Theater, down busy Olav V's Gate or Roald Amundsen Gate (passing one of Oslo's tourist information offices on Fridtjof Nansens plass 5 on the way), lies Oslo Rådhuset (Oslo City Hall) and the open space of Rådhusplassen. Adjoining this square is Rådhusbrygge (City Hall Pier) and the local ferryboat dock on Pipervika inlet. The ferry to the Bygdøy peninsula operates at this dock from April through September.

Exploring Oslo

Central Oslo is easily explored on foot, but you should become familiar with the transportation system so you can take one of the many day trips within easy reach. Public transportation is very efficient and easily understood; travel on city trams is a relaxing experience in itself. Visit the outlying Bygdøy peninsula, with its clutch of outstanding museums, or Frognerparken (Frogner Park) and Vigelandsparken (Vigeland Park), Norway's most visited attraction (see page 368).

Oslo's main street, Karl Johans Gate, is full of stores of all kinds, including David-Andersen AS at No. 20 (☎ 24 14 88 00; www.david-andersen.no), Scandinavia's largest jewelry store. The Paléet shopping mall has a mix of

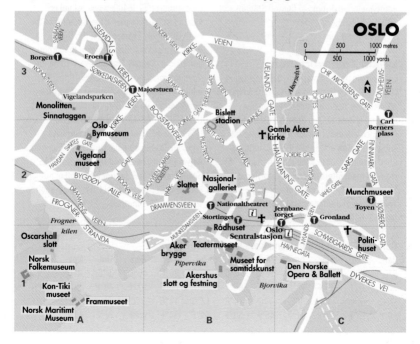

fashion boutiques and restaurants. Stop for coffee and pastries at the Grand Café (see page 486) at the Grand Hotel, one of Henrik Ibsen's former haunts.

A short distance north of the Royal Palace is the busy shopping street of Hegdehaugsveien and its continuation, Bogstadveien. Down at the harbor, on the western side of Pipervika inlet in the converted shipyard buildings, is Aker Brygge, a modern complex with numerous stores, restaurants, cafés and entertainment venues. The area's attractive waterside setting adds to the character.

Eating out in Oslo offers a variety of local and international cuisine. Try traditional restaurants such as the excellent Engebret Café (see page 486) on Bankplassen, where you can enjoy Norwegian specialties. Feast on excellent music too, in the Oslo Konserthus on Munkedamsveien, a little to the north of Aker Brygge.

The Oslo experience is a relaxed one, because of the compactness of the city center and because of the ease with which you can reach the outlying attractions and surrounding countryside. The openness of the city is reflected in the people, who are brisk but friendly in their attitude. English is a second language, especially to younger Norwegians, and you are never far away from advice and guidance to help you make the most of your stay.

Essential Information

Tourist Information
VisitOSLO
Fridtjof Nansens plass 5 (next to Oslo City Hall)
☎ 81 53 05 55;
www.visitoslo.com
Jernbanetorget 1 (next to Central Station)
☎ 81 53 05 55;
www.visitoslo.com

Urban Transportation
Oslo's main railroad station is Sentralstasjon (Central Station), known as Oslo S. Oslo has an efficient bus and tram network. The bus terminal is next to Oslo Sentralstasjon. Six tramlines run east to west. The city also has a subway system, called the T-bane, with six lines running east to west identified by a "T" sign. Its main intersection is at Stortinget Station. For more information contact Trafikanten at Jerbanetorget 1, by Oslo S (daily 8–8, May–Sep.; Mon.–Fri. 7 a.m.–8 p.m.,

Sat.–Sun. 8–6, rest of year); for travel outside Oslo visit www.trafikanten.no). Taxis are available from Oslo Taxi (☎ 02323).

Airport Information
Oslo Airport (☎ 06400; www.osl.no) is located at Gardermoen, 31 miles north of the city. An Airport Express Train (FlyToget; www.flytoget.no) runs between the airport and Oslo S (Central Station) every 10 minutes; no night services; the trip takes 19 to 22 minutes. Regular train services stop at the airport and take less than 30 minutes to Oslo S. The SAS Airport Express buses (☎ 22 80 49 71 or 117 [within Norway]; www.flybussen.no/oslo) run every 20 minutes between the airport and the Radisson SAS Scandinavia Hotel (journey time 50 minutes) via the Oslo Bussterminal (Oslo Bus Station; travel time 40 minutes).

Climate – average highs and lows for the month

Jan.	Feb.	Mar.	Apr.	May	Jun.	Jul.	Aug.	Sep.	Oct.	Nov.	Dec.
0°C	0°C	4°C	9°C	16°C	19°C	22°C	20°C	16°C	9°C	4°C	0°C
32°F	32°F	39°F	48°F	61°F	66°F	72°F	68°F	61°F	48°F	39°F	32°F
-7°C	-7°C	-3°C	1°C	7°C	10°C	12°C	12°C	7°C	3°C	-2°C	-5°C
19°F	19°F	27°F	34°F	45°F	50°F	54°F	54°F	45°F	37°F	28°F	23°F

Oslo Sights

Akershus slott og festning

Akershus slott (Akershus castle) stands
on a rocky height on the eastern side of
the harbor inlet of Pipervika. It was
founded in 1299 as a royal residence,
but by the end of the 17th century it had
been transformed into the powerful
festning (fortress).

The Norges Hjemmefrontmuseum
(Norwegian Resistance Museum) here
is a compelling record of Norway's
experiences in World War II, when
the Nazi occupation headquarters were
at Akershus.

Also of interest is the Forsvarsmuseet
(Armed Forces Museum).

Slott 🕇 B1 ✉ Oslo mil/Akershus ☎ 23 09 35 53;
www.akershusfestning.no ◷ Mon.–Sat. 10–4, Sun.
12:30–4, May–Aug.; Sat.–Sun. 12:30–4, Thu. guided
tour only (in English) at 1, rest of year. Closed during
official engagements 🚇 Stortinget 🚊 Tram 10, 12
🍴 Engebret Café, see page 486 💷 $$$
Festning ✉ Oslo mil/Akershus ☎ 23 09 39 82;
www.nasjonalefestningsverk.no ◷ Outdoor area:
daily 6 a.m.–9 p.m. Information center: Mon.–Fri. 9–6,
Sat.–Sun. 11–5, May–Aug.; Mon.–Fri. 10–4, Sat.–Sun.
11–5, rest of year 🚇 Stortinget 🚊 Tram 10, 12
🍴 Engebret Café, see page 486 💷 Free guided tours
Norges Hjemmefrontmuseum ✉ Oslo mil/Akershus
☎ 23 09 31 38; www.nhm.mil.no ◷ Mon.–Fri. 10–5,
Sat.–Sun. 11–4, Jun.–Aug.; Mon.–Fri. 10–4, Sat.–Sun.
11–4, rest of year 🚇 Stortinget 🚊 Tram 10, 12
🍴 Engebret Café, see page 486 💷 $$
Forsvarsmuseet ☎ 23 09 35 82 ◷ Mon.–Fri. 10–5,
Sat.–Sun. 11–5, May–Aug.; Tue.–Fri. 11–3, Sat.–Sun.
11–4, rest of year. Closed Easter and Whit Sat.–Sun.
💷 Free

Frammuseet

The centerpiece of the Frammuseet
(Fram Museum) is the preserved Arctic
exploration vessel *Fram*, with a bow like
a battering ram and a hull as solid as a
castle wall. The *Fram* was launched in
1892 and was used by Norwegian
explorers Fridtjof Nansen, Otto
Sverdrup and Roald Amundsen in polar
expeditions. Go aboard the vessel to see
its sturdiness and get a sense of the
tough, determined life that its crew led.
🕇 A1 ✉ Bygdøynesveien 36, Bygdøynes ☎ 23
28 29 50; www.fram.museum.no/en ◷ Daily 9–6,
Jun.–Aug.; 10–5 in May and Sep.; 10–4, Mar.–Apr. and
in Oct.; Mon.–Fri. 10–3, Sat.–Sun. 10–4, rest of year
🚌 30 ⛴ Bygdøynes Boat 91, from Rådhusbrygge 3
(Apr.–Sep.) 💷 $$$

Kon-Tiki museet

The Kon-Tiki museet (Kon-Tiki
Museum) is a colorful celebration of
Thor Heyerdahl's amazing voyages.

This museum complements the general
maritime themes of the adjacent Fram
Museum and the Norwegian Maritime
Museum. Heyerdahl's ethos of
adventure, linked to environmentalism
and international cooperation, is vividly
expressed. The *Kon-Tiki* balsa wood raft
of his 1947 Pacific crossing and the
papyrus vessel *Ra II* of his 1970 Atlantic
crossing both reflect the Norwegian
genius for maritime exploration.
🕇 A1 ✉ Bygdøynesveien 36, Bygdøynes ☎ 23
08 67 67; www.kon-tiki.no ◷ Daily 9:30–5:30,
Jun.–Aug.; 10–5, Apr.–May and in Sep.; 10:30–4 in
Mar. and Oct.; 10:30–3:30, rest of year 🚌 30
⛴ Bygdøynes Boat 91, from Rådhusbrygge 3
(Apr.–Sep.) 💷 $$$

Munch-museet

The Munch-museet (Munch Museum)
is a fitting celebration of Norway's most
famous artist. Edvard Munch's *The
Scream* (one of two versions, the other
is in the National Gallery, see page 368),
on display here, is a world-famous
cultural icon.

Munch produced a huge body of work,
and the Munch Museum provides an
insight into the complex personality of
this fascinating artist.
🕇 C2 ✉ Tøyengata 53 ☎ 23 49 35 00;
www.munch.museum.no ◷ Daily 10–6, Jun.–Aug.;

Tue.–Fri. 10–4, Sat.–Sun. 11–5, rest of year 🚇 Tøyen 🚌 20 🍴 Café 🎟 $$$ (free Oct.–Mar.) ℹ Guided tours (free) in English daily at 1, Jul.–Aug.

Nasjonalgalleriet

Oslo's Nasjonalgalleriet (National Gallery) has works by painters such as Georges Braque and Pablo Picasso, but its main collection is of work from 1800 up to 1950 by Norwegian masters such as Christian Krohg, Johan Christian Dahl, Thomas Fearnley and Edvard Munch. Highlights include Krohg's lively portrait *Oda Krohg, the Painter*, a charming rendition of artist Oda Krohg in vivid red and blue clothes. The Romantic Fjordland paintings of Johan Christian Dahl and Thomas Fearnley will entice you to visit the fjords. Look on the top floor for Ernst Josephson's *The Spanish Blacksmiths*. The room devoted to Munch shows some classic masterpieces, including a version of *The Scream*, the powerful *Dance of Life*, the sensual *Day After* and the most ravishing *Madonna*.

🔆 B2 ✉ Universitetsgata 13 ☎ 21 98 20 00; www.nationalmuseum.no 🕐 Tue.–Fri. 10–6 (also Thu. 6–7 p.m.), Sat.–Sun. 10–5 🚇 Nationaltheatret 🚌 Buses to Nationaltheatret; tram 10, 11, 13, 17, 18, 19 🍴 Café 🎟 Free, except during special exhibitions

Norsk Folkemuseum

The Norsk Folkemuseum (Norwegian Folk Museum) gives an excellent portrayal of Norway's folk culture. The museum includes a lovely parklike area consisting of 155 traditional buildings and some reconstructed 19th-century village streets.

The main buildings display crafts, folk costumes and examples of rural interiors. There also is an exhibition on the culture of the Sami, the indigenous people of northern Scandinavia.

🔆 A1 ✉ Museumsveien 10, Bygdøy ☎ 22 12 37 00; www.norskfolkemuseum.no 🕐 Daily 10–6, mid-May to mid-Sep.; Mon.–Fri. 11–3, Sat.–Sun. 11–4, rest of year 🚌 30 🚢 Bygdøynes Boat 91, from Rådhusbrygge 3 (Apr.–Sep.) 🍴 Café 🎟 $$$ (less expensive mid-Sep. to mid-May)

Norsk Maritimt Museum

Norsk Maritimt Museum (Norwegian Maritime Museum), located on the tip of the Bygdøy peninsula, overlooks the calm waters of the Oslofjorden. In the main hall Christian Krogh's great marine painting, *Leiv Eriksson's Discovery of America*, sets the scene for exhibits on all things to do with shipping and the sea. The basement theater shows a video on Norway's great maritime history. On the main floor is the escape boat, secretly (and daringly) made from rough planking by Norwegian sailors while imprisoned aboard ships in West Africa by the Germans during World War II.

🔆 A1 ✉ Bygdøynesveien 37, Bygdøynes ☎ 24 11 41 50; www.norsk-sjofartsmuseum.no 🕐 Daily 10–6, mid-May to Aug. 31; 10:30–4 (also Thu. 4–6), rest of year 🚌 30 🚢 Bygdøynes Boat 91, from Rådhusbrygge 3 (Apr.–Sep.) 🍴 Cafés 🎟 $$ ℹ Audio tours

Den Norsk Opera & Ballett

The massive, white building, designed by the Norwegian company Snøhetta, has captured several awards for its contemporary architecture. Looking like an iceberg at the very end of the Oslo fjord, it's a "must see."

🔆 C1 ✉ Kirsten Flagstad plass 1 ☎ 21 42 21 00; www.operaen.no 🕐 Guided tours in English: daily at 2, Jun.–Sep., Fri.–Mon. at 2, May–Jun., Sat.–Sun. at 2, rest of year 🚇 Oslo-S 🎟 $$$

Vigelandsparken

One of Norway's most visited attractions, Vigelandsparken (Vigeland Park) represents the life's work of the Norwegian sculptor Gustav Vigeland (1869–1943) and is the world's largest sculpture park accomplished by a single artist. At the southern end of the park the Vigeland-museet (Vigeland Museum) displays much of his work.

🔆 A3 ✉ Off Kirkeveien. Museum: Nobels gate 32 ☎ 23 49 37 00; www.vigeland.museum.no 🕐 Daily 24 hours. Museum: Tue.–Sun. 10–5, Jun.–Aug.; Tue.–Sun. noon–4, rest of year 🚇 Majorstuen 🚌 20; tram 12 🍴 Café 🎟 Park: free; Museum: $$ (free Oct.–Mar.)

Fjord and Mountain Line

Most visitors to Norway go to the western fjords during their stay. Even if your time is limited you can still make the famous "Norway in a nutshell" journey by train, bus and boat through some of the most magnificent scenery in western Norway. The trip can be completed in one to three days, depending on how much time you have available, at any time of the year. It starts from Oslo, Bergen or Voss aboard the scenic Bergen Railway, the 292-mile rail link between Oslo and Bergen, northern Europe's highest railroad, rising at one point to 4,009 feet.

At Myrdal you'll transfer to the famous Flåmsbana (Flåm Railway), one of the high points of the tour. The stylish train, with its comfortable accommodations, takes 55 minutes to travel 12.5 miles down the wild Flåm valley, affording views of some of the most magnificent mountain scenery in Norway.

At Flåm (pronounced Flum) there is time to eat and to wander around before continuing the trip by boat on the Aurlandsfjord and into the Nærøyfjord, the narrowest fjord in Europe and on the UNESCO World Heritage List. Surrounded by mountains up to 5,900 feet high, the boat glides past small traditional farms clinging to the mountainsides. You will see goats grazing along the edge of the fjord and, if you're lucky, seals lying on rocks before the boat docks at Gudvangen.

The next stage of the trip is the bus ride up Stalheimskleiva (the steepest road in northern Europe – not passable October through April). Through 13 spectacular hairpin bends, offering views of the spectacular waterfalls Stalheimfossen and Sivlefossen, you'll arrive at the Stalheim Hotel, where there is a short stop before the trip carries on to Voss. From Voss you can continue your exploration by train to Bergen or Oslo for the last leg of one of the world's great round trips.

The Norway in a nutshell tour can be booked through Fjord Tours, Strømgaten 4, 5015 Bergen, ☎ 81 56 82 22; www.fjordtours.com or Rail Europe (☎ 08448 484 064; general reservations team; www.raileurope.com/us).

Tumbling in several steep cascades, a waterfall crashes into Sognefjord in fjord country

Portugal

Opposite: Colorful boats in the fishing village of Sesimbra, south of Lisbon

Portugal

Portugal, lying on the western edge of the Continent and overshadowed by Spain, its larger neighbor to the east, was for many years considered the poor relation of southwestern Europe.

Political turmoil and poverty have long hindered development, but after joining the European Union in 1986, billions of dollars have poured into the country, helping to modernize its economy.

The Land

For travelers who knew Portugal a few decades ago, some things have changed beyond recognition; others remain stubbornly the same. In rural areas Portugal is still old-fashioned and underdeveloped, a real bonus for visitors seeking something a little different from mainstream European travel.

The country is small, geographically diverse and beautiful. Stretching 350 miles from north to south, it is packed with mountains, plateaus, river valleys, flat dry plains, rolling forested hills and a truly beautiful coastline. Portugal borders the Atlantic, and weather conditions can range from hot and sunny to stormy and wet. In the northern Trás-os-Montes region, winter temperatures drop well below freezing; in summer, it is not uncommon for the thermometer to top 100 degrees.

The Algarve, a popular vacation area on the southern coast that's often visited by northern Europeans, enjoys a Mediterranean climate, and the vegetation is subtropical. On the whole, summers are warm and dry, winters mild and wet, although it can be cold in the mountains. Mainland Portugal's highest mountain is the imposing, granite Torre, in the wilds of the Serra da Estrela, which rises above 6,500 feet. The Tagus (Tejo) river divides the country roughly in half. The Tagus and two other important rivers, the Douro and the Guadiana, rise in Spain, and Portugal must share their waters with its bigger neighbor, a factor which sometimes leads to difficulties in supply and environmental problems.

Portuguese Empire

It's easy to forget that Portugal was once at the head of a powerful empire. Beginning in the early 15th century, Portuguese explorers pushed far into the unknown, challenging the traditional view that the world ended somewhere west of Gibraltar. Madeira and the Azores were the first to be discovered, and these islands remain part of Portugal. Portuguese ships rounded the

More Top Destinations in Portugal

View over Lisbon from Esplanada da Igreja da Graça

Cape of Good Hope in 1488, and in 1497 Vasco da Gama reached Calicut, India. By 1560, Portugal had claimed Brazil and had an empire stretching east as far as Japan, with missionary and trading posts in Africa, India, Malaysia, Macao and Timor.

Despite strong rivalry between Portugal and Spain over discoveries in the Americas, the 16th century was a Golden Age, with spices, slaves and gold making Portugal hugely rich. But the voyages and maintenance of an overseas empire were extremely costly, and the

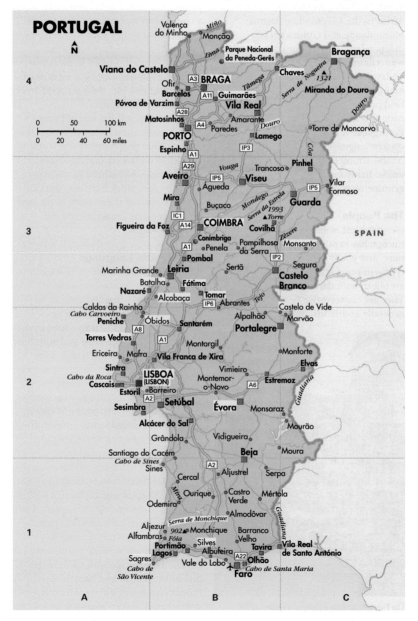

PORTUGAL

N

Valença do Minho
Monção
Miño
Lima
Parque Nacional da Peneda-Gerês
Bragança

Viana do Castelo
Ofir
A3 BRAGA
Tâmega
Chaves
Serra de Nogueira
1321
Miranda do Douro

4

Barcelos
A11 Guimarães
Vila Real

Póvoa de Varzim
A28
Matosinhos
A4
Amarante
Paredes
Douro
Torre de Moncorvo

0   50   100 km
0   20   40   60 miles

PORTO

Espinho
A1
Lamego
IP3

A29
Vouga
Trancoso
Pinhel

Aveiro
IP5
Viseu

Mira
Águeda
Buçaco
Mondego
Serra da Estrela
1993
Guarda
IP5
Vilar Formoso

IC1
A14 COIMBRA
Torre
Covilhã
Zêzere

3

Figueira da Foz
Conímbriga
A1 Penela
Pampilhosa da Serra
Monsanto
SPAIN

Pombal
Sertã
IP2
Segura

Marinha Grande
Leiria
Castelo Branco

Batalha
Fátima
Nazaré
Alcobaça
Tomar
IP6 Abrantes
Tejo
Castelo de Vide

Caldas da Rainha
Cabo Carvoeiro
Peniche
Óbidos
Santarém
Alpalhão
Marvão
Portalegre

Torres Vedras
A8
Montargil
Monforte

Ericeira
Mafra
A1
Vila Franca de Xira
Vimieiro
Elvas

Sintra
Cabo da Roca
Cascais
LISBOA (LISBON)
Montemor-o-Novo
A6
Estremoz

2

Estoril
Barreiro
A2
Setúbal
Évora
Monsaraz
Guadiana

Sesimbra
Alcácer do Sal
Mourão

Grândola
Vidigueira

Santiago do Cacém
Cabo de Sines
Sines
A2
Beja
Moura

Cercal
Aljustrel
Serpa

Ourique
Castro Verde
Mértola

Odemira
Mira
Almodôvar
Guadiana

1

Aljezur
Serra de Monchique
902 Monchique
Barranco Velho

Alfambras
Fóia
Silves
Tavira
Vila Real de Santo António

Portimão
Lagos
Albufeira
A22
Olhão

Sagres
Cabo de São Vicente
Vale do Lobo
Cabo de Santa Maria
Faro

A   B   C

home economy was worsening. By 1580, Philip II of Spain had claimed the throne, becoming Philip I of Portugal the following year. Within 100 years, many of the overseas possessions had fallen to the English and Dutch.

The legacy of the empire still exists, however. Portugal extricated itself from Africa in the 1970s, when Angola, Mozambique and Guinea became independent; East Timor in Indonesia was relinquished at the same time. Today there are buildings, churches and monuments wherever the Portuguese held power, but language became the country's most important legacy. Portuguese is the seventh most widely spoken language in the world. Brazil retains strong ties with Portugal and, unlike many former colonies, there is genuine respect between the countries.

The People

Geographical isolation from most of Europe has kept Portuguese bloodlines pure, and you'll notice a definite racial type – in provincial areas, most people are short, with dark eyes, skin and hair. They are conservative people who are generally courteous and respectful.

The Elevador da Bica climbs up a Lisbon street

Northerners, with a harsher climate and historically poorer living conditions, tend to be less easygoing than people in the south, and more religious. Even so, the Catholic church continues to hold great sway everywhere.

Approximately 40 percent of the population still lives in rural areas, with a large urban increase occurring in the 1970s, when people came home from former African colonies following independence. In Lisbon in particular, many Afro-Portuguese have integrated into Portuguese life; there's a good level of interracial harmony.

The country still has one of Europe's highest emigration rates, with more than three million people living and working abroad. With few natural resources, many people in northern Portugal are forced to seek work overseas; you can see the results of their labors in the new houses and cars found in even the poorest villages.

Society and Language

Being polite and friendly will smooth your path as you travel through Portugal. The Portuguese tend to be welcoming and unhurried, so be prepared for things to take a long time. There are traditional ideas and attitudes toward women, and the farther away from major towns you travel the more obvious this becomes. It's sometimes considered disrespectful to wear skimpy clothing, and it is customary to speak formally and politely until you get to know the people you are talking to.

One of the major hurdles in getting to know the Portuguese is the language barrier. Don't try your Spanish in Portugal. Despite – or because of – proximity to Spain, the Portuguese don't appreciate being addressed in Spanish. However, if you can read Spanish you'll have no problem reading Portuguese. It's a romance language with Latin roots, similar to Spanish and Italian. Pronunciation is a different matter altogether, however, and spoken

A detail of the elaborate carving at the Mosteiro dos Jerónimos in the Belém district of Lisbon

Portuguese, with its sibilants, nasal vowels and guttural consonants, reminds some people of Russian and Slavic languages.

The Portuguese are excellent linguists; you'll find English spoken in major tourist areas, and in the countryside among the younger generation. Do try and tackle one or two words; your efforts will be appreciated and faces will light up when you try to communicate.

Changing Portugal

Since the watershed of 1986, huge changes have occcured in Portugal. Once one of the poorest countries in Western Europe, Portugal had one of the highest economic growth rates in the 1990s. While unemployment plummeted, the cost was a widening gap between rich and poor, noticeable wherever you travel.

The enlargement of the EU since 2004, however, poses several challenges. As countries farther east in Europe have swelled the ranks, Portugal lost its advange of relatively cheap labor costs, and a high proportion of national earnings comes from overseas – a global market that becomes ever more challenging. Agriculture in Portugal is still relatively unproductive due to lack of investment and the difficulty of using modern methods and large equipment on much of the terrain. Education levels are low by European standards, with a surprising percentage of the population having literacy problems.

By 2005 Portugal had dropped to 18th in the GDP (Gross Domestic Product) table of European countries. As the world financial crisis broke in 2008, economic growth stalled at 0 percent and as yet it has failed to recover with GDP hovering at -0.5 percent in early 2011. However, Portugal does export large amounts of certain products including cork, tomato paste and wine. It also earns through foreign tourism, an industry that continues to develop. Portugal has become a much-loved holiday destination for many Europeans. For visitors, the blend of old and new is alluring. Investment in infrastructure through the early 2000s has improved the visitor experience, while the rustic way of life is still evident away from the major cities and towns.

Timeline

1000 BC to AD 400	Occupation by Phoenicians, Carthaginians, Iberians, Celts, Romans and Visigoths.
AD 713	Moors control most of the country and remain in power for 400 years.
1179	Pope recognizes Kingdom of Portugal.
1255	Afonso III makes Lisbon the capital of Portugal.
1480–1500s	Age of Discovery.
1488	Bartolomeu Dias rounds Cape of Good Hope.
1580	End of Golden Age with invasion by Philip II of Spain, who declares himself Philip I of Portugal.
1668	Treaty of Lisbon recognizes Portuguese independence.
1755	Lisbon earthquake.
1910	Portuguese monarchy overthrown and replaced by republic.
1916–18	Portugal joins Allies in World War I.
1933	Estado Novo (New State) established. Falls in 1974.
1939–45	Portugal neutral throughout World War II.
1960s	Portuguese colony of Goa occupied by India; local nationalist uprisings in Angola, Guinea and Mozambique.
1976	New constitution drawn up after the fall of the Estado Novo.
1986	Portugal admitted to European Union; start of period of huge economic growth and social reform.
2001	Porto is named European Capital of Culture for 2001.
2004	Portuguese Prime Minister José Manuel Barroso is appointed President of the European Union.
2005–2006	Portugal's driest summer on record brings drought and forest fires.
2006	Social Democrat Anibel Cavaco Silva wins the presidential elections.
2008–2011	The Portuguese economy struggles on the verge of collapse as EU enlargement and the world credit crisis take their toll.
2011	Anibel Cavaco Silva is reelected as President.

Prince Henry the Navigator

The impetus for the great Portuguese "Age of Discovery" of the late 15th century came from the son of João I, Prince Henry, who was born in 1394. He can be credited with transforming Portugal into a great maritime power whose success was based on a scientific approach to exploration, navigation and cartography. At his base in the Algarve, Henry gathered together accomplished shipbuilders, sailors, navigators, instrument makers and astronomers, encouraging them to prepare for long voyages into the unknown. A new type of ship, the highly successful caravel, was designed: a speedy vessel that made the great voyages possible. Motivated by religion as well as commerce, Henry's ships sailed ever farther south, rounding Cape Bojador in West Africa, then thought to be the end of the world, in 1434. By Henry's death in 1460, the Portuguese had reached Sierra Leone, and the known world had become a bigger place.

Survival Guide

- The Portuguese are committed wine drinkers. Generally, when you order house wine in restaurants you'll get something very drinkable, even though it may appear in an earthenware jug in rustic eateries.

- Water available everywhere is safe to drink, although sometimes it may taste less than delicious. Avoid tap water in the Algarve during the summer and drink bottled water instead, to be on the safe side. It is readily available.

- In more rural areas, the modest Portuguese are often shocked by scanty clothes, especially men without shirts, except at the beach. If you are wearing a sleeveless top, take along a scarf to wrap around your shoulders as needed, particularly if you intend to visit churches. Do not enter while a service is in progress.

- Portuguese drivers are among Europe's worst; the country has one of the highest accident rates in Europe.

- Telephone calls from your hotel room are expensive, but Portugal's telephone system is state-of-the-art. The on-street "Credifone," which accepts coins, credit cards and plastic phone cards, offers an easy way to connect. You can buy phone cards from street kiosks.

- Be prepared for Portugal to be different in many ways from its neighbor, particularly if you've already visited Spain. Despite their proximity, the two countries are very different.

- Public restrooms are few and far between, but it's acceptable – even if you're not a customer – to ask to use hotel or restaurant facilities. Men's toilets are marked "H" and women's are marked "S."

- Try not to let any apparent grime or shabbiness in some cities affect you; look for the positive qualities, such as elaborate period architecture.

- Don't be surprised by the sometimes startling amount of garbage in rural areas.

- It is increasingly easy to find luxury accommodations and excellent service away from major tourist centers, with the opening of a large number of spas, fine country hotels and boutique-style bed-and-breakfast places.

- Portuguese food is traditionally rustic and served in hearty portions. Some dishes require an adventurous spirit, alternatively you can enjoy roasted meats, grilled fish and chicken.

- Leave small change in a bar; otherwise about 5–10 percent is an adequate tip.

- *Pousadas* offer many interesting accommodations options when traveling in Portugal. These are state-owned but privately run, deluxe establishments located in historic or beautiful places such as former monasteries, palaces and castles. Advance reservations are highly recommended.

Shoppers and diners at the café terraces in Rua Augusta in Baixa, Lisbon

Lisbon

Lisbon (Lisboa) is a beguiling city. It has a great past and a promising future. Its backstreets may easily strike the visitor as old-fashioned and crumbling – but these elements also are an essential part of its charm. Look for the positive: the port city's vigor and life; its great colonial past; the atmospheric old trams; and the evocative sights, sounds and scents – laundry flapping in the wind, shoeshine men hawking their trade, the melancholy strains of *fado* music, the aroma of roasting coffee and chestnuts.

Most sights of interest are within walking distance of downtown, with the exception of the glorious attractions of suburban Belém, to the west of the old city, a train, bus or tram ride away.

Lisbon Flavors and *Bacalhau*

Lisbon has a wide range of restaurants at every price level, with the emphasis on traditional Portuguese cooking, although fast-food outlets are easy to find as well. Breakfast consists of small cakes and pastries, and hotels usually offer a continental-style breakfast buffet. Lunch is more substantial than in other European cities.

Heavy soups are popular, salads, although sometimes limited in

ingredients, are readily available as is freshly squeezed orange juice. Lisbon inhabitants eat a lot of fish and seafood, including *bacalhau* (a dried, salted codfish), and the warming winter stews are excellent.

The Lisbon Earthquake

On All Saints' Day (November 1), 1755, the Lisbon earthquake struck. Churches were packed for this major feast day, and thousands of lighted candles toppled during the tremors, starting fires that were as destructive as the quake. A massive tidal wave followed, swallowing Lisbon's fleet and flooding the already-destroyed lower city. During the aftermath hospitals opened, prices were fixed and a tax levied to cover rebuilding costs, including the lower city, today known as the Baixa district. Although Lisbon largely recovered, 1755 marked the end of its role as Europe's leading port city.

You may be surprised at the number of pastry and cake shops; the Portuguese are notoriously sweet-toothed, and Lisbon has many tempting, old-fashioned shops selling traditional specialties like the delicious *pastéis de* *Belém* (pastries filled with custard). Portugal makes very good red and white wine, national and foreign beers are everywhere, and all the usual spirits and aperitifs are available. It is known for the fortified wine, port.

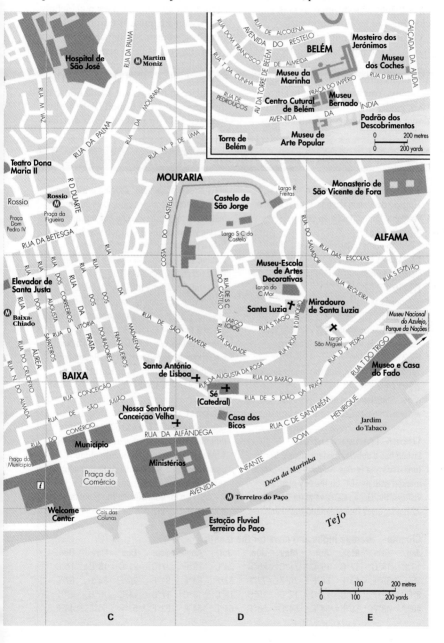

Souvenirs from Lisbon

Shopping is great fun in Lisbon, and there are many stores selling lovely Portuguese crafts. The area known as the Chiado, in downtown Lisbon, is the most fashionable shopping district, with streets lined with numerous classy clothing and jewelry boutiques.

Carpets from Arraiolos are a superb buy, as is the porcelain manufactured by Vista Alegre. Linen and cotton sheets and tablecloths are another Portuguese specialty. You have the lovely glazed tiles, *azulejos*, made to order, or track down something made from cork.

Film, Music and *Fado*

Lisbon offers a variety of music, theater, ballet and movies. Films are all shown in their original language with subtitles. *Fado*, a unique style of Portuguese music, is heard at its best in Lisbon and should be experienced. This melancholy and passionate music is traditionally sung by a woman, accompanied by guitar. Its origins lie in history, a mix of Moorish and African elements, and can be described as a kind of operetta. The best place to hear it is at a *fado* house in the Upper Town of Lisbon (Bairro Alto, see page 381), or in the Alfama district.

Essential Information

Tourist Information

Turismo de Lisboa (Lisbon Tourist Office)
Welcome Center, Praça do Comércio
☎ 210 312 810
Santa Apolónia (railway station)
☎ 218 821 606
Lisbon International Airport (arrivals)
☎ 218 450 660
Jerónimos Monastery Quiosque
☎ 213 658 435
Rua Augusta Quiosque ☎ 213 259 131
Palácio Foz, Praça dos Restauradores
☎ 213 463 314
Youth Tourist Office, Rua Jardim do Regedor
☎ 213 472 134
www.visitlisboa.com or
www.askmelisboa.com

Urban Transportation

Lisbon has a subway system, buses, trams, funiculars and ferries. Subway stations are marked with an "M" on the city map. For visitors, the Lisboa Card, valid for 24, 48 or 72 hours, gives free unlimited travel and free entry into 26 attractions. Zapping is a replenishable electronic card, valid on buses, metro and ferries, or you can buy bus and tram tickets when boarding, and subway tickets from a machine or office at the subway station. The modern tram 15 is a useful line. Ferry tickets are available from offices at the ferry stations; a ferry trip is recommended as part of your sightseeing. Prepaid taxi vouchers to various zones and destinations are available at three tourist information centers – the airport, Lisboa Welcome Center and Palácio Foz. There are taxi stands on the Rossio and the Praça da Figueira, or you can call a cab (☎ 217 932 756 and 218 119 000).

Airport Information

Lisbon Airport (☎ 218 413 500 for flight information, or online at www.ana.pt) is about 4 miles (a 20-minute drive) north of the downtown area. The No. 91 Aero-Bus shuttle service leaves every 20 minutes daily 7 a.m.–11 p.m. from outside the terminal to downtown Lisbon.

Climate – average highs and lows for the month

Jan.	Feb.	Mar.	Apr.	May	Jun.	Jul.	Aug.	Sep.	Oct.	Nov.	Dec.
13°C	15°C	17°C	19°C	21°C	25°C	28°C	29°C	27°C	21°C	18°C	14°C
55°F	59°F	63°F	66°F	70°F	77°F	82°F	84°F	81°F	70°F	64°F	57°F
8°C	9°C	10°C	12°C	12°C	15°C	18°C	18°C	17°C	14°C	10°C	9°C
46°F	48°F	50°F	54°F	54°F	59°F	64°F	64°F	63°F	57°F	50°F	48°F

Lisbon Sights

Bairro Alto

The Bairro Alto (Upper Town) is one of the five areas that constitute Lisbon's historic center and the atmospheric jumble of streets and squares tumble down steep slopes to the Baixa (the Lower Town) below. At night it's one of the city's liveliest quarters, where in *fado* houses you can hear melancholic, evocative Portuguese songs.

The Elevador de Santa Justa, a wonderfully clunky elevator built in 1902, takes people from the Baixa up to the Chiado and Bairro Alto.

🞣 Off map at A3 ✉ Area on slopes to west of Baixa
🅠 Restauradores, Baixa-Chiado 🚌 758, 790; tram 28

Baixa and Rossio

Rossio Square, properly known as Praça Dom Pedro IV, and the grid of streets forming the Baixa district will repeatedly draw you back. The Teatro Nacional (National Theater) and a soaring column topped by a statue of Dom Pedro IV dominate the spacious Rossio, which is lined with stores and cafés.

The square has an ancient history and was the scene of Inquisition burnings in the 16th century. Between Rossio and the waterfront lies the Baixa, a perfect example of rational 18th-century planning, erected at the Marquês de Pombal's instigation after the 1755 earthquake. The orderly streets are lined with lovely old stores, modern chain stores, gracious buildings and decorative tiled facades.

🞣 C3, B4 ✉ Praça Dom Pedro IV and streets between it and Praça do Comércio 🅠 Baixa-Chiado, Rossio
🚌 All services to Rossio and Praça do Comércio

Castelo de São Jorge

Visible from many parts of Lisbon, the Castelo de São Jorge (St. George's Castle) stands on the site of the earliest settlement. Fortified sucessively by the Romans, Visigoths and Moors, it was besieged in 1147 by Afonso Henriques and his Christian army and finally fell after 17 weeks – a turning point in the struggle to evict the Moors from Portugal. The Moorish battlements still stand, offering superb views over the rooftops to the river. Today, extensive restoration within the main structure has made a verdant, cool oasis, with terraces, pools and fountains.

The Câmara Escura observation tower offers 360-degree views of Lisbon and the Tagus. The Alfama district around the palace is worth exploring.

🞣 D4 ✉ Rua Santa Cruz do Castelo ☎ 218 800 620; www.castelosaojorge.pt 🕐 Daily 9–9, Mar.–Oct.; daily 9–6, rest of year (last entry 30 minutes before closing)
🚌 737; tram 12, 28 🅤 $$$

An equestrian statue of King José I on Praça do Comércio, near the Triumphal Arch in the Baixa district

Mosteiro dos Jerónimos

The stunning architectural ensemble of the Mosteiro dos Jerónimos (Jerónimos Monastery), a UNESCO World Heritage Site, stands on the site of an earlier chapel, visited by Portuguese explorers before their great voyages.

Building began on the present church in 1501 to celebrate Vasco da Gama's successful voyage to the Indies. It took almost 100 years to complete, by which time various architectural fashions had come and gone. As a result, the church and adjoining cloisters are a glorious mix of Gothic, Renaissance and Manueline styles.

Pause first at the magnificent south door. Its intricate carving includes the figure of Henry the Navigator; the west door, equally splendid, features Manuel I, who started the construction. The soaring interior contains the simple tomb of Vasco da Gama, a contrast to the surrounding riot of stonework. The cloisters are equally elaborately carved, a combination of delicacy and strength.

➕ See map inset ✉ Praça do Império ☎ 213 620 034; www.mosteirojeronimos.pt 🕐 Tue.–Sun. 10–6:30, May–Sep.; 10–5, rest of year (last entry 30 minutes before closing) 🚊 Train: Belém 🚌 28, 714, 727, 729, 751; tram 15 🚢 Belém 🍴 O Caseiro, see page 487 💶 $$$; free Sun. and national holidays until 2 p.m.

Museu Calouste Gulbenkian

Portugal's greatest museum, the Museu Calouste Gulbenkian (Calouste Gulbenkian Museum) was financed by a bequest from the Armenian magnate, whose private collection makes up the bulk of the exhibits. It consists of two sections: European art and artifacts, and Oriental and ancient pieces. The museum is not vast, but everything it contains is of the highest quality.

Most visitors are particularly enthralled by the Lalique jewelry and glass, distinctive art deco pieces displayed in a darkened room.

➕ Off map at A5 ✉ Avenida de Berna 45A ☎ 217 823 000; www.museu.gulbenkian.pt 🕐 Tue.–Sun.

10–6 (last entry at 5:45) 🚇 S. Sebastião or Praça de Espanha 🚌 16, 56, 718, 726, 742 🍴 Restaurant and café in museum 💶 $$; free to all Sun.

Museu de Marinha

The Museu de Marinha (Maritime Museum) is one of the best of its kind in Europe. It's a huge collection, with full-size boats, royal barges, paintings, uniforms and archaic navigational instruments. Most evocative, perhaps, is the attractive wooden statue of the Archangel Raphael, said to have accompanied Vasco da Gama on his epic voyage to the Indies in 1497.

➕ See map inset ✉ Praça do Império ☎ 213 620 019; http://museu.marinha.pt 🕐 Tue.–Sun. 10–6, May–Sep.; 10–5, rest of year 🚊 Train: Belém 🚌 28, 201, 714, 727, 729, 751; tram 15 💶 $$; free on Sun. 10–1

Museu Nacional do Azulejo

Throughout Lisbon and Portugal, you'll notice the exquisite tiles, or *azulejos*, adorning the walls of countless buildings. The Museu Nacional do Azulejo (National Tile Museum) traces the history of the painted glazed tile, which has been used in Portugal since the 15th century. You can see how the art developed from simple early tiles to complex, multicolored examples. Blue and white has predominated since Chinese porcelain arrived in Europe; the wonderful tiled view of Lisbon, made in 1738, is a fine example.

➕ Off map at E2 ✉ Rua da Madre de Deus 4 ☎ 218 100 340; http://mnazulejo-imc-ip.pt 🕐 Wed.–Sun. 10–6, Tue. 2–6 (last entry 30 minutes earlier) 🚌 794 🍴 Café in museum 💶 $$; free on Sun. 10–2

Padrão dos Descobrimentos

The eye-catching white mass of the Padrão dos Descobrimentos (Monument to the Discoveries) soars up from the water's edge at Belém, serving as a reminder of Portugal's great maritime past. It was erected in 1960 to mark the 500th anniversary of the death of Henry the Navigator, and has an angular front and curving form that represents a ship's

Lisbon Life

Everyday life in Lisbon, a relatively small and atmospheric city, is far more relaxed than in other capitals. The day starts around 7:30, when commuters are on the move and children make their way to school. Trams, the subway and buses are all crowded. Some people travel to town on the ferries that crisscross the Tagus. Many grab breakfast in a bar before work. Breakfast is usually coffee, with one of the cloyingly sweet pastries so loved by the Portuguese.

Lunch in Lisbon is taken seriously, and many people eat a full meal rather than a snack, although they eat it fast, often standing at a bar counter. Workers also use the lunch hour to shop for food or browse in stores. At the end of the afternoon, commuters head home but will often reemerge later to meet friends for a drink or more tea or coffee and cakes. Midweek evenings are often spent at home, although in the summertime the streets will be thronged for a few hours as people stroll around and chat outside.

Weekends are a different matter; people head for the Upper Town to eat and drink before going to concerts, movies or the theater, while young Portuguese enjoy the old district's waterfront clubs.

Saturday and Sunday are popular shopping days when crowds flock to huge malls on the outskirts of the city, which stay open late. Sundays, too, are high points for soccer fans, with the big matches attracting large crowds. Lisbon is blessed by its proximity to a beautiful coastline, and it's easy in summer to drive or catch a train to the coast for a day at the beach and dinner in an excellent fish restaurant. In midsummer, an outing to the cool green countryside around Sintra (see page 385), some 15 miles away, is another pleasant weekend option.

The exterior of the Teatro São Carlos in Lisbon's Chiado district

prow and sails. Figures crowd the prow, led by Henry, who holds a ship. An elevator rises more than 435 feet to the top, offering panoramic views. Below, a mosaic map traces the Portuguese voyages of exploration.

➕ See map inset ✉ Avenida de Brasília ☎ 213 031 950; www.padraodescobrimentos.egeac.pt 🕐 Daily 10–7, May–Sep.; Tue.–Sun. 10–6, rest of year (last entry 30 minutes earlier) 🚇 Train: Belém 🚌 28, 714, 727, 729, 751; tram 15 🍽 O Caseiro, see page 487 💶 $ (temporary exhibitions free); free on Sun. 10–2

Parque das Nações

The Parque das Nações (Park of the Nations) is used for trade fairs and exhibitions. Striking buildings, moorings, landscaped gardens, street cafés and restaurants front the Tagus. From the water rises the Oceanário (Oceanarium). This state-of-the-art aquarium is one of Europe's largest. It features a vast central tank, surrounded by four others representing the main oceans. Marine mammals and seabirds thrive, as well as fish, underwater creatures and vegetation, making this one of Lisbon's most impressive sights.

➕ Off map at E2 ✉ Parque das Nações ☎ 218 919 333 (Oceanarium); www.portaldasnacoes.pt; www.oceanario.pt 🕐 Oceanarium: daily 10–8, Apr.–Oct.; 10–7, rest of year (last admission 1 hour before closing) 🚇 Oriente 🚌 759, 782, 794 💶 Park free; Oceanarium $$$

Praça do Comércio

One side of the spacious Praça do Comércio (Commercial Square) opens on the water, emphasizing its original purpose as an imposing gateway to the city from the sea. To experience its original perspective, take the five-minute ferry trip from nearby Terreiro do Paço

(Palace Square) across the Tagus to the suburb of Cacilhas. The vista of the square and the triumphal arch leading to the streets of the Baixa opens up to buildings, churches and monuments, giving a flavor of the city's past.

➕ C2 ✉ Praça do Comércio 🚇 Baixa-Chiado 🚌 All buses to Praça do Comércio; tram 15 ⛴ Terreiro do Paço for ferries to Cacilhas

Sé

Construction of the Sé (Cathedral) started in 1150, soon after the expulsion of the Moors. It was the city's first church, a solid and harmonious Romanesque edifice. Its two massive towers are a city landmark. It largely escaped damage in the 1755 earthquake, making it a symbol of Lisbon's history. Inside, be sure to see the font where St. Anthony of Padua was baptized.

➕ D2 ✉ Largo da Sé ☎ 218 876 628 🕐 Church: Mon.–Sat. 9–7, Sun. 9–5. Museum and cloister: Tue.–Sat. 9–noon and 2–7 🚇 Rossio 🚌 737; tram 12, 28 💶 Museum and cloister $

Torre de Belém

In the nearby suburb of Belém, the Torre de Belém (Belém Tower) rises beside the Tagus river. This exquisite honey-colored stone tower is a symbol of Portugal's maritime past. Built between 1515 and 1520, it was designed by Francisco de Arruda, a Portuguese architect whose earlier Moroccan travels influenced his style. His work shows delightful Moorish elements – little domes topping the battlements, corner towers, and arcaded windows and loggias. Built as a bastion against pirate attack, it later served as a prison, and has been designated a World Heritage Site by UNESCO.

➕ See map inset ✉ Avenida de Brasília ☎ 213 620 034 🕐 Tue.–Sun. 10–6:30, May–Sep.; 10–5, rest of year (last entry 30 minutes before closing) 🚇 Train: Belém 🚌 28, 714, 727, 729, 751; train 15 🍽 O Caseiro, see page 487 💶 $$; free Sun. and hollidays until 2 p.m.

Visitors in a shady loggia of the Torre de Belém

Sintra

By far the most popular day trip from Lisbon is to beautiful Sintra, a small town packed with delights, set in lush and mountainous country some 15 miles northwest of Lisbon. Once there, the attractions are scattered over a wide area, so unless you have plenty of time, it makes sense to take a tour or rent a car and drive from the city. Alternatively, take the train from Lisbon and make use of the efficient Sintra buses which cover the main sites. As a bonus, most tour operators include a detour to Cabo da Roca, the Continent's westernmost point.

For more than 500 years Sintra was the summer resort of Portuguese kings – a legacy that is apparent in the town's two astounding palaces. The National Palace (Palácio Nacional) was first built by João I in the 15th century and remained in use until the end of the 19th century.

Architecturally imposing, it's nevertheless a muddle of mainly Gothic and Manueline styles. The interior is worth exploring. Note the superb ceramic tiles, as well as the elaborately decorated ceilings: one is painted with gold-collared swans and another with magpies.

The other main palace is the Pena National Palace (Palácio Nacional da Pena), built in the 1840s by Ferdinand of Saxe-Coburg-Gotha, husband of Queen Maria II. It's a creation rivaling the best of Disney, complete with towers, turrets and battlements. Inside is a riot of flamboyant furniture, wall hangings and paintings, including a whole room of nudes. Nearby is the eighth-century Castelo dos Mouros, a ruined Moorish stronghold.

The other outstanding attractions in Sintra are its gardens and parks. The warm, damp climate is ideal for a profusion of exotic trees, shrubs and roses, and you'll see everything from rhododendrons and camellias to tree ferns and palms. The Pena Gardens, below the Pena National Palace, are lovely, with lakes and mock temples. But the highlight is the Monserrate Gardens, west of Sintra. Two Englishmen laid out the gardens between 1790 and 1860, and they ramble over 74 acres.

Around Sintra lies the Sintra-Cascais Natural Park (Parque Natural Sintra-Cascais), a wonderful area stretching from the tree-clad mountains of Sintra down to the dramatic Atlantic coastline at Guincho.

Tour Operators

Cityrama-Grayline ✉ Avenida João XXI 7BE ☎ 213 191 090; www.grayline.com

Lisboasightseeing ✉ Rua Pascoal de Melo 3 ☎ 976 086 536 or 800 208 513 (toll free); www.lisboasightseeing.com

Inside Lisbon ✉ Avenida Forças Armadas 103 ☎ 968 412 612; www.insidelisbon.com

Diana Tours ✉ Campo Grande 30B ☎ 217 998 540; www.dianatours.pt

The Pena National Palace is a storybook castle with turrets and towers

Porto

Porto, Portugal's second-largest city with about 200,000 residents and about 1.7 million in the greater Porto area, is located on the steep and rocky north bank of the Douro river, just a couple of miles from its outlet on the Atlantic. The city suburbs sprawl down to the coast. Many visitors encounter Porto on their way up the beautiful Douro valley. The city also is known for its long association with port wine, which has been shipped from Vila Nova de Gaia, a suburb of Porto, since the 17th century. It has long been referred to as "Oporto," a name never used by the Portuguese and now declining in use elsewhere.

Development of Porto

Founded in pre-Roman times, the city of Porto gave its name to the country, and was the birthplace of Prince Henry the Navigator, son of João I of Portugal and Philippa of Lancaster, granddaughter of Edward III of England, in 1394. Traditionally liberal, its residents have always had a strong rebellious streak, which goes well with the city's industrious and down-to-earth image.

Porto is a refreshing antidote to the faded elegance of Lisbon – a bustling, no-nonsense city lying at the center of Portugal's most important economic area, its layout inextricably entwined with the history of the port trade. Grandiose buildings testify to 18th- and 19th-century wealth, but the true spirit of the city lies in the maze of narrow streets below the cathedral, the old docks and the waterfront houses. Pockets throughout the city are endowed with *azulejos* (glazed ceramic tiles) decoration.

Suggested Itineraries

Two or three days is sufficient to see Porto. Nearly everything of interest is within a short walk or bus ride from the city center. The streets are steep and hilly, so wear comfortable shoes.

If you're just passing through on your way up the Douro valley, make time to visit the port lodges in Vila Nova de Gaia, Porto's main tourist attraction.

If you've got more time, the city can be neatly divided into cultural itineraries, focusing on medieval, baroque and neoclassic monuments and churches. And for a state-of-the-art attraction, Porto now boasts a world-class arts center, the Casa da Música.

The heart of modern Porto centers around Avenida dos Aliados, a broad avenue with the monumental town hall at one end and the Praça da Liberdade, a transportation hub, at the other. This stretch is a good place to observe locals going about their daily business. The main shopping areas are east and north of this avenue. You can use the river to help orient yourself to the city.

Porto Flavors

The people of Porto have traditionally been known as *tripeiros*, or "tripe-eaters," allegedly because they sacrificed all their meat except the tripe to their army during a legendary battle – an historic indicator that refined cooking doesn't top the culinary priority list. Expect hearty, tasty meals, plenty of fish, the much-beloved *bacalhau* (dried, salted codfish) and super-sweet desserts on every menu at any time of the day. On the other hand, a glass of smooth, silky and subtle port – drunk on its native soil – may convert even the most inveterate port-hater.

An especially atmospheric place to dine is beside the river at Ribeira, in the heart of the oldest part of Porto. Until the early 1990s it was run-down and decayed, but most of the area has now been given a face-lift, and it is filled with dozens of good, lively restaurants, cafés and bars under the medieval arches, with tremendous tourist appeal.

Crafts and Shopping

Porto is the place to track down northern handicraft specialties, fine port, locally made shoes and traditional gold filigree jewelry from the villages of the Minho.

The city's wonderfully old-fashioned stores, many of which still retain their early 20th-century facades and details, are worth a visit even if you're not buying. Highlights include the Lello and Irmão bookstore on Rua das Carmelitas, with its superb double staircase and somber wooden paneling, and Cardoso Cabeleireiro on Rua do Bonjardim, a shop specializing in wigs and toupees. Similar stores cluster together in Porto, so you'll find streets packed with hardware stores, seed merchants, jewelers and linen stores. Marques Soares, a chic department store on Rua das Carmelitas, carries exquisite leather goods.

Excursions and Entertainment

There are several marine operators that run cruises on the Douro river, varying

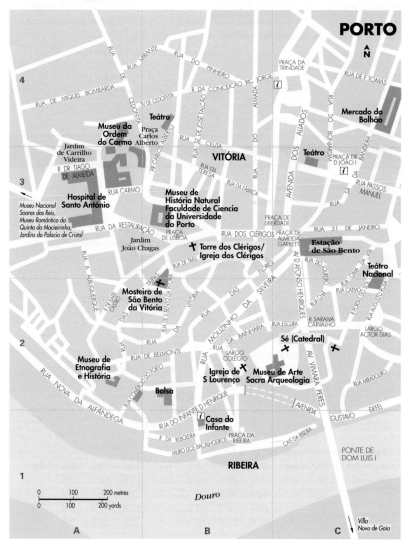

PORTO

The Igreja and Torre dos Clérigos tower over Porto

rabelo, the glorious old boats once used to carry barrels of port downstream from the vineyards. Sections of the 19th-century narrow-gauge railway still operate in the Douro valley – this is a fun way to do a little exploring. Tour operators also run bus trips in, around and out of Porto; Diana Tours (☎ 217 998 540; www.dianatours.pt) is a reliable operator with English-speaking guides. Alternatively, tickets may be bought at the tourist office. Be sure to visit the port lodges in Vila Nova de Gaia (see page 390), an essential stop on any Porto visit.

in price and ranging from a week-long trip up the river on a luxury cruiser taking in the sights along the riverbank, to a couple of hours puttering around the lower reaches in a reproduction of a

For evening entertainment, locals attend theaters, concerts and the movies, although many people prefer to while away the hours of warm, balmy evenings at a terrace café or simply strolling along the riverbank.

Essential Information

Tourist Information
Turismo do Porto (Porto Tourism).
Casa da Camâra, Terreiro da Sé
☎ 223 325 174
Rua Clube dos Fenianos 25
☎ 223 393 472; www.portoturismo.pt
Rua do Infante D Henrique 63
☎ 222 060 412

Urban Transportation
The Sociedade de Transportes Colectivos do Porto (STCP) issues a Mapa de Transportes showing both day and nighttime bus, tram and metro routes (available from tourist offices). Pay as you get on the bus or the tram or buy a 24-hour "Andante" card from one of the many kiosk outlets, which is also valid on the city's tram and metro system (details at www.metrodoporto.pt). Porto Tourism issues a Porto Card, valid for 1, 2 or 3 days, which offers free public transportation around the city as well as free entrance to many attractions. Taxis are inexpensive; there is an additional charge to cross the river to Gaia. For bus information ☎ 225 071 000; www.stcp.pt

Airport Information
Francisco Sá Carneiro International Airport (☎ 229 432 400; www.ana.pt) is about 12 miles northwest of central Porto. Porto Metro (☎ 808 20 50 60; www.metrodoporto.pt) line E links the airport with Trinidade station in the city center, running from 6 a.m. to 1 a.m. Travel time is 35 minutes. Bus services 601 and 602 serve the airport, but the metro is best.

Climate – average highs and lows for the month

Jan.	Feb.	Mar.	Apr.	May	Jun.	Jul.	Aug.	Sep.	Oct.	Nov.	Dec.
13°C	13°C	15°C	17°C	18°C	22°C	23°C	23°C	23°C	19°C	17°C	14°C
55°F	55°F	59°F	63°F	64°F	72°F	73°F	73°F	73°F	66°F	63°F	57°F
6°C	7°C	7°C	9°C	10°C	13°C	14°C	14°C	14°C	12°C	8°C	7°C
43°F	45°F	45°F	48°F	50°F	55°F	57°F	57°F	57°F	54°F	46°F	45°F

Porto Sights

Igreja e Torre dos Clérigos

The soaring Torre dos Clérigos (Tower
of Clérigos), attached to an 18th-century
granite church (Igreja dos Clérigos), is a
Porto landmark, and most visitors climb
it to admire the views. Nicolau Nasoni
designed the oval church, with its
elaborately festooned facade of swags
and garlands, in the 1730s in Italian
baroque style.

➕ B3 ✉ Rua São Felipe de Nery ☎ 222 001 729
🕐 Church: daily 8:45–12:30 and 3:30–7. Tower: daily
10–7 in Aug.; 9:30–1 and 2–7, Apr.–Jul. and Sep.–Oct.;
10–12 and 2–5, rest of year (last entry 30 minutes
before closing) 🚇 D line: São Bento 🚌 All Praça da
Liberdade services 🎫 Church free; Tower $

Jardins do Palácio de Cristal

The Jardins do Palácio de Cristal
(Crystal Palace Gardens) offer one of
the best vantage points in Porto. A lime
tree-lined avenue leads from pools and
fountains past magnolias, camellias
and rhododendrons to rose gardens and
terraces high above the river. Summer
concerts are held in the park's pavilion.

➕ Off map at A3 ✉ Rua de Dom Manuel II
☎ 226 081 000 🕐 Tue.–Sat. 10–6, Sun. 2–dusk
🚌 200, 201, 207, 302,303, 501 🍴 Cafeteria in
gardens

Museu Nacional Soares dos Reis

The Museu Nacional Soares dos Reis
(Soares dos Reis National Museum),
named after the 19th-century sculptor,
is Porto's most important museum.
Housed in an impressive 1795 neoclassic
edifice, it was occupied in the early
1800s during the Peninsular War by first
the French and then the English. The
museum emphasizes works by dos Reis,
with fine exhibits of glass and porcelain;
look for pieces from the famous Vista
Alegre factory.

➕ Off map at A3 ✉ Rua Dom Manuel II 44 ☎ 223
393 770; http://mnsr-ipmuseus.pt 🕐 Wed.–Sun. 10–6,
Tue. 2–6 (last entry at 5:30) 🚌 200, 201, 207, 301,
303, 501 🎫 $$; free on Sun. until 2 p.m.

Museu Romântico da Quinta da Macieirinha

For an insight into how the prosperous
bourgeois of Porto lived in the 19th
century, visit the Museu Romântico da
Quinta da Macieirinha (Romantic
Museum) in a pretty villa overlooking
the river. Admire the furniture and
paintings; many of the furnishings have
connections with the last king of
Piedmont, who lived here in exile. The
basement houses the Solar do Vinho do
Porto (Port Wine Rooms), where you
can sample a selection of ports.

➕ Off map at A3 ✉ Rua de Entrequintas 220
☎ 226 057 033 🕐 Tue.–Sat. 10–12:30 and 2–5:30,
Sun. 2–5:30 (last entry 30 minutes before closing)
🚌 200, 201, 207, 301, 303, 501 🎫 $; free Sat.–Sun.

Ponte do Dom Luís I

Five bridges span the Douro river, all
built high above the water over the
gorge cut by the lower reaches of the
river. The most impressive is the Ponte
do Dom Luís I (Luis I Bridge), a striking
bi-level iron construction designed by
Théophile Seyring (one of Gustave
Eiffel's collaborators) and dating from
1886. The bridge effectively links four
city areas and has undergone renovation
to accommodate the metro line, as well
as motor and pedestrian traffic.

➕ C1 ✉ Ponte do Dom Luís I 🚇 D line: São Bento
🚌 900, 901, 906

Praça da Ribeira

The waterfront Praça da Ribeira (Ribeira
Square) is the focal point of the Ribeira
district, by far the most atmospheric area
of Porto and designated a UNESCO
World Heritage Site. Many of the
buildings were erected between 1776
and 1782. Although you can approach
the area by descending the steep Rua da

Alfândega past Casa do Infante (House of the Prince), Prince Henry the Navigator's reputed birthplace, the easiest way is to walk through the warren of canyon-like streets tumbling down to the river from the cathedral.

There's no better place to experience historic Porto than in this district. While you're here, visit the Casa do Infante and drop into their shop, Loja do Infant, which sells a wonderful range of traditional northern handicrafts.

Casa do Infante ✚ B1 ✉ Rua da Alfândega 10, Ribeira ☎ 222 060 400 ◉ Exhibition Room: Mon.–Fri. 10–12 and 2–5, Sat.–Sun. 10–12:30 and 2–5:30. Museum: Tue.–Sun. 10–1 and 2–5:30 (last entry 30 minutes before closing) 🚊 D line: São Bento 🚌 202, 500, 900, 901, 904, 906 💵 $; free Sat.–Sun.

Loja do Infante ✉ Rua Infante Don Henrique, Ribeira ☎ 222 060 400 ◉ Tue.–Sun 10–1 and 2–5:30 🚌 202, 500, 900, 901, 904, 906

Sé

Porto's Sé (Cathedral) stands high above the slopes leading to the river. Built in the 12th century as a fortress church, it was extensively altered in the 1700s in the baroque style, although the vast silver altarpiece in the north transept dates from the mid-16th century.

The two-story cloisters are more appealing than the cathedral itself; the solid granite lines are enlivened with beautiful tiles, and there are good views over the town. A museum in the treasury houses archeological finds from pre-Roman to Gothic times, plus liturgical objects from the 15th to 19th centuries.

✚ C2 ✉ Terreiro da Sé ☎ 222 059 028 ◉ Church: daily 8:45–12:30 and 2:30–7, Apr.–Oct.; 8:45–12:30 and 2:30–6, rest of year. Cloisters: Mon.–Sat. 9–12:15 and 2:30–6:30, Sun. 2:30–6:30, Apr.–Oct.; Mon.–Sat. 9–12:15 and 2:30–5:30, Sun. 2:30–5:30, rest of year 🚊 D line: São Bento 🚌 207, 303, 400, 900, 901, 904, 905, 906, ZH 💵 Church free; Cloisters $$

Vila Nova de Gaia

A separate municipality, Vila Nova de Gaia lies across the Douro river from Porto itself. Its name is synonymous with port, for until 1987 all port had to be matured here to be so named. The riverside slopes are dominated by the solid granite buildings of the port warehouses, or lodges. There are many opportunities for free tours and tastings. This is the place to buy port; the white aperitif variety is hard to find abroad.

The huge complex high above the river is the old monastery of Serra do Pilar, now a military installation and closed to the public.

✚ Off map at C1 ✉ Vila Nova de Gaia ◉ Most lodges open Mon.–Fri. 10–noon and 2–6 (also Sat. in summer) 🚊 D line: Jardim do Morro 🚌 900, 901, 906

The cathedral cloisters are lined with blue-and-white *azulejos* **(glazed ceramic tiles)**

Port Wine

Port, one of Portugal's glories, is drunk all over the world, as an aperitif and a digestive aid. In the 18th century, its production area was the world's first demarcated wine zone, helping to make port one of the few wines with a flavor that has remained untouched for centuries. Be sure to try it in Porto, a city more associated with port than any other.

Port is a fortified wine, which means that brandy is added to the grapes during the production process. This both "fortifies" the wine, making it stronger, and halts the fermentation process, leaving half the natural grape sugar in the wine. These two factors give port its strength, sweetness and smoothness; its complex flavors come from the soil and climate where the grapes are grown.

To people accustomed to the lush vineyards of other countries, those in the upper Douro valley, which produce port, are a revelation. It's a stony, barren area, a microclimatic zone where temperatures reach extremes of heat and cold. The soil is a thin layer on top of schist, and the vine roots must force their way through the rock, sometimes as much as 20 feet, to find water. The Portuguese insist, probably rightly, that these conditions are what gives port its unique character.

The vineyards grow on steep terraces, so much of the harvesting is done by hand, and until recently the grapes were still even trodden by foot. (Treading the grapes by foot enables the flavor to be released without crushing the grape seed, which would add a bitter taste to the port.) Today more than 90 percent are crushed and fermented at a controlled temperature, sometime between mid-September and mid-October. The new wine is stored up-river in a lodge or *armazém*, to clear until the following spring. In March it's ready for transport. Following strict tradition, until as recently as 1987 it could not be called port unless the maturation had taken place in Vila Nova de Gaia, across the Douro from Porto. Increasingly, as is now allowed, it is matured on site due to space consideration and transportation costs.

Port comes in several varieties: white, a semi-sweet light wine; ruby, a clear, intense red; tawny, which is older and more complex; and vintage and late bottled vintage port. Vintage port is aged in the bottle and comes from grapes from a single year; late bottled is matured for up to four years before further maturing after bottling.

Barrels of port are stored at Solar do Vinho do Porto (Port Wine Rooms) in the Romantic Museum

Spain

Opposite: Casa Batlló designed by Gaudí is in the L'Eixample district of Barcelona

Spain

Spain is a country of diverse landscapes, climates, peoples and cultures, forged over the centuries into a political unity. Physically separated from the rest of Europe by the Pyrenees mountain chain, Spain also found itself isolated internationally during General Francisco Franco's dictatorship (1939–75). Since Franco's death, however, and with the restoration of its parliamentary monarchy (currently King Juan Carlos I and Queen Sofía), Spain has regained its place politically, economically and culturally within Europe.

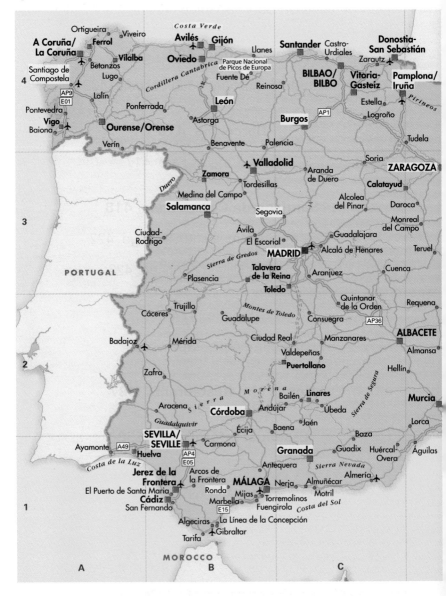

But despite the rate of progress, many aspects of Spanish life remain untouched, and Spain retains much of its traditional character.

Spain Today

Spain's long and checkered history peaked in the Golden Age of the 16th century, when it was one of the most influential nations of the world. It had immense power across Europe and possessed many overseas colonies. The following centuries saw a gradual decline and increasing isolation from the rest of Europe, culminating in the bitter Civil War (1936–39) and Franco's long dictatorship.

In Spain today, political, cultural and artistic life flourishes, along with national confidence. In 1992 Madrid was chosen as the Cultural Capital of Europe, the same year that dynamic Barcelona hosted the Olympic Games and Seville the World Fair. Other Spanish cities awarded the title of European Capital of Culture were Santiago de Compostela, in 2000, and Salamanca, in 2002. The Americas Cup has been hosted by Valencia on two occasions (2007 and 2010).

From Pyrenees to Portugal

One of Europe's most mountainous countries, Spain occupies much of the Iberian peninsula, stretching southwest from the Pyrenees. Much of the land area is covered by the mighty Meseta, a little populated agricultural plateau surrounded by long mountain ranges. These ranges stretch from the Sierra Nevada in the south to the Cordillera Cantábrica in the north, and give Spain an average altitude of 2,100 feet. The

More Top Destinations in Spain

- Burgos C4
- Córdoba B2
- Costa Brava E3–E4
- Costa de la Luz A1
- Costa Verde B4
- Granada C1
- León B4
- Monestir de Poblet E3
- Pamplona C4
- Parque Nacional de los Picos de Europa B4
- Peñíscola D3
- Ronda B1
- Salamanca B3
- Segovia C3
- Sierra de Montserrat E3
- Zaragoza D3

A passionate flamenco display in Madrid

highest mainland peak is the 11,424-foot Mulhacén in the Sierra Nevada, although Mount Teide on the Canary island of Tenerife is nearly 1,000 feet higher.

The mild, moist Atlantic coast of the Costa Verde in the north contrasts with the sun-baked Mediterranean beaches of the southern Costa del Sol. The grandeur of the Pyrenees is more than rivaled by the dramatic peaks of the Asturian mountains on Spain's northern coast, which some consider the most beautiful region in Spain. East of Asturias the Ebro valley slashes southeast toward the Mediterranean, where it bisects the coastal plain southwest of Barcelona.

The fertile gardens of Murcia and the agricultural flatlands of the Guadalquivir yield harvests rivaled only by the tourist crop drawn from the golden sands of the Mediterranean beaches.

The Mediterranean coast ends on the northern shore of the Straits of Gibraltar, only 9 miles from Africa. Such diversity is echoed in Spain's climate, which varies from the mild, wet weather of the northern Atlantic coast to the typical Mediterranean hot, dry summers and mild, wet winters in the south. Winter inland can be very cold.

The island groups of the Balearics (Mallorca, Menorca, Ibiza and small Formentera) and the Canaries (including Gran Canaria, Tenerife, Lanzarote and the tiny La Gomera) have their own geographical and climatic characteristics.

Diversities of Spain

Regional differences are reflected in the Spanish people, their looks, their character, their attitudes and, above all, their cuisine. The 800 years of Moorish occupation, the eventual unification of a number of small kingdoms, and the power and wealth of 16th-century colonial Spain have all played their part in the evolution of diverse provincial characteristics.

The concept of centralized power is alien to many Spaniards, and regionalism is very strong in Spain. It has its base in the peninsula's linguistic groups: Galician, spoken in the northwest; Basque, another northern language; Castilian, also known as Spanish; and Catalan, based in the northeast, with Valencian and Mallorcan variations of this. These are all co-official languages in Spain.

In 1977, when the present constitution was established, various regional groups were provided for through the establishment of 17 autonomous governments. The Basque Country and Catalonia are the two regions in Spain having the most autonomy, although Basque extremists continue to push for independence.

Spanish Characters

There are physical differences between Spaniards from different parts of the peninsula. With a population of 47 million, there's room for diversity; contrary to popular belief, not all

Spaniards are dark-eyed and olive-skinned. The Moorish genetic legacy is strongest in Andalucia, where many are delicate-featured and dark, personifying the Spanish stereotype.

Spaniards are sometimes thought of as an exuberant, passionate and light-hearted people, much like the Italians, but nothing could be further from the truth. They are certainly passionate, but there's a strong streak of self-control and melancholy in the national character. History has given them loyalty and tolerance. Kindness to children and respect for the elderly are the norm.

Young Spaniards enjoy a freedom and lifestyle their grandparents could never have imagined, yet society is still in a state of flux, and there are huge contrasts between different regions, towns and rural areas. But wherever you go you'll find the same level of hospitality and friendliness, particularly if you speak a little Spanish. English is widely spoken along the Mediterranean coast and by hotel staff in big cities, but very rarely elsewhere.

Cities, Towns and Villages

For visitors the three great cities are Madrid, Barcelona and Seville, but in Spanish eyes the industrial centers of Valencia and Bilbao are of equal importance, and the inhabitants of each region claim their capital as the most beautiful in Spain.

Andalucia, with the architectural treasures of Granada and Córdoba, is rich in Moorish history.

The region of Castille has Christian castles built during the struggle to oust the Moors.

A view along the seafront to Cádiz's cathedral, bathed in the golden light of the setting sun

The Mediterranean coast has many remains from centuries of Roman occupation, while the Atlantic port of Cádiz boasts 2,000 years of maritime history. Rural Spain continues largely unchanged; agriculture is more mechanized with the inevitable introduction of some modern harvesting equipment, but the way and pace of life are still deeply rooted in the past.

As in other European countries, however, the young are abandoning rural villages in favor of city life, and now more than 70 percent of Spain's population lives in urban areas.

Spanish Lifestyle

Daily life in Spain differs in one major way from other southern European countries; mealtimes are very late. Breakfast in hotels is served from around 7:30 until 9:30 or 10. Most Spaniards rise early and eat very little first thing, so they are ready for a snack around 11. This delays lunch until 2 at the earliest, and therefore dinner is often around 9:30 p.m. or later.

An early start means you can take advantage of the cool mornings, vital in a country where air-conditioning is not universal. Virtually everything – stores, offices, churches and museums – closes from 1:30 or 2 p.m. until 4 or 5, and most people sleep or take a break after lunch for an hour on the weekends, during the fabled siesta.

This break in the day bypasses the worst heat and leaves people ready to stay up late and enjoy the comparatively fresh evening air. It's a pleasure to sit at a café or restaurant table until 1 or 2 in the morning, as long as you've had a midday rest.

You'll find that most entertainment begins very late, around 10 p.m., and clubs don't get going until the early hours of the morning. Along the Mediterranean coast things are more geared toward foreigners, and you should be able to have dinner soon after 8:30 p.m.

Spain is traditionally a Catholic country. When you visit churches, cover the tops of your arms and shoulders and avoid wearing shorts. The local fiestas held in every town and village are always in honor of the Virgin or some favorite local saint, and if you get the chance to watch one, you will see how religion plays an integral part in everyday life.

Traveling in Spain

The economic boom of the last few decades resulted in a good infrastructure. Spain has an excellent network of well-marked toll roads and highways. Spaniards drive fast but safely, and you should have no problems if you rent a car. Public transportation is good, with a choice of internal flights, fast and punctual trains, and long-distance buses going to even the most remote corners.

Hotels are graded and inspected by the government, so you are guaranteed a clean and adequate room no matter how little you pay. Try to spend at least a few nights at one of the *paradores*. These are state-owned hotels in historic buildings such as castles and monasteries, often furnished with antiques and offering a high standard of comfort and service.

Spanish Passions

Spaniards are a passionate people and throw themselves wholeheartedly into eating out, shopping, going to a soccer match or spending a day on the beach. Their most famous and controversial passion is bullfighting, but soccer has more supporters. Huge crowds follow the fortunes of teams such as Real Madrid and F.C. Barcelona.

Spain has some of Europe's finest golf courses, chiefly along the Mediterranean coast, where you'll also find excellent marinas and watersports facilities, as well as untouched wilderness areas. Young people travel from all over Europe to experience Spain's club scene, at its most frenetic on the island of Ibiza.

Moorish-style decoration on a house in Alicante

Timeline

15,000–12,000 BC	Caves at Altamira painted; earliest sign of habitation.
218–210 BC	Rome begins conquest of Iberian peninsula.
AD 411	Visigoths invade and establish powerful kingdom at Toledo.
711	Moors defeat Visigoths and begin period of occupation.
1478–79	Spanish Inquisition against Jews, Moors and Protestants.
1492	Christopher Columbus discovers New World.
1519	Spanish conquistadores move across America.
1588	Spanish Armada is sent against Protestant England; fleet destroyed and maritime preeminence lost.
1704	British capture Gibraltar.
1808–14	Peninsular War (War of Independence) sees expulsion of French and defeat of Napoleon.
1898	Philippines and Cuba rebel against Spanish rule; the United States occupies Puerto Rico; end of Spanish Empire.
1914–18	Spain remains neutral in World War I.
1936–39	Spanish Civil War; General Francisco Franco leads Nationalist troops from Morocco against Republicans.
1939	Franco becomes head of state; Spain enters period of isolation and remains neutral throughout World War II.
1955	Spain joins United Nations.
1975	Death of Franco; Juan Carlos becomes king.
1986	Spain joins the European Commmunity (later known as the European Union.
1992	Barcelona hosts Olympic Games; Madrid declared Cultural Capital of Europe; Seville is the venue for Expo '92.
2004	Madrid suffers its worst terrorist attack on March 11, resulting in 191 deaths.
2004–2008	Spanish Socialist Worker's Party, led by Zapatero, wins general election in 2004. Zapatero reelected in 2008.
2010	Spanish unemployment reaches 20 percent, the highest of any industrialized nation. Catalonia becomes the first Spanish region to ban bullfighting.

The Moorish Occupation

In AD 711 a faction of the ruling Visigoth tribe in Spain went to Islamic Africa to seek help with some domestic political problems. They returned with an army of 7,000; after victory at Cádiz, the Moors encountered little resistance in taking over all but a small strip of northern Spain over the next 30 years. Their tactics were a blend of intelligent strategy and diplomacy; they never demanded religious subordination, as long as Christians paid taxes. Beginning in AD 744, however, resistance against the invaders spread south from the small, unoccupied northern territory, fueled by the legend of St. James the Moorslayer. El Cid succeeded in capturing Toledo from the Moors in 1085, and despite some setbacks, a coalition of Christian armies was finally victorious at the Battle of Navas de Tolosa in 1212, the last great battle between Moors and Christians. The Moorish occupation left important legacies, however – they brought mathematics, papermaking, oranges, spices and rice to Spain, which were then introduced to the rest of Europe.

Sampling *tapas* at a market is a must on any visit to Spain

Survival Guide

- English is not widely spoken, even in large cities. Keep in mind that the Spanish you may have learned in high school differs in accent, pronunciation and some vocabulary from that spoken in Spain.
- It's best not to discuss politics, since Spaniards are very proud and the subject could be sensitive.
- Beachwear, shorts and revealing necklines are not acceptable away from coastal resorts.
- Public restrooms are few except in museums, but it's acceptable to use the facilities in a bar; leave a small tip on the counter or stop and have a cup of coffee while you're there.
- Inebriation is frowned on in Spain; the Spanish drink alcohol every day, but in moderation.
- The Spanish are formal and polite; it is best to ask, in Spanish, if the person you're addressing speaks English before you start to speak, and shake hands at the end of casual conversations.
- Water is a precious commodity in many parts of Spain; you may find that hotel bathrooms have a shower rather than a tub. Shower pressure is generally low.

- You can safely drink the water throughout Spain, although you may prefer to drink bottled mineral water, which is inexpensive and served chilled. Ice is not generally served in drinks unless you ask.
- Throughout Spain, especially along the Mediterranean, bars specialize in *tapas*, delicious selections of hot or cold savory mouthfuls served with drinks. Be sure to try some of the dozens available: fish, smoked ham, stewed peppers, salads, *tortilla*, anchovies, local almonds, olives. Two or three little dishes will make a delicious lunch.
- All large cities have malls, usually away from the town center; downtown department stores; and a range of antiques stores, designer boutiques, local craft and souvenir shops, gourmet food stores, and clothing and bric-a-brac markets.
- Prices in Spain are comparable to the rest of Europe; meals are a little cheaper.
- Try to arrange your trip so that it coincides with one of the major local festival. Spain has some of the most colorful and exotic celebrations in Europe.

Madrid

Unlike most European capital cities, Madrid did not evolve as the nation's capital. It was chosen. In 1561, Philip II settled the court permanently in Madrid, as much for its position in the center of Spain as for political reasons. Today Madrid is fascinating, noisy, vibrant and chaotic – a city of great wealth and grueling poverty, but still the country's financial capital.

Like so much of Spain, Madrid's spirit is elusive and diffused, and will surprise you repeatedly. Plan to stay in the city center, so you can easily reach your hotel in the middle of the day, when many museums and monuments are closed for the siesta. The best way to tackle sightseeing is to concentrate on

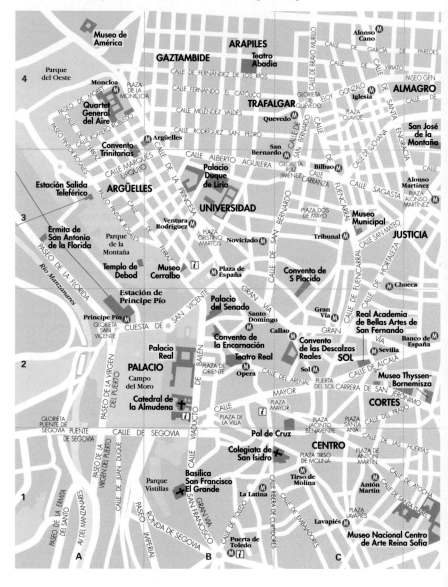

one section at a time. There are three historical areas of interest in the vicinity of the city's main plaza, Puerta del Sol; Old Madrid (Viejo Madrid), centering on the Plaza Mayor; the Eastern Quarter (Barrio de Oriente), by the Palacio Real; and Bourbon Madrid, the heart of which is the sweeping avenues and sparkling fountains around the Prado Museum.

A convenient tourist bus (*bus turistico*;

☎ 902 50 78 50; www.emtmadrid.es), links all three, allowing passengers to get on and off when they want to. Tickets are valid for one or two days, and there's English commentary. Turismo de Madrid organizes walking and bicycling tours in the city. Bookings should be made at the tourist office in Plaza Mayor 27 (☎ 91 588 1636; www.esmadrid.com). The city also has an efficient subway system. Take along a good English-Spanish dictionary, as English is not widely spoken here.

Dining Out

Eating is a pleasure in Madrid, and there is much to choose from. Local specialties include tripe, but there many regional restaurants feature traditional dishes from all over Spain. The cuisine of the Basque country and Galicia is very good, or you could try a Latin-American restaurant, where even the meat is imported from Argentina. Fast-food outlets abound and offer hamburgers, *tortillas* or even paella to go.

Most restaurants have a fixed-price lunch menu Monday through Friday. Usually a good value, it includes a choice of first and second courses, a dessert and drink. Madrid has innumerable bars where you'll find everything from tea and coffee to beer, champagne and exotic cocktails. In summer, bar life moves onto the sidewalks, with hundreds of outdoor venues (*terrazas*) crowded until dawn.

Malls and Markets

The central department stores, such as the nationwide chain El Corte Inglés, are clustered in the commercial area around the Puerta del Sol. If you're looking for malls, the large Príncipe Pio occupies an attractive 19th-century station near the Royal Palace; the ABC Serrano, between Serrano and Castellana in the center of Madrid, is smaller and more upscale.

The most fashionable shopping area is the Salamanca district around the streets of Calle de Serrano and Goya, where you'll find expensive stores. Madrid is a good place for Spanish souvenirs, and there are many antiques stores – the Salamanca district alone has more than 50. Visit the Rastro flea market on Sunday morning and public holidays and browse in the tiny boutiques.

Evening Entertainment

Classical music, opera and theater thrive in Madrid, and the tourist office publishes a monthly guide, *es Madrid* magazine, with excellent listings. It is available from tourist offices and hotels, or can be downloaded from www. esmadrid.com. You might enjoy a *zarzuela* performance, a traditional form of musical, combining elements of opera, vaudeville and melodrama. Jazz is very popular, or, if you're looking for flamenco, there are several clubs *(tablaos)* where it is staged. Madrid has an exceptional nightclub scene and a number of movie theaters.

Essential Information

Tourist Information

Oficinas de Información Turística (Tourist Information Offices).
Calle Duque de Medinaceli 2
☎ 91 429 4951
Plaza Mayor 27 ☎ 91 588 1636
Aeropuerto de Madrid-Barajas (airport), Terminals 2 and 4 ☎ 91 588 1636
Plaza de Colón (underground passage)
☎ 91 588 1636
Information points on Paseo del Prado and by the Atocha railroad station, both
☎ 91 588 1636
www.turismomadrid.es
www.descubremadrid.com
www.esmadrid.com
SATE (Foreign Tourist Assistance Service)
The tourist police with translators available to help visitors in trouble
Calle Leganitos 19
☎ 91 548 8537, open daily 9 a.m.–midnight

Urban Transportation

Getting around Madrid is simple on the subway (metro) and bus systems. Subway stations are marked on the Madrid city map by the letter "M" on a blue back-ground inside a red diamond. The subway has 12 lines and runs daily 6 a.m.–2 a.m. Purchase tickets from machines or ticket offices in the stations or go online at www.metromadrid.es. The Metrobús ticket, valid for 10 trips on the subway and bus systems, is available from metro stations, tobacconists *(estancos)* and Municipal Transport Company (EMT) booths at some bus stops. Buses run daily 6 a.m.– midnight, with a limited all-night service that is not as frequent as the daytime one. Pay the driver or stamp your pass in the machine when you board. Taxis are plentiful and can be hailed on the street. To call a taxi dial Tele-Taxi (☎ 90 250 1130).

Airport Information

Madrid's Barajas Airport (☎ 902 404 704) is 8 miles northeast of the city center, about a 30-minute drive. Express buses run every 20 minutes between the airport and Atocha railroad station. There is a subway (metro) line from the airport (with two stops, one for Terminals 1, 2, and 3, and another for Terminal 4) to Nuevos Ministerios (metro station of the same name).

Climate – average highs and lows for the month

Jan.	Feb.	Mar.	Apr.	May	Jun.	Jul.	Aug.	Sep.	Oct.	Nov.	Dec.
9°C	12°C	15°C	18°C	21°C	27°C	32°C	31°C	26°C	19°C	13°C	10°C
48°F	54°F	59°F	64°F	70°F	81°F	90°F	88°F	79°F	66°F	55°F	50°F
1°C	2°C	4°C	6°C	9°C	14°C	17°C	17°C	13°C	9°C	4°C	2°C
34°F	36°F	39°F	43°F	48°F	57°F	63°F	63°F	55°F	48°F	39°F	36°F

Madrid Sights

> **Key to symbols**
> ✚ map coordinates refer to the Madrid map on pages 402–403 💷 admission charge: $$$ more than €6, $$ €3–€6, $ less than €3
> See page 5 for complete key to symbols

A statue in the grounds of the America Museum

Convento de las Descalzas Reales

The oddly named Convento de las Descalzas Reales (Convent of the Royal Barefoot Nuns) was founded in 1557 as a convent for aristocratic ladies seeking the religious life. They and their families decorated 33 chapels with treasures by mainly Spanish artists.

✚ C2 ✉ Plaza de las Descalzas Reales 3 ☎ 91 454 8800 🕐 Tue.–Sat. 10:30–12:45 (also Tue.–Thu. and Sat. 4–5:45), Sun. and holidays 11–1:45 🚇 Sol, Callao or Opera 💷 $$ ✚ Admission by guided visit only

Iglesia de San Jerónimo el Real

San Jerónimo et Real (St. Jerome the Royal) is the beautiful royal church where princes were crowned and monarchs married until King Alfonso XIII married Queen Victoria in 1878. Rebuilt in 1505 by King Ferdinand for his queen, Isabella, this Gothic church is less flamboyant than other churches in the country. The cloister has been incorporated into the modern extension to the Museo del Prado (see page 406).

✚ D2 ✉ Calle Moreto 4 ☎ 91 420 3578 🕐 Mon.–Sat. 10–1 and 5–8, Sun. and holidays 9:30–2:30 and 5:30–8:30 🚇 Atocha

Museo de América

The Museo de América (America Museum) is devoted to pre-Columbian and Hispanic artifacts telling the story of European ties with America. The information is in Spanish, but anyone can appreciate the Quimbayas Treasure and the Cortesiano Codex, which records in Mayan runes the arrival of the Spaniards in the New World.

✚ A4 ✉ Avenida Reyes Católicos 6 ☎ 91 549 2641; http://museodeamerica.mcu.es 🕐 Tue.–Sat. 9:30–8, Sun. 10–3, May–Oct.; Tue.–Sat. 9:30–6, Sun. 10–3, rest of year; closed on public holidays 🚇 Moncloa or Islas Filipinas 💷 $$; free Sun.

Museo Nacional Centro de Arte Reina Sofía

The Museo Nacional Centro de Arte Reina Sofía (Queen Sofía National Art Center), the city's spectacular modern art museum, is housed in the former Hospital de San Carlos. Exterior glass elevators whisk you up to the permanent exhibitions. Visitors flock to Pablo Picasso's *Guernica*. When it was commissioned his only instruction was to paint a big picture; this black-and-white composition has become a symbol of antiwar sentiment.

Other highlights in the museum include paintings by Salvador Dalí and Joan Miró.

✚ D1 ✉ Calle Santa Isabel 52 ☎ 91 774 1000; www.museoreinasofia.es 🕐 Mon. and Wed.–Sat. 10–9, Sun. 10–2:30; closed on public holidays 🚇 Atocha 🍴 Café and restaurant 💷 $$ (senior citizens and under 18 free; free to all Mon. and Wed.–Fri. 7 p.m.–9 p.m., Sat. after 2:30 p.m. and Sun.)

The Museo del Prado displays its collection of Spanish art to great effect in its large, well-lit rooms

Museo del Prado

The Museo del Prado (Prado Museum), with its unrivaled collection of Spanish paintings, is among the world's finest. Once the royal collection, the Prado represents the personal taste of the Spanish monarchs, with a noticeable emphasis on religious and courtly paintings. Space limitations allow only about 1,000 of the 18,000 works to be displayed; get an up-to-date floor plan as you arrive. Some works, particularly those by Diego Velázquez and Francisco Goya, attract huge crowds.

Highlights include Velázquez' *Las Meninas*, often described as "the finest painting in the world." Goya's work occupies many rooms; look for his *Majas*, two paintings thought to be of the Duchess of Alba, one demure and clothed, the other sensuously naked. His *pinturas negras*, the dark pictures, stand in stark contrast; disturbing and pessimistic, they represent the apocalyptic vision of a man on the edge of madness. The Spanish monarchs were fascinated by the surreal work of Hiëronymous Bosch; his *Garden of Earthly Delights*, with its wealth of weird detail, is one of his finest works.

✚ D1–D2 ✉ Paseo del Prado ☎ 902 107 077; www.museodelprado.es ⏲ Tue.–Sun. 9 a.m.–8 p.m. 🚇 Banco de España or Atocha 🍴 Café 💵 $$$ (free Tue.–Sat. 6–8 p.m., Sun. 5–8 p.m and all day on certain national holidays. Senior citizens and under 18 free)

Museo de la Real Academia de Bellas Artes de San Fernando

Art lovers will enjoy the peaceful Real Academia de Bellas Artes de San Fernando (Royal Academy of Fine Arts), founded in the 18th century to emulate art venues in Paris and London. The academy has some fine paintings by Francisco Goya and a good Diego Velázquez portrait of Philip IV. The highlight is *Spring* by Italian artist Giuseppe Arcimboldo, a portrait in which the sitter's features are entirely composed of fruit and vegetables.

✚ C2 ✉ Calle Alcalá 13 ☎ 91 524 0864; http://rabasf.insde.es ⏲ Tue.–Sat. 9–3, Sun. and public holidays 9–2:30 🚇 Sol or Sevilla 💵 $$ (senior citizens and under 18s free)

Museo Thyssen-Bornemisza

Acquired in 1993 for about $350 million, the art collection of the Museo Thyssen-Bornemisza (Thyssen-Bornemisza Museum) includes much of

The existing majestic Palacio Real (Royal Palace) was built in the 18th century

the best of Western art produced in the last 800 years. It contains around 2,000 works, all acquired since the 1920s by Baron Heinrich and his son, Baron Hans-Heinrich Thyssen-Bornemisza. The Carmen Thyssen-Bornemisza Collection was incorporated in 2004.

Western paintings from the 13th to 20th centuries are arranged chronologically, so start on the top floor and work down. Early portraits and Renaissance works are grouped together, followed by Dutch interiors. Nineteenth-century American paintings feature a portrait of George Washington's cook by Gilbert Stuart and a sea scene by Winslow Homer. The 20th century is well represented by Joan Miró, Salvador Dalí and Mark Rothko. Expressionist artists include German Otto Kirchner and Norwegian Edvard Munch.

🚼 D2 ✉ Paseo del Prado 8 ☎ 91 369 0151; www.museothyssen.org 🕐 Tue.–Sun. 10–7. Temporary exhibitions until 11 p.m. on Sat. 🚇 Banco de España 🍴 Café and restaurant in museum 💷 $$$ (separate fee for temporary exhibition)

Palacio Real

The vast white bulk of the Palacio Real (Royal Palace) looks striking from the Campo del Moro, a peaceful garden behind the palace. After a fire destroyed the Moorish original, the palace was planned to be three times its existing size. In the 18th century, architect Francisco Sabatini began to rebuild and extend the palace. Funds ran out, and the present structure was completed in 1764. In use until 1931, it is now occasionally used for state receptions. Everything is opulent and large. The 1993 Cathedral of the Almudena nearby offers panoramic views from its vast dome; the Plaza de Oriente is a grand, café-lined square across the road, home to the Teatro Real (Opera Theatre).

🚼 B2 ✉ Calle Bailén ☎ 91 454 8800; www.patrimonionacional.es 🕐 Daily 10–8, Apr.–Sep.; Mon.–Sat. 9:30–6, Sun. 9–4, rest of year. Closed when official events are held 🚇 Opera 💷 $$$ (free to E.U. citizens on Wed.)

Parque del Retiro

The Parque del Retiro was laid out in the 1630s as part of the French-style pleasure gardens surrounding the Buen Retiro Palace. The building itself was destroyed during the Napoleonic Wars. Today the park is bright with flowers. Many people head for the lake, with its

Relaxing under the shady parasols of a café in the stunning Plaza Mayor

statue of Alfonso XII; other attractions include the Palacio de Cristal (Crystal Palace), a 19th-century glass palace.

A wood, the Bosque de Recuerdo, was laid out in memory of victims of the 2004 bomb atack on Madrid.

🟥 E1 ✉ Main entrance: Plaza de la Independencia 🕐 Daily dawn–dusk 🚇 Retiro or Ibiza 🎟 Free

Plaza Mayor

One of Europe's most dazzling squares, the present Plaza Mayor (Main Square) stands on the site of the medieval market, the Plaza del Arrabal (Outskirts Square), so called because it was outside the city walls. When Madrid became Spain's capital, Philip III ordered it to be rebuilt as the focal point, and it was completed in 1620, the work of architect Gómez de Mora. Harmonious brick facades are punctuated with stonework and arcades. The plaza was used for fiestas, bullfights and proclamations, and was also the scene of executions during the later days of the Inquisition.

🟥 C2 ✉ Plaza Mayor 🚇 Sol

Plaza de Toros Monumental de las Ventas

Madrid's Plaza Monumental de Toros de las Ventas (Las Ventas Bullring) was opened in 1934, and for aficionados is the most important bullring in the world. The Museo Taurino (Bullfight Museum), devoted to some famous names, features posters, paintings, memorabilia and the "suit of lights" worn by the legendary Manolete in 1947 when he was gored in the leg.

🟥 Off map at E3 ✉ Alcalá, 237 Plaza de las Ventas ☎ 902 150 025; www.las-ventas.com; (Museo Taurino: 91 725 1857) 🕐 Museo Taurino: Tue.–Sun. 9:30–2:30

(10–1 on bullfighting days) 🚇 Ventas 🎨 Museum $$$; tickets for fights $$$ ❗ Guided tours of bullring in English Tue.–Sun. 10–2 ($$$). For information ☎ 91 556 9237

Plaza de la Villa

Despite their different dates, the three main stone buildings around this plaza (Town Square) coexist harmoniously. The Gothic Torre de los Lujanes (Lujanes Tower), a 15th-century structure, is balanced by the Casa de Cisneros, a restored 1537 Plateresque-style palace. The Casa del Ayuntamiento was the meeting place for the town council from 1640 until 2008.

🟥 B2 ✉ Plaza de la Villa 🕐 Buildings: guided tour ($$) Mon. at 5 p.m. 🚇 Sol or Opera ❗ Reserve tours at Centro de Turismo, Plaza Mayor 27, or check online www.esmadrid.com

Puerta de Alcalá

Surrounded by roaring traffic, the Puerta de Alcalá (Alcalá Gate) is a symbol of Madrid, along with the equally splendid Plaza de la Cibeles, a street away. Designed in 1778 as the main entrance to the Spanish court, it's a monumental gateway, with five arches topped by lion heads, cherubim and coats of arms.

🟥 D2 ✉ Plaza de la Independencia 🚇 Retiro

Puerta del Sol

Puerta del Sol has been a plaza since 1570, when the original gate was demolished. This is the heart of Madrid. The headquarters of the regional government are housed on the south side, where a stone in the sidewalk marks Kilometer Zero, from which all distances in Spain are measured.

🟥 C2 ✉ Puerta del Sol 🚇 Sol

Monasterio de El Escorial

Twenty-five miles northwest of Madrid, on the southern slopes of the Sierra da Guadarrama mountain range, stands the massive religious complex known as El Escorial, easily visited on a day-trip by train or tour bus. One of the most impressive monuments in Spain, the complex is easily accessible from Madrid and gives true insight into the extraordinary wealth and power of the 16th-century Spanish monarchy.

In 1557 the Spanish forces of Philip II defeated the French at St. Quentin. To give thanks to God, Philip conceived the idea of building a monastery dedicated to St. Lawrence (San Lorenzo), which would also serve as a royal palace and burial place. The vast complex was principally designed in 1584 by the architect Juan de Herrera, and it took 1,500 laborers to complete the work. It has more than 1,200 doors, 2,600 windows and 16 courtyards, and is nearly 670 feet long. The granite stone accentuates the severe lines of the building, which is built on a grid plan. The clear air has kept the stone and tiles pristine. Later Bourbon monarchs left their stamp on the palace through decoration, furnishings and pictures.

El Escorial Today

Philip II's modest private apartments contrast with his throne room. He lived in a suite of small rooms with direct access to the chapel.

Later Bourbon monarchs extended these impressive royal Habsburg apartments near the church to the third floor. You will find sumptuously painted ceilings, frescoes and a wonderful tapestry collection. A frescoed courtyard gives access to the marbled staircase leading down to the Royal Pantheon (Panteón de los Reyes), where virtually all of the Spanish kings and queens from the time of Charles V onward are buried.

The church itself is on a monumental scale. Its 100-foot-high altarpiece with onyx, marble and jasper columns is punctuated by bronze sculptures. Move on to the equally opulent library, with its shelves made from rare types of wood, marble tables and ornate ceiling.

One of the highlights is the art museum. Among numerous paintings by Peter Paul Rubens, Titian and Jacopo Tintoretto are Rogíer van der Weyden's thought-provoking *Calvary* and the acidic angularity of El Greco's *Martyrdom of St. Maurice*.

➕ C3 ✉ El Escorial ☎ 91 890 5903 🕐 Tue.–Sun. 10–8, Apr.–Sep.; 10–6, rest of year. Closes for official events 🚆 Trains from Atocha (train line C-8 (☎ 902 240 202) 🚌 Autobuses Herranz (☎ 91 890 4122); buses 661 and 664 leave from the terminus at Madrid's Moncloa subway station 💲 $$$

The harmonious facade of El Escorial stretches for almost 670 feet

Barcelona

Barcelona, the capital of the autonomous Spanish region of Catalonia (Catalunya), is one of the Mediterranean's most vibrant cities. Catalonia is Spain's leading economic region, the most innovative and prosperous area of the country, with a proud history, an independent spirit and a strong sense of identity.

In 1975 King Juan Carlos restored Catalonia's status as an autonomous region, which marked the beginning of Barcelona's renaissance. The pride and self-confidence engendered by a thriving economy and urban renewal culminated in the Barcelona Olympic Games of 1992. Since then, the city has continued to forge ahead. With its 2,000-year-old history, exhilarating atmosphere and superb architecture from nearly every age, it can't fail to please.

The City and Its People

Wherever you stay, the excellent public transportation system gives easy access to the entire city. For atmosphere, you might want to be somewhere near the avenue La Rambla or in the old town, and thus within easy walking distance of many of the main sights and the waterfront. The architecturally interesting L'Eixample area is more spacious, with excellent shopping and restaurants; other hotels are relatively far out of the city center. Barcelonins are exceptionally helpful and polite, with an ability to combine efficiency with a relaxed Mediterranean attitude.

English is not widely spoken, although most hotel staff speak it adequately. There are two official languages in Catalonia: Spanish and Catalan, which are both romance languages with Latin roots. Catalan is widely spoken, and street signs are exclusively in Catalan.

Barcelonan Themes

Since there's so much to see in Barcelona, concentrate on specific areas and themes. Spend a day on the waterfront taking in the Old Port district, Barceloneta and the ultra-modern Olympic Port. There's a choice of boat tours around the harbor and up the coast, which is the best way to admire the port.

Head for l'Eixample, the Passeig de Gràcia and the Sagrada Família to enjoy the fabulous Modernista architecture for which the city is so well known. Barcelona is blessed with two hills, Montjuïc and Tibidabo; each offers a refuge from the summer noise and heat and has magnificent views over the city and sea.

Barcelona has more than 50 museums and galleries. The Maritime Museum, the Pedralbes Monastery, the F.C. Barça Museum, the City History Museum, the Picasso Museum and Joan Miró Foundation cater to a wide range of interests, and are all fascinating. Modern art lovers should visit the Contemporary Art Museum, and the MNAC (see page 415) is a must for lovers of medieval art.

If time is short, there are plenty of English-language guided tours and excursions that take in the main city sights by day and night, and also offer a chance to explore some of the other parts of Catalonia.

Gaudí

Antoni Gaudí was born in Barcelona in 1852, and lived and worked in the city throughout his life. His architectural vision was unique and flamboyant, and guided by the premise that there are no straight lines in nature, he designed some of Barcelona's most outstanding Modernist buildings. Curved lines, pinnacles, organically inspired stone and towers are his trademarks, seen at their best in the remarkable Holy Family Temple (Temple Expiatori de la Sagrada Família, see page 416). He was run over by a tram in 1926 and died, unrecognized, in a hospital. When his body was identified, the people of Barcelona lined the streets for his funeral.

Parks and Pools

Barcelona is rich in relaxing parks. The Parc de la Ciutadella, near the Old Town and waterfront, is a haven of tranquility with shady trees, a lake and Spain's best zoo and is a great place for a picnic or to go boating.

Other parks in the city include the Parc Joan Miró, with its ceramic sculpture, and several green, flower-filled gardens on the slopes of Montjuïc. Good beaches are within easy reach, and the city also has excellent public swimming pools.

Where to Shop

Prosperous Barcelona is a great shopping center. You'll find serious shopping along the Passeig de Gràcia and on its surrounding streets, which have all the big fashion names, expensive antiques stores and enticing interior design outlets. The wide avenue of Diagonal is lined with good stores, while the Plaça de Catalunya has a large branch of the department store El Corte Inglés.

For Spanish souvenirs, try the stores around Portal de l'Àngel and La Rambla. For local crafts head to the Born area. Mercat dels Encants is a secondhand market on the Plaça de les Glòries on Monday, Wednesday and Friday (7–6).

Nightlife

Classical music, jazz, rock, dance, theater and movies are popular forms of entertainment; there are comprehensive listings in the *Guía del Ocio* and *Time*

The Three Graces fountain on Plaça Reial

Out, both available from newsstands. Dancing is very popular, and the club scene is one of the best in Spain, ranging from the elegant to the avant-garde. As everywhere in the country, nightlife reaches its peak around 2 a.m. and continues until dawn.

Barcelona has some superb festivals throughout the year, often featuring decorated floats, fireworks and processions of dragon and demon figures known as *capgrossos*, or "big heads." The biggest and best festival is La Mercè at the end of September.

Essential Information

Tourist Information

Barcelona Turisme (Barcelona Tourism)
Plaça de Catalunya 17-S
Plaça Sant Jaume
Estació Barcelona-Sants (railroad station)
Barcelona Airport (terminals 1 and 2B))
☎ For all inquiries: 93 285 3834
www.barcelonaturisme.com

Urban Transportation

Getting around is easy on the subway and bus systems. Subway stations are marked on the Barcelona city map by the letter "M" in a red circle. There are 11 color-coded lines on the subway; trains run Mon.–Thu. 5 a.m.– midnight, Fri. 5 a.m.–2 a.m., Sat. 24 hrs, Sun. 6 a.m.–midnight. The T10 ticket offers 10 rides on metro, trains and buses. Combination tourist tickets valid for 1, 2, 3, 4 or 5 days give unlimited use of the bus, tram, subway and urban trains; tickets and maps are available from subway stations. Validate tickets by stamping them at the turnstile before boarding trains, or when you get on the bus or tram. Bus Turístic operates daily 9–7:45 all year and

has two routes, plus a summer-only route, that cover Barcelona's main attractions, taking you closer to the sights than the regular city service. A cable car links La Barceloneta and Montjuïc, and there are two funiculars, serving Montjuïc and Tibidabo; the latter also is served by tram. You can pick up a black-and-yellow taxi at a stand, hail one on the street, or call Radio Taxi (☎ 93 303 3033).

Airport Information

Barcelona International Airport (☎ 902 404 704) connects to most major European cities and is 11 miles southwest of the city center, about a 20-minute drive. A train connects to Estació Barcelona-Sants and Passeig de Gràcia station, daily 5:30 a.m.–11 p.m. (6 a.m.– 11:30 p.m. from the airport); journey time 20 minutes. The Aerobus (A1 for Terminal 1 and A2 for Terminal 2) runs to and from Plaça de Catalunya every 6 minutes daily 5:30 a.m.– 1 a.m. Travel time is 30 minutes. The two terminals are linked by shuttle bus. The last bus from the airport leaves at 1 a.m. and 0:15 a.m. from Plaça de Catalunya.

Climate – average highs and lows for the month

Jan.	Feb.	Mar.	Apr.	May	Jun.	Jul.	Aug.	Sep.	Oct.	Nov.	Dec.
13°C	14°C	15°C	17°C	21°C	24°C	28°C	28°C	25°C	21°C	17°C	14°C
55°F	57°F	59°F	63°F	70°F	75°F	82°F	82°F	77°F	70°F	63°F	57°F
5°C	6°C	8°C	10°C	12°C	17°C	20°C	20°C	19°C	13°C	9°C	8°C
41°F	43°F	46°F	50°F	54°F	63°F	68°F	68°F	66°F	55°F	48°F	46°F

Barcelona Sights

> **Key to symbols**
> ✚ map coordinates refer to the Barcelona map on page 411 💷 admission charge: $$$ more than €6, $$ €3–€6, $ less than €3
> See page 5 for complete key to symbols

The Passion Facade of the Sagrada Família

La Barceloneta

The district of La Barceloneta (Little Barcelona) occupies a triangle of reclaimed land between the harbor and the sea. Developed in the 18th century to house seamen, fishermen and dockworkers, this delightful neighborhood retains its maritime atmosphere. This is a great place to eat at the many seafood restaurants.

✚ C1 ☒ La Barceloneta 🚇 Barceloneta
🚌 14, 17, 39, 64

Barri Gòtic

A maze of narrow streets and squares make up this area, built within the old Roman walls when Barcelona was one of the richest and most important Mediterranean trading cities. At its heart the Barri Gòtic (Gothic Quarter) is centered around the Catedral and Plaça Sant Jaume. This plaza, once the power center of Catalonia's kings, is still the site of the city hall and buildings of the government of Catalonia. The Plaça del Rei, formerly the medieval marketplace, is said to be where King Ferdinand and Queen Isabella welcomed Christopher Columbus home from America in 1493. Nearby is the Plaça Reial, an arcaded square built in 1848. Gothic mansions line the streets, and you'll find museums, churches, and plenty of bars and restaurants.

✚ B2 ☒ Bounded by Rambla, Universitat, Laietana and Ferran 🚇 Jaume I 🚌 14, 17, 19 🍴 Onofre, see page 489

Catedral

Nothing more strongly represents Barcelona's historic past than the great Catedral (Cathedral). It was built

between the 13th and 15th centuries (with a 19th-century neo-Gothic facade), and the soaring space beneath the Catalan Gothic arches and numerous side chapels houses a wealth of treasures. The tranquil 14th-century cloister, with its fountains, magnolias and palms, is beautiful.

✚ C2 ☒ Plaça de la Seu ☎ 93 310 7195; www.catedralbcn.org 🕐 Church: daily 8–12:45 and 5:15–7; Cloister 9–12:30 and 5–7; Museum: 10–12:30 and 5:15–7 🚇 Jaume I 🚌 17, 19, 40, 45
💷 Cathedral free (roof $; choir $; Museum $). Admission by guided tour only ($$) 1–4:30 (2–4:30 Sun.)

L'Eixample

Between 1860 and 1920 Barcelona expanded into a grid of uniform streets parallel to the sea, an area known as l'Eixample (the Extension). Today this is a residential, commercial and business district, divided in half by the Diagonal, a grand avenue cutting through the grid at a 45-degree angle.

An interesting example of innovative town planning, it contains Barcelona's finest Modernist buildings. Some of the best are in the Passeig de Gràcia; look for No. 43, Gaudí's Casa Batlló, with a

Ventilation chimneys on the roof of Casa Mila, also known as La Pedrera and designed by Antoni Gaudí

mosaic facade and wavy roofline that represent St. George's dragon. The block at No. 92 is known as La Pedrera, Gaudí's last secular work, built without a single straight line or sharp corner.

⊞ C3 ⓢ Diagonal, Catalunya or Passeig de Gràcia

Fundació Joan Miró

More than 200 instantly recognizable and vibrantly colored paintings, along with sculptures, tapestries and drawings, are displayed in the white, bright space of the Fundació Joan Miró (Joan Miró Foundation).

Born in Barcelona in 1893, Miró spent most of his life in the city before retiring to Mallorca in 1956. In 1971 he established the foundation to house the largest collection of his works and to promote contemporary art.

⊞ A2 ✉ Avenida Miramar, Parc de Montjuïc
☎ 93 443 9470; www.fundaciomiro-bcn.org
ⓞ Tue.–Sat. 10–8 (also Thu. 8–9:30 p.m.), Sun. 10–2:30, Jul.–Sep.; Tue.–Sat. 10–7 (also Thu. 7–9:30 p.m.), Sun. 10–2:30, rest of year ⓢ Espanya
🚍 50, 55, 193; Montjuïc funicular to Miramar from metro station Paral.lel 🍴 Café in museum 💵 $$$

Mercat de la Boquería

Make time to visit the glorious Mercat de la Boquería (Boquería Market), housed since the 1830s in a covered hall just off La Rambla. If you arrive at lunchtime, take advantage of the snack bars.

The scents and colors of the fish, hams, freshly picked fruit and vegetables, and the babble of noise from the area will proabably be one of the most enduring memories of your visit to Barcelona.

⊞ B2 ✉ Plaça de la Boquería ⓞ Mon.–Sat. 8 a.m.–8:30 p.m. (fish stalls are closed on Mon.)
ⓢ Liceu 🚍 14, 59, 91

Montjuïc

The green hill of Montjuïc, 698 feet high, dominates Barcelona's southern suburbs. Once known as the "Mountain of the Jews," Montjuïc today is a pleasant recreational area, dotted with gardens, museums and sports facilities. The most impressive approach is through the monumental Plaça d'Espanya to the Font Màgica (Magic Fountain). The fountain stands below the pavilions built for the 1929 International Exhibition.

Also here is the 1992 Olympic complex, the Anella Olímpica.

⊞ A1 ✉ Montjuïc ⓞ Font Màgica displays: Thu.–Sun. 9 p.m.–11:30 p.m., May–Sep.; Fri.–Sat. 7 p.m.–9 p.m., rest of year ⓢ Subway to Paral.lel station, then funicular to Parc de Montjuïc and the telefèric cable car to Mirador and Castell; subway to Espanya for the fountains 🚍 13, 50, 55, 61

Museu F.C. Barcelona

F.C. Barcelona are one of the most popular and successful soccer teams in the world, with a massive international following. This museum celebrates their achievements with video footage of match highlights, displays of trophies and a visitor's book inscribed with the names of illustrious fans. A visit includes a tour of the Camp Nou stadium.

🔢 Off map at A4 ✉ Camp Nou, Avda Aristides Maillol s/n ☎ 93 496 3600; www.fcbarcelona.com 🕐 Mon.–Sat. 10–8, Sun. 10–2:30, Apr.–Oct.; Mon.–Sat. 10–6:30 p.m., Sun. 10–2:30, rest of year 🚇 Les Cortes 🚌 15, 54 💲 $$$

Museu d'Història de Barcelona

The fascinating Museu d'Història de Barcelona (Barcelona City History Museum) covers more than two millennia of history. It is built above the subterranean ruins of Roman Barcino, where you can still walk along ancient roads rutted by 2,000-year-old cart wheels, and admire the faded remnants of mosaics from long-gone villas. Above ground, the visit continues in the magnificent Saló del Tinell, a Gothic throne room spanned by vast stone arches. This is where Isabella and Ferdinand received Columbus after his second transatlantic voyage. Adjoining the throne room is the Capella de Santa Àgata, a dainty Gothic chapel built in 1302, which is dedicated to St. Agatha.

🔢 C2 ✉ Plaça del Rei s/n ☎ 93 256 21 00; www.museuhistoria.bcn.es 🕐 Tue.–Sat. 10–7, Sun. 10–8, Apr.–Oct.; Tue.–Sat. 10–6, Sun. 10–8, rest of year 🚇 Jaume I or Li 🚌 17, 19, 40, 45 💲 $$

Museu Nacional d'Art de Catalunya (MNAC)

The Museu Nacional d'Art de Catalunya (National Museum of Catalonian Art) contains a vast collection, spanning more than a millennium. The highlight is the medieval art collection, one of the finest in the world. Catalan Romanesque art, with its solid rounded forms and stunning simplicity, is represented by sculpture and carving, gold, enamel and textiles. The outstanding treasures are the 11th- and 12th-century murals, from isolated country churches. The superb Gothic collection features ornately gilded paintings and altarpieces, while the Modernista section displays furnishings by Gaudí as well as artwork.

These collections are compemented by the Thyssen-Bornemisza bequest of about 100 masterworks by Fra Angelico, Raphael and Titian among others.

🔢 A2 ✉ Palau Nacional, Parc de Montjuïc ☎ 93 622 0376; www.mnac.es 🕐 Tue.–Sat. 10–7, Sun. 10–2:30 🚇 Espanya 🚌 9, 13, 37, 50, 55, 56, 57, 65, 109, 157 🍴 Café and restaurant in museum 💲 $$$ (free for seniors and free for all first Sun. of the month); guided tours by appointment

Museu Picasso

Pablo Picasso, born in Andalucia in 1881, lived in Barcelona from 1895 until 1904, and he held his first exhibition in the city in 1900. The Museu Picasso (Picasso Museum) is the most important collection of his early works in Spain. Set in five splendid palaces, it also hosts excellent temporary exhibitions.

🔢 C2 ✉ Calle Montcada 15–23 ☎ 93 256 3000; www.museupicasso.bcn.es 🕐 Tue.–Sun. 10–8 🚇 Jaume I 🚌 14, 17, 19, 39, 40, 45, 51, 59 🍴 Café-restaurant in museum 💲 $$ (free first Sun. of the month) ℹ Guided tours in English on Tue. and Thu. at 4 p.m. by reservation

A series of unique tiles by Gaudí in Parc Güell

Parc Güell

Parc Güell (Güell Park) boasts lovely views and wide green spaces and has architectural elements by Antoni Gaudí scattered across its 50 acres. Planned as a residential landscaped area by Gaudí's main patrons, the Güell family, only the grand entrance, the plaza, the paths and the steps were completed. These are interspersed with weirdly shaped sculptures, fountains and columns, many decorated with tiny pieces of colorful broken ceramics (*trencadís*). Inside the park is the Casa Museu Gaudí (tel: 93 219 3811; open daily 10–8, Mar.–Oct.; 10–6 rest of year; $$).

✚ C4 ✉ Calle Olot ☎ 93 213 0488 🕒 Daily 10–9, May–Aug.; 10–8, Apr. and Sep.; 10–7, Mar. and Oct.; 10–6, rest of year 🚇 Vallcarca or Lessops 🚌 24, 31, 32

Poble Espanyol

The streets and squares of the Poble Espanyol (Spanish Village), built for the 1929 World Exhibition, give a glimpse of the country's many architectural styles. Reproductions range from the white houses of Andalucia to the flat granite facades of Galicia, all blended to form one "village." The buildings house workshops where you'll find crafts and artifacts from all over Spain, while evening brings live music and flamenco.

✚ A2 ✉ Avenida de Marquès de Comillas ☎ 93 508 6300 🕒 Mon. 9–8, Tue.–Thu. 9 a.m.–2 a.m., Fri. 9 a.m.–4 a.m., Sat. 9 a.m.–5 a.m., Sun. 9 a.m.–midnight 🚇 Espanya 🚌 13, 23, 50, 55, 61 🎫 $$$

Port Vell

The Port Vell (Old Port) district, once run-down, was transformed for the 1992 Olympics. An integral part of the city again, it is a busy recreation area, with a modern marina and elegant bridges and walkways connecting its attractions. The centerpiece is Maremagnum, a shopping, eating and leisure center, complete with an IMAX movie theater and one of Europe's largest aquariums.

✚ B1 ✉ Port Vell 🚇 Drassanes or Barceloneta 🚌 17, 19, 36, 64

Las Ramblas

Las Ramblas, Barcelona's most famous street, runs from Plaça de Catalunya to the waterfront. It's an exuberant tree-lined promenade effectively joining the old and new parts of the city, divided into seven distinctive sections. The name Rambla is Arabic, from *ramla*, "a torrent," a reminder that the street follows an old watercourse. Here is the Liceu opera house, restored after a fire in 1994. From here head to the statue of Christopher Columbus on a 164-foot iron plinth near the waterfront; take the elevator to an observation deck.

✚ B1–B2 ✉ Las Ramblas 🚇 Catalunya, Drassanes or Liceu 🚌 14, 38, 59, 91

Santa Maria del Mar

Built between 1329 and 1384 at the height of Barcelona's medieval prestige, the beautiful Gothic church of Santa Maria del Mar (Our Lady of the Sea) is tucked away in the Ribera district. Its stark, serene interior allows the elegant architecture to speak for itself.

✚ C2 ✉ Plaça de Santa Maria ☎ 93 310 2390 🕒 Daily 9–1:30 and 4:30–8 🚇 Jaume I 🚌 14, 17, 51

Temple Expiatori de la Sagrada Família

The famous Catalan Modernist architect Antoni Gaudí worked on the Temple Expiatori de la Sagrada Família (Expiatory Temple to the Holy Family) for over 40 years. He envisioned a vast cathedral, with facades to show the birth, death and resurrection of Christ, and 18 towers to represent the Twelve Apostles, the Four Evangelists, the Virgin and Christ. At his death in 1926 only the nativity facade, the crypt and one of the towers was complete. In 2010 Pope Benedict XVI consecrated the as-yet-unfinished temple. The plan is to finish this magnificent building by 2026.

✚ C3 ✉ Plaça de la Sagrada Família ☎ 93 207 3031; www.sagradafamilia.cat 🕒 Daily 9–8, Apr.–Sep.; 9–6, rest of year 🚇 Sagrada Família 🚌 19, 33, 34, 43, 44, 50, 51 🎫 $$$; guided tours $$

Catalan Fare

You can eat as well in Barcelona as anywhere in Spain, sampling local Catalan dishes, fresh fish and seafood, and specialties from other parts of Spain and abroad. Dinner is served slightly earlier here than elsewhere in Spain.

Fish and Seafood

Be sure to try some fish dishes during your visit, preferably in one of Barceloneta's restaurants where it is a specialty. Appetizers often include a selection of shellfish, tiny grilled sardines or giant prawns. Local main fish dishes are often a type of *sarsuela*, fish stew, or *suquet de peix*, a soupy fish and potato casserole. Although not the home of paella (that's Valencia), there are wonderful *arròs* dishes, where rice, subtly flavored with vegetables and spices, is combined with fish and its stock. Try *fideuà*, cooked like paella but using fine pasta in place of rice.

Mar i Muntanya

Mar i muntanya (sea and mountain), or surf 'n' turf, has inspired some of Catalonia's best recipes. Using local ingredients, cooks have created combination dishes featuring rabbit, shrimp, prawns, chicken and pork. Look for *mar i cel* (sea and sky) on local menus, or try some of the excellent pork products. Main dishes are usually accompanied by intensely flavored vegetables, a saffron sauce, a garlic mayonnaise or a crisp salad. The local bread, baked several times a day, is crisp and light, a reminder of Barcelona's proximity to the French border. Cured ham, spicy sausages and garlic snails are often part of a *tapas* lunch, a good time to try a variety of tastes.

Thirst-quenchers

Bars serve tea, coffee, soda and fruit juice as well as every conceivable form of alcohol. You'll find many familiar drinks and a range of Spanish beers and wines.

  Beer is available in bottles or on tap, and you can buy wine by the glass as well as by the bottle. Local red, white and rosé wines come from the Penedès area; Torres and Masia Bach are good, reliable labels. Cava makes a great aperitif; a light sparkling dry wine, it's produced in the same way as champagne.

While in Barcelona you should eat at one of the excellent seafood restaurants

Santiago de Compostela

Tucked away in the green fringes of Galicia, in northwest Spain, is the beautiful granite city of Santiago de Compostela – one of the great shrines of medieval Christendom. Millions of pilgrims braved hazardous journeys to worship at the shrine of St. James, the patron saint of Spain. People still come here on pilgrimages, especially during holy years, which occur when St. James' Day (July 25) falls on a Sunday.

Santiago is a perfect medieval city – a mix of religious and secular buildings, with an ancient and thriving university and a unique spiritual atmosphere. It is also home to the parliament of Galicia, which is an autonomous region, and there is a lively and prosperous modern town surrounding the central core.

Old Santiago

The historic heart is pedestrian-only and can be traversed on foot in less than a

half-hour; everything you'll want to see lies within this small area. Santiago offers quality, not quantity, so most visitors find a stay of a few days ample.

The two main streets, Rúa do Franco and Rúa do Vilar, lead south from the cathedral square and are lined with bustling stores, bars and restaurants. Pick up a map at the tourist office; it's easy to lose your bearings.

Santiago Flavors

Galician cooking is delicious and relies on the excellent quality of local ingredients. Seafood and shellfish are extensively farmed in the *rias*, deeply indented coastal inlets, and are of superb quality. Regional specialties include *pulpo* (octopus) cooked in various ways; blood puddings and sausages; and *empanadas*, flat pies with a meat or fish filling. Local lamb and beef are particularly good. Santiago has many pastry shops, where you'll find wonderful cakes and cookies.

Local wine varieties include Ribeiro and Albariño, straightforward whites,

and the excellent red Amandi and Condado. If the weather's cold try a cup of hot chocolate; thick enough to eat, it's some of the best in Spain.

Souvenirs and Entertainment

Santiago's streets are lined with stores selling all types of pilgrim souvenirs – medals, rosaries, key rings, holy pictures and statues, many decorated with the image of St. James and his scallop shell emblem. The traditional material for pilgrimage souvenirs is jet, polished and cut, or fashioned into the *figa*, a clenched-fist amulet. The guild of silversmiths, hugely important in the past, is still active and makes fine pieces.

This is a university town with a thriving cultural life, and there are year-round classical concerts, as well as the clubs frequented by students. You'll often hear bagpipes, Galicia's national instrument, played on the streets; this continues to be a favorite way for students to make extra cash to pay their way through university.

Santiago Festivals

Santiago's biggest festival is on July 25, the Fiesta de Santiago (feast of St. James), when the city is packed with pilgrims, tourists and local people. The night before sees the Fuego del Apóstol (Apostle's Fire), a spectacular fireworks display in front of the cathedral (detail picture opposite). The feast itself represents a solemn Mass, with music, choirs and Galician bagpipes. The huge incense burner, the *botafumeiro*, is swung in the cathedral. The feast falls in the middle of Santiago's folklore festival, a two-week celebration of Galician culture, with street music, parades, concerts and markets. An international music festival is held in July and draws crowds from across Europe.

Essential Information

Tourist Information

Turismo de Santiago
Rúa do Vilar 63 ☎ 98 155 5129
Plaza de Galicia ☎ 981 573 990
Airport, Sala B ☎ 98 154 7704;
www.santiagoturismo.com

Urban Transportation

Santiago's historic center is pedestrian-only; vehicular access is for taxis and delivery vehicles. It takes 15 to 20 minutes to walk from one end of the center to the other, and everything you'll want to see is within this area, even most of the hotels. If you are staying outside the historic center, take a taxi to the edge of the old town and then walk.

Taxis can be found at stands outside the old city, or you can call them (☎ 98 156 9292, 98 156 1028 or 98 159 5964). Eurotaxis (☎ 98 153 5154) operate wheelchair-adapted taxis.

Airport Information

Santiago-Lavacolla International Airport (☎ 902 404 704), with services to many European cities, is 7 miles east of the city, about a 15- to 30-minute drive. Buses into Santiago run every 30 minutes from the terminal,daily 6:45 a.m.–12:45 a.m. (travel time 30 minutes). Buses run from the bus station and other central stops to the airport from 6 a.m.–midnight. Taxis also leave from the terminal.

Climate – average highs and lows for the month

Jan.	Feb.	Mar.	Apr.	May	Jun.	Jul.	Aug.	Sep.	Oct.	Nov.	Dec.
13°C	14°C	15°C	17°C	19°C	22°C	25°C	25°C	24°C	20°C	17°C	14°C
55°F	57°F	59°F	63°F	66°F	72°F	77°F	77°F	75°F	68°F	63°F	57°F
5°C	6°C	7°C	8°C	10°C	14°C	16°C	16°C	14°C	12°C	9°C	7°C
41°F	43°F	45°F	46°F	50°F	57°F	61°F	61°F	57°F	54°F	48°F	45°F

Santiago de Compostela Sights

Barrio Antiguo

The Barrio Antiguo (Old Quarter) of Santiago is packed with beautiful, historic buildings. The main streets are lined with arcaded old granite houses in the traditional Galician style.

East of the cathedral, the spacious Praza da Quintana is surrounded by notable buildings, including the arcaded Casa da Conga (Canon's Residence). This faces a gracious flight of steps leading up to the 17th-century Casa da Parra (House of the Bunch of Grapes). On the third side is the austere facade of San Paio de Antealtares Monastery, founded in the ninth century. Opposite, the Puerta del Perdón (Door of Pardon) opens onto the east end of the cathedral – this is only used during holy years. On the cathedral's north side stands the huge complex of the Monasterio de San Martín Pinario, with its church and three cloisters. Behind the monastery lies the 17th-century Convento de San Francisco, commemorating a pilgrimage by St. Francis of Assisi in 1213. It is now a museum devoted to the Holy Land and incorporates a hotel.

➕ A2–B2 ✉ Barrio Antiguo

Catedral

The present Catedral (Cathedral) dates from the 11th to 13th centuries. The simple Romanesque lines of the interior provide a superb contrast to the ornate facade, added in 1750, at the cathedral's main entrance. Here stands the 12th-century triple doorway known as

the Pórtico da Glória (Doorway of Glory), one of the sculptural marvels of Spain. Prophets and Apostles surround Christ the Savior and the Four Evangelists, all carved with exceptional imagination and fluidity. Behind the worn entrance pillar and the statue of St. James is a figure said to be Maestro Mateo, the cathedral's designer. It was customary to bump your head against his in the hope that some of his genius would rub off, but it's now protected.

You'll notice a pulley system high above the transept; this operates the botafumeiro, a monster incense burner used during major feasts, which requires eight men to swing it through a huge arc above the transept. The silverwork and gilded figures of the High Altar glitter under the lights of the candelabra.

➕ A2 ✉ Praza do Obradoiro ☎ 981 583 548; www.catedraldesantiago.es 🕐 Daily 7 a.m.–9 p.m.; hours sometimes vary

Museo das Peregrinacións

The Museo das Peregrinacións (Pilgrimage Museum) tells the story of pilgrimage in general, and the Santiago pilgrimage in particular. Exhibits show how the cathedral and town grew around the apostle's tomb, how the routes west across Europe developed, what the pilgrims wore and how they traveled. There's a facsimile of the fascinating *Codex Calixtinus*, a 13th-century guide to the route, full of tips about travel and information about Santiago (the original is in the cathedral, but not on display). Look for the collection of souvenirs 14th-century pilgrims took home.

➕ B2 ✉ Rúa San Miguel 4 ☎ 981 581 558; www.mdperegrinacions.com 🕐 Tue.–Fri. 10–8, Sat. 10:30–1:30 and 5–8, Sun. 10:30–1:30 💷 $ (pilgrims, senior citizens and under 18 free; free to all Sat. afternoon and Sun.)

Museo do Pobo Galego

Santiago is more than a noted shrine, it's also one of the main towns in Galicia. The Museo do Pobo Galego (Museum of the Galician People), set in the old convent of San Domingo, explains Galicia and the traditional way of life in this part of Spain. There are displays of pottery, costumes, tools, handicrafts and musical instruments, as well as exhibits on Galicia's dolmens, stone circles and hill forts. The museum's galleries encircle the 17th-century cloister; in one corner a superb staircase, with three intertwining flights of steps, rises through the building.

➕ B2 ✉ Rúa de San Domingo de Bonaval ☎ 981 583 620; www.museodopobo.es 🕐 Tue.–Sat. 10–2 and 4–8, Sun. 11–2 ✋ Free

Museo y Tesoro de la Catedral

The Museo y Tesoro de la Catedral (Cathedral Museum and Treasury) is housed around the magnificent 16th-century cloisters adjoining the cathedral. It also includes the Romanesque Old Cathedral (a crypt beneath the Pórtico da Glória) and the Chapel of San Fernando, which opens off the interior of the cathedral. In the latter you can see gem-encrusted gold crucifixes and statues still used for important feasts. The museum includes a fine collection of tapestries from the most prestigious workshops. The cloisters, a lovely blend of Castilian-Gothic and Renaissance architecture, are some of the largest in Spain. Stairs lead up to the gallery, completed in 1590, which offers a good vantage point over the cathedral square. The interesting building adjoining the left of the cathedral is the old Bishop's Palace.

➕ A2 ✉ Praza do Obradoiro ☎ 981 569 327 🕐 Mon.–Sat. 10–2 and 4–8, Sun. 10–2, Jun.–Sep.; Mon.–Sat. 10–1:30 and 4–6:30, Sun. 10–1:30, rest of year ✋ $$

Praza do Obradoiro

The sweeping expanse of Praza do Obradoiro (Obradoiro Square), in front of the cathedral, is surrounded on its other sides by three harmonious buildings. These are the Hostal Reyes Católicos (Hostel of the Catholic Monarchs), the Colegio de San Jerónimo (College of St. Jerome) and the Pazo de Raxoi, or Ayuntamiento (City Hall). The oldest building is the hostel (now a *parador* hotel, see page 489), originally founded by Ferdinand and Isabella as a pilgrims' lodging house. It has an elegantly plain facade centered by a superb Plateresque doorway. Inside, the building is laid out around four patios.

Across from the hostel is the college and its charming balcony, which dates mainly from the 17th century – although its doorway is 200 years younger. Facing the cathedral, the 18th-century City Hall seems to unite the whole ensemble.

➕ A2 ✉ Praza do Obradoiro 🍴 El Caballo Blanco, see page 489

The baroque facade of the cathedral

St. James and Santiago

To medieval Europeans, a pilgrimage *(peregrinación)* was a means of earning extra grace and thus attaining entry to heaven faster. Pilgrimages were made to many holy places, but the great goals were Jerusalem, Rome and Santiago de Compostela. The apostle St. James is known as "Sant Iago" in Spanish. The city which bears his name also is the site of his shrine and burial place. According to legend, he had preached in Spain before returning to martyrdom in Judea in AD 44. His disciples brought his body back to Spain, where it lay hidden until AD 844.

Legend tells that he appeared in a vision to Christian leaders and led them to victory against the Muslim invaders, earning him the title of *Matamoros*, the Moorslayer. His body and relics were rediscovered at Compostela, which became the center of devotion for Spain's new patron saint. By the 11th century, pilgrims arrived from all over Europe.

The *Camino de Santiago*

Pilgrims traveled from France, Britain, Germany, Italy and Scandinavia, as well as Spain and Portugal, many taking years to complete their journey. By the mid-12th century, between 500,000 and two million people were on the move annually, a vast number in relation to the total population.

Roads to Spain threaded their way across the Continent, but once over the Pyrenees they converged into a well-organized route across northern Spain. This became known as the *Camino de Santiago*, the Way of St. James. Administered by a religious military order, the *camino* was policed and marked along its length with hostels, inns and churches offering practical and spiritual sustenance to travelers. Towns grew up around the stopping points, with their own churches, hospitals and hospices.

Dressed in sandals and heavy capes and armed with stout staffs, pilgrims also wore the scallop shell emblem of the saint on their broad-brimmed hats. On arrival in Santiago, the custom was to enter the cathedral and embrace the golden effigy of the saint placed above his tomb, while giving alms and thanks in gratitude for the safe completion of the pilgrimage.

The *Camino* Today

The custom of walking the *camino* died out during the 16th century, but was revived around 1880. Today thousands of people make the journey to Santiago, by car, train, plane and on foot. Those who complete the journey on foot, or by bicycle or horseback, and have fulfilled certain requirements, can receive a certificate called "La Compostela."

The Cathedral of St. James with its soaring towers dominates the city skyline

A Day in Santiago

A Spiritual Morning

Your first stop should be a visit to the excellent Pilgrimage Museum (Museo das Peregrinacións, see page 420), where you can learn about the fascinating history of pilgrimage. It provides a sense of perspective and will pave the way for a visit to the cathedral, which should be next on the list. The worn stones of the entrance pillar show where pilgrims once touched them as a gesture on their arrival, but the stones are now protected and touching is no longer allowed.

Spend time admiring the architecture and artistic treasures, then join the line and mount the steps behind the altar to embrace the effigy of St. James, as pilgrims have done for more than 1,000 years. You could time your visit to coincide with the daily Pilgrims' Mass at noon.

A Secular Afternoon

Head up Rúa do Franco or Rúa do Vilar, Santiago's main streets, and choose one of the many restaurants for lunch – shellfish or octopus are both traditional Galician specialties. After lunch, you could head back toward the cathedral and visit the Museo y Tesoro de la Catedral (Cathedral Museum and Treasury, see page 421) before walking back across town to the Museo do Pobo Galego (Museum of the Galician People, see pages 420–421). At about 6 p.m. the streets begin to fill with shoppers and university students, and the bars become busy.

A Peaceful Evening

There's no problem finding an excellent restaurant for dinner; try some fish, such as bass, hake or turbot, or one of the flavorful Galician meat dishes, often pork-based, with potatoes and turnip tops. Be sure to order some of the local dome-shaped cheese, and finish with a slice of *tarta de Santiago*, a special almond pastry made only here. As you wander through the ancient streets after dinner, you'll probably hear the strains of bagpipes echoing through some hidden courtyard. For the walking route, see the city map on page 418.

A terrace of restaurants in Rua San Clemente in Santiago de Compostela

Seville

Some of Spain's quintessential images are of whitewashed streets, Moorish architecture, flamenco dresses, orange trees and proud horsemen.

This mental picture actually reflects Andalucia and its capital, Seville (Sevilla). It is the fourth-largest city in Spain, the seat of a university founded in the early 16th century, an important industrial city and the center of a rich agricultural region.

The Exposition building in Plaza de España

Renowned for architectural treasures, great festivals and a relaxed lifestyle, Seville has attracted visitors for many years, and cares for them far better than many other Spanish cities.

Seville on Foot

In Seville, every building, garden and street is designed as an escape from the sun. If you're visiting in summer, take lengthy siestas during the hottest hours. The central old core is relatively small, and you'll be able to walk to many of the main sights. The narrow, twisting streets can be confusing, so always take a city map with you; maps are free and available at the tourist office and many hotels. Blue-and-white signs direct visitors to the main sights. There's plenty of information in English, and helpful multilingual guides – often university students – offer assistance at all of the main attractions.

There's plenty to see in Seville besides the main attractions. The range of museums, fine churches and civic buildings attracts many visitors: the Casa de Pilatos, an elegant private palace, is a favorite. Also look for the Tobacco Factory (Fabrica de Tabacos), now part of the university but also where Carmen (of opera fame) worked.

Walking is only one option. Visitors can take an open-carriage drive from outside the cathedral that takes in many of the sights. Alternatively, 30-minute cruises run from the Torre del Oro on the Guadalquivir river, one of Spain's greatest waterways, and this is a relaxing way to admire Seville.

Festivals in Seville

Seville has two major festivals: the *Semana Santa* (Holy Week), the last week of Lent, and the *Feria de Abril* (April Festival), held the last week in April. If you plan to visit the city during either of these events, reserve a room far in advance as the city will be packed. Holy Week is a deeply religious time, celebrated by *pasos* processions held by rival brotherhoods in Seville's different districts. *Pasos* are huge carriers supporting religious statues, richly decorated and carried by up to 60 men.

The April Festival is secular, a weeklong celebration of Andalucia's love affair with horses, music and beautiful women. Carriages filled with girls in ruffled dresses, accompanied by horseback riders in traditional dress, parade the streets, and the graceful *sevillanas* is danced all night.

Eating Southern Style

Eating is a pleasure in Seville, with a wide range of restaurants and *tapas* bars. More than almost anywhere else in Spain, *tapas* has a special place here. There's a fabulous choice of dishes, traditionally eaten with a glass of *fino*, or sherry, the fortified wine from Jerez de la Fontera – a city south of Seville.

Mealtimes are late, particularly in summer, with lunch often finishing around 4 or 5 and dinner starting at

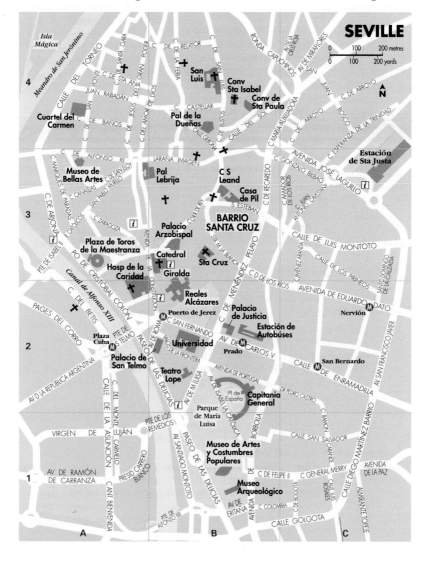

Spain

11 p.m. or midnight. The more cosmopolitan restaurants are geared to foreigners' dining habits. Andalucian coffee is very strong, so it's best to ask for a *café Americano* if you like it weaker.

Mantillas and Castanets

Shoppers throng Calle Sierpes – "the Serpent" – the winding pedestrian-only street running north from near the cathedral. Stroll around and enjoy the traditional storefronts; it's a good place to shop for Sevillian fans, mantillas, shawls, flamenco dresses, castanets and gourmet candies. You'll find attractive pottery at tiny stores in Santa Cruz or across the river in the Triana district, where they also make fine wrought-iron goods, saddles and guitars.

Flamenco

Flamenco is a synthesis of dance and music, ideally performed spontaneously to express joy and sorrow about everyday life, religion and work. Its heartland lies in Andalucia, but its origins stretch as far afield as Egypt and India. It reaches its zenith in the soulful songs known as *cante jondo* (deep song), expressions of deep feelings. The profound meaning of flamenco is hard for foreigners to grasp, but the music, played on guitars *(toque)* and dance, the distinctive costume, the rythmic hand-clapping *(palmas)* and the click of castanets can be enjoyed by all. In 2010 UNESCO added flamenco to its list of Masterpieces of the Oral and Intangible Heritage of the World – encouragement for local communities to maintain this heritage.

Essential Information

Tourist Information

Oficinas Municipales de Turismo (Municipal Tourist Offices)
Plaza del Triunfo 1 ☎ 95 421 0005
Plaza de San Francisco 19 ☎ 95 459 5288
Paseo de las Delicias 9 ☎ 95 423 4465/95 459 2915; www.sevilla.org

Urban Transportation

Since 2009, Seville has a new subway line, and three other lines are to be added over the next few years. The city has an efficient bus system that services the residential suburbs. Some city-center routes run past the cathedral to the Plaza Nueva, and other lines terminate at Plaza de la Encarnación. Maria Luisa Park and the surrounding area is well served from the center. Buy single tickets when you board, or show your 1- or 3-day tourist pass, available at newsstands or from the Tussam bus office.

A tram called Metrocentro in the city center provides rapid transport from Plaza Nueva to Prado de San Sebastian (pedestrian-only route). There's a tourist bus, run by Sevirama (☎ 95 456 0693). This hop-on-and-off service covers the main sights; tickets are valid all day. White-and-yellow taxis can be hailed on the street or at a stand, or call Radio Taxi (☎ 95 458 0000), Radio Taxi Giralda (☎ 95 467 5555) or Tele-Taxi (☎ 954 622 222).

Airport Information

Seville International Airport (☎ 90 240 4704), with connections to major European cities, is 6 miles northeast of the city, a 15- to 30-minute drive. An airport bus runs every 30 minutes from the terminal to Prado de San Sebastian, Mon.–Fri. 6 a.m.–1 a.m.; less often on weekends. Take taxis from outside the terminal.

Climate – average highs and lows for the month

Jan.	Feb.	Mar.	Apr.	May	Jun.	Jul.	Aug.	Sep.	Oct.	Nov.	Dec.
15°C	16°C	18°C	22°C	27°C	32°C	35°C	35°C	32°C	25°C	20°C	16°C
59°F	61°F	64°F	72°F	81°F	90°F	95°F	95°F	90°F	77°F	68°F	61°F
5°C	7°C	8°C	10°C	13°C	17°C	18°C	19°C	18°C	14°C	10°C	4°C
41°F	45°F	46°F	50°F	55°F	63°F	64°F	66°F	64°F	57°F	50°F	39°F

Seville Sights

> **Key to symbols**
> ➕ map coordinates refer to the Seville map on
> page 425 💶 admission charge: $$$ more than €6,
> $$ €3–€6, $ less than €3
> See page 5 for complete key to symbols

La Giralda, the bell tower of Seville's cathedral

Barrio de Santa Cruz

The whitewashed Barrio de Santa Cruz
(Santa Cruz Quarter), with its narrow
streets, ironwork grilles and sun-
splashed squares shaded by orange
trees, typifies Seville and draws many
visitors. Originally the Jewish quarter,
until the Jews were expelled from Spain
in 1492, it was popular with 17th-
century nobility, who added mansions
along its alleyways.
➕ B3 ✉ Santa Cruz 🚊 21, 22, 23, 24, 25, 26, 30, 31,
33, 34, 41, 42, C3, C4

Catedral

Seville's magnificent Catedral
(Cathedral), on the site of the Moorish
mosque, is the third largest in Europe.
It was built between 1401 and 1507, a
blend of Gothic austerity and Spanish
flamboyance. Almost as wide as it is
long, the interior is dominated by the
chancel, the Capilla Mayor, its
splendidly carved Flemish altarpiece
glistening with gold leaf behind
immense grilles. Opposite lie the choir
stalls. Stand between the two and look
up at the transept roof, 184 feet above
your head; this riot of stone filigree is
supported by massive arches and
columns, but even these are dwarfed
by the scale of the cathedral.

Other highlights include Christopher
Columbus' tomb in the south transept;
the treasury and sacristy, packed with
paintings and precious altar vessels; and
the domed Royal Chapel, the burial
place of Alfonso X of Castille.
➕ B3 ✉ Plaza Virgen de los Reyes ☎ 95 456 3150;
www.catedraldesevilla.org 🕐 Mon.–Sat. 11–4:30,
Sun. 2:30–6:30, Jul.–Aug.; Mon.–Sat. 11–5:30, Sun.
2:30–6:30, rest of year (ticket office closes 30 minutes
before closing) 🚊 21, 22, 23, 24, 25, 26, 30, 31, 34, 41,
42, C3, C4 💶 $$$ (combined ticket for Cathedral and
La Giralda)

Giralda

When Christians destroyed the mosque
to build the cathedral, they kept the
minaret and transformed it into the new
cathedral's bell tower. Nicknamed the
Giralda, the "weather-vane," the
322-foot-tall tower was built in the
12th century. Instead of stairs, you
climb a series of interior ramps; 17 levels
lead to the top, from which there are
views over Seville.

Below the tower lies the lovely Patio de
los Naranjos (Courtyard of the Orange
Trees), once part of the mosque.
➕ B3 ✉ Plaza Virgen de los Reyes ☎ 95 456 3150
🕐 Open same days and hours as the Catedral, via the
same entrance and with the same ticket 🚊 21, 22, 23,
24, 25, 26, 30, 31, 34, 40, 41, 42, C3, C4 💶 $$$
(combined ticket for Cathedral and Giralda)

Isla Mágica

Seville hosted Expo '92 on the Isla de la
Cartuja, an island between two branches
of the Guadalquivir river. This is now
the site of Isla Mágica, a theme park
devoted to the Spanish discovery of the

New World in the 15th and 16th centuries. Roller coasters, a 4D cinema and the world's largest virtual-reality theater are among the attractions.

🚉 A4 ✉ Avenida Camino de los Descubrimientos ☎ 902 16 17 16; www.islamagica.es ⏰ Daily 11–11 (midnight on Sat.), Jul. 1 to mid-Sep.; days and times vary, Apr.–Jun. and mid-Sep. to early Jan. 🚌 C1, C2 💵 $$$ (reduction for evening)

Museo de Artes y Costumbres Populares

The Museo de Artes y Costumbres Populares (Museum of Arts and Popular Traditions), located in one of the 1929 International Exhibition pavilions, the Mudéjar Pabellón (Mudéjar Pavilion), is devoted to everyday life in Andalucia. There are reconstructions of workshops where you can see how guitars and castanets are made, old agricultural implements, pottery, furniture and much more. Upstairs are embroidered costumes, painted fans and delicate lace. You also can learn about Seville's great Spring Festival, the *Fiesta Primaverales*.

🚉 B1 ✉ Plaza de América, Parque de María Luisa ☎ 95 471 2391 ⏰ Tue.–Sat. 9–8:30, Sun. 9–2:30 🚌 1, 30, 31, 33, 34, 36 💵 $

Museo de Bellas Artes

Seville's Museo de Bellas Artes (Fine Arts Museum), housed in an 18th-century convent, concentrates on the Golden Age of Spanish painting. The former church is devoted to the Spanish religious painter Bartolomé Murillo, and the highlight is his painting, *Immaculate Conception*. Francisco de Zurbarán, another great master, also is represented with works such as *La Virgen de las Cuevas* and *San Hugo en el Refectorio*.

🚉 A3 ✉ Plaza del Museo 9 ☎ 95 478 6500 ⏰ Tue.–Sat. 9–8:30, Sun. 9–2:30 🚌 6, 43, C3, C4, C5 🍴 Bar Eslava, see page 490 💵 $

Plaza de España and Parque de María Luisa

Built as the centerpiece for the 1929 International Exhibition, the Plaza de España overlooks Parque de María Luisa (María Luisa Park). Traditionally styled and lavishly decorated with thousands of colored tiles, the 650-foot-wide plaza is framed by a semicircular range of buildings and encircled by a canal. The park, laid out in the 19th century, is a tranquil area. It plays a central part in Seville's Spring Festival, when hundreds of horsemen accompany carriages of silk-robed girls around the park.

🚉 B1–B2 ✉ Plaza de España 🚌 6, 34, C1, C2

Plaza de Toros de la Real Maestranza

Seville's Plaza de Toros (Bullring) is one of the oldest and most prestigious in Spain. Once built of wood, the present 14,000-seat ring was designed around the Prince's Balcony and is oval rather than round. Tours include the Museo Taurino, stables, chapel and paintings.

🚉 A3 ✉ Paseo Colón 12 ☎ 95 422 4577; www.realmaestranza.com ⏰ Museum and Plaza daily 9:30–8, May–Oct.; 9:30–7, rest of year. Daily 9:30–3 on bullfight days 🚌 5, 41, C3, C4 💵 $$

Reales Alcázares

The unforgettable Reales Alcázares (Royal Palace) epitomizes the elegance of Mudéjar secular architecture. Little remains of the original Moorish Alcaza. Most of the palace you see today was built by Pedro the Cruel in the 1360s, long after the Moors left Spain, but the builders were Christianized Moors, the inventors of Mudéjar style, and this "Arabian Nights" complex is one of the purest examples of their art remaining today. It's a labyrinth of courtyards, delicate stucco and tile rooms, terraces and coffered chambers, fountains and arched patios. From here you pass into the 16th-century Palace of Charles V, with its tapestries and lavish rooms. Outside are gardens with terraces, pools and shady magnolia and orange trees.

🚉 B2 ✉ Patio de Banderas ☎ 95 450 2324; www.patronato-alcazarsevilla.es ⏰ Tue.–Sun. 9:30–7, Apr.–Sep.; 9:30–5, rest of year 🚌 21, 23, 25, 26, 30, 31, 32, 34, 40, 41, 42, C3, C4 💵 $$$ (free to students and senior citizens)

Active Spain

Spain is a superb destination for active visitors – whether you want to ski in the Pyrenees, hike through the rugged hills of Mallorca or sail around pristine Galician islands, Spain has it all. Useful websites include www. spain.info and http://reddeparquesnacionales.mma.es/parques/index.htm

Skiing and Winter Sports
Spain boasts Europe's most southerly ski resort in the glorious Sierra Nevada, near Granada in Andalucía. There are more ski stations in the Sierra de Guadarrama near Madrid, and in the Picos de Europa. However, the finest skiing can be had in the lofty peaks of the Catalan Pyrenees, particularly the smart resort of Baqueira-Beret, which is where the Spanish royal family spend their winter vacations. The ski season is relatively short, and is best between mid-December and late February.

Hiking
The European network of long distance paths, called GR (*Gran Recorrido* in Spanish), provide some of the most spectacular treks in Spain. Particularly striking are the GR11, which tranverses the Pyrenees from coast to coast, and the GR7, which runs the entire length of the Mediterranean coastline. Spain's 14 national parks are superb destinations for hiking. Spring and autumn are usually the best times, as summer can be overpoweringly hot, unless hiking in the cooler mountainous areas – but access may be restricted during the winter.

Sailing and Watersports
Spain's extensive coastline is dotted with marinas, while sailing, water-skiing, jet-skiing, snorkelling and diving are just some of the sports commonly offered at the main resorts along the Costa Brava, Costa Blanca, the Costa del Sol, Mallorca, Menorca and Ibiza. There are more marinas along the Atlantic coast to the north, which is also a mecca for surfers. The marine reserves at Illes Medes (Costa Brava), the Illes Cies (Galicia) and the Cap de Creus (Catalunya) are ideal for sailing, snorkelling and diving.

Other Activities
Golf is popular throughout Spain, with numerous world-class courses. Facilities for horseback-riding, fishing and tennis are found throughout the country.

The clear waters off Las Salinas beach in Ibiza are popular with watersports enthusiasts

Sweden

Opposite: Kornhamnstorg square, in the Gamla Stan area of Stockholm, with the spire of Tyska Kyrkan behind

Sweden

Sweden is the largest of the Scandinavian countries, famed for the perceived efficiency of its people and the pragmatism of its government. This is a land of wide-open spaces, where even a large city like Stockholm seems to merge urban and rural elements in a way that benefits the people.

Swedish Landscapes

Southern Sweden is an area of forests and farmland punctuated by a vast number of lakes, of which two – Vänern and Vättern – dominate the landscape. The south also is the center of Sweden's industrial powerhouse. The main cities are Gothenburg (Göteborg) and Malmö on the southwest coast.

The southernmost province, Skåne, is a rich farming area where you will find a hint of Danish features, in the people, architecture and landscape; the area was long occupied by the Danes. This is Sweden's vacation land. Off the east coast, the islands of Gotland and Öland in the Baltic Sea have superb beaches that benefit from calm waters and warm summer sunshine.

Stockholm lies on the east coast of Sweden, within a beautiful mosaic of inland lakes and offshore islands. In the surrounding provinces there is a richly varied countryside centered on mighty Lake Mälaren. North of Stockholm is Sweden's ancient capital, the university town of Uppsala. This area is accessible by ferries and cruise boats that ply a network of waterways and lakes.

Northern Sweden is known as Norrland, with similarities to northern Finland, and it enjoys the same "Land of the Midnight Sun" tag. It is a country of vast forests and tumbling rivers that are fed by icy, crystal waters from the mountains. Lapland, or Sápme (see page 434), is a vast and magnificent wilderness of mountains, moorland, birch forest and tundra.

Travel and Climate

Sweden has an extensive road network, but public transportation throughout the country also is a very efficient and convenient way to get around. Trains are modern and comfortable, and buses serve even the most remote northern parts of the country.

Sweden's climate is similar to that of its neighbors, but the country is generally much drier than Norway's western regions. Summers can be as warm and sunny as anywhere else in northern Europe, and along the southern coast you may even find yourself enjoying a Scandinavian heat wave. Conversely, visitors need to be prepared for wet weather in Sweden's maritime climate.

A remarkable number of Swedes are fluent in English, and most people in the cities have at least some command of English. The people are generally very helpful, and have a great awareness of the world in general; they are politely curious about visitors and are lively conversationalists, once their initial reserve is overcome.

Swedes are conservative by nature, and may seem overly serious about life. They are very aware that their society operates on the basis of willingness and co-operation and accepting the norm.

You may mistake Swedish directness for impatience, especially in Stockholm, but this simply reflects a national confidence about how things work.

Old merchants' houses in Gamla Stan

SWEDEN

N

| 0 | 100 | 200 | 300 km |
| 0 | | 100 | 200 miles |

5

Abisko
Kiruna
2111
Kebnekaise
Malmberget
Gällivare
Jokkmokk

E10

FINLAND

Arjeplog
Haparanda
Boden
Strimasund
Arvidsjaur
Luleå
Piteå

E4

4
Stotuman
Skellefteå
Lycksele
Vilhelmina

E12
Doroteå
Åsele
Umeå

NORWAY
Strömsund

B
C
Örnsköldsvik
Östersund

Härnösand

E14
Sundsvall

E15
Ljusdal
E4
3
Sveg
Hudiksvall
Särna
Söderhamn

Mora
Rättvik
Siljan
Stöllet
Leksand
Gävle
Norra Ny
Borlänge
Falun
Sandviken
Avesta
Uppsala

Västerås
STOCKHOLM
Karlstad
Örebro
E18
Köping
E18
Södertälje
Katrineholm
2
Vänern
E20
E4
Nyköping
Uddevalla
Skara
Motala
Norrköping
Vättern
Trollhättan
Skövde
Linköping
Falköping
Visby
Göteborg
Borås
Granna
Gotland
Jönköping
Västervik
Bredaryd
Oskarshamn
Varberg
Ljungby
Växjö
Öland
Halmstad
Borgholm
Tylösand
E4
Älmhult
Kalmar
Båstad
Helsingborg
Karlskrona
Kristianstad
1
Landskrona
Malmö
Lund
Falsterbo
Ystad
BALTIC
Trelleborg
SEA

DENMARK
A

POLAND

Sweden's Geography

Like its neighbors Norway and Finland, Sweden is a long, narrow country, but uniform in breadth. It shares its longest border with Norway, with the Scandinavian mountain chain running along this frontier for more than 1,000 miles. Northern Sweden borders Finland, with the Arctic Circle sweeping across the farthest reaches of the land, part of an area known as the "Nordic Cap." East of Sweden is the Gulf of Bothnia, which eventually gives way to the Baltic Sea in the southeast. To the southwest, a shorter coastline borders the North Sea within the protective shadow of neighboring Norway and the northern reaches of Denmark.

More Top Destinations in Sweden

- Göteborg A2
- Gotland B2
- Kalmar A1
- Lund A1
- Malmö A1
- Siljan A3
- Uppsala B2

Timeline

8000 BC	Hunter-gatherers move throughout Scandinavia in the wake of retreating ice sheets; the Sami (Lapp) people are thought to descend from these early settlers.
1500 BC	Germanic tribes in southern Sweden develop trading links with the European lands to the south, from which they came.
AD 750	The legendary Battle of Bråvalla; the Svear emerge as the dominant tribe and give their name to the country Sverige.
800–1000	Swedish "Vikings" travel east via the great rivers of eastern Europe, as far as Constantinople.
1397	Union of Kalmar unites Denmark, Sweden and Norway under Queen Margaret of Denmark.
1523	Gustav Vasa establishes Sweden's independence; becomes King Gustav I; Lutheran Protestantism becomes the country's main religion.
1658	Treaty of Roskilde secures all of southern Swedish mainland from Danish control.
1814	Sweden wins control of Norway from Denmark.
1905	Norway achieves independence from Sweden.
1914–18	Sweden remains neutral during World War I.
1939–45	Sweden again remains neutral during World War II.
1946	Sweden maintains neutrality but joins the United Nations.
1989	The Sami people are granted their own parliament, known as the Sametinget.
1995	Sweden joins the European Union.
2000	The 10-mile Öresund tunnel and bridge linking Malmö and Copenhagen opens.
2003	In a referendum, the majority of Swedes reject the euro.
2008	Sweden hosts key UN forum on Iraq.

The Sami

The Sami are the indigenous people of Sápme, the area popularly called Lapland. They are known historically as Lapps, but this is not a native name and is one that the Sami themselves feel is derogatory. The ancient name Sápme, a form of Sami which is said to mean "the people of the interior," is now considered accepted usage. Sápme covers the Scandinavian Arctic region from the Russian Kola peninsula to the northwest coast of Norway, and extends down either side of the Norwegian-Swedish border to the central area of both countries. There are an estimated 70,000 Sami people today, of which some 20,000 live in Sweden. A minority of Sami are reindeer herders, but the Sami also are developing alternative livelihoods while strengthening their self-awareness and political position within Scandinavia. Tourism is increasing in Scandinavian Lapland, but some Sami people are concerned about what they believe is too much intrusion on their fragile environment and culture.

Survival Guide

■ For lunch you must experience *smörgåsbord*, a Scandinavian institution, although less common these days. The name translates as *smörgås* for "bread," *bord* for "table." The reality of a true *smörgåsbord* means much more than this simple image implies. There may be more than 100 different dishes in a true *smörgåsbord*, with items ranging from gravad *lax* (salmon slices in herbs) to *köttbullar* (tasty meatballs), *sillbullar* (herring rissoles) or *kåldolmar* (stuffed cabbage rolls).

■ Sweden has the same tight control over alcohol sales as do Norway and Finland, and alcohol is expensive. The government-controlled liquor monopoly, *Systembolaget*, has branches throughout the country, which are generally open Mon.–Fri. 10–6, Sat. 10–3. They sell spirits, wines and strong beers; the minimum age to purchase is 20. Light beers can be purchased at grocery stores and supermarkets. Try some *aquavit* with your food. The beverage is distilled from grain or potatoes and flavored with spices or herbs. Drink small quantities, consumed in one gulp. Note: Light beer is sold to people age 18 or older.

■ July is a popular month to travel in Sweden. The countryside and coast are very busy, populated with Swedes also on vacation.

■ Swedish design is world famous, especially in silver, ceramics, glassware and stainless steel. The Småland area in southeast Sweden is particularly noted for its fine glassware. Stores such as NK in Stockholm's Hamngatan have good selections of glassware, as does Nordiska Kristall, a delightful store in Kungsgatan and Österlånggatan.

■ Home furnishings are a Swedish specialty. Visit the world's biggest IKEA store at Kungens Kurva, south

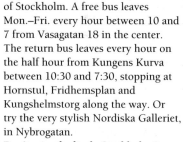

Lake Kallston in the north of the country

of Stockholm. A free bus leaves Mon.–Fri. every hour between 10 and 7 from Vasagatan 18 in the center. The return bus leaves every hour on the half hour from Kungens Kurva between 10:30 and 7:30, stopping at Hornstul, Fridhemsplan and Kungshelmstorg along the way. Or try the very stylish Nordiska Galleriet, in Nybrogatan.

■ Don't miss the lively Stockholm Jazz Festival (www.stockholmjazz.com), a three- to four-day event held in mid-June. People flock to Skansen, Stockholm, to listen to world-famous Swedish and international artists and groups playing jazz, blues, soul and Latin American music.

■ In big cities there are public restrooms along some main streets, in main subway stations and department stores. Signs are *Damer* for ladies and *Herrar* for men. If there is an attendant, the charge can be between 1SKr and 5SKr.

Stockholm

Stockholm is one of the world's most beautiful capitals, probably the only city in the world where you can catch a salmon at a busy road intersection under the walls of a royal palace, and where the city's subway stations double as eye-catching art galleries. The salmon thrive in Stockholm's clean waters at the very heart of the city, and local anglers fish from the Strömbron bridge. The artwork that enlivens subway stations is just one expression of the vigorous cultural life that makes Stockholm one of the world's most civilized cities.

City of Islands

Modern Stockholm is a large, exhilarating city. The scale of its public buildings is monumental, the bustle of its streets all-embracing, yet the city is given a uniquely open character by the 24,000 islands in its archipelago and by the mirror images of lakes that pepper its hinterland. Stockholm stands on 14 interlocking islands; the city is a mosaic of land, lake and waterway stitched together by 50 bridges, making it a vibrant urban environment.

Gamla Stan lies at the heart of old Stockholm, a dramatic and fascinating expression of heritage and tradition. It stands on an island in the middle of the narrow bottleneck channel between the salty Baltic Sea and the inland freshwater lake of Mälaren, the third-largest lake in Sweden, after Vänern and Vättern. To the south is the hilly island of Södermalm, a suburban area with generous expanses of grass and trees. North of Gamla Stan and the buildings of state (the Royal Palace and the Parliament House) is Norrmalm, the business and commercial district. This is the heart of the modern city – glass, steel, concrete and good Swedish design – a cityscape of towering buildings, stylish shopping malls, busy streets and traffic-free concourses that satisfy the demands of both vehicles and pedestrians. East of Norrmalm is the residential district of Östermalm and the city's island park, Djurgården, the world's first National City Park. To the west is Kungsholmen, one of the many islands that inhabit the expanse of Lake Mälaren, Stockholm's "inland" sea.

Compass Bearings

Most visitors arrive at the city's big, bustling central railroad station in Norrmalm, and the experience can be disorienting at first. Just east of the railroad station along Klarabergsgatan is the big sunken square of Sergels Torg, with its landmark Kristall tower of glass and steel and a huge glass facade on the south side. This is Stockholm's contemporary hub. You can orient yourself here and relax in spite of the surrounding traffic and noise. Running north and south of Sergels Torg are busy shopping streets, such as the pedestrian-only Drottninggatan. The northern section of Drottninggatan runs past many additional stores.

Continuing east from Sergels Torg into the street of Hamngatan takes you past elegant NK, the best name in Swedish shopping. This huge department store has floor after floor of fine selections and

---

Subway Art

Subway art in Stockholm is not freelance graffiti but spectacular and eclectic art. When the Stockolm *Tunnelbana* was built in the late 1940s (68 miles long) a decision was made to decorate each station with individual artworks. T-Centralen, the hub of the system, has the most, with examples ranging from terrazzo sofas to wrought-iron gates and ceramic figures on a white-stone background. Visit the Blue Line's amazing Kungsträdgården station; not only is it very deep, but it also has outstanding sculptures, some modern and some dating back several centuries. A guide to subway art is available from transportation and tourist offices, and guided tours are regularly arranged.

such fashionable restaurants as Bobergs Matsal, where Greta Garbo is said to have whiled away the time. Also in Hamngatan is Gallerian, a big shopping mall. Farther along are the offices of the Stockholm Tourist Centre and the great open swath of the Old Royal Gardens (Kungsträdgården). They sweep south to the waters of Strömmen, the magnificent Kungliga Slottet (Royal Palace) and enchanting Gamla Stan.

Seeing Stockholm

For all its size, Stockholm is a city that can be enjoyed on a human scale. You can see it by tour bus, sightseeing boat or you can book a knowledgeable personal guide or a taxi tour, although the latter can be very expensive. Try a boat trip for the wider view of Stockholm's islands, and visit some attractions, such as Djurgården and Drottningholm Palace, by ferry boat.

Ask at the tourist center about the Stockholmskortet (Stockholm Card). Once purchased, it offers free admission, for one, two or three days (425, 550 and 650SKr respectively), to around 80 museums and attractions; a free sightseeing boat trip (Jun.–Aug.); free public transportation in Stockholm and the surrounding area, including hop-on/hop-off boats (May and early Sep.) and other benefits.

Stockholm is neatly packaged into separate entities because of its island

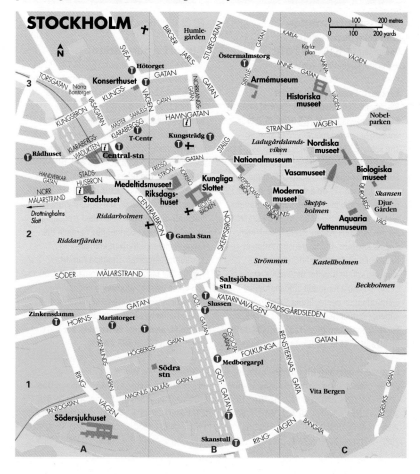

STOCKHOLM

Sweden

nature, making it easy to plan your visit one day at a time. At night the city becomes even more majestic when it is lit up and vibrant with music and lively entertainment.

Stockholmers

Stockholm's confidence is infectious. Listen closely to advice and don't be afraid to ask for clarification or guidance. Then let the magic of the city take over and relax. Stockholmers have created one of the most endearing and enchanting cities in the world, and know how to enjoy it.

The setting sun casts a glow on Stockholm

Essential Information

Tourist Information

Stockholm Tourist Centre
Vosagatan 14 ☎ 08 508 285 08;
www.stockholmtown.com/en

Urban Transportation

Stockholm Centralstationen (Central Station) BKlarabergsviadukten (☎ 0771 75 75 75; www.sj.se), is the main railroad station. The subway (Tunnelbana) is known as T-Bana; there are three lines: green, red and blue. Subway stations are indicated by signs bearing a blue "T" on a white background. On the Stockholm city map subway stations are marked with the letter "T" in a red circle. An efficient bus system serves Stockholm and its environs. Public transportation in Stockholm has a unified ticket system, allowing you to transfer between systems. SL, responsible for public transportation, has an information center in the T-Centralen subway station (☎ 08 600 10 00; www.sl.se). For information on taxis: Taxi Kurir ☎ 08 30 00 00 and 0771 86 00 00, Taxi Stockholm

☎ 08 15 00 00 or Taxi 020 ☎ 020 20 20 20.

Airport Information

Stockholm-Arlanda Airport (☎ 08 797 60 00; www.arlanda.se) is 28 miles north of the city and is Stockholm's main air terminal. The Arlanda Express train (☎ 771 720 200; www.arlandaexpress.com) links the airport and Central Station at 10- or 15-minute intervals daily 4:35 a.m.–00:35 a.m. from Stockholm and 5:05 a.m.–1:05 a.m. from Arlanda. The trip takes 20 minutes. The Flygbussarna airport buses (☎ 08 588 228 28; www.flygbussarna.se) run at 10-minute intervals during peak times (less frequently at night) and take 35 minutes to reach the Cityterminalen (City Terminal) at Klarabergsviadukten. Bromma Airport (☎ 08 797 68 00; www.brommaairport.se) is 5 miles west of Stockholm and handles domestic and some international flights. Buses run between the airport and the City Terminal; travel time 20 minutes. For information ☎ 08 588 228 28.

Climate – average highs and lows for the month

Jan.	Feb.	Mar.	Apr.	May	Jun.	Jul.	Aug.	Sep.	Oct.	Nov.	Dec.
-1°C	-1°C	3°C	8°C	15°C	19°C	21°C	20°C	15°C	9°C	4°C	0°C
30°F	30°F	37°F	46°F	59°F	66°F	70°F	68°F	59°F	48°F	39°F	32°F
-5°C	-6°C	-3°C	0°C	5°C	11°C	13°C	13°C	9°C	4°C	1°C	-2°C
23°F	21°F	27°F	32°F	41°F	52°F	55°F	55°F	48°F	39°F	34°F	28°F

Stockholm Sights

Drottningholms Slott

Drottningholms Slott (Drottningholm Palace) is on Lovön island. The palace, home of Sweden's royal family since 1981, is a superb 17th-century baroque building in the style of Versailles. It overlooks Lake Mälaren amid its own gardens, a mix of French and English styles. On the grounds is the 18th-century Kina Slott (Chinese Pavilion), where Asian meets rococo.

Nearby is the 18th-century baroque Slottsteater (Palace Theater), which is a venue for opera from late May to mid-August. A museum showcases the work of Dutch sculptor Adriaen de Vries (1556–1626).

Drottningholms Slott ➕ Off map at A2
✉ Drottningholm ☎ 08 402 62 80;
www.royalcourt.se ⏰ Daily 10–4:30, May–Aug.;
daily 11–3:30 in Sep.; Sat.–Sun. 11–3:30 in Apr. and
Oct.; Sat.–Sun. noon–3:30, rest of year

Kina Slott ✉ Drottningholm ☎ 08 402 62 70;
www.royalcourt.se ⏰ Daily 11–4:30, May–Aug.;
noon–3:30, in Sep.

Slottsteater ✉ Drottningholm ☎ 771 707 070 (box
office); www.dtm.se ⏰ Guided tours daily 11–4:30,
May.–Aug.; 1–3:30 in Sep.

Drottningholms Slott, Kina Slott and Slottsteater:
🚇 T-Brommaplan; then bus 301 or 323 🚌 177, 178
🚢 Stadshuskajen (in summer) 🖲 $$$ for each part
(includes guided tour); a combined ticket is also
available in summer saving 305Kr

Kungliga Slottet

The monumental Kungliga Slottet (Royal Palace), the official residence of the king and queen, is a stunning mix of classical styles developed throughout the 18th century on the site of the original Castle of Three Crowns. The Representationsvåningarna (Royal Apartments) in the palace are a fine expression of French baroque, rococo and imperial styles. There are several museums within the palace, including the Tre Kronor Museum, with remnants of the Tre Kronor Castle; the Skattkammaren (Treasury), where state regalia are on display; Gustav III's Antikmuseum (Gustav III's Museum of Antiquities), with a collection of classical sculptures; and the Livrustkammaren (Royal Armory), where Sweden's 500-year military history is depicted.

**Representationsvåningarna, Tre Kronor Museum,
Skattkammaren and Gustav III's Antikmuseum**
➕ B2 ✉ Slottsbacken ☎ 08 402 61 30;
www.royalcourt.se ⏰ Daily 10–5, late May to late
Sep.; Tue.–Sun. noon–4, rest of year, depending on
official royal receptions; see website for details.
Gustav III's Antikmuseum: daily 10–5, mid-Mar. to late
Sep. 🚇 Gamla Stan 🚌 2, 3, 43, 53, 55, 71, 76
🖲 $$$ for each attraction (includes guided tours).
A combined ticket is also available, valid for 30 days,
costing 140SKr for admission to all three attractions

One of a series of bronze statues outside City Hall

Livrustkammaren ✉ Slottsbacken 3 ☎ 08 402 3030; www.livrustkammaren.se 🕓 Daily 10–6, Jul.–Aug.; 11–5, May–Jun.; Tue.–Sun. 11–5 (also Thu. 5–8) rest of year 🚇 Gamla Stan 🚌 3, 43, 46, 53, 55, 59, 62, 65 💷 $$ 🚹 Guided tours

Medeltidsmuseet

The Medeltidsmuseet (Museum of Medieval Stockholm) is a fascinating attraction, enhanced by its underground location below the Riksdagshuset (Parliament House) on the tiny island of Helgeandsholmen, between Gamla Stan and the main city. Here, in the late 1970s, layers of medieval remains were uncovered during excavations for an underground parking lot. Admirably, the parking plan was abandoned in favor of preservation.

Depicting the history of Stockholm from the 1250s to the 1520s, the museum is entered via steps leading down from Norrbro, the bridge between Gustav Adolfs Torg and Gamla Stan.
➕ B2 ✉ Strömparterren ☎ 08 508 317 90; www.medeltidsmuseet.stockholm.se 🕓 Daily noon–5, Jul.–Aug.; Wed. noon–7, Tue.–Sun. noon–5, rest of year 🚇 Gamla Stan, T-Centralen or Kungsträdgården 🚌 43 💷 Free 🚹 Guided tours in English daily at 2, Jul.–Aug.

Moderna museet

The collection of contemporary art at Stockholm's Moderna museet (Modern Museum) includes works by Andy

The 14 islands of Stockholm are superb for sailors

Warhol, Willem de Kooning, René Magritte and Pablo Picasso. Don't miss Salvador Dalí's startling *The Enigma of William Tell* and Marcel Duchamp's *Fountain*. There also are compelling works by Swedish artists Vera Nilsson and Siri Derkert.
➕ B2 ✉ Slupskjulsvägen 7–9, Skeppsholmen ☎ 08 519 552 89; www.modernamuseet.se 🕓 Tue.–Sun. 10–6 (also Tue. 6–8) 🚇 Kungsträdgården 🚌 65 ⛴ Slussen 🍴 Restaurant and café 💷 $$$ (includes guided tour and audio tour)

Nationalmuseum

The Nationalmuseum (National Museum) is a dignified Italianate building on little Blasieholmen peninsula, across the water east of Gamla Stan and facing the Royal Palace. The museum has a superb collection of Swedish, international and applied art from the late Middle Ages to the early 20th century. Among the paintings are works by Rembrandt, Goya and Paul Gauguin. Swedish art includes superb watercolors by Carl Larsson and fine works by Anders Zorn. The design and applied art section is a feast of furnishings and artifacts, including Swedish 20th-century design classics.
➕ B2 ✉ Södra Blasieholmshamnen ☎ 08 519 543 00; www.nationalmuseum.se 🕓 Tue. and Thu. 11–8, Wed. and Fri.–Sun. 11–5, Sep.–May; Tue. 11–8, Wed.–Sun. 11–5, Jun.–Aug. 🚇 Kungsträdgården 🚌 2, 55, 62, 65, 76 🍴 Restaurant and café 💷 $$$ (ground floor free; under 19s free) 🚹 Audio tours

Nordiska museet

The building housing the Nordiska museet (Northern Museum) is a splendid work in its own right. Standing at the entrance to Djurgården, its gabled facade of brick and stone has elegant turrets and a handsome central steeple. The exhibits illustrate Swedish and general Nordic cultural life from the medieval period onward. There is an excellent section depicting the life of the Sami (Lapp) people (see page 434) and exhibits of Swedish traditional dress. Note as you enter the oak statue of

Gustav Vasa, the 16th-century warrior who established the Swedish state and became King Gustav I.

🔷 C2–C3 ✉ Djurgårdsvägen 6–16, Djurgården ☎ 08 519 546 00; www.nordiskamuseet.se ◉ Daily 10–5, Jun.–Aug.; Mon.–Fri. 10–4 (Wed. also 4–8), Sat.–Sun. 11–5, rest of year ⓠ Karlaplan 🚌 44, 69, 76; tram 7 from Nybroplan and Norrmalmstorg ⛴ Slussen 🍴 Restaurant 💵 $$$ (free Wed. 4–8, Sep.–May.) 🎧 Audio tours (free)

Skansen

The Skansen open-air museum is located on Djurgården, Stockholm's island park. This area was the old hunting domain of Swedish royalty and is now preserved as an urban escape zone for Stockholmers and visitors. Individual attractions on Djurgården include the Vasamuseet (Vasa Museum, see below) and the Nordiska Museet (Northern Museum, see page 440), but the island offers many diversions. Enjoy the woodland walks or a stroll alongside the quiet waters of the Djurgärdsbrunnsviken. At the heart of Djurgården, Skansen features more than 150 traditional buildings from the 18th to 20th centuries, and is a lively working environ-ment in summer for artisans. You can sample traditional Swedish delicacies, such as *smörgåsbord* and waffles with cream and cloudberries. Skansen's other attraction is its zoo, which boasts elk, brown bear and lynx as well as an aquarium. There are several smaller museums and art galleries scattered around Djurgården, and fun for everyone at Gröna Lunds Tivoli amusement park.

🔷 C2 ✉ Djurgårdsslätten 49–51, Djurgården ☎ 08 442 80 00; www.skansen.se ◉ Daily 10–10, Jul.–Aug.; daily 10–8, May–Jun. and Sep.; daily 10–4, Apr. and in Oct.; Mon.–Fri. 10–3, Sat.–Sun. 10–4 in Nov. 🚌 44; tram 7 from Norrmalmstorg or Nybroplan ⛴ Slussen (year-round); Nybroplan (early Aug.–early Oct.) 🍴 Restaurants and cafés 💵 $$–$$$ (varies during year)

Stadshuset

Stockholm's Stadshuset (City Hall) is perhaps the city's finest example of early 20th-century Scandinavian Romantic Nationalistic style. This was the same style that produced the Jugend buildings of Helsinki (see page 163). Built of red brick and with a magnificent Italianate tower, it stands on the shore of Lake Mälaren. The City Hall Tower (Stadshustornet) tapers to an upper platform and lantern that supports the gleaming Tre Kroner, the three crowns symbol of the city. Interiors are no less striking; the highlight is the Golden Hall with its marble floor. Admission to City Hall is by guided tour only. From April to September you can climb the 348-foot tower – or take the elevator halfway – for fine views over the city.

🔷 B2 ✉ Hantverkargartan 1 ☎ 08 508 290 58 (for tours) or 08 508 29349 (Tower, May–Sep.); www.stockholm.se/stadshuset ◉ Guided tours in English daily at 10, 11, 12, 1, 2 and 3, though subject to change; additional tours Jun.–Aug. Tower: daily 9–5, Jun.–Aug.; 10–4 in May and Sep.; Sat.–Sun. 10–4 in Apr. ⓠ Råduset 🚌 3, 62 🍴 Restaurant 💵 City Hall $$$ ($$ Nov.–Dec.); Tower $

Vasamuseet

The Vasamuseet (Vasa Museum) celebrates a unique historical event. The focus of the museum is the sailing ship *Vasa*, which sank spectacularly in Stockholm harbor within minutes of starting its maiden voyage in 1628. At 230 feet long and fully restored and rigged, the *Vasa* is the only intact 17th-century ship in the world. The ship was ornamental and functional, and its finest features were preserved in the muddy Baltic waters for more than 330 years. The museum tells the story of the people who salvaged the Vasa in 1961, and exhibits 12,000 recovered artifacts.

🔷 C2 ✉ Galärvarvsvägen 14, Djurgården ☎ 08 519 548 00 or 08 519 558 10; www.vasamuseet.se ◉ Daily 8:30–6, Jun.–Aug.; 10–5 (also Wed. 5–8), rest of year ⓠ Karlaplan 🚌 44; tram 7 from Norrmalmstorg ⛴ Slussen (all year); Nybroplan (early Aug.–early Oct.) 🍴 Restaurant 💵 $$$ (less expensive Wed. 5–8 p.m., Sep.–May) 🎧 Guided tours in English Mon.–Fri. 11:30, 1:30 and 3:30., Sat.–Sun. 10:30, 11:30, 1:30 and 3:30 included in admission fee

A Stroll Around Gamla Stan

Stockholm's Gamla Stan (Old Town) – or *staden mellan broarna*, "the city between the bridges," as it is more lyrically known to Swedes – is not a perfectly preserved medieval townscape by any means. Disastrous fires in 1407 and 1640 destroyed the original wooden buildings of medieval Gamla Stan. But the island nature of the settlement, its small area and its crowded layout have spared Gamla Stan from too much modernization. What remains today is a superb enclave of attractive old stone buildings dating from the 15th to the 18th centuries.

You can wander at will through the Old Town without getting lost. On this tiny island you are never far from the waterside or a bridge to reorient yourself. It is best experienced on foot, so pick up a large-scale Gamla Stan map, widely available in stores, restaurants and tourist venues, to help you find specific places.

There are many easily missed treasures hidden away from the main streets of Västerlånggatan and Österlånggatan. Pay a visit to the Cathedral of Stockholm (Storkyrkan). Dating from the 13th century, it is the city's oldest building and is just south of the courtyard of the Royal Palace. The church's finest artifact is the oak- and elkhorn-gilded sculpture of *St. George and the Dragon*, a 15th-century Gothic masterpiece of thorny carving by sculptor Bernt Notke. You may catch a lunchtime organ recital or musical performance in the church. The Riddarholmskyrkan is the memorial place and royal burial ground for past Swedish kings.

From the church, walk along the narrow street of Trångsund and then turn left past a charming old phone booth to reach Stortorget (Great Square). This was the scene in 1520 of the notorious Stockholm "Blood Bath," when Christian II of Denmark slaughtered 82 Swedish nobles and citizens in a bid to seal with blood his overlordship of Sweden. This brutal act inspired Gustav Vasa, son of a murdered nobleman, to rebel successfully against Denmark and to secure Sweden's independence. On the west side of Stortorget is a row of fine gabled houses with little cafés and restaurants on their ground floors. The 18th-century Bourse, or Stock Exchange, commands the north side of the square and contains the Nobelmuseet (Nobel Museum, open daily 10–6 (Tue. also 6–8), May–Sep.; Wed.–Sun. 11–5, Tue. 11–8, rest of year). The Swedish Academy, the body that selects Nobel prize winners, meets at the Bourse.

Leave the square via the east side and walk down Köpmangatan, "Street of the Merchants," the oldest street in the Old Town and home to several

Café terraces are popular gathering spots in summer

fine antiques shops with attractively painted ceilings. At the end of Köpmangatan, in the little square of Köpmantorget, is a dramatic reprise of the Great Church's statue of *St. George and the Dragon*, this time in bronze but just as powerful. Farther east is Österlånggatan, a long, winding street that was once the Old Town's shoreline. Here you'll find many stores selling authentic Gustavian furniture.

Bear right, down the short slope of Köpmanbrinken street, and then keep right along Österlånggatan, past stylish restaurants, antiques and craft stores, and fashion salons. There are lots of gift possibilities here, especially for children, in shops such as Textilarna, Kalikå and Tomtar & Troll, which has a wonderful array of painted wooden handicrafts. The narrow streets running east to the sea, such as Drakens Gränd, Ferkens Gränd and Packhusgränd, mark the old piers of the early medieval era. Near the end of Österlånggatan is the well-known restaurant Den Gyldene Freden (see page 491).

Soon you reach Järntorget (Iron Square), a name probably derived from the days when the Old Town's fortunes were built on its status as the main outlet for the Swedish iron and copper trade. Here, against the wall of the old Central Bank, is the remarkably lifelike statue of Swedish poet and songwriter Evert Taube, a popular performer who died in 1976. Built in the late 17th century, the Riksbank is thought to be one of the oldest bank buildings in Europe. Take a break at the nearby Sundbergs Konditori, a well-known institution (established 1785 and the oldest bakery in the city), selling coffee and delicious pastries.

From Järntorget, turn right onto Västerlånggatan, the busiest street in the Old Town, especially in the summer, crammed with stores and tempting restaurants and cafés. On the right, just past the Mårten Trotzig restaurant, you'll pass the narrow entrance to Mårten Trotzigs Gränd, reputed to be the narrowest alleyway in Stockholm and named after a German medieval copper trader who had a business here. In fact, German architectural influence can be easily identified in many of the winding streets and buildings of the Old Town.

All the way along Västerlånggatan you will be tempted by souvenir stores and Swedish craft stores, such as Handkraft Svea Rike at No. 24 (☎ 08 200 636). Note the glass-paneled ceilings of many of the stores.

Wandering along the delightful side streets is equally rewarding. To end your excursion, stroll to where the bridge over the canal Stallkanalen leads through the arched passage to the gate at Riksgatan. Follow this back into Stockholm via the shopping street of Drottninggatan.

Switzerland

Opposite: The Lauterbrunnen Valley in the Bernese Oberland

Switzerland

With stunning Alpine scenery, lush meadows, a medley of beautiful lakes and attractive and neat cities and towns, Switzerland has a wonderful variety of natural and man-made attractions.

Neutral Territory

The Swiss Constitution, modeled on that of the United States, was drawn up in 1848 and revised in 1874; it is still in force today. Modern Switzerland is a federation of democracies (cantons), and neutrality has traditionally been the cornerstone of state policy. Switzerland has interfered in no foreign conflicts and has made no alliances, although it became a member of the United Nations in 2002.

Remaining neutral through both world wars, Switzerland emerged in 1945 as a powerful commercial player. Banking has long thrived here due to the political stability of the country and because of Swiss financial acumen. The superb infrastructure of railroads, tunnels and roads has overcome the daunting mountainous terrain and allows the country to exploit a trading position at the center of Europe.

The Swiss Landscape

Europe's continental watershed runs through Switzerland, a landlocked country, with a central lowland sandwiched between the tree-clad slopes of the Jura mountains to the north and the mighty Alps to the south. The mountain glaciers and peaks of the Swiss Alps occupy around 60 percent of the country. Dense forests cover another quarter of the land and the rest is a delightful picture-postcard mix of lakes, winding rivers and green meadow pasture.

Switzerland's weather is typical of central Europe; Ticino canton, south of the Alps, has a pleasant, Mediterranean climate, and on some days the *föhn* – a warm, dry wind – blows from the northern slopes of the Alps.

SWITZERLAND

| 0 | 20 | 40 | 60 | 80 km |
| 0 | 10 | 20 | 30 | 40 | 50 miles |

FRANCE

Porrentruy · Delémont

La Chaux-de-Fonds · Biel

Neuchâtel

Lac de Neuchâtel

Yverdon-l-B · Fribourg

Bulle

Morges · Lausanne

Nyon · Lac Léman · Gstaad

Montreux

Château de Chillon · Aigle · Villars

Genève (Geneva) · Sion

Champéry

Martigny

FRANCE

A   B

More Top Destinations in Switzerland

- Ascona C1
- Baden C3
- Basel B3
- Bern B2
- Brienz C2
- Château de Chillon B1
- Engelberg C2
- Fribourg B2
- Grindelwald C2
- Gstaad B2
- Interlaken C2
- Lausanne A2
- Montreux B1
- St.-Moritz E2
- Schaffhausen C3
- Villars B1
- Wilderswil C2
- Zermatt B1

Language and Manners

Reflecting Switzerland's location in central Europe, the Swiss speak four different languages: Schwyzerdütsch, a number of Swiss-German dialects (although German is used for reading and writing); French; Italian; and Romansch (Rhaeto-Romanic), an ancient Latin tongue. This linguistic diversity results in very different types of people; you'll notice this as you travel.

On the whole, the Swiss are extremely law-abiding, and consider punctuality very important. They have a reputation for being aloof, but this is a misunderstanding. Manners are formal, with hand-shaking and serious toasts in all social circumstances. Efficient, civic-minded and polite, they make Switzerland a very best-run country.

Vacationing in Switzerland

The fabled Swiss efficiency has many positive benefits for visitors: trains run punctually, hotels are clean and comfortable, opening times for attractions are reliable, and everyone connected with tourism speaks English.

You will also discover that Switzerland is very expensive, so if you're watching your budget, don't plan on staying here too long.

There's something to enjoy throughout the year – skiing in the mountains during the winter, walking, sailing and other outdoor pursuits all summer. Late spring sees the countryside at its best, with carpets of mountain and meadow wildflowers; fall, when the leaves turn and the first snow whitens the lower peaks, also is magnificent.

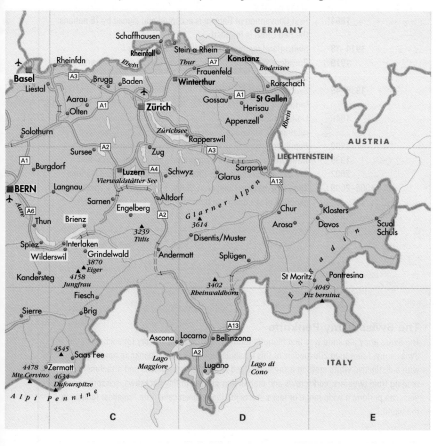

Timeline

3,000 BC	Evidence of earliest neolithic settlers by Lake Neuchâtel.
circa 100 BC	Romans invade from the south, incorporating Helvetic tribes.
circa AD 400	Romans expelled southward; Burgundians occupy western areas (modern French-speaking Switzerland) and Alemans the north and east (German-speaking Switzerland).
1032	Existing country incorporated into Holy Roman Empire, followed by gradual emergence of powerful independent nobles.
1515	Defeat at Battle of Marignano inaugurates neutrality.
1526	Zwingli's Reformation takes hold in Zurich, continued by John Calvin in Geneva beginning in 1536.
1648	Treaty of Westphalia recognizes Swiss neutrality and independence of 13 cantons.
1798	French invasion and rule under Napoleon, who establishes Helvetic Republic.
1815	Congress of Vienna guarantees Swiss independence.
1848	Adoption of Swiss Constitution, which defines political organization of the country.
1864	First Convention of Geneva is accepted and signed by 16 nations; the Red Cross is founded.
1914–18	Switzerland remains neutral during World War I.
1919	President Woodrow Wilson chooses Geneva as headquarters of the League of Nations.
1939–45	Switzerland remains neutral during World War II, but image is tarnished by pro-Nazi activities.
1946	United Nations takes over role of League of Nations; Geneva retained as European headquarters.
1990	Population votes to freeze nuclear power development.
1999	Ruth Dreifuss becomes Switzerland's first woman president.
2002	Switzerland becomes the 190th member of the United Nations.
2008–2009	The Large Hadron Collider at CERN is switched on, a vast scientific experiment set up to run between Switzerland and France.

The Swiss Army Penknife

The Swiss army penknife was first manufactured in 1891 as an accessory for soldiers in the Swiss army. More than 200 models of this versatile world-renowned penknife now exist, each with a distinctive white cross in a shield on a red background. Its blades and attachments, ranging from tweezers, corkscrews and magnifying glasses to tiny hacksaws, scissors and nail files, can perform a wide range of tasks. It has justifiably been called the "smallest toolbox in the world."

A restaurant and communications tower at the summit of Uetliberg mountain overlook Zurich

Survival Guide

■ Keep more money available than you think you will need; cash seems to be spent alarmingly fast throughout Switzerland. Credit cards are widely accepted.

■ Although most Swiss are excellent linguists, it's polite to ask if they speak English before starting a conversation or asking a question.

■ Be polite to everyone – *bitte, prego* or *je vous en prie* is the equivalent of "you're welcome," and it's important to use one of these expressions when you're thanked. When you use public transportation, it's customary to give up your seat for elderly people, pregnant women and people with disabilities.

■ Be punctual; if you're likely to be checking in to your hotel later than planned, let them know you've been held up.

■ In cities other than Zurich, Basel and Bern it is considered rude to eat or drink on the street. If you purchase food to go, find somewhere to sit down and eat it.

■ Don't drop litter; it is a finable offense. When getting rid of trash, make sure you put it in the compartment designated for that particular type of waste.

■ Although informality is the norm in active, health-conscious Switzerland, very casual clothing – like beachwear – isn't usually seen in cities.

■ There is no state medical health service in Switzerland; treatment must be paid for on the spot. Therefore, it is very important to carry medical travel insurance valid in Switzerland. Many drugs can be bought over the counter. If you require a prescription drug, the prescription must be written by a Swiss doctor.

■ In large towns and cities, stores are often closed on Monday mornings. Museums are usually closed on Mondays.

■ Always cross the street at designated crossings, and wait for the green man symbol.

■ Each canton (state) and community is responsible for its own laws and law enforcement. The police uniform differs widely from place to place, as do local bylaws. Respect authority at all times, even if you see no point in what you are being requested to do.

■ Use the superbly efficient public transportation system rather than the inordinately expensive taxis.

■ You'll save money by eating and drinking in smaller establishments away from the more upscale areas.

■ There is no need to tip in Switzerland; a service charge is automatically added to all bills.

Switzerland

Geneva

Sparkling Geneva (Genève), beautifully situated by the shores of the crescent-shaped Lake Geneva (Lac Léman) and backed by the Jura mountains and the Alps, is indeed an elegant city. With its key role as an important international meeting place, many visitors are in the city on business, but others come to enjoy the scenic location, excellent museums, stores, restaurants and the lively cultural life.

The Modern City

Strategically positioned at the head of the Rhône river, Geneva joined the Swiss Confederation in 1815, after Napoleon's downfall. Since then the city has grown, prospered and become increasingly cosmopolitan.

Today Geneva hosts meetings, exhibitions, conventions and many organizations involved with humanitarian and social causes. It plays a major part in Swiss industry, finance and commerce, but has succeeded in retaining much of its French style and attitude, resulting in a pleasing blend of charm and efficiency.

An important university and scientific center, Geneva also is home to CERN, the European Center of Nuclear Research. The city is ringed with attractive countryside – the ski slopes of the French Alps are less than an hour away, and Lake Geneva offers superb watersports facilities.

Old Town and Beyond

Geneva is used to foreign visitors, and it's an easy city with which to become familiar. Getting around by public transportation is simple, and the center of the city is small enough to cover on foot, with much of the Old Town pedestrian-only. It's worth spending a couple of hours getting your bearings by walking around the town center, which lies on either side of the Rhône river.

Much of what you'll want to see is in or around the Old Town and is well marked, although with more than 30 museums to choose from, you are likely to take a bus at some point. Tourist trams run through the Old Town,

A pleasure boat on Lake Geneva (Lac Leman), with mountains rising up behind the city

leaving from the place Neuve every half-hour; they're a relaxing way to enjoy the city, although guided walking tours are available.

Tour buses travel to Lausanne and Château de Chillon, and into the Alps to Mont Blanc and Gstaad. Many lake cruises are offered, most lasting from one to three hours and many with commentary in English.

Gourmet Geneva

Like all Swiss cities, Geneva has a wide range of restaurants offering cuisine from around the world. It also has its own specialties, many of which have more in common with France than the rest of Switzerland. Eating out can be expensive, although away from the city center you'll find friendly neighborhood restaurants prices are considerably lower and the food is just as good.

Many places serve Swiss specialties such as fondue, sausage and *rösti*, but you can choose from French, Italian, Thai, Japanese, Korean, Chinese,

Festivals and Fun

Geneva's biggest traditional festival is the *Escalade*, a December commemoration of a 1602 battle. A wonderful parade in 17th-century costumes marches through the Old Town, and the whole city is out in the streets to celebrate. The *Bol d'Or* annual sailing regatta, the biggest lake sailing race in Europe, is held in June, when more than 600 boats and their crews take over the lakeshore, and at the beginning of August the city is lit up by musical fireworks displays during the renowned *Fêtes de Genève*, with hundreds of concerts performed all over the canton.

Russian, Spanish, Australian, Moroccan and many more.

You'll find all the usual fast-food outlets in the center, and it's fun to shop for a picnic to enjoy in one of the lakeside parks.

There's a plethora of bars throughout the city; the nicest are in the Old Town and also along the lakeside.

Designer Style and Souvenirs

Geneva stores do not usually close at lunchtime and are open until 8 p.m. on Thursdays. There are vast malls on the city outskirts, but it's likely you'll be shopping in the downtown city area, where the most attractive and elegant stores are all located. You will find many of them along the rue du Rhône, the rue du Mont Blanc and other elegant neighboring streets.

Don't miss Globus in the Grand Passage, a large department store that's a Geneva institution. You'll find watches, expensive jewelry, high fashion and superb leather goods from stylish outlets such as Boucheron and Piaget, Christian Dior, Giorgio Armani, Gucci, Hermès and Chanel.

If you're looking for gifts or souvenirs to take home, try the tourist boutique in Globus in the Grand Passage, Swiss Corner on the rue des Alpes, or l'Ours de Berne on the place du Port.

Essential Information

Tourist Information

Genève Tourisme (Geneva Tourism)
Rue du Mont-Blanc 18 🌐 Mon. 10–6,
Tue.–Sun. 9–6
☎ 022 909 7000;
www.geneve-tourisme.ch

Urban Transportation

Geneva is efficiently served by swift and punctual trolley buses and buses that cover the city's various areas; it's likely you'll be traveling mainly inside Zone 10, which covers the city center. You buy and validate your ticket from the machines at each bus stop, which also have route maps and clear instructions about using the system. A ticket for one zone is valid for 30 minutes; two zones, 60 minutes. The best ticket is the Geneva Transport Card, which is free when visitors check in at their hotel, hostel or campsite and allows use of all public transportation. To board or leave the bus, press the red button

near the door; the doors will open and close automatically. For information contact the Transports Publics Genevois (TPG) head office, route de la Chapelle 1, or call the Mobility Call Center (☎ 0900 022 021, CHF1.19 per minute). Taxis are at stands in the city center and also can be hailed on the street or called from your hotel. Call Taxiphone SA Genève (☎ 022 331 4133).

Airport Information

The Aéroport Internationale de Genève-Cointrin (Geneva International Airport, ☎ 022 717 7111) is 3 miles north of the city center. It is linked to the central railroad station by trains departing every 15 minutes, daily 6:30 a.m.–12:30 a.m., with a 6-minute journey time. Bus No. 10 (free) runs about every 10 minutes between the airport and the city and takes 20–25 minutes. Taxis are available outside the airport terminal. Fares between the airport and the city range from CHF30 to CHF35.

Climate – average highs and lows for the month

Jan.	Feb.	Mar.	Apr.	May	Jun.	Jul.	Aug.	Sep.	Oct.	Nov.	Dec.
4°C	5°C	10°C	13°C	18°C	22°C	25°C	25°C	20°C	13°C	8°C	4°C
39°F	41°F	50°F	55°F	64°F	72°F	77°F	77°F	68°F	55°F	46°F	39°F
-2°C	0°C	2°C	3°C	7°C	12°C	14°C	14°C	11°C	6°C	2°C	0°C
28°F	32°F	36°F	37°F	45°F	54°F	57°F	57°F	52°F	43°F	36°F	32°F

Geneva Sights

> **Key to symbols**
> ➕ map coordinates refer to the Geneva map on page 451 💶 admission charge: $$$ more than CHF10, $$ CHF7–CHF10, $ less than CHF7
> See page 5 for complete key to symbols

Cathédrale St-Pierre

The vast and austere Cathédrale St-Pierre (St. Peter's Cathedral) has been a Protestant church since 1536.

It was built in the 12th and 13th centuries, and its current neoclassic facade was added in the 18th century. This is where John Calvin preached; his seat is still in the north aisle. Climb the 157 steps up the tower for views over Geneva and the lake. The cathedral has a long-standing musical tradition; the Clémence, the largest bell in the tower, weighs more than 6 tons and was placed there in 1407. The carillon changes monthly, and there are summer organ recitals starting at 6 p.m. on Saturdays from June through September.

➕ B2 ✉ cour de St.-Pierre ☎ 022 311 7575; tours 022 310 2929 🕐 Cathédrale: Mon.–Sat. 9:30–6:30, Sun. noon–6:30, Jun.–Sep.; Mon.–Sat. 10–5:30, Sun. noon–5:30, rest of year. Site archéologique: Tue.–Sun. 10–5 🚌 3, 5, 17; tram 12 💶 Cathedral free; site archéologique $$

Fondation Baur

An elegant 19th-century mansion houses the Fondation Baur (Baur Foundation), the extensive Asian art collection of connoisseur Alfred Baur (1865–1951). Among the many exhibits you'll find exquisite Chinese ceramics and samples of jade, snuff bottles from the 10th to the 19th centuries, prints and *netsuke* (Japanese carved toggles), and intricate Japanese and Chinese lacquerwork dating from the 8th to the 18th centuries.

Spend some time lingering over the porcelain and marveling at the depth and translucency of the yellow and celadon-green glazes.

➕ B2 ✉ rue Munier-Romilly 8 ☎ 022 704 3282 🕐 Tue.–Sun. 2–6 (Wed. also 6–8) 🚌 1, 8, 36 💶 $$

Jardin Anglais

Statues, trees and a riot of colorful flowers help make the lakeside Jardin Anglais (English Garden) and its mountain views the perfect place to escape the city's bustle. Admire the 1862 fountain, with numerous reclining nymphs, before spending a few minutes at the Floral Clock. This huge timepiece, made entirely of 6,500 flowers and plants, was installed in 1955 as a symbol of the Geneva watch industry. From the garden, Geneva's most prominent landmark, the Jet d'Eau, a towering spray of water over the lake, can be seen. A short walk along the lake will bring you to Parc de la Grange, a lovely rose garden seen at its best in mid-June.

➕ B2–C2 ✉ promenade du Lac 🕐 Daily dawn–dusk 🚌 6, 8, 29 🍴 Cafés and restaurants

Musée Ariana

The Musée Ariana is Switzerland's only public museum dedicated entirely to ceramics and glass. With some 20,000 objects, this collection is one of Europe's largest, covering seven centuries of European, Middle Eastern and Asian ceramic and glass manufacture. The main techniques represented are pottery, stoneware, faïence and porcelain.

➕ Off map at A3 ✉ avenue de la Paix 10 ☎ 022 418 5450 🕐 Tue.–Sun. 10–6 🚌 5, 8, 11, 13, 18, 22, F, V, Z 💶 Free; temporary exhibitions $

Musée d'Art et d'Histoire

Behind the grandiose facade of Geneva's Musée d'Art et d'Histoire (Museum of Art and History) lies a dauntingly large collection of paintings, archeological finds and objets d'art. Ancient history fans will enjoy the Egyptian, Greek, Roman and Etruscan rooms. With 400 paintings, the galleries cover the full range of European painting, but concentrate on Swiss specialties, such as Ferdinand Hodler's powerful work *The Drinkers* or Konrad Witz's 1444 altarpiece; its background is one of Europe's first accurate landscape representations. Other rooms contain applied arts collections, examples of fine furniture, silver and porcelain.

➕ B1 ✉ rue Charles-Galland 2 ☎ 022 418 2600 🕐 Tue.–Sun. 10–6 🚌 1, 2, 3, 5, 7, 8, 16, 17, 36 🍴 Restaurant 💷 Free; temporary exhibitions $

Musée Barbier-Mueller

Situated in the heart of the Old Town, the Barbier-Mueller Museum was founded in 1977 to conserve, restore and exhibit an extensive collection of works of art begun by Josef Mueller in 1907. The collection consists of more than 7,000 pieces of tribal and classical art and ornaments from primitive civilizations, and includes pieces collected by Mueller's son-in-law, Jean Paul Barbier. The museum has earned an international reputation for its traveling exhibitions, loans to museums and the publication of catalogues and art books.

➕ B2 ✉ rue Jean-Calvin 10 ☎ 022 312 0270; www.barbier-mueller.ch 🕐 Daily 11–5 🚌 2, 7, 12, 16, 17 💷 $$

Muséum d'Histoire Naturelle

The splendid Muséum d'Histoire Naturelle (Natural History Museum) is immensely popular and can be very crowded, so get there early. The exhibits cover everything from the history of the Earth through the dinosaur age to comprehensive displays of animals, birds, reptiles and fish from all over the world. It's all excellently displayed, with some very realistic sound effects to help your imagination. If you have time, don't miss the relief map of Switzerland on the fifth floor.

➕ C1 ✉ route de Malagnou 1 ☎ 022 418 6300; www.ville-ge.ch/musinfo/mhng 🕐 Tue.–Sun. 10–5 🚌 1, 8, 20, 27; trams 12, 16, 17 🍴 Café and snack bar 💷 Free, except some temporary exhibitions

Musée International de la Croix Rouge et du Croissant Rouge

It's well worth visiting the state-of-the-art Musée International de la Croix-Rouge et du Croissant-Rouge (International Red Cross and Red Crescent Museum), which explains the principles and history of the organization during some of the most serious crises of the 20th century.

➕ Off map at A3 ✉ avenue de la Paix 17 ☎ 022 748 9525; www.micr.org 🕐 Wed.–Mon. 10–5 🚌 8 🍴 Restaurant 💷 $$ ℹ️ Guided tours by appointment (☎ 022 748 9506)

Palais des Nations

Built between 1929 and 1936 to house the League of Nations, the Palais des Nations (Palace of Nations) is now the European seat of the United Nations. The U.N.O.G. (United Nations Office Geneva) has 1,600 people on staff and hosts more than 8,000 meetings each year. The vast marble and travertine-stone complex is beautifully situated on the slopes above the lake, with views of Mont Blanc. You can tour some of the interior and see the Salle des Pas-Perdus, a room decorated with marble donated by United Nations member countries, and the 2,000-seat Salle des Assemblées, one of the world's most active conference centers. After the tour, learn more through the multilingual interactive games.

➕ Off map at A3 ✉ avenue de la Paix (Porte 39) ☎ 022 917 4896 or 022 917 4539; www.unog.ch/ 🕐 Mon.–Fri. 10–noon and 2–4, Apr.–Jun.; daily 10–noon and 2–4, Sep.; daily 10–5, Jul.–Aug. 🚌 5, 8, 11, 13, 15, F, V, Z 🍴 Café 💷 $$$ ℹ️ Passport or identity card required for entry

Place du Bourg-de-Four

Bourg-de-Four square is the heart of Old Geneva, historically the site of the Roman market, medieval trade fairs, and political and religious meetings. Today the square and its surrounding streets are a lovely place to enjoy a drink. Many of the fine buildings date from the 16th century; note their extra floors, added later to accommodate the flood of Protestant religious exiles.

➕ B1 ✉ place du Bourg-de-Four 🚌 8, 17 🍴 Cafés and restaurants nearby

The Red Cross

In 1859, Jean Henri Dunant (1828–1910), son of a prominent Genevan family, set off to appeal to Napoleon III of France on a personal matter. Dunant caught up with Napoleon the day after the Battle of Solferino, where he saw more than 40,000 wounded men desperately in need of care and attention.

Dunant returned to Geneva and wrote a moving book, *Souvenir of Solferino*, in which he proposed the establishment of a body of volunteer male nurses to impartially care for the wounded in wartime. He further suggested that these men be recognized through an international agreement. Three friends added their support, the book was published and the International Committee of Help for the Wounded in Case of War (Comité Internationale de Secours aux Blessées en Cas de Guerre) was set up.

In 1864, the First Convention of Geneva was accepted and signed by 16 nations; a revised version of its standards of treatment for prisoners of war is still in effect today. An easily recognizable logo for the new movement was needed, and a reverse version of the colors of the Swiss flag was used; a red cross on a white background, rather than a white cross on a red background – a symbol now known the world over.

The Red Cross, present in more than 50 countries throughout the world, works hand in hand with the Red Crescent, an identical body functioning in Muslim and other non-Christian countries. Jean Henri Dunant was awarded the first Nobel Peace Prize in 1901, along with Frédéric Passy.

The Red Cross functions at both international and national levels. The international headquarters are in Geneva, and it is from here that major humanitarian relief work is coordinated. Each participating country has its own national committee that deals with day-to-day work in that particular country. The Red Cross is still manned largely by volunteers, who cover everything from terrorist attacks and natural disasters to organizing collections for war victims and refugees, as well as training the public in emergency aid procedures.

The headquarters of the International Red Cross in Geneva

Zurich

Primarily a business center, with an emphasis on international finance and banking, this prosperous and clean city has plenty for visitors to enjoy. It is dotted with fine buildings, museums, historic churches and green spaces, the perfect background for affluent stores, elegant cafés and well-dressed citizens.

Lakeside City

Zurich surrounds the northern end of Zürichsee (Lake Zurich), from which the Limmat river flows to bisect the city. The oldest part lies on either side of the river, with the 19th-century grandeur of the Bahnhofstrasse area on the west. East of the river, hills rise to the university complex, while boulevards, parks and gardens run along the lake.

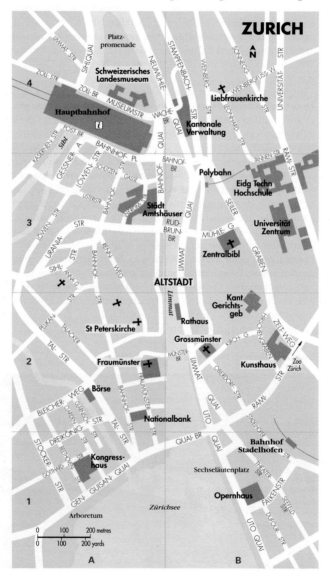

ZURICH

A tram ride is an essential experience; these vehicles ensure that city streets are virtually traffic-free. You can borrow a free bike from four places in the city, including the main railroad station (daily 8 a.m.–9:30 p.m., ID and deposit of CHF20 required); www.zuerirollt.ch.

Evenings Out

There's a range of excellent restaurants in Zurich, most of them expensive. You can eat well and relatively cheaply on the east side of the river. You'll find fast-food outlets, cafés and tea rooms, and cozy taverns and wine cellars.

Notice boards all over the city list movie theaters (often showing American films in English), concerts, theater and opera. For a relaxed evening with the locals, you'll find plenty of packed bars, open late, in and around the Limmatquai; on summer nights there is an array of street performers. Zurich also has a number of cabarets and discos.

Chocolates and Watches

Bahnhofstrasse is one of Europe's great shopping streets. Lined with expensive stores, you'll find luxury items here. Schweizer Heimatwerk store specializes in Swiss handicraft. Don't miss Sprüngli, a mouthwatering chocolate shop. The narrow old streets on each side of the river are packed with antiques stores.

Essential Information

Tourist Information

Zürich Tourism

Im Hauptbahnhof (in Central Station) ☎ 044 215 4000; fax 044 215 4080; www.zuerich.com Ⓒ Daily; call for times

Urban Transportation

Zurich's efficient tram and bus system runs daily 4:30 a.m.–12:30 a.m. It is easy to use, fast and never late. Tickets must be purchased and validated before boarding; all bus stops have ticket machines with transportation maps and instructions for buying and validating your ticket. Blue ticket machines accept cash or credit cards. You can buy a Zürich Card for unlimited travel in the city for 1–3 days. These are valid for trams, buses, local trains and some boats and offer discounts to museums, shops and restaurants. Numbers and stops (which are named) are displayed on the front of the vehicles as well as inside. Press the red button on the door to open it before

getting off; it will close automatically. For information about public transportation ☎ 0848 988 988; www.zvv.ch. Taxis are an expensive option; call Alpha Taxi (☎ 044 777 7777) or Taxi 44 AG (☎ 044 444 4444). Boats run on Lake Zurich April through October. Their timetables are listed at departure points; call Wassertaxi (☎ 044 928 1811).

Airport Information

Zurich-Kloten Airport (☎ 043 816 2211, or for flight information ☎ 0900 300 313 toll call; www.flughafen-zuerich.ch) is about 6 miles north of the city center. Trains run every 10 minutes from the Hauptbahnhof, daily 5:30 a.m.–12:30 a.m., with a ride time of around 10 minutes. There are two arrivals terminals, 1 and 2, which are interconnected. Taxis are available from outside the terminals; the journey from the airport to downtown costs CHF60, or call Airport Taxi (☎ 0848 850 852).

Climate – average highs and lows for the month

Jan.	Feb.	Mar.	Apr.	May	Jun.	Jul.	Aug.	Sep.	Oct.	Nov.	Dec.
2°C	3°C	8°C	12°C	16°C	19°C	22°C	22°C	18°C	12°C	6°C	3°C
36°F	37°F	46°F	54°F	61°F	66°F	72°F	72°F	64°F	54°F	43°F	37°F
-2°C	-2°C	2°C	4°C	8°C	11°C	14°C	14°C	11°C	7°C	2°C	0°C
28°F	28°F	36°F	39°F	46°F	52°F	57°F	57°F	52°F	45°F	36°F	32°F

Zurich Sights

Altstadt
The narrow streets and peaceful squares on either side of the Limmat river make up the Altstadt (Old Town) with its well-preserved old buildings. Take in the Lindenhof, a square planted with lime trees on the site of the original Roman settlement, then cross the river to amble down the east side's lively Niederdorfstrasse and Hirschengasse.
🔡 A3–B3 ✉ Altstadt ☎ 044 215 4088 (tours) 🕐 Mon.–Fri. 3, Sat.–Sun. 3, 11, Apr.–Oct.; Wed. and Sun. 11, Sat. 11, 3, rest of year 🚌 4, 6, 7, 15 💰 Tours: $$$

Fraumünster
The graceful spire of the Fraumünster (Our Lady's Minster Church), founded in the 9th century by two German princesses, rises near the west riverbank in the Old Town. The interior dates from 1250 and earlier; against its gray stone serenity, Marc Chagall's stained-glass choir windows vibrate with green, blue and yellow. Augusto Giacometti designed the transept glass.
🔡 A2 ✉ Am Münsterhofplatz ☎ 076 372 3911 🕐 Mon.–Sat. 10–6, Sun. 11:15–6, Apr.–Oct.; 10–4, Nov.–Mar. Sun. service at 10 a.m. 🚃 Trams 4, 15 💰 Free ℹ For guided tours ☎ 044 221 2063; for guided organ tours ☎ 044 363 1905

Grossmünster
Grossmünster (Great Cathedral) played a major part in Zurich's Reformation (a 16th-century movement which aimed at reforming the Roman Catholic Church and resulted in the establishment of Protestant churches). It was here that Ulrich Zwingli, the father of Swiss Protestantism, preached and taught. He transformed this Catholic foundation into a theological college that became the focal point of the University of Zurich. The church, galleries and three naves were built between 1100 and 1260, a superb Romanesque basilica with some outstanding sculpture on the capitals of its columns.

Be sure to visit the tranquil cloister, where exhibits tell the story of the Reformation, and then climb the tower for views over Zurich and the lake.
🔡 B2 ✉ Grossmünsterplatz ☎ 044 252 5949 🕐 Mon.–Sat. 10–6, Sun. noon–6, Mar.–Oct.; daily 10–5, rest of year. Open Sun. after services. Tower closed Tue. 🚃 4, 15 💰 $

Kunsthaus
Zurich's Kunsthaus (Art Gallery), a lively museum that often mounts important temporary exhibitions, is mainly devoted to 19th- and 20th-century paintings and artworks. Earlier times are represented by a clutch of Venetian paintings, as well as some splendid Dutch works.

The exhibits of modern art are housed in the newer wing. Here you'll find the largest collection of Edvard Munch outside Scandinavia, paintings by Marc Chagall, and a good cross-section of modern work by Mark Rothko, Francis Bacon and Roy Lichtenstein, whose contribution is a baked potato oozing with butter.
🔡 B2 ✉ Heimplatz 1 ☎ 044 253 8484 🕐 Tue. and Sat.–Sun. 10–6, Wed.–Fri. 10–8 🚃 31; trams 3, 5, 8, 9 🍴 Café and restaurant 💰 $$$

St. Peterskirche
The oldest church foundation in Zurich, St. Peterskirche (St. Peter's Church), stands in a quiet square at the heart of the Old Town, its restrained baroque interior typifying the city's God-fearing prosperity.

Four churches predate the existing one, which preserves the late Romanesque choir and 13th-century tower. All is harmony and balance, from the richly carved choir stalls to the superb plasterwork. The clock in the

A street dominated by the clock tower of St. Peter's Church

tower is Europe's largest clock-face, measuring some 28.5 feet across.

➕ A2 ✉ St. Peterhofstatt 6 ☎ 044 211 2588 🕐 Mon.–Fri. 8–6, Sat. 10–4, Sun. noon–5 and service at 10 a.m. 🚊 Trams 4, 15 💵 Free

Schweizerisches Landesmuseum

Housed in a bizarre-looking castle complete with towers and turrets, the Schweizerisches Landesmuseum (Swiss National Museum) should top your sightseeing list. This is the place to learn about Switzerland's history and development, and it is one of Europe's best organized museums.

Beginning in prehistoric times, you can follow the flowering of Swiss civilization through frescoes, religious wood carvings and exquisite jewelry, wood-paneled interiors, and furniture and costumes from every corner of the land. The 16th-century globes, showing all that had so far been discovered, and

the reconstruction of rooms from different eras, are fascinating.

➕ A4 ✉ Museumstrasse 2 ☎ 044 218 6511; www.musee-suisse.ch 🕐 Tue.–Sun. 10–5 (also Thu. 5–7) 🚉 Beside main station 🍴 Café and restaurant 💵 $$

Zoo Zürich

Zurich's zoo enjoys a parkland setting on a hill overlooking the city. More than 2,000 animals are exhibited, with emphasis on species from South America, Africa and Asia. If you're traveling with kids, arrange to be here at 10 a.m. when the elephants and monkeys enjoy their daily bath.

The zoo has a successful breeding program; a board near the entrance gives information about any new arrivals.

➕ Off map at B2 ✉ Zürichbergstrasse 221 ☎ 044 254 2505; www.zoo.ch 🕐 Daily 9–6, Mar.–Oct.; 9–5, rest of year 🚌 39; tram 6 🍴 Cafés and restaurant on zoo grounds 💵 $$$

Swiss Flavors

Switzerland has a range of regional dishes – German, French and Italian – rather than a national cuisine. With many foreigners working in the country, there's plenty of choice, and in the cities you'll find everything from Japanese to Tex-Mex. The Swiss call a restaurant menu the *karte* or *carte*; *menu* means the "dish of the day."

Swiss Cheese Specials
The country's best-known specialty, fondue, is made by melting a selection of Swiss hard cheeses, such as Gruyère, Emmentaler and Vacherin, in white wine spiked with garlic and then adding spices and kirsch. The bubbling pot sits in the middle of the table on a little brazier, and you help yourself by dipping forkfuls of bread into the thick mixture. Be careful not to drop the bread in the pot – traditionally the culprit has to buy the next bottle of wine. Fondues also are made by cooking cubed beef in either hot oil *(fondue bourguignonne)* or beef stock *(fondue chinoise);* these are served with a variety of tasty dipping sauces. The traditionally French *raclette* is undergoing a revival and is popular throughout Switzerland, particularly with large groups. A whole block of cheese is cut into slices and melted under a grill and then draped over boiled potatoes to be eaten with gherkins, smoked ham and sausage. It's delicious!

Main Dishes
Bündnerfleisch – raw, dried smoked beef – is well worth sampling, as are the many kinds of *wurst*, sausages eaten raw, grilled or boiled. The traditional accompaniment is *rösti*, a crisp potato cake studded with onions and bacon. Hungry diners might enjoy the *Berner Platte*, a groaning plate of sausage, beef and ham served with potatoes and sauerkraut. The Swiss also are fond of liver, pork and veal. Traditional fish recipes in this landlocked country involve lake trout, carp and perch.

A Little Something Sweet
Chocolate and cream feature heavily in Swiss desserts; in addition to the ubiquitous Nestlé and Cailler, Lindt, Sprüngli, Teuscher and Tobler are varieties worth sampling. There are some splendid local cakes; try *leckerli* (spiced bread with honey), meringues, and delicious kirsch-flavored cakes and fruit breads. Start the day with a breakfast bowl of muesli, a tasty mixture of grains, fruit and nuts.

Skiers build up a hearty appetite on the mountains for the delicious local fare

Hotels and Restaurants

Hotels and Restaurants

The hotels and restaurants in this book were selected by on-site contributing authors. Since price is often the best indication of the level of facilities and quality of service guests can expect, a three-tiered price guide appears at the beginning of the listings for each city. Prices vary widely depending on the country. Because variable rates will affect the amount of foreign currency that can be exchanged for dollars, price ranges are given in the local currency.

Although price ranges and any given days/times restaurants are closed were accurate at press time, this information is always subject to change. If you are interested in an establishment, it is always advisable to call ahead and verify amenities or hours of operation, but not all establishments will have phones.

Facilities suitable for travelers with disabilities vary greatly and you are strongly advised to contact an establishment directly. Buildings in the old areas of city centers may not be suitable for visitors with limited or impaired mobility.

Accommodations

Accommodations have been selected with two considerations in mind: a particularly attractive character or sense of local flavor, or a central location. Establishments in different price ranges are included for each city.

Map Coordinates

Map coordinates given in each listing relate to the city maps and give an idea of the approximate area in which each establishment is located. Although you may be able to find some of the street locations on these maps, it is always a good idea to pick up a more detailed city map from the local tourist office to help you find places.

City-center hotels fill up quickly, especially during summer; make reservations well in advance. In-room bathrooms (usually referred to as "en-suite facilities") may not be available in smaller budget hotels.

European hotels normally provide a light breakfast of rolls or croissants and coffee (if not, the listing description is "room only"). Breakfast in British and Irish hotels, however, can be a filling meal of bacon, sausages, eggs, fried potatoes and toast.

Some hotels offer a price for their overnight accommodations that includes an evening meal (known as "half-board" in Britain and Ireland and *demi-pension* in French-speaking countries).

Eating Out

Listed restaurants range from upscale places to small cafés. Some are close to attractions; where this is the case, there is a cross-reference under the attraction listing. Other possibilities are the cafeterias and restaurants on the premises of museums and galleries.

Be sure to sample the amazing variety of indigenous European fast-food: *crêpes* (filled pancakes) in France; tasty hot *Wurst* (sausages) in Germany and Austria; fish and chips (fish fillets and french fries) in Britain; savory tapas appetizers served in Spanish bars; and pizzas in Italy – served crusty and piping hot from charcoal ovens or *al taglio* (sliced to go) on street corners.

Many European hotels, especially the larger ones in big cities, are not only options for an overnight stay but also for a meal. Their lounges and bars often are comfortable, quiet places to relax.

Alcoholic beverages have a rich European heritage. France, Germany and Spain produce memorable wines; beers in the Czech Republic, Belgium and Britain are justly famed; and Guinness, of course, is an Irish institution. The nonalcoholic fruit juices (*portokalada freska*) served in Greece are wonderfully refreshing.

Cities are shown in the order that they appear in the book.

<hr>**VIENNA HOTELS**<hr>

Price guide: (double room with breakfast for two people)
$ €50–€70
$$ €70–€150
$$$ over €150

Best Western Premier Schlosshotel Römischer Kaiser $$–$$$

This is an exotically furnished hotel with crimson fabrics and sparkling chandeliers. The 24 rooms are comfortable and have WiFi. A generous buffet breakfast is served. The hotel is family owned and occupies a 17th-century baroque palace close to the old town.
27 D2   Annagasse 16
01 51 27 75 10   Stephansplatz
1, 71, D   AX, DC, MC, VI

Grand Hotel Wien $$$

This is the ultimate in luxury, combining the style and service of a majestic old European hotel with modern comforts and high standards of hospitality. Ask about the packages which typically include a champagne buffet breakfast, dinner for two in the hotel's award-winning restaurant Le Ciel, and tickets to concerts, exhibitions or museums.
27 D2   Kärntner Ring 9
01 51 58 00   Tram 1, 2, D, J
AX, DC, MC, VI

Kärntnerhof $$

The Kärntnerhof, situated in the city center, is convenient for sightseeing. It occupies a 19th-century building with a roof garden and sits quietly on a cul-de-sac, where a gate leads to the beautiful courtyard of Heiligenkreuzerhof.
27 D3   Grashofgasse 4
01 51 21 923   Stephansplatz, Schwedenplatz   AX, DC, MC, VI

König von Ungarn $$$

A hotel since 1815, this building has rooms set around a covered central courtyard, which has been converted into an elegant bar/sitting room. The restaurant serves traditional Viennese meals in the vaulted dining rooms. It's very close to St. Stephen's Cathedral and next to the Figarohaus (Figaro House), where Mozart composed his opera *The Marriage of Figaro*.

27 D2   Schulerstrasse 10
01 51 58 40   Stephansplatz
1A   AX, DC, MC, VI

Pension Felicitas $

Hidden away on a quiet side street in Josefstadt, just behind the parliament building, this accommodation is for those who like a personal hotel touch: it feels a little as if you're staying in somebody's home, perfect after a day's sightseeing.
27 C2   Josefsgasse 7
01 40 57 21 20   U2 to Rathaus
No credit cards

<hr>**VIENNA RESTAURANTS**<hr>

Price guide: (dinner per person, excluding drinks)
$ €10–€15
$$ €15–€22
$$$ over €22

Augustinerkeller $$

Delicious Austrian- and Viennese-style dishes are complemented by good, locally produced wines. It's popular with foreign visitors.
27 D2   Augustinerstrasse 1
01 533 1026   U1, U2, U4 to Karlsplatz   AX, DC, MC, VI

Café Drechsler $$

This café opens at 3 a.m. and thus has an interesting mix of customers, including people on their way home from a night out and stall owners on their way to the market. Expect a quiet atmosphere and billiard tables. Hot dishes are served throughout the day. International newspapers are available for patrons.
27 C2   Linke Wienzeile 22
01 581 2044   Tue.–Sat. 3 a.m.–2 a.m., Sun. 3 a.m.–midnight, Mon. 8 a.m.–2 a.m.   U1, U2, U4
4A, 59A   No credit cards

Do & Co Im Haas-Haus $$$

Shellfish, Thai and Japanese dishes are specialties at this trendy top-floor restaurant in the glass-fronted Haas-Haus building.
27 D2   7th floor, Haas-Haus, Stephansplatz 12   01 53 53 969
U1, U3   AX, DC, MC, VI

Plachutta $$–$$$

This is one of the best restaurants for original Viennese dishes in the Old Town. Typical items include *Wiener Tafelspitz* (boiled rump of beef with apple and horseradish sauce),

delicious sautéed pike or perch with garlic butter, and pork with dumplings and cabbage. Reservations are advisable.
27 D2   Wollzeile 38
01 512 1577   U3 Stubentor
AX, DC, MC, VI

Steirereck am Stadtpark $$$

This intimate (22 tables) restaurant is ideal for a special occasion or a relaxing lunch. The food here is a mix of traditional, new, regional and international, and there is an outstanding wine list from the vaulted cellars. Reservations are necessary at this popular place.
27 D2   Am Heumarkt 2A
01 71 33 168   Closed Sat.–Sun. and holidays   U4 to Stadtpark
AX, DC, MC, VI

<hr>**INNSBRUCK HOTELS**<hr>

Price guide: (double room with breakfast for two people)
$ €50–€70
$$ €70–€150
$$$ over €150

Best Western Hotel Goldener Adler $$–$$$

At this charming hotel in the heart of old Innsbruck, modern comfort combines with Tyrolean character. There are two excellent restaurants to choose from.
35 A2   Herzog-Friedrichstrasse 6   0512 571111   A, O, C, Airport Bus; trams 1, 3   AX, DC, MC, VI

Central $$

This centrally located hotel is big on comfort and service and has a wide range of facilities, including a sunning terrace, sauna, steam bath and fitness room.
35 B2   Gilmstrasse 5   0512 5920   4, O   AX, DC, MC, VI

Grand Hotel Europa $$$

Innsbruck's top hotel has a wide range of rooms at varying prices, some elegant public areas, and a friendly and welcoming staff.
35 C1   Südtirolerplatz 2
0512 5931   Tram 3
AX, DC, MC, VI

Maximilian $$

On the edge of Old Town, this modern hotel combines comfort with traditional service and atmosphere. There is free WiFi access in the business center.

KEY TO SYMBOLS

⊞	map page number and coordinates
✉	address
☎	telephone number
◷	days/times closed
Ⓢ	nearest subway station
Ⓑ	nearest bus/trolley bus/tram/funicular route
⛴	ferry
$$$	expensive
$$	moderate
$	inexpensive
AX	American Express
DC	Diners Club
MC	MasterCard
VI	VISA

⊞ 35 A2 ✉ Marktgraben 7–9
☎ 0512 59967 Ⓑ A, C, D, E, J, O;
tram 1, 3 AX, DC, MC, VI

Weisses Kreuz $–$$

Mozart and his father once stayed at this 15th-century Old Town hotel, which combines Tyrolean charm with modern comfort. Rooms at the lower prices can be small. Restaurants are on the premises.

⊞ 35 A2 ✉ Herzog-Friedrichstrasse 31 ☎ 0512 594790 Ⓑ Tram 3 AX, MC, VI

INNSBRUCK RESTAURANTS

Price guide: (dinner per person, excluding drinks)

$	€10–€15
$$	€15–€22
$$$	over €22

Dengg $$

Known for its international cooking, this Old Town restaurant offers good vegetarian dishes.

⊞ 35 B2 ✉ Riesengasse 13
☎ 0512 582347 ◷ Closed Sun. and holidays Ⓑ A, O; tram 1 AX, DC, MC, VI

Ottoburg $

This historic restaurant was established around 1745 in a building that some say is the oldest in Innsbruck. Dishes take in standard classics with fish, meat and noodles, but there are some innovative additions to the menu.

⊞ 35 A2 ✉ Herzog-Friedrichstrasse 1 ☎ 0512 584338 ◷ Closed Mon. and holidays Ⓑ Tram 1, 3 AX, DC, MC, VI

Restaurant Goldener Adler $$

Its decor and friendly staff make this traditional hotel restaurant popular with locals and tourists alike. The menu of hearty Tyrolean specialties includes steak with onions and braised saddle of lamb. The desserts are delicious

⊞ 35 A2 ✉ Herzog-Friedrichstrasse 6 ☎ 0512 571111 Ⓑ A, O, C, Airport bus; trams 1, 3 AX, DC, MC, VI

Stiftskeller $$

In the heart of the Old Town, this restaurant with several dining rooms serves filling Tyrolean and Austrian specialties.

⊞ 35 A2 ✉ Burggraben 31
☎ 0512 583490 Ⓑ A, O AX, DC, MC, VI

Eating in Innsbruck

Most of Innsbruck's best – and most expensive – restaurants are located in a tiny area of Old Town, along with some excellent cafés and coffee houses. Many serve meals all day, so you can eat when you feel like it, a bonus if you've been skiing or hiking. Maria-Theresien-Strasse has a number of self-service and fast-food restaurants if you're looking for a quick lunchtime snack. For lunch with a view, take the Hungerburgbahn to Hoch-Innsbruck, where there are several restaurants with pretty terraces, or ride the cable car up to Seegrube mountain and eat on the terrace while enjoying a superb mountain panorama. The daily market, held in the Markthalle building beside the river, is an excellent place to buy provisions for a picnic.

SALZBURG HOTELS

Price guide: (double room with breakfast for two people)

$	€50–€70
$$	€70–€150
$$$	over €150

Altstadthotel Wolf-Dietrich $$–$$$

This family-run hotel near the city's historic center has a good restaurant, an indoor swimming pool, where a "jet stream" provides resistance for a good workout, and a spa and sauna. Rooms include family suites for up to five people.

⊞ 40 C4 ✉ Wolf-Dietrich-Strasse 7 ☎ 0662 871 275 Ⓑ 2 AX, DC, MC, VI

Am Dom $$–$$$

Reserve ahead to ensure one of just 13 rooms at this restored boutique hotel in the heart of Salzburg's historic center.

⊞ 40 C2 ✉ Goldgasse 17 ☎ 0662 842 765-55 ◷ Closed Feb. Ⓑ 3, 5, 6, 25 AX, DC, MC, VI

Goldener Hirsch $$$

This luxurious, baronial-style hotel is one of Salzburg's oldest and most famous accommodations, and provides service to match. Rooms and suites are finished in vibrant colors with several rooms in the renovated Festival Wing.

⊞ 40 B3 ✉ Getreidegasse 37 ☎ 0662 80 84 0 AX, DC, MC, VI

Radisson Blu Altstadt $$$

This renovated luxury hotel, in one of Salzburg's oldest buildings, in the heart of the Old Town, has 62 lovely rooms and an excellent restaurant serving classic Austrian and international dishes. The rooms all have excellent views and offer high-speed internet connections

⊞ 40 C2 ✉ Rudolfskai 28/Judengasse 15 ☎ 0662 848 571 AX, DC, MC, VI

Schloss Mönchstein $$$

This luxury-class hotel is beautifully situated in thickly wooded grounds high above the old center of Salzburg. Sumptuous rooms are complemented by gleaming marble bathrooms. There is a choice of dining venues, including an intimate four-seater dining room.

⊞ 40 A3 ✉ Mönchsberg Park 26
☎ 0662 848 555-0
Ⓑ Mönchsberglift AX, DC, MC, VI

SALZBURG RESTAURANTS

Price guide: (dinner per person, excluding drinks)
$ €10–€15
$$ €15–€22
$$$ over €22

Augustiner Bräu $

This huge restaurant and summer beer garden serves beer, *Wurst* and simple Austrian fare in wood-paneled halls and is very popular with tourists.

✚ 40 A4 ✉ Lindhofstrasse 7 ☎ 0662 431 2460 🚋 7, 8, 20, 21, 24, 27, 28 No credit cards

Restaurant Zur Festung Hohensalzburg $$

Located in the Hohensalzburg Fortress (see page 84), this restaurant has panoramic views of the Salzburg area and serves good Austrian cooking (reservations required for dinner Jul.–Aug.).

✚ 40 B2 ✉ Hohensalzburg, Am Mönchsberg 34 ☎ 0662 841 780 🕐 Closed mid-Jan. to end of Feb. and in Nov. 🚋 Festungbahn funicular AX, DC, MC, VI

Stiftskeller St. Peter $$

Said to be Europe's oldest restaurant, Stiftskeller is a popular beer cellar serving reasonably priced beer, wine and local dishes.

✚ 40 B2 ✉ Stiftsbezirk 1–4 ☎ 0662 841 2680 🚋 1, 4 AX, MC, VI

BRUSSELS HOTELS

Price guide: (double room with breakfast for two people)
$ under €75
$$ €75–€175
$$$ over €175

Amigo $$$

This charming hotel near the Grand' Place, now part of the Rocco Forte group, is luxurious, offers perfect service, and is both lively and relaxed with an excellent Italian restaurant, which also serves Belgian specialties. Rooms have excellent central views.

✚ 56 B2 ✉ rue del'Amigo 1–3 ☎ 02 547 4747 🚇 Gare Centrale 🚋 48, 94; trams 3, 52, 55, 56 AX, DC, MC, VI

Le Dixseptième $$$

This luxurious and stylish boutique hotel, in a grand 17th-century house behind the Grand-Place, was once the residence of the Spanish ambassador. The old part of the hotel houses the breakfast room and several suites, while the modern addition has 12 comfortable rooms.

✚ 56 B2 ✉ rue de la Madeleine 25 ☎ 02 517 1717 🚇 Gare Centrale AX, DC, MC, VI

Métropole $$

Built in 1895, the Métropole Hotel's glorious and flamboyant facade and ground floor are now a protected monument. The hotel has a fine restaurant, L'Alban Chambon, a beautiful bar, and a fitness center.

✚ 56 B3 ✉ place De Brouckère 31 ☎ 02 217 2300 🚇 De Brouckère 🚋 Trams 29, 38, 46, 47, 63, 66, 71, 86, 88 AX, DC, MC, VI

Warwick Barsey $$

One of Brussels' few boutique hotels, this is elegantly decorated with rich textiles and objets d'art. This is a choice venue for visiting celebrities and a perfect location for those who have shopping in mind.

✚ 56 off B1 ✉ avenue Louise 381–383 ☎ 02 649 9800 🚇 Louise then tram 94 AX, DC, MC, VI

Welcome $$

This charming small hotel has 17 rooms, each one decorated in the style of a different country. The buffet breakfast is served in a lovely room. Guests have access to WiFi.

✚ 56 B3 ✉ quai au Bois à Brûler ☎ 02 219 9546 🚇 St.-Catherine DC, MC, VI

BRUSSELS RESTAURANTS

Price guide: (dinner per person, excluding drinks)
$ under €30
$$ €30–€50
$$$ over €50

Belgaqueen $$–$$$

The superb Hôtel de la Poste, with its grand entrance hall and late 19th-century stained-glass windows, is now a trendy dining complex serving classic Belgian food.

✚ 56 B3 ✉ rue Fosse aux Loups 32 ☎ 02 217 2187 🚇 Gare Centrale, De Brouckère AX, DC, MC, VI

Bonsoir Clara $$

Trendy brasserie on Brussels' hippest shopping street. The menu includes mainly light Mediterranean-style dishes, but you also can get an excellent Belgian *steak frites* or delicious caramelized duck.

✚ 56 A3 ✉ rue Antoine Dansaert 22–26 ☎ 02 502 0990 🚇 Bourse 🚋 Tram 23, 52, 55, 56, 81 AX, MC, VI

La Clef des Champs $$

A tiny bistro with a very traditional and accomplished French menu – there's a choice of six or so starters or mains, ensuring the dishes are seasonal and fresh. One of the city's must-visit restaurants.

✚ 57 B2 ✉ rue de Rollebeek 23 ☎ 02 512 1193 🕐 Closed Mon., Sun. dinner 🚇 Petit Sablon 🚋 Tram 92, 93, 94 AX, DC, MC, VI

Comme Chez Soi $$$

Brussels' top gastronomic experience can be savored at this celebrated restaurant. New Belgian cuisine with traditional specialties is featured; reserve well in advance.

✚ 56 A2 ✉ place Rouppe 23 ☎ 02 512 2921 🕐 Closed Sun.–Mon., Wed. lunch, mid-Jul. to mid-Aug., Apr. 16, All Saints' Day 🚋 Tram 23, 52, 55, 56 AX, DC, MC, VI

Falstaff $$

This beautiful and original art nouveau brasserie serves excellent Belgian cuisine plus a range of lighter dishes, which are perfect at lunchtime. Drop in for a beer and marvel at the decor.

✚ 56 B3 ✉ rue Henri Maus 19 ☎ 02 511 8789 🕐 Daily 11 a.m.– 11 p.m. 🚇 Bourse AX, MC, VI

Taverne du Passage $$

This hugely popular and staunchly Belgian brasserie, founded in 1928, serves all the key Belgian dishes in style. Specialties include *croquettes au crevettes* (shrimp croquettes) and *moules* (mussels) when in season, but the menu is extensive and should satisfy most appetites.

✚ 56 B3 ✉ Galerie de la Reine 30 ☎ 02 512 3731 🕐 Daily noon–midnight 🚇 Gare Centrale AX, DC, MC, VI

Vincent $$–$$$

A traditional Bruxellois restaurant, where skilled waiters prepare specialties like *steak flambée* or *steak tartare* at your table. Entrance to the atmospheric, old-fashioned tiled dining room is through the kitchen.

✚ 56 B3 ✉ 8–10 rue des Dominicains, off rue des Bouchers ☎ 02 511 2607 🕐 Closed Jan. 1–12 and Aug. 1–15 🚇 De Brouckère, Gare Centrale AX, DC, MC, VI

KEY TO SYMBOLS

✛	map page number and coordinates
✉	address
☎	telephone number
◎	days/times closed
⊜	nearest subway station
☒	nearest bus/trolley bus/tram/funicular route
⛴	ferry
$$$	expensive
$$	moderate
$	inexpensive
AX	American Express
DC	Diners Club
MC	MasterCard
VI	VISA

Chocolates Galore

By far the best chocolate shop in Bruges is the family-run Speghelaere at Ezelstraat 92. The house specialty is bunches of chocolate grapes filled with marzipan or *pralinée*. Here you can see the daily production of fresh chocolate in a workshop where traditional methods are used – from the preparation of the chocolate in melting cauldrons to the hand-making process, in which white, milk and dark chocolate are fashioned into a variety of forms. Choco-Story is a fascinating chocolate museum at St. Jansplein (Wijnzakstraat 2; ☎ 050 612 237, daily 10–5). It explains the history of chocolate and the process of making chocolates. Finish your visit with a taste of freshly made chocolates by one of Belgium's master *chocolatiers*. The Museum of Cocoa and Chocolate in Brussels is at 9–11 rue de la Tête d'Or (off Grand Place) ☎ 02 514 2048, Tue.–Sun., 10–4:30 (also open Mon. 10–4:30 during the national holidays).

Price guide: (double room with breakfast for two people)
$	under €75
$$	€75–€175
$$$	over €175

Hotel Fevery $$

This small family-owned eco-label hotel has lots of loyal clients. It is centrally located and also offers gluten-free breakfast options and private parking.
✛ 62 B3 ✉ Collaert Mansionstraat 3 ☎ 050 331 269 ☒ 4, 14 MC, VI

Marie Paul $

There are three rooms in this ivy-clad house in a courtyard with views of a windmill. Their breakfasts are excellent.
✛ 62 C4 ✉ Oostproosse 14 ☎ 050 339 246 ☒ 4 No credit cards

Martin's Orangerie $$$

One of Bruges' most lauded hotels is within this 15th-century canalside building, with views of the tree-lined Dijver walkway. Guests have use of the pool and sauna of the De Tuilerieën Hotel.
✛ 62 B2 ✉ Kartuizerinnensstraat 10 ☎ 050 341 649 ☒ 1, 6, 11, 16 AX, DC, MC, VI

The Pand Hotel $$$

This hotel is hidden away on a backwater close to the Markt. Rooms are luxurious and tastefully decorated. The owners also own an antiques and objets d'art shop, Kasimir's Antique Studio.
✛ 62 B2 ✉ Pandreitje 16 ☎ 050 340 666 ☒ 1, 6, 11, 16 AX, DC, MC

Price guide: (dinner per person, excluding drinks)
$	under €30
$$	€30–€50
$$$	over €50

Bistro den Huzaar $–$$

Chef Willy Bostyn serves a mix of French and Flemish dishes including smoked eel soup and stews flavored with beer. There's a terrace for summer dining.
✛ 62 B2 ✉ Vlamingstraat 36 ☎ 050 333 797 ◎ Closed Wed. and Thu. ☒ All buses for Markt MC, VI

Den Dijver $$

This atmospheric, old-fashioned Flemish restaurant, furnished with

---

antiques, specializes in local dishes cooked in beer. Excellent cuisine.
✛ 62 B2 ✉ Dijver 5 ☎ 050 336 069 ◎ Closed Wed. and Thu. MC, VI

In't Nieuw Museum $$

An informal relaxed restaurant with a range of French-style steaks and salads, but famed for the "all-you-can-eat" ribs special.
✛ 62 C2 ✉ Hooistraat 42 ☎ 050 331 280 ☒ 6, 16 MC, VI

Kardinaalshof $$$

This intimate restaurant serves a set menu of exceptional French cuisine. The chef has a Michelin star for his innovative dishes. Menus change regularly and reflect what's in season.
✛ 62 B2 ✉ Sint Salvatorstraat 14 ☎ 050 341 691 ◎ Closed Wed., Thu. lunch ☒ All buses for the Markt AX, MC, VI

Rock Fort $$

This wonderful, contemporary restaurant is run by two men who put on the menu only the things they like to eat: their favorite Belgian dishes are all perfectly prepared, with more than a touch of the Mediterranean.
✛ 62 B2/C2 ✉ Langestraat 15 ☎ 050 334 113 ◎ Closed Sat. and Sun. ☒ 4, 6 AX, MC, VI

Price guide: (double room with breakfast for two people)
$	under €75
$$	€75–€175
$$$	over €175

The Boatel $$

This converted canal barge with seven rooms, moored on a canal a 10-minute walk away from the city center, offers an unusual Ghent hotel experience. A hearty breakfast is served on deck, weather permitting.
✛ 70 off C3 ✉ Voorhoutkaai 44 ☎ 09 267 1030 MC, VI

Gravensteen $$

Housed in a 19th-century mansion, this comfortable hotel is near the Castle of the Counts and other city attractions. Try to get a reservation in the tower room, which has one of the best views over Ghent.
✛ 70 A3 ✉ Jan Breydelstraat 35 ☎ 09 225 1150 ☒ Trams 1, 10, 11, 12 AX, DC, MC, VI

Hotel Erasmus $$

This charming family-run hotel is in an impressive town house, right in the center of town, but you will not be disturbed by noise. The 10 bedrooms are furnished in authentic Flemish style. Friendly service.
➕ 70 A3 ✉ Poel 25 ☎ 09 224 2195 🚋 Trams 1, 11, 12 AX, DC, MC, VI

Hotel Harmony $$

A contemporary interior wrapped in two canalside town houses, the Harmony combines history with modern facilities, including a simming pool. The lovely courtyard garden is an added bonus.
➕ 70 B4 ✉ Kraanlei 37 ☎ 09 324 2680 🚋 Tram 1 AX, MC, VI

NH Gent Belfort $$

This is a large luxury hotel in the historic heart of the city, opposite the Town Hall. Its many amenities, including a restaurant and fitness room, make it a decent value.
➕ 70 B3 ✉ Hoogpoort 63 ☎ 09 233 3331 🚋 16, 17, 18, 19, 38; trams 12, 41 AX, DC, MC, VI

Price guide: (dinner per person, excluding drinks)
$ under €30
$$ €30–€50
$$$ over €50

Belgaqueen $$–$$$

Set in a converted 13th-century grain storehouse, which now also houses a restaurant, a beer bar, an oyster bar and a cigar lounge. The food is good and the atmosphere is lively. It has a sister restaurant in Brussels (see page 465).
➕ 70 A3 ✉ Graslei 10 ☎ 09 280 0100 🕐 Daily 🚋 1, 11, 12 AX, DC, MC, VI

Bij den Wijzen en den Zot $$–$$$

One of Ghent's best and most atmospheric restaurants is set in the charming neighborhood of the Patershol. Flemish traditional dishes are prepared here, including the famous Ghent *waterzooi* with fish.
➕ 70 B4 ✉ Hertogstraat 42 ☎ 09 223 4230 🕐 Tue.–Sat. lunch and dinner DC, MC, VI

De Blauwe Zalm $$–$$$

Delightful restaurant with a contemporary feel, with tables set up in an impressive courtyard.

Specialties of the house are fresh seafood and fish.
➕ 70 B4 ✉ Vrouwebroerstraat 2 ☎ 09 224 0852 🕐 Closed Sun. and lunch Mon. and Sat.; late Dec.–early Jan. 🚋 Trams 1, 11, 12, 40, 42 AX, DC, MC, VI

Brasserie Pakhuis $$

Set in a large and spectacular warehouse (*pakhuis* in Flemish) is this wonderful restaurant, popular with locals for the mouthwatering French-Italian cuisine.
➕ 70 A3 ✉ Schuurkenstraat 4 ☎ 09 223 5555 🚋 Trams 1, 11, 12 AX, DC, MC, VI

Nestor $$

Set on one of Ghent's prettiest historic streets, Nestor is a contemporary eatery with a menu concentrating on charcoal-grilled meat and fish.
➕ 70 B4 ✉ Kraanlei 17 ☎ 02 225 1880 🕐 Closed Sun. 🚋 Trams 1, 10, 11, 13 AX, MC, VI

Price guide: (double room with breakfast for two people)
$ £50–£100
$$ £100–£150
$$$ over £150

The Dorchester $$$

Favored by celebrities, this world-class hotel offers guests the very best in luxury accommodations. Nonguests can enjoy the famous afternoon tea.
➕ 86 B2 ✉ Park Lane ☎ 020 7629 8888 🚇 Hyde Park Corner or Green Park AX, DC, MC, VI

The Gallery $$–$$$

Housed in two restored Georgian houses in South Kensington, The Gallery is a good choice for a comfortable base close to the Natural History Museum.
➕ 86 A1 ✉ 8–10 Queensberry Place ☎ 020 7915 0000 🚇 South Kensington AX, DC, MC, VI

London Marriott Hotel County Hall $$$

The large London Marriott occupies a prime South Bank riverside location. Many rooms have superb views of the city and the river.
➕ 87 D2 ✉ County Hall, Westminster Bridge Road ☎ 020 7928 5200 🚇 Waterloo AX, DC, MC, VI

The Mandeville $$$

This quiet hotel, popular with foreign visitors, is a short walk from the stores on Oxford Street. There is a range of rooms through single to the Terrace Suite with balcony dining.
➕ 86 B3 ✉ Mandeville Place ☎ 020 7935 5599 🚇 Bond Street AX, DC, MC, VI

The Ritz London $$$

Luxurious Louis XVI interiors and all the expense and style that goes with the name are the details you can expect at this top hotel.
➕ 86 C2 ✉ 150 Piccadilly ☎ 020 7493 8181 🚇 Green Park AX, DC, MC, VI

Price guide: (dinner per person, excluding drinks)
$ £10–£15
$$ £15–£30
$$$ over £30

Le Caprice $$

Featuring modern European dishes on an exciting but simple menu, this is a favorite celebrity dining choice close to Piccadilly and London's West End. The service is excellent. Le Caprice's three-course set menu available for both lunch and dinner is a good value
➕ 86 C2 ✉ Arlington House, Arlington Street ☎ 020 7629 2239 🕐 Closed Jan. 1, dinner Dec. 24, Dec. 25–26 and Aug. public holiday 🚇 Green Park AX, DC, MC, VI

Hélène Darroze at The Connaught $$$

The hotel's restaurant serves gourmet delights overseen by one of France's most distinguished chefs.
➕ 86 C3 ✉ 16 Carlos Place, Mayfair ☎ 020 3147 7200 🚇 Bond Street or Green Park AX, DC, MC, VI

Pied à Terre $$$

This restaurant's stylish yet simple ambience combines with highly refined French cuisine.
➕ 86 C3 ✉ 34 Charlotte Street ☎ 020 7636 1178 🕐 Closed Sun. and 2 weeks around Dec. 25 and Jan. 1 🚇 Goodge Street or Tottenham Court Road AX, DC, MC, VI

Quaglino's $$–$$$

One of London's most glamorous eateries, superbly designed and stylish. Modern European cuisine served; reservations are advised.

KEY TO SYMBOLS

➕ map page number and coordinates
✉ address
☎ telephone number
◷ days/times closed
Ⓜ nearest subway station
🚍 nearest bus/trolley bus/ tram/funicular route
⛴ ferry
$$$ expensive
$$ moderate
$ inexpensive
AX American Express
DC Diners Club
MC MasterCard
VI VISA

➕ 86 C2 ✉ 16 Bury Street
☎ 020 7930 6767 ◷ Closed Sun.
Ⓜ Green Park AX, MC, VI

Restaurant Gordon Ramsay $$$

London's finest temple of gastronomy. Supreme modern French cuisine from Britain's most famous A-list celebrity chef. Reservations are essential. The head chef here is Clare Smyth, one of Britain's most accomplished chefs.
➕ 86 B1 ✉ 68 Royal Hospital Road
☎ 020 7352 4441 ◷ Closed Sat.–Sun., 2 weeks at Christmas and public holidays Ⓜ Sloane Square AX, DX, MC, VI

EDINBURGH HOTELS

Price guide: (double room with breakfast for two people)
$ £50–£100
$$ £100–£150
$$$ over £150

Abbey Hotel $–$$

Situated on the north side of Calton Hill, this small hotel in a Georgian town house offers good views to the Firth of Forth from the top floors and has an in-house bar. The public areas have been refurbished.
➕ 99 E3 ✉ 9 Royal Terrace
☎ 0131 557 0022 🚍 City-center buses AX, MC, VI

The Balmoral Hotel $$$

This classic Edwardian building dominates the east end of Princes Street with views over the city. The rooms and suites are elegantly furnished and air conditioned.
➕ 98 D3 ✉ 1 Princes Street
☎ 0131 556 2414 🚍 City-center buses AX, DC, MC, VI

Ivy Guest House $–$$

This friendly guesthouse occupies an elegant Victorian town house a short distance from the city center. The bedrooms have been redecorated.
➕ 99 off the map ✉ 7 Mayfield Gardens ☎ 0131 667 3411 🚍 3, 31, 36, 37, 37a, 69, 80, 81 MC, VI

Old Waverley Hotel $$$

This long-established hotel, a landmark in the heart of the city on famous Prices Street, enjoys fine views of Edinburgh Castle and the Scott Monument.
➕ 98 C2 ✉ 43 Princes Street
☎ 0131 556 4648 🚍 City-center buses AX, MC, VI

Roxburghe Hotel $$–$$$

Traditional Scottish hospitality prevails at this upscale hotel in the heart of Georgian Edinburgh, with amenities and extras to match its status. A few minutes in the lap pool can be followed by relaxing sessions in the steam and sauna rooms
➕ 98 B2 ✉ 38 Charlotte Square
☎ 0844 879 9063 or 0131 240 5555
🚍 City-center buses AX, DC, MC, VI

EDINBURGH RESTAURANTS

Price guide: (dinner per person, excluding drinks)
$ £10–£15
$$ £15–£30
$$$ over £30

Café St. Honore $$$

French-style café on a delightful cobbled lane. Buzzing at lunchtime, cozy and candlelit at night. The food is built on Scottish foundations.
➕ 99 C3 ✉ 34 NW Thistle Lane ☎ 0131 226 2211 ◷ Closed 3 days around Jan. 1 and Dec. 24–26
🚍 City-center buses AX, DC, MC, VI

Dubh Prais Restaurant $$

Snug cellar restaurant that offers truly fine Scottish fare. The menu is full of local produce, such as the Inverawe platter of smoked meats, and the desserts are particularly special. There's a wide range of malt and vintage whiskeys, too.
➕ 99 D2 ✉ 123b High Street
☎ 0131 557 5732 ◷ Dinner only; closed Sun. and Mon. 🚍 23, 27, 35, 41, 42, 45 MC, VI

The Restaurant at the Bonham $$$

Contemporary decor provides the backdrop to the modern European cuisine served in this hotel restaurant, which makes good use of seasonal organic produce. Located at the west end of Princes Street.
➕ 98 A2 ✉ 35 Drumsheugh Gardens ☎ 0131 274 7444 🚍 13, 19, 36, 37, 41, 47 AX, DC, MC, VI

Stac Polly $$$

A small, city-center eatery, just off the Royal Mile, with the charm of a country restaurant. The traditional Scottish and British cuisine feature some global touches. Reservations are advised.
➕ 98 D2 ✉ 38 St. Mary's Street
☎ 0131 557 5754 ◷ Closed Sat. and Sun. lunch, Jan. 1 and Dec. 25
🚍 10, 11, 15, 16 AX, DC, MC, VI

Gentse Feesten

Ghent has several festivals during which it is important to make sure that you have a firm hotel reservation, including Gent Jazz Festival (early July), Ten Days Off (mid-July), International Festival of Flanders (mid-September to early October) and International Film Festival (late October). However, the most important one of these is Gentse Feesten. Taking place over 10 days in late July, around 2 million people visit the city to enjoy the performances, making it one of the Top 10 festivals in Europe. Book rooms early if you intend to visit the city at this time.

Britain

The Witchery by the Castle $$–$$$

Located by the gates of Edinburgh Castle and lit by hundreds of candles which reflect off the Gothic furnishings, tapestries and hand-painted timber ceilings. The contemporary menu features traditional Scottish fare. Reservations are advised.

✚ 99 C2 ✉ 352 Castlehill
☎ 0131 225 5613 🕐 Closed Dec. 25–26 🚌 23, 27, 35, 41, 42, 45 AX, DC, MC, VI

OXFORD HOTELS

Price guide: (double room with breakfast for two people)
$ £50–£100
$$ £100–£150
$$$ over £150

The Balkan Lodge Hotel $

Located east of Oxford but with easy access to the city center. One of the attractive bedrooms has a four-poster bed and Jacuzzi. Breakfasts are hearty and willl set you up for a day of sightseeing.

✚ 107 off map ✉ 315 Iffley Road
☎ 01865 244524 🚌 4 MC, VI

Macdonald Randolph Hotel $$–$$$

Top-of-the-line landmark hotel with neo-Gothic architectural features and elegant interiors, very comfortable rooms and luxury service. Visit the spa for treatments or its sauna and Jacuzzi. The Randolph is near the Ashmolean Museum.

✚ 107 A2 ✉ Beaumont Street
☎ 0844 879 9132 🚌 City-center buses AX, MC, VI

Manor House Hotel $

A small, recently refurbished, family-run hotel in a Victoria-era building 1 mile from the center with a comfortable lounge, bar and dining facilities.

✚ 107 off map ✉ 250 Iffley Road
☎ 01865 727627 🚌 3, 4 AX, MC, VI

Mercure Eastgate Hotel $$–$$$

A charming mid-size hotel occupying the site of the medieval East Gate of the city. Rooms are light and bright. The restaurant menu features locally sourced, seasonal produce in its modern European dishes. Very convenient to the city center and historic university buildings.

✚ 107 C1 ✉ 73 High Street
☎ 0870 400 8201 or 01865 248332
🚌 City-center buses AX, DC, MC, VI

Old Bank Hotel $$$

This skillfully restored former bank is a place of tranquility away from the bustle of High Street, yet within walking distance of all central sights and shops. The Quod Brasserie and Bar (see below) is on the premises.

✚ 107 B2 ✉ 91–94 High Street
☎ 01865 799599 🚌 City-center buses AX, DC, MC, VI

OXFORD RESTAURANTS

Price guide: (dinner per person, excluding drinks)
$ £10–£15
$$ £15–£30
$$$ over £30

Brasserie Blanc $$–$$$

A popular and stylish yet friendly brasserie owned by the renowned French chef Raymond Blanc. Ingredients are seasonal and of the finest quality.

✚ 107 off the map ✉ 71–72 Walton Street ☎ 01865 510999 🕐 Closed Dec. 25 🚌 2, 6 AX, MC, VI

Gee's Restaurant $$–$$$

This conservatory restaurant serving modern British food is a 20-minute walk from the city center. Live jazz is played every Sunday evening, accompanied by a special set menu.

✚ 107 off the map ✉ 61 Banbury Road ☎ 01865 553540 🚌 2, 6, 7A, 10, 14, 27 AX, MC, VI

Kazbar $–$$

Popular, chilled-out and inexpensive *tapas* restaurant with a souk-inspired setting and great wines from a long list. Sip a glass of Rioja while nibbling on *gambas pil pil* (prawns in chili and garlic) or oven-roasted pork ribs.

✚ 107 off map C1 ✉ 25–27 Cowley Road ☎ 01865 202920 🕐 Closed lunch Mon.–Fri. 🚌 5 MC, VI

Quod Brasserie and Bar $–$$

This trendy and hugely popular all-day hotel bar and grill serves breakfast and later a choice of meat and pasta dishes with a distinctly Italian accent.

✚ 107 B2 ✉ Old Bank Hotel, 92–94 High Street ☎ 01865 202505 🕐 Closed Dec. 25–26 🚌 City-center buses AX, MC, VI

Turf Tavern $

Traditional English pub-restaurant, in the heart of the university area. Experience British dishes like hand-battered cod and chips, pork in cider and beef and beer pie.

✚ 107 B2 ✉ 4 Bath Place
☎ 01865 243235 🚌 1, 4, 5, 7A, 8, 9, 10, 13, 15, U1, U5 AX, MC, VI

YORK HOTELS

Price guide: (double room with breakfast for two people)
$ £50–£100
$$ £100–£150
$$$ over £150

The Alhambra Court Hotel $–$$

This attractive Georgian building is on a quiet side road within walking distance of central York. Pleasantly furnished, with home-style cooking. The family who run the hotel strive to ensure that guests have a comfortable time with them.

✚ 113 A3 ✉ 31 St. Mary's, Bootham ☎ 01904 628474 🚌 1, 56 AX, MC, VI

Best Western Dean Court Hotel $$–$$$

A handsome Victorian building in an unsurpassed location, with views of the Minster from upper front rooms. Stylish, first-class facilities include an award-winning, upscale restaurant. Rooms have fine Egyptian bed linen and free WiFi.

✚ 113 B3 ✉ Duncombe Place
☎ 01904 625082 🚌 1 AX, DC, MC, VI

The Groves Hotel $

The Groves is in a quiet tree-lined area. It offers a good standard of accommodation and service, as well as excellent home-style cooking.

✚ 113 off the map ✉ 15 St. Peter's Grove ☎ 01904 559777 🚌 29, 30, 31X MC, VI

Lady Anne Middleton's Hotel $

This city-center hotel, created from six historic buildings, all renovated to the highest standards, features an adjoining leisure club (the pool is popular and booking ahead is recommended). The bedrooms were refurbished in 2010 and some rooms can accommodate families.

✚ 113 B1 ✉ Skeldergate
☎ 01904 611570 🚌 10, 11, 12, 13 AX, MC, VI

KEY TO SYMBOLS

✚	map page number and coordinates
✉	address
☎	telephone number
◷	days/times closed
Ⓜ	nearest subway station
🚌	nearest bus/trolley bus/tram/funicular route
⛴	ferry
$$$	expensive
$$	moderate
$	inexpensive
AX	American Express
DC	Diners Club
MC	MasterCard
VI	VISA

English Pubs

The traditional English pub, from the term "public house," is another of those treasured institutions by which an entire culture is measured. The great thing about traditional pubs is their spirit of easygoing informality. Pubs were always the focus of local life, places where people exchanged views and took their hard-earned leisure. It is no coincidence that village pub and village church often stand cheek by jowl. In medieval times, churches and monasteries often owned the local pub, or "hostelry." In and around Oxford you will find traditional pubs that have not compromised with modern fashion, while still maintaining the highest standards of comfort and service. Try The Chequers, off High Street; the King's Arms, on Holywell Street; the Turf Tavern, in Bath Place; the Isis Tavern on the towpath at Iffley Lock; or The Rose and Crown on North Parade Avenue.

The Royal York $$–$$$

This magnificent, top-quality Victorian hotel near the railroad station offers easy access to the city center and provides excellent service.
✚ 113 A2 ✉ Station Parade ☎ 01904 653681 🚌 1, 5, 6 AX, DC, MC, VI

YORK RESTAURANTS

Price guide: (dinner per person, excluding drinks)
$	£10–£15
$$	£15–£30
$$$	over £30

The Blue Bicycle $$–$$$

One of York's best-loved restaurants exudes old charm and offers a wide-ranging, modern European menu and an excellent wine list. Situated alongside the River Foss.
✚ 113 C2 ✉ 34 Fossgate ☎ 01904 673990 ◷ Closed first 2 weeks Jan. and Dec. 24–26 🚌 6, 11, 12, 13, 13a, X64 MC, VI

Ivy Brasserie $$

This hotel restaurant has beautifully set tables and serves contemporary and classic dishes, with an emphasis on seafood.
✚ 113 off the map ✉ The Grange Hotel, 1 Clifton ☎ 01904 644744 ◷ Closed Mon.–Sat. lunch 🚌 2 Park & Ride, 31X AX, MC, VI

Melton's Restaurant $$

Attractively presented modern British cuisine, and generous portions are on offer here. There is an appealing fixed-price lunch as well as an early evening menu.
✚ 113 off the map ✉ 7 Scarcroft Road ☎ 01904 634341 ◷ Closed Sun. and Mon. lunch and Dec. 23–Jan. 9 🚌 11 MC, VI

Middlethorpe Hall and Spa $$$

Modern British fare is served in an oak-paneled restaurant in this restored William III house, only 1.5 miles from the center of York.
✚ 113 off the map ✉ Bishopthorpe Road, Middlethorpe ☎ 01904 641241 ◷ Closed Dec. 25 and 31 🚌 11 AX, MC, VI

One 19 The Mount $$

Georgian elegance prevails in this formal restaurant, with polished wooden floors, overlooking a delightful garden. The menu is good and there is also a daily chef's menu.

✚ 113 off the map ✉ Mount Royale Hotel, 119 The Mount ☎ 01904 619444 ◷ Closed Sun. and Jan. 1–6 🚌 4, 12, 13, 13a, X64 MC, VI

PRAGUE HOTELS

Price guide: (double room with breakfast for two people)
$	1,000Kč–2,500Kč
$$	2,500Kč–4,500Kč
$$$	over 4,500Kč

Czech Inn $

This upscale hostel is an acceptable budget option for travelers of all ages. In addition to standard dorm accommodations, they offer clean private singles, doubles and triples. The decor is chic, minimalist modern; the staff is helpful; and the full buffet breakfast is almost worth the price of the room itself.
✚ 24–125 off the map ✉ Francouzska 76 ☎ 267 267 000 Ⓜ Náměstí Miru 🚌 Trams 4, 22 AX, MC, VI

Penzion U Medvídků $$

The name of this 15th-century former brewery tavern means "The Little Bears." There are 33 rooms in two categories: all have bathrooms, but the "historic rooms" cost more. There's a breakfast buffet.
✚ 124 C3 ✉ Na Perštýně 7 ☎ 224 211 916 Ⓜ Národní třída 🚌 Trams 6, 9, 18, 21, 22 AX, DC, MC, VI

Savoy $$$

A relaxed atmosphere prevails at this stunning, five-star top Prague hotel, located behind Prague Castle. Rooms are well designed and modernized, making it a perfect base.
✚ 124 off the map ✉ Keplerova 6 ☎ 224 302 430 Ⓜ Malostranská 🚌 Tram 22 AX, DC, MC, VI

Sax $$

On the steep hill leading to Prague Castle (just off Nerudova, near the bustling Charles Bridge), this reasonable hotel has a funky, retro-inspired interior and well-equipped, comfortable rooms.
✚ 124 A4 ✉ Jánský vršek 3 ☎ 257 531 268 Ⓜ Malostranská 🚌 Trams 12, 20, 22 AX, DC, MC, VI

U Zlaté Studně $$$

This luxury boutique hotel, perched on a hill overlooking Malá Strana, has won excellence awards around the world, meaning you will have to plan your stay well in advance. It is

worth it, though, for the 19th-century period charm, the quiet and the chance to dine on the terrace.
🚩 124 B4 ✉ U Zlaté Studně 4 ☎ 257 011 2137 🚇 Malostranská 🚊 Trams 12, 20, 22 AX, DC, MC, VI

PRAGUE RESTAURANTS

Price guide: (dinner per person, excluding drinks)
$	100Kč–200Kč
$$	200Kč–600Kč
$$$	over 600Kč

Aromi $$–$$$

Aromi has been turning out arguably Prague's best high-end Italian cooking for the past couple of years and shows no sign of letting up. The setting in residential Vinohrady is elegant without being stuffy. The chef prides himself on the fish choices, but everything is delicious and a good value. Reservations are a good idea in the evening.
🚩 Off map ✉ Mánesova 78 ☎ 222 713 222 🚇 Jiřího z Poděbrad 🚊 Trams 12, 20, 22 AX, DC, MC, VI

Lokál $

Solid Czech pub fare, including good roasted pork and Wienerschnitzel, plus arguably the best beer in Prague make this a tough table to get during meal times. Book in advance or try off-peak times (before 11:30 a.m. for lunch, before 6 p.m. for dinner). This great location is just five minutes on foot from Old Town Square.
🚩 124 D4 ✉ Dlouhá 33 ☎ 222 316 265 🚇 Staroměstská No credit cards

Lví dvůr $$

The name means "Lion's Court," after the lions that were once kept here, close to Prague Castle. Traditional Czech fare is served, including roasted suckling pig – a specialty. There is a special venison menu, too
🚩 124 A5 ✉ U Prašného mostu 6 ☎ 224 372 361 🚇 Malostranská 🚊 12, 20, 22 AX, DC, MC, VI

Plzenská Restaurace $$$

This stylish art nouveau, Czech-style pub, in the cellar of the landmark Obecní dům (Municipal House), offers traditional specialties, including roast duck. Live music is played nightly.
🚩 124 E4 ✉ Náměstí Republiky 5 ☎ 222 002 770 🚇 Náměstí Republiky 🚊 Trams 5, 8, 14 AX, DC, MC, VI

U Zlaté Hrušky $$$

Excellent Czech specialties, including pâté, duck and venison, and good wines are served in an attractive house with rustic furniture. The name means "At The Golden Pear."
🚩 Off the map page 124 ✉ Nový svět 3 ☎ 220 941 244 🚇 Malostranská or Hradčanska 🚊 Tram 22 AX, DC, MC, VI

COPENHAGEN HOTELS

Price guide: (double room for two people)
$	DKr400–DKr700
$$	DKr700–DKr1,200
$$$	over DKr1,200

Axel Hotel Guldsmeden $$–$$$

The Axel is the most luxurious of the appealing chain of small, laid-back, eco-friendly Guldsmeden hotels. Very close to the central railroad station, and individually decorated in modern-chic Balinese style, all rooms have four-poster beds and flat-screen TVs. Breakfasts are delicious and the on-site organic spa luxurious.
🚩 140 B1 ✉ Helgolandsgade 11 ☎ 33 31 69 70 🚇 S train Kobenhavn H AX, MC, VI

Best Western Hotel City $$–$$$

This attractive, comfortable, modernized hotel in an old Copenhagen town house is near the center of things, but in a quiet location. Only breakfast is served.
🚩 140 D2 ✉ Peder Skrams Gade 24 ☎ 33 13 06 66 🚇 Kongens Nytorv 🚊 27 AX, MC, VI

Copenhagen Admiral Hotel $$$

This waterfront hotel, in a superbly renovated, 18th-century, red-brick granary warehouse, is located close to Amalienborg Plads. Regular rooms and family suites are available; a restaurant (breakfast is extra) and sauna are on the premises.
🚩 140 D3 ✉ Toldbodgade 24–28 ☎ 33 74 14 14 🚇 Kongens Nytorv 🚊 1A, 15, 26, 29 AX, DC, MC, VI

Copenhagen Plaza $$–$$$

Located in the heart of the city across from Tivoli, the luxurious, modern Plaza has superbly furnished rooms. The Library Bar encourages literary browsing over drinks, and there's a good restaurant.
🚩 140 B1 ✉ Bernstorffsgade 4

☎ 1866 332 3590 (from U.S. and Canada), 00 800 97 33 42 26 (from Europe) 🚇 S-train København H 🚊 8, 250S AX, MC, VI

Hotel Nimb $$$

One of Copenhagen's newest hotels, Nimb is magically placed in the Tivoli Gardens in the Moorish Palace building. With just 13 rooms, of which eight are suites and seven overlook the gardens, this is one of Copenhagen's most luxurious and exotic sleeping options. The Michelin-starred restaurant is just downstairs; there is also a recommended brasserie.
🚩 140 B1 ✉ Bernstorffsgade 5 ☎ 88 70 00 00 🚇 S train Kobenhavn H 🚊 1A, 11A AX, DC, MC, VI

COPENHAGEN RESTAURANTS

Price guide: (dinner per person, excluding drinks)
$	DKr100–DKr250
$$	DKr250–DKr300
$$$	over DKr300

Nyhavns Færgekro $$

One of the best restaurants on canalside Nyhavn, with a nautical theme that includes model boats hanging from the ceiling. Superb lunchtime buffets featuring a variety of herring dishes are a great deal; the Danish, French and Italian dinner menu is more expensive.
🚩 140 D2 ✉ Nyhavn 5 ☎ 33 15 15 88 🚇 Kongens Nytorv 🚊 1A, 15, 350S DC, MC, VI

Peder Oxe $$

Built on the foundation of an old monastery, this noted restaurant/cellar bar is on Grey Brothers Square. Traditional cuisine emphasizes hearty helpings of meat; the lunchtime smørrebrød is very good. Food is locally sourced where possible.
🚩 140 C2 ✉ Gråbrødretorv 11 ☎ 33 11 00 77 🚇 Kongens Nytorv DC, MC, VI

Restaurant Els $$–$$$

Original painted wall panels from the 1850s add style to this popular Nyhavn restaurant, situated on a street leading off Kongens Nytorv square. Excellent fish specialties and fine wines are served. Reservations are advised.
🚩 140 D2–D3 ✉ Store Strandstræde 3 ☎ 33 14 13 41 🚇 Kongens Nytorv 🚊 1, 6, 10 AX, DC, MC, VI

Denmark, Finland, France

KEY TO SYMBOLS

- ✚ map page number and coordinates
- ✉ address
- ☎ telephone number
- 🕐 days/times closed
- Ⓜ nearest subway station
- 🚌 nearest bus/trolley bus/tram/funicular route
- ⛴ ferry
- $$$ expensive
- $$ moderate
- $ inexpensive
- AX American Express
- DC Diners Club
- MC MasterCard
- VI VISA

Danish Smørrebrød

Like their fellow Scandinavians, Danes are great believers in hearty lunches, and nothing is more mouthwatering or filling than *smørrebrød*, which translates simply as "buttered bread." If it sounds like "smothering," then that's exactly what happens to the large slice of rye bread that is the basis of *smørrebrød* when it is piled high with a tasty mix of salads and garnishes, shrimp and chunks of fish, beef or pork. You can accompany this mini-banquet with a Danish lager and a small glass of chilled *akvavit* (aquavit). You also can enjoy the Danish *kolt bord*, or cold table, an array of meat and fish dishes, salads and savory dips, hot dishes, and a selection of bread and rolls.

RizRaz $–$$

RizRaz takes its inspiration from world cuisine and offers delicious low-fat, healthy options. There's plenty of choice, but especially popular is its all-you-can-eat fresh, seasonal salad buffet, to which you can add prime steak, salmon or kebabs cooked over an open-flame grill. There are two restaurants – the one at Kannikstraede 19 has a large courtyard open in summer.
✚ 140 C2 ✉ Kompagnistræde 20 ☎ 33 15 05 75 Ⓜ Nørreport 🚌 1A, 2A, 5A, 6A, 350S DC, MC, VI

Skt. Gertruds Kloster $$$

Housed in an ancient monastery building, this stylish, candlelit restaurant has a vaulted cellar and atmospheric dining rooms. Fish dishes are the specialty here, with everything from mussels to lobster, and there's a comprehensive selection of wines. Reservations are advised.
✚ 140 C3 ✉ Hauser Plads 32 ☎ 00800 333 333 from Europe (toll free) 🕐 Closed for lunch Ⓜ Nørreport AX, MC, VI

ODENSE HOTELS

Price guide: (double room with breakfast for two people)
$ DKr400–DKr700
$$ DKr700–DKr1,200
$$$ over DKr1,200

City Hotel Odense $$

A comfortable, modern hotel handily located near the Hans Christian Andersen Museum, this in the heart of the Old Town.
✚ 146 C2 ✉ Hans Mulesgade 5 ☎ 66 12 12 58 AX, DC, MC, VI

First Hotel Grand $$–$$$

This is one of Odense's most expensive hotels and is situated in a wonderfully handsome old building just across from the Fyns Kunstmuseum (Funen Art Museum), close to the city center.
✚ 146 B2 ✉ Jernbanegade 18 ☎ 66 11 71 71 AX, DC, MC, VI

Hotel Domir $–$$

The friendly, medium-size Dormir, with comfortable rooms and plenty of amenities, is conveniently located in the city center, minutes from the railroad station and within easy walking distance of the Town Hall.
✚ 146 A3 ✉ Hans Tausensgade 19 ☎ 66 12 14 27 AX, DC, MC, VI

Pjentehus $

Located just outside the city center, this is a small, very comfortable bed-and-breakfast housed in a pleasant villa near the Hans Christian Andersen Museum.
✚ 146 C3 ✉ Pjentedamsgade 14 ☎ 66 12 15 55 🕐 Mar.–Nov. No credit cards

Radisson Blu H. C. Andersen Hotel $$$

A very luxurious, modern hotel, close to the Hans Christian Andersen Museum and next door to the Concert Hall and the Carl Nielsen Museum, the Radisson has its own restaurant. Amenities include sauna, solarium, billiards room and casino.
✚ 146 C2 ✉ Claus Bergs Gade 7 ☎ 66 14 78 00, from US (toll free): (0800) 333 3333, from Europe (toll free) AX, DC, MC, VI

ODENSE RESTAURANTS

Price guide: (dinner per person, excluding drinks)
$ DKr100–DKr250
$$ DKr250–DKr300
$$$ over DKr300

Den Gamle Kro $$$

This restaurant occupies a magnificent 1683 building. Meals are served in several rooms, including the brick-vaulted cellar. Expect excellent Danish cuisine.
✚ 146 B2–C2 ✉ Overgade 23 ☎ 66 12 14 33 AX, DC, MC, VI

Den Grimme Ælling $–$$

This charming little restaurant, The Ugly Duckling, is on a cobbled lane, just across the main road from the Hans Christian Andersen Museum. It is known for its extravagant buffets based on a range of meats.
✚ 146 B2 ✉ Hans Jensens Stræde 1 ☎ 65 91 70 30 AX, MC, VI

Jensens Bøfhus $

This popular lunchtime grill and evening favorite serves steaks with lavish salads. A favorite for families.
✚ 146 A2 ✉ Kongensgade 10 ☎ 66 14 59 59 AX, MC, VI

Kvægtorvets $$$

Located just outside the city center, this is a stylish restaurant. The good, set menu has a choice of three, four or five courses.
✚ 146 A3 ✉ Rugårdsvej 25 ☎ 65 91 50 01 🕐 Closed Sun. AX, DC, MC, VI

Restaurant Air Pub $–$$
This pub and restaurant has a good atmosphere to go along with hearty Danish cooking and a decent selection of beers. There is a good choice of lighter dishes.
🔲 146 A2 ✉ Kongensgade 41
☎ 66 14 66 08 ⊙ Closed Sun. AX, MC, VI

Price guide: (double room with breakfast for two people)
$ €50–€100
$$ €100–€150
$$$ over €150

Hotel Anna $$–$$$
This comfortable hotel is conveniently located within walking distance of the Esplanade and yet is relatively peaceful, being on one of the quiet streets of the city center. Its moderate size, with just 64 rooms, contributes to a friendly and relaxed atmosphere.
🔲 159 C3 ✉ Annankatu 1 ☎ 09 616 621 🚌 2N, 14, 14B, 16, 20; trams 3B, 6, 9, 10 AX, DC, MC, VI

Helka $–$$
Located in the heart of the city, this hotel was renovated in 2006 and is finished in a cool Finnish style. It offers good service, good value and a sauna. Special weekend rates.
🔲 158 B4 ✉ Pohjoinen Rautatiekatu 23 ☎ 09 613 580 🚌 All buses from Kamppi bus station and 14, 14B, 32, 39, 45, 47; trams 3B, 3T AX, DC, MC, VI

Hotel Linna $$–$$$
Formerly known as the Hotel Lord, this 48-room, Jugend-style hotel is part of the upscale Palace Kämp group of hotels and restaurants. The hotel has thick granite walls and cool modern furnishings. Breakfast is served in the cozy cellar.
🔲 159 C4 ✉ Lönnrotinkatu 29 ☎ 010 344 4100 🚌 20, 20N; tram 6 AX, DC, MC, VI

Scandic Grand Marina Hotel $$–$$$
You can step from ferry to foyer, if you travel to Helsinki by Viking Line, and stay in this large hotel on the western side of the harbor. Rooms are elegant and there are several bars and a restaurant. Kids stay free.
🔲 158 D4 ✉ Katajanokanlaituri 7 ☎ 09 16661 🚌 Tram 4 AX, DC, MC, VI

Scandic Marski Hotel $$–$$$
This large, modern hotel is conveniently located right at the heart of things on busy Mannerheimintie Street.
🔲 158 C4 ✉ Mannerheimintie 10 ☎ 09 68061 🚌 16, 20, 24; trams 3B, 3T, 6, 9, 10 AX, DC, MC, VI

Price guide: (dinner per person, excluding drinks)
$ €10–€25
$$ €25–€35
$$$ over €35

G. W. Sundmans $$$
Located in the 19th-century house of a naval captain, this restaurant serves modern Finnish dishes such as brill with shrimp and lobster and fillet of reindeer.
🔲 159 D3 ✉ Eteläranta 16 ☎ 09 6128 5400 ⊙ Closed Sat. lunch and Sun. 🚌 Trams 1, 3B, 3T AX, DC, MC, VI

Kappeli $$–$$$
This is a stylish restaurant and café, with outside terraces on the Esplanade, in a pavilion of cast iron and glass dating from 1867. Good Finnish and Scandinavian dishes are offered, with an emphasis on fresh seasonal produce. In summer there are concerts at the nearby bandstand.
🔲 158 C4 ✉ Eteläesplanadi 1 ☎ 010 766 3880 🚌 13, 64S, 77S; tram 1, 1A AX, MC, VI

Nuevo $$$
This top-quality restaurant in the "Street Museum" serves Spanish cuisine; fish specialties are offered when in season. The *tapas* menu is a good choice for lunch.
🔲 158 C4 ✉ Sofiankatu 4 ☎ 09 6128 5900 ⊙ Closed Sat. before 2 p.m. and Sun. 🚌 Trams 1, 2, 4, 7, 3B, 3T AX, DC, MC, VI

Ravintola Lyon $$–$$$
Good-quality French cuisine using the finest local ingredients is presented in this unassuming and friendly restaurant perfectly positioned opposite the Helsinki Opera House. The roasted breast of goose is a favorite.
🔲 159 C5 ✉ Mannerheimintie 56 ☎ 09 408 131 ⊙ Closed lunch and Mon.–Sun. 🚌 Trams 4, 10 AX, DC, MC, VI

Price guide: (double room with breakfast for two people)
$ under €150
$$ €150–€225
$$$ over €225

Bristol Paris $$$
The Louis XV-style rooms affirm the elegance of this hotel, which boasts a rooftop indoor swimming pool, pampering spa and superb restaurant.
🔲 174 B3 ✉ 112 rue du Faubourg-St.-Honoré ☎ 01 53 43 43 00 🚇 Miromesnil AX, DC, MC, VI

Hôtel des Deux-Îles $$
A peaceful hotel, beautifully housed in a 17th-century dwelling, with understated charm and elegance. Rooms have been renovated to a good standard. Breakfast is served in a stone-arched room.
🔲 175 D2 ✉ 59 rue St.-Louis-en-l'Île ☎ 01 43 26 13 35 🚇 Pont-Marie AX, MC, VI

Hôtel des Grandes Écoles $
This typically French hotel has pretty bedrooms and is set in a garden on a narrow street in the Latin Quarter.
🔲 174 D1 ✉ 75 rue Cardinal-Lemoine ☎ 01 43 26 79 23 🚇 Cardinal-Lemoine MC, VI

Hôtel New Orient $–$$
Newly refurbished, small and personal, this is a little gem for the room prices and is located 10 minutes on foot from the Opera.
🔲 174 B4 ✉ 16 rue de Constantinople ☎ 01 45 22 21 64 🚇 Villiers AX, DC, MC, VI

Pavillon de la Reine $$$
A romantic and luxurious hotel, complete with four-poster beds. The rooms and suites have individual decor. The spa offers a range of treatments and massages.
🔲 175 E2 ✉ 28 place des Vosges ☎ 01 40 29 19 19 🚇 Saint-Paul AX, DC, MC, VI

Price guide: (dinner per person, excluding drinks)
$ under €35
$$ €35–€60
$$$ over €60

Bistro Poulbot $$
This cozy restaurant is decorated with pictures of Montmartre. The

France

KEY TO SYMBOLS

- ⊞ map page number and coordinates
- ✉ address
- ☎ telephone number
- ◷ days/times closed
- Ⓜ nearest subway station
- 🚌 nearest bus/trolley bus/ tram/funicular route
- ⛴ ferry
- $$$ expensive
- $$ moderate
- $ inexpensive
- AX American Express
- DC Diners Club
- MC MasterCard
- VI VISA

Russian Restaurants

You can sample authentic Russian cuisine in Helsinki at one of the city's several Russian restaurants. Russian food is not noted for its lightness of touch, but it can be innovative and is extremely filling. You can even start with caviar and sour cream if you want, before plunging into hearty meat dishes – lamb is a specialty – with cakes, fruit pies and ice cream for dessert. Two notable choices to try are Kasakka at Meritullinkatu 13 (☎ 06 135 6288), and Bellevue at Rahapajankatu 3 (☎ 09 179 560).

---

owner-chef's cuisine is refined – bistro style at lunch and gourmet at dinner. A *prix-fixe* menu is also available.

⊞ 174 D4 ✉ 39 rue Lamarck ☎ 01 46 06 86 00 ◷ Closed Sun. and Mon. Ⓜ Lamarck-Caulaincourt VI

Chez Paul $–$$

Chez Paul is a genuine old bistro with original early 1900s period decor. The menu is filled with excellent French staples and portions are generous and the wine list is long.

⊞ 174 E2 ✉ 13 rue de Charonne, 75011 ☎ 01 47 00 34 57 Ⓜ Bastille AX, DC, MC, VI

La Coupole $$

This sprawling art deco brasserie, renowned in the 1920s, serves seafood, fish and steaks. Sole *meunière* and sweetbreads are among the specialties.

⊞ 175 C1 ✉ 102 boulevard du Montparnasse ☎ 01 43 20 14 20 Ⓜ Vavin AX, DC, MC, VI

Le Dôme $$$

The specialties at this famous Montparnasse brasserie are seafood and fish. Service is efficient.

⊞ 175 C1 ✉ 108 boulevard du Montparnasse ☎ 01 43 35 25 81 Ⓜ Vavin AX, MC, VI

Le Grizzli $$

In the heart of the Marais, this old-fashioned bistro serves dishes from central and southwest France.

⊞ 174 D3 ✉ 7 rue St.-Martin ☎ 01 48 87 77 56 Ⓜ Hôtel-de-Ville AX, MC, VI

Nos Ancêtres les Gaulois $$

This picturesque island restaurant offers a *prix-fixe* menu in convivial 17th-century surroundings.

⊞ 175 D2 ✉ 39 rue St.-Louis-en-l'Île ☎ 01 46 33 66 07 ◷ Closed Mon.–Sat. lunch Ⓜ Pont-Marie AX, DC, MC, VI

LYON HOTELS

Price guide: (double room with breakfast for two people)
$ under €125
$$ €125–€200
$$$ over €200

Collège Hôtel $$

Styled around the theme of an old college dorm, this new hotel is delightfully quirky. Rooms are

brilliant white and have terraces with lovely views of the city.

⊞ 186 A4 ✉ 5 place St.-Paul ☎ 04 72 10 05 05 Ⓜ St.-Paul, Vieux Lyon (St.-Jean) AX, DC, MC, VI

Hotel Sofitel Lyon Bellecour $$–$$$

This deluxe hotel, centrally located on the Rhône river, is a good choice. There are two restaurants on site.

⊞ 186 B1 ✉ 20 quai Gailleton ☎ 04 72 41 20 20 Ⓜ Bellecour AX, DC, MC, VI

Mercure Beaux-Arts Tradition $–$$

An early 20th-century building houses this comfortable hotel in the center of the Presqu'Île.

⊞ 186 B3 ✉ 75 rue Président Édouard-Hérriot ☎ 04 78 38 09 50 Ⓜ Cordeliers or Bellecour AX, DC, MC, VI

St.-Paul $

Consider staying at this excellent budget choice in the Old Town. It has simple, clean and airy rooms.

⊞ 186 B3 ✉ 6 rue Lainerie ☎ 04 78 28 13 29 AX, DC, MC, VI

La Villa Florentine $$$

A former convent, this deluxe hotel with many amenities – including a pretty garden – stands above the Old Town, on the slopes of Fourvière.

⊞ 186 A3 ✉ 25–27 montée St.-Barthélémy ☎ 04 72 56 56 56 Ⓜ Hôtel de Ville or Vieux Lyon AX, DC, MC, VI

LYON RESTAURANTS

Price guide: (dinner per person, excluding drinks)
$ under €35
$$ €35–€60
$$$ over €60

L'Assiette du Marche $

An excellent lively Lyonnaise bistro serving great-value typical lunches and evening meals in a modern *bouchon* environment – service is brisk and it's always busy. Choose from a full set menu or from a choice of dishes.

⊞ 186 off A4 ✉ 21 Grand rue de Vaise ☎ 04 78 83 84 90 ◷ Closed Sun. lunch, Sun.–Thu. dinner MC, VI

L'Auberge du Pont de Collonges $$$

The height of French haute cuisine (three Michelin stars). Chef Paul

Bocuse offers exceptional dishes and exemplary formal service. You will need to reserve a table.

🔶 186 off the map ✉ 40 rue de la Plage, Collonges (2.5 miles north of Lyon city) ☎ 04 72 42 90 90 🕐 Daily lunch and dinner AX, DC, MC, VI

Chabert et Fils $

Sophisticated Lyonnais specialties served here include a chicken-liver gâteau and delicate soups.

🔶 186 C2 ✉ 11 rue des Marronniers ☎ 04 78 37 01 94 🚇 Bellecour AX, DC, MC, VI

Le Petit Glouton $

This tiny *bouchon* is "old-school," serving good Lyon cuisine without fancy prices and fancy table settings.

🔶 186 A3 ✉ 56–58 rue St.-Jean ☎ 04 78 37 30 10 🕐 Closed Aug. 🚇 Vieux Lyon No credit cards

Têtedoie $$$

Rich but light specialties are on the menu at this elegant and professionally staffed restaurant, with large windows giving wonderful views of the city.

🔶 186 A2 ✉ Montée du Chemin Neuf ☎ 04 78 29 40 10 🕐 Closed Sat. lunch, Sun. all day, Mon. lunch; Aug. 🚇 Vieux Lyon AX, DC, MC, VI

Price guide: (double room with breakfast for two people)
$ under €125
$$ €125–€200
$$$ over €200

Elysée Palace $$–$$$

The excellent facilities include a rooftop pool at this modern luxury hotel on the famous promenade des Anglais.

🔶 194 B1 ✉ 59 promenade des Anglais ☎ 04 93 97 90 90 🚌 8, 11, 98, 52, 59, 60, 62, 70, 94 AX, DC, MC, VI

Gounod $–$$

This moderately priced belle époque choice is in a quiet location, and is a 10-minute walk from the sea.

🔶 194 B1 ✉ 3 rue Gounod ☎ 04 93 16 42 00 🕐 Closed late Nov.–late Dec. 🚌 7, 9, 10, 14, 22, 38 AX, DC, MC, VI

Négresco $$$

This is one of the world's great hotels in the flamboyant belle époque style; superb comfort, service and facilities.

🔶 194 B1 ✉ 37 promenade des Anglais ☎ 04 93 16 64 00 🚌 8, 11, 52, 59, 60, 62, 70, 94, 98, 99 AX, DC, MC, VI

Villa Eden $

This hotel is housed in a converted mansion built for a Russian countess, half a block inland from the seafront. Some sea views.

🔶 194 A1 ✉ 99 bis promenade des Anglais ☎ 04 93 86 53 70 🚌 8, 11, 52, 59, 60, 62, 70, 94 AX, DC, MC, VI

Windsor $$

This famous hotel is centrally located and has a garden pool and beautifully frescoed rooms, each with sound-proofing.

🔶 194 B1 ✉ 11 rue Dalpozzo ☎ 04 93 88 59 35 🚌 3, 7, 8, 9, 10, 14, 22, 52, 59, 94 AX, DC, MC, VI

Price guide: (dinner per person, excluding drinks)
$ under €35
$$ €35–€60
$$$ over €60

L'Ane Rouge $$$

Typical Provençal dishes from land and sea. There's a lovely view over the old harbor from the terrace.

🔶 195 E1 ✉ 7 quai des 2 Emmanuel ☎ 04 93 89 49 63 🕐 Closed Wed. lunch and dinner, Thu. lunch 🚌 3, 7, 20, 30, 70, 81, 100 AX, DC, MC, VI

Boccaccio $$–$$$

Located in the city center, this restaurant offers mouthwatering seafood specialties; in summer you can dine on the terrace.

🔶 195 C1 ✉ 7 rue Masséna ☎ 04 93 87 71 76 🚌 3, 7, 8, 9, 10, 14, 22, 52, 59; Tram Masséna AX, DC, MC, VI

Le Chantecler $$$

Nice's finest restaurant, and one of the best in France, is housed in the opulent Hôtel Négresco, and serves traditional French food. Reservations are advised.

🔶 194 B1 ✉ Hôtel Négresco, 37 promenade des Anglais ☎ 04 93 16 64 00 🕐 Wed.–Sat. dinner, Sun. lunch and dinner 🚌 8, 11, 52, 59, 60, 62, 70, 94 AX, DC, MC, VI

La Coupole $$

This popular restaurant in the town center specializes in seafood and fish dishes.

🔶 194 C1 ✉ 4 rue de France ☎ 04 93 87 14 15 🚋 Tram Massena MC, VI

La Petite Maison $–$$$

Join the regulars and enjoy good home cooking from a menu that features seasonal specialties and a fantastic range of hors d'oeuvres. Reservations are advised.

🔶 195 D1 ✉ 11 rue St.-François-de-Paule ☎ 04 93 92 59 59 🕐 Closed Sun. 🚌 5, 6, 8, 16, 18, 25, 37, 38, 88 AX, DC, MC, VI

Price guide: (double room with breakfast for two people)
$ under €125
$$ €125–€200
$$$ over €200

Cardinal de Rohan $–$$

This pretty hotel on a picturesque and historic street close to the cathedral is an easy stroll from the main sights and several good restaurants.

🔶 200 B1 ✉ 17–19 rue du Maroquin ☎ 03 88 32 85 11 🚌 10, 14, 21, 24; trams A, D AX, DC, VI

Cathédrale $–$$

This excellent hotel is close to Strasbourg's main sights and some of the city's best restaurants. Rooms are air-conditioned and soundproof and there is a small bar.

🔶 200 B2 ✉ 12–13 place de la Cathédrale ☎ 03 88 22 12 12 🚌 14, 21, 24; tram A, D AX, DC, VI

Maison Kammerzell $$

Situated opposite the cathedral, this comfortable, traditional hotel has a lovely terrace and good restaurant. It's an excellent vacation choice.

🔶 200 B2 ✉ 16 place de la Cathédrale ☎ 03 88 32 42 14 🚌 10, 21, 24; trams A, D AX, DC, VI

Mercure Strasbourg Centre $$

This convenient and comfortable hotel, located in the historic center, has large, soundproof rooms.

🔶 200 B2 ✉ 25 rue Thomann ☎ 03 90 22 70 70 🚌 4, 6; trams A, B, C, D AX, DC, MC, VI

Quality Suites Victoria Gardens $

This good-value hotel lies close to the train station and has simple rooms with modern decor and facilities.

KEY TO SYMBOLS

- ⊞ map page number and coordinates
- ⊠ address
- ☎ telephone number
- ◷ days/times closed
- Ⓠ nearest subway station
- ⊟ nearest bus/trolley bus/tram/funicular route
- ⛴ ferry
- $$$ expensive
- $$ moderate
- $ inexpensive
- AX American Express
- DC Diners Club
- MC MasterCard
- VI VISA

The *Belle Époque* in Nice

The *belle époque*, or "beautiful era," was the name the French gave to the early 20th century. During this period Nice's fame soared with the influx of up to 150,000 wealthy English and Russians who came here to while away northern winters in elegance. They expected luxury, and it was for them that sumptuous and grandiose hotels and villas were built. Some buildings survive along the promenade des Anglais. The Hôtel Négresco is the most famous; enjoy a drink there in Edwardian style.

⊞ 200 off the map ⊠ 9 rue du Magasins ☎ 03 90 22 43 43 ⊟ 2, 6, 10 AX, DC, MC, VI

STRASBOURG RESTAURANTS

Price guide: (dinner per person, excluding drinks)

$	€20–€30
$$	€30–€45
$$$	over €45

Aux Armes de Strasbourg $–$$

Interesting local dishes and a huge variety of beers are served at this atmospheric restaurant.
⊞ 200 B1 ⊠ 9 place Gutenberg ☎ 03 88 32 85 62 ⊟ 14, 21, 24; trams A, D AX, DC, MC, VI

Au Bon Vivant $–$$

One of the few remaining traditional family-run restaurants in the city center is this winner, serving local specialties in a relaxed atmosphere.
⊞ 200 B1 ⊠ 7 rue du Maroquin ☎ 03 88 32 77 81 ◷ Closed Thu. dinner and all day Fri. ⊟ 14, 21, 24; trams A, D AX, MC, VI

Le Baeckeoffe d'Alsace $

An old timbered building in the loveliest part of the Old Town is the setting for this *winstub* (wine room). Naturally, they serve *Baeckeoffe*, a slow-cooked stew of beef, lamb and pork in wine.
⊞ 200 A1 ⊠ 14 rue des Moulins ☎ 03 88 23 05 40 ⊟ 14, 21, 24; trams A, D AX, MC, VI

Au Petit Tonnelier $$

This family-run restaurant, on one of the Old Town's prettiest streets, serves seasonal and regional dishes.
⊞ 200 B1 ⊠ 16 rue des Tonneliers ☎ 03 88 32 53 54 ⊟ 14, 21, 24; trams A, D AX, MC, VI

BERLIN HOTELS

Price guide: (double room with breakfast for two people)

$	under €75
$$	€75–€150
$$$	over €150

Alsterhof $$

This is a small 1960s hotel, behind the KaDeWe department store. In spite of the plain exterior, it is stylish inside, with 200 rooms, a chic restaurant and annex conservatory.
⊞ 216 B2 ⊠ Augsburger Strasse 5 ☎ 030 212 420 Ⓠ U-Bahn to Augsburger Strasse, or

Wittenbergplatz; S-Bahn to Zoologischer Garten AX, DC, MC, VI

Hotel Kronprinz Berlin $$$

This elegant hotel, in a 70-room (all nonsmoking) late 19th-century house surrounded by chestnut trees, is only a few steps from the Ku'damm and has an attractive terraced beer garden.
⊞ 216 off the map ⊠ Kronprinzendamm 1 ☎ 030 896 030 Ⓠ S-Bahn to Halensee ⊟ 109, M19, M29 AX, DC, MC, VI

Kempinski Hotel Bristol $$$

This hotel, formerly on Unter den Linden, has a famous name and a traditional style, with formal furnishings, chandeliers and deep-pile carpets. There are 252 rooms and 52 suites, and an elaborate menu in the restaurant.
⊞ 216 B2 ⊠ Kurfürstendamm 27 ☎ 030 884 340 Ⓠ U-Bahn to Uhlandstrasse; U-Bahn/S-Bahn to Zoologischer Garten AX, DC, MC, VI

Transit $

Pleasant rooms in an attractive part of the Kreuzberg quarter. The English-speaking staff is very welcoming and helpful.
⊞ 217 D1 ⊠ Hagelberger Strasse 53–54 ☎ 030 789 0470 Ⓠ U-Bahn to Mehringdamm ⊟ M19 AX, MC, VI

BERLIN RESTAURANTS

Price guide: (dinner per person, excluding drinks)

$	under €15
$$	€15–€30
$$$	over €30

Alt Luxemburg $$$

What you get at one of the city's best restaurants is German food by chef Karl Wannemacher, some of the country's best. Each month they have a special four-course menu.
⊞ 216 A2 ⊠ Windscheidstrasse 31 ☎ 030 323 8730 ◷ Mon.–Sat. from 5 p.m. Ⓠ U-Bahn to Sophie-Charlotte-Platz AX, DC, MC, VI

Berliner Stube $$

Berliner Leber (calf's liver) is the specialty at this restaurant near the Ku'damm in the Steigenberger Hotel; international dishes also are on the menu.
⊞ 216 B2 ⊠ Los-Angeles-Platz 1 ☎ 030 212 7750 ◷ Daily noon–3

and 6–10 🚇 Kurfürstendamm
AX, DC, MC, VI

Borchardt $$$

Stylish Berliners and politicians love
this attractive, 1920s-style bistro, a
lunch spot where "new" and
international cuisine is featured.
➕ 217 D2 ✉ Französische
Strasse 47 ☎ 030 8188 6262
🚇 Französische Strasse AX, MC, VI

Dressler $$–$$$

Fine German and French cuisine
can be enjoyed inside this
sophisticated art deco restaurant or
outside on the sun terrace. Seasonal
cuisine includes game and young
herring.
➕ 216 B2 ✉ Kurfürstendamm
207–208 ☎ 030 883 35 30
🚇 Kurfürstendamm or Uhlandshasse
AX, MC, VI

Zum Nussbaum $

The name of this inexpensive
pub-style restaurant, or Gasthaus, in
the Nikolaiviertal area means "The
Nut Tree."
➕ 217 E3 ✉ Am Nussbaum 3
☎ 030 242 3095 🚇 Alexanderplatz
MC, VI

COLOGNE HOTELS

Price guide: (double room with
breakfast for two people)
$ under €75
$$ €75–€150
$$$ over €150

Buchholz Downtown $$

This privately owned and family-run
hotel with a friendly staff has 18
bedrooms. The central but quiet
location is a real added bonus. A
shuttle service to the airport can be
provided for customers on request.
➕ 225 C4 ✉ Kunibertsgasse 5
☎ 0221 16083-0 🚇 Dom/Hbf
DC, MC, VI

CityClass Hotel Europa am Dom $$

Conveniently located directly
opposite the cathedral, this hotel is
close to most museums. Nonsmoking
rooms are available.
➕ 225 B3 ✉ Am Hof 38–46
☎ 0221 2058-0 🚇 Dom/Hbf
AX, DC, MC, VI

Das Kleine Stapelhäuschen $–$$

Two adjacent town houses, in
historically interesting buildings on
the Rhine promenade, house a
friendly hotel with a comfortable
wine bar that's just a short walk
from the cathedral.
➕ 225 C3 ✉ Fischmarkt 1–3
☎ 0221 272 7777 🚋 Trams 1, 7, 9
MC, VI

Sofitel Mondial am Dom $$–$$$

Despite its dull exterior, this is a,
stylish hotel, situated between the
impressive cathedral and the river
and ideally placed for exploring the
Old Town. There's also a restaurant
serving international and regional
cuisine.
➕ 225 B3 ✉ Kurt-Hackenberg-Platz
1 ☎ 0221 20630 🚇 Dom/Hbf
AX, DC, MC, VI

Viktoria $$

This turn-of-the-20th-century
Jugendstil building by the Rhine
offers some rooms with river views
and a generous breakfast buffet.
➕ 225 off the map ✉ Worringer
Strasse 23 ☎ 0221 973 1720
🚇 Reichensperger Platz AX, DC,
MC, VI

COLOGNE RESTAURANTS

Price guide: (dinner per person,
excluding drinks)
$ under €15
$$ €15–€30
$$$ over €30

Bosporus $$$

Located in the multicultural quarter
of Weidengasse, Bosporus has four
set menus offering a wide range of
Turkish dishes. The nearby Eigelstein
quarter is equally lively.
➕ 225 B4 ✉ Weidengasse 36
☎ 0221 125 265 🚋 Trams 15, 16, 18
AX, DC, MC, VI

Brauhaus Sion $$

This busy side-street brewery-tavern,
near the cathedral, is especially
popular for lunch and coffee, and for
strong Kölsch beer. Traditionally
dressed waiters roll out the barrels.
➕ 225 B3 ✉ Unter Taschenmacher
5–7 ☎ 0221 257 8540 🚋 Trams 1,
7, 9 MC, VI

Kintaro $$–$$$

Japanese dishes are served in this
popular sushi restaurant, where
particularly good entrées include
seaweed (*hijiki*) and octopus, and
cucumber and seaweed in vinegar
(*tako su*). Reservations are advised.

➕ 225 A3 ✉ Friesenstrasse 16
☎ 0221 135 255 🚇 Friesenplatz
AX, DC, MC, VI

Pfaffen Brauerei Max Päffgen $$

This pub, belonging to Cologne's
smallest brewery, is conveniently
located close to the city's main
attractions. Tasty regional dishes
and Kölsch beer are served in a
congenial atmosphere.
➕ 225 C2 ✉ Heumarkt 62
☎ 0221 257 7765 🕐 Closed Mon.
🚋 Trams 1, 7, 9 No credit cards

MUNICH HOTELS

Price guide: (double room with
breakfast for two people)
$ under €75
$$ €75–€150
$$$ over €150

Hotel Gästehaus Englischer Garten $$

This hotel, at the edge of the English
Garden in Schwabing, is housed in a
converted water mill. You'll really
feel as if you're relaxing in the heart
of the country, especially when
eating the breakfast buffet, served in
the garden in summer.
➕ 230 off the map
✉ Liebergesellstrasse 8 ☎ 089
383 9410 🚇 Münchner Freiheit
AX, DC, MC, VI

Mandarin Oriental, Munich $$$

Celebrity guests including Madonna
and Prince Charles have stayed at
the city's newest luxury hotel, with
73 rooms, including some luxurious
suites.
➕ 231 C2 ✉ Neuturmstrasse 1
☎ 089 29 09 80 🚇 Marienplatz
🚋 Tram 19 AX, DC, MC, VI

Opéra $$$

This 56-bed hotel, housed in an old
mansion with elegant arcades and a
Renaissance courtyard, is convenient
to Munich's upscale shopping.
➕ 231 D2 ✉ St. Anna-Strasse 10
☎ 089 210 4940 🚇 Lehel
🚋 Tram 19 AX, MC, VI

Splendid-Dollmann $$$

Rooms at this bed-and-breakfast in
the city center are decorated in a
range of styles, from baroque to
Bavarian.
➕ 231 D2 ✉ Thierschstrasse 49
☎ 089 23 80 80 🚇 Lehel
AX, MC, VI

KEY TO SYMBOLS

✚	map page number and coordinates
✉	address
☎	telephone number
◎	days/times closed
Ⓜ	nearest subway station
🚍	nearest bus/trolley bus/ tram/funicular route
⛴	ferry
$$$	expensive
$$	moderate
$	inexpensive
AX	American Express
DC	Diners Club
MC	MasterCard
VI	VISA

Strasbourg Specials

Visualize French flair and imagination combined with high-quality ingredients and German influences, and you'll begin to understand the gastronomic delights that await you in Strasbourg. This is the home of foie gras, fatted goose liver eaten whole or made into pâté; *choucroute* (sauerkraut), assorted meats and spicy sausages served with mounds of pickled cabbage; and *kougelhupf*, yeast cake traditionally eaten for breakfast. There are other, less well-known regional dishes; look for *bæckeoffe*, a slow-cooked casserole featuring three different meats, and *tarte flambée*, a rich hot onion tart. The smooth, pungently aromatic Munster is Strasbourg's local cheese.

Torbräu $$$

Munich's oldest hotel has been in the heart of the Old Town for more than five centuries. On the premises are an Italian restaurant, café and 91 quiet, individually styled rooms.
✉ 231 C2 ✉ Tal 41 ☎ 089 24 23 40 Ⓜ Marienplatz or Isartor AX, MC, VI

MUNICH RESTAURANTS

Price guide: (dinner per person, excluding drinks)

$	under €15
$$	€15–€30
$$$	over €30

Augustiner $

Munich's oldest surviving brewery produced its own beer until 1897, and now serves Bavarian dishes in the large dining hall. There's a beer garden in the courtyard.
✉ 231 B2 ✉ Neuhauser Strasse 27 ☎ 089 23 18 32 57 Ⓜ Karlsplatz AX, MC, VI

Halali $$$

Unpretentious regional cooking is offered here. Game dishes such as venison are served with touches like cranberry or wild mushroom sauce.
✉ 231 C3 ✉ Schönfeldstrasse 22 ☎ 089 28 59 09 ◎ Closed Sat. lunch, Sun. and holidays
Ⓜ Odeonsplatz AX, MC, VI

Ratskeller $$

Hearty local dishes are served in the Ratskeller tavern, situated in the New Town Hall's vaulted cellars.
✉ 231 C2 ✉ Marienplatz 8 ☎ 089 21 99 89-0 Ⓜ Marienplatz AX, MC, VI

Schlosscafé im Palmenhaus $$–$$$

This elegant café is located in the palm house at Nymphenburg Palace.
✉ 230 off the map ✉ Schloss Nymphenburg, entrance 43 ☎ 089 17 53 09 🚍 51, trams 12, 16, 17 No credit cards

Spatenhaus an der Oper $$$

The atmosphere is relaxed and the service good at this favored after-theater restaurant, which serves a traditional Bavarian menu as well as a range of regional and international dishes.
✉ 230 C2 ✉ Residenzstrasse 12 ☎ 089 290 7060 Ⓜ Marienplatz, Odeonsplatz; tram 19 AX, MC, VI

ATHENS HOTELS

Price guide: (double room with breakfast for two people)

$	€50–€80
$$	€80–€140
$$$	over €140

Attalos Hotel $$

Clean and comfortable, mid-range choice halfway between Omonia and Monastiraki squares. The roof garden/bar has good views of the Acropolis, which is only a 15-minute walk away.
✉ 244 B3 ✉ 29 Athinas ☎ 210 321 2801-3 Ⓜ Omonia, Monastiraki AX, DC, MC, VI

BabyGrand $$

This fun boutique hotel sports rooms decorated by local artists and has the first champagne bar in Athens.
✉ 244 off the map ✉ 65 Athinas ☎ 210 325 0900 Ⓜ Omonia AX, DC, MC, VI

Grande Bretagne $$$

The Grande Bretagne is Athens' most historic, grandest and very traditional hotel, offering the highest level of service and amenities.
✚ 244 C2 ✉ Syntagmatos ☎ 210 333 0000 🚍 1, 18, 15 AX, DC, MC, VI

Phaedra $

A location at the quieter end of Pláka makes up for one or two fairly small rooms at this pleasant hotel.
✚ 244 C2 ✉ Cherefontos 16 & Adrianou ☎ 210 323 8461
Ⓜ Akrópoli 🚍 9, 11, 15 AX, DC, VI

Saint George Lycabettus $$$

Beautifully situated on the quiet, shady slopes of Lykabettus Hill, this first-class hotel offers lovely views from its rooftop restaurant. Rooms have good, modern facilities.
✚ 244 D3 ✉ 2 Kleomenous-Dexamini ☎ 210 729 0711
🚍 3, 8, 13 AX, DC, MC, VI

ATHENS RESTAURANTS

Price guide: (dinner per person, excluding drinks)

$	€10–€15
$$	€15–€30
$$$	over €30

Archeon Gefsis $$$

Dine at this imaginative restaurant that offers meat and fish dishes prepared from classical recipes.

➕ 244 A4 ✉ Kodratou 22
☎ 210 523 9661 Ⓜ Metaxourghio
AX, DC, VI

O Platanos $

This friendly Plaka *taverna* serves simple and delicious food at both indoor and outdoor tables.
➕ 244 B2 ✉ 4 Diogenous, Pláka
☎ 210 322 0666 🚌 1, 9, 11, 18
No credit cards

Psaras $$

Tucked below the Acropolis on one of Pláka's prettiest streets is this 100-year-old *taverna*, serving home-cooked traditional dishes.
➕ 244 B2 ✉ 16 Erekteos and Erotokritou Pláka ☎ 210 321 8733
Ⓜ Thission 🚌 1, 9, 11, 18 AX, DC, MC, VI

Saita $

This popular basement restaurant in the Pláka has good food and friendly service. (The sidewalk tables close to the door belong to another restaurant.)
➕ 244 B2 ✉ 21 Kidathineon
☎ 210 322 6671 🚌 1, 5, 9, 18
No credit cards

Spondi $$$

To sample state-of-the-art Greek cooking, eat at the Michelin-starred Spondi and sample their "Discovery" tasting menu. It gets no better than this
➕ 244 B3 ✉ 5 Pyrronos ☎ 210 756 4021 Ⓜ Agios Ioannis AX, DC, MC, VI

Price guide: (double room with breakfast for two people)
$ under Ft17,500
$$ Ft17,500–Ft44,500
$$$ over Ft44,500

Carlton $$

This is a spacious and simple hotel at the foot of Castle Hill. Of the 95 rooms – all with excellent facilities – only those on the upper floor have good views.
➕ 258 B2 ✉ Apor Péter utca 3
☎ 1 224 0999 Ⓜ Battyány tér
AX, DC, MC, VI

Danubius Hotel Astoria $$–$$$

Set on a busy intersection in the center of Pest, this is a splendid hotel in an old building with a relaxing atmosphere. It was the

headquarters of the Soviet army during the 1956 revolution.
➕ 258 C2 ✉ Kossuth Lajos utca 19–21 ☎ 1 889 6000 Ⓜ Astoria AX, DC, MC, VI

Hilton Budapest $$$

This modern building, in a prime position on Castle Hill, incorporates the ruins of a 13th-century Dominican cloister and a 17th-century Jesuit cloister. You'll get spectacular views over the Danube. Facilities include cafés, shops and a courtyard concert area.
➕ 258 A3 ✉ Hess András tér 1–3
☎ 1 889 6600 Ⓜ Moszkva tér, then Várbusz (Castle Bus) AX, DC, MC, VI

Kempinski Hotel Corvinus Budapest $$$

This luxury hotel with an unusual postmodern design includes two presidential apartments. It's popular with business travelers and has a good fitness center and pool.
➕ 258 C2 ✉ Erzsébet tér 7–8 ☎ 1 429 3777 Ⓜ Deák tér AX, DC, MC, VI

Victoria $$

Marvelous views across to the Pest bank are a feature at this comfortable 27-room hotel on the Buda bank, overlooking Chain Bridge and convenient to many tourist sights.
➕ 258 B2 ✉ Bem rakpart 11
☎ 1 457 8080 Ⓜ Battyány tér
🚌 16; tram 19 AX, DC, MC, VI

Price guide: (dinner per person, excluding drinks)
$ under Ft3,000
$$ Ft3,000–Ft6,000
$$$ over Ft6,000

Alabárdos $$$

This stylish, formal restaurant serves Hungarian dishes in ancient vaulted dining rooms. Presentations are beautiful and the staff attentive. There are only a few tables, so it's always best to reserve in advance.
➕ 258 A3 ✉ Országház utca 2
☎ 1 356 0851 🕐 Closed Sun.
Ⓜ Moszkva tér, then Várbusz (Castle Bus) AX, DC, MC, VI

Gundel $$$

Traditional Hungarian meals are served in this 100-year-old restaurant in City Park. The owner, George Lang, also owns the Café des Artistes in New York.

➕ 259 D4 ✉ Állatkerti út 2
☎ 1 468 4040 Ⓜ Hősök tere
AX, DC, MC, VI

Mirror $$

The grand restaurant in the impressive, early 20th-century Hotel Astoria serves first-class Hungarian and international dishes and good wines. A pianist entertains evening diners, and there's also an atmospheric café.
➕ 258 C2 ✉ Kossuth Lajos utca 19–21 ☎ 1 889 6022 Ⓜ Astoria AX, DC, MC, VI

Művész Kávéház $

This coffeehouse, opposite the Opera House, has retained the ambience of Budapest's golden era of café society.
➕ 258 C3 ✉ Andrássy út 29 ☎ 1 352 1337 Ⓜ Opera No credit cards

Panorama $$

In the art nouveau Danubius Hotel Gellért, this well-known restaurant, over a thermal spring at the foot of Gellért Hill, has fine river views. Pike, perch and veal are specialties. A gypsy band entertains in the evenings.
➕ 258 C1 ✉ Gellért tér 1 ☎ 1 889 5500 🕐 Closed Mon. and Sun. dinner 🚌 Trams 18, 19, 47, 49 AX, DC, MC, VI

Price guide: (double room with breakfast for two people)
$ under €100
$$ €100–€180
$$$ over €180

The Clarence $$$

This is an individual and tasteful hotel owned by Bono and The Edge, of Irish rock group U2. The two-bedroom penthouse is superb. There is a good restaurant.
➕ 274 B3 ✉ 6–8 Wellington Quay
☎ 01 407 0800 🚌 Most cross-city buses AX, DC, MC, VI

Harding Hotel $

A stone's throw from Temple Bar and opposite Christ Church Cathedral, this small, friendly hotel offers roomy en-suite bedrooms with modern furnishings. The downstairs bar/restaurant hosts live music on some evenings.
➕ 274 A3 ✉ Copper Alley, Fishamble Street ☎ 01 679 6500
🚌 49, 50, 56A, 123 MC, VI

KEY TO SYMBOLS

🔶 map page number and coordinates
✉ address
☎ telephone number
⊘ days/times closed
Ⓜ nearest subway station
🚌 nearest bus/trolley bus/ tram/funicular route
⛴ ferry
$$$ expensive
$$ moderate
$ inexpensive
AX American Express
DC Diners Club
MC MasterCard
VI VISA

The Schoolhouse Hotel $$–$$$

This former schoolhouse has been converted into a comfortable hotel with spacious rooms in a leafy part of town, and with free parking. There's also a restaurant and a pub on-site.

🔶 Off map at 274 C2 ✉ 2–8 Northumberland Avenue ☎ 01 667 5014 Ⓜ DART Pearse Street Station 🚌 25, 25A, 26, 49X, 50X MC, VI

The Shelbourne $$$

This elegant Dublin institution saw a major renovation in 2007, restoring much of its former glory while maintaining the highest of standards. Bedrooms are first-class, some with views over St. Stephen's Green, and facilities include a spa, leisure suite, fine dining and the legendary afternoon tea.

🔶 274 C2 ✉ 27 St. Stephen's Green ☎ 01 633 4500 Ⓜ DART Pearse Station; LUAS St. Stephen's Green 🚌 10, 11, 11A, 15A, 25X, 32X, 46X AX, DC, MC, VI

Waterloo Lodge $–$$

Set back from the road, with parking at the front, this Georgian town house provides quality bed-and-breakfast accommodations at a reasonable price. Rooms are spacious and contemporary, and the hearty breakfasts will set you up for a day's sightseeing.

🔶 274 off the map at C1 ✉ 3 Waterloo Road ☎ 01 668 5380 Ⓜ DART Lansdowne Road; LUAS St. Stephen's Green MC, VI

DUBLIN RESTAURANTS

Price guide: (dinner per person, excluding drinks)
$ €15–€30
$$ €30–€45
$$$ over €45

Chapter One $$$

This literary-themed restaurant located in the Dublin Writers Museum has French cuisine with an Irish influence. Just the place to discuss Shaw over salmon or Joyce over venison.

🔶 274 B4 ✉ 18–19 Parnell Square ☎ 01 873 2266 ⊘ Closed Sun.–Mon. and Sat. lunch Ⓜ DART Connolly Station 🚌 10, 11, 13, 16, 19 AX, DC, MC, VI

Cornucopia $$

This good-value restaurant serves imaginative vegetarian food.

🔶 274 B3 ✉ 19 Wicklow Street ☎ 01 677 7583 Ⓜ LUAS St. Stephen's Green 🚌 46A and other cross-city buses MC, VI

Gallagher's Boxty House $$

This is just the place to sample authentic Irish cuisine, from traditional Irish potato boxty pancake and Irish stew to Baileys cheesecake.

🔶 274 B3 ✉ 20–21 Temple Bar ☎ 01 677 2762 🚌 78, 79, 90, 92, 15X, 49X, 50X, 58X, 65X MC, VI

Restaurant Patrick Guilbaud $$$

This highly regarded restaurant has a reputation for outstanding modern classic cuisine. It's superbly understated, stylish and very expensive. It also contains a wonderful collection of Irish art.

🔶 274 C2 ✉ Merrion Hotel, 21 Upper Merrion Street ☎ 01 676 4192 ⊘ Closed Sun. and Mon. Ⓜ DART Pearse Station 🚌 7, 7A AX, DC, MC, VI

ROME HOTELS

Price guide: (double room with breakfast for two people)
$ under €125
$$ €125–€225
$$$ over €225

66 Imperial Inn $–$$

This central bed-and-breakfast, near the Roma Opera theater, was completely renovated in 2011, and transformed into a delightful Maison de Charme. Its five bedrooms are all decorated in a quirky, colorful style and facilities include Jacuzzi showers and plasma TVs.

🔶 293 D3 ✉ Via del Viminale 66 ☎ 06 4825 648 or 3388 531264 (cell) Ⓜ Termini station MC, VI

Campo de Fiori $$–$$$

You'll find comfortable rooms, renovated in 2006, and a roof garden at this pretty and moderately priced hotel near one of Rome's liveliest squares.

🔶 292 C2 ✉ Via del Biscione 6 ☎ 06 6880 6865 🚌 40, 46, 62, 64, 116, 190, 571, 916 AX, DC, VI

Casa Howard $$

This stylish boutique hotel is split into two houses, offerig elegantly furnished rooms, opulent with silky fabrics, fresh flowers and a Turkish bath. Both establishments, the work

---

Water in Greece

It's important not to waste water in Greece, especially on the islands, where it often has to be shipped in by tankers. Although Athens' tap water is drinkable, bottled water is cheap and tastes better. Greeks are water connoisseurs, discussing the flavor and mineral properties of favorite spring varieties. Glasses of water are served alongside every drink you order in cafés: Drink it, or pour it in your ouzo and watch the clear spirit turn milky white. Since it's often hot and most places are not air-conditioned, it's important to drink plenty of water.

of interior designer Tommaso Ziffer, are near the Spanish Steps. The good-value room rates for such luxurious living are hard to beat in Rome. Breakfast costs extra.
🔢 292 C3 ✉ Via Capo le Case 18 ☎ 06 6992 4555 🚇 Spagna MC, VI

Hotel de Russie $$$
A glorious, luxurious establishment, very close to Piazza del Popolo, distinguished by its chic design. The rooms and suites are stylish, bright and airy and most have views of the delightful gardens. Dining alfresco in the highly acclaimed Jardin de Russie is a great delight.
🔢 292 C4 ✉ Via del Babuino 9 ☎ 06 328 881 🚇 Flamino AX, DC, MC, VI

Navona $–$$
This comfortable, simple and friendly hotel is a just few minutes' stroll from the delightful Piazza Navona. Be sure to make reservations ahead of time.
🔢 292 C2 ✉ Via dei Sediari 8 ☎ 06 6830 1252 🚌 30, 70, 81, 87, 116, 130, 186, 492 AX, VI

Westin Excelsior $$$
A stay at this world-class luxury hotel, with its high standard of service and elegance, is among Rome's most sybaritic experiences.
🔢 292 D3 ✉ Via Vittorio Veneto 125 ☎ 06 47081 🚇 Barberini 🚌 52, 53, 95 AX, DC, MC, VI

ROME RESTAURANTS
Price guide: (dinner per person, excluding drinks)
$ under €25
$$ €25–€40
$$$ over €40

Da Baffetto $$
For a quintessential Roman experience and the best pizza in town, stand in line to get a table at this tiny pizzeria. Great for partygoers, it stays open until 1 a.m.
🔢 292 B3/C3 ✉ Via del Governo Vecchio 114 ☎ 06 686 1617 🚌 30, 70, 81, 87, 116, 130, 186, 492, 628 No credit cards

Checchino dal 1887 $$$
This long-established restaurant specializes in the traditional Roman dishes of tripe, brains and offal. Reservations are essential.
🔢 292 C1 ✉ Via Monte Testaccio 30 ☎ 06 574 3816 or 06 5474 6318

🕐 Closed Sun.–Mon., Aug. and Dec. 25 🚌 719 AX, DC, MC, VI

Life $$
A very popular contemporary eatery combines restaurant/pizzeria/wine bar. Come for a formal or casual meal or a glass or two of local wine.
🔢 292 C3 ✉ Via delle Vite ☎ 06 6938 0948 🚌 All routes down Via del Corso MC, VI

Da Lucia $
A tiny, typical Trastevere trattoria, Da Lucia has a friendly family atmosphere and great pasta.
🔢 292 B2 ✉ Vicolo del Mattonato 2b ☎ 06 580 3601 🕐 Closed Mon. and 2 weeks in Aug. 🚌 125 No credit cards

Papà Giovanni $$$
Reservations are advised to enjoy this popular restaurant's light and innovative cooking and excellent wine list.
🔢 292 C2 ✉ Via dei Sediari 4 ☎ 06 686 5308 🕐 Closed Sun and Aug. 🚌 30, 70, 81, 87, 116, 130, 186, 492, 628 AX, MC, VI

Da Paris $$–$$$
You can eat outside in summer at this popular Trastevere restaurant serving fine pasta and fish dishes.
🔢 292 B2 ✉ Piazza San Calisto 7a ☎ 06 581 5378 🕐 Closed Sun. evening, Mon. and 3 weeks in Aug. 🚌 790, H AX, DC, MC, VI

FLORENCE HOTELS
Price guide: (double room with breakfast for two people)
$ under €150
$$ €150–€250
$$$ over €250

Brunelleschi $$–$$$
Reserve ahead to stay in this comfortable hotel, with tastefully decorated rooms, situated around a medieval tower in the heart of Florence.
🔢 302 C3 ✉ Piazza Santa Elisabetta 3 ☎ 055 27370 🚶 In the pedestrian zone. C2, C3 AX, DC, MC, VI

Casci $
This excellent mid-range hotel is just two minutes from the Duomo. The charming owners keep clean, well-appointed rooms.
🔢 302 B4 ✉ Via Cavour 13 ☎ 055 211 686 🚌 10,11, 25, 31, 82, C1 AX, DC, MC, VI

481

Firenze $–$$
This good budget choice, located close to the center of Florence, is popular with younger travelers.
🔢 303 D2–D3 ✉ Piazza dei Donati 4 ☎ 055 214 203 🚶 In the pedestrian zone. C1, C2 DC, VI

Monna Lisa $$
Housed in a 15th-century palace, this hotel has grand public rooms and a tranquil garden; be sure to request a quiet bedroom.
🔢 303 E3 ✉ Borgo Pinti 27 ☎ 055 247 9751 🚌 6, 14, 23, 71 AX, DC, MC, VI

Relais Santa Croce $$$
Part of the luxury Baglioni group, this elegant small hotel in the ehart of Florence blends tradition with cutting-edge design. Opulent furnishings, frescoed ceilings, Murano chandeliers and marbled walls feature in the rooms. Next door, belonging to the hotel, is Florence's only 3-Michelin-starred restaurant, the Enoteca Pinchiorri.
🔢 303 E2 ✉ Via Ghibellina 87 ☎ 055 234 2230 🚌 14, 23, C1, C2, C3 AX, DC, MC, VI

FLORENCE RESTAURANTS
Price guide: (dinner per person, excluding drinks)
$ under €25
$$ €25–€35
$$$ over €35

Alle Murate $$$
The charismatic owner Umberto Montana has moved his restaurant to this historic palazzo, formerly belonging to the Judges and Notaries Guild, where there are fine frescoes to admire. Admirable, too, is the contemporary regional cuisine, including fine classic dishes such as *bistecca alla Fiorentina* (Florentine T-bone steak) – or treat yourself to the tasting menu.
🔢 303 D2 ✉ Via del Proconsolo 16r ☎ 055 240 618 🕐 Closed Mon. and lunchtimes 🚌 14, 23, C1, C3 AX, DC, MC, VI

Cantinetta Antinori $$$
Enjoy Tuscan food with superb wine within the 15th-century Palazzo Antinori, which belongs to this great wine-producing family. Dress in appropriate attire.
🔢 302 B3 ✉ Piazza Antinori 3r ☎ 055 292 234 🕐 Closed Sat.–Sun. 🚌 6, 22, C1 AX, DC, MC, VI

Dublin, Rome, Florence

KEY TO SYMBOLS

⊞ map page number and coordinates
⊠ address
☎ telephone number
Ⓓ days/times closed
Ⓜ nearest subway station
🚌 nearest bus/trolley bus/ tram/funicular route
⛴ ferry
$$$ expensive
$$ moderate
$ inexpensive
AX American Express
DC Diners Club
MC MasterCard
VI VISA

Il Carmine $$

This family-run restaurant serves good traditional Tuscan food in a friendly atmosphere.

⊞ 302 A2 ⊠ Piazza del Carmine 18r ☎ 055 218 601 Ⓓ Closed Sun. 🚌 6, D AX, DC, VI

Il Cibrèo $$$

This legendary restaurant run by owner/chef Fabio Picchi is among Florence's best. Traditional Tuscan specialties are served, including the Florentine favorite *trippa* (tripe), which if never tempting before could convert you here. There is no grilled meat or pasta, but the culinary creations are delicious and inventive. The attentive staff is multilingual.

⊞ 303 E2 ⊠ Via A. del Verrocchio 8r ☎ 055 2341 1000 Ⓓ Closed Sun.–Mon., Dec. 31–Jan. 6 and Aug. 🚌 6, 14, 19, 23 AX, DC, MC, VI

Osteria de' Benci $

A genuine Florentine osteria. Start with *crostini* (Tuscan *bruschetta* – toasted bread served with spreads, cheeses and cold meats), then choose from a daily menu.

⊞ 303 D2 ⊠ Via dei Benci 13r ☎ 055 234 4923 Ⓓ Closed Sun. 🚌 23, 71, C3 AX, DC, VI

Ponte Vecchio $$$

Head to this restaurant for some local cooking; it's popular with tourists, but is none the worse for that.

⊞ 302 C2 ⊠ Lungarno Archibusieri 8r ☎ 055 292 289 🚌 In the pedestrian zone AX, DC, MC, VI

NAPLES HOTELS

Price guide: (double room with breakfast for two people)
$ under €125
$$ €125–€225
$$$ over €225

Britannique $

This quietly situated and comfortable hotel has a secluded garden and lovely views over the Bay of Naples.

⊞ 309 A2 ⊠ Corso Vittorio Emanuele 133 ☎ 081 761 4145 🚌 V1 AX, DC, MC, VI

Canada $

You'll have to reserve well in advance to get one of the sea-view rooms at this small and friendly hotel, near the harbor at Mergellina.

⊞ 309 off the map ⊠ Via Mergellina 43 ☎ 081 680 952 🚌 R3 AX, DC

Excelsior $$–$$$

A grand hotel, in the elegant Chiaia district; where rooms have period furnishings and views of Capri.

⊞ 309 A1 ⊠ Via Partenope 48 ☎ 081 764 0111 🚌 R3 AX, DC, VI

Grand Hotel Santa Lucia $$

This elegant and prestigious waterfront hotel near the Castel dell'Ovo has spacious and well-furnished rooms.

⊞ 309 A1 ⊠ Via Partenope 46 ☎ 081 764 0666 🚌 R3 AX, DC, MC, VI

Renaissance Naples Hotel Mediterraneo $$$

This large, modern hotel is conveniently located near the waterfront, and has good facilities and a lovely rooftop terrace.

⊞ 309 B3 ⊠ Via Nuova Ponte di Tappia 25 ☎ 081 797 0001 🚌 R2, R3 AX, DC, VI

NAPLES RESTAURANTS

Price guide: (dinner per person, excluding drinks)
$ under €20
$$ €20–€35
$$$ over €35

Al 53 $$

Naples' oldest restaurant, complete with 17th-century furnishings and original mosaic floor, serves great appetizers, seafood pasta and delicious Neapolitan desserts.

⊞ 309 B3 ⊠ Piazza Dante 53 ☎ 081 549 9372 🚌 R1, 24 DC, MC, VI

Amici Miei $$

The elegant, friendly Amici Miei restaurant serves excellent appetizers, risotto and pasta dishes.

⊞ 309 A2 ⊠ Via Monte di Dio 78 ☎ 081 764 6063 Ⓓ Closed Sun. dinner and Mon. 🚌 R1, R3 AX, DC, VI

La Cantinella $$$

This seafront restaurant specializes in creative fish cooking, which you can enjoy on the terrace. The wine list is outstanding.

⊞ 309 B1 ⊠ Via Cuma 42 ☎ 081 764 8684 Ⓓ Closed Sun. (except Nov.–May) and part of Aug. 🚌 R3 AX, DC, MC, VI

Trattoria Medina $$

This cheerful restaurant, packed with locals, serves authentic Neapolitan

dishes, seafood and pizzas accompanied by live music.
➕ 309 B2 ✉ Via Medina 32 ☎ 081 551 5233 🚌 R3 AX, DC, MC, VI

Trianon $
Naples' finest and most popular pizzeria, offering numerous combinations, has been in business for more than 70 years.
➕ 309 C4 ✉ Via P. Colletta 46 ☎ 081 553 9426 🕐 Closed Sun. lunch 🚌 R2, 14, 110 No credit cards

Price guide: (double room with breakfast for two people)
$ under €150
$$ €150–€250
$$$ over €250

Canada $–$$
This is one of the best budget bets in Venice, near the Rialto. You will need to reserve in advance.
➕ 313 D3 ✉ Campo San Lio, Castello 5659 ☎ 041 522 9912 🚤 1, 2 AX, DC, MC, VI

Cipriani $$$
This is one of the most famous luxury hotels in the world, with every comfort and impeccable service. It is located amid beautiful gardens on the Giudecca – a chain of islets just a short boat ride from central Venice.
➕ 314 off the map ✉ Giudecca 10 ☎ 041 520 7744 🕐 Closed Nov.–Mar. 🚤 2, or use hotel's private launch AX, DC, MC, VI

Danieli $$$
Widely considered to be Venice's finest hotel, the Danieli has style, elegance and class. Book a room in the older part for the full experience.
➕ 314 C2 ✉ Riva degli Schiavoni, Castello 4196 ☎ 041 522 6480 🚤 1 AX, DC, MC, VI

Hotel Agli Alboretti $$
Book well in advance to stay at this pleasant hotel, conveniently situated on a tree-lined street between the Accademia and the Záttere.
➕ 315 B2 ✉ Rio Terrà Antonio Foscarini, Dorsoduro 884 ☎ 041 523 0058 🚤 1, 2 AX, DC, MC, VI

Pensione Seguso $–$$
This is a wonderfully atmospheric, old-fashioned *pension* overlooking the Giudecca Canal. Rooms feature painted ceilings.
➕ 324 off map ✉ Fondamenta ai

Gesuati, Dorsoduro 779 ☎ 041 528 6858 🚤 1, 2, 51, 61 AX, DC, VI

San Clemente Palace $$$
This hotel is set on its own island close to St. Mark's, It is an oasis of tranquility, recalling its monastic heritage, with cloisters and flower-filled courtyards. The stylish, rooms are spacious and elegantly furnished.
➕ 314 off C1 ✉ Isola di San Clemente ☎ 041 244 5001 🚤 Complimentary private shuttle boat, 10 to 15 minutes to San Marco AX, DC, MC, VI

Price guide: (dinner per person, excluding drinks)
$ under €25
$$ €25–€45
$$$ over €45

Alla Madonna $$
This big, noisy fish restaurant, one of the most traditional in Venice, is hugely popular.
➕ 314 C3 ✉ Calle della Madonna, San Polo 594 ☎ 041 522 3824 🕐 Closed Wed., Jan. and 2 weeks in Aug. 🚤 1, 2, N AX, MC, VI

Da Franz $$$
Situated near the Giardini Pubblici, this excellent fish and seafood restaurant has a summer terrace for enjoyable outdoor dining.
➕ 314 off the map ✉ Fondamenta San Giuseppe, Castello 745 ☎ 041 522 0861 🕐 Closed Tue. in winter 🚤 1, 41, 42, 51. 52, 61, N AX, DC, MC, VI

Dona Onesta $
The decor is simple and the Venetian dishes straightforward yet of excellent quality at this friendly local restaurant; reservations are advised.
➕ 314 B2 ✉ Calle della Dona Onesta, Dorsoduro 3922 ☎ 041 710 586 🕐 Closed Sun. 🚤 1, 2 AX, VI

La Mascareta $
A traditional and long-established wine bar and restaurant for snacks, seafood and light meals.
➕ 314 D3 ✉ Calle Lunga Santa Maria Formosa, Castello 5183 ☎ 041 523 0744 🕐 Closed Wed. 🚤 1, 41, 42, 51, 52 AX, MC, VI

Taverna San Trovaso $$
This lively neighborhood restaurant and pizzeria is always busy serving

Venetian families and tourists. The dishes are not expensive for the area.
➕ 314 B2 ✉ Fondamenta Priuli, Dorsoduro 1016 ☎ 041 520 3703 🕐 Closed Mon. 🚤 1 AX, DC, MC, VI

Price guide: (double room with breakfast for two people)
$ under €90
$$ €90–€150
$$$ over €150

Français $$
Ideal for strolling to the Old Town, this hotel is at the heart of the city and has its own restaurant, with a terrace on the central square.
➕ 329 B3 ✉ 14 place d'Armes ☎ 47 45 34 🚌 All city-center buses AX, DC, MC, VI

Golden Tulip Central Molitor $$
This modernized business and tourist hotel is located between tourist attractions and the railway station.
➕ 329 B2 ✉ 28 avenue de la Liberté ☎ 48 99 11 🚌 9 AX, DC, MC, VI

Grand Hôtel Cravat $$$
Place d'Armes is a few steps from this stylish hotel overlooking the Pétrusse valley. It is part of the well-known restaurant association Luxembourg à la Carte, and its own restaurant Le Normandy offers the best French and traditional Luxembourg cuisine.
➕ 329 B3 ✉ 29 boulevard F. D. Roosevelt ☎ 22 19 75 🚌 All city-center buses AX, DC, MC, VI

Italia $–$$
Just off the place de Paris, this pleasant hotel, in the heart of the business center, is conveniently close to the city center. Its good restaurant specializes in Italian cuisine.
➕ 329 B2 ✉ 15–17 rue d'Anvers ☎ 48 66 26-1 🚌 9 AX, DC, MC, VI

Price guide: (dinner per person, excluding drinks)
$ under €20
$$ €20–€40
$$$ over €40

Les Caves Gourmandes $$–$$$
This popular and atmospheric place in the Îlot Gastronomique complex is within part of the Old Town wall. The French cuisine features breast of

KEY TO SYMBOLS

⊞ map page number and coordinates
✉ address
☎ telephone number
⊘ days/times closed
Ⓜ nearest subway station
🚍 nearest bus/trolley bus/tram/funicular route
⛴ ferry
$$$ expensive
$$ moderate
$ inexpensive
AX American Express
DC Diners Club
MC MasterCard
VI VISA

duck with figs and *crème brûlée* for dessert.
⊞ 329 C3 ✉ Îlot Gastronomique, 32 rue de l'Eau ☎ 46 11 24
⊘ Closed Sat. lunch and Sun.
🚍 All buses AX, MC, VI

La Lorraine $$$

Located on place d'Armes, this bright, attractive restaurant offers French cuisine with excellent fish dishes. You can choose your lobster from a tank by the door.
⊞ 329 B3 ✉ 7 place d'Armes
☎ 47 14 36 🚍 All city-center buses AX, DC, MC, VI

Maison des Brasseurs $$–$$$

This popular restaurant on Grand-Rue serves classic country cooking such as *Judd mat Gaardebounen* (roast and smoked pork). There also are vegetarian dishes on the menu.
⊞ 329 B3 ✉ 48 Grand-Rue ☎ 47 13 71 ⊘ Closed Sun. and public holidays 🚍 All city-center buses DC, MC, VI

Speltz $$$

This beautifully appointed restaurant has a pleasant outdoor eating area and an excellent wine menu to accompany the top-quality French and Luxembourg cuisine. The menu might include turbot or scorpion fish. There is a good cheese selection.
⊞ 329 B3 ✉ 8 rue Chimay
☎ 47 49 50 ⊘ Closed Sun., Mon., 1 week at Easter, 2 weeks in early Aug. and 1 week at Christmas 🚍 All city-center buses AX, DC, MC, VI

AMSTERDAM HOTELS

Price guide: (double room with breakfast for two people)
$ €75–€150
$$ €150–€300
$$$ over €300

Ambassade Hotel $$

On the splendid Herengracht, the most elegant canal, this beautifully furnished hotel offers comfortable rooms and a good breakfast.
⊞ 342 B2 ✉ Herengracht 341
☎ 020 555 0222 🚍 Trams 1, 2, 5 AX, DC, MC, VI

Hotel de L'Europe $$$

The private boat landing at this expensive luxury hotel on the Amstel river says it all. It has a fine Victorian exterior, and inside it has been

renovated to offer every modern amenity. The finest *haute cuisine* and wine list will be found at the hotel's Bord d'Eau restaurant.
⊞ 342 C2 ✉ Nieuwe Doelenstraat 2–8 ☎ 020 531 1777 🚍 Trams 4, 9, 14, 16, 24, 25 AX, MC, VI

Nova Hotel $$

This family-run hotel has a central location but is sheltered from street noise. Spotless en-suite rooms and friendly, efficient service make this a good budget choice.
⊞ 342 C3 ✉ Nieuwezijds Voorburgwal 276 ☎ 020 623 0066 🚍 Trams 1, 2, 5 AX, DC, MC, VI

Hotel Pulitzer $$$

This stylish hotel recaptures some of the spirit of old Amsterdam within its complex of 25 17th-century canal houses on Prinsengracht. Relax in the art nouveau Garden Room or the 17th-century Saxenburg Room.
⊞ 342 B2 ✉ Prinsengracht 315–331 ☎ 020 523 5235
🚍 Trams 6, 13, 14, 17 AX, MC, VI

Singel Hotel $

A short walk from Centraal Station along the Singel Canal, this 32-room hotel occupies three converted canalside houses. It has an historic feel but modern amenities.
⊞ 342 C2 ✉ Singel 13–17
☎ 020 626 3108 Ⓜ Amsterdam Centraal 🚍 Trams 1, 2, 5, 13 17 AX, DC, MC, VI

AMSTERDAM RESTAURANTS

Price guide: (dinner per person, excluding drinks)
$ €10–€20
$$ €20–€30
$$$ over €30

Christophe $$$

For more than 20 years, Christophe's has retained its reputation as one of the best eating experiences in the city, its inventive French/Mediterranean cuisine served in a stylish yet relaxed atmosphere.
⊞ 342 B3 ✉ Leliegracht 46
☎ 020 625 0807 ⊘ Closed Mon. and lunch Tue.–Sat. 🚍 13, 14, 17 AX, DC, MC, VI

In de Waag $–$$

Come to this friendly restaurant for late-night Continental cuisine, when it is lit by hundreds of candles. The generous three-course lunch and early evening menu offer good value.

Plan Ahead for Venice

To enjoy a stress-free visit in Venice it is absolutely necessary to make hotel reservations ahead of time. Reservations for June to September should be made during the previous fall, as should those for the two weeks in February in which Carnival falls (although you may be able to get something closer to the time of your visit if you hunt around). Three months ahead should be enough time for other months. If you would like to eat at a specific restaurant it's also advisable to make reservations; your hotel concierge will be happy to call and set them up.

🚫 342 C3 ✉ Nieuwmarkt 4
☎ 020 422 7772 🚇 Nieuwmarkt
AX, DC, MC, VI

New Dorrius $$$

In the Crowne Plaza Amsterdam City Centre, this is the place for a taste of Dutch cuisine with a dash of French flair. Try the oysters and eel or salted cod and a light cheese soufflé.
🚫 342 C3 ✉ Nieuwendijk 60 Voorburgwal 5 ☎ 020 420 2224
🚇 Centraal Station 🚋 Tram 1, 2, 5, 13, 17 AX, DC, MC, VI

De Silveren Spiegel $$$

Located in a restored, redbrick building dating from 1614, this restaurant has a varied menu, from Dutch cuisine to fish.
🚫 342 C4 ✉ Kattengat 4–6 ☎ 020 624 6589 🕐 Closed lunch and Sun.
🚇 Centraal Station 🚋 Tram 1, 2, 5, 6, 11, 13, 17 AX, DC, MC, VI

Toscanini $$

This stylish Jordaan district restaurant features excellent Italian food. Homemade *biscotti* is a particular specialty.
🚫 342 B4 ✉ Lindengracht 75
☎ 020 623 2813 🕐 Closed lunch and Sun. 🚋 Tram 3, 10 AX, DC, MC, VI

Price guide: (double room with breakfast for two people)
$ €75–€150
$$ €150–€300
$$$ over €300

Best Western Delft Museumhotel and Residence $$

While in Delft, spend at least one night in this tastefully furnished hotel overlooking a tranquil canal.
🚫 350 off the map ✉ Oude Delft 189 ☎ 015 215 3070 🚇 Delft Centraal station 🚋 Tram 1 AX, DC, MC, VI

Carlton Ambassador Hotel $$–$$$

This luxury hotel in an elegant neighborhood is within easy walking distance of the city center.
🚫 350 B2 ✉ Sophialaan 2
☎ 070 363 0363 🚋 4, 5, 22; tram 10 AX, DC, MC, VI

Hotel Mozaic $$

This renovated hotel is a short distance from the city center but it is

a good option as there are good tram connections. A good budget choice.
🚫 350 B2 ✉ Laan Copes van Cattenburch 38 ☎ 070 352 2335
🚋 Trams 1, 9 AX, DC, MC, VI

Mercure Hotel Den Haag Central $–$$

This modern hotel is located near the railroad station and city center. It also has a restaurant.
🚫 350 C1 ✉ Spui 180 ☎ 070 363 6700 🚋 4, 18, 22, 25; trams 1, 9, 15, 16 AX, DC, MC, VI

Steigenberger Kurhaus Hotel $$–$$$

If you are in Scheveningen and want a hotel with a sun lounge and terrace overlooking the beach, consider this Old European-style hotel, built in the 1880s. Some rooms have a balcony.
🚫 350 A4 ✉ Gevers Deynootplein 30, Scheveningen ☎ 070 416 2636
🚋 14, 22, 23; trams 1, 9 AX, DC, MC, VI

Price guide: (dinner per person, excluding drinks)
$ €10–€20
$$ €20–€30
$$$ over €30

Bodega De Posthoorn $$

This restaurant is housed in an attractive building in the stylish Lange Voorhout. Reserve ahead.
🚫 350 C2 ✉ Lange Voorhout 39a
☎ 070 360 4906 🚋 4; trams 1, 9, 16 AX, VI

Le Café Hathor $$

Set beside a quiet stretch of canal, near the center, this well-established bar and restaurant is not fancy, but serves modern Dutch-style food.
🚫 350 C2 ✉ Maliestraat 22 ☎ 070 346 40 81 🕐 Closed Sun. 🚋 Trams 9, 10, 16, 17 No credit cards

It Rains Fishes $$$

High-quality, expensive seafood is served in this intimate restaurant. Reservations are advised.
🚫 350 B2 ✉ Noordeinde 123
☎ 070 365 2598 🕐 Closed Sat. lunch and Sun. 🚋 Trams 7, 8 AX, DC, MC, VI

Les Ombrelles $$

In attractive, historic Denneweg, this restaurant, with a terrace for summer, serves good seafood dishes.
🚫 350 C2 ✉ Hooistraat 4a ☎ 070

365 8789 🕐 Closed Sat. and Sun. lunch 🚋 Tram 2, 6, 8, 16 AX, DC, MC, VI

Stadsherberg 't Goude Hooft $$$

Rebuilt in the 17th century, this popular inn serves good food.
🚫 350 B1 ✉ Dagelijkse Groenmarkt 13 ☎ 070 346 9713 🚋 Trams 1, 2, 3, 6, 10, 17 AX, MC, VI

Price guide: (double room with breakfast for two people)
$ Kr800–Kr1,000
$$ Kr1,000–Kr1,400
$$$ over Kr1,400

Best Western Anker Hotel $$–$$$

Comfortable 3-star hotel, a few minutes' walk from Oslo Central Station and Karl Johan gate.
🚫 365 C2 ✉ Storgata 55 ☎ 22 99 75 00 🚇 Jernbanetorget 🚋 30, 31, 32; trams 12, 13 AX, DC, MC, VI

Hotel Continental $$$

Located between the Royal Palace and City Hall, this is a top-quality, inexpensive hotel. A member of "The Leading Hotels of the World," with four good restaurants and cafés.
🚫 365 B1 ✉ Stortingsgaten 24–26
☎ 22 82 40 00 🚇 Nationaltheatret
🚋 Trams 13, 19 AX, DC, MC, VI

First Hotel Grims Grenka $$–$$$

Norway's most fashionable hotel, boasting deluxe rooms and suites, is in the center of Oslo.
🚫 365 B1 ✉ Kongens gate 5 ☎ 23 10 72 00 🚇 Stortinget 🚋 Trams 12 AX, DC, MC, VI

Grand Hotel $$$

This 19th-century hotel is one of Oslo's most prestigious places to stay with well-appointed rooms, good restaurants, bars and an inviting rooftop sauna and pool.
🚫 365 B1 ✉ Karl Johans gate 31
☎ 23 21 20 00 🚇 Stortinget
🚋 Trams 11, 17, 18 AX, DC, MC, VI

Thon Hotel Bristol $$$

This elegant luxury hotel in central Oslo has superb furnishings and decorations, bars and restaurants.
🚫 365 B2 ✉ Kristian IV's gate 7
☎ 22 82 60 00 🚇 Stortinget 🚋 30, 31, 32, 37; trams 10, 11, 12, 17, 18 AX, DC, MC, VI

KEY TO SYMBOLS

- ✚ map page number and coordinates
- ✉ address
- ☎ telephone number
- ⏰ days/times closed
- Ⓜ nearest subway station
- 🚌 nearest bus/trolley bus/tram/funicular route
- ⛴ ferry
- $$$ expensive
- $$ moderate
- $ inexpensive
- AX American Express
- DC Diners Club
- MC MasterCard
- VI VISA

Weekend Treats

As in other Scandinavian cities, Oslo hotels cater to business people on weekdays. This makes weekday room rates some of the most expensive in Europe. On weekends and during the holiday summer months fewer reservations are made, and hotels often offer discounts. You can stay in a luxury hotel from Friday night through Monday morning for a substantially reduced rate. Outside the height of summer this can also mean that there are few fellow guests, making your weekend stay seem even more exclusive. The high standard of service does not diminish with the price. Reduced rates on weekends and during holiday periods are common in many major European cities – it's always worth asking at the hotel you are interested in.

OSLO RESTAURANTS

Price guide: (dinner per person, excluding drinks)

$	Kr50–Kr80
$$	Kr80–Kr200
$$$	over Kr200

Café Christiania $$$

Traditional Norwegian food is served in museumlike surroundings. In summer you can dine on the terrace overlooking the Parliament building. Enjoy afternoon tea after noon.
✚ 365 B1 ✉ Nedre Vollgate 19 ☎ 22 01 05 10 ⏰ Closed Sun. year-round, Mon. in Jul. Ⓜ Stortinget 🚌 Trams 11, 18, 19 AX, DC, MC, VI

D/S Louise Restaurant and Bar $$$

Located in the Aker Brygge complex, with views across the harbor to Akershus Castle, this nautically themed restaurant serves traditional and international dishes.
✚ 365 B1 ✉ Stranden 3 ☎ 22 83 00 60 ⏰ Closed Sun., Oct.–Mar. 🚌 21, 54; tram 12 AX, DC, MC, VI

Engebret Café $$

Founded in 1857 by Engebret Christoffersen, this restaurant still maintains a strong tradition. Norwegian and international cuisine, including traditional fish dishes.
✚ 365 B1 ✉ Bankplassen 1 ☎ 22 82 25 25 ⏰ Closed Sat. lunch and Sun. Ⓜ Stortinget 🚌 Tram 12 AX, DC, MC, VI

Grand Café $$$

A great heritage, including visits by Ibsen in his day, makes this restaurant in the Grand Hotel (see page 485) a favorite with locals. Norwegian cuisine, from elk stew to *lutefisk* (marinated dried fish), is available.
✚ 365 B1 ✉ Karl Johans gate 31 ☎ 23 21 20 00 Ⓜ Stortinget 🚌 Trams 11, 17, 18 AX, DC, MC, VI

Restaurant Det Gamle Rådhus $$

In the 17th-century building next to Akershus Castle, this restaurant is billed as Oslo's oldest eating establishment. International cuisine and fish specialties are served. It is very popular so reservations are strongly advised.
✚ 365 B1 ✉ Nedre Slottsgate 1 ☎ 22 42 01 07 ⏰ Closed Sun. and 3 weeks in Jul. Ⓜ Stortinget 🚌 Tram 12 AX, DC, MC, VI

LISBON HOTELS

Price guide: (double room with breakfast for two people)

$	under €125
$$	€125–€200
$$$	over €200

As Janelas Verdes $$–$$$

This small hotel, in an 18th-century town house, offers large and luxurious rooms. Its location, west of the center, is the only real drawback.
✚ 378 off A1 ✉ Rua das Janelas Verdes 47 ☎ 213 968 143 🚌 28, 713, 727, 760; trams 15, 18, 25 AX, DC, MC, VI

Britânia $$–$$$

This friendly, art deco-style hotel, just east of Avenida da Liberdade, was refurbished in the 1990s.
✚ 378 off A5 ✉ Rua Rodrigues Sampaio 17 ☎ 213 155 016 Ⓜ Avenida 🚌 All buses for Avenida Liberdade AX, DC, MC, VI

Duas Nações $

Although only some rooms have private bathrooms, this hotel – in a 19th-century building – is a superb budget choice, located in the heart of the historic Baixa district.
✚ 379 C3 ✉ Rua da Vitória 41 ☎ 213 460 710 Ⓜ Rossio, Baixa-Chiado AX, DC, MC, VI

Four Seasons Ritz $$$

One of Lisbon's most luxurious hotels, with sumptuously decorated large rooms and suites, and exceptional service. Visit the spa for some pampering.
✚ 378 off A5 ✉ Rua Rodrigo da Fonseca 88 ☎ 213 811 400 Ⓜ Marquês de Pombal 🚌 All buses for Marquês de Pombal AX, DC, MC, VI

International Design Hotel $$

Situated on the Rossio and easily recognized by its violet color, this hotel offers design-oriented rooms, some of which are decorated in vibrant hues.
✚ 379 B4 ✉ Rua Betesga 30 ☎ 213 240 990 🚌 All buses for Rossio Ⓜ Rossio AX, DC, MC, VI

LISBON RESTAURANTS

Price guide: (dinner per person, excluding drinks)

$	under €20
$$	€20–€30
$$$	over €30

100 Maneiras $$$

Book in advance to savor 100 Maneiras' innovative 10-course tasting menu with ingredients sourced from the Ribeira market.
🚇 378 A4 ✉ Rua do Teixeira 35
☎ 210 990 475 or 910 307 575
🕐 Closed Mon.–Sat. lunch and Sun.
🚌 758, 790 🚋 Restauradores and Gloria elevator AX, DC, MC, VI

Bocca $$–$$$

Great reviews have made Bocca popular; its crisp interior and sophisticated menu do not disappoint. There are fixed-price two- and three-course lunch menus and four- to five-course tasting menus in the evening.
🚇 379 off A5 ✉ Rua Rodrigo da Fonseca 87D, 1250-190 Lisboa
☎ 213 808 380 🕐 Closed Mon.
🚌 All services to Marquês de Pombal
🚋 Marquês de Pombal AX, DC, MC, VI

O Caseiro $$

Close to the Jerónimos monastery, O Caseiro serves excellent air-cured hams and traditional cheese, grilled fish and roasted meats.
🚇 379 inset ✉ Rua de Belém 35
☎ 213 638 803 🕐 Closed Sun.
🚋 Train: Belém 🚌 28, 714, 727, 729, 751, tram 15 AX, DC, MC, VI

Gambrinus $$$

There's an old-fashioned ambience at this deluxe, formal restaurant, where fish and seafood are the specialties. Reservations advised.
🚇 378 B5 ✉ Rua das Portas de Santo Antão 23 ☎ 213 421 466
🚋 Rossio AX, MC, VI

Tágide $$$

Great views, charming atmosphere and excellent food make this one of Lisbon's classiest restaurants.
🚇 379 B2 ✉ Largo da Academia Nacional de Belas Artes 18–20
☎ 213 404 010 🕐 Closed Sun. and Mon. 🚋 Baixa-Chiado 🚌 758, 790; tram 28 AX, DC, MC, VI

Terra $$

This mostly vegetarian and vegan restaurant is an excellent addition to Lisbon's culinary scene, with a creative menu, a traditional tiled dining room and a garden for alfresco meals.
🚇 379 off A5 ✉ Rua da Palmeira 15
☎ 707 108 108 🕐 Closed Mon.
🚌 92, 758, 773, 790 AX, DC, MC, VI

PORTO HOTELS

Price guide: (double room with breakfast for two people)
$ under €100
$$ €100–€175
$$$ over €175

Boavista $

This peaceful, quiet hotel in the suburb of Foz is very comfortable and has great ocean views.
🚇 387 off the map ✉ Esplanada do Castelo 58 ☎ 225 320 020 🚌 500; tram 1 AX, DC, MC, VI

Hotel da Bolsa $

Friendly service and spacious rooms await at this comfortable hotel in the heart of the historic center.
🚇 387 B2 ✉ Rua Ferreira Borges 101 ☎ 222 026 768 🚌 500, 900, 901, 906 AX, DC, MC, VI

Hotel Teatro $–$$

Decorated in a theatrical theme with draped curtains and stage-like spotlights, rooms are well equipped and location central.
🚇 387 C3 ✉ Rua Sá da Bandeira 84
☎ 220 409 620 or 1 800 33746 85 (toll free from U.S.) 🚋 São Bento
🚌 All Avenida dos Aliados services AX, DC, MC, VI

Infante de Sagres $$

Porto's landmark hotel has a pretty terrace and some lovely bedrooms.
🚇 387 B3 ✉ Praça Filipa de Lencastre 62 ☎ 223 398 500
🚌 All buses for Praça da Liberdade
🚋 Aliados AX, DC, MC, VI

Pestana Porto $$–$$$

In the heart of the Ribeira district, within a UNESCO heritage site, this boutique hotel offers comfortable rooms with river views and friendly staff.
🚇 387 B1 ✉ Praça da Ribeira 1
☎ 223 402 300 🚌 500, 900, 901, 906 AX, DC, MC, VI

PORTO RESTAURANTS

Price guide: (dinner per person, excluding drinks)
$ under €15
$$ €15–€25
$$$ over €25

Abadia $–$$

With huge portions of hearty Portuguese food, Abadia, operating since 1939, has been a local favorite for many years. The food is the real draw here, not the setting.

🚇 387 C3 ✉ Rua do Ateneu Comercial do Porto 22 🕐 Closed Sun.
☎ 222 008 757 🚌 All buses for Praça da Liberdade 🚋 Aliados AX, MC, VI

Boca do Lobo $$$

The restaurant at the Hotel Infante Sagres is one of Porto's best and most elegant, serving Portuguese and international dishes. Specialties are seafood, including salmon (try the roasted loin) and tuna.
🚇 387 B3 ✉ Praça Filipa de Lencastre 62 ☎ 223 398 500
🚌 All buses for Praça da Liberdade
🚋 Aliados AX, DC, MC, VI

Galeria de Paris $$

Once a textile warehouse, the converted Galeria de Paris retains its original character but now offers light *tapas*-style snacks, buffet lunches and full meals.
🚇 387 B3 ✉ Rua Galeria de Paris 56 ☎ 934 210 792 🕐 Closed Sun.
🚌 201, 302 or 501 from Boavista area AX, DC, MC, VI

Mercearia $$–$$$

This traditional restaurant on the riverbank in Old Porto specializes in seafood, soup and *bacalhau*.
🚇 387 B1 ✉ Cais da Ribeira 32–33A
☎ 222 004 389 🕐 Closed Tue., Oct.–Mar. AX, DC, MC, VI

Pedro Lemos $$–$$$

Head to the seafront district of Foz do Douro and this fine-dining restaurant set in a traditional town house. A *tapas* menu and afternoon tea are also available.
🚇 387 off the map ✉ Rua Padre Luis Cabral 974, Fox do Douro
☎ 220 115 986 🕐 Closed Sun. dinner and Mon.–Tue. lunch
🚌 500; tram 1 AX, DC, MC, VI

MADRID HOTELS

Price guide: (double room with breakfast for two people)
$ €50–€100
$$ €100–€150
$$$ over €150

Hospedaje A. Romero $

An affordable, central, family-run guesthouse with well-kept rooms.
🚇 402 B2 ✉ Gran Vía 64, 6th floor
☎ 92 559 76 61 🚋 Gran Vía MC, VI

Hotel de las Letras $$$

An elegant hotel with a fabulous roof terrace, which enjoys extraordinary

KEY TO SYMBOLS

✚	map page number and coordinates
✉	address
☎	telephone number
🕐	days/times closed
Ⓜ	nearest subway station
🚌	nearest bus/trolley bus/tram/funicular route
⛴	ferry
$$$	expensive
$$	moderate
$	inexpensive
AX	American Express
DC	Diners Club
MC	MasterCard
VI	VISA

Eating in Portugal

The Portuguese do not eat at the same hours as their Spanish neighbors, so you won't have to wait until 10 p.m. for dinner. Many people eat dinner as early as 7:30, and restaurants remain open until about 10:30; many close on Sunday evenings and/or Mondays. Breakfast is usually a light meal, and lunch starts around 12:30. The daily menu (*ementa turística*) is an excellent value and normally offers a decent variety. Meals often start with a selection of appetizers, which arrive automatically and are added to your bill if you eat them. Portuguese helpings are big, but often you can ask for a half portion.

---

views and is the perfect place to unwind after a day's sightseeing.
✚ 402 C2 ✉ Gran Via 11 ☎ 91 523 79 80 Ⓜ Gran Vía AX, MC, VI

Hotel Petit Palace Embassy $$

A stylishly modernized 19th-century town house in the upmarket Salamanca district, with bright, modern accommodation. Rooms are all equipped with computers, and they also offer family rooms and rooms adapted for wheelchair users.
✚ 403 D4 ✉ Calle Serrano 46 ☎ 91 431 3060 Ⓜ Serrano AX, MC, VI

Room Mate Alicia $$

This is part of a rapidly expanding chain of cheap-and-chic hotels, and has a fabulous central location right on the Plaza Santa Ana.
✚ 402 C1 ✉ Calle Prado 2 ☎ 91 389 60 95 Ⓜ Sevilla AX, MC, VI

Westin Palace $$$

This grand, century-old hotel, with fitness center, sauna and solarium, is ideally situated within walking distance of Madrid's main attractions. It hosts brunch with opera on Sunday.
✚ 402 D2 ✉ Plaza Cortes 7 ☎ 91 360 8000 Ⓜ Banco de España AX, MC, VI

MADRID RESTAURANTS

Price guide: (dinner per person, excluding drinks)

$	€10–€25
$$	€25–€50
$$$	over €50

El Bodegon $$$

A long-estalished classic, El Bodegon offers a set menu at dinner and an à la carte lunch menu, alongside excellent service.
✚ 402 D4 ✉ Pinar 15 ☎ 91 562 3137 🕐 Closed Sat. lunch, Sun., public holidays and Aug. Ⓜ Gregorio Marañón AX, DC, MC, VI

La Bola $$

This long-established tavern specializes in Madrid *cocido*, stews cooked slowly in traditional pots.
✚ 402 B2 ✉ Bola 5 ☎ 91 547 6930 🕐 Closed Sun. dinner Ⓜ Santo Domingo No credit cards

Le Cabrera $$

This fashionable new gastro-bar is split into two equally glamorous

sections: upstairs serves outstanding *tapas* and *raciones*, while the more intimate downstairs bar is dedicated to divine cocktails. It's located in a handsome palace, which now contains the Casa de América cultural center.
✚ 402 D2 ✉ Paseo de Recoletos 2 ☎ 91 577 59 55 🕐 Closed Sun. and Mon. Ⓜ Colón AX, MC, VI

Casa Patas $$

One of the best flamenco venues in town. Here you can enjoy traditional dishes or *tapas* at the bar. Daily flamenco shows (extra charge).
✚ 402 C1 ✉ Cañizares, 10 ☎ 91 369 0496 🕐 Closed Sun. Ⓜ Antón Martín AX, MC, VI

Mercado de San Miguel $–$$

The century-old, wrought-iron Mercado (Market) de San Miguel has been transformed into the gastronomic hub of the old city. As well as the stalls selling the finest gourmet produce (including oils, hams, cheeses, seafood and conserves), it has several wonderful bars serving fine wines accompanied by all manner of delicious treats. Some stalls may take credit cards.
✚ 402 B2 ✉ Plaza de San Miguel ☎ 91 542 4936 🕐 Open daily 10 a.m. to midnight, until 2 a.m. Fri.–Sun. Ⓜ Sol

BARCELONA HOTELS

Price guide: (double room with breakfast for two people)

$	€60–€120
$$	€120–€180
$$$	over €180

Arts $$$

This 44-story, luxury waterfront hotel, with superb views across the city is still the city's premier address.
✚ 411 A1 ✉ Calle de la Marina 19–21 ☎ 93 221 1000 Ⓜ Ciutadella/Vila Olímpica AX, DC, MC, VI

Hotel Banys Orientals $

This budget boutique hotel enjoys a superb location in the fashionable Born neighborhood.
✚ 411 C1 ✉ Carrer Argenteria 37 ☎ 93 269 84 60 Ⓜ Jaume I AX, MC, VI

Colón $$$

Opposite the cathedral, this hotel combines an old-fashioned and friendly atmosphere with comfort. Some rooms overlook the cathedral.

✚ 411 B1/C1 ✉ Avenida de la Catedral 7 ☎ 93 301 1404 Ⓜ Jaume I AX, MC, VI

Hotel Neri $$$

One of the ciy's finest boutique hotels, hidden away in the Gothic heart of old Barcelona.

✚ 411 B1 ✉ Calle Sant Sever 5 ☎ 93 304 06 55 Ⓜ Liceu AX, MC, VI

The Praktik $$

A cheap-and-chic hostel, just off Passeig de Gràcia, with limited services but elegant interiors. Beds are extra large and there is free WiFi.

✚ 411 C2 ✉ Diputacío, 325 ☎ 93 467 3115 Ⓜ Passeig de Gràcia AX, DC, MC, VI

Café de l'Acadèmia $$

Perfect for a romantic dinner, particularly on the pretty terrace on the lovely square, this restaurant serves some of the best Catalan fare in the city. The cod dishes are tasty.

✚ 411 C2 ✉ Lledó 1, Plaça Sant Just ☎ 93 319 8253 🕙 Closed Sat.–Sun. and 3 weeks in Aug. AX, MC, VI

Kaiku $$

This is one of the best seafood restaurants in the city, although you'd never guess it from the plain exterior. It's most famous for the *arròs del xef*, a paella-style dish made with smoked rice, but this is complemented each day by a range of fabulously fresh seafood. Book a table on the terrace, and enjoy a long languid lunch with sea views.

✚ 411 C1 ✉ Plaça del Mar 1 ☎ 93 221 9082 🕙 Closed dinner and Mon. Ⓜ Barceloneta MC, VI

Onofre $

This bodega, down a side street near the Palau de la Música, offers good wines accompanied by platters of top-quality hams and cheeses.

✚ 411 C2 ✉ Calle Magdalenes 18 (off Calle Comtal) ☎ 93 317 69 37 Ⓜ Urquinaona 🕙 Closed Sun. and Aug. MC, VI

Set Portes $$–$$$

One of Barcelona's best and most historic restaurants serves a wide range of excellent Catalan food and fine wines. It is famous for the quality of its paella.

✚ 411 C1 ✉ Passeig de Isabel II 14 ☎ 93 319 3033 Ⓜ Barceloneta AX, DC, MC, VI

Tapaç 24 $$

The perfect combination of traditional *tapas* and modern cuisine is served here. Open for breakfast through to dinner.

✚ 411 C3 ✉ Diputació, 269 ☎ 93 488 0977 Ⓜ Passeig de Gràcia AX, MC, VI

Hotel Costa Vella $

Enchanting hotel overlooking a beautiful garden on the edge of Santiago de Compostella's old quarter. Bedrooms are comfortable.

✚ 418 B3 ✉ Calle Porta de Pena 17 ☎ 981 56 95 30 MC, VI

Hotel A Quinta da Agua $$

Just outside the city, on the banks of the River Sar, this small and wonderfully luxurious hotel is set amid extensive gardens.

✚ 418 off A2 ✉ Paseo da Amaia 2b, Urbanización Brandia, Vidán ☎ 981 53 46 36 AX, DC, MC, VI

Hostal Alfonso $

For location, comfort and price, it's hard to beat this friendly little *hostal* which is run by a charming couple. The rooms are simple, but immaculately kept, and some have views across the square to the cathedral. Book well in advance – with just six rooms, it fills up quickly.

✚ 418 off A2 ✉ Calle Pombal 40 ☎ 981 585 686 MC, VI

Hostal Reis Católicos $$$

This *parador* is considered by many to be the finest deluxe hotel in Spain. It is magnificently situated in the cathedral square, in a beautiful 15th-century cloistered building. You will need to book months in advance.

✚ 418 A3 ✉ Praza do Obradoiro 1 ☎ 981 582 200 AX, DC, MC, VI

San Miguel $$

A beautiful hotel in an historic building near the cathedral, this has light-filled, modern rooms set around a pretty garden courtyard. The excellent restaurant, with tables out on the terrace, is perfect for relaxing after a long day's sightseeing.

✚ 418 B2 ✉ Plaza de San Miguel Dos Agros 9 ☎ 981 555 779 AX, DC, MC, VI

El Caballo Blanco $

This relaxed *tapas* bar in the heart of the old town, is a big favourite with locals thanks to its terrace. Plates are heaped high and prices are low.

✚ 418 B2 ✉ Praza Pescadería Vella 5 ☎ 981 56 40 98 🕙 Closed Sun. eve. and Mon. No credit cards

Casa Marcelo $$$

This is one of the best restaurants in Galicia. The intimate dining room offers a single fixed-price menu of creative Galician cuisine.

✚ 418 A2 ✉ Hortas 1 ☎ 981 558 580 🕙 Closed Sun. and Mon.; Tue. and Wed. dinner AX, DC, MC, VI

Don Gaiferos $$$

In the heart of the old center, this restaurant serves wonderful fresh shellfish, seafood and traditional Galician dishes.

✚ 418 A2 ✉ Rua Nova 23 ☎ 981 583 894 🕙 Closed Sun. dinner and Mon. dinner AX, DC, MC, VI

Pedro Roca $$

One of Santiago's best kept secrets. Here you'll sample creative cooking in a tranquil environment.

✚ 418 off A1 ✉ Domingo García Sabell 1 ☎ 98 158 5776 🕙 Closed Sun. dinner AX, DC, MC, VI

Alfonso XIII $$$

Seville's top hotel, set in an attractive palm-shaded garden, offers every comfort in its elegant, luxurious

KEY TO SYMBOLS

✚	map page number and coordinates
✉	address
☎	telephone number
◐	days/times closed
Ⓜ	nearest subway station
🚌	nearest bus/trolley bus/ tram/funicular route
⛴	ferry
$$$	expensive
$$	moderate
$	inexpensive
AX	American Express
DC	Diners Club
MC	MasterCard
VI	VISA

Andalucian Cuisine

Simplicity is all in Andalucian cooking, in which the superb quality of the ingredients, combined with a Moorish legacy of spices, almonds and oranges, has created one of Spain's most enjoyable cuisines. *Tapas* originated here, as did *gazpacho*, the cold summer soup, and sherry, a fortified wine that is drunk and used in cooking. There are tasty stews and soups, both thickened with lentils and potatoes, and every dish is redolent with olive oil, garlic and tomatoes. Excellent bread and rich Arab-inspired pastries and desserts complete the picture.

---

rooms with exceptional service. Reopens spring 2012 after a major renovation.
✚ 425 B2 ✉ San Fernando 2 ☎ 95 491 7000 🚌 21, 23, C3, C4 AX, DC, MC, VI

Casas de la Judería $$$

This atmospheric hotel, located in the heart of Santa Cruz, features peaceful courtyards with fountains.
✚ 425 B3 ✉ Callejón de dos Hermanas 7 ☎ 95 441 5150 🚌 5, C3, C4 AX, DC, MC, VI

Hotel Casa 1800 $$–$$$

This 19th-century *palacete* (small palace), in an atmospheric neighbourhood, has been converted into a boutique hotel. Rooms are sumptuously decorated, and touches include free afternoon tea on the patio. From the roof terrace, you can enjoy views of the cathedral. You will need to take a taxi and then walk the final 55 yards to the hotel.
✚ 425 B3 ✉ Calle Rodrigo Caro 6 ☎ 954 56 1800 AX, DC, MC, VI

Hotel Alminar $

This modest hotel has just a dozen rooms in an ideal location near the cathedral. Although decor is a little dated, this is more than made up for by the welcoming staff, and thoughtful touches such as the library of travel guides. Street noise can be a problem, so pack ear plugs.
✚ 425 A3 ✉ Calle Álvarez Quintero 52 ☎ 954 293 913 🚌 21–26, 30, 31, 34, 41, 42, C3, C4 MC, VI

Hostal Callejon del Agua $

Definitely one of the nicest budget bets in town, this charming *hostal* is located in a 19th-century town house in the old quarter. The elegantly furnished bedrooms are set around a plant-filled patio. There are good views from the roof terrace.
✚ 425 B3 ✉ Calle Corral del Rey 23 ☎ 954 954 21 91 89 AX, MC, VI

Price guide: (dinner per person, excluding drinks)
$	€10–€25
$$	€25–€50
$$$	over €50

Bar Eslava $

The setting is very simple at this popular bar and the focus is firmly on the fabulously fresh *tapas* which are chalked up on the blackboard.

✚ 425 A4 ✉ Carrer Eslava 3 ☎ 954 90 65 68 ◐ Closed Sun. eve. and Mon. MC, VI

Becerrita $$

This long-established restaurant serves traditional Andalucian food and prides itself on its desserts.
✚ 425 B3 ✉ Recaredo 9 ☎ 95 441 2057 ◐ Closed Sun. dinner and 2 weeks in Aug. 🚌 10, 11, C1, C2 AX, DC, MC, VI

Casa Román $

This delightfully old-fashioned tavern, complete with hanging hams, has been going strong since the 1930s. Select from a wide range of classic *tapas*, and hope for a table overlooking the delightful square.
✚ 425 B2/C2 ✉ Plaza Venerables 1 ☎ 954 228 483 No credit cards

Taberna del Alabardero $$–$$$

A mixture of innovative and traditional Spanish cuisine is offered here in the beautiful surroundings of an elegant 19th-century house.
✚ 425 A3 ✉ Zaragoza 20 ☎ 95 450 2721 🚌 43, C1, C2, C3, C4 AX, DC, MC, VI

El 3 de Oro $$

This lively and friendly restaurant in Santa Cruz serving Andalucian dishes is always packed with locals.
✚ 425 B3 ✉ Santa María la Blanca 34 ☎ 95 442 2759 🚌 1, C3, C4 AX, MC, VI

Price guide: (double room with breakfast for two people)
$	800SKr–1,500SKr
$$	1,500SKr–2,200SKr
$$$	over 2,200SKr

Diplomat $$–$$$

This comfortable hotel in a handsome early 20th-century building overlooks the waterfront on the road to Djurgården. The on-site T/BAR is a delightful place to stop for tea.
✚ 437 C2 ✉ Strandvägen 7C ☎ 08 459 68 00 ◐ Östermalmstorg 🚌 47, 69 AX, DC, MC, VI

First Hotel Reisen $$–$$$

A popular hotel on the east side of the Old Town, within easy walking distance of the city center.
✚ 437 B2–C2 ✉ Skeppsbron 12 ☎ 08 22 32 60 ◐ Gamla Stan 🚌 2, 43, 55, 71, 76 AX, DC, MC, VI

Grand Hôtel Stockholm $$$

This top-quality hotel stands across from the Royal Palace. Facilities, including a spa, are luxurious; the restaurants serve international and local cuisine and the hotel is famous for its *smörgåsbord*.

✚ 437 C2 ✉ Södra Blasieholmshamnen 8 ☎ 08 679 35 00 🚇 Kungsträdgården 🚌 2, 43, 55, 62, 76 AX, DC, MC, VI

Mälardrottningen $–$$

Once owned by Woolworth heiress Barbara Hutton, this 1920s converted yacht, on the west side of the Old Town, is a hotel with a difference. The restaurant serves excellent international and Swedish cuisine.

✚ 437 B2 ✉ Riddarholmen ☎ 08 545 187 80 🚇 Gamla Stan 🚌 3, 53 AX, DC, MC, VI

Radisson Blu Strand Hotel $$–$$$

This comfortable hotel with modern facilities is in a fine old building on the southwest side of Nybroviken inlet. Enjoy views across the water from the top-floor restaurant.

✚ 437 B2 ✉ Nybrokajen 9 ☎ 08 506 640 00, or 800 3333 3333 in Europe (toll free) 🚇 Kungsträdgården or Östermalmstorg 🚌 2, 62, 65, 69, 71, 76, 91, 96 AX, DC, MC, VI

Price guide: (dinner per person, excluding drinks)
$ 50SKr–200SKr
$$ 200SKr–400SKr
$$$ over 400SKr

Den Gyldene Freden $$$

Established in 1722, this famous Old Town restaurant attracts the rich and famous, including Nobel Prize selection committee members. Even the restroom has 18th-century poetry on the wall. The cuisine is excellent. Reservations are definitely required.

✚ 437 B2 ✉ Österlånggatan 51 ☎ 08 24 97 60 🕐 Closed Sun. 🚇 Gamla Stan, Slussen 🚌 2, 3, 53, 55 AX, DC, MC, VI

Hermans $

This vegetarian restaurant has a glassed-in terrace and open garden overlooking Stockholm Harbour and Djurgården island. Its buffet features dishes from Asia, Mexico, the Mediterranean, the Middle East and India. Delicious desserts.

✚ 437 C2 ✉ Fjällgatan 23B ☎ 08 643 94 80 🚇 Gamla Stan MC, VI

Mathias Dahlgren $$$

The luxury restaurant of the Grand Hôtel Stockholm (see left) offers a daily changing menu with Swedish and global influences, based on fresh, natural products.

✚ 437 C2 ✉ Grand Hôtel Stockholm, Södra Blasieholmshamnen 8 ☎ 08 679 35 84 🚇 Kungsträdgården 🚌 2, 43, 55, 62, 76 AX, DC, MC, VI

Pontus $$$

Trendy and busy, Pontus's superb fish dishes, sauces and great service make it worth the money. In addition to the restaurant there is an oyster bar and a cocktail bar

✚ 437 B3 ✉ Brunnsgatan 1 ☎ 08 545 273 00 🕐 Closed Sun., Dec. 25 and public holidays 🚇 Östermalmstorg or Hötorget 🚌 All city center buses AX, DC, MC, VI

Villa Källhagen $$

Scandinavian specialties are served on a terrace overlooking the former royal hunting grounds in Djurgården, five minutes from the city.

✚ 437 C2 ✉ Skeppsbron 44 ☎ 08 665 03 00 🕐 Closed Sun. dinner 🚇 Karlaplan 🚌 56, 69 AX, DC, MC, VI

Price guide: (double room with breakfast for two people)
$ SF100–SF250
$$ SF250–SF400
$$$ over SF400

Beau Rivage $$$

Founded in 1865 on the shore of Lac Léman (Lake Geneva), the Beau Rivage is one of the most famous and luxurious hotels in the world. Its elegance and perfect service embody the dream and the qualities of "Old Europe."

✚ 451 B3 ✉ quai du Mont Blanc 13 ☎ 022 7166 6666 🚌 5, 8, 11 AX, DC, MC, VI

Edelweiss Manotel $$

A popular choice with tourists, this chalet-style hotel near the lakeside has 42 attractive, comfortable rooms and stages frequent folklore evenings.

✚ 451 B3 ✉ place de la Navigation 2 ☎ 022 544 5151 🚌 1 AX, DC, MC, VI

Eden $$$

In a quiet area near Mon Repos park and the lake, this comfortable hotel has a good restaurant and a friendly, relaxed atmosphere.

✚ 451 off the map ✉ rue de Lausanne 135 ☎ 022 716 3700 🚌 4, 18 AX, DC, MC, VI

Hôtel Central $

This is a friendly, family-run hotel in the heart of the city and at the foot of the old town, near Lake Geneva.

✚ 451 B2 ✉ rue de la Rôtisserie 2 ☎ 022 818 8100 🚌 10; tram 16 AX, DC, MC, VI

Hôtel de Genève $

This traditional, centrally located hotel is an excellent budget choice and is nonsmoking throughout.

✚ 451 A3 ✉ place Isaac-Mercier 1 ☎ 022 908 5400 🚌 7; trams 13, 14, 15, 16 AX, DC, MC, VI

Tiffany $$$

This newly renovated hotel in the heart of Geneva is furnished in *belle époque* style, with comfortable rooms, a bar and a restaurant.

✚ 451 A2 ✉ rue de l'Arquebuse 20 ☎ 022 708 1616 🚌 13 AX, DC, MC, VI

Price guide: (dinner per person, excluding drinks)
$ SF25–SF45
$$ SF45–SF60
$$$ over SF60

Auberge de Coutance $$$

This elegant restaurant provides exceptional service and top-quality French cuisine.

✚ 451 A2–A3 ✉ rue de Coutance 25 ☎ 022 732 7919 🕐 Closed Sun. 🚌 1 AX, DC, MC, VI

Auberge de Savièse $

Enjoy a selection of Swiss specialties at this friendly restaurant, which features different types of fondue.

✚ 451 B3 ✉ rue du Pâquis 20 ☎ 022 732 8330 🚌 1 AX, DC, MC, VI

Brasserie Lipp $$$

This popular French restaurant in the Confédération Centre shopping mall is named after a Parisian brasserie.

✚ 451 B2 ✉ rue de la Confédération 8 ☎ 022 318 8030 🚌 12, 16, 17; trams 1, 2, 3, 5, 7, 9, 10, 19, 20, 29 AX, DC, MC, VI

KEY TO SYMBOLS

- 🗺 map page number and coordinates
- ✉ address
- ☎ telephone number
- 🕐 days/times closed
- 🚇 nearest subway station
- 🚍 nearest bus/trolley bus/ tram/funicular route
- ⛴ ferry
- $$$ expensive
- $$ moderate
- $ inexpensive
- AX American Express
- DC Diners Club
- MC MasterCard
- VI VISA

Swiss Food and Wine Festivals

From summer through fall, there are food and wine festivals held in every region of Switzerland. The grape harvests during August prompt wonderful festivities in Anzère, the Lake Geneva region and eastern Switzerland, while Locarno, Ascona and the Ticino area also celebrate the chestnut harvest. In Charmey, Jaun and Fribourg *la bénichon* culinary feast features a special mustard, and at the Basel Autumn Fair, the delicious confectionary *mässmogge* is a must-try.

La Coupole $$$

Choose from classic French rotisserie specials or Tuscan cuisine at this stylish restaurant on the Left Bank.

🗺 451 B2 ✉ rue Pierre Fatio 15 ☎ 022 787 5010 🕐 Closed Sun. 🚍 1, 8; tram 12 AX, DC, VI

Le Patara $$$

This is the best Thai restaurant in Geneva. Expect impeccable service in tasteful surroundings.

🗺 451 B3 ✉ Hôtel Beau Rivage, quai du Mont-Blanc 13 ☎ 022 731 5566 🚍 5, 8, 11 AX, DC, MC, VI

Restaurant des Vieux-Grenadiers $$

A typical Genevan restaurant, this specializes in regional dishes and fondues. It has a pretty summer terrace and occasional live jazz.

🗺 451 off the map ✉ rue de Carouge 92 ☎ 022 320 1327 🕐 Closed Sun. 🚍 Trams 12, 13 AX, MC, VI

Price guide: (double room with breakfast for two people)

$	SF150–SF250
$$	SF250–SF400
$$$	over SF400

Eden au Lac $$$

Stay at this elegant lakeside hotel, built in 1909, for the ultimate in comfort, luxury and service.

🗺 456 B1 ✉ Utoquai 45 ☎ 044 266 2525 🚍 Tram 4 AX, DC, MC, VI

Franziskaner $$

This reasonably priced hotel, overlooking a pretty square, has comfortable rooms and a restaurant.

🗺 456 B2 ✉ Niederdorfstrasse 1 ☎ 044 250 5300 🚍 Trams 4, 15 AX, DC, MC, VI

Garni Hotel Bristol $$

This is a comfortable hotel near the railroad station, with modern and functional rooms.

🗺 456 B4 ✉ Stampfenbachstrasse 34 ☎ 044 258 4444 🚍 Trams 11, 14 AX, DC, MC, VI

Krone Unterstrass $–$$

This well-equipped hotel caters to business travelers in a residential area 10 minutes fom the city center.

🗺 456 off the map ✉ Schaffhauserstrasse 1 ☎ 044 360 5656 🚍 Trams 11, 14 AX, DC, MC, VI

Rössli $$

The Rössli is a comfortable and imaginatively designed hotel with well-equipped rooms.

🗺 456 B2 ✉ Rössligasse 7 ☎ 044 256 7050 🚍 Trams 4, 15 AX, DC, MC, VI

Price guide: (dinner per person, excluding drinks)

$	SF25–SF45
$$	SF45–SF60
$$$	over SF60

Adler's Swiss Chuchi $

This friendly restaurant in the Hotel Adler serves meat and cheese fondue, *raclette* and *rösti* (grated potatoes cooked in a skillet), as well as veal specialties.

🗺 456 B2 ✉ Rosengasse 10 ☎ 044 266 9666 🚍 Trams 4, 15 AX, DC, MC, VI

Haus Zum Rüden $$$

Overlooking the Limmat river, this historic restaurant serves the best of Swiss specialties.

🗺 456 B2 ✉ Limmatquai 42 ☎ 044 261 9566 🕐 Closed Sat.–Sun. 🚍 Tram 4 AX, DC, MC, VI

Kronenhalle $$$

This long-established restaurant offers traditional dishes beneath artworks by Picasso and Matisse.

🗺 456 B2 ✉ Rämistrasse 4 ☎ 044 262 9900 🚍 Trams 4, 11 AX, DC, MC, VI

Restaurant zum Kropf $$

This cheerful restaurant has been serving generous portions of local dishes since 1888.

🗺 456 A2 ✉ In Gassen 16 ☎ 044 221 1805 🕐 Closed Sun. 🚍 Trams 6, 7, 11, 13 AX, MC , VI

Mère Catherine $

This central garden restaurant serves fish and seafood, with an accent on Mediterranean and Provençal dishes.

🗺 456 B2 ✉ Nägelihof 3 ☎ 044 250 5940 🚍 Trams 4, 15 AX, DC, MC, VI

Münsterhof $–$$

Historic, renovated Monte Primero Münsterhof serves traditional Swiss specialties at good prices and also has a garden.

🗺 456 A2 ✉ Münsterhof 6 ☎ 044 262 3300 🕐 Closed Sun. 🚍 Trams 4, 15 AX, DC, MC, VI

Essential Information

Austria

National Flag

Essential for Travelers*

● **Required** ● **Recommended** ● **Not required**

Passport	●
Visa (check regulations before you travel)	●
Travel, medical insurance	●
Round-trip or onward airline ticket	●
Local currency	●
Traveler's checks	●
Credit cards	●
First-aid kit and medicines	●
Inoculations*	●

*see also *Health* section

Essential for Drivers*

Driver's license	●
International Driving Permit	●
Car insurance (for nonrental cars)	●
Car registration (for nonrental cars)	●

*see also *Driving* section

Important Addresses

Austrian National Tourist Office
P.O. Box 1142
New York, NY 10018-1142
☎ (212) 944-6880
Fax (212) 730-4568
www.austria.info

Österreich Werbung
Österreich (Austrian National Tourist Office)
Margaretenstrasse 1
A-1040 Vienna, Austria
☎ 01 588 66-0
Fax 01 588 66-40
www.austria-info.at

American Citizen Services
Parkring 12A
A-1010 Vienna, Austria
☎ 01 31 339-7535
Fax 01 512 5835
www.usembassy.at
Mon.–Fri. 8–5:30 (outside these hours
☎ 01 313 39)

Customs

✔ **Duty-free limits on goods brought in from non-European Union countries:**
200 cigarettes, 100 cigarillos, 50 cigars or 250 g. tobacco; 1 L. alcohol over 22% volume; or 2 L. alcohol under 22% volume or 2 L. sparkling wine; 2 L. wine; 25 ml. perfume or toilet water; plus any other duty-free goods (including gifts) to the value of €175. Personal allowance from Czech Republic, Slovakia, Hungary or Slovenia: €125 (unless you arrive by air, when it is €175, as above). This information applies to visitors age 17 and over. There are no currency regulations. There is no limit on the importation of tax-paid goods purchased within the European Union, provided they are for your own personal use.

✘ No unlicensed drugs, weapons, ammunition, obscene material, pets or other animals, counterfeit money or copied goods, meat or poultry.
For customs limits for returning U.S. citizens see page 16.

Money

Austria's currency is the euro (€), a currency shared by 16 other European Union countries. The euro is divided into 100 cents (¢). The denominations of euro bills are 5, 10, 20, 50, 100, 200 and 500. There are coins of 1, 2, 5, 10, 20 and 50¢ and €1 and €2. You can exchange dollars or traveler's checks *(Reiseschecks)* at a bank *(Bank)*, exchange office *(Wechselbüro)*, post office *(Postamt)* and at hotels. Credit cards are widely accepted.

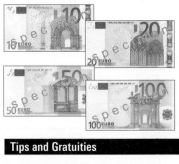

Tips and Gratuities

Tips *(Trinkgeld)* are welcomed and expected in restaurants and cafés.

Restaurants (even when service is included)	10%
Cafés/bars	10%
Taxis	10%
Porters	at your discretion
Chambermaids	at your discretion
Hairdressers (and change to shampooer)	5%

Vienna	New York	Chicago	Denver	Los Angeles	Time zones
12:00 noon	– 6 hrs	– 7 hrs	– 8 hrs	– 9 hrs	

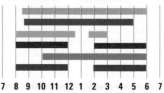

495

Austria

Communications

Post Offices

Buy stamps *(Briefmarken)* at a post office *(Postamt)*, or newsstand/tobacconist *(Tabak Trafik)* or from a hotel.

Post offices can be recognized by a golden trumpet symbol and can often be found close to the main square or railroad station. Hours for out-of-town post offices may vary. Mailboxes are yellow or orange.

Telephones

Use cash or prepaid phone cards *(Wertkarte)* to make a call. Telephones have direct dialing for national and international calls.

Buy phone cards from gas stations, newsstands, post offices and hotels. Some booths take credit cards.

Phoning inside Austria
All Austrian telephone numbers in this book include an area code: dial the number that is listed. To call the operator dial 11 88 77.

Phoning Austria from abroad
The country code for Austria is 43. Note that Austrian numbers in this book do not include the country code; you will need to prefix this number if you are phoning from another country. To phone Austria from the United States or Canada, omit the first zero from the Austrian number, and add the prefix 011 43. (Note that the number of digits in Austrian area codes varies.) Example:
01 12 23 34-4 becomes 011 43 1 12 23 34-4.

Phoning from Austria
To phone the United States or Canada from Austria, prefix the area code and number with 00 1. Example: (111) 222-3333 becomes 00 1 111 222-3333. To call National and European information dial 11 88 77. To call overseas information dial 0900 11 88 77.

Emergency telephone numbers
Police *(Polizei)* **133**   Fire service *(Feuerwehr)* **122**
Ambulance *(Krankenwagen)* **144**
Mountain rescue service *(Bergrettung)* **140**
Emergency calls are free from phone booths.
General emergency number within the E.U. **112**

Hours of Operation

- Stores Mon.–Sat.
- Offices Mon.–Fri.
- Banks Mon.–Fri.
- Post Offices Mon.–Fri.
- Museums/Monuments
- Pharmacies

7 8 9 10 11 12 1 2 3 4 5 6 7

Saturday is early closing day; shops close between noon and 5 p.m. Thursday or Friday is late-night shopping (until 7 or 8).
Banks stay open until 5:30 p.m. on Thursday.
Post offices may also open 8–10 on Saturday.
Main and station post offices in larger cities are open 24 hours, including weekends and public holidays.
Pharmacies usually follow store opening hours with a 2-hour lunch break. There is always one pharmacy open late in each city: details are displayed in pharmacy windows.
Facilities at tourist resorts may have special hours of operation.

National Holidays

Banks, businesses and most stores close on these days. Also, some museums may be closed or have restricted hours.

Jan. 1	New Year's Day
Jan. 6	Epiphany
Mar./Apr.	Easter Monday
May 1	Labor Day
May	Ascension Day
May/Jun.	Pentecost Monday
May/Jun.	Corpus Christi
Aug. 15	Assumption of the Virgin
Oct. 26	National Day
Nov. 1	All Saints' Day
Dec. 8	Immaculate Conception
Dec. 25	Christmas Day
Dec. 26	St. Stephen's Day

Photography

Magnificent and varied subject matter awaits the photographer in Austria. Away from the city, the Alpine peaks give enormous scope for landscape photography, and the light is generally very good. Camera batteries are readily available and there are many places offering download and CD services for digital cameras. Most museums will not allow you to take pictures; check first.

Austria

Health

Medical Insurance

The cost of medical treatment in Austria is high, and private medical insurance is recommended. The Austrian Medical Society can suggest a doctor *(Arzt)* or hospital *(Krankenhaus):* Höfergasse 13/1 (corner of Lazarettgasse), Vienna, ☎ 01 405 45 68; www.ameso.at. The south and east are home to *Zecken* – a kind of tick that can transmit encephalitis. This disease is potentially lethal, and it is essential to seek medical advice if you are bitten. An inoculation is available.

Dental Services

Dentists *(Zahnarzt)* will charge for any treatment given. Dental work is expensive, so check that it is covered by your medical insurance. Dentists are listed in the telephone directory, or ask for English-speaking dentists at your embassy, a tourist office or hotel.

Sun Advice

Austria has strong sun during the summer months so sun protection is needed. Wear a hat, cover shoulders, drink plenty of fluids and use sunscreen.

Drugs

Pharmacies *(Apotheken)* can dispense prescriptions. Many assistants speak English, and a schedule displayed on the door enables you to find a late-opening or 24-hour pharmacy in every town.

Safe Water

Tap water is safe to drink throughout Austria. Mineral water *(Mineralwasser)* is widely available.

Restrooms

Public restrooms *(Toiletten/WC)* are generally easy to find and immaculately clean. A small charge is levied.

Electricity

Austria has a 220-volt power supply. Electrical sockets take plugs with two round pins. American appliances will need a plug adapter and will require a transformer if they do not have a dual-voltage facility.

National Transportation

Train *(Zug)*

The Austrian Federal Railways (Österreichische Bundesbahnen or ÖBB) runs a comfortable and efficient service, with connections to all European countries. If you like a slower pace try a steam train journey through valleys along lakesides or a cable-car trip; local tourist offices can give details. For rail information ☎ 05 1717.

Bus *(Bus)*

Austria has a good network of local, federal and private bus companies. Bus travel is slower but less expensive than the train; for information contact Austria Info ☎ 0810 10 18 18, Mon.–Fri. 9–5:30.

Ferry *(Fähre)*

From Easter to the end of October you can enjoy steamer services on the Danube; some continue into neighboring countries. Steamers ply the larger Austrian lakes from May to September. Wien-Tourismus can supply details on steamer companies: ☎ 01 24-555.

Driving

Drive on the right

Speed Limits

Police impose on-the-spot fines (for which receipts are issued), although a foreign motorist may refuse and instead be asked to make a surety payment.

 Limited-access highways *(Autobahnen)*
130 k.p.h. (80 m.p.h.)

 Main roads
100 k.p.h. (62 m.p.h.)

 Urban areas
50 k.p.h. (31 m.p.h.)

Seat Belts

Must be worn in front and back seats at all times. Children under 14 are not allowed to use a front seat, unless in a child safety seat.

Blood Alcohol

The legal blood alcohol limit is 0.05%. Random breath tests on drivers are carried out frequently, especially late at night, and the penalties for offenders are severe.

Driving (continued)

Tolls

To use toll highways, purchase a windshield sticker *(Vignette)* at automobile clubs in Austria or abroad, or at a border crossing, gas station, post office or tobacconist. There are charges for some other major roads. Nonpayment of tolls results in a fine.

Car Rental

The leading rental firms have offices at airports and train stations. Hertz offers discounted rates for AAA members (see page 15). For reservations:

	United States	Austria
Alamo	(800) 462-5266	01 866 1610 (Europcar)
Avis	(800) 230-4898	0800 0800 8757
Budget	(800) 527-0700	01 7007 32711
Hertz	(800) 654-3001	0800 20 11 11

Fuel

Many gas stations *(Tankstelle)* are self-service, and 24-hour facilities are common. Unleaded gas *(Bleifrei)* is available at 95 and 98 octane. Diesel is available.

AAA Affiliated Motoring Club

Österreichischer Automobil-, Motorrad-und Touring Club (ÖAMTC) Schubertring 1-3, A-1010 Vienna ☎ 01 711 1530, fax 01 711 99 1352. If you break down while driving, phone ☎ 120 (ÖAMTC breakdown service). Not all automobile clubs offer full services to AAA members.

Breakdowns and Accidents

There are 24-hour emergency phones at regular intervals on highways. All accidents involving personal injury must be reported to the police (☎ 133). Most car rental firms provide their own free rescue service; if your car is rented, follow the instructions given in the documentation. Use of a car repair service other than those authorized by your rental company may violate your agreement. You must carry a first-aid kit, warning triangle and a fluorescent vest in case of a breakdown or accident.

Other Information

The minimum age for driving a car is 18 (may be higher for some car rental firms). An International Driving Permit (IDP) is recommended; some rental firms require them, and they can speed up formalities if involved in an accident. A Green Card (international motor insurance certificate) is recommended if driving a private car (see page 15). Only hands-free phone use is permitted while driving. In winter, snow tires or chains are essential, and are legal Nov. 1–Apr. 15. Rent chains at automobile clubs and border crossings.

Useful Words and Phrases

The official language in Austria is German, although Austrians are very proud of their brand of the language *(Österreichisch)*, and are offended if it is treated as a mere dialect of "standard" German *(Hochdeutsch)*. On paper, the differences between the two varieties are not obvious, but the Austrian accent is distinctive, and especially strong in rural regions.

There are numerous words that are peculiar to Austria and the south of Germany. The Austrian diminutive is *-el* or *-lein* compared with the German *-chen*, so *Mädchen* (girl) in German becomes *Mädel* in Austrian. A small number of Austrian words, such as *Fauteil* (armchair) and *Plafond* (ceiling), are in fact of French origin.

See page 525 for a pronunciation and basic vocabulary guide to the German language; the following list is an eclectic sample of words peculiar to Austrian German.

Everyday life

friend, guy	*haberer*
funny	*hetzig*
goodbye	*pfiat di*
guitar	*klampfe*
hello	*Grüss Gott*
legs	*haxen*
policeman	*gendarm*
slippers	*schlapfen*
work	*hockn*

Food and drink

blood sausage	*blunzn*
carrot	*karotte*
corn	*kukuruz*
croissant	*kipferl*
doughnut	*krapfen*
green beans	*fisole*
green salad	*häuplsalat*
lemonade	*kracherl*
milky coffee	*melange*
mushroom	*schwammerl*
potato	*erdäpfel*

Common words and phrases

breakfast	*frühstück*
closed	*geschlossen*
excuse me	*Entschuldigen*
how much?	*Wieviel kostet es?*
I don't understand	*Ich verstehe nicht*
I'd like	*Ich möchte*
key	*schlüssel*
no smoking	*nicht rauchen*
open	*geöffnet*
please	*bitte*
room	*zimmer*
shower	*dusche*
thank you	*danke*
where is…?	*Wo ist…?*

Belgium

National Flag

Essential for Travelers

● Required ● Recommended ● Not required

Passport	●
Visa (check regulations before you travel)	●
Travel, medical insurance	●
Round-trip or onward airline ticket	●
Local currency	●
Traveler's checks	●
Credit cards	●
First-aid kit and medicines	●
Inoculations	●

Essential for Drivers*

Driver's license	●
International Driving Permit	●
Car insurance (for nonrental cars)	●
Car registration (for nonrental cars)	●

*see also *Driving* section

Important Addresses

Belgian Tourist Office
220 East 42nd Street, Suite 3402 (34th floor)
New York, NY 10017
☎ (212) 758-8130 Fax (212) 355-7675
www.visitbelgium.com

Belgian Tourist Office Information Office
Flanders Belgium (Flemish-speaking areas)
Grasmarkt 61, 1000 Brussels, Belgium
☎ 02 504 0390 Fax: 02 513 0475;
www.visitflanders.com
Wallonie Bruxelles (French-speaking areas)
rue Saint Bernard 30, 1060 Brussels, Belgium
☎ 070 221 021; www.wallonie-tourisme.be

American Embassy
boulevard du Régent 27/Regentlaan 2,
1000 Brussels, Belgium
☎ 02 811 4000 Fax 02 811 4500
http://Belgium.usembassy.gov. Open Mon.–Fri. 9–6

American Embassy Consular Service
☎ 02 811 4300
Open Mon., Wed., Fri. 1:30–3:30, Tue., Thu.
11–12:30, by appointment apart from in emergency

Customs

✓ **Duty-free limits on goods brought in from non-European Union countries:**
200 cigarettes or 100 cigarillos or 50 cigars or 250 g. tobacco; 1 L. alcohol over 22% volume or 2 L. alcohol under 22% volume; 2 L. wine; 50 ml. perfume; 250 ml. toilet water; plus any other duty-free goods (including gifts) to the value of €430 for visitors entering the EU (and France) by air or by sea or €300 if arriving by other means. There is no limit on the importation of tax-paid goods, for personal use, purchased within the E.U. Visitors must declare cash over the value of $10,000 (or equivalent).

✗ No unlicensed drugs, weapons, ammunition, obscene material, pets or other animals, counterfeit money or copied goods, meat or poultry.
For customs limits for returning U.S. citizens see page 16.

Money

Belgium's currency is the euro (€), a currency shared by 16 other European Union countries. The euro is divided into 100 cents (¢). The denominations of euro bills are 5, 10, 20, 50, 100, 200 and 500. There are coins of 1, 2, 5, 10, 20 and 50¢ and €1 and €2. Credit cards are widely accepted, but can be unwelcome for small amounts.

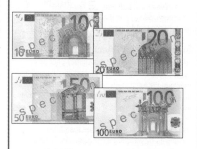

Tips and Gratutities

Tips are not obligatory; a service charge is usually included for restaurants, cafés and taxis.

Restaurants (where service is not included)	10%
Cafés/bars	change
Taxis	change
Porters	€1 per item
Chambermaids	€1 per day
Cloakroom attendants	€1–€2

Brussels	New York	Chicago	Denver	Los Angeles	Time zones
12:00 noon	− 6 hrs	− 7 hrs	− 8 hrs	− 9 hrs	

499

Belgium

Communications

Post Offices

Buy stamps *(timbres/ postzegels)* at a post office *(bureau de poste/ postkantoor)*, a tobacconist or newsstand *(tabac/ tabaksverkoper)*, or from a vending machine. Allow a week for mail to reach the United States. Mailboxes are painted red. Hours for out-of-town post offices may vary.

Telephones

There are some coin-operated public phones but phone card booths are more common. Phone cards *(télécartes/telefoonkaart)* are available from Belgacom Teleboutiques, post offices, railroad stations, bookstores and some newsstands, from €5 and up. Phones accepting credit cards are available at certain tourist sites. Instructions in English are often displayed in public booths.

Phoning in Belgium
All Belgian phone numbers in this book include an area code: dial the entire number. To call the operator dial 0800 89 0320 for Auto Belgium Direct or 0800 89 0010 for Belgium Pre-Paid.

Phoning Belgium from abroad
The country code for Belgium is 32. Belgian numbers in this book do not include the country code; you will need to prefix this number if you are phoning from another country. To phone Belgium from the United States or Canada, dial 011 32 then omit the first zero from the Belgian number. (Note that Belgian area codes have two or three digits.) Example: 01 122 3344 becomes 011 32 1 122 3344.

Phoning from Belgium
To phone the United States or Canada from Belgium, prefix the area code and number with 00 1. Example: (111) 222-3333 becomes 00 1 111 222-3333. To call international directory assistance, dial 1304; for local directory assistance in English, dial 1405.

Emergency telephone numbers
Police *(police)* **101**
Fire service *(pompiers)* **100**
Ambulance *(ambulance)* **100**
Red Cross ambulance **105**
General emergency number within the E.U. **112**

Hours of Operation

- Stores Mon.–Sat.
- Offices Mon.–Fri.
- Banks Mon.–Fri.
- Post Offices Mon.–Fri.
- Museums/Monuments
- Pharmacies Mon.–Sat.

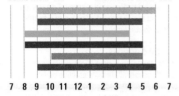

7 8 9 10 11 12 1 2 3 4 5 6 7

While Sunday is the official closing day, souvenir shops in many towns stay open, usually 10–4.

Many **bakeries and patisseries** open at 7:30 or 8 a.m. and also open on Sunday morning.

Department and other major stores often stay open until 7 p.m. on weekdays and 8 or 9 p.m. on Friday.

Smaller stores and **out-of-town post offices** and **banks** may close for lunch.

Some **city post offices and banks** open on Saturday morning. Post offices and banks outside cities and large towns may close for 2 hours at lunch.

It is common for **museums** to close on Monday (except for some small museums) and open later one evening a week. Many close for 2 hours at lunch.

National Holidays

Banks, businesses and most stores close on these days. Most cities, towns and villages celebrate their patron saint's day, but most places stay open.

Jan. 1	New Year's Day
Mar./Apr.	Easter Monday
May 1	Labor Day
May	Ascension Day
May/Jun.	Pentecost Monday
Jul. 21	National Day
Aug. 15	Assumption of the Virgin
Nov. 1	All Saints' Day
Nov. 11	Armistice Day
Dec. 25	Christmas Day

Photography

Camera batteries are readily available and there are many places offering digital equipment, download services for digital cameras and rapid developing services. Most museums will not allow you to take pictures; check first.

Belgium

Health

Medical Insurance

Private medical insurance is recommended. Visitors from non-European Union countries can receive treatment in a hospital emergency room but are charged if admitted to a hospital *(hôpital/ziekenhuis)*.

Dental Services

Dental treatment is not available free of charge; all dentists practice privately. A list of dentists *(dentiste/tandarts)* can be found in the yellow pages *(pages jaunes/Gouden Gids)*. Check that dental treatment is covered by your private medical insurance.

Sun Advice

The warmest months are July and August, with average daytime temperatures of 60°F. Belgian weather can be unpredictable and although the sun is not often very fierce, protection is still required.

Drugs

Prescription and nonprescription medicines are available from a pharmacy *(pharmacie/apotheek)*. If you need a medicine outside regular hours, the addresses of 24-hour facilities are posted on the door of all pharmacies.

Safe Water

Tap water is safe to drink and mineral water *(eau minérale/mineraalwater)* is widely available. The origin of the English word "spa" is in fact the Belgian town of Spa, especially popular during the 19th century for its mineral springs.

Restrooms

Public restrooms *(toilettes/toiletten)* are not always easy to find but are usually clean. If you need to use the facilities at a restaurant or café purchase a drink first. Restrooms in the larger restaurants and cafés sometimes have attendants; you should tip them 25–50 cents, which goes toward their wages.

Electricity

Belgium has a 220-volt power supply. Electrical sockets take plugs with two round pins; American appliances will need a plug adapter and will require a transformer if they do not have a dual-voltage facility.

National Transportation

Train *(Train/Trein)*

The national rail network is the SNCB/NMBS (Société Nationale des Chemins de Fer Belges in French, and Nationale Maatschappij der Belgische Spoorwegen in Flemish). Information is available and reservations can be made online at www.b-rail.be or by phone ☎ 02 528 28 28. The Eurostar trains from London arrive in the Gare du Midi (☎ 079 79 79 79; www.eurostar.com). Brussels has good connections with the Thalys network that operates high-speed trains to Paris, Amsterdam, Cologne and Geneva (☎ 079 79 79 79; www.raileurope.com or www.thalys.com).

Bus *(Bus/Bus)*

The local bus service is good; details and timetables are available from local tourist offices. Open the door yourself on buses and trams; where there is no handle, press the black strip or button. Low-cost international buses to most European capitals are operated by Eurolines (☎ 02 274 13 50; www.eurolines.com).

Driving

Drive on the right

Speed Limits

Police impose on-the-spot fines (receipts are issued), although a foreign motorist may refuse and instead be asked to make a surety payment.

Limited-access highways *(autoroutes/autoweg)* **120 k.p.h. (74 m.p.h.)** Minimum speed on straight, level stretches **70 k.p.h. (43 m.p.h.)**

Main roads
90 k.p.h. (56 m.p.h.)

Urban areas
50 k.p.h. (31 m.p.h.)

Seat Belts

Must be worn in front and back seats at all times; children under 10 must travel in the rear. If a child is sitting in the front, a seat belt/child restraint appropriate to his or her size/weight must be used.

Blood Alcohol

The legal blood alcohol limit is 0.05%. Random breath tests on drivers are carried out frequently, especially late at night, and the penalties for offenders are severe.

Belgium

Driving (continued)

Tolls

There are no tolls on Belgian highways, but there is a toll on the Liefkenshoek Tunnel to the north of Antwerp.

Car Rental

The leading rental firms have offices at airports, train stations and ferry terminals. Hertz offers discounted rates for AAA members (see page 15). For reservations:

	United States	Belgium
Alamo	(877) 222-9075	31 02 721 0592
Avis	(800) 331-1212	070 223 001
Budget	(800) 472-3325	02 721 5097
Hertz	(800) 654-3001	02 717 3201

Fuel

Gasoline *(essence/benzine)* and diesel are priced in liters and are expensive. There are two grades of unleaded gas *(sans plomb/loodvrij)*: normal (95 octane) and super (98 octane). Most gas stations are self-service, and 24-hour facilities are common.

AAA Affiliated Motoring Club

Touring Club Belgium (TCB) 44 rue de la Loi, 1040 Brussels ☎ 02 233 2202; www.touring.be. If you break down while driving, phone ☎ 070 344 777 (TCB breakdown service) or, on a limited-access highway, use one of the emergency telephones located every 1.2 miles. Ask for *"Touring-Secours."* Not all automobile clubs offer full services to AAA members.

Breakdowns and Accidents

Most car rental firms have their own free rescue service; if your car is rented, follow the instructions given in the documentation. Use of a car repair service other than those authorized by your rental company may violate your rental agreement. If you are involved in an accident phone ☎ 101 for police assistance. You must carry a warning triangle and a fluorescent vest in your car.

Other Information

The minimum age for driving a car is 18 (may be 21 for some car rental firms). An International Driving Permit (IDP) is recommended; some rental firms require them, and they can speed up formalities if you are involved in an accident. A Green Card (international motor insurance certificate) is recommended if you are driving a private car; see page 15 for more information. Drivers must yield the right of way to vehicles approaching from the right (except on major roads) and to vehicles on rails and public transport buses. Beware of cobbled roads, which can be slippery in wet weather.

Useful Words and Phrases

A linguistic battle has existed in Belgium for many centuries; settlers have long entered from neighboring countries, and as a result there are three distinct language communities: French, Dutch and German.

The two dominant languages are Walloon (a form of French, spoken in the south) and Flemish (related to Dutch, spoken in the north). Passions run deep between the two groups; prosperity has moved back and forth between them over the centuries, and their relationship is still difficult to this day. The Flemish fear their language is being diminished, aware of the strength that French has as a world language. In addition, German is spoken in the east.

Both Walloon and Flemish hold equal status as official languages, and although the bilingual signs can be confusing to the visitor, English is widely spoken.

In Brussels, where Flemish and French are both spoken, the street signs also are in both languages. Place-names are not usually a problem, since the Flemish and French proper names have similarities, but there can be differences.

Following is a selection of locations:

English	Flemish	French
Aalst	Aalst	Alost
Antwerp	Antwerpen	Anvers
Bruges	Brugge	Bruges
Brussels	Brussel	Bruxelles
Ghent	Gent	Gand
Jodoigne	Geldenaken	Jodoigne
Kortrijk	Kortrijk	Courtrai
Liège	Luik	Liège
Louvain	Leuven	Louvain
Mechelen	Mechelen	Malines
Mons	Bergen	Mons
Mouscron	Moeskroen	Mouscron
Nivelles	Nijvel	Nivelles
Ostend	Oostende	Ostende
Roeselare	Roeselare	Roulers
Ronse	Ronse	Renaix
Scheldt	Schelde	Escaut
Tongeren	Tongeren	Tongres
Tournai	Doornik	Tournai
Veurne	Veurne	Furnes
Ypres	Ieper	Ypres

For useful phrases in French, see page 521; for phrases in German, see page 525; for phrases in Dutch, see page 549.

National Flag

Essential for Travelers

● Required ● Recommended ● Not required

Passport	●
Visa (check regulations before you travel)	●
Travel, medical insurance	●
Round-trip or onward airline ticket	●
Local currency	●
Traveler's checks	●
Credit cards	●
First-aid kit and medicines	●
Inoculations	●

Essential for Drivers*

Driver's license	●
International Driving Permit	●
Car insurance (for nonrental cars)	●
Car registration (for nonrental cars)	●

*see also *Driving* section

Important Addresses

VisitBritain
www.visitbritain.us

British and London Visitor Centre
1 Regent Street
Piccadilly Circus
London
SW1Y 4XT
U.K.
(personal callers only)
www.visitbritain.co.uk
Mon. 9:30–6:30, Tue.–Fri. 9–6:30, Sat. 9–5,
Sun. 10–4, Apr.–Sep.; Mon. 9:30–6, Tue.–Fri. 9–6,
Sat. 10–4, Sun. 10–4, rest of year

American Embassy
24 Grosvenor Square
London W1A 1AE
U.K.
☎ 020 7499 9000
Fax 020 7495 5012
www.usembassy.org.uk

Customs

✓ **Duty-free limits on goods brought in from non-European Union countries:**
200 cigarettes or 100 cigarillos or 50 cigars or 250 g. tobacco; 2 L. wine; 1 L. of alcohol over 22% volume or 2 L. of alcohol under 22% volume; 60 ml. perfume; 250 ml. toilet water; plus any other duty-free goods (including gifts) to the value of £390. There is no limit on the importation of any currency or of tax-paid goods purchased within the European Union, provided the goods are for your own personal use.

✗ No unlicensed drugs, weapons, obscene material, counterfeit and copied goods, meat or poultry.
For customs limits for returning U.S. citizens see page 16.

Money

Britain's currency is the pound sterling (£), which is divided into 100 pence (p). The denominations of pound bills are 1 (Scotland only), 5, 10, 20, 50 and 100 (Scotland only). There are coins of 1, 2, 5, 10, 20 and 50p and £1 and £2. You can exchange dollars or traveler's checks at banks, main post offices, exchange offices and some travel agencies. Buy traveler's checks in pounds sterling, so you do not lose money every time you change them. Credit cards are widely accepted throughout Britain, and ATMs are very common in shopping areas. When sightseeing, it is a good idea to carry a mix of large and small denominations.

Tips and Gratuities

Restaurants (where service is not included)	10–15%
Cafés/bars	change
Taxis	10–15%
Porters	£1
Hairdressers	10%
Tour guides	£1–£2
Chambermaids	change
Cloakroom attendants (where no charges)	30p–50p

London	New York	Chicago	Denver	Los Angeles	Time zones
12:00 noon	− 5 hrs	− 6 hrs	− 7 hrs	− 8 hrs	

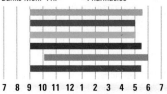

503

Britain

Communications

Post Offices

 Buy stamps at post offices, gas stations, tobacconists and supermarkets. Out-of-town post offices often close 1–2. Mailboxes

("pillar-boxes") are red, and are usually free-standing, though some may be set into walls. Pillar-boxes show who was monarch at the time of their installation (ER II, for instance, stands for Elizabeth Regina II).

Telephones

 Public telephones are easy to find, although the traditional red booths are rare in towns and cities. Use cash, a credit or debit card. Most public telephones accept 10p, 20p, 50p, £1 and £2 coins, but only unused coins are returned. There is a minimum charge of 60p, which allows up to 30

minutes (then 10p for each subsequent 15 minutes) for a local or national call (i.e. all numbers commencing 01 or 02). If using a credit card there is a £1.20 minimum fee and a charge of 20p per minute for local and national calls.

Phoning in Britain
All British numbers in this book have an area code: dial the number listed. To call the operator dial 100.

Phoning Britain from abroad
The country code for Britain is 44. British numbers in this book do not include the country code; you need to prefix it if you are phoning from another country. To phone Britain from the United States or Canada, omit the first zero from the British number, and add the prefix 011 44. Example: 011 2233 4455 becomes 011 44 11 2233 4455.

Phoning from Britain
To phone the United States or Canada from Britain, prefix the area code and number with 00 1. Example: (111) 222-3333 becomes 00 1 111 222-3333. To call the international operator dial 155.

Emergency telephone numbers
Police **999** or **112**
Fire service **999** or **112**
Ambulance **999** or **112**
Emergency calls are free from phone booths.

Hours of Operation

- ■ Stores Mon.–Sat.
- ■ Offices Mon.–Fri.
- ■ Banks Mon.–Fri.
- ■ Post Offices Mon.–Fri.
- ■ Museums/Monuments
- ■ Pharmacies

7 8 9 10 11 12 1 2 3 4 5 6 7

The times above are traditional hours of operation. Many malls and city-center **stores** open for longer hours (late-night hours one day a week, usually Wednesday or Thursday) and also open on Sunday (11–5). Convenience grocery stores stay open until late in the evening.

Main town **banks** and **post offices** open on Saturday mornings.

Museum opening times vary. Some major sights close on Monday and open later one evening a week; more modest sights of interest may close off season, so it is advisable to check with the local tourist office.

Note that many restaurants do not open for dinner until around 6 or 7 p.m. Before then, chain restaurants and fast-food outlets are usually the only places serving meals.

National Holidays

Banks, businesses and smaller stores close on these days, although larger stores may remain open.

Jan. 1	New Year's Day
Jan. 2	Bank Holiday (Scotland only)
Mar./Apr.	Good Friday
Mar./Apr.	Easter Monday (not in Scotland)
First Mon. of May	May Day
Last Mon. of May	Spring Bank Holiday
First Mon. of Aug.	Summer Bank Holiday (Scotland only)
Last Mon. of Aug.	Summer Bank Holiday
Dec. 25	Christmas Day
Dec. 26	Boxing Day

When December 25 and 26 fall on a weekend, the following Monday and Tuesday are public holidays. If January 1 falls on a weekend, usually the first Monday in January is a public holiday.

Photography

 Memory cards and camera batteries are readily available and there are many places offering download and CD services for digital cameras.

Britain

Health

Medical Insurance

Private insurance is recommended. Visitors can receive treatment in emergency rooms but are charged if admitted to a hospital. You can seek advice from a doctor at a surgery or health center; you must make an appointment, and will be charged. Doctors are listed in the *Yellow Pages*, or ask at your hotel or a tourist office.

Dental Services

Dentists charge for consultations or treatment. Emergency treatment is available after hours in towns and cities (see the *Yellow Pages*). Check if it is covered by your medical insurance.

Sun Advice

Although not renowned for very warm weather, Britain does have its moments, and it is not unheard of for July and August to be as hot as the Mediterranean. Visiting historic sights can involve being outside for prolonged periods, so cover up, apply sunscreen and drink plenty of fluids.

Drugs

Prescription and nonprescription medicines are available from pharmacies (chemists). Pharmacists can advise on medication for common ailments. Notices in all pharmacy windows give details of emergency facilities open outside regular hours.

Safe Water

Tap water is safe to drink, even in remote areas. Mineral water is widely available but is usually quite expensive, particularly in restaurants.

Restrooms

Public restrooms (toilets, lavatories, WCs or, in everyday parlance, "loos") are generally easy to find and maintained to a high standard. Most are free, but there may be a charge for those at major rail stations (about 20p).

Electricity

Britain has a 240-volt power supply. Electrical sockets take plugs with three square pins, so an adapter is needed for American appliances. A transformer is also required for appliances operating on 110 or 120 volts.

National Transportation

Train

Rail services are good in Britain. First class is comfortable but more expensive than standard. Intercity (high-speed) trains connect cities. For frequent rail use, rail cards offer discounts: contact Rail Europe ☎ 08448 484 064; www.raileurope.com. Once you are in Britain, Rail Rover passes are good value for regional rail travel: ☎ 08457 484950; www.nationalrail.co.uk

Bus

It is cheaper to travel by bus than by rail. The main operator for long-distance bus/coach travel in Britain is National Express. For details ☎ 08717 818181; www.nationalexpress.com. Euroline's buses operate from Britain to the rest of Europe: ☎ 08717 818181; www.eurolines.co.uk

Ferry

The busiest ferries run between southeast England and France (a high-speed train also shuttles passengers and cars through the Channel Tunnel). Service is frequent, especially in summer. Ferries also serve the smaller British islands, plus Ireland, Spain, Belgium, The Netherlands and Denmark.

Driving

Drive on the left

Speed Limits

British speed limits are stringently enforced by police patrols and also by strategically positioned cameras that detect speeding motorists.

Limited-access highways (motorways); divided highways (dual carriageways)
70 m.p.h

Main roads
50 or 60 m.p.h.

Urban areas
20, 30 or 40 m.p.h.

Seat Belts

Must be worn in front and rear seats at all times.

Blood Alcohol

The legal blood alcohol limit is 0.08%. Random breath tests on drivers are carried out frequently. Penalties are severe.

Driving (continued)

Tolls

Limited-access highways are free except for the M6 Toll Road (junction 4 to 11a). Some bridges or tunnels levy a toll. In central London there is a weekday congestion charge (see page 16). Phone 0845 900 1234 or visit www.tfl.gov.uk for payment information.

Car Rental

The leading rental firms have offices at airports, train stations and ferry terminals. Hertz offers discounted rates for AAA members (see page 15). For reservations:

	United States	Britain
Alamo	(800) 462-5266	0870 556 5656
		(Europcar)
Avis	(800) 331-1212	08445 445566
Budget	(800) 527-0700	08445 443439
Hertz	(800) 654-3131	0870 599 6699

Fuel

Gasoline (petrol) and diesel are priced in liters and are expensive. There are two grades of unleaded gas: super (98 octane) and premium (95 octane). Most gas stations are self-service, and 24-hour facilities are common.

AAA Affiliated Motoring Club

The Automobile Association (AA) Ltd., Fanum House, Basing View Basingstoke, Hampshire RG21 4EA
☎ 08705 448866; www.theAA.com

AAA members staying in the U.K. for up to 3 months get free AA Breakdown Service. If you break down while driving a privately owned car in the U.K. call ☎ 0800 887766 (AA Breakdown Service). If you're driving a rental car, contact the rental company's assistance partner. If you're staying for longer than 3 months, call the AA on 0800 085 2721 when you arrive in the U.K. to obtain AA Breakdown Service. You also can purchase the service online: www.theAA.com

Breakdowns and Accidents

There are emergency telephones at intervals on limited-access and divided highways. If you have an accident ☎ 999 or 112 for police, fire and ambulance. Most car rental firms provide their own rescue service; if your car is rented, follow the company's instructions. Use of an unauthorized car repair service may violate your rental agreement.

Other Information

The minimum age for driving a car is 17. An International Driving Permit (IDP) is recommended. A Green Card (international motor insurance certificate) is recommended if you are driving a private car; see page 15 for more information.

Useful Words and Phrases

Spotting the differences between American and British English is fun, especially as some regional accents are almost incomprehensible to the untrained ear! Britons have become familiar with Americanisms through American television shows, but it is still possible to make a blunder. Below are some illustrations of the "Atlantic divide."

American	British
ATM	*cashpoint*
ball-point pen	*biro*
to call collect	*to reverse the charges*
check	*cheque*
check (in a restaurant)	*bill*
elevator	*lift*
first/second floor (etc.)	*ground/first floor (etc.)*
movie theater	*cinema*
phone booth	*phone box*
reserve (reservation)	*book (reservation)*
restroom	*toilet/loo (colloquial)*
Scotch™ tape	*sticky tape/Sellotape™*
trash or garbage can	*dustbin or rubbish bin*
Food and drink	
(soft hamburger) bun	*bap*
beer	*bitter (dark),*
	lager (light)
candy	*sweets*
(potato) chips	*crisps*
cookies	*biscuits*
corn	*sweetcorn*
cotton candy	*candyfloss*
eggplant	*aubergine*
french fries	*chips*
grocery store	*supermarket*
Jell-O™	*jelly*
jelly	*jam*
liquor store	*off-licence*
oatmeal	*porridge*
Saranwrap™	*cling film*
zucchini	*courgette*
Fashion	
bangs	*fringe*
pants	*trousers*
pantyhose	*tights*
suspenders	*braces*
undershirt	*vest*
vest	*waistcoat*
Getting around	
hood (of a car)	*bonnet*
one-way trip	*single*
parking lot	*car park*
paved shoulder	*lay-by*
rotary/traffic circle	*roundabout*
round trip	*return ticket*
sidewalk	*pavement*
stick shift	*manual*
subway	*tube/underground*
truck	*lorry*
trunk (of a car)	*boot*

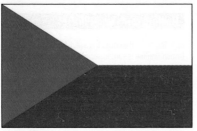

National Flag

Essential for Travelers

● Required ● Recommended ● Not required

Passport	●
Visa* (check regulations before you travel)	●
Travel, medical insurance	●
Round-trip or onward airline ticket	●
Local currency	●
Traveler's checks	●
Credit cards	●
First-aid kit and medicines	●
Inoculations	●

*U.S. citizens can stay in the Czech Republic for up to 90 days without a visa. For stays of longer than 90 days, visas must be obtained from an embassy outside the Czech Republic.

Essential for Drivers*

Driver's license	●
International Driving Permit	●
Car insurance (for nonrental cars)	●
Car registration (for nonrental cars)	●

*see also *Driving* section

Important Addresses

Czech Tourist Authority CzechTourism
Czech Center, 1109 Madison Avenue
New York, NY 10028
☎ (212) 288-0830 ext. 101
Fax (212) 288-0971
www.czechtourism.com

CzechTourism
Vinohradská 46, P.O. Box 32
120 41, Praha 2, Czech Republic
☎ 221 580 611
Fax 222 514 421
www.czechtourism.com

American Embassy
Tržiště 15
118 01 Praha 1, Czech Republic
☎ 257 022 000
Fax 257 022 809
www.usembassy.cz

Customs

✔ **Duty-free limits on goods brought in from non-European Union countries:**
200 cigarettes or 100 cigarillos or 50 cigars or 250 g. tobacco; 1 L. alcohol more than 22% volume or 2L. less than 22% volume; 2 L. non-sparkling wine; 50 ml. perfume or 250 ml. toilet water; plus any other duty-free goods (including gifts) to the value of €175. Persons importing alcohol must be 18 and over, for cigarettes and tobacco products 16 and over. There is no restriction on the import or export of Czech or foreign currencies, but amounts in excess of €15,000 must be declared.

✘ No unlicensed drugs, firearms, ammunition, offensive weapons, obscene material, unlicensed animals, counterfeit or copied goods, meat and poultry.
For customs limits for returning U.S. citizens see page 16.

Money

The Czech Republic's currency is the Koruna česká (Kč) – or Czech crown – which is divided into 100 haléřů (h) – or hellers – although you won't find many of the latter around. The denominations of Kč bills are 100, 200, 500, 1,000, 2,000 and 5,000. There are coins of 1, 2, 5, 10, 20 and 50Kč. You can exchange dollars at a bank *(banka)*, exchange office *(směnárna)*, post office *(pošta)* or hotel; you may be asked to show ID. Traveler's checks can usually only be exchanged at banks. It is an offense to change money through black-market money dealers; in any case, they rarely offer an attractive rate.

Tips and Gratuities

Tips are welcomed in restaurants and cafés, although service is normally included.

Restaurants (even when service is included)	5–10%
Cafés/bars	5–10%
Taxis	10%
Porters	40Kč
Hairdressers	10%
Tour guides	20Kč

Communications

Post Offices

 Buy stamps *(známky)* at a post office *(pošta)*, a newsstand/kiosk *(trafika/tabák)* or from a hotel. The postal service is generally reliable and not expensive.

Mailboxes are orange. Hours for out-of-town post offices may vary.

Telephones

 Pay phones either accept coins (less common, usually in more remote locations) or telephone cards *(telefonní karta or TRICK)* which cost 200 or 300Kč, and which can be bought from newsstands, tobacconists, post offices, shops, hotels and travel agencies. Most card phone booths have English instructions.

Phoning inside the Czech Republic
There are no area codes in the Czech Republic; all numbers are nine digits: dial the number that is listed. For national directory inquiries dial 1180.

Phoning the Czech Republic from abroad
The country code for the Czech Republic is 420. You will need to prefix this number to the numbers in this book if you are phoning from another country. To phone the Czech Republic from the United States or Canada dial the prefix 011 420. Example: 112 233 445 becomes 011 420 112 233 445.

Phoning from the Czech Republic
To phone the United States or Canada from the Czech Republic, prefix the number with 00 1. Example: (111) 222-3333 becomes 00 1 111 222-3333. To call international information dial 1181.

Emergency telephone numbers
All Emergencies **112**
Police – national *(Policie Česká republiky)* **158**
City police *(Městská policie)* **156**
Fire service *(požár)* **150**
Ambulance (ambulance) **155**
Emergency calls are free from phone booths.

Hours of Operation

- Stores Mon.–Sat.
- Offices Mon.–Fri.
- Banks Mon.–Fri.
- Post Offices Mon.–Fri.
- Museums/Monuments
- Pharmacies Mon.–Sat.

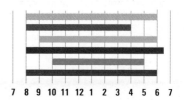

7 8 9 10 11 12 1 2 3 4 5 6 7

Stores close early on Saturday; many close at noon or 1. Some stores close for an hour for lunch, normally between noon and 1 p.m.

Food stores in the large cities open at 7 a.m., and large stores and shopping centers stay open until 8 or 10 p.m. (4 p.m. on Saturday). In Prague, most stores open all day Saturday and Sunday.

Banks may close earlier on Friday, though some stay open until 7 p.m. some days, and some are open Saturday morning. Some post offices open on Saturday morning. Some tourist resorts may have special opening times.

Museums often close on Monday and days following public holidays, and opening times may be reduced during the winter.

National Holidays

Banks, businesses and most stores close on these days. Monuments, museums and galleries usually open on public holidays (except Jan. 1, Easter, and Dec. 25 and 26) but are closed the following day.

Jan. 1	New Year's Day and Day of Restoration of Independent Czech State
Mar./Apr.	Easter Monday
May 1	Labor Day
May 8	Liberation Day
Jul. 5	SS Cyril and Methodius' Day
Jul. 6	Jan Hus Day
Sep. 28	Czech Statehood Day
Oct. 28	Independence Day
Nov. 17	Day of Fight for Freedom and Democracy
Dec. 24	Christmas Eve
Dec. 25	Christmas Day
Dec. 26	St. Stephen's Day

Photography

Czechs are enthusiastic photographers and you will have no difficulty in finding spare equipment for your digital camera, including memory cards, batteries and accessories. Several shops in Prague will do on-the-spot digital printing. An excellent shop is Foto Škoda at Vodičkova 47.

Czech Republic

Health

Medical Insurance

 Private medical insurance is recommended. U.S. and Canadian visitors can receive treatment in a hospital emergency and accident unit, but you will be charged if you are admitted to a hospital *(nemocnice)*. You may be asked to show your passport when seeking hospital treatment. The following clinics in Prague have English-speaking doctors: Na Homolce Hospital, Roentgenova 2 ☎ 257 271 111, and Canadian Medical Care, Veleslavínská 30 ☎ 235 360 133.

Dental Services

A dentist *(zubař)* will charge for any treatment given. Check if it is covered by your medical insurance. For an English-speaking dentist, ask at your hotel or embassy or at a tourist office or the American Dental Associates, V Celnici 4 ☎ 221 181 121.

Sun Advice

June through August is the sunniest period, when adequate sun protection should be applied.

Drugs

A pharmacy *(lékárna)* is the only place you can buy over-the-counter medicines. Pharmacies also dispense many drugs normally available only by prescription in other Western countries. However, it is advisable to bring supplies of your own medicines with you. If you need a pharmacy after regular hours, information about the nearest all-night facility is posted at some pharmacies.

Safe Water

Tap water is safe but may have an unpleasant taste. Bottled water is available everywhere.

Restrooms

Public restrooms *(WC)* are scarce and usually require a payment of 5–10Kč. Metro stations in Prague will have a reasonably clean restroom. The best bet is to use the facilities of a hotel or restaurant.

Electricity

The Czech Republic has a 230-volt power supply. Electrical sockets take plugs with two round pins; American appliances will need a plug adapter, and will require a transformer if they do not have a dual-voltage facility.

National Transportation

Train *(Vlak)*

Czech Railways (České dráhy, CD) is extensive and inexpensive, but often crowded. The fast trains stop at major cities; local trains stop everywhere but usually provide only second-class service. All long-distance trains have two classes; some have dining carriages and overnight services. Reserve seats on express trains. For information: ☎ 840 112 113 (24-hours); www.cd.cz

Bus *(Autobus)*

Inexpensive and popular with Czechs. Reserve for weekends, national holidays or early morning. Tickets are purchased from the bus station kiosk or the driver. For information ☎ 900 144 444 (daily 24-hours); www.florenc.cz. Large items of luggage will be stowed for a small charge. Euroline's buses connect to other countries: ☎ 245 005 245; www.eurolines.cz

Ferry *(Prévos)*

 From April to September boats cruise the Vltava river as far as Troja Château to the north of Prague and Slapy Dam to the south: ☎ 224 810 030; www.evd.cz

Driving

Drive on the right

Speed Limits

Police can give on-the-spot fines. If this should happen to you, ask for a receipt.

 Limited-access highways *(dalnice)* **130 k.p.h. (80 m.p.h.).**
Minimum speed **80 k.p.h. (49 m.p.h)**

 Main roads
90 k.p.h. (56 m.p.h.)

Urban areas
50 k.p.h. (31 m.p.h.)

Seat Belts

Must be worn in front and back seats at all times. Children under 4 feet 11 inches or 79 pounds must not travel in the front

Blood Alcohol

The legal blood alcohol limit is zero. Random breath tests on drivers are carried out frequently, especially late at night, and the penalties for offenders are severe.

Driving (continued)

Tolls

A tax is levied for use of highways and express roads. A sticker *(vignette)* must be purchased and displayed; failure to do so will result in a fine. Stickers can be bought for one week, one month or one year at the Czech border, ÚAMK offices, gas stations or post offices.

Car Rental

The leading rental firms have offices at airports and train stations. Hertz offers discounted rates for AAA members (see page 15). For reservations:

	United States	Czech Republic
Alamo	(877) 222-9075	224 811 290 (Europcar)
Avis	(800) 230-4898	221 851 225
Budget	(800) 527-0700	220 560 443
Hertz	(800) 654-3131	225 345 031

Fuel

Gas, sold in liters, is unleaded *(natural)* sold as 95 and 98 octane, diesel *(nafta)* or LPG *(autoplyn or plyn)*. Some out-of-town stations *(benzinová pumpa)* close for lunch and after 6 p.m. There are 24-hour gas stations in cities and along highways.

AAA Affiliated Motoring Club

Ústřední automotoklub České republiky (ÚAMK; CR) Na Strži 9, CZ-140 02 Prague 4 ☎ 261 104 111; fax: 261 104 278; www.uamk.cz. If you break down while driving phone ☎ 1230 (24-hours; ÚAMK breakdown service). Not all automobile clubs offer full services to AAA members.

Breakdowns and Accidents

There are 24-hour emergency phones at regular intervals on highways or ☎ 158 for police assistance. Most car rental firms provide their own free rescue service; if you have an accident, follow the rental documentation instructions supplied with the car. Use of an unauthorized repair company may violate your agreement. You must carry a first-aid kit and a warning triangle in the car.

Other Information

The minimum age for driving a car is 18 (may be higher for some car rental firms). An International Driving Permit (IDP) is formally required, though police and rental car companies will usually accept a U.S. state driver's license. A Green Card (international motor insurance certificate) is required for a private car; see page 15 for more information. You are required by law to use dimmed headlights at all times when driving.

Useful Words and Phrases

The official language of the Czech Republic is Czech *(česky)* – a highly complex Slav tongue. Czech sounds and looks daunting, but apart from a few special letters, each letter and sound is pronounced as it is written – the key is to stress the first syllable of a word.

Any attempt to speak Czech will be heartily appreciated, although English is spoken by many involved in the tourist trade. Below are a few words that may be helpful.

Do you speak English?	*Mluvíte anglicky?*
What is your name?	*Jak se jmenujete?*
hello, goodbye (casual)	*ahoj*
good morning	*dobré ráno*
goodbye	*na shledanou*
good night	*dobrou noc*
How much?	*Kolik?*
excuse me	*promiňte*
I am American	*Jsem Američan(ka)*
I would like	*Chtěl(a) bych*
I don't understand	*Nerozumím*
no smoking	*kouření zakazano*
okay	*dobře*
open	*otevřeno*
closed	*zavřeno*
please	*prosím*
thank you	*děkuji*
ticket	*lístek*
(one-way/round trip)	*(jednosměrnou/ zpáteční)*
Where is...?	*Kde je...?*
yes/no	*ano/ne*
you're welcome	*prosím*
the hotel	***hotel***
breakfast	*snídaně*
reservation	*reservaci*
key	*klíč*
room	*pokoj*
single/double room	*jednolužkový dvoulužkový pokoj*
Where is the toilet?	*Kde je toalet?*
shower	*sprcha*
bathroom	*koupelna*
the restaurant	***restaurace***
beef	*hovězí*
beer	*pivo*
bread	*chleb*
the check	*účet*
chicken	*kuře*
coffee	*káva*
dessert	*moučnik*
dish of the day	*nabídka dne*
fish	*ryba*
lamb	*jehněcí*
meat	*maso*
pork	*vepřové maso*
seafood	*mořské ryby*
starter	*předkrm*
wine	*víno*

National Flag

Essential for Travelers*

● Required ● Recommended ● Not required

Passport	●
Visa (check regulations before you travel)	●
Travel, medical insurance	●
Round-trip or onward airline ticket	●
Local currency	●
Traveler's checks	●
Credit cards	●
First-aid kit and medicines*	●
Inoculations	●

*see also *Health* section

Essential for Drivers*

Driver's license	●
International Driving Permit	●
Car insurance (for nonrental cars)	●
Car registration (for nonrental cars)	●

*see also *Driving* section

Important Addresses

VisitDenmark
PO Box 4649
Grand Central Station
New York, NY 10163-4649
☎ (212) 885-9700
Fax (212) 885-9726
www.visitdenmark.com

VisitDenmark
Islands Brygge 43, 3rd Floor
DK-2300 København S, Denmark
☎ 32 88 99 00
Fax 32 88 99 01
www.visitdenmark.com

American Embassy
Dag Hammarskjölds Allé 24
DK-2100 København Ø, Denmark
☎ 33 41 71 00
Fax 35 43 02 23
http://denmark.embassy.gov

Customs

✔ **Duty-free limits on goods brought in from non-European Union countries:**
200 cigarettes or 100 cigarillos or 50 cigars or 250 g. tobacco; 2 L. wine; 1 L. alcohol over 22% volume; 2 L. alcohol under 22% volume; 50 ml. perfume; 250 ml. toilet water; plus any other duty-free goods (including gifts) to the value of DKr1,350. There is no limit on the importation of tax-paid goods purchased within the European Union, provided they are for your own personal use. Limits for alcohol and tobacco products apply to visitors aged 17 or over. There are no currency regulations.

✗ No unlicensed drugs, weapons, ammunition, obscene material, pets or other animals, counterfeit money or copied goods, meat or poultry.
For customs limits for returning U.S. citizens see page 16.

Money

Denmark's currency is the krone (DKr), which is divided into 100 øre. The denominations of krone bills are 50, 100, 200, 500 and 1,000. There are coins of 25 and 50 øre and 1, 2, 5, 10 and 20DKr. Banks may not exchange foreign bank notes of high denominations. Tourists coming from the euro zone may use a euro credit card; the exchange rate does not fluctuate. Most international credit cards are accepted in larger stores, for which a fee will be charged. Senior citizens and holders of International Student Identity Cards (ISIC) can often obtain discounts on travel and entrance fees.

Tips and Gratuities

Tips are not expected, but may be given for outstanding service.

Restaurants (service is always included)	change
Cafés/bars	change
Taxis (tips included in fare)	change
Porters	change
Chambermaids	change
Cloakroom attendants	change

Communications

Post Offices

Stamps *(frimerker)* can be bought at a post office *(postkontoret)*, newsstand *(aviskiosk)* or stationer *(papirhandel)*.

Mailboxes *(postkasse)* are red with a horn and crown detail. Hours for out-of-town post offices may vary. For postal service inquiries telephone Post Danmark ☎ 80 20 70 30; www.postdanmark.dk.

Telephones

Danish public telephones *(telefon)* work efficiently for national and international calls, but do not refund your money if the call is not answered. Some phones require coins to be

inserted after dialing – DKr1, DKr2, DKr5, DKr10 and DKr20 coins. Some phones also accept euro coins (10, 20 and 50 cents and €1 and €2). Phone card booths are also available; buy the cards (DKr30, DKr50 or DKr100) from a post office, train station, newsstand or gas station.

Phoning inside Denmark

All telephone numbers are 8 digits and include the regional code. Dial all digits when making a call. To call the operator dial 110; to call collect dial 115; for the long-distance operator dial 114.

Phoning Denmark from abroad

The country code for Denmark is 45. Note that Danish numbers in this book do not include the country code. To phone Denmark from the United States or Canada add the prefix 011 45. Example: 11 22 33 44 becomes 011 45 11 22 33 44.

Phoning from Denmark

To phone the United States or Canada from Denmark, prefix the area code and number with 00 1. Example: (111) 222-3333 becomes 00 1 111 222-3333. To call directory inquiries in Denmark dial 118. To call international information dial 113.

Emergency telephone numbers

Police *(politi)* **112**
Fire service *(brandvæsen)* **112**
Ambulance *(sygevogn)* **112**
Emergency calls are free from phone booths

Hours of Operation

■ Stores Mon.–Sat. ■ Post Offices Mon.–Fri.
■ Offices Mon.–Fri. ■ Museums/Monuments
■ Banks Mon.–Fri. ■ Pharmacies Mon.–Fri.

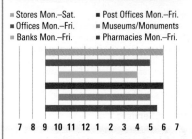

7 8 9 10 11 12 1 2 3 4 5 6 7

Although Sunday is the official closing day, souvenir shops in many towns, supermarkets and grocery stores in summer vacation areas stay open during the high season.

Many bakeries and patisseries also open on Sunday morning.

On Friday **stores** stay open until 7 or 8 p.m. Most shops close at 1, 2 or 4 p.m. on Saturday afternoon, but many shops in Copenhagen are open until 5 p.m.

Department stores and supermarkets often stay open later than 5:30/6 p.m.

Large gas stations sell convenience foods seven days a week.

Banks in Copenhagen are open until 5 p.m. On Thursday all banks are open until 6 p.m.

Post offices open at 9 or 10 and close at 5 or 6; some post offices open Saturday 9 or 10–noon or 2.

National Holidays

Banks, businesses and most stores close on these days.

Jan. 1	New Year's Day
Mar./Apr.	Maundy Thursday
Mar./Apr.	Good Friday
Mar./Apr.	Easter Monday
Apr. /May	Great Prayer Day
May/Jun.	Ascension Day
May/Jun.	Pentecost Monday
Jun. 5	Constitution Day
Dec. 24	Christmas Eve
Dec. 25	Christmas Day
Dec. 26	St. Stephen's Day
Dec. 31	New Year's Eve

Photography

Denmark is not renowned for its sunshine and the winter months have short daylight hours. Batteries are sold throughout the city and there are plenty of places to download and print digital images. Some museums may not allow photography.

Health

Medical Insurance

Private medical insurance is recommended. In an emergency, visitors from the U.S. and Canada can receive free temporary treatment in a hospital *(hospitalet)*. You will be charged for more extensive treatment. Health offices *(kommunes social og sundhedforvaltning)* have lists of hospitals and doctors, or ask at your hotel.

Dental Services

Dentists *(tandlægen)* will charge for any treatment given. They are listed in the telephone directory, and after-hours treatment is available in some clinics. Advice can be sought at tourist and health offices. Be sure that treatment is covered by your medical insurance.

Sun Advice

The warmest months are July and August. The sun in Denmark is not fierce, but sun protection is still advised, especially on boats or near the water.

Drugs

To obtain a prescription medicine at a pharmacy *(apotek)* it must be prescribed by a Scandinavian doctor, so make sure that your supply of prescribed medicines will last your stay. Additionally, some preparations available over the counter in the U.S. may be obtained in Denmark only with a prescription. After regular hours, the nearest all-night facility is posted at all pharmacies.

Safe Water

Tap water is safe to drink, and mineral water *(mineralvand)* is widely available.

Restrooms

Public restrooms *(toiletterne)* are easy to find, clean, well equipped and usually free. They are often indicated by a symbol, or marked WC or *Damer* (women) and *Herrer* (men).

Electricity

Denmark has a 220-volt power supply. Electrical sockets take plugs with two round pins. American appliances will need a plug adapter and will require a transformer if they do not have a dual-voltage facility.

National Transportation

Train *(Tog)*

Copenhagen is an important meeting point for trains between Europe and the rest of Scandinavia. Danish State Railways, Danske Statsbaner (DSB), runs an efficient service with trains linking to Germany and, via the Øresund Link, to Sweden. Most domestic trains have refreshment facilities; seat reservations are recommended. For information (☎ 70 13 14 15; press 3 for English-language version, 1 for information and tickets, 2 for international routes) www.dsb.dk

Bus *(Bus)*

The domestic bus service is good; ask for details at local tourist offices. Eurolines services run between other European countries (☎ 33 88 70 00; www.eurolines.dk).

Ferry *(Færge)*

There are numerous ferry services from Denmark, with year-round connections to many northern European countries. DFDS Seaways has an office in Denmark, ☎ 33 42 30 00 (Mon.–Fri. 8–5); www.dfdsseaways.com

Driving

Drive on the right

Speed Limits
Police can impose on-the-spot fines.

Limited-access highways *(motorvej)* **130 (80 m.p.h.)** or **110 k.p.h. (68 m.p.h.)**

Main roads **80 k.p.h. (49 m.p.h.)** Minimum speed **40 k.p.h. (24 m.p.h.)**

Urban areas **50 k.p.h. (31 m.p.h.)** but **40 k.p.h. (24 m.p.h.)** in central Copenhagen

Seat Belts

Must be worn in front and back seats at all times.

Blood Alcohol

The legal blood alcohol limit is 0.05%. Random breath tests on drivers are carried out frequently, especially late at night, and the penalties for offenders are severe.

Driving (continued)

Tolls

There are no tolls on highways. However, the *Storebælt* (Great Belt) tunnel and bridge from Korsør to Nyborg and the impressive 10-mile Øresund tunnel and bridge from Copenhagen to Malmö (Sweden) both levy a toll.

Car Rental

The leading car rental companies have offices at airports, principal railroad stations and ferry terminals. Hertz offers discounted rates for AAA members (see page 15). For reservations:

	United States	Denmark
Alamo	(877) 222-9075	98 17 53 55
Avis	(800) 230-1898	33 26 80 80
Budget	(800) 527-0700	33 55 05 00
Hertz	(800) 654-3131	33 17 90 00

Fuel

Gas *(benzin)* is sold in liters; unleaded gas *(blyfri)* comes in 92 and 95 octane ratings. Self-service gas stations *(tank selv* or *selvbetjening)* are common, except on limited-access highways. Most gas stations take credit cards, and some have automatic pumps for DKr50 and DKr100 bills.

AAA Affiliated Motoring Club

Forenede Danske Motorejere (FDM) Firskovvej 32, P.O. Box 500, 2800 Kgs. Lyngby ☎ 45 27 07 07; www.fdm.dk. Not all automobile clubs offer full services to AAA members.

Breakdowns and Accidents

Report accidents to the Dansk Forening for International Motorkøretøjsforsikring (DFIM), Philip Heymans Allé 3, DK-2900 Hellerup (☎ 41 91 90 69, 10 a.m.–3 p.m.; fax 41 91 91 92).

Most car rental firms provide their own free rescue service; if your car is rented, follow the instructions given in the documentation. Use of a car repair service other than those authorized by your rental company may violate your agreement. You must carry a warning triangle in your car.

Other Information

The minimum legal age for driving a car is 18 (may be 20 to 25 for some car rental firms).

An International Driving Permit (IDP) is recommended; some rental firms require them, and they can speed up formalities if you are involved in an accident. A Green Card (international motor insurance certificate) is recommended if you are driving a private car; see page 15 for more information. Use dimmed headlights at all times.

Useful Words and Phrases

Danish is a Germanic language, close to Swedish and Norwegian, but it is tricky to pronounce because some letters *(d, g)* are silent in the middle or at the end of words, *h* before a *v* becomes silent, and some specifically Scandinavian vowels *(å, ø, and æ)* are awkward to say correctly. But Danes are aware of this, and most of them speak very good English. In addition, menus are often in English or German.

In the Danish alphabet, the following letters come after *z: å, ø* and *æ*. (Århus, for example, comes at the end of the alphabet.) *Å* is used in place of aa, although the city of Aalborg prefers to write the two vowels out in full.

The following words and phrases should help you:

Do you speak English?	*Taler de Engelsk?*
excuse me	*undskyld*
hello/goodbye	*hej/farvel*
how much is...?	*hvor meget koster det?*
I am American	*jeg er Amerikaner*
I'd like...	*jeg vil gerne have...*
I don't understand	*jeg forstår det ikke*
open/closed	*åben/lukket*
please/thank you	*værså venlig/tak*
ticket (one-way/ round trip)	*billet (enkeltbillet/ en tur-retur)*
where is/are...?	*hvor er...?*
yes/no	*ja/nej*
the hotel	***hotel***
breakfast	*morgenmad*
key	*nøgle*
for one/two nights	*en nat/to nætter*
for one person/ two people	*enkeltværelse/ dobbeltværelse*
room	*værelse*
shower	*brusebad*
the restaurant	***restaurant***
beef	*bøf*
bread	*brød*
butter	*smør*
cheese	*ost*
the check	*regningen*
chicken	*kylling*
cod	*torsk*
coffee/tea	*kaffe/the*
Danish pastry	*Wienerbrød*
dessert	*dessert*
fish	*fisk*
fruit salad	*frugtsalat*
herring	*sild*
pork	*suinkød*
potatoes	*kartofler*
shellfish	*skaldyr*
shrimps	*rejer*
starter	*forret*
trout	*ørred*
vegetables	*grøntsager*
wine	*vin*

Finland

National Flag

Essential for Travelers

● **Required** ● **Recommended** ● **Not required**

Passport	●
Visa (check regulations before you travel)	●
Travel, medical insurance	●
Round-trip or onward airline ticket	●
Local currency	●
Traveler's checks	●
Credit cards	●
First-aid kit and medicines	●
Inoculations	●

Essential for Drivers*

Driver's license	●
International Driving Permit	●
Car insurance (for nonrental cars)	●
Car registration (for nonrental cars)	●

*see also *Driving* section

Important Addresses

Finnish Tourist Board (MEK)
297 York Street
Jersey City
NJ 07302
☎ (917) 863 5484
Fax (212) 885 9710
www.visitfinland.com/us

Finnish Tourist Board (MEK)
P.O. Box 625
Töölönkatu 11
FIN-00101 Helsinki, Finland
☎ 010 60 58 000
Fax 010 60 58 333
www.mek.fi

American Embassy
Itäinen Puistotie 14B
FIN-00140 Helsinki, Finland
☎ 09 616 250 (embassy);
citizen services ☎ 40 140 5957
Fax 09 616 2 5800
Telephone to make appointments
Telephone inquiries Mon.–Thu. 2–4

Customs

✓ **Duty-free limits on goods brought in from non-European Union countries:**
200 cigarettes or 100 cigarillos or 50 cigars or 250 g. tobacco; 1 L. alcohol over 22% volume or 2 L. alcohol under 22% volume; 2 L. wine; 16 L. beer; 50 ml. perfume; 250 ml. toilet water; plus any other duty-free goods (including gifts) to the value of a175. Tax-free allowances for goods purchased within the European Union: 200 cigarettes or 50 cigars or 250 g. tobacco or 100 cigarillos; 1 L. alcohol over 22% volume; 2 L. alcohol under 22% volume; 2 L. sparkling wine; 16 L. beer. There are no currency regulations. Pets are allowed if vaccinated against rabies between one and 12 months prior to date of arrival.

✗ No unlicensed drugs, weapons, ammunition, obscene material, counterfeit money or copied goods.
For customs limits for returning U.S. citizens see page 16.

Money

Finland's currency is the euro (€), a currency shared by 16 other European Union countries. The euro is divided into 100 cents (¢). The denominations of euro bills are 5, 10, 20, 50, 100, 200 and 500. There are coins of 5, 10, 20 and 50¢ and €1 and €2. Exchange dollars and traveler's checks at a bank *(pankki)* or an exchange office, as the exchange rate in city hotels may be poor.

Tips and Gratuities

Tips are welcomed, but not expected.

Restaurants	change
Cafés/bars	change
Taxis; hairdressers	none
Porters; restroom attendants	change
Chambermaids	change
Cloakroom attendants; hotel/restaurant doormen	€1

Helsinki **12:00 noon** | New York **− 7 hrs** | Chicago **− 8 hrs** | Denver **− 9 hrs** | Los Angeles **− 10 hrs** | Time zones

515

Finland

Communications

Post Offices

Most post offices are open Mon.–Fri. 9–6. Hours for out-of-town post offices may vary. Stamps *(postimerkki)* can be bought at post offices, bookstores, newsstands (R-kiosks), railroad and bus stations, and some hotels. Mailboxes are usually yellow and set into walls. (This white and blue mail box is on Aland Island.)

Telephones

The Finnish public telephone system is efficient and accepts mostly credit cards and prepaid telephone cards. Phone cards are available from R-kiosks, telephone company (Sonera) shops and some post offices. Most people have cell phones; you can rent one for the length of your stay.

Phoning inside Finland

All Finnish telephone numbers in this book include an area code: dial the number listed. To call the operator dial 115; for directory assistance information dial 118.

Phoning Finland from abroad

The country code for Finland is 358; to phone Finland from the United States or Canada, omit the first zero from the Finnish number and prefix with 011 358. (Finnish area codes have two or three digits including the first zero.) Example: 01 122 3344 becomes 011 358 1 122 3344.

Phoning from Finland

To phone the United States or Canada from Finland, prefix the area code and number with 00 1. (There are other numbers to dial out of the country depending on what telephone system you are using: 990, 994 or 999, followed by 1.) Example: (111) 222-3333 becomes 00 1 111 222-3333. For national information, dial 02 02 02; for international information, dial 02 02 08.

Emergency telephone numbers

Police *(poliisi)* **112**
Fire service *(palokunta)* **112**
Ambulance *(ambulanssi)* **112**
Emergency calls are free from phone booths.

Hours of Operation

- Stores Mon.–Sat.
- Offices Mon.–Fri.
- Banks Mon.–Fri.
- Post Offices Mon.–Fri.
- Pharmacies Mon.–Fri.

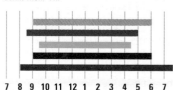

7 8 9 10 11 12 1 2 3 4 5 6 7

Many stores close at 2 or 3 on Saturday, but department **stores** and shopping malls stay open until 5 or 6. During the week, large stores extend their hours to 8 or 9, and open on Sunday from June through August and during December. Grocery stores stay open until 8 or 9. Some supermarkets and convenience stores open on Sunday.

Some **gas stations** close on Sunday.

Out-of-town post offices and banks may have shorter hours, and some city post offices and banks stay open into the evening.

Museum and **monument** opening times vary according to the season. Check opening times with the local tourist office.

Some **pharmacies** *(apteekki)* close early on Saturday. In Helsinki, the Apteekki Yliopiston, Mannerheimintie 96, ☎ 0300 20200, is open 24 hours.

National Holidays

Banks, businesses and most stores close on these days.

Jan. 1	New Year's Day
Jan. 6	Epiphany
Mar./Apr.	Good Friday
Mar./Apr.	Easter Monday
May	Ascension
Jun. 21–22	Midsummer's Day Eve and Midsummer's Day
Nov. 1	All Saints' Day
Dec. 6	Independence Day
Dec. 24	Christmas Eve
Dec. 25	Christmas Day
Dec. 26	St. Stephen's Day

Photography

Camera batteries are readily available and there are many places offering digital equipment and download services for digital cameras. Bring a tripod if you hope to photograph the northern lights *(aurora borealis)*. Check whether photography is permitted in museums.

Finland

Health

Medical Insurance

Private medical insurance is recommended. All treatment in a hospital (sairaala) has to be paid for. Foreign visitors can receive good service at a private hospital or health center *(lääkäriasema);* for 24-hour medical advice ☎ 0910023. For private medical care contact Mehiläinen, Runeberginkatu 47A, Töölö, Helsinki ☎ 010 414 3030 (24 hours).

Dental Services

Dentists *(hammaslääkäri)* charge for treatment and can be expensive, so find out if treatment is covered by your medical insurance. City hospitals have 24-hour clinics.

Sun Advice

Southeast Finland has the highest summer temperature in Scandinavia, so precautions are necessary. Use a suitable sunscreen and cover up sensitive skin.

Drugs

Prescription and nonprescription medicines are available from pharmacies *(apteekki)*. If you need a pharmacy outside regular hours, information about the nearest all-night facility is posted at all pharmacies.

Safe Water

Tap water is safe to drink, and mineral water *(kivennäisvesi)* is widely available.

Restrooms

Public restrooms are easy to find, immaculately clean and modern, and are designated by *Miehille/Miehet* (men) and *Naisille/Naiset* (women). There may be a small charge, but many are free. Attendants welcome loose change as a tip.

Electricity

Finland has a 220-volt power supply. Electrical sockets take plugs with two round pins. American appliances will need a plug adapter and will require a transformer if they do not have a dual-voltage facility.

National Transportation

Train *(Juna)*

The Finnish Railway (Valtion Rautatiet, or VR) extends north to southern Lapland. For timetable *(Suomen kulkuneuvot)* information ☎ 0600 41 902; www.vr.fi. If you are planning extensive rail travel, buy a FinnRailpass, which can be bought at main railroad stations or Finnish travel agencies. For information ☎ 0600 41 902. In the U.S. you can buy a Eurail Scandinavia Pass from Rail Europe ☎ 1 800 622 8600; www.raileurope.com.

Bus *(Bussi)*

Bus lines run to even the most remote corners of Finland. Bus passes (discount cards) are available for those traveling long distances (valid 2 weeks). For information ☎ 0200 4000.

Ferry *(Laiva)*

There are many excursions exploring Finland's eastern lake system and the country's canal network. Trips into Russia, Estonia, Latvia and Lithuania are possible; check with the tour operator whether a short-term visa is required. These can be obtained through the country's embassy or a travel agent. Contact Tallink Silja ☎ 358 600 15 700 (outside Europe) or 49 451 58 99 222 (within Europe) and Viking Line ☎ 0600 41577.

Driving

Drive on the right

Speed Limits

Minor fines can be imposed on the spot, but not collected. Payment can be made at banks.

 Limited-access highways *(moottoritie)*
120 k.p.h. (74 m.p.h.) in summer
100 k.p.h. (62 m.p.h.) in winter
Divided highways **100 k.p.h. (62 m.p.h.)**

 Main roads
80 k.p.h. (49 m.p.h.)

Urban areas
40–60 k.p.h. (24–37 m.p.h.)

Seat Belts

Must be worn in front and back seats at all times.

Blood Alcohol

 The legal blood alcohol limit is 0.05%. Random breath tests on drivers are carried out frequently, especially late at night, and the penalties for offenders are severe.

Driving (continued)

Tolls

 There are no highway tolls in Finland.

Car Rental

The leading rental firms have offices at airports and train stations. Hertz offers discounted rates for AAA members (see page 15). For reservations:

	United States	Finland
Alamo	(877) 222-9075	40 30 62 819
Avis	(800) 230-4898	09 859 8333
Budget	(800) 527-0700	0207 466 600
Hertz	(800) 654-3131	0200 112 233

Fuel

There is no leaded gas in Finland. There are two grades of unleaded gas, 95 and 98 octane. Diesel is also available. Gas stations are open Mon.–Sat. 7 a.m.–9 p.m., shorter hours on Sunday. Credit cards are acccepted at most filling stations; check with your card issuer for usage in Finland.

AAA Affiliated Motoring Club
Autoliitto (AL) P.O. Box 35, Hämeentie 105A, FIN-00551 Helsinki
☎ 09 7258 4400; fax 09 7258 4460
If you break down while driving, call ☎ 02 00 80 80 (24 hours) for the AL breakdown service.
Not all automobile clubs offer full services to AAA members.

Breakdowns and Accidents

There are 24-hour emergency phones at regular intervals on highways. If you are involved in an accident, phone ☎ 112 for police, fire or ambulance. Accidents should be reported without delay to: Finnish Motor Insurers' Center (Liikenne-vakuutuskeskus), Bulevardi 28, FIN-00120 Helsinki ☎ 040 450 4750 (administration); fax 040 450 4696 (insurance).

Most car rental firms provide their own free rescue service. Use of a car repair service other than those authorized by your rental company may violate your agreement. You must carry a warning triangle and a fluorescent vest in your car.

Other Information

The minimum age for driving a car is 18 (19–25 for car rental firms). An International Driving Permit (IDP) is recommended; some rental firms require them, and they can speed up formalities if you are involved in an accident. A Green Card (international motor insurance certificate) is recommended if you are driving a private car; see page 15 for more information. Dimmed headlights must be used at all times. In winter, snow tires or chains are essential. From December through February, winter tires

Driving (continued)

(with or without studs) or tires intended for year-round use are compulsory. You can buy or rent winter driving equipment from Autoliitto. Watch out for signs warning of elk and reindeer crossing roads, indicating the approximate length of danger zones – these animals are more active at dusk.

Useful Words and Phrases

Finnish is a complex and difficult language to learn, and bears little or no resemblance to neighboring languages. However, Swedish is Finland's second, more accessible language, and most people speak some English.

Finnish uses compound words, which are pronounced exactly as they are written. The first syllable of a word is always stressed, and each letter is pronounced individually.

Do you speak English?	*Puhutteko englantia?*
excuse me	*anteeksi*
hello	*terve*
goodbye	*näkemiin*
how much?	*kuinka paljon?*
how are you?	*kuinka voitte?*
Is it near?	*Onko se lähellä?*
I'd like…	*Haluaisin…*
I don't understand	*en ymmärrä*
nonsmoking	*tupakointi kielletty*
okay	*ja lyh*
open/closed	*avoinna/suljettu*
please/thank you	*olkaa hyvä/kiitos*
ticket (one-way/ round trip)	*menolippu meno-paluulippu*
where is…?	*missä on…?*
yes/no	*kyllä or joo/ei*
the hotel	***hotelli***
breakfast	*aamiainen*
key	*avain*
room	*huone*
shower	*suihku*
it's too expensive	*se on liian kallis*
the restaurant	***ravintola***
beef	*nauta*
bread	*leipä*
chicken	*kana*
coffee	*kahvi*
dessert	*jälkiruoka*
fish	*kala*
lamb	*karitsa*
main course	*pääruoka*
milk	*maito*
pork	*sianliha*
seafood	*äyrläisiä*
soup	*keitto*
steak	*pihvl*
wine	*vini*

France

National Flag

Essential for Travelers

● **Required** ● **Recommended** ● **Not required**

Passport	●
Visa (check regulations before you travel)	●
Travel, medical insurance	●
Round-trip or onward airline ticket	●
Local currency	●
Traveler's checks	●
Credit cards	●
First-aid kit and medicines	●
Inoculations	●

Essential for Drivers*

Driver's license	●
International Driving Permit	●
Car insurance (for nonrental cars)	●
Car registration (for nonrental cars)	●

*see also *Driving* section

Important Addresses

**Maison de la France
(French Government Tourist Office)**
79–81 rue de Clichy, 75009 Paris
(not open to the public)
☎ 01 42 96 70 00
www.franceguide.com

American Embassy
2 avenue Gabriel, 75008 Paris, France
☎ 01 43 12 22 22
Fax 01 42 66 97 83
http://france.usembassy.gov

American Consulate for American Citizen Affairs
4 avenue Gabriel, 75008 Paris, France
☎ 01 43 12 22 22 or 0892 238 472 (information),
0810 26 46 26 (live service operator)
Open by appointment only

French Embassy USA
4101 Reservoir Road, N.W.
Washington D.C., 20007
☎ (202) 944-6000
www.info-france-usa.org

Customs

✔ **Duty-free limits on goods brought in from non-European Union countries:**
200 cigarettes or 100 cigarillos or 50 cigars or 250 g. tobacco; 2 L. wine; 1 L. alcohol over 22% volume; 2 L. alcohol under 22%; 60 ml. perfume; 250 ml. toilet water; plus any other goods (including gifts) to the value of €400 (see www.ec.europa.eu/taxation_customs/travellers/enter_eu/index_en.html for details). There is no limit on the importation of tax-paid goods purchased within the European Union provided they are for your own personal use. Unlimited currency may be taken into France, but large amounts must be declared if it is to be reexported.

✘ No unlicensed drugs, weapons, ammunition, obscene material, pets or other animals, counterfeit money or copied goods, meat or poultry.
For customs limits for returning U.S. citizens see page 16.

Money

France's currency is the euro (€), a currency shared by 16 other European Union countries. The euro is divided into 100 cents (¢). The denominations of euro bills are 5, 10, 20, 50, 100, 200 and 500. There are coins of 1, 2, 5, 10, 20 and 50¢ and €1 and €2. You can exchange dollars or traveler's checks *(chèques de voyage)* at a bank *(banque)* or an exchange office *(bureau de change)*.

Tips and Gratuities

Tips *(pourboires)* are welcomed, but not expected.

Restaurants (service is almost always included)	change
Cafés/bars (service is almost always included)	change
Taxis	€1–€2
Porters	€1–€2
Chambermaids	€2–€10
Hairdressers	€1–€2
Cloakroom attendants	50¢–€1

Paris	New York	Chicago	Denver	Los Angeles	Time zones
12:00 noon	− 6 hrs	− 7 hrs	− 8 hrs	− 9 hrs	

519

France

Communications

Post Offices

Buy stamps *(timbres-poste)* at a post office *(la poste)*, newsstand *(marchand de journaux)* or tobacconist *(tabac)*.

Hours of out-of-town post offices may vary. Mailboxes are yellow and wall-mounted or free-standing; there are separate compartments for local mail *(départemental)*, for elsewhere in France, and abroad *(autres départements/destinations)*.

Telephones

The telephone system in France is efficient, and phone booths with instructions in English are easy to find. Most phones are operated solely with a phone card *(télécarte)*, which can be bought for 50 or 120 units from post offices, France Telecom offices, newsstands, tobacconists *(tabacs)*, and SNCF *(railway)* counters. Some booths accept credit cards.

Phoning inside France
All telephone numbers are 10 digits, and include the regional code. Paris and Île de France numbers begin with 01; the rest of France is divided into four zones (02, 03, 04 and 05). Dial all digits when making a call.

Phoning France from abroad
The country code for France is 33. Note that French numbers in this book do not include the country code; you need to prefix this number if you are phoning from another country. To phone France from the United States or Canada, omit the first zero from the French number, and add the prefix 011 33. Example: 01 22 33 44 55 becomes 011 33 1 22 33 44 55.

Phoning from France
To phone the United States or Canada from France, prefix the area code and number with 00 1. Example: (111) 222-3333 becomes 00 1 111 222-3333. For directory inquiries dial 118 008. For international directory inquiries dial 118 008.

Emergency telephone numbers
Police *(police)* 17; Fire service *(pompiers)* 18
Ambulance *(ambulance)* 15
112 (pan-European emergency number)
Emergency calls are free from phone booths

Hours of Operation

- Stores Mon.–Sat.
- Offices Mon.–Fri.
- Banks Mon.–Fri.
- Post Offices Mon.–Sat.
- Museums/Monuments Tue.–Sun.
- Pharmacies Mon.–Fri.

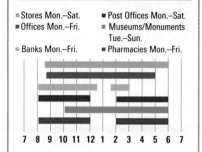

Many **stores** close on Sunday and all day or a half-day Monday, although some food establishments, especially bakeries, open Sunday mornings. Hypermarkets (large all-purpose stores) are open Mon.–Sat. 9 a.m.– 9 or 10 p.m., although many close Monday morning. Opening hours are longer in resort areas and major towns and cities.

Out-of-town **banks** may stay closed on Monday, while city banks may open on Saturday morning. Post offices close at noon on Saturday.

Museum times vary considerably, and it is best to check before a visit. Municipal museums close on Monday, while national museums close on Tuesday (except Versailles, Trianon Palace and Musée d'Orsay, which close on Monday). Many museums close on national holidays.

National Holidays

Banks, businesses and most stores close on these days.

Jan. 1	New Year's Day
Mar./Apr.	Easter Monday
May 1	May Day
May 8	VE Day
May	Ascension Day
May/Jun.	Pentecost Monday
Jul. 14	Bastille Day
Aug. 15	Assumption of the Virgin
Nov. 1	All Saints' Day
Nov. 11	Armistice Day
Dec. 25	Christmas Day

Photography

The range of subjects to photograph in France is enormous. All sizeable towns will have a camera store with digital equipment and photo developing facilities, though development may not be the same day and will be expensive.

Some museums and churches will allow you to photograph inside, but permission for flash photography is usually required.

France

Health

Medical Insurance

Private medical insurance is recommended. Visitors from non-E.U. countries have to pay for all medical treatment; keep all receipts and medicine labels to claim on your travel insurance. If you wish to see an English-speaking doctor *(médecin)* ask at your consulate or hotel.

Dental Services

A dentist *(dentiste)* charges for treatment. Emergency help is available from dentists listed in the yellow pages *(pages jaunes)*. Make sure that your private medical insurance covers dental treatment.

Sun Advice

The yearly average for sunshine is high: 2,500 hours (3,000 hours along the coast). Summers, particularly July and August, can be dry and hot, especially in the south. When outside wear a hat and drink plenty of fluids. On the beach a high-SPF sunscreen is essential.

Drugs

Prescription medicines and medical advice can be obtained from a pharmacy *(pharmacie)*, designated by a green cross sign. If you need medicines after regular hours, information about the nearest 24-hour facility is posted on the door of all pharmacies.

Safe Water

It is safe to drink tap water, but never drink from a fountain marked *"eau non potable"* ("not drinking water"). Many French people prefer the taste of bottled mineral water *(eau minérale en bouteille)*, which is widely available. A less expensive alternative is *eau de source*, which is spring water.

Restrooms

It is not difficult to find a restroom *(toilettes* or *WC,* pronounced *vay-say* in French), although you may still find the old-fashioned "squat" variety. Hygiene is usually of a reasonable standard. There is a small fee to use facilities in rail stations. If you need to use the restroom in a café or bar, buy a drink first.

Electricity

France has a 220-volt power supply. Electrical sockets take plugs with two round pins (occasionally with three round pins. American appliances will need a plug adapter and will require a transformer if they do not have a dual-voltage facility.

National Transportation

Train *(Train)*

The state rail company is the Société Nationale des Chemins de Fer Français (SNCF): ☎ 3635; www.sncf.com. Trains are fast, reliable and comfortable, with numerous discounts available. A round-the-clock car-carrying service from Calais (Le Shuttle) to Folkestone, England, and a Paris–London passenger train, Eurostar (☎ 08432 186 186, toll call; www.eurostar.com) both run through the tunnel under the English Channel.

Bus *(Autobus)*

Bus services in cities are excellent, but rural areas may be less well served. Long-distance bus stations are usually close to railroad stations, and major train and bus services usually co-ordinate (a long-distance bus is called a *car)*. Bus services shown on train timetables are run by the SNCF, and rail tickets are often valid for them. The Eurolines international bus network operates in France (☎ 08 92 89 90 91, toll call; www.eurolines.com).

Ferry *(Ferry)*

There are frequent traditional and fast ferry sailings to Britain from ports along the English Channel. A car-carrying train service also operates – see **Train** above. Some Mediterranean ferries operate in summer only and may need reservations in advance.

Driving

Drive on the right

Speed Limits

Traffic police can impose severe on-the-spot fines.

 Limited-access toll highways *(autoroutes à peage)* **130 k.p.h. (80 m.p.h.)**
Outer lane minimum **80 k.p.h. (49 m.p.h.)**
On wet roads **110 k.p.h. (68 m.p.h.)**
In fog with visibility less than 50m (55 yards) **50 k.p.h. (31 m.p.h.)**
Toll-free highways *(autoroutes)* and divided highways **110 k.p.h. (68 m.p.h.)**

 Main roads **90 k.p.h. (56 m.p.h.)**
On wet roads **80 k.p.h. (49 m.p.h.)**

Urban areas. **50 k.p.h. (31 m.p.h.),** sometimes reduced to **30 k.p.h. (18 m.p.h.)**

France

Driving (continued)

Seat Belts
Must be worn in front and back seats at all times.

Blood Alcohol
The legal blood alcohol limit is 0.05%. Random breath tests on drivers are carried out frequently, and the penalties for offenders are severe.

Tolls
There are tolls on many limited-access high-ways *(autoroutes à péage)*. Collect a ticket on entry and keep it in a safe place: you must show the ticket and pay when exiting. Cash and credit cards are accepted.

Car Rental
The leading rental firms have offices at airports and train stations. Hertz offers discounted rates for AAA members (see page 15). For reservations:

	United States	**France**
Alamo	(877) 222-9075	08 25 16 15 18
		(Europcar)
Avis	(800) 331-1212	08 20 05 05 05
Budget	(800) 527-0700	08 20 61 16 20
Hertz	(800) 654-3001	08 25 88 97 55

Fuel
Gas stations are generally easy to find, and highway service areas are open 24 hours. Gas *(essence)* is unleaded *(sans plomb)* and sold in liters. Credit cards are accepted at most fillling stations; many pumps read cards directly, so the customer does not have to pay at the counter; check with your card issuer for usage in France.

AAA Affiliated Motoring Club
Automobile Club de L'Ile de France (FFAC)
14 Avenue de la Grande Armée, Paris
01 40 55 43 00; fax 01 43 80 90 51;
www.automobileclub.org. Not all automobile clubs offer full services to AAA members.

Breakdowns and Accidents
If you are involved in an accident, phone 17 or 112 for police assistance. There are orange emergency telephones every 2 km (1.2 miles) on highways. Most car rental firms provide their own free rescue service; follow the instructions given in the rental documentation. Use of a car repair service other than those authorized by your rental company may violate your agreement. In the event of a breakdown you must put on a fluorescent vest when you are outside your vehicle. You must carry a warning triangle.

Driving (continued)

Other Information
The minimum age for driving a car is 18 (may be higher, usually between 21 and 25, for some car rental firms). An International Driving Permit (IDP) is recommended; some rental firms require them, and they can speed up formalities if you are involved in an accident. A Green Card (international motor insurance certificate) is recommended if you are driving a private car; see page 15 for more information. In built-up areas you must yield the right-of-way to vehicles coming from a side street on the right.

Useful Words and Phrases

You'll be well received if you try to pronounce words correctly. Final consonants are seldom pronounced. For instance, the masculine adjective *ouvert* (open) is pronounced [oo-ver]; the feminine *ouverte* [oo-vert]. The final consonant in a word like *vin, bon* or *grand* alters the last vowel, making it nasal.

h is silent	*hôtel* [o-tel]
th is *t* (but *ch* is *sh*)	*thé* [tay]; *chaud* [show]
ou is full	*tout* [too]
u is tight, as in cupola	*tu* [tu], *menu* [meuh-nu]
c and *g* hard before	*car* [car], *guide* [geed]
a, o, u,	
c and *g* soft before	*cigarette, age* [arzh]
i or *e*	
ç is soft (before an a)	*français* [frahn-say]
gn as in union	*agneau* [an-yo]
Do you speak English?	*Parlez-vous anglais?*
excuse me	*excusez-moi*
hello/goodbye	*bonjour/au revoir*
How much is this?	*C'est combien?*
I am American	*Je suis Américain/e*
I'd like...	*je voudrais...*
I don't understand	*Je ne comprends pas*
open/closed	*ouvert/fermé*
please/thank you	*s'il vous plaît/merci*
ticket	*billet*
(one-way/round trip)	*(simple/aller-retour)*
where is...?	*où est...?*
yes/no	*oui/non*
you're welcome	*de rien*
the hotel	***l'hôtel***
breakfast	*petit déjeuner*
I have a reservation	*j'ai réservé*
for one/two nights	*pour une/deux nuit(s)*
one/two people	*une/deux personne(s)*
room	*une chambre*
shower	*une douche*
with en-suite bathroom	*avec salle de bains*
the restaurant	***le restaurant***
beef	*boeuf*
bread	*pain*
the check	*l'addition*

Germany

National Flag

Essential for Travelers

● **Required** ● **Recommended** ● **Not required**

Passport	●
Visa (check regulations before you travel)	●
Travel, medical insurance	●
Round-trip or onward airline ticket	●
Local currency	●
Traveler's checks	●
Credit cards	●
First-aid kit and medicines	●
Inoculations	●

Essential for Drivers*

Driver's license	●
International Driving Permit	●
Car insurance (for nonrental cars)	●
Car registration (for nonrental cars)	●

*see also Driving section

Important Addresses

German National Tourist Office
122 East 42nd Street, Suite 2000
New York, NY 10168-0072
☎ (212) 661-7200, (800) 651-7010
Fax (212) 661-7174
www.cometogermany.com

**Deutsche Zentrale für Tourismus e.V
(German National Tourist Office)**
Beethovenstrasse 69
60325 Frankfurt am Main, Germany
☎ 069 974 64-0
Fax 069 751 903
www.deutschland-tourismus.de

American Embassy
Clayallee 170
14195 Berlin, Germany
☎ 030 832-9233 (Mon.–Fri. 2–4) or 030 8305-0
(emergencies only)
Fax 030 8305-1215
American Citizen Services
Mon.–Fri. 8:30–noon; closed on German and
American holidays
www.usembassy.de

Customs

✔ **Duty-free limits on goods brought in from
non-European Union countries:**
200 cigarettes or 100 cigarillos or 50 cigars or
250 g. tobacco; 1 L. alcohol over 22% volume and
2 L. alcohol under 22% or 2 L. sparkling or fortified
wine and 2 L. still wine; 50 ml. perfume; 250 ml.
toilet water; plus any other duty-free goods
(including gifts) to the value of S175. There is no
limit on the importation of tax-paid goods
purchased within the European Union, provided
they are for your own personal use. There are no
currency regulations.

✗ No unlicensed drugs, weapons,
ammunition, obscene material, pets
or other animals, counterfeit money or copied
goods, meat or poultry.
**For customs limits for returning U.S. citizens
see page 16.**

Money

Germany's currency is the euro (€), a currency
shared by 16 other European Union countries.
The euro is divided into 100 cents (¢). The
denominations of euro bills are 5, 10, 20, 50, 100,
200 and 500. There are coins of 1, 2, 5, 10, 20 and
50¢ and €1 and €2. You can exchange dollars or
traveler's checks *(Reiseschecks)* at a bank *(Bank)*
or an exchange office *(Wechselbüro)*.

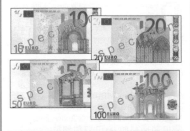

Tips and Gratuities

Restaurants (where service is not included)	10%
Cafés/bars (where service is not included)	10%
Taxis	10%
Porters	change
Chambermaids	change
Hairdressers	change
Restroom attendants	change
Cloakroom attendants	change

Berlin	New York	Chicago	Denver	Los Angeles	Time zones	**523**
12:00 noon	− 6 hrs	− 7 hrs	− 8 hrs	− 9 hrs		

Germany

Communications

Post Offices

Buy stamps *(Briefmarken)* at a post office *(Postamt)*. Hours for out-of-town post offices may vary. Mailboxes are bright yellow.

Telephones

Black telephones have instructions in English, and most operators are bilingual. Increasingly fewer phones accept coins; most are

operated by telephone cards *(Telefonkarten)*, which can be bought at any post office. International calls can be made from any booth.

Phoning inside Germany

German telephone numbers in this book include an area code: dial the number listed.

To call the operator dial 0180 200 10 33 (extra cost).

Phoning Germany from abroad

The country code for Germany is 49. Note that German numbers in this book do not include the country code; you will need to prefix this number if you are phoning from another country. To phone Germany from the United States or Canada, omit the first zero from the German number, and add the prefix 011 49. (Note that the number of digits in German area codes varies.) Example: 011 22 33 44 becomes 011 49 11 22 33 44.

Phoning from Germany

To phone the United States or Canada from Germany, prefix the area code and number with 00 1. Example: 111 222-3333 becomes 00 1 111 222-3333. National information for Germany: dial 11833. To call international information dial 11834.

Emergency telephone numbers

Police *(Polizei)* **110**
Fire service *(Feuerwehr)* **112**
Ambulance *(Krankenwagen)* **112**
Emergency calls are free from phone booths

Hours of Operation

- Stores Mon.–Sat.
- Offices Mon.–Fri.
- Banks Mon.–Fri.
- Post Offices Mon.–Sat.
- Museums/Monuments. Tue.–Sun.
- Pharmacies Mon.–Fri.

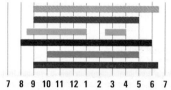

| 7 | 8 | 9 | 10 | 11 | 12 | 1 | 2 | 3 | 4 | 5 | 6 | 7 |

Store opening hours vary considerably, so even within cities there is no standard rule. In larger cities, some stores stay open as late as 10 p.m., but generally they close around 8 p.m.

Pharmacies tend to close earlier during the week and at 4 p.m. on Saturday.

Banks stay open until 6 p.m. on Thursday.

Post offices open 8–noon on Saturday. Post offices at airports and railway stations sometimes operate longer hours.

Government offices close promptly at 4, or at 2 on Friday.

Museums often close on Monday and open late on Thursday; some outside cities close for lunch.

National Holidays

Banks, businesses and most stores close on these days.

Jan. 1	New Year's Day
Jan. 6	Epiphany (Bavaria, Baden Württemberg and Saxony only)
Mar./Apr.	Good Friday
Mar./Apr.	Easter Monday
May 1	Labor Day
May	Ascension Day
May/Jun.	Pentecost Monday
Aug. 15	Assumption of the Virgin (Bavaria and Saarland only)
Oct. 3	Day of German Unity
Nov. 1	All Saints' Day (Baden-Württemberg, Bavaria, North Rhine-Westphalia, Rhineland-Palatinate and Saarland only)
Dec. 25	Christmas Day
Dec. 26	St. Stephen's Day

Photography

For conventional photography, quality brand-name batteries are easy to find. There are stores for digital equipment and facilities for downloading and printing. Photography is generally forbidden in museums and churches or needs special permission.

Health

Medical Insurance

➕ U.S. and Canadian visitors must pay for medical treatment from a doctor or at a hospital *(Krankenhaus)*. Keep all receipts to claim on your travel insurance. For details on emergency, weekend or English-speaking doctors, ask your hotel or consulate.

Dental Services

A dentist *(Zahnarzt)* always charges for treatment. Emergency help is available from dentists listed in the local telephone directory. Find out if your private medical insurance covers dental treatment.

Sun Advice

Germany's Continental climate brings cold, clear winters and warm summers, when sun protection is needed. Use sunscreen; children and those with fair skin should be vigilant.

Drugs

Prescription medicines and advice can be obtained from a pharmacy *(Apotheke)*; cosmetics and toiletries at a *Drogerie*. If you need medicine outside regular hours, information about the nearest 24-hour facility is posted on the door of all pharmacies.

Safe Water

Water is safe to drink in Germany, but you may prefer to drink bottled mineral water *(Mineralwasser)*, which is widely available.

Restrooms

Finding a restroom *(Toilette)* is not difficult; they are usually identified by symbols, or are designated *Herren* (men) and *Damen* or *Frauen* (women). Most toilets in restaurants, bars and coffee shops are free. Public toilets, however, are not free and often are operated by a 20¢ coin. If there is an attendant, small change is appreciated as a tip.

Electricity

Germany has a 220-volt power supply. Electrical sockets take plugs with two round pins or sometimes three pins in a vertical row. American appliances will need a plug adapter and will require a transformer if they do not have a dual-voltage facility.

National Transportation

Train *(Zug)*

 Germany's fast, efficient rail network is operated by Deutsche Bahn (DB). ICE is a modern service of long-distance, high-speed trains. IC and EC trains operate between major towns and cities. Regional (IR) trains are modern and comfort-able, and connect with long-distance services. Local services are called SE or S-Bahn. There are many fare reductions available; for bookings and information, phone 📞 11861 (24 hours; toll call).

Bus *(Bus)*

 Towns and villages not served by the rail network usually have bus links, with timetables and routes coordinating with trains. German towns have their own buses, and one ticket is often good for other types of city transportation. The Eurolines (Deutsche Touring GmbH) international bus service operates in Germany: 📞 069 7903 501.

Ferry *(Fähre)*

 Ferries from the ports of Lübeck, Kiel and Rostock in the north connect to Denmark, Norway, Sweden, Finland and the Baltic countries. Boats also offer a service on many German lakes, rivers and canals. Ask for details at your travel agency or a local tourist office, where reservations can often be made.

Driving

Drive on the right

Speed Limits

Traffic police can impose severe on-the-spot fines.

Limited-access highways *(Autobahn)*: unless signposted there is no speed limit but the suggested limit is **130 k.p.h. (80 m.p.h.)**

Main roads **100 k.p.h. (62 m.p.h.)**

Urban areas **50 k.p.h. (31 m.p.h.)** or **30 k.p.h. (18 m.p.h.)**

Seat Belts

Seat belts must be worn at all times. Children must use a suitable restraint or seat.

Blood Alcohol

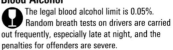 The legal blood alcohol limit is 0.05%. Random breath tests on drivers are carried out frequently, especially late at night, and the penalties for offenders are severe.

Driving (continued)

Tolls

There are no highway tolls.

Car Rental

The leading rental firms have offices at airports and train stations. Hertz offers discounted rates for AAA members (see page 15). For reservations:

	United States	Germany
Alamo	(800) 462-5266	01805 462526
Avis	(800) 331-1212	01805 217702
Budget	(800) 527-0700	01805 217711
Hertz	(800) 654-3001	01805 333535

Fuel

Gas *(Benzin)* and diesel fuel are sold in liters. Gas stations are easy to find, and most highway services are open 24 hours. Self-service stations are called *Selbstbedienung* or *SB-Tanken,* and credit cards are widely accepted.

AAA Affiliated Motoring Club

Allgemeiner Deutscher Automobil-Club E.V. (ADAC) Am Westpark 8, 81373 Munich ☎ 089 76 76-0; fax 089 76 76-25 00. If you break down while driving, phone ☎ 01802 22 22 22 (ADAC breakdown service). Not all automobile clubs offer full services to AAA members.

Breakdowns and Accidents

Most car rental firms provide their own free rescue service; if your car is rented, follow the instructions given in the documentation. Use of a car repair service other than those authorized by your rental company may violate your agreement. If you are involved in an accident, phone ☎ 110 for police.

Other Information

The minimum age for driving a car is 18 (may be higher for some car rental firms). You must keep an official translation with your driver's license; your embassy or a tourist office can help. An International Driving Permit (IDP) is recommended; some rental firms require them, and they can speed up formalities if you are involved in an accident. A Green Card (international motor insurance certificate) is recommended if you are driving a private car; see page 15 for more information. On-the-spot fines can be imposed if you run out of gas on a highway. Using a cell phone while driving is not permitted.

Useful Words and Phrases

German has many dialects. Language in the north is descended from Old Saxon, and in the south from Old High German. Their differences were resolved by Standard German *(Schriftdeutsch)*, created by Martin Luther when he translated the Bible in the 16th century.

Germans are helpful to visitors who attempt to communicate in German, although English is widely spoken.

ü is like the u in cupola	*über* (over)
ie sounds like heat	*Sie* (you)
ei sounds like height	*Eingang* (entrance)
ch is a harsh rasp…	*J. S. Bach*
j is like the English y	*ja* (yes)
r is a guttural sound	*Fräulein* (Miss)
w sounds like English v	*wo* (where)
z is like English ts	*Zeit* (time)
Do you speak English?	*Sprechen Sie Englisch?*
excuse me	*Verzeihung*
hello	*Guten Tag*
goodbye	*Auf Wiedersehen*
How much is…?	*Wieviel kostet…?*
I am American	*Ich bin Amerikaner (in)*
I'd like…	*Ich hätte gerne*
I don't understand	*Ich verstehe nicht*
nonsmoking	*Nichtraucher*
open/closed	*offen/geschlossen*
please/thank you	*bitte/danke*
one-way ticket	*einfache Fahrkarte*
round-trip ticket	*Rückfahrkarte*
where is…?	*wo ist…?*
yes/no	*ja/nein*
you're welcome	*bitte*
the hotel	***das Hotel***
breakfast	*Frühstück*
reservation	*Reservieren/ Reservierung*
key	*Schlüssel*
for one/two nights	*für eine Nacht/ zwei Nächte*
for one/two people	*für eine Person/ zwei Personen*
room	*Zimmer*
shower	*Dusche*
the restaurant	***das Restaurant***
beefsteak	*Steak*
bread	*Brot*
the check	*Rechnung*
chicken	*Hähnchen*
coffee	*Kaffee*
dish of the day	*Tagesgericht*
dessert	*Dessert*
entree	*Hauptgericht*
first courses	*Vorspeisen*
fish	*Fisch*
lamb	*Lamm*
pork	*Schweinefleisch*
seafood	*Meeresfrüchte*
wine	*Wein*

Greece

National Flag

Essential for Travelers*

• Required • Recommended • Not required

Passport	•
Visa (check regulations before you travel)	•
Travel, medical insurance	•
Round-trip or onward airline ticket	•
Local currency	•
Traveler's checks	•
Credit cards	•
First-aid kit and medicines*	•
Inoculations	•

*see also *Health* section

Essential for Drivers*

Driver's license	•
International Driving Permit	•
Car insurance (for nonrental cars)	•
Car registration (for nonrental cars)	•

*see also *Driving* section

Important Addresses

Greek National Tourism Organization
Olympic Tower
9th Floor
645 Fifth Avenue
New York, NY 10022
☎ (212) 421-5777
Fax (212) 826-6940
www.greektourism.com

Hellenic Tourism Organization
(Greek National Tourism Organization)
Tsoha 24
11521 Athens, Greece
☎ 210 870 7000
www.gnto.gr

American Embassy
91 Vassilissis Sophias Avenue
10160 Athens, Greece
☎ 210 721 2951
Mon.–Fri. 8:30–5
http://athens.usembassy.gov

Customs

✓ **Duty-free limits on goods brought in from non-European Union countries:**
200 cigarettes or 100 cigarillos or 50 cigars or 250 g. tobacco; 2 L. wine; 1 L. alcohol over 22% volume; 2 L. alcohol under 22% volume; 50 ml. perfume; 250 ml. toilet water; plus any other duty-free goods (including gifts) to the value of €175. There is no importation limit for tax-paid goods purchased within the European Union for personal use. Foreign currency over $200 (U.S.) or the equivalent must by law be declared at the customs entry point. Up to $1,000 in foreign currency may be exported by visitors.

✗ No unlicensed drugs, weapons, ammunition, obscene material, pets or other animals, counterfeit money or copied goods, meat or poultry.
For customs limits for returning U.S. citizens see page 16.

Money

The Greek currency is the euro (€), a currency shared by 16 other European Union countries. The euro is divided into 100 cents (¢). The denominations of euro bills are 5, 10, 20, 50, 100, 200 and 500. There are coins of 1, 2, 5, 10, 20 and 50¢ and €1 and €2. Traveler's checks are widely accepted, and some gift stores accept dollars. Exchange dollars or traveler's checks *(taxithiotiki epitayi)* at a bank *(trapeza)* or an exchange office *(sarafiko)*. You can get cash at a bank with a credit card, but there is usually a charge.

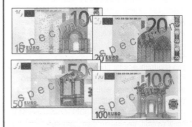

Tips and Gratuities

Tips are welcomed, but not expected or obligatory.

Restaurants (where service is not included)	10–15%
Cafés/bars	change
Taxis	change
Porters	€2
Chambermaids	€2 per day
Cloakroom attendants	change

Athens	New York	Chicago	Denver	Los Angeles	Time zones
12:00 noon	− 6 hrs	− 7 hrs	− 8 hrs	− 9 hrs	

527

Greece

Communications

Post Offices

Buy stamps *(ghramatósima)* at a post office *(takhithromio)*, distinguished by a yellow "OTE" sign. Lines can be long at post office counters; if you simply need stamps, check whether there's a window that sells stamps. A corner kiosk *(periptero)* will sell stamps if you are buying postcards. Hours for out-of-town post offices may vary.

Telephones

Most public telephones take phone cards available from kiosks, local stores and OTE *(Organismos Tilepikoinonion Ellados,* pronounced *O-tay)* offices. If your calls are short and local, use a street kiosk *(periptero)* where you pay after the call. With the advent of cell phones, coin-operated phones are increasingly hard to find in the more urban and resort areas of Greece.

Phoning inside Greece

All Greek telephone numbers in this book include an area code: dial the number that is listed. To call the operator dial 132 (or 131 in Athens).

Phoning Greece from abroad

The country code for Greece is 30. Note that Greek numbers in this book do not include the country code; you will need to prefix this number if you are phoning from another country. To call a Greek number from the United States or Canada, omit the first zero and add the prefix 011 30. Example: 210 122 3344 becomes 011 30 210 122 3344.

Phoning from Greece

To phone the United States or Canada from Greece, prefix the area code and number with 00 1. Example: (111) 222-3333 becomes 00 1 111 222-3333. To call international information dial 00 162.

Emergency telephone numbers

All emergencies **112**
Police *(astínomia)* **100**
Tourist police (Athens only) **171**
Fire service *(fotyá)* **199**
Ambulance *(asthenoforo)* **166**
Emergency calls are free from phone booths

Hours of Operation

- Stores Mon.–Sat.
- Offices Mon.–Fri.
- Banks Mon.–Fri.
- Post Offices Mon.–Fri.
- Museums/Monuments
- Archaeological sites
- Pharmacies Mon.–Fri.

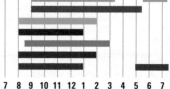

In tourist areas **stores** open at 8 a.m. and close late; they have shorter hours off-season, and some close completely in winter.

Banks close at 1:30 Fridays. They may stay open longer hours at peak season in resort areas.

Post offices close at noon on Saturday.

Archaeological sites usually close in the afternoon; some reopen in the evening in the summer, but all sites vary their hours depending on the time of year. It is best to check locally. Many archaeologcal sites, museums and monuments close on Monday.

Restaurants open all day in resort areas but may close off-season.

National Holidays

Banks, businesses and most stores and museums close on these days, but restaurants and some stores in tourist areas may stay open.

Jan. 1	New Year's Day
Jan. 6	Epiphany
Feb./Mar.	Shrove Monday
Mar. 25	Independence Day
*Apr./May	Good Friday
*Apr./May	Easter Monday
May 1	Labor Day
May/Jun.	Pentecost Monday
Aug. 15	Assumption of the Virgin
Oct. 28	Óchi Day
Dec. 25	Christmas Day
Dec. 26	St. Stephen's Day

* Greece observes the Orthodox calendar, and the date on which Easter falls may differ from that observed by other Western nations.

Photography

Note that the sun in Greece is strong. Camera batteries are widely available. Digital equipment and printing facilities are available in cities and large towns.

Never take photos near military bases, and ask first in museums and churches.

Greece

Health

Medical Insurance

Private medical insurance is recommended. Visitors from non-E.U. countries can receive basic treatment at hospital emergency rooms. Admittance to a hospital *(nosokomío)* or consultation with a doctor *(iatrós)* will entail a fee. Ask your hotel, consulate or the tourist police for information on English-speaking doctors.

Dental Services

Dentists *(odhondoyatrós)* always charge for treatment, so find out if your medical insurance covers it; keep all receipts for insurance purposes. Treatment is available from English-speaking dentists listed in the telephone directory, or ask at your hotel.

Sun Advice

Summer, particularly July and August, can be oppressively hot and humid. Seek shelter inside a museum, or cover up, apply a sunscreen and drink plenty of fluids. Be especially careful on boats or near the water.

Drugs

A pharmacy *(farmakío)*, distinguished by a green cross, has staff qualified to offer medical advice and provide a wide range of prescription medicines. Information about the nearest all-night facility is usually posted at pharmacies. Note that codeine is banned and you can be fined for carrying it.

Safe Water

Tap water is safe to drink but because of the high level of minerals it can cause upsets. Bottled water *(metaliko nero)* is available everywhere at a reasonable cost.

Restrooms

Finding a clean restroom *(toualéta)* away from tourist areas can be difficult. It is advisable to use facilities in cafés and restaurants after buying a drink. Restrooms are free. The Greek sewage system does not take toilet tissue, even in café and restaurant facilities; use the wastebin provided.

Electricity

Greece has a 220-volt power supply. Electrical sockets take plugs with two round pins. American appliances will need a plug adapter and will require a transformer if they do not have a dual-voltage facility.

National Transportation

Train *(Tréno)*

Greek trains are run by Organismos Sidirodromon Ellados (OSE), a service restricted to the mainland. The network is limited, and a reservation is essential on most express trains. For rail information in Athens: 145 (domestic services) or 147 (international services).

Bus *(Leoforío)*

Buses are popular and frequent; few villages or ferry ports are without a bus link. Buy city-to-city tickets from the bus station; in rural areas tickets *(isitirio)* are issued by a conductor on the bus. For bus information in Athens: 185.

Ferry *(Féribot)*

Ferries serve all of the Greek islands, and boat excursions run from May to October. You can take a boat from the port of Piréas to most islands, but check the length of the trip on the timetable – some ferries stop at every island. You can usually buy a ticket on the day of travel unless you are reserving a cabin or taking a car. You may need to reserve in advance in mid-August and over the Easter period; ask at a travel agency or tourist office.

Driving

Drive on the right

Speed Limits
Police can impose on-the-spot fines but they cannot collect them.

Limited-access highways
130 k.p.h. (80 m.p.h.)

Main roads
90 k.p.h. (56 m.p.h.) or
110 k.p.h. (68 m.p.h.)

Urban areas
50 k.p.h. (31 m.p.h.)

Seat Belts

Must be worn in the front seat at all times and in the rear seat where fitted. Children over three years and under 1.5 meters are not allowed to travel in the front seat.

Blood Alcohol

The legal blood alcohol limit is 0.05%. Random breath tests on drivers are carried out frequently, especially late at night, and the penalties for offenders are severe.

Driving (continued)

Tolls

There are some, but not many, highway tolls in Greece.

Car Rental

The leading rental firms have offices at airports, train stations and principal ferry terminals. Hertz offers discounted rates for AAA members (see page 15).

For reservations:

	United States	Greece
Alamo	(877) 222-9075	210 353 3323
Avis	(800) 331-1212	210 322 4951
Budget	(800) 527-0700	210 898 1444
Hertz	(800) 654-3001	210 353 4900

Fuel

Gas *(venzini)* is sold in liters and usually comes in five grades: super *(sooper)*, regular *(apli)*, unleaded *(amolyvdhi)*, super unleaded *(sooper amolyvdhi)* and diesel *(petrelaio)*. There are few stations in remote areas; they are less likely to be open on weekends and may not take credit cards.

AAA Affiliated Motoring Club

Automobile and Touring Club of Greece (ELPA) 395 Messogion Street, 153 43 Agia Paraskevi, Athens ☎ 201 606 8800; fax 201 606 8800; www.elpa.gr. If you break down while driving, phone ☎ 10400 (ELPA breakdown service). Not all automobile clubs offer full services to AAA members.

Breakdowns and Accidents

There are emergency telephones at regular intervals on highways. If you are involved in an accident, phone ☎ 100 for police. Most car rental firms provide their own free rescue service; if your car is rented, follow the instructions given in the documentation. Use of a car repair service other than those authorized by your rental company may violate your agreement.

Other Information

The minimum age for driving a car is 18 (may be higher for some car rental firms). An International Driving Permit (IDP) is recommended; some rental firms require them, and they can speed up formalities if you are involved in an accident. A Green Card (international motor insurance certificate) is recommended if you are driving a private car; see page 15 for more information. You can be fined for unnecessary use of the horn. You must carry a fire extinguisher, a first-aid kit and a warning triangle in your car.

Useful Words and Phrases

The Greek language can be daunting to the visitor; it uses a different alphabet and is spoken with staccato rapidity. The way words and place-names are converted into English varies considerably according to which transliteration system a translator happens to prefer.

With patience and a keen ear, you should be able to recognize what sounds these unfamiliar letters stand for. Learning the Greek alphabet may enable you to deduce the meaning of signs and notices. The easiest thing to do, however, is to learn a few basic courtesy phrases.

The Greeks realize how difficult their language appears to foreigners, and they appreciate visitors' attempts to speak it.

Do you speak English?	*milate angliká?*
excuse me	*signomi*
hello/goodbye	*yásou/chérete*
how much?	*póso?*
I'd like	*tha íthela*
I do not understand	*dhen katalavéno*
nonsmoking	*khoros ya mi kapnízondes*
okay	*endáysi*
open/closed	*aniktos/klistos*
please/you're welcome	*parakaló*
thank you	*efharistó*
ticket	*isitíro*
one-way/round trip	*apló/isitiro met epistrofis*
where is...?	*poo íne...?*
yes/no	*né/óhi*
the hotel	***xenodochio***
breakfast	*proino*
key	*klidhí*
for one/two nights	*ya mía/dhıo vradhiés*
for one/two people	*yiá éna/dhıo átoma*
room	*éna dhomátio*
shower	*doos*
the restaurant	***estiatorio***
beans	*fasólia*
beer	*bira*
bread	*psomi*
the check	*logariasmós*
chicken	*kotópoulo*
coffee	*kafé*
dessert	*glikisma*
food	*fagitó*
lamb	*arnáki*
lobster	*astakós*
meat balls	*kefthédes*
olives	*eliés*
pork	*hirino*
red mullet	*barboúnia*
squid	*kalamarákia*
starter	*proto piato*
stuffed vine leaves	*dolmadakia*
water	*neró*
wine	*krasí*

National Flag

Essential for Travelers

● **Required** ● **Recommended** ● **Not required**

Passport	●
Visa (check regulations before you travel)	●
Travel, medical insurance	●
Round-trip or onward airline ticket	●
Local currency	●
Traveler's checks	●
Credit cards	●
First-aid kit and medicines	●
Inoculations	●

Essential for Drivers*

Driver's license	●
International Driving Permit	●
Car insurance (for nonrental cars)	●
Car registration (for nonrental cars)	●

*see also *Driving* section

Important Addresses

Hungarian National Tourist Office
447 Broadway, 5th Floor
New York, NY 10113
☎ (212) 695-1221
www.gotohungary.com

Tourinform (Hungarian National Tourist Office)
v. Sütő utca 2
H-1548 Budapest
Hungary
☎ 1 438 8080 (24 hours) or 00 800 36 00 00 00
24 hours, toll free from United States
www.tourinform.hu

American Embassy
H-1054 Budapest
Szabadság tér 12
Hungary
☎ 1 475 4400 (8 a.m.–5 p.m.); 1 475 4703 or
1 475 4924 (5 p.m.–8 a.m.; U.S. citizens only)
www.hungary.usembassy.gov

Customs

✔ **Duty-free limits on goods brought in from non-European Union countries:**
200 cigarettes or 100 cigarillos or 50 cigars or 250 g. tobacco; 2 L. still wine; 1 L. spirits or strong liqueurs over 22% volume or 2 L. fortified wine, sparkling wine or other liqueurs; 50 ml. perfume; 250 ml. toilet water; plus any other duty-free goods (including gifts) up to a value of Ft48,000 (€175). There is no limit on the importation of tax-paid goods purchased within the European Union, provided the goods are for your own personal use. If you are bringing in cash or traveler's checks to the value of $14,800, customs must be notified and proof of ownership will be required.

✘ No unlicensed drugs, weapons, ammunition, obscene material, pets or other animals, counterfeit money and copied goods, meat or poultry.
For customs limits for returning U.S. citizens see page 16.

Money

Hungary's currency is the forint (Ft or HUF), which is divided into 100 fillérs, although fillérs are no longer legal tender. The denominations of forint bills are 200, 500, 1,000, 2,000, 5,000, 10,000 and 20,000. There are coins of 5, 10, 20, 50, 100 and 200 forints. You can exchange dollars or traveler's checks *(utazasi csekket)* at a bank *(bank)*, exchange office *(penzvalto)*, post office *(posta)* and some hotels. Credit card acceptance is limited; although they are increasingly common, they are not accepted everywhere.

Tips and Gratuities

Tips *(borravaló)* are welcomed, but not expected, where service is not included.

Restaurants	10–20%
Cafés/bars	10–20%
Taxis	10%
Porters	to reflect quality of service
Chambermaids	to reflect quality of service
Hairdressers	10%
Gas station attendants	change
Cloakroom attendants	change

| Budapest | New York | Chicago | Denver | Los Angeles | Time zones | **531** |
| 12:00 noon | – 6 hrs | – 7 hrs | – 8 hrs | – 9 hrs | | |

Hungary

Communications

Post Offices

Buy stamps *(bélyeg)* at a post office *(posta)*, newsstand/tobacconist *(dohanyaruda)* or from a hotel. Hours for out-of-town post offices may vary. Mail boxes are wall-mounted and red with a calling-horn emblem.

Telephones

You can use cash and prepaid phone cards to make a call in Hungary. For direct dialing for national and international calls, use Ft20, Ft50 and Ft100 coins (minimum Ft20). International calls can be made from red phone booths. Phone cards of 50 and 100 units can be bought from newsstands/tobacconists, gas stations, post offices and hotels.

Phoning inside Hungary
Hungarian telephone numbers include an area code of one or two digits (there is no initial zero). For long-distance calls within Hungary precede the number with 06. Numbers in Budapest are seven digits, not including the area code; the area code is 1. To call the operator dial 191.

Phoning Hungary from abroad
The country code for Hungary is 36. Note that Hungarian numbers in this book do not include the Hungarian country code; you will need to enter the country code if you are phoning from another country. To phone Hungary from the United States or Canada, add the prefix 011 36 before the area code and number. Example: 1 122 3344 becomes 011 36 1 122 3344.

Phoning from Hungary
To phone the United States or Canada from Hungary, prefix the area code and number with 00 1. Example: (111) 222-3333 becomes 00 1 111 222-3333. To call the international operator dial 190; for international directory inquiries dial 199.

Emergency telephone numbers
Any emergency **112**
Police *(rendörség)* **107** or **112**; Fire service *(tüzoltéóság)* 105 or 112; Ambulance *(mentök)* 104 or 112

Hours of Operation

- Stores Mon.–Sat.
- Offices Mon.–Fri.
- Banks Mon.–Fri.
- Post Offices Mon.–Fri.
- Museums/Monuments
- Pharmacies

7 8 9 10 11 12 1 2 3 4 5 6 7

Department **stores** are open Mon.–Fri. 10–6, Sat. 9–1. Saturday afternoon they close early, and few stores remain open after 1 or 2 p.m. Thursday is late-night shopping until 7 or 8 p.m.

Grocery stores and other food stores have longer hours and also open on Sunday morning. In large cities, some stores stay open 24 hours.

In smaller towns, stores close over lunchtime. Large shopping centers in cities are open Mon.–Sat. 10–9, Sun. 10–6.

The National **Bank** of Hungary is open Mon.–Fri. 10:30–2. Most other banks close at 1 p.m. on Friday. Banks are closed Dec. 24 and 31.

Post offices close at 1 p.m. on Saturday.
Many **museums** close on Monday.

National Holidays

Banks, businesses and most stores are closed on these days. If a public holiday falls on a Tuesday or a Thursday, the day between it and the weekend also becomes a holiday.

Jan. 1	New Year's Day
Mar. 15	Day of the Nation (anniversary of 1848 revolution)
Mar./Apr.	Easter Monday
May 1	Labor Day
May/Jun.	Pentecost Monday
Aug. 20	Constitution Day
Oct. 23	Day of the Proclamation of the Republic
Nov. 1	All Saints' Day
Dec. 25	Christmas Day
Dec. 26	St. Stephen's Day

Photography

Hungary has spectacular landscapes, including the Danube bend north of Budapest, one of the most beautiful stretches of this great river, and romantic Lake Balaton, framed by vineyards. Digital camera equipment and printing services are available in towns and cities.

Hungary

Health

Medical Insurance

Private medical insurance is recommended. U.S. and Canadian visitors can receive free essential first-aid and emergency treatment. All further treatment and care has to be paid for. Fees for medical care are set by the individual hospital or practice. There is a 24-hour private medical care service with English-speaking doctors in Budapest: SOS Hungary. It also has its own ambulance service ☎ 1 240 0475; www.soshungary.hu.

Dental Services

Dentists *(forgovos)* charge for any treatment, but quality dental work is relatively inexpensive. Check to be sure it is covered by your medical insurance. Dentists are listed in the yellow pages; ask for English-speaking dentists at your embassy or hotel, or at a tourist office. There is a 24-hour dental service in Budapest: SOS Dental Service ☎ 1 267 9602.

Sun Advice

Hungary has up to 2,500 hours of sun annually, one of the highest levels in Europe. In summer, 9 or 10 hours a day can be expected, so protection is essential.

Drugs

A pharmacy *(gyógyszetár* or *patica)* sells both prescription and nonprescription medicines (bring your own medication if you need a specific product). Most are cheaper than similar U.S. products. Information about the nearest 24-hour facility is posted at all pharmacies.

Safe Water

Although tap water is safe, you may find it causes mild upsets. Bottled mineral water *(ásvány víz)* and soda water *(szoda víz)* are widely available and advised.

Restrooms

Public restrooms *(mosdó)* are fairly easy to find, and are usually indicated by a symbol or marked WC, and designated by *férfi* for men and *nöi* for women. There may be a charge of between Ft50 and Ft200.

Electricity

Hungary has a 220/230-volt power supply. Electrical sockets take plugs with two round pins. American appliances will need a plug adapter and will require a transformer if they do not have a dual-voltage facility.

National Transportation

Train *(Vonat)*

The state railroad, MÁV-Start, serves most towns. Express trains link Budapest with provincial centers; it may be quicker to go via the capital for cross-country journeys. Fares are low, and MÁV-Start offers many discounted fares and passes, including rail cards for unlimited travel; ☎ 06 40 49 49 49 (international ☎ 1 444 4499); www.mav-start.hu.

Bus *(Busz)*

Long-distance buses are expensive, but can be quicker than trains. The main Budapest terminal is at Erzsébet tér. The main operator is state-owned Volánbusz, whose yellow buses serve even very small communities. Volánbusz is a member of Eurolines, who operate an international bus service; ☎ 1 382 0888 (domestic and international); www.volanbusz.hu.

Ferry *(Komp)*

Ferries run from spring to late autumn on Lake Balaton, the Danube between Budapest and Esztergom, and the Tisza river (for Sárospatak, Tokaj, Szolnok, Csongrád and Szeged). Information is available from Mahart at the Vigadó tér landing stage; ☎ 1 484 4013; www.mahartpassnave.hu.

Driving

Drive on the right

Speed Limits

On-the-spot fines of up to Ft10,000 can be imposed by the police. Receipts must be issued.

 Limited-access highways *(autópályára)*
130 k.p.h. (80 m.p.h.)
Divided highways **110 k.p.h. (68 m.p.h.)**

Main roads
90 k.p.h. (56 m.p.h.)

Urban areas
50 k.p.h. (31 m.p.h.)
Some resorts and residential zones
30 k.p.h. (18 m.p.h.)

Seat Belts

Must be worn in front and rear seats at all times.

Blood Alcohol

The legal blood alcohol limit is zero. Random breath tests on drivers are carried out frequently, especially at night.

Fire Service 105 or 112
(Tűzoltéóság)

Ambulance 104 or 112
(Mentők)

533

Hungary

Driving (continued)

Tolls

There are tolls on most sections of M numbered highways (M0 through M70). Toll stickers (valid for nine days, one month or a year) can be purchased at toll booths or at fuel stations.

Car Rental

The leading rental firms have offices at airports and railroad stations. Hertz offers discounted rates for AAA members (see page 15). For reservations:

	United States	Hungary
Alamo	(800) 327-9633	1 505 4404
		(Europcar)
Avis	(800) 331-2112	1 318 4240
Budget	(800) 527-0700	1 296 8197
Hertz	(800) 654-3080	1 296 0999

Fuel

Unleaded fuel (ólommentes benzine) is graded 95 octane. Diesel can be bought along major routes and in cities. Many gas stations (benzinkút) are self-service, although you may not be able to use a credit card in smaller stations. A map of rural gas stations is available from MAK (see below).

AAA Affiliated Motoring Club

Magyar Autóklub (MAK) H-1024 Budapest, Rómer Flóris u 8 ☎ 1 345 1800. If you break down while driving, phone ☎ 188 or 1 345 1755 (MAK breakdown service). Not all automobile clubs offer full services to AAA members.

Breakdowns and Accidents

If you have an accident, phone ☎ 107 for police, and ask for an interpreter at the scene. You are legally required to report personal injury. Most car rental firms provide their own free rescue service; if you break down follow the instructions given in the documentation. Use of an unauthorized car repair service may violate your agreement. Vehicles with damaged bodywork may only leave the country with an official certificate.

Other Information

The minimum age for driving a car is 18 (21 for some car rental firms). An International Driving Permit (IDP) is recommended; some rental firms require them, and they can speed up formalities if you are involved in an accident. A Green Card (international motor insurance certificate) is needed if you are driving a private car; see page 15 for more information. Dimmed headlights must be used by cars at all times outside built-up areas. You must have a first-aid kit, a warning triangle and a fluorescent vest in your car.

Useful Words and Phrases

Hungarian, called Magyar by its speakers, is a difficult language, related to Finnish and Estonian. German is traditionally the second language, but English is gradually replacing it, especially among the younger generation.

Apart from a few international words (posta, telefon), Hungarian offers few clues as to its meaning. However, pronunciation is regular – letters consistently stand for the same sounds. By learning basic words, street signs, notices and labels will begin to make sense.

Do you speak English?	*Beszél angolul?*
What is your name?	*Hogy hívnak?*
excuse me	*elnézést*
hello	*jó napot kivanok*
goodbye	*viszontlátásra*
yes/no	*igen/nem*
how much?	*mennyibe kerul?*
I am American	*Amerikai vagyok*
I don't understand	*nem értem*
nonsmoking	*nem domanyzo*
open	*nyitva*
closed	*zárva*
please	*kérem*
thank you	*köszönöm*
ticket	*jegy*
(one-way/round trip)	*(egyiranyu/retur)*
where is...?	*hol van...?*
the hotel	***szálloda***
you're welcome	*szívesen*
Where is the restroom?	*Hol a mosdó?*
breakfast	*reggeli*
reservation	*foglalás*
key	*kulcs*
room	*szoba*
shower	*zuhany*
the restaurant	***étterem/vendeglo/etkezde***
beef	*marha*
beer	*sör*
bread	*kenyer*
the check	*szamla*
coffee/tea	*kávé/tea*
dessert	*édesség*
fish	*hal*
fruit	*gyümölcs*
ice cream	*fagylalt*
meat	*hús*
pork	*sertés*
potato	*burgonya*
poultry	*csirke*
starter	*elöételek*
vegetable	*zöldség*
wine	*bor*

National Flag

Essential for Travelers

● **Required** ● **Recommended** ● **Not required**

Passport	●
Visa (check regulations before you travel)	●
Travel, medical insurance	●
Round-trip or onward airline ticket	●
Local currency	●
Traveler's checks	●
Credit cards	●
First-aid kit and medicines	●
Inoculations	●

Essential for Drivers*

Driver's license	●
International Driving Permit	●
Car insurance (for nonrental cars)	●
Car registration (for nonrental cars)	●

*see also *Driving* section

Important Addresses

Tourism Ireland (Republic of Ireland and Northern Ireland)
345 Park Avenue, New York, NY 10154
☎ (212) 418 0800
www.discoverireland.ie/us
Fáilte Ireland – Irish Tourist Board
Amiens Street, Dublin 1, Republic of Ireland
☎ 01 890 525 525
www.failteireland.ie
American Embassy (Republic of Ireland)
42 Elgin Road, Ballsbridge
Dublin 4, Republic of Ireland
☎ 01 668 8777
http://dublin.usembassy.gov
American Citizens Services: Mon.–Tue. and
Thu.–Fri. 8:30–11:30
Belfast Welcome Centre
47 Donegall Place, Belfast BT1 5AD
Northern Ireland
☎ 028 9024 6609
www.gotobelfast.com
American Consulate (Northern Ireland)
Danesfort House, 223 Stranmills Road
Belfast BT9 5GR
☎ 028 9038 6100
www.usembassy.org.uk, Mon.–Fri. 8:30–5

Customs

✓ **Duty-free limits on goods brought in from non-European Union countries**:
200 cigarettes or 100 cigarillos or 50 cigars or 250 g. tobacco; 4 L. still wine or 16 L. of beer; 1 L. spirits or strong liqueurs over 22% volume or 2 L. fortified wine, sparkling wine or other liqueur; 60 ml. perfume; 250 ml. toilet water; plus any other duty-free goods (including gifts) to the value of €430. There is no limit on the importation of tax-paid goods bought within the E.U., if they are for your own personal use. There are no currency regulations.

✗ No unlicensed drugs, weapons, ammunition, obscene material, pets or other animals, counterfeit money or copied goods, meat or poultry.
For customs limits for returning U.S. citizens see page 16.

Money

The Republic of Ireland's currency is the euro (€), a currency shared by 16 other European Union countries. The euro is divided into 100 cents (¢). The denominations of euro bills are 5, 10, 20, 50, 100, 200 and 500. There are coins of 1, 2, 5, 10, 20 and 50c and €1 and €2. Credit cards are accepted in hotels, large stores and upscale restaurants; check first in small or rural establishments. Exchange dollars or traveler's checks at a bank, exchange office, post office or a large hotel. For information about currency in Northern Ireland, see page 502.

Tips and Gratuities

Restaurants (if service is not included)	10–15%
Cafés/bars (if service is not included)	10%
Taxis	10%
Porters	€1 (IR) or £1 (NI) per bag
Hairdressers	€2 (IR) or £1 (NI)
Tour guides	€2 (IR) or £1 (NI)
Cloakroom attendants	€1 (IR) or £1 (NI)

Communications

Post Offices

 Buy stamps at post offices, newsstands/tobacconists, large grocery stores and hotels. Hours for out-of-town post offices may vary. Mailboxes are green in the Republic of Ireland and red in Northern Ireland (as in Britain).

Telephones

Public phone booths are either blue and cream or the newer glass-booth style, although many are now glass and metal. They take cash or prepaid phone cards bought from

 newsstands, post offices and local stores. Some city phones take credit cards. For phone calls made to or from Northern Ireland, except calling Northern Ireland from the Republic (see below), follow the instructions for Britain on page 503.

Phoning inside Ireland

All Irish phone numbers in this book include the area code; dial the number listed. To call the operator dial 10 (Republic), 100 (NI).

Phoning the Republic of Ireland from abroad

The country code for the Republic of Ireland is 353. To phone the Republic from another country, prefix 353 to the number given. To phone the Republic from the United States or Canada, omit the first zero from the Irish number, and add the prefix 011 353. (The number of digits in Irish area codes varies.) Example: 01 122 3344 becomes 011 353 1 122 3344.

Phoning from Ireland

To phone the United States or Canada from Ireland, prefix the area code and number with 00 1. Example: (111) 222-3333 becomes 00 1 111 222-3333. To phone Northern Ireland from the Republic of Ireland, replace the code 028 with 048. Example: 028 1122 3344 becomes 048 1122 3344. To call international directory inquiries dial 11818 (Republic), 118505 (NI).

Emergency telephone numbers

Any emergency **112**.
Police (gardaí) **999**. Fire service **999**.
Ambulance **999** Emergency calls are free from phone booths.

Hours of Operation

- Stores Mon.–Sat.
- Offices Mon.–Fri.
- Banks Mon.–Fri.
- Post Offices Mon.–Fri.
- Museums/Monuments
- Pharmacies Mon.–Fri.

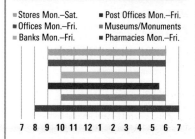

7 8 9 10 11 12 1 2 3 4 5 6 7

Hours in chart refer to the Republic of Ireland; hours for Northern Ireland may differ slightly.
Some **stores** stay open until 8 or 9 on Thursday or Friday. On Sunday some bigger stores and many supermarkets open from noon until 5 or 6. In smaller towns and rural areas stores close in the afternoon on one day of the week.

Pharmacies may close earlier on Saturday.

Some **banks** in small towns close 12:30–1:30. Banks open until 5 p.m. one day a week (Thursdays in Dublin and Belfast). Nearly all banks are closed on Saturday and Sunday.

In larger cities and towns, **post offices** stay open during lunchtime and until 5 on Saturdays. In suburban and rural areas, they typically close for lunch (1–2:15) and are closed on Saturdays.

Hours for **museums** and tourist sights vary; always check with the local tourist office. Some places close from October to March, although most major sights are open all year.

National Holidays

Banks, businesses and most stores close on these days. Museums also may have restricted hours.

Jan. 1	New Year's Day
Mar. 17	St. Patrick's Day
Mar./Apr.	Good Friday
Mar./Apr.	Easter Monday (also day after in NI)
1st Mon. in May	May Bank Holiday
Last Mon. in May	Spring Bank Holiday (NI)
1st Mon. in Jun.	June Bank Holiday (ROI)
Jul. 12	Battle of the Boyne (NI)
1st Mon. in Aug.	August Bank Holiday (ROI)
Last Mon. in Aug.	Summer Bank Holiday (NI)
Last Mon. in Oct.	October Bank Holiday (ROI)
Dec. 25	Christmas Day
Dec. 26	St. Stephen's Day

Photography

The light is frequently poor. Bring a tripod for landscape work. Digital equipment and printing facilities are widely available. Camera batteries are also available countrywide.

Ireland

Health

Medical Insurance

Private medical insurance is recommended. U.S. and Canadian visitors can receive treatment in emergency rooms, but are charged if admitted to a hospital bed. A general practitioner also will charge for services.

Dental Services

Dental work is expensive, so check to see if it is covered by your medical insurance. Dentists are listed in the *Golden Pages* (IR) or *Yellow Pages* (NI), or ask at your hotel or embassy. For the Irish Dental Association call ☎ 01 295 0072.

Sun Advice

The sunniest months are May and June, with 5–6.5 hours of sun a day (the extreme southwest is the sunniest). July and August are the warmest. During these months you should take sensible precautions against the sun.

Drugs

Pharmacies (also called chemists) sell a range of prescription and nonprescription medicines. If you need medicine outside regular hours, information about the nearest 24-hour facility should be posted on the door of all pharmacies.

Safe Water

Tap water is safe to drink throughout Ireland. If, however, you prefer mineral water you will find it widely available.

Restrooms

Identify restrooms by *Fir* (men) and *Mná* (women). A small charge is levied in restrooms at some railroad stations, but most other facilities are free. The standards of hygiene are moderate. You will be welcomed into any local pub if you need to use their facilities, but stop for a drink and a talk while you are there.

Electricity

The Republic of Ireland has a 230-volt and Northern Ireland a 240-volt power supply.

Electrical sockets either take plugs with two round pins or three square pins. American appliances will need a plug adapter and will require a transformer if they do not have a dual-voltage facility.

National Transportation

Train

The Republic of Ireland's rail company is Iarnród Éireann (IÉ or Irish Rail). Trains are the fastest way of covering long distances and are generally reliable and comfortable, but the network is limited and one-way tickets cost almost as much as round-trip tickets. Midweek is less expensive than weekends, and there are many special offers on fares. For information: ☎ 01 850 366 222; www.irishrail.ie. For Northern Ireland call Translink ☎ 028 9066 6630 for rail schedules and fares; www.translink.co.uk

Bus

Bus Éireann (Irish Bus) operates a network of express bus routes serving most of the country (some run summer only). For information: ☎ 01 836 6111; www.buseireann.ie. For Northern Ireland call Translink ☎ 028 9066 6630 for information.

Ferry

A car ferry runs between Ballyhack (County Wexford) and Passage East (County Waterford); ☎ 051 382 480, saving 60 miles on the road trip. Another serves Killimer (County Clare) and Tarbert (County Kerry); ☎ 065 905 3124. There also are ferries to several islands; ask for details at a local tourist office. There are regular ferries from Belfast, Larne, Dublin, Dun Laoghaire and Rosslare to ports on the mainland of Britain, and from Cork and Rosslare to France.

Driving

Drive on the left

Speed Limits

Traffic police can impose on-the-spot fines.

 Limited-access highways (motorways/blue) **120 k.p.h. (74 m.p.h.)**

 Main roads (national/green) **100 k.p.h. (62 m.p.h.)**; in some areas **80 k.p.h. (49 m.p.h.)** Regional/local/white **80 k.p.h. (49 m.p.h.)**

 Urban areas (RI) **50 k.p.h. (31 m.p.h.)** Northern Ireland: **50–60 k.p.h (31–37 m.p.h.)**

Seat belts

 Must be worn in front and back seats at all times.

Driving (continued)

Blood Alcohol
The legal blood alcohol limit is 0.08%. Random breath tests on drivers are carried out frequently, especially late at night, and the penalties for offenders are severe.

Tolls
Tolls are charged at some locations: Dublin Port Tunnel; M50 (radial route around Dublin); East Link Bridge and West Link Bridge (both Dublin); M1 (Drogheda By-Pass); M4 (Kinnegad-Enfield-Kilcock); N8 (Rathcormac/Fermoy By-Pass). There are no tolls on other highway or national routes.

Car Rental
The leading rental firms have offices at airports, railroad stations and large ferry terminals. Hertz offers discounted rates for AAA members (see page 15).

Advise the car rental company if you plan on traveling between the Republic and Northern Ireland. For reservations:

	United States	Republic of Ireland
Alamo/ National	(800) 426-5266	061 206 088
Avis	(800) 331-1212	021 428 1111
Budget	(800) 527-0700	090 662 7711
Hertz	(800) 654-3131	01 676 7476

Fuel
Gas is unleaded and sold in liters; diesel also is easily purchased. Gas stations in villages stay open until 8 or 9 p.m. and usually open after Mass on Sunday.

AAA Affiliated Motoring Club
AA Ireland 56 Drury Street, Dublin 2
☎ 08457 887766. If you break down while driving, phone ☎ 1800 66 77 88 (AAI breakdown service). Not all automobile clubs offer full services to AAA members. Northern Ireland: see Britain section (page 505).

Breakdowns and Accidents
There are 24-hour emergency phones at regular intervals on highways. ☎ 999 if involved in an accident. Most car rental firms provide their own free rescue service; if your car is rented, follow the instructions given in the documentation. Use of a car repair service other than those authorized by your rental company may violate your agreement.

Other Information
The minimum age for driving a car is 17 (may be higher for some car rental firms). An International Driving Permit (IDP) is recommended; some rental firms require it, and it can speed up formalities if

Driving (continued)

you are involved in an accident. A Green Card (international motor insurance certificate) is recommended if you are driving a private car; see page 15 for more information.

In the Republic of Ireland road signs are marked in kilometers, but you may find old signs in miles. In Northern Ireland all road signs are in miles.

Useful Words and Phrases

Although the Republic of Ireland is officially bilingual, and the Irish language (Gaelic or Gaeilge) is learned by all schoolchildren, English is more commonly spoken. There are around 90,000 native speakers of Irish, making it Europe's least widespread official language.

Because it often reflects expressions in Gaelic, Irish English is famed for its picturesque turns of phrase, much more poetic than American or British English.

The Gaelic language is enjoying a revival: radio, television and the Internet all stir up interest in the old language. There are Gaelic-speaking clubs as far away as the U.S. West Coast.

Following are pronunciations of words you may come across:

Bord Fáilte (Irish Tourist Board)	bord falt-cha
Ceilidh (traditional dance night)	kaylee
Gaeilge (the Irish language)	gale-geh
Gaeltacht (Irish-speaking country)	gale-tackt
Garda (policeman)	gawrdah
Fleadh (traditional music evening)	flah
Taoiseach (prime minister)	teeshock

Numbers:

1	*a haon*	a hay-on
2	*a dó*	a doe
3	*a trí*	a tree
4	*a ceathair*	a ca-hir
5	*a cuíg*	a koo-ig
6	*a sé*	a shay
7	*a seacht*	a shocked
8	*a hocht*	a huct
9	*a naoi*	a neigh
10	*a deich*	a de

Other words:

good day	*lá maith*	law mah
goodbye	*slán*	slawn
goodnight	*oíche mhaith*	ee-ha vah
How are you?	*Conas taio?*	co-nus tee?
please	*más é do thoil é*	maws eh duh hull eh
thanks	*gusmaith agat*	gurrah mah a-gut
pub	*tábhairne*	taw-er nay
water	*uisce*	ishkek
whiskey	*fuisci*	fwishgee
yes	sea	shah

Italy

National Flag

Essential for Travelers

● Required ● Recommended ● Not required

Passport	●
Visa (check regulations before you travel)	●
Travel, medical insurance	●
Round-trip or onward airline ticket	●
Local currency	●
Traveler's checks	●
Credit cards	●
First-aid kit and medicines	●
Health inoculations	●

Essential for Drivers*

Driver's license	●
International Driving Permit	●
Car insurance (for private cars)	●
Car registration (for private cars)	●
*see also Driving section	

Important Addresses

Italian Government Tourist Board
630 Fifth Avenue
Suite 1565, Rockefeller Center
New York, NY 10111
☎ (212) 245-5618 or (212) 245-4822
(brochure hotline)
🕐 Mon.–Fri. 9–5
www.italiantourism.com

Ente Nazionale Italiano per il Turismo (Italian State Tourist Board)
Via Marghera 2/6
00185 Rome, Italy
☎ 06 49711
www.enit.it

American Embassy
Via Vittorio Veneto 119/a
00187 Rome, Italy
☎ 06 46741 or 06 4674 2420
www.rome.usembassy.gov
Non-emergency services are available through an online appointment system or ☎ 899 343 432

Customs

✓ **Goods brought into Italy from non-European Union countries limited to:**
200 cigarettes or 100 cigarillos or 50 cigars or 250 g. tobacco; 2 L. wine; 1 L. alcohol over 22% volume or 2 L. alcohol under 22% volume; 50 ml. perfume; 250 ml. toilet water; plus any other duty-free goods (including gifts) to the value of €300 if arriving by land, €430 if arriving by sea or air. There is no limit on the importation of tax-paid goods purchased within the European Union, provided they are for your own personal use. Foreign or local currency in excess of $10,000 must be declared on arrival.

✗ No unlicensed drugs, weapons, ammunition, obscene material, pets or other animals, counterfeit money or copied goods, meat or poultry.
For customs limits for returning U.S. citizens see page 16.

Money

Italy's currency is the euro (€), a currency shared by 16 other European Union countries. The euro is divided into 100 cents (¢). The denominations of euro bills are 5, 10, 20, 50, 100, 200 and 500. There are coins of 1, 2, 5, 10, 20 and 50¢ and €1 and €2. Exchange dollars or traveler's checks *(assegni turistici)* at a bank *(banca)* or exchange office *(ufficio di cambio)*. Hotels may exchange traveler's checks, but stores do not. ATMs *(sportello automatico)* are fairly common and accept major credit cards.

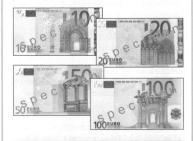

Tips and Gratuities

Restaurants (service usually included but add 50¢ per person)	
Cafés/bars	small change
Taxis	15%
Porters	€1
Chambermaids	€1 per day
Restrooms	minimum
Cloakroom attendants	50¢

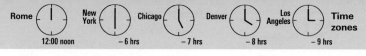
Communications

Post Offices

Buy stamps *(francobolli)* at a post office *(ufficio postale)* or at a tobacconist *(tabaccaio)*. Mailboxes (red or blue) often have two slots, one for local mail *(per la città)*, the other for out-of-town mail *(tutte le altre destinazioni)*. Mail can take up to three weeks; to speed delivery send it priority *(posta prioritaria)* or recorded *(raccomandata)* post.

Telephones

Pay phones can be found in bars and other public places. Prepaid cards *(carta or scheda telefonica)* for card-operated phones are

available from tobacconists, bars, post offices, newsstands, railroad stations and dispensers showing a Telecom Italia (TI) logo. Use a prepaid card for international calls; tear the corner off before using it. Calls from hotel rooms are expensive.

Phoning inside Italy
All telephone numbers in Italy include an area code that must always be dialed. To call the operator dial 10.

Phoning Italy from abroad
The country code for Italy is 39. Note that Italian numbers in this book do not include the country code; you will need to prefix this number if you are phoning from another country. To call Italy from the United States or Canada dial the prefix 011 39. Include the first zero of the regional code. There is no standard number of digits in Italian numbers. Example: 01 122 3344 becomes 011 39 01 122 3344.

Phoning from Italy
To phone the United States or Canada from Italy, prefix the area code and number with 00 1. Example: (111) 222-3333 becomes 00 1 111 222-3333. To call international information dial 4176.

Emergency telephone numbers
Police *(policia)* 113 (local) or 112 (national)
Fire service *(pompieri)* 115 or 112
Ambulance *(ambulanza)* 118 or 112
Emergency calls are free from phone booths.

Hours of Operation

- Stores Mon.–Sat.
- Offices Mon.–Fri.
- Banks Mon.–Fri.
- Post Offices Mon.–Fri.
- Museums/Monuments
- Architectural sites
- Churches/Pharmacies

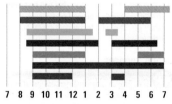

7 8 9 10 11 12 1 2 3 4 5 6 7

Department **stores**, some grocery stores and stores in major cities and tourist areas may not close at lunchtime, and sometimes stay open until later in the evening. Some stores close on Monday morning and may close on Saturday afternoon in summer; most stores close on Sunday. Many stores, especially in Rome, Florence and Venice (less so in Naples) now stay open from 1 to 4.

Some **banks** close at 2 and do not reopen later in the afternoon.

Post office times may vary slightly; some may be open Saturday 8:30–noon.

Many **museums** are open in the late afternoon (typically 4–7), others are open all day, and a few stay open late into the evening. Many museums close early on Sunday (around 1), and many are closed on Monday.

National Holidays

Banks, businesses and most stores and museums close on these days. Most cities, towns and villages celebrate their patron saint's day, but generally most establishments remain open.

Jan. 1	New Year's Day
Jan. 6	Epiphany
Mar./Apr.	Easter Monday
Apr. 25	Liberation Day 1945
May 1	Labor Day
Jun. 2	Anniversary of the Republic
Aug. 15	Assumption of the Virgin
Nov. 1	All Saints' Day
Dec. 8	Immaculate Conception
Dec. 25	Christmas Day
Dec. 26	St. Stephen's Day

Photography

Digital equipment is available in towns and cities. The light in Italy is usually good. Photography may be banned in museums and churches.

Health

Medical Insurance

✚ Private medical insurance is strongly recommended. Visitors from non-European Union countries can receive treatment in a hospital accident and emergency room, but will be charged if admitted to a bed. A general practitioner *(medico)* can deal with less urgent cases, but also will charge.

Dental Services

Emergency dental treatment is available from English-speaking dentists listed in the yellow pages *(pagine gialle; www.paginegialle.it)*. A fee will be charged, so check that you are covered for treatment on your private medical insurance.

Sun Advice

In summer, especially July and August, it can be oppressively hot and humid in cities. On sunny days cover your head and shoulders and use a sunscreen. Cathedrals and other stone buildings can be refreshingly cool. Take frequent breaks in the shade and drink plenty of fluids.

Drugs

A pharmacy *(farmacia)* displays a green cross symbol and has staff who can provide prescription medicines and offer advice on minor ailments. Information about the address of the nearest 24-hour facility is normally posted at every pharmacy.

Safe Water

In isolated rural areas it is not advisable to drink tap water. However, across most of the country tap water is perfectly safe, although most Italians prefer to drink bottled mineral water *(acqua minerale)*, which is inexpensive and widely available.

Restrooms

Finding a restroom *(gabinetto/bagno)* can be difficult away from airports, rail and bus stations, highway service areas and museums. Leave a tip (about 50¢) for the attendant. If using the facilities in a bar you will be expected to buy a drink. Some bars have separate restrooms for men *(signori)* and women *(signore)*.

Electricity

Italy has a 220-volt power supply (in some areas, 125 volts). Electrical sockets take plugs with two round pins or three pins in a vertical row. American appliances will need a plug adapter and will require a transformer if they do not have a dual-voltage facility.

National Transportation

Train *(Treno)*

 Italian State Railways (Trenitalia call center in Italy ☎ 89 2021; www.trenitalia.com) provides an efficient range of services. *Regionale* and *Interregionali* trains are slow for long journeys; Intercity and Intercity Plus trains, which do not make stops at each station *(stazione)*, cost more but are faster; the Eurostar and Eurostar City are the fastest and most expensive.

Bus *(Autobus)*

 There is no national bus company, but each major city has its own company for short-, medium- and some long-distance bus travel. International Eurolines buses run from the main Italian cities: ☎ 086 155 4014; www.eurolines.it

Ferry *(Traghetto)*

 Genoa and Naples are the main Mediterranean ports, with regular services to Sicily and Sardinia. Naples also has services to Capri and other islands. Many services are reduced off-season, and some are cut altogether. Reserve well in advance for car ferries.

Driving

Drive on the right

Speed Limits

Police can demand up to a quarter of an imposed fine to be paid on the spot.

 Limited-access highways *(autostrada)*
130 k.p.h. (80 m.p.h.)
Some designated stretches of *autostrada* have a **150 k.p.h. (93 m.p.h.)** limit.

 Main roads
90–110 k.p.h. (56–68 m.p.h.)

Urban areas
50 k.p.h. (31 m.p.h.)

Seat Belts

Must be worn in front and back seats at all times.

Blood Alcohol

The legal blood alcohol limit is 0.05%. Random breath tests are carried out frequently, especially late at night.

Driving (continued)

Tolls

You will be issued a toll-card on entering nearly every limited-access highway *(autostrada)*: pay on leaving. You can buy a prepaid card *(viacard)* at tollbooths, service areas, tourist offices and tobacconists.

Car Rental

The leading rental firms have offices at airports, railroad stations and ferry terminals. Hertz offers discounted rates for AAA members (see page 15).
For reservations:

	United States	Italy
Avis	(800) 331-1084	199 100 133
Budget	(800) 472-3325	06 7290 7739 (Rome)
Europcar	(877) 940-6900	06 9670 9592
Hertz	(800) 654-3001	199 112 211

Fuel

Gas *(benzina)* is unleaded *(senza piombo)* 95 and 98 octane. Outside urban areas, stations are open daily 7–12:30 and 3–7:30. Highway services are open 24 hours. Credit cards are accepted at most filling stations.

AAA Affiliated Motoring Club

Automobile Club D'Italia (ACI) Via Marsala 8, 00185 Rome ☎ 803116 in Italy (24 hours a day); or 06 491 115 or 800 000 116 (toll-free in Italy); www.aci.it. If you break down while driving, phone ☎ 803116. Not all automobile clubs offer full services to AAA members.

Breakdowns and Accidents

There are emergency phones at regular intervals on all highways. If you are involved in an accident, phone ☎ 112. Most car rental firms provide their own free rescue service; if you have an accident, follow the rental documentation instructions. Use of an unauthorized repair company may violate your agreement. In the event of a breakdown, you must put on a fluorescent vest when you are outside your vehicle. You must carry a warning triangle in your vehicle.

Other Information

The minimum age for driving a car is 18 (may be higher for some car rental firms). An International Driving Permit (IDP) is recommended; some rental firms require it, and it can speed up formalities if you are involved in an accident. A Green Card (international motor insurance certificate) is recommended if you are driving a private car (see page 15). Dimmed headlights are required by law at all times outside built-up areas and when visiblity is poor. Many historic downtown areas have a Zone a Traffico Limitato (ZTL) with automatic fines for non-approved vehicles.

Useful Words and Phrases

Italian pronunciation is consistent with spelling, and vowels are always pronounced. The letter h is always silent, but can modify the sound of letters c and g. As a general rule, accentuate the next-to-last syllable.

c is hard before a, o, u, h	*medico; Chianti*
c is soft before i or e	*ciao* [chow]
g is hard before a, o, u, h	*Gucci*, Lamborghini
g is soft before i or e	*gelati*
	[jel-ah-tee]
gl as in Amelia	*figlia* [fee-lyah]
gn as in union	*gnocchi*
	[nyee-ok-kee]
sc before i or e is soft	*prosciutto*
	[pro-shoot-toh]

Where two consonants appear together, each belongs to a different syllable.

Do you speak English?	*Parla inglese*?
excuse me	*mi scusi*
goodbye	*arrivederci*
hello	*buongiorno*
How much is…?	*Quanto costa…?*
I am American	*sono Americano/-a*
I'd like…	*vorrei…*
I don't understand	*non capisco*
nonsmoking	*per non fumatori*
okay	*va bene*
open/closed	*aperto/chiuso*
please/thank you	*per favore/grazie*
ticket (one-way/	*biglietto (andata*
round trip)	*sola/andata ritorno*)
where is…?	*dov'è…?*
yes/no	*si/no*
you're welcome	*prego*
the hotel	***l'albergo***
breakfast	*prima colazione*
I have a reservation	*ho una prenotazione*
key	*una chiave*
for one/two nights	*per una/due notte/-i*
one/two people	*una/due persona/-e*
room	*una camera*
shower	*una doccia*
with en-suite bathroom	*con bagno privato*
the restaurant	***il ristorante***
starter	*l'antipasto*
entrée	*il secondo*
beef	*il manzo*
bread	*il pane*
chicken	*il pollo*
coffee	*il caffè*
dish of the day	*il piatto del giorno*
seafood	*i frutti di mare*
fish	*il pesce*
lamb	*l'agnello*
pork	*il maiale*
wine	*il vino*
dessert	*il dolce*
the check	*il conto*

National Flag

Essential for Drivers

● **Required** ● **Recommended** ● **Not required**

Passport	●
Visa (check regulations before you travel)	●
Travel, medical insurance	●
Round-trip or onward airline ticket	●
Local currency	●
Traveler's checks	●
Credit cards	●
First-aid kit and medicines	●
Inoculations	●

Essential for Drivers*

Driver's license	●
International Driving Permit	●
Car insurance (for nonrental cars)	●
Car registration (for nonrental cars)	●

*see also *Driving* section

Important Addresses

Luxembourg National Tourist Office
17 Beekman Place
New York, NY 10022
☎ (212) 935-8888
www.visitluxembourg.com

**Office National du Tourisme
(Luxembourg National Tourist Office)**
P.O. Box 1001
L-1010 Luxembourg
☎ 42 82 82 20
www.ont.lu or www.visitluxembourg.lu

Embassy of the United States
22 boulevard Emmanuel Servais
L-2535 Luxembourg
☎ 46 01 23
http://luxembourg.usembassy.gov
Mon.–Fri. 8:30–5:30

Customs

✔ **Duty-free limits on goods brought in from non-European Union countries:**
200 cigarettes or 100 cigarillos or 50 cigars or 250 g. tobacco; 2 L. wine; 1 L. alcohol over 22% volume or 2 L. alcohol under 22% volume; 50 ml. perfume; 250 ml. toilet water; plus any other duty-free goods (including gifts) to the value of €175 (€90 for children under 15). There is no limit on the importation of tax-paid goods purchased within the European Union, provided they are for your own personal use. There are no restrictions on the import or export of cash or traveler's checks in euros or foreign currency.

✘ No unlicensed drugs, weapons, ammunition, obscene material, pets or other animals, counterfeit money or copied goods, meat or poultry.
For customs limits for returning U.S. citizens see page 16.

Money

Luxembourg's currency is the euro (€), a currency shared by 16 other European Union countries. The euro is divided into 100 cents (¢). The denominations of euro bills are 5, 10, 20, 50, 100, 200 and 500. There are coins of 1, 2, 5, 10, 20 and 50¢ and €1 and €2.

Exchange dollars and traveler's checks *(cheques de voyage)* at a bank *(banque)* or an exchange office *(bureau de change)*.

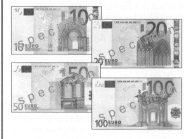

Tips and Gratuities

Restaurants, cafés and bars (service usually included)	
	round up to nearest €1 or €2
Taxis	15%
Porters, chambermaids	€1–€2
Hairdressers	€2
Restroom attendants	20¢
Cloakroom attendants	50¢ per coat

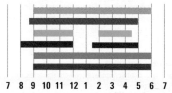

City of Luxembourg	New York	Chicago	Denver	Los Angeles	Time zones
12:00 noon	– 6 hrs	– 7 hrs	– 8 hrs	– 9 hrs	

543

Luxembourg

Communications

Post Offices

Buy stamps *(timbres-poste)* at a post office *(poste)*, newsstand/tobacconist *(tabac-journaux)*, or at a bookstore. Mailboxes are yellow, and are attached to walls and post offices. Luxembourg City's main post office is ✉ 25 rue Aldringen ☎ 4765-4451 🕐 Mon.–Fri. 7–7, Sat. 7–5. Another is ✉ 38 place de la Gare ☎ 4088-7610 🕐 Mon.–Fri. 6 a.m.– 7 p.m., Sat. 6–noon.

Hours for out-of-town post offices may vary.

Telephones

Finding a public telephone *(cabine téléphonique)* is easy. Phone booths usually have pictorial instructions, with French and German text. You can use most denominations of coins, or buy a prepaid phone card *(télécarte)* from a post office or railroad station. International phone booths display a yellow sign showing a telephone dial with a receiver in the center.

Phoning inside Luxembourg

There are no area codes in Luxembourg; dial the number that is listed. To call the operator dial 118 171. To call the international operator dial 11816.

Phoning Luxembourg from abroad

The country code for Luxembourg is 352. Note that Luxembourg numbers in this book do not include the country code; you will need to prefix this number if you are phoning from another country. To phone Luxembourg from the United States or Canada, add the prefix 011 352.
Example: 11 22 33 becomes 011 352 11 22 33.

Phoning from Luxembourg

To phone the United States or Canada from Luxembourg, prefix the area code and number with 00 1. Example: (111) 222-3333 becomes 00 1 111 222-3333.

Emergency telephone numbers

Police *(police)* **112** or **113**
Fire service *(pompiers)* **112**
Ambulance *(ambulance)* **112**
Emergency calls are free from phone booths

Hours of Operation

- Stores Mon.–Sat.
- Offices Mon.–Fri.
- Banks Mon.–Fri.
- Post Offices Mon.–Fri.
- Museums/Monuments
- Pharmacies Tue.–Sat.

| 7 | 8 | 9 | 10 | 11 | 12 | 1 | 2 | 3 | 4 | 5 | 6 | 7 |

Some **stores** open at 8 a.m. Many stores and **pharmacies** do not open until noon on Monday, and most are closed on Sunday. Many establishments have long lunch breaks (typically noon–2)

Provincial **post offices** and **banks** may have shorter hours, but some stay open at lunchtime and open on Saturday morning. Some post offices open earlier and stay open in the evening.

Opening times for **museums** and **monuments** vary; they are frequently closed on Monday – check with the local tourist office.

National Holidays

Banks, businesses and most stores close on these days.

Jan. 1	New Year's Day
Feb./Mar.	Carnival Day
Mar./Apr.	Easter Monday
May 1	May Day
May/Jun.	Ascension Day
May/Jun.	Whit Monday
Jun. 23	National Day
Aug. 15	Assumption of the Virgin
First Mon. in Sep.	Luxembourg City Fete (City of Luxembourg only)
Nov. 1	All Saints' Day
Dec. 25	Christmas Day
Dec. 26	St. Stephen's Day

National holidays falling on a Sunday are normally observed on the following Monday.

Photography

Luxembourg enjoys a temperate climate, and the light is good. Make sure that photography is permitted before taking pictures in museums. Camera batteries can be bought from tourist stores. Digital equipment and printing facilities are available in major towns.

Luxembourg

Health

Medical Insurance

Private medical insurance is recommended; U.S. and Canadian visitors can be treated in emergency rooms, but are charged if admitted to a hospital *(hôpital)*. Phone ☎ 112 for 24-hour information on hospitals and English-speaking doctors.

Dental Services

A dentist *(dentiste)* will charge a fee for treatment, so check whether this is covered by your medical insurance. Emergency clinics are available in city hospitals. To find a dentist look in the yellow pages *(pages jaunes)* or ask at your hotel.

Sun Advice

You will not experience extremes of temperature in Luxembourg, but the sunshine during summer months can burn, so good sun protection is essential.

Drugs

Prescription medicines and advice can be obtained from a pharmacy *(pharmacie)*, identified by a green cross. Information about the nearest 24-hour facility is posted at all pharmacies.

Safe Water

Tap water is safe to drink, and bottled mineral water *(eau minérale)* is widely available.

Restrooms

Restrooms *(toilettes)* are usually clean, modern and easy to find. They may also be called "WC" (pronounced *vay-say*). Coin-operated facilities exist; those with an attendant usually charge 50¢ or €1.

Electricity

Luxembourg has a 220-volt power supply. Electrical sockets take plugs with two round pins. American appliances will need a plug adapter and will require a transformer if they do not have a dual-voltage facility.

National Transportation

Train *(Train)*

The national rail company is the Societé Nationale des Chemins de Fer Luxembourgeois (CFL; www.cfl.lu). Most services run through the city of Luxembourg. Combined train and bus one-day travel cards (the "Oeko-Pass") are good value at €4 and are valid until 8 a.m. the following day. "Short distance" train and bus tickets are available for €1.50 and are valid for 2 hours or 6 miles. At Luxembourg City train station there is an information office (🕐 daily 5 a.m.–9.30 p.m.). National information and tickets ☎ 2489-2489.

Bus *(Bus)*

Long-distance, CFL-operated buses complement the rail network (☎ 24 89 24 89; www.cfl.lu). The Eurolines European bus network serves Luxembourg, arriving at place de la Gare, in front of Gare Centrale.

River Boat *(Bateau-mouche)*

There are many excursions (mostly Easter to October) exploring Luxembourg's magnificent Moselle river. For details, contact Entente Touristique de la Moselle Luxembourgeoise, 115 route du Vin, P.O. Box 33, L-6701 Grevenmacher ☎ 75 84 12; www.visitmoselle.lu

Driving

Drive on the right

Speed Limits

Police impose minor on-the-spot fines.

Limited access highways *(autoroutes)*
130 k.p.h. (80 m.p.h.), 110 k.p.h. (68 m.p.h. when wet or in snow conditions

Main roads
90 k.p.h. (56 m.p.h.)

Urban areas
50 k.p.h. (31 m.p.h.)

Seat Belts

Must be worn in front and back seats at all times. Children aged 3 to 18 years and/or under 4 feet 11 inches in height must use an appropriate child restraint system.

Blood Alcohol

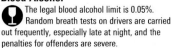
The legal blood alcohol limit is 0.05%. Random breath tests on drivers are carried out frequently, especially late at night, and the penalties for offenders are severe.

Driving (continued)

Tolls

There are no highway tolls in Luxembourg.

Car Rental

The leading rental firms have offices at airports and train stations. Hertz offers discounted rates for AAA members (see page 15). For reservations:

	United States	Luxembourg
Alamo	(877) 222-9075	40 42 28 (Europcar)
Avis	(800) 331-1212	43 51 71
Budget	(800) 527-0700	43 75 75
Hertz	(800) 654-3001	43 46 45

Fuel

Most gas stations *(stations de service)* are self-service, and 24-hour facilities are common. Stations on highways often have café services. The price of gas is fixed by the government, but self-service stations often offer discounts. Major credit cards are accepted.

AAA Affiliated Motoring Club

Automobile Club du Grand-Duché de Luxembourg (ACL) 54 route de Longwy, L-8007 Bertrange, ☎ 45 00 45-1 (Mon.–Fri. 8:30–6); www.acl.lu. If you break down while driving, phone ☎ 26000 (ACL 24-hour breakdown service). Not all automobile clubs offer full services to AAA members.

Breakdowns and Accidents

There are emergency phones at regular intervals on highways. If you are involved in an accident, phone for emergency assistance (☎ 112 or 113 for police or ☎ 112 for fire or ambulance). Most car rental firms provide their own free rescue service; if your car is rented, follow the instructions given in the documentation. Use of a car repair service other than those authorized by your rental company may violate your agreement. In the event of a breakdown, you must put on a fluorescent vest when you are outside your vehicle. You must carry a warning triangle in your vehicle.

Other Information

The minimum age for driving a car is 18 (may be higher for some car rental firms). An International Driving Permit (IDP) is recommended; some rental firms require them, and they can speed up formalities if you are involved in an accident. A Green Card (international motor insurance certificate) is recommended if you are driving a private car; see page 15 for more information.

Useful Words and Phrases

Because the Grand Duchy of Luxembourg is tucked between Belgium, France and Germany, Luxembourgers often slip unconsciously between different languages.

The official language (and, unofficially, the language of the elite) is French, but German is used for many situations. In addition to this, there is a third, everyday language: Lëtzebuergesch, a symbol of both national identity and Luxembourg's ability to assimilate other cultures.

The roots of Luxembourg's own language are Germanic, but it has evolved into a dialect that Germans no longer understand. The use of Lëtzebuergesch is primarily an oral tradition. It was only in 1984 that its spelling was decreed by law; up until then Luxembourgers spelled words more or less as they pleased.

French, German and Lëtzebuergesch are taught in schools, and English also is widely spoken, especially among the young and those working in the tourist trade. Don't expect Luxembourgers in rural areas to have mastered a fourth language, however!

Lëtzebuergesch is resilient enough to exist side-by-side with such widely spoken languages as French and German, but as the patois of a tiny, landlocked duchy it's evidently not very exportable. So if you have the opportunity to speak a word or two of this country's uniting language you'll raise a smile and a welcome.

good morning/hello	*moien*
goodbye	*eddi*
thank you (very much)	*merci (villmols)*
sorry	*pardon*
excuse me	*entschellegt*
please	*wanneschglift*
I don't understand	*ech verstin nët*
Food and drink	
apple cake	*Äppelkuch*
blood sausage	*Trèipen*
cheesecake	*Kéiskuch*
chicken in Riesling sauce	*Hong am Rèisleck*
coffee	*Kaffi*
crayfish	*Kriibsen*
green bean soup	*Bou'neschlupp*
nettle soup	*Brennesselszopp*
pike in green liquor	*Hiecht mat Kraïderzooss*
pork in aspic	*Jhelli*
potato dumplings	*Gromperekniddeln*
potato soup	*Gromperenzopp*
tripe	*Kuddelfleck*
trout in Riesling sauce	*F'rell am Rèisleck*

For useful phrases in French, see page 521; for phrases in German see page 525.

National Flag

Essential for Travelers

● **Required** ● **Recommended** ● **Not required**

Passport	●
Visa (check regulations before you travel)	●
Travel, medical insurance	●
Round-trip or onward airline ticket	●
Local currency	●
Traveler's checks	●
Credit cards	●
First-aid kit and medicines	●
Inoculations	●

Essential for Drivers*

Driver's license	●
International Driving Permit	●
Car insurance (for nonrental cars)	●
Car registration (for nonrental cars)	●

*see also *Driving* section

Important Addresses

The Netherlands Board of Tourism
355 Lexington Avenue, 19th floor
New York, NY 10017
☎ (212) 370-7360
www.goholland.com

**Nederlands Bureau voor Toerisme & Congressen
– NBTC (Netherlands Board of Tourism
& Conventions – NBTC)**
Vlietweg 15, 2266 KA Leidschendam
The Netherlands
☎ 070 370 5705
www.holland.com

American Embassy
Lange Voorhout 102
2514 EJ The Hague, The Netherlands
☎ 070 310 2209
http://thehague.usembassy.gov

Customs

✔ **Duty-free limits on goods brought in from non-European Union countries:**
200 cigarettes or 100 cigarillos or 50 cigars or 250 g. tobacco; 2 L. wine; 1 L. alcohol over 22% volume or 2 L. alcohol under 22% volume; 50 ml. perfume; 250 ml. toilet water; plus any other duty-free goods (including gifts) to the value of €45. There is no limit on the importation of tax-paid goods purchased within the European Union, provided they are for your own personal use. There are no currency regulations.

✗ No unlicensed drugs, weapons, ammunition, obscene material, pets or other animals, counterfeit money or copied goods, meat or poultry.
For customs limits for returning U.S. citizens see page 16.

Money

The Dutch currency is the euro (€), a currency shared by 16 other European Union countries. The euro is divided into 100 cents (¢). The denominations of euro bills are 5, 10, 20, 50, 100, 200 and 500. There are coins of 1, 2, 5, 10, 20 and 50¢ and €1 and €2. You can change dollars and traveler's checks *(reischeques)* at a bank, a GWK exchange office or other exchange office or the larger VVV (tourist information center) bureaus.

Tips and Gratuities

Restaurants (service is always included)	change
Cafés/bars (service is always included)	change
Taxis (service is always included)	change
Porters	change
Hairdressers	change
Chambermaids	change
Restroom attendants	50¢
Cloakroom attendants	none

| The Hague | New York | Chicago | Denver | Los Angeles | Time zones |
| 12:00 noon | − 6 hrs | − 7 hrs | − 8 hrs | − 9 hrs | |

547

The Netherlands

Communications

Post Offices

Buy stamps *(postzegels)* at a post office *(postkantoor* or *TNT Post)*, tobacco shop, newsstand, souvenir shop or vending machines in

post offices. If you are buying from a counter make sure you are in a line for stamps. Mailboxes have two slots; foreign mail should be dropped into the slot marked *Overige*. Hours for out-of-town post offices may vary.

Telephones

You can use cash (uncommon), credit cards and prepaid phone cards *(kaarttelefhoon)* to make telephone calls. Phone cards can be bought from GWK–Holland Welcome Service offices, post offices, VVV tourist offices and shops displaying the phone card symbol. Orange-and-gray-colored booths, located at most railroad stations, require a

different phone card, available from GWK– Holland Welcome Service offices, Wizzl shops and railroad ticket offices. Calls also can be made from post offices and *Telehouse* booths.

Phoning inside The Netherlands
All Dutch telephone numbers in this book include an area code; dial the number listed. To call the operator dial 0800 0410.

Phoning The Netherlands from abroad
The country code for The Netherlands is 31. Dutch numbers in this book do not include the country code; include the country code if you are phoning from another country. To phone The Netherlands from the United States or Canada, omit the first zero from the Dutch number and dial the prefix 011 31. Example: 011 223 3445 becomes 011 31 11 223 3445.

Phoning from The Netherlands
To phone the United States or Canada, prefix the area code and number with 00 1. Example: (111) 222-3333 becomes 00 1 111 222-3333. To call international information dial 0900 8418 (toll call). For directory inquiries dial 0900 8008 (toll call).

Emergency telephone numbers
Police *(politie)* 112
Fire service *(brandweer)* 112
Ambulance *(ziegenwagen)* 112
Emergency calls are free from phone booths

Hours of Operation

- Stores Mon.–Sat.
- Offices Mon.–Fri.
- Banks Mon.–Fri.
- Post Offices Mon.–Fri.
- Museums/Monuments. Mon.–Sat..
- Pharmacies Mon.–Fri.

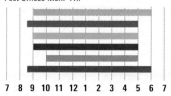

7 8 9 10 11 12 1 2 3 4 5 6 7

Stores open at 11 a.m. on Monday and close at 5 on Saturday. In Amsterdam many stores open Sunday noon–7 and in The Hague and Rotterdam noon–5. In other Dutch cities stores open one Sunday a month. Larger city stores stay open until 9 p.m. on Thursday or Friday. In rural areas many stores close for lunch.

Banks generally open at 1 p.m. Monday.

Post offices also are open 9–noon or 12:30 on Saturday. Some city post offices stay open into the evening (Thursday or Friday).

Museums and **monuments** usually are open 1–5 on Sunday; some may close on Monday. In rural areas they may be closed October through March.

National Holidays

Banks, businesses and most stores close on these days, except for Good Friday, when most shops remain open.

Jan. 1	New Year's Day
Mar./Apr.	Good Friday
Mar./Apr.	Easter Monday
Apr. 30	Queen's Birthday
May 5	Liberation Day (occurs every 5 years; next in 2014)
May/Jun.	Ascension Day
May/Jun.	Pentecost Monday
Dec. 25	Christmas Day
Dec. 26	St. Stephen's Day

Photography

The Dutch climate is essentially maritime; conditions for outdoor photography are gentle but changeable. Some museums do not allow photography; check before taking pictures. Camera batteries are widely available. Digital equipment and printing services are available in towns and cities.

The Netherlands

Health

Medical Insurance

Private medical insurance is recommended. U.S. and Canadian visitors can receive emergency treatment, but are charged if admitted to a hospital *(ziekenhuis)*. Doctors *(dokter)* are listed at the beginning of the telephone directory; English is widely spoken throughout the medical profession.

Tourist Medical Service: doctor ☎ 020 592 3355.

Dental Services

Dentists charge for treatment and can be expensive. Look in the telephone directory, or ask about local dentists at your hotel or embassy.

Sun Advice

The Netherlands' maritime climate is not one of extremes, but precautions against sunburn should be taken from June through August.

Drugs

For nonprescription medicines go to a pharmacy *(drogisterij)*. If you need prescription medicines you will have to go to an *apotheek*, where staff also are trained to treat minor ailments. If you need medicine after regular hours, information about all-night facilities is posted at all pharmacies.

Safe Water

Tap water is safe to drink throughout The Netherlands. Mineral water is widely available.

Restrooms

There are not many public restrooms, although you will usually find adequate and clean facilities in museums, department stores and roadside service areas. Cafés provide restrooms for the use of customers; buy a drink if you need to use them.

Electricity

The Netherlands has a 220-volt power supply. Electrical sockets take plugs with two round pins. American appliances will need a plug adapter and will require a transformer if they do not have a dual-voltage facility.

National Transportation

Train *(Trein)*

Netherlands Railways, or *Nederlandse Spoorwegen (NS)*, network is fast, clean, modern, punctual and inexpensive. Information in English is widely available from stations; ☎ 0900 9296 (toll call) for international train service, ☎ 0900 9292 (toll call) for all domestic transportation services; www.ns.nl.

Bus *(Bus)*

Bus travel is well-organized, with many connections to trains (bus and railroad stations are usually next to each other). If you're planning several trips ask for the *Nationale Buswijer*, which provides maps and full route details; ☎ 0900 9292 (toll call) for information. The Eurolines European bus network operates in The Netherlands ☎ 020 560 8787.

Ferry *(Veerboot)*

There are ferry services from the mainland across the Waddenzee to the Wadden islands (from Den Helder for Texel; Harlingen for Vlieland and Terschelling; Holwerd for Ameland; and Lauwersoog for Schiermonnikoog), and in summer services between the islands. For details about canal trips, contact VVV tourist information centers.

Driving

Drive on the right

Speed Limits

Police can impose on-the-spot fines.

Limited-access highways *(autoweg)* **100 k.p.h. (62 m.p.h.)** or **120 k.p.h. (74 m.p.h.)**

Main roads **80 k.p.h. (49 m.p.h.)**

Urban areas **50 k.p.h. (31 m.p.h.)**

Seat Belts

Must be worn in front and back seats at all times. Children must use a suitable restraint system for their height/weight.

Blood Alcohol

The legal blood alcohol limit is 0.05%. Random breath tests on drivers are carried out frequently, especially late at night, and the penalties for offenders are severe.

The Netherlands

Driving (continued)

Tolls

There are no highway tolls in The Netherlands, but there are tolls for the Dordtse Kil tunnel near Dordrecht and the Westerschelde tunnel.

Car Rental

The leading rental firms have offices at airports and train stations. Hertz offers discounted rates for AAA members (see page 15). For reservations:

	United States	Netherlands
Alamo	(877) 222-9075	020 316 4190 (Europcar)
Avis	(800) 331-1212	020 655 6050
Budget	(800) 527-0700	020 604 1349
Hertz	(800) 654-3001	020 502 0240

Fuel

Many gas stations are self-service and 24-hour facilities are common. Unleaded gas *(Super-Plus* and *Euro-Super)*, lead-replacement fuel and diesel are available, and credit cards are accepted at most garages.

AAA Affiliated Motoring Club

Koninklijke Nederlandse Toeristenbond (ANWB) Wassenaarseweg 220, 2596 The Hague ☎ 088 269 2999; www.anwb.nl. If you break down while driving, telephone ☎ 088 269 2888 (ANWB breakdown service, toll free). Not all automobile clubs offer full services to AAA members.

Breakdowns and Accidents

There are yellow 24-hour emergency phones at regular intervals on highways. All accidents involving personal injury must be reported to the police; ☎ 112. Most car rental firms provide their own free rescue service; if your car is rented, follow the instructions given in the documentation. Use of a car repair service other than those authorized by your rental company may violate your agreement.

Other Information

The minimum age for driving a car is 18 (usually between 21 and 25 for car rental firms). An International Driving Permit (IDP) is recommended; some rental firms require them, and they can speed up formalities if you are involved in an accident. A Green Card (international motor insurance certificate) is recommended if you are driving a private car; see page 15 for more information. Drivers should yield to vehicles approaching from the right. In built-up areas, trams and buses have the right of way when leaving bus stops. Beware of cyclists and skaters.

Useful Words and Phrases

It is not easy to reproduce the guttural sounds that make up the Dutch language. There are many similarities between German and Dutch, although the Dutch go to lengths to point out the differences. English is spoken fluently by a large proportion of the population, who learn foreign languages from an early age.

Dutch pronunciation is similar to English, with some variations:

j as in *y*ellow
v like an f as in *f*ar
w like a v as in *v*at
ng as in bri*ng*
nj as in o*ni*on

Double consonants keep their separate sounds: for instance, k and n together are never pronounced as in the English "know."

Some letters and diphthongs are tricky. If the letter is doubled, the vowel sound is lengthened. For example:

a as in s*a*p,	*aa* as in *a*rt
e as in l*e*t,	*ee* as in f*a*te
o as in m*o*p,	*oo* as in m*o*pe
oe as in f*oo*d	
au, *ou* and *ui* as in h*ow*	
ei and *ij* as in l*i*ne	
ch as in Ba*ch*	
tje as in *ch*urch	
tie as in *tee*	

Do you speak English?	*Spreekt u Engels?*
excuse me	*pardon*
hello	*hallo or dag*
goodbye	*tot ziens*
yes/no	*ja/nee*
how much is?	*wat kost?*
I want…	*ik wil…*
I don't understand	*Ik begrijp het niet*
open/closed	*open/gesloten*
please	*alstublieft*
thank you	*bedankt*
ticket (one-way/ round trip)	*enkele reis retour*
where's the…?	*waar is het…?*
airport	*vliegveld*
room	*kamer*
breakfast	*ontbijt*
dinner	*diner*
May I order?	*Mag ik even bestellen?*
steak	*biefstuk*
bread	*brood*
chicken	*kip*
coffee/tea	*koffie/thee*
sandwich	*broodje*
dish of the day	*daschotel*
lamb	*lamsvlees*
pork	*fricandeau*
wine	*wijn*

Norway

National Flag

Essential for Travelers

● **Required** ● **Recommended** ● **Not required**

Passport	●
Visa (check regulations before you travel)	●
Travel, medical insurance	●
Round-trip or onward airline ticket	●
Local currency	●
Traveler's checks	●
Credit cards	●
First-aid kit and medicines	●
Inoculations	●

Essential for Drivers*

Driver's license	●
International Driving Permit	●
Car insurance (for nonrental cars)	●
Car registration (for nonrental cars)	●

*see also *Driving* section

Important Addresses

Innovation Norway
655 Third Avenue, Suite 1810
New York, NY 10017-9111
☎ (212) 885-9700
www.visitnorway.com

Innovation Norway
P.O. Box 448, Sentrum
N-0104 Oslo, Norway
☎ 22 00 25 00
www.visitnorway.com

American Embassy
Henrik Ibsens gate 48
N-0255 Oslo, Norway
☎ 22 44 85 50 or 21 30 85 40
http://norway.usembassy.gov
◑ Mon.–Fri. 7:30–5

Customs

✓ **Duty-free limits on goods brought in from non-European countries:**
200 cigarettes or 250g. tobacco and 200 cigarette papers; 1 L. alcohol 23–60%; 1.5 L. alcohol up to 22%; 2 L. beer. If you have no alcohol 23–60% you are allowed 1.5 L. extra of alcohol up to 22%, or 5L. beer if no other alcohol. Also goods to the value of Kr6,000, which must include your tobacco and alcohol allowances. You must be 20 and over to bring in spirits and 18 and over to bring in wine, beer and tobacco products. You may import or export local or foreign currency to the value of Kr25,000. Larger amounts must be declared to the customs authorities. This does not apply to traveler's checks.

✗ No unlicensed drugs, weapons, ammunition, fireworks, obscene material, pets, or other animals, counterfeit money or copied goods, alcohol over 60%, meat or poultry.
For customs limits for returning U.S. citizens see page 16.

Money

Norway's currency is the krone (NOK or Kr), which is divided into 100 øre. The denominations of krone bills are 50, 100, 200, 500 and 1,000. There are coins of 50 øre and Kr1, Kr5, Kr10 and Kr20. You can exchange dollars or traveler's checks *(reisesjekk)* at a bank *(bank)*, exchange office *(vekslekontor)*, post office *(posten)* or hotel; you will need ID. Credit cards *(kredittkort)* are widely accepted in hotels, main stores and more expensive restaurants.

Tips and Gratuities

Restaurants (service is included)	5–10%
Cafés/bars (service is included)	5–10%
Taxis (service is included)	10% (optional)
Porters	Kr5 per bag
Hairdressers	change
Chambermaids	Kr5
Restroom attendants	Kr3
Cloakroom attendants	change

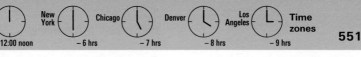

Oslo	New York	Chicago	Denver	Los Angeles	Time zones
12:00 noon	− 6 hrs	− 7 hrs	− 8 hrs	− 9 hrs	

551

Norway

Communications

Post Offices

Buy stamps *(frimerker)* at a post office (posten), a newsstand/ tobacconist such as Narvesen or MIX or from a hotel. Hours for out-of-town post offices may vary. Mailboxes are red.

Telephones

You can use cash or a credit card to make a call in Norway. Most phone booths have direct dialing for international calls. Use Kr1, Kr5, Kr10 and Kr20, or S1 or S2 coins (minimum charge

Kr5 or S1). Some card phones accept credit cards. International phone calls are provided by BBG, call (toll-free) 800 33 200 and follow instructions.

Phoning inside Norway
There are no area codes in Norway; all numbers are eight digits: dial the number that is listed.
To call the operator dial 117; for directory inquiry information (Norway, Sweden and Denmark) dial 1881.

Phoning Norway from abroad
The country code for Norway is 47. Note that Norwegian numbers in this book do not include the country code; you will need to prefix this number if you are phoning from another country. To phone Norway from the United States or Canada, simply add the prefix 011 47. Example: 11 22 33 44 becomes 011 47 11 22 33 44.

Phoning from Norway
To phone the United States or Canada from Norway, prefix the area code and number with 00 1. Example: (111) 222-3333 becomes 00 1 111 222-3333. To call international information dial 1882. For the international operator dial 115.

Emergency telephone numbers
Police *(politi)* **112**
Fire service *(brannvesen)* **110**
Ambulance *(ambulanse)* **113**
Sea emergency **120**
Emergency calls are free from phone booths

Hours of Operation

- Stores Mon.–Sat.
- Offices Mon.–Fri.
- Banks Mon.–Fri.
- Post Offices Mon.–Fri.
- Museums/Monuments
- Pharmacies Mon.–Fri.

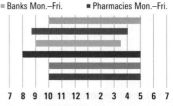

7 8 9 10 11 12 1 2 3 4 5 6 7

On Thursday most **stores** open at 9 and remain open until between 6 and 8 p.m. On Saturday most stores shut between 1 and 3.

Supermarkets are generally open Mon.–Fri. 9–8 or 9, Sat. 9–4 or 6. Many shopping complexes are open until 8 p.m. (4 or 6 p.m. on Sat.). Kiosks are open daily and stay open until 10 or 11 p.m. Most stores are closed on Sunday. Stores around tourist attractions may have special hours.

Offices usually close at 3 p.m. in summer.

Banks generally close half an hour earlier from mid-May to mid-September, but stay open until 5 on Thursday all year and are closed weekends.

Some **post offices** may not open until 9 and close at 4. They are open 9–1 on Saturday.

Museums often close on Monday, and hours of operation may be reduced during the winter.

Pharmacies are open the same hours as stores.

National Holidays

Banks, businesses and most stores close on these days.

Jan. 1	New Year's Day
Mar./Apr.	Maundy Thursday
Mar./Apr.	Good Friday
Mar./Apr.	Easter Monday
May 1	Labor Day
May 17	Constitution Day
May	Ascension Day
May/Jun.	Pentecost Sunday and Monday
Dec. 25	Christmas Day
Dec. 26	St. Stephen's Day

Photography

Spectacular shots are possible in fjord country if the weather is right (bear in mind that Norway is susceptible to poor light, especially during the winter). Photography is not permitted in some museums and places of historic interest – check before taking pictures. Camera batteries are readily available in towns. Digital photography equipment and facilities for downloading and printing are also widely available.

Health

Medical Insurance

U.S. and Canadian visitors will be charged for medical assistance, including treatment in a hospital *(sykehus)* emergency room. For medical emergency service in Oslo contact Oslo kommune Legevakt, ☎ 22 93 22 93 (24 hours). For general practitioners, see *Lege* in the phone directory.

Dental Services

A dentist *(tannlege)* will charge you for treatment, so check your medical insurance coverage. Many dentists speak English; ask a tourist office or your hotel to find one for you. For after-hours emergency treatment *(tannlegevakten)* in Oslo contact Oslo kommunale Tannlegevakt (☎ 22 67 30 00).

Sun Advice

Despite its northerly location, Norway has warm weather during the summer months. Use an appropriate sunscreen.

Drugs

A pharmacy *(apotek)* sells prescription medicines; many pharmacists speak English. Information about the nearest late-night or 24-hour facility is posted at all pharmacies. For a 24-hour pharmacy in Oslo go to Jernbanetorgets Apotek, Jernbanetorget 4B, near Oslo Central Station (☎ 23 35 81 00).

Safe Water

Tap water is safe to drink throughout Norway. Mineral water *(mineralvann)* is widely available.

Restrooms

Public restrooms *(toaletter)* are easy to find. Facilities are separate for men *(herrer)* and women *(damer)*, and are identified by symbols or a "WC" sign. They are invariably clean and modern, and a small charge (usually Kr5) may be made.

Electricity

Norway has a 220-volt power supply. Electrical sockets take plugs with two round pins. American appliances will need a plug adapter and will require a transformer if they do not have a dual-voltage facility.

National Transportation

Train *(Tog)*

The Norges Statsbaner (NSB) network operates as far north as the Arctic Circle. Travel is comfortable but not cheap. Reservations are recommended on train trips and compulsory on long-distance and overnight trains; ask about discounts when booking (☎ 81 50 08 88, then dial 4 for an English-speaking operator, or www.nsb.no).

Bus *(Buss)*

Buses are an inexpensive way to travel in Norway. NOR-WAY Bussekspress (☎ 81 54 44 44; www.nor-way.no) is the national operator. Buy your ticket on board; it is not necessary to book in advance.

Ferry *(Ferje)*

Norway relies heavily on ferries and express boats/catamarans, which connect with trains and buses. Car ferries operate on a first-come, first-served system; payment is made on board. Some waterways have ferry services. *Hurtigruten*, a grand coastal steamer, links Bergen with Kirkenes, in northern Norway, calling at 34 ports en route over 11 days round trip (☎ 81 00 30 30; www.hurtigruten.com).

Driving

Drive on the right

Speed Limits

Speed controls are stringent. Police can impose on-the-spot fines.

 Limited-access highways *(motorvei)* **90 k.p.h. (56 m.p.h.)** or **100 k.p.h. (62 m.p.h.)**

Main roads **80 k.p.h. (49 m.p.h.)**

Urban areas **50 k.p.h. (31 m.p.h.)**; usually **30 k.p.h. (18 m.p.h.)** in residential areas

Seat Belts

 Must be worn in front and back seats at all times. Children under 4 feet 5 inches or 79 pounds must use child safety equipment.

Blood Alcohol

 The legal blood alcohol limit is 0.02%. Random breath tests on drivers are carried out frequently, especially late at night, and the penalties for offenders are extremely severe.

Driving (continued)

Tolls

There are tolls to enter Bergen, Oslo, Stavanger and Trondheim, as well as some highways, bridges and tunnels.

Car Rental

The leading rental firms *(bilutleie)* have offices at airports and train stations. Hertz offers discounted rates for AAA members (see page 15). For reservations:

	United States	Norway
Alamo	(877) 222-9075	23 24 54 30
Avis	(800) 331-1212	81 53 30 44
Budget	(800) 527-0700	81 56 06 00
Hertz	(800) 654-3001	67 81 05 50

Fuel *(Olje)*

Unleaded gas is 95 and 98 octane; diesel is also available. Gas stations *(bensinstasjon)* have varying opening hours and there are few in remote areas, so keep your eye on the gauge.

AAA Affiliated Motoring Club

Norges Automobil-forbund (NAF)
Østensjøveen 14, Postboks 6682, Etterstad, NO-0609 Oslo ☎ 08505 (from abroad: 926 08505); www.naf.no. If you break down while driving, call ☎ 08 505 (24-hour NAF breakdown service). A fee is charged for the service. Not all automobile clubs offer full services to AAA members.

Breakdowns and Accidents

NAF patrols main roads and mountain passes mid-June to mid-August. There are 24-hour emergency phones on all highways. All accidents involving personal injury must be reported to the police (☎ 112). Most car rental firms provide their own free rescue service; if you break down follow the instructions given in the documentation. Use of an unauthorized car repair service may violate your agreement. You must carry a warning triangle in your car.

Other Information

The minimum age for driving a car is 18 (may be higher for car-rental firms). An International Driving Permit (IDP) is recommended; some rental firms require them, and they can speed up formalities if you are involved in an accident. A Green Card (international motor insurance certificate) is highly recommended if you are driving a private car (see page 15 for more information). You are required by law to use dimmed headlights at all times when driving. Snow tires and chains are advised from November 1 until the first Sunday after Easter (mid-Oct. through Apr. 30 in northern Norway); rent tires and chains from NAF or at border crossings.

Useful Words and Phrases

There are two official, and similar forms of Norwegian. Riksmal, or Bokmal ("book language"), is an old form of Norwegian. Athough many bureaucrats speak in Bokmal, it is mostly used in its written form. Landsmal, or Nynorsk, has its roots in Old Norse dialects but developed out of the wave of Norwegian nationalism in the 19th century. You will encounter both during your stay; it is not uncommon for speakers to use a combination of both, but writing rarely mixes styles. The phrases below are translated into Bokmal:

Do you speak English?	*Snakker du engelsk?*
excuse me	*unnskyld meg*
hello	*god dag*
goodbye	*ha det bra*
how much?	*hvor mye?*
I would like	*Jeg vil gjerne*
I don't understand	*Jeg forstår ikke*
nonsmoking	*røyking forbudt*
open/closed	*åpen/stengt*
please	*vaer så snill*
thank you	*takk*
ticket (one-way/ round trip)	*enkeltbillett/ tur-returbillett*
Where is...?	*Hvor er...?*
yes/no	*ja/nei*
early/late	*tidlig/sent*
hot/cold	*varm/kald*
big/small	*stor/liten*
good/bad	*god/dårlig*
airport	*flyplass*
you're welcome	*vaer så god*
the restaurant	**restaurant**
beef	*oksekjøtt*
bread	*brød*
breakfast	*frokost*
the check	*regningen*
chicken	*kylling*
coffee/tea	*kaffe/te*
cookies	*kjeks*
cranberries	*tranebær*
dessert	*dessert*
entree	*hovedrett*
fish	*fisk*
herring	*sild*
hot-dog	*pølse*
ice cream	*is*
lamb	*lammekjøtt*
lobster	*hummer*
pork	*svinekjøtt*
salad	*salat*
sandwich	*smørbrød*
seafood	*sjømat*
starter	*forrett*
waffles	*vafler*
wine	*vin*

Portugal

National Flag

Essential for Travelers

● Required ● Recommended ● Not required

Passport	●
Visa (check regulations before you travel)	●
Travel, medical insurance	●
Return or onward ticket	●
Local currency	●
Traveler's checks	●
Credit cards	●
First-aid kit and medicines	●
Inoculations	●

Essential for Drivers*

Driver's license	●
International Driving Permit	●
Car insurance (for nonrental cars)	●
Car registration (for nonrental cars)	●

*see also *Driving* section

Important Addresses

Portuguese National Tourist Office
590 Fifth Avenue, 4th Floor
New York, NY 10036-4702
☎ (646) 723-0200
www.visitportugal.com

Turismo de Portugal (Portugal Tourist Office)
Rua Ivone Silve, Lote 6, 1050-124 Lisboa
☎ 211 140 200
www.visitportugal.com

American Embassy
Avenida Forças Armadas
1600-081 Lisbon, Portugal
☎ 217 273 300
http://portugal.usembassy.gov
🕐 Mon.–Fri. 8–5

Customs

✔ **Duty-free limits on goods brought in from non-European Union countries:**
200 cigarettes or 100 cigarillos or 50 cigars or 250 g. tobacco; 4 L. wine; 1 L. alcohol over 22% volume or 2 L. alcohol under 22% volume; 60 ml. perfume; 250 ml. toilet water; plus any other duty-free goods (including gifts) to the value of €440. Local or foreign currency (including coins, notes, traveler's checks or other monetary securities) exceeding €12,000 must be declared on entry and when leaving the country. There is no limit on the importation of tax-paid goods purchased within the European Union if they are for personal use.

✗ No unlicensed drugs, weapons, ammunition, obscene material, pets or other animals, counterfeit money or copied goods, meat or poultry.
For customs limits for returning U.S. citizens see page 16.

Money

Portugal's currency is the euro (€), a currency shared by 16 other European Union countries. The euro is divided into 100 cents (¢). The denominations of euro bills are 5, 10, 20, 50, 100, 200 and 500. There are coins of 1, 2, 5, 10, 20 and 50¢ and €1 and €2. You can change dollars or traveler's checks *(cheques de viagem)* at a bank *(banco)* or an exchange office *(casa de cambio)*.

Tips and Gratuities

Restaurants (where service is not included)	5–10%
Cafés/bars (where service is not included)	change
Taxis	10%
Porters	50¢–€1
Hairdressers	€3–€5
Chambermaids	€3–€5
Restroom attendants	50¢
Cloakroom attendants	50¢

The Portuguese are not big tippers although, naturally, tips are always appreciated.

Communications

Post Offices

Buy stamps *(selos)* at a post office *(correios)*, identified by a sign showing a white horse on a red background. You may also see the words "Correios." Hours for out-of-town post offices may vary.

Telephones

You can use coins or a phone card, available from post offices, in a phone booth *(cabine telefónico)*. Public phones are easily found on the street and in cafés, main post offices

and at some newsstands and tourist offices. Most public phones also take international credit cards.

Phoning inside Portugal
All Portuguese telephone numbers in this book include an area code; dial the number listed. To call the international operator dial 120. To call information dial 118.

Phoning Portugal from abroad
The country code for Portugal is 351. Note that Portuguese numbers in this book do not include the country code; you will need to prefix this number if you are phoning from another country. To phone Portugal from the United States or Canada dial the prefix 011 351. Example: 111 223 344 becomes 011 351 111 223 344.

Phoning from Portugal
To phone the United States or Canada from Portugal, prefix the area code and number with 00 1. Example: (111) 222-3333 becomes 00 1 111 222-3333. For an international operator dial 120. To call international information dial 1820.

Emergency telephone numbers
Police *(polícia)* **112**
Fire service *(bombeiros)* **112**
Ambulance *(ambulância)* **112**
Emergency calls are free from phone booths

Hours of Operation

▪ Stores Mon.–Sat.   ▪ Post Offices Mon.–Fri.
▪ Offices Mon.–Fri.   ▪ Museums/Monuments
▪ Banks Mon.–Fri.   ▪ Pharmacies Mon.–Fri.

7 8 9 10 11 12 1 2 3 4 5 6 7

Most **stores** and **pharmacies** close at 1 p.m. on Saturday and are not open on Sunday. Stores in large malls are open Mon.–Sun. from 10 a.m. until midnight. Grocery stores are usually open until 9 p.m.

Post offices and **banks** in rural areas often close for lunch. A few banks in Lisbon stay open until 6 p.m.

Museums generally close on Monday (others close on Wednesday), and the smaller sights may have shorter hours of operation off-season.

National Holidays

Banks, businesses and most stores close on these days. Additionally, there are many local festivals when everything comes to a halt and a whole town takes part in events.

Jan. 1	New Year's Day
Feb./Mar.	Shrove Tuesday
Mar./Apr.	Good Friday
Apr. 25	Liberty Day
May 1	Labor Day
May/Jun.	Corpus Christi
Jun. 10	Portugal Day
Aug. 15	Assumption of the Virgin
Oct. 5	Republic Day
Nov. 1	All Saints' Day
Dec. 1	Independence Day
Dec. 8	Immaculate Conception
Dec. 25	Christmas Day

Photography

Finding adequate light is rarely a problem in Portugal; rise early for atmospheric shots of fishing ports, villages, castles and the mountains. You will not be permitted to photograph at airports or military areas, and ask permission before taking pictures in museums and churches. Digital peripherals and commercial digital printers are widely available at camera stores, along with popular brands of batteries.

Medical Insurance

 U.S. and Canadian visitors will be charged for emergency medical treatment, consultation with a doctor and/or admittance to a hospital *(hospital)*. Ask at a tourist office or your hotel to find an English-speaking doctor.

Dental Services

Dental treatment is charged for in Portugal. Ask at a tourist office or your hotel for a list of English-speaking dentists. Check whether dental treatment is covered by your medical insurance.

Sun Advice

The sun is strong during summer, particularly in the south. Do not be deceived by the cooling breeze off the Atlantic. Avoid prolonged exposure and protect yourself with a sunscreen or cover up.

Drugs

Prescription medicines are available from a pharmacy *(farmácia)*, distinguished by a large green cross. Pharmacists can prescribe remedies for minor ailments, and many speak English. Information about the nearest late-night or 24-hour facility is posted at all pharmacies.

Safe Water

Tap water is generally safe, but does not always taste too pleasant. It is advisable to drink bottled water *(agua mineral)*, especially in rural areas; *sem gas* means noncarbonated, *com gas* means carbonated.

Restrooms

Public restrooms *(casa de banho* or *lavabos)* are easy to find. Ladies' *(senhoras)* restrooms may occasionally charge a small fee and are generally clean. Men's *(homens)* restrooms are usually free.

Electricity

Portugal has a 220-volt power supply. Electrical sockets take plugs with two round pins. American appliances will need a plug adapter and a transformer if they do not have a dual-voltage facility.

National Transportation

Train *(Comboios)*

 The Caminhos de Ferro Portugueses (CP) operates three types of service: *regional* and *Intercidade* (which both stop at most stations) and *Alfo Pendular* (express between Braga in the north and Faro in the south). For information ☎ 808 208 208 (national toll number); www.cp.pt.

Bus *(Autocarros)*

 Rede Expressos operates a network to all major destinations with connections to smaller towns (☎ 707 223 344; www.rede-expressos.pt). Buses are modern and comfortable. Several companies also maintain an extensive network in the regions of the country.

Ferry *(Barcos)*

 Ferries cross the Rio Tejo from Cais do Sodré to Cacilhas, Seixal, Montijo, Terreiro do Paço to Barreiro and Belém to Trafaira (www.transtejo.pt). From Setúbal ferries cross the Rio Sado to the Tróia peninsula. Tickets can be bought at the boat stations' ticket offices.

Driving

Drive on the right

Speed Limits

Police can impose on-the-spot fines.

 Limited-access highways *(autoestrada)* **120 k.p.h. (74 m.p.h.)**. Minimum speed **50 k.p.h. (31 m.p.h.)** Divided highways **100 k.p.h. (62 m.p.h.)**

 Main roads **90 k.p.h. (56 m.p.h.)**

 Urban areas **50 k.p.h. (31 m.p.h.)**

Seat Belts

Must be worn in front and back seats at all times.

Blood Alcohol

The legal blood alcohol limit is 0.05%. Random breath tests on drivers are carried out frequently, especially late at night, and the penalties for offenders are severe.

Driving (continued)

Tolls

There are tolls on highways *(auto-estradas)* in Portugal. Highway numbers are prefixed by A.

Car Rental

The leading rental firms have offices at airports and train stations. Hertz offers discounted rates for AAA members (see page 15). For reservations:

	United States	Portugal
Alamo	(877) 222-9075	219 407 790 (Europcar)
Avis	(800) 230-4898	800 201 002
Budget	(800) 472-3325	808 25 26 27
Hertz	(800) 654-3001	808 202 038

Fuel *(Gasolina)*

Gas and diesel are sold in liters, and many stations *(posto de gasolina)* are often self-service. Gas stations, generally open daily 7 a.m.– 8 p.m. (some 24 hours), are not as common in the more remote northern areas, and credit cards are mostly accepted.

AAA Affiliated Motoring Club

Automóvel Club de Portugal (ACP) Rua Rosa Araújo 24–26, 1250–195 Lisbon ☎ 213 180 100 or 707 509 510 for 24-hour global assistance; www.acp.pt. Not all automobile clubs offer full services to AAA members.

Breakdowns and Accidents

There are 24-hour emergency phones at regular intervals on highways. If you are involved in an accident ☎ 112 for police assistance. Most car rental firms provide their own free rescue service; if your car is rented, follow the instructions given in the documentation. Use of a car repair service other than those authorized by your rental company may violate your agreement.

Other Information

The minimum age for car rental is 21 (some rental firms stipulate 23). An International Driving Permit (IDP) is a good idea; some rental firms require them, and they can speed up formalities if you are involved in an accident. A Green Card (international motor insurance certificate) is essential if you are driving a private car; see page 15 for more information. You are required by law to carry photographic ID at all times.

Useful Words and Phrases

Portuguese is a Latin language, so an acquaintance with French, Spanish or Italian makes written Portuguese quite easy to understand. Understanding spoken Portuguese, however, is more difficult. Although on paper Portuguese words look similar to Spanish, they actually sound very different. English is widely spoken in tourist areas, but using a few Portuguese words will make your trip more rewarding.

Do you speak English?	*Fala Inglês?*
I'm sorry	*desculpe*
hello/goodbye	*olá/adeus*
yes/no	*sim/näo*
how much?	*quanto?*
I am American	*sou Americano*
I would like a	*queria um/uma*
I don't understand	*não entendo*
nonsmoking	*não fumadores*
okay	*está bem*
today/tomorrow	*hoje/amanhã*
open/closed	*aberto/fechado*
right/left	*direita/esquerda*
near/far	*perto/longe*
big/little	*grande/pequeno*
cheap/expensive	*barato/caro*
please	*se faz favor*
thank you	*obrigado (m.)/ obrigada (f.)*
ticket	*bilhete*
one way/return	*ida/ida e volta*
where is…?	*onde é…?*
the hotel	**hotel**
breakfast	*pequeno almoço*
lunch	*almoço*
dinner	*jantar*
I have a reservation	*tenho uma marcação*
key	*chave*
for one night	*para uma noite*
room	*quarto*
shower	*duche*
with bathroom	*com casa de banho*
the restaurant	**restaurante**
beef	*bife*
bread	*pão*
cheese	*queijo*
the check	*a conta*
chicken	*frango*
coffee/tea	*café/chà*
dessert	*sobremesa*
dish of the day	*prato do dia*
fish	*peixe*
ham	*fiambre*
lamb	*carneiro*
pork	*porco*
starter	*entrada*
veal	*vitela*
wine	*vinho*
Is the service included?	*O serviço está incluido?*

National Flag

Esential for Travelers

● Required ● Recommended ● Not required

Passport	●
Visa (check regulations before you travel)	●
Travel, medical insurance	●
Round-trip or onward airline ticket	●
Local currency	●
Traveler's checks	●
Credit cards	●
First-aid kit and medicines	●
Inoculations	●

Essential for Drivers*

Driver's license	●
International Driving Permit	●
Car insurance (for nonrental cars)	●
Car registration (for nonrental cars)	●

*see also *Driving* section

Important Addresses

Tourist Office of Spain
60 East 42nd Street, Suite 5300
New York, NY 10165
☎ (212) 265-8822
www.spain.info
Visitors by appointment only

Turespaña (Tourist Office of Spain)
Calle José Lázaro Galdiano 6
28036 Madrid, Spain
☎ 91 343 3500
www.tourspain.es

American Embassy
Serrano 75
28006 Madrid, Spain
☎ 91 587 2200
http://spanish.madrid.usembassy.gov
Personal inquiries: Mon.–Fri. 8:30–1
Emergencies: ☎ 91 587 2200

Customs

✔ **Duty-free limits on goods brought in from non-European Union countries:**
200 cigarettes or 100 cigarillos or 50 cigars or 250 g. tobacco; 2 L. wine; 1 L. alcohol over 22% volume; 2 L. alcohol under 22% volume; 50 ml. perfume; 250 ml. toilet water; plus any other duty-free goods (including gifts) to the value of €200. The import of currency of any denomination exceeding €6,010 must be declared on arrival in Spain. There is no limit on the importation of tax-paid goods purchased within the European Union if they are for personal use.

✘ No unlicensed drugs, weapons, ammunition, obscene material, pets or other animals, counterfeit money or copied goods, meat or poultry.
For customs limits for returning U.S. citizens see page 16.

Money

Spain's currency is the euro (€), a currency shared by 16 other European Union countries. The euro is divided into 100 cents (¢). The denominations of euro bills are 5, 10, 20, 50, 100, 200 and 500. There are coins of 1, 2, 5, 10, 20 and 50¢ and €1 and €2. Exchange dollars or traveler's checks *(cheques de viaje)* at a bank *(banco)* or exchange office *(oficina de cambio)*.

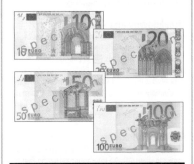

Tips and Gratuities

Locals rarely tip, though they may add a couple of euros to a large bill. There are different expectations of visitors, however. If you receive good service, consider tipping as follows. Most hotel, restaurant and café checks will include a service charge.

Restaurants (service is normally included)	5–10%
Cafés/bars (service is normally included)	change
Taxis	5%
Porters, chambermaids	€1
Cloakroom attendants	change

Madrid	New York	Chicago	Denver	Los Angeles	Time zones
12:00 noon	− 6 hrs	− 7 hrs	− 8 hrs	− 9 hrs	

559

Spain

Communications

Post Offices

Buy stamps *(sellos)* at a post office *(correos)*, a tobacconist *(estancos)* denoted by a "T" or at some hotels. Hours for out-of-town post offices may vary.

Telephones

Few public telephones (except those in bars) still accept coins. Most now operate with phone cards, available from post offices, tobacconists, newsstands and authorized retailers for 6 or 12 euros. Many public phone booths are modern, with instructions in English and lists of

national and international dialing codes posted inside them. In major cities, telecommunications stores offer facilities such as faxing and e-mail.

Phoning inside Spain
All Spanish phone numbers in this book include an area code; dial the number that is listed. To call the operator dial 11818.

Phoning Spain from abroad
The country code for Spain is 34. Note that Spanish numbers in this book do not include the Spanish country code; you will need to prefix this number if you are phoning from another country. To phone Spain from the United States or Canada dial the prefix 011 34. (Note that the number of digits in Spanish area codes varies.) Example: 11 122 3344 becomes 011 34 11 122 3344.

Phoning from Spain
To phone the United States or Canada from Spain, prefix the area code and number with 00 1. Example: (111) 222-3333 becomes 00 1 111 222-3333. To call international information dial 11825.

Emergency telephone numbers
All emergencies **112**
Police *(policía)* **091**
Fire service *(bomberos)* **080**
Ambulance *(ambulancia)* **061**
Emergency calls are free from phone booths

Hours of Operation

- Stores Mon.–Sat.
- Offices Mon.–Fri.
- Banks Mon.–Fri.
- Post Offices Mon.–Fri.
- Museums/Monuments Tue.–Sat.
- Pharmacies Mon.–Fri.

7 8 9 10 11 12 1 2 3 4 5 6 7

Department **stores** and grocery stores may operate the hours shown, especially in summer. Department **stores** are open Mon.–Sat. 10–10, and in Madrid also open the first Sun. of each month. In December stores in big towns also are open on Sundays. Business hours vary depending on season; many companies work *horas intensivas* (shorter, more intensive hours) from 8 to 3 in summer.

Some **banks** are open Saturdays 9–1 in winter.

Most **museums** and **monuments** are closed on Monday, but many are open 9–2 on Sunday.

National Holidays

Banks, businesses and most stores close on these days. Days marked (*) are not national holidays but are celebrated in Catalonia, when shops and offices may close.

Jan. 1	New Year's Day
Jan. 6	Epiphany
Mar. 19	St. Joseph's Day (not Catalonia)
Mar./Apr.	Good Friday
***Mar./Apr.**	Easter Monday
May 1	Labor Day
***May/Jun.**	Pentecost Monday
***Jun. 24**	St. John's Day
Aug. 15	Assumption of the Virgin
***Sep. 11**	National Day (Catalonia)
***Sep. 24**	Our Lady of Mercy Day
Oct. 12	National Day
Nov. 1	All Saints' Day
Dec. 6	Constitution Day
Dec. 8	Immaculate Conception
Dec. 25	Christmas Day
***Dec. 26**	St. Stephen's Day
Dec 31	New Year's Eve (only some close in the afternoon)

Photography

Take your pictures early in the morning or late in the evening. Ask permission before taking pictures in museums and churches. Digital camera equipment and printing facilities are widely available.

Health

Medical Insurance

U.S. and Canadian visitors can receive treatment in a hospital emergency room, but are charged if admitted to a bed. There also are private clinics, such as Unidad Médica (Conde de Aranda, Madrid ☎ 91 435 1823; www.unidadmedica.com), where English is spoken.

Dental Services

You will be charged for dental treatment, so check whether it is covered by your medical insurance. Dentists *(dentista)* are listed in the yellow pages.

Sun Advice

The sun is strong during summer, particularly in the south. Dress sensibly, avoid prolonged exposure and protect yourself with a sunscreen.

Drugs

Prescription medicines are available from pharmacies *(farmacias)*, designated by a red or green cross. Information about the nearest late-night or 24-hour facility is posted at all pharmacies.

Safe Water

Tap water is generally safe, although it can be heavily chlorinated. Mineral water *(agua mineral)* is inexpensive and is sold *con gas* (carbonated) and *sin gas* (noncarbonated). Drink plenty of fluids during hot weather.

Restrooms

Public restrooms *(servicios)* can usually be found in large department stores, museums and other places of interest to visitors. Elsewhere, restrooms may not be easy to find, but there is no charge. If you use the facilities in a bar you will be expected to buy a drink. Spanish words are *señores* for men and *señoras* for women.

Electricity

Most of Spain has a 220-volt power supply. Electrical sockets take plugs with two round pins. American appliances will need a plug adapter, and either a dual voltage facility or a transformer.

National Transportation

Train *(Tren)*

The Red Nacional de los Ferrocarriles Españoles (RENFE) rail network is inexpensive to use. There are express services for long-distance travel: Alaris, Talgo 200 and AVE (reservations required/advisable for all three). For information and reservations ☎ 902 320 320 (24 hours); www.renfe.com.

Bus *(Autobus)*

Spain has a good bus system, and the Spanish Tourist Board publishes a guide to domestic services. Ask at a tourist office for details. The Eurolines international bus service operates in Spain: ☎ 91 506 3360 (Madrid); 93 490 4000 (Barcelona); www.eurolines.es.

Ferry *(Transbordador)*

Barcelona is the Mediterranean's biggest port and offers a regular ferry service to the Balearic islands. One of the largest ferry operators is Acciona Transmediterránea: ☎ 902 45 46 45. "Mini-cruises" of two or three days operate from northern Spain to and from Britain; obtain details from a travel agent.

Driving

Drive on the right

Speed Limits

Police can impose on-the-spot fines.

 Limited-access highways *(autopistas)*
110 k.p.h. (68 m.p.h.).
Divided highways **100 k.p.h. (62 m.p.h.)**

 Main roads
90 k.p.h. (56 m.p.h.)

 Urban areas
40 k.p.h. (25 m.p.h.)

Seat belts

Must be worn in front and back seats at all times.

Blood Alcohol

The legal blood alcohol limit is 0.05% (the limit is 0.03% for drivers with less than 2 years' driving experience). Random breath tests on drivers are carried out frequently, especially late at night, and the penalties for offenders are severe.

Driving (continued)

Tolls

A toll *(peaje)* is levied on limited-access highways; a toll highway is signed *autopista de peage* (AP). Take a ticket when you enter and pay when exiting.

Car Rental

The leading rental firms have offices at airports and train stations. Hertz offers discounted rates for AAA members (see page 15). For reservations:

	United States	Spain
Alamo	(800) 222-9275	91 323 7232
Avis	(800) 331-1212	902 13 55 31
Budget	(800) 527-0700	902 11 25 85
Hertz	(800) 654-3080	902 402 405

Fuel

Gas *(gasolina)* and diesel are sold in liters. Many gas stations *(gasolineras)* in towns and cities and on highways are open 24 hours.

AAA Affiliated Motoring Club

Real Automóvil Club de España (RACE). Parque Tecnológico de Madrid ☎ 902 40 45 45. If you break down while driving, phone ☎ 902 30 05 05 (RACE breakdown service). Not all automobile clubs offer full services to AAA members.

Breakdowns and Accidents

There are 24-hour emergency phones on highways. If you are involved in an accident, phone ☎ 112. Most car rental firms provide their own free rescue service; if your car is rented, follow the instructions given in the documentation. Use of a car repair service other than those authorized by your rental company may violate your agreement. In the event of a breakdown, you must put on a fluorescent vest when you are outside your vehicle. You must carry a warning triangle in your vehicle.

Other Information

The minimum age for driving a car is 18 (may be higher for most car rental firms). An International Driving Permit (IDP) is recommended; some rental firms require them, and they can speed up formalities if you are involved in an accident. A Green Card (international motor insurance certificate) is recommended if you are driving a private car; see page 15 for more information. The police may impound your car if you fail to produce a Green Card after an accident.

Useful Words and Phrases

Castilian is the main language in Spain, with three important regional languages: Catalan, spoken in Catalonia, the Balearics and Valencia; Basque, the official language of the Basque north; and Galician, spoken in the northwest.

Catalan is closely related to Occitan (or Provençal), and Galician has noticeable links with Portuguese. The Basque tongue is unique, having no connection with any language in Europe.

The following words and phrases are in Castilian:

Do you speak English?	*¿Habla usted inglés?*
excuse me	*perdone*
hello	*hola*
goodbye	*adiós*
yes/no	*si/no*
how much?	*¿cuánto?*
I would like	*me gustaría*
I don't understand	*no entiendo*
no smoking	*no fumadores*
okay	*vale*
open/closed	*abierto/cerrado*
today/tomorrow	*hoy/mañana*
here/there	*aquí/allí*
more/less	*más/menos*
please	*por favor*
thank you	*gracias*
you're welcome	*de nada*
how/what	*cómo/qué*
left/right	*izquierda/derecha*
What time is it?	*¿Qué hora es?*
travel ticket	*el billete*
one way/return	*ida/ida y vuelta*
where is…?	*¿donde está…*
the hotel	**el hotel**
breakfast	*desayuno*
lunch	*la comida*
dinner	*la cena*
I have a reservation	*Tengo una reserva*
key	*la llave*
room	*la habitación*
shower	*la ducha*
the restaurant	**restaurante**
beef	*la carne de vaca*
bread	*el pan*
the check	*la cuenta*
cheese	*el queso*
chicken	*el pollo*
coffee	*el café*
dessert	*el postre*
dish of the day	*el plato del día*
fish	*el pescado*
fixed-price lunch menu	*el menú del dia*
pork	*la carne de cerdo*
starter	*el primer plato*
wine, red/white	*el vino tinto/blanco*

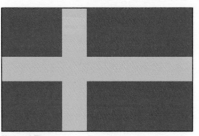

National Flag

Essential for Travelers

● **Required** ● **Recommended** ● **Not required**

Passport	●
Visa (check regulations before you travel)	●
Travel, medical insurance	●
Round-trip or onward airline ticket	●
Local currency	●
Traveler's checks	●
Credit cards	●
First-aid kit and medicines	●
Inoculations	●

Essential for Drivers*

Driver's license	●
International Driving Permit	●
Car insurance (for nonrental cars)	●
Car registration (for nonrental cars)	●

*see also *Driving* section

Important Addresses

VisitSweden
P.O. Box 4649, Grand Central Station
New York, NY 10163-4649
☎ (212) 885-9700
www.visitsweden.com

Stockholm Visitors Board
Sverigehuset (Sweden House)
Hamngatan 27
Kungsträdgården
103 27 Stockholm
☎ 08 508 28 508
http://beta.stockholmtown.com/en
www.visitsweden.com

American Embassy
Dag Hammarskjölds Väg 31
SE-115 89 Stockholm, Sweden
☎ 08 783 53 00
http://stockholm.usembassy.gov

Customs

✔ **Duty-free limits on goods brought in from non-European Union countries:**
200 cigarettes or 100 cigarillos or 50 cigars or 250 g. tobacco; 1 L. alcohol over 22% volume or 2 L. alcohol under 22% volume; 2 L. fortified or sparkling wine; 32 L beer; a reasonable quantity of perfume or toilet water; plus any other duty-free goods (including gifts) to the value of 1,700SKr. Thre are no longer restrictions on the importation of tax-paid goods purchased within the European Union. You must be 18 years or over to import tobacco products and 20 or over to import alcohol. There is no restriction on the import of Swedish or foreign currencies, but amounts in excess of €10,000 must be declared.

✘ No unlicensed drugs, weapons, ammunition, obscene material, pets or other animals, counterfeit money or copied goods, meat, poultry, fish or shellfish.
For customs limits for returning U.S. citizens see page 16.

Money

Sweden's currency is the krona (SEK, SKr or Kr; plural kronor), which is divided into 100 öre. The denominations of krona bills are 20, 50, 100, 500 and 1,000. There are coins of 50 öre, and 1, 5 and 10SKr. Exchange dollars and traveler's checks *(resechecker)* at a bank or an exchange office. "Forex" exchange offices have distinctive yellow signs and offer favorable exchange rates. Although a member of the European Union, Sweden chose not to adopt the euro as its official currency on January 1, 1999. However, it is possible for tourists coming from the euro zone to pay with a euro credit card.

Tips and Gratuities

Tips are welcomed but not expected or obligatory. In restaurants it is usual to round off the check to the nearest 10SKr.

Restaurants, cafés/bars (service is included)	change
Taxis	10%
Hairdressers, chambermaids	none
Porters, restroom attendants	change
Cloakroom attendants	5SKr

Sweden

Communications

Post Offices

 Buy stamps *(frimärken)* at a post office *(postkontoret)*, supermarket, newsstand *(nyhetsbyra)*, stationer *(handel)* or kiosk displaying

 a blue-and-yellow post sign. Hours for out-of-town post offices may vary.

Telephones

You can use prepaid phone cards or credit cards only to make a call from a public phone *(telefon)* in Sweden. A telephone card *(telefonkort)* can be bought from newsstands, stores, hotels or magazine kiosks (e.g. *Pressbyrån)*.

Post offices do not have telephone facilities. Long-distance calls can be made from offices called *Telebutik*, marked "*Tele*." Operators speak English.

Phoning inside Sweden
All Swedish numbers in this book include an area code; dial the number that is listed. To call the operator dial 90130; for directory assistance dial 118118.

Phoning Sweden from abroad
The country code for Sweden is 46. Note that Swedish numbers in this book do not include the Swedish country code; you will need to prefix this number if you are phoning from another country. To phone Sweden from the United States or Canada, omit the first zero from the Swedish number and add the prefix 011 46. For example: 01 122 33 44 becomes 011 46 1 122 33 44.

Phoning from Sweden
To phone the United States or Canada from Sweden, prefix the area code and number with 00 1. Example: (111) 222-3333 becomes 00 1 111 222-3333. For national operator assistance dial 0018. For international operator assistance dial 07977.

Emergency telephone numbers
Police *(polis)* **112**
Fire service *(brandkår)* **112**
Ambulance *(ambulans)* **112**
Emergency calls are free from phone booths

Hours of Operation

- Stores Mon.–Sat.
- Offices Mon.–Fri.
- Banks Mon.–Fri.
- Post Offices Mon.–Fri.
- Museums/Monuments
- Pharmacies Mon.–Fri.

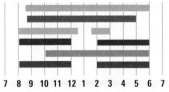

7 8 9 10 11 12 1 2 3 4 5 6 7

In large towns, department **stores** stay open until 7 or 10 p.m., and some also are open Sunday from around noon to 4. Stores often close on Saturday afternoon between 2 and 4 p.m., and usually close early the day before a public holiday. Some smaller stores may close for lunch.

Banks also are open on Thursday until 4 or 5:30 p.m. and in some cities Monday to Friday until 6 p.m. All banks are closed on weekends.

Post offices may stay open later in main cities. They also are open Sat. 9–1. The post office at Centralstationen (Central Station) in Stockholm is open Mon.–Fri. 7 a.m.–10 p.m., Sat.–Sun. 9–6.

Some **museums** close on Monday and stay open late one or two nights a week.

Some **pharmacies** *(apotek)* in major cities are open 24 hours.

National Holidays

Banks, businesses and most stores close on these days; they also may be closed or close earlier the day before a holiday.

Jan. 1	New Year's Day
Jan. 5–6	Epiphany
Mar./Apr.	Good Friday
Mar./Apr.	Easter Monday
May 1	Labor Day
May	Ascension Day
May/Jun.	Pentecost Monday
Jun. 6	Sweden's National Day
Jun.	Midsummer's Eve (Fri. before Jun. 21)
Jun.	Midsummer's Day (Sat. nearest Jun. 21)
Nov. 1	All Saints' Day
Dec. 24	Christmas Eve
Dec. 25	Christmas Day
Dec. 26	St. Stephen's Day
Dec. 31	New Year's Eve

Photography

Poor light conditions occcur in winter. Taking photographs in museums may be forbidden; check first. Digital photography equipment, and printing services are available.

Sweden

Health

Medical Insurance

Private medical insurance is recommended. There are no general practitioners; go straight to a hospital clinic *(Akutmottagning* or *Vårdcentral)*, taking your passport with you. You will be charged for treatment (free for under 16s). For information contact Stockholm Care AB, ☎ 08 672 24 00; www.stockholmcare.se

Dental Services

Dentists *(tandläkeren)* always charge for treatment. Emergency treatment is available after hours in major cities. Clinics are indicated by *"Tandläkare"* or *"Folktandvård"* signs.

Sun Advice

The Gulf Stream dictates Sweden's temperate climate of warm sunshine during July and August. Although the sun is not fierce, good sun protection is necessary. Take precautions near the water.

Drugs

Prescription and nonprescription drugs and medicines are available from a pharmacy *(apotek)*. Information about the nearest all-night facility is posted at all pharmacies. A 24-hour service is available in most cities.

Safe Water

Tap water is safe to drink, and mineral water *(mineralvatten)* is widely available.

Restrooms

Public restrooms *(toalett)* are easy to find. There is a charge of 1SKr–5SKr to use some restrooms. Separate facilities for men *(Herrar)* and women *(Damer)* are always clean and modern.

Electricity

Sweden has a 220-volt power supply. Electrical sockets take plugs with two round pins. American appliances will need a plug adapter and will require a transformer if they do not have a dual-voltage facility.

National Transportation

Train *(Tåg)*

The Swedish rail network is operated by several companies: Statens Järnvägar (SJ), Tågkompaniet, BK Tåg, LINX, Connex and Inlandsbanan. It is an efficient and extensive system extending above the Arctic Circle. General information (timetables, prices, etc) is available at www.resplus.se or from any station *(järnvägsstation)*. On some trains reservations are necessary. To obtain tickets for travel with SJ call ☎ 0771 75 75 75; www.sj.se.

Bus *(Buss)*

Travel by bus in Sweden is inexpensive and trouble-free. There is an excellent network of express services between larger towns and cities in south and central Sweden and between Stockholm and the north. The largest bus operator is Swebus Express ☎ 0771 218 218; www.swebus.se, with 300 destinations. International Euroline buses operate to 27 destinations in Sweden ☎ 08 30 12 45; www.eurolines.se.

Ferry *(Farja)*

There are ferry services in Sweden, and you can get various island-hopping boat passes or coupons. Most depart from Stockholm. Passes are available from Waxholmsbolaget, on Strömkajen in Stockholm; ☎ 08 679 58 30; www.waxholmsbolaget.se.

Driving

Drive on the right

Speed Limits

Police can impose on-the-spot fines, but cannot collect them. Pay particular attention to road signs as speed limits also are based on the quality and safety of the actual road.

Limited-access highways
110 k.p.h. (68 m.p.h.)
Divided highways **90 k.p.h. (56 m.p.h.)**

Main roads
70 k.p.h. (43 m.p.h.)

Urban areas
50 k.p.h. (31 m.p.h.), reduced to **30 k.p.h. (18 m.p.h.)** around schools

Seat Belts

Must be worn in front and rear seats at all times.

Driving (continued)

Blood Alcohol

The legal blood alcohol limit is 0.02%. Random breath tests on drivers are carried out frequently, especially late at night, and the penalties for offenders are severe.

Tolls

There are no highway tolls in Sweden except when crossing the Oresund Bridge between Sweden and Denmark.

Car rental

The leading rental firms have offices at airports and train stations. Hertz offers discounted rates for AAA members (see page 15). For reservations:

	United States	Sweden
Alamo	(877) 222-9075	85 55 98 400
Avis	(800) 230-4898	910 733 330
Budget	(800) 527-0700	0770 11 00 12
Hertz	(800) 654-3131	0771 21 12 12

Fuel

Gas *(bensin)* is sold unleaded *(blyfri)* in 95 and 98 octane. Diesel is also available. Most gas stations are self-service, and on highways and in main towns they are open 24 hours. Major credit cards are usually accepted.

AAA Affiliated Motoring Club

Motormännens Riksförbund (M)
Fridhemsgatan 32, Stockholm. ☎ 08 690 38 00; fax 08 690 38 24; www.motormannen.se. Not all automobile clubs offer full services to AAA members.

Breakdowns and Accidents

There are 24-hour emergency phones at regular intervals on highways. If you are involved in an accident, phone ☎ 112 for police. If you break down while driving, contact Assistancekåren: ☎ 020 912 912 (toll-free). Most car rental firms provide their own free rescue service; if your car is rented, follow the instructions given in the documentation. Use of a car repair service other than those authorized by your rental company may violate your agreement.

Other Information

The minimum age for driving a car is 18 (may be higher for some car rental firms). An International Driving Permit (IDP) is recommended; some rental firms require them, and they can speed up formalities if you are involved in an accident.

A Green Card (international motor insurance certificate) is recommended if you are driving a private car; see page 15 for more information.

Driving (continued)

Dimmed headlights must be turned on year-round, even during daylight hours. Be aware of moose, roe deer and reindeer appearing on roads, especially at dawn or dusk.

Useful Words and Phrases

Any effort made to speak Swedish is appreciated although most Swedes also speak English. German, Danish and Norwegian are understood.

In Swedish, a vowel sound is usually long when it is the final syllable, and verbs are the same regardless of person. Definite articles are determined by the ending of the noun: -en and -et for singular nouns and -na or -n for plural. There are an additional three letters in the Swedish alphabet – å, ä and ö – which always appear at the end in alphabetical lists.

There are two words for "you": *du* and *ni*. Ni is the polite form, du is the familiar form. Unlike some other European countries, it is not necessarily impolite to address a complete stranger with the familiar form. In fact, many Swedes consider the polite form to be old-fashioned.

Do you speak English?	*Talar ni Engelska?*
excuse me	*ursäkta mig*
hello	*hej*
goodbye	*adjö/hej då*
yes/no	*ja/nej*
how much is it?	*hur mycket kostar den?*
I am American	*Jag är från U.S.A.*
I'd like	*Jag skulle vilja ha*
I don't understand	*Jag förstår inte*
nonsmoking	*rökning förbjuden*
open	*öppen/öppet*
closed	*stängt*
please	*snälla, vänligen*
thank you	*tack*
(one-way) ticket	*en enkelbiljett*
the hotel	***hotell***
breakfast	*frukost*
lunch	*lunch*
dinner	*middag*
key	*nyckel*
room	*rum*
shower	*dusch*
the restaurant	***restaurang***
beef	*nötkött, oxkött*
beer	*öl*
bread	*bröd*
chicken	*kyckling*
coffee/tea	*kaffe/te*
dessert	*efterrätt*
fish	*fisk*
lamb	*lammkött*
pork	*fläsk*
wine	*vin*
please bring the check	*notan tack*

National Flag

Essential for Travelers

● **Required** ● **Recommended** ● **Not required**

Passport	●
Visa (check regulations before you travel)	●
Travel, medical insurance	●
Round-trip or onward airline ticket	●
Local currency	●
Traveler's checks	●
Credit cards	●
First-aid kit and medicines	●
Inoculations	●

Essential for Drivers*

Driver's license	●
International Driving Permit	●
Car insurance (for nonrental cars)	●
Car registration (for nonrental cars)	●

*see also Driving section

Important Addresses

Switzerland Tourism
Swiss Center, 608 Fifth Avenue
New York, NY 10020
☎ (877) 794-8037 (toll free), 011800 100 200 30
(international toll free)
www.myswitzerland.com

Schweiz Tourismus (Switzerland Tourism)
Postfach 695
8027 Zürich, Switzerland
☎ 00800 100 200 30 (toll free)
www.myswitzerland.com

American Embassy
Sulgeneckstrasse 19
CH-3005 Bern, Switzerland
☎ 031 357 7011 (Mon.–Fri. 9–11 and 1:30–5)
031 357 7011 (office hours) or 031 357 7777
http://bern.usembassy.gov

Customs

✔ **Duty-free limits on goods brought in from non-European countries:**
400 cigarettes or 100 cigarillos or cigars or 500 g. tobacco; 2 L. alcohol under 15% volume and 1 L. alcohol over 15% volume; plus any other duty-free goods (including gifts) to the value of SF100. These limits apply to visitors aged 17 and over. There are no currency regulations. There is no limit on the importation of tax-paid goods purchased within the European Union if they are for personal use.

✘ No unlicensed drugs, weapons, ammunition, obscene material, pets or other animals, counterfeit money or copied goods, meat or poultry.
For customs limits for returning U.S. citizens see page 16.

Money

Switzerland's currency is the Swiss franc (SF), which is divided into 100 centimes or "Rappen." The denominations of franc bills are 10, 20, 50, 100, 200, 500 and 1,000. There are coins of 5, 10, 20 and 50 centimes and 1, 2 and 5SF. Exchange dollars or traveler's checks *(Reiseschecks)* at a bank *(Bank)*, exchange office *(Wechselbüro)*, post office *(Postamt)* or hotel. Swiss Bankers traveler's checks (in Swiss francs) can be obtained from various overseas branches of most Swiss banks as well as branches of American Express, and are accepted in Switzerland at their face value and without a commission fee.

Tips and Gratuities

Tips are welcomed but not expected, as a service charge is always included. A small tip is accepted for exceptional service.

Restaurants, cafés/bars (service included)	change
Taxis (usually includes service)	change
Porters, chambermaids	change
Hairdressers	change
Restroom/cloakroom attendants	change

Zurich	New York	Chicago	Denver	Los Angeles	Time zones
12:00 noon	– 6 hrs	– 7 hrs	– 8 hrs	– 9 hrs	**567**

Switzerland

Communications

Post Offices

Buy stamps *(Briefmarken)* at a post office *(Postamt)*, newsstand *(Zeitungsstand)* or from a hotel. Hours for out-of-town post offices may vary.

Telephones

You can use cash or a prepaid phone card *(Kartentelefon)* to make a call in Switzerland. Most telephones have direct dialing

for international calls; if you need to go through an operator dial 114. A Taxcard (phone card) can be bought from newsstands, gas stations, railroad stations and post offices for 5, 10 and 20SF. Check that the phone booth is equipped with a Taxcard reader. You also can make a call with 1 5SF and 5SF coins.

Phoning inside Switzerland
All Swiss telephone numbers in this book include an area code; dial the number that is listed. To call national information dial 111.

Phoning Switzerland from abroad
The country code for Switzerland is 41. Note that Swiss numbers in this book do not include the country code; you will need to prefix this number if you are phoning from another country. To phone Switzerland from the United States or Canada, omit the first zero from the Swiss number and add the prefix 011 41. (Note that Swiss area codes are either one or two digits.) Example: 01 122 33 44 becomes 011 41 1 122 33 44.

Phoning from Switzerland
To phone the United States or Canada from Switzerland, prefix the area code and number with 00 1. Example: (111) 222-3333 becomes 00 1 111 222-3333. To call international information dial 1811.

Emergency phone numbers
Police *(Polizei)* **117**
Fire service *(Feuerwehr)* **118**
Ambulance *(Krankenwagen)* **117** or **144**
Emergency calls are free from phone booths

Hours of Operation

- Stores Mon.–Sat.
- Offices Mon.–Fri.
- Banks Mon.–Fri.
- Post Offices Mon.–Fri.
- Museums/Monuments
- Pharmacies Mon.–Sat.

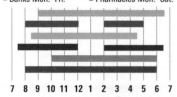

7 8 9 10 11 12 1 2 3 4 5 6 7

Stores close on Saturday afternoon at 4 or 5. In large towns stores may close on Monday morning, while out-of-town stores often close on a Wednesday or Thursday afternoon; some also may close for lunch (noon–1:30).

The hours of operation for **banks** are varied and complicated depending on the town; ask at your hotel or a tourist office.

Post offices close at 11 on Saturday morning except for some major offices in cities, which close later; small offices have briefer hours of operation.

Museums often close on Monday and hours vary, so check locally.

National Holidays

Banks, businesses and most stores close on these days. Various cantons observe other national holidays such as Jan. 2, May 1, Corpus Christi and All Saints' Day.

Jan. 1	New Years' Day
Mar./Apr.	Good Friday
Mar./Apr.	Easter Monday
May	Ascension Day
May/Jun.	Pentecost Monday
Aug. 1	National Day
Dec. 25	Christmas Day
Dec. 26	St. Stephen's Day

Photography

Digital camera equipment and developing services are available in towns and cities. Photography is prohibited in some military areas, which includes some public footpaths, parks and forest areas. It is quite common to come across the Swiss army when you are walking, hiking or mountain biking. Some footpaths are closed during maneuvers, and temporary barriers set up by the army should be observed at all times. Photography may be forbidden in some churches and museums; ask if you need to obtain permission to take pictures.

Switzerland

Health

Medical Insurance

Private medical insurance is recommended. U.S. and Canadian visitors will have to pay for all medical treatment, including emergency assistance, consultation or admittance to a hospital *(Krankenhaus)*. If you are planning to take part in winter sports, special sports policies are widely available. For information on medical issues dial Anglo-Phone, ☎ 157 5014 (toll call), from anywhere in Switzerland.

Dental Services

A dentist *(zahnarzt)* will charge for any treatment; dental work is expensive, so check whether it is covered by your medical insurance. Dentists are listed in the telephone directory. You also can ask for English-speaking dentists at your embassy or hotel, or at a tourist office.

Sun Advice

Conditions vary considerably; no country in Europe combines within so small an area such marked climatic contrasts. The sun can be deceptively strong in the mountains; protection is essential. The warmest part of Switzerland is south of the Alps, which is under the influence of the Mediterranean. Sun protection is needed; it is advisable to wear a hat and apply a sunscreen.

Drugs

Pharmacies sell a range of medicines and drugs and dispense prescriptions. Many pharmacists speak English. At least one pharmacy in every town stays open late; information is displayed on store doors.

Safe Water

Tap water is safe to drink throughout Switzerland. Mineral water *(sprudelwasser)* is widely available.

Restrooms

Most toilets *(Toiletten)* are clean and well maintained. They are indicated by a variety of signs, such as "WC" or *Toiletten*. Women's restrooms are designated *Damen, Frauen, Femmes, Dames, Signore or Donne;* men's as *Herren, Männer, Hommes, Messieurs, Signori or Uomini*.

Electricity

Switzerland has a 220-volt power supply. Electrical sockets take plugs with two round pins; American appliances will need a plug adapter and will require a transformer if they do not have a dual-voltage facility.

National Transportation

Train *(Zug)*

Swiss Federal Railways is Chemins de Fer Fédéreaux (CFF) in French, Schweizerische Bundesbahnen (SBB) in German, and Ferrovie Federali Svizzere (FFS) in Italian. It runs a fast, clean and efficient service. Express trains only stop at major cities. *Regionalzuge* are slow trains usually running the same routes. To reach an English-speaking operator, ☎ 0900 300300 (toll call). There are various good-value rail passes available. Inquire at tourist offices or any large railroad station.

Bus *(Bus)*

The bus service takes passengers to mountainous regions where railroads are unable to go. Mail bus routes encounter magnificent scenery joining villages and towns, occasionally even delivering the mail. There are many special offers; passes and cards that combine train, bus and boat travel are available at reduced rates. Eurolines operates in Switzerland; ☎ 0900 573747 (toll call).

Ferry *(Fähre)*

There are many excursions on Switzerland's lakes. Regional tourist offices in different cantons can offer information, and some take reservations.

Driving

Drive on the right

Speed Limits

Police can impose on-the-spot fines, for which a receipt is issued. Fines are severe.

 Limited-access highways *(Autobahn)*
120 k.p.h. (74 m.p.h.)
Divided highways **100 k.p.h. (62 m.p.h.)**

Main roads
80 k.p.h. (49 m.p.h.)

Urban areas
50 k.p.h. (31 m.p.h.) or
30 k.p.h. (18 m.p.h.)

Seat Belts

 Must be worn in front and back seats at all times. Children under 7 are not allowed in a front seat.

Fire Service 118
(Feuerwehr)

Ambulance 117 or 144
(Krankenwagen)

569

Switzerland

Driving (continued)

Blood Alcohol

The legal blood alcohol limit is 0.05%. Random breath tests on drivers are carried out frequently, especially late at night, and the penalties for offenders are severe.

Tolls

An annual road tax of SF40 is levied on all cars and motorcycles using Swiss highways. Permits *(vignettes)*, available at border crossings, post offices and service areas in Switzerland, are valid for multiple re-entry into Switzerland within the duration of the license period. To avoid border delays, it is advisable to buy the permit in advance from a Swiss tourist office.

Car Rental

The leading rental firms have offices at airports and train stations. Hertz offers discounted rates for AAA members (see page 15). For reservations:

	United States	Switzerland
Alamo	(800) 462-5266	022 717 8430
Avis	(800) 331-1212	0848 81 18 18
Hertz	(800) 654-3001	0848 822 020

Fuel

Gas and diesel are sold in liters. There are 24-hour gas stations on highways and in cities; many have refreshment facilities and stores. Credit cards are accepted for payment.

AAA Affiliated Motoring Club

Touring Club Suisse (TCS) Chemin de Blandonnet 4, CH-1214 Vernier/Geneva, Switzerland ☏ 0844 888 111. If you break down while driving ☏ 140 (TCS breakdown service). Not all automobile clubs offer full services to AAA members.

Breakdowns and Accidents

There are 24-hour emergency phones at regular intervals on highways. If you are involved in an accident ☏ 117 for police. Most car rental firms provide their own free rescue service; if your car is rented, follow the instructions given in the documentation. Use of a car repair service other than those authorized by your rental company may violate your agreement. You must use a warning triangle in the event of an accident or breakdown; this must be kept within easy reach (not in the trunk).

Other Information

The minimum age for driving a car is 18 (may be higher for some car rental firms). An International Driving Permit (IDP) is recommended; some rental firms require them, and they can speed up formalities if you are involved in an accident.

A Green Card (international motor insurance certificate) is recommended if you are driving a private car; see page 15 for more information.

Dimmed headlights must be used when passing through tunnels. Yellow mail buses have priority at all times, as do vehicles ascending mountain roads. Many mountain pass roads are closed from October through June. For road conditions ☏ 163. For other general information ☏ 111.

Useful Words and Phrases

There are four official languages spoken in Switzerland: German, French, Italian and Romansch. About 18 percent of the population in southwest Switzerland speak French. South of the Alps, Italian (12 percent) is predominant throughout Ticino and parts of the Grisons (also known as the Graubünden). Most Swiss (65 percent) speak German. A Swiss-German dialect with a variety of local variations is used in everyday conversation; traditional German is used for business purposes.

The fourth language is Romansch, an ancient hybrid of Celtic and Latin tongues spoken by about 40,000 people in the Surselva region of southeastern Switzerland.

This coexistence of distinct languages results in a true "European" nation. The Romansch area is probably the most "Swiss" part of the country. French influence is evident in Lausanne, while Lugano exhibits both Italian and Swiss influences.

Every Swiss child learns two or three languages. English is spoken throughout the country, but an attempt to say a few words in any of Switzerland's languages will always be appreciated.

See page 521 for French words, page 525 for German and page 541 for Italian.

European Distance Chart

Road distances, in kilometers (km), are calculated by the shortest or quickest routes (highways, main roads) from center to center and do not take into account seasonal weather conditions.

Miles	Km
1	1.6
10	16
20	32
30	48
40	64
50	80
100	160
200	320
300	480
400	640
500	800
1000	1600

Column/row cities (diagonal headers):

1. Amsterdam (NL)
2. Athina (Athens) (GR)
3. Barcelona (ES)
4. Berlin (DE)
5. Brugge/Bruges (BE)
6. Brussel/Bruxelles (BE)
7. Budapest (HU)
8. Den Haag (The Hague) (NL)
9. Dublin (IE)
10. Edinburgh (GB)
11. Firenze (Florence) (IT)
12. Genève (CH)
13. Gent (BE)
14. Helsinki (FI)
15. Innsbruck (AT)
16. København (Copenhagen) (DK)
17. Köln (Cologne) (DE)
18. Lisboa (Lisbon) (PT)
19. London (GB)
20. Luxembourg (LU)
21. Lyon (FR)
22. Madrid (ES)
23. München (Munich) (DE)
24. Nápoli (Naples) (IT)
25. Nice (FR)
26. Odense (DK)
27. Oslo (NO)

Distance matrix (values per row, from left):

Athina	1736
Barcelona	1600 1591
Berlin	653 1577 1889
Brugge/Bruges	269 1680 1372 832
Brussel/Bruxelles	210 1568 1403 773 101
Budapest	1413 1521 2085 874 1473 1368
Den Haag	64 1755 1574 697 211 180 1432
Dublin	959 2350 1958 1522 704 791 2163 930
Edinburgh	1092 2483 2091 1655 837 924 2296 1063 538
Firenze	1387 544 1103 1228 1331 1219 1085 1406 2001 2134
Genève	1004 973 809 1119 769 724 1276 896 1355 1488 606
Gent	221 1635 1367 783 52 56 1423 191 742 875 1286 764
Helsinki	1542 2864 2929 1013 1748 1689 2449 1586 2438 2571 2515 2159 1700
Innsbruck	1001 832 1381 750 1061 956 731 1021 1751 1884 483 574 1011 2037
København	926 2248 2313 397 1132 1073 1833 970 1822 1955 1899 1543 1084 620 1421
Köln	262 1481 1419 569 315 210 1158 282 1005 1138 1132 749 265 1502 747 886
Lisboa	2370 2847 1258 2908 2161 2168 3340 2341 2747 2880 2359 2065 2156 3841 2637 3225 2345
London	482 1873 1481 1045 227 314 1686 453 463 665 1524 878 265 1961 1274 1345 528 2270
Luxembourg	410 1356 1190 759 324 212 1193 384 1014 1147 1007 512 279 1697 677 1081 230 2222 537
Lyon	932 1069 652 1233 779 734 1429 906 1365 1498 693 153 774 2272 727 1656 751 1908 888 522
Madrid	1809 2188 630 2347 1600 1607 2681 1779 2186 2319 1700 1406 1595 3279 1978 2663 1784 625 1709 1660 1249
München	834 990 1396 583 894 789 690 854 1584 1717 641 587 844 1870 163 1254 580 2677 1107 566 740 1993
Nápoli	1859 594 1577 1700 1803 1691 1557 1878 2473 2606 474 1080 1758 2987 955 2371 1604 2833 1996 1479 1167 2174 1113
Nice	1396 910 681 1347 1268 1223 1403 1394 1853 1986 421 541 1263 2551 700 1935 1142 1937 1376 1011 472 1278 858 895
Odense	765 2086 2151 599 911 911 1671 809 1660 1793 1737 1381 922 781 1260 165 724 3063 1183 919 1495 2502 1093 2209 1774
Oslo	1510 2832 2897 981 1716 1657 2417 1554 2406 2539 2483 2127 1668 530 2005 588 1470 3809 1929 1665 2241 3247 1838 2954 2519 749
	589 1980 1588 1152 334 421 1793 560 396 598 1631 985 372 2068 1381 1452 635 2377 90 644 995 1816 1214 2103 1483 1290 2036
	509 1508 1067 1047 300 307 1494 480 888 1021 1141 542 295 1980 953 1364 484 1856 411 376 466 1295 831 1614 954 1202 1948
	2170 2647 1213 2708 1961 1968 3140 2141 2547 2680 2159 1865 1956 3641 2437 3025 2145 318 2070 2022 1708 564 2477 2632 1737 2863 3609
	967 1375 1754 343 1027 922 531 987 1717 1850 1026 984 977 1377 549 761 713 2895 1240 747 1098 2333 382 1498 1243 957 1345
	1663 521 1381 1504 1607 1495 1362 1683 2277 2410 278 885 1562 2791 759 2175 1409 2637 1800 1283 971 1978 917 219 700 2014 2759
	977 1007 1535 726 1037 932 553 997 1727 1860 658 725 987 2013 180 1397 723 2791 1250 722 879 2132 139 1129 875 1236 1981
	2078 2555 1166 2616 1869 1876 3048 2049 2454 2587 2067 1773 1864 3549 2345 2933 2053 549 1977 1930 1616 646 2385 2540 1645 2771 3517
	2354 2599 1041 2892 2145 2152 3092 2325 2733 2866 2111 1817 2140 3825 2389 3209 2329 408 2256 2206 1660 543 2404 2584 1689 3047 3793
	1542 2864 2929 1013 1748 1689 2449 1586 2438 2571 2515 2159 1700 1800 2037 620 1502 3841 1961 1697 2273 3279 1870 2986 2551 781 530
	628 1133 1147 753 543 431 1063 602 1213 1346 784 401 498 1793 471 1177 354 2335 736 219 491 1744 360 1256 794 1015 1761
	1345 537 1256 1126 1289 1177 847 1364 1959 2092 256 584 1244 2413 381 1797 1090 2512 1482 965 701 1853 539 728 574 1636 2381
	1157 1124 1843 637 1217 1112 244 1176 1907 2040 843 1020 1167 2193 475 1577 902 3084 1430 937 1174 2440 434 1315 1161 1415 2161
	805 2196 1804 1368 550 637 2009 776 322 311 1847 1201 588 2284 1597 1668 851 2593 339 860 1211 2032 1430 2319 1699 1506 2252
	831 940 1095 844 775 663 996 851 1446 1579 591 285 730 1986 284 1370 577 2351 969 451 439 1692 306 1062 600 1209 1954

European Distance Chart

	Oxford (GB)	Paris (FR)	Porto (PT)	Praha (Prague) (CZ)	Roma (Rome) (IT)	Salzburg (AT)	Santiago de Compostela (ES)	Sevilla (Seville) (ES)	Stockholm (SE)	Strasbourg (FR)	Venézia (Venice) (IT)	Wien (Vienna) (AT)	York (GB)	Zürich (CH)
518
2177	1656
1347	1049	2695
1907	1419	2437	1303
1347	987	2591	377	934
2084	1564	231	2603	2345	2499
2363	1840	679	2762	2389	2543	910
2068	1982	3641	1377	2791	2013	3548	3827
843	489	2135	618	1060	516	2042	2157	1793
1589	1119	2312	816	532	436	2219	2266	2413	742
1537	1238	2884	294	1119	297	2791	2853	2193	807	605
295	734	2393	1563	2123	1573	2300	2579	2284	1059	1805	1753
1076	664	2151	712	867	445	2058	2105	1986	229	548	740	1292

576

Acknowledgments

The Automobile Association wishes to thank the following photographers and organizations for their assistance in the preparation of this book.

Abbreviations for the picture credits are as follows – (t) top; (b) bottom; (l) left; (r) right; (c) centre; (AA) AA World Travel Library

3 AA/J Tims; 18 AA/J Smith; 22 Jon Arnold Images Ltd/Alamy; 23 AA/J Smith; 25 AA/J Smith; 29 AA/J Smith; 30 AA/D Noble; 31 AA/M Siebert; 32 AA/D Noble; 33 AA/J Smith; 34 Aivar Mikko/Alamy; 37 Kutti -Travel/Alamy; 38 Martin Siepmann/Photolibrary; 39 AA/M Jourdan; 43 AA/A Baker; 45 AA/J Smith; 47 AA/J Smith; 48 AA/A Kouprianoff; 52 AA/A Kouprianoff; 53 Arterra Picture Library/Alamy; 55 PCL/Alamy; 57 imagebroker/Alamy; 59 AA/A Kouprianoff; 61 eye35.com/Alamy; 63 AA/A Kouprianoff; 65 Hideo Kurihara/Alamy; 66 Groeningemuseum, Bruges, Belgium/Peter Willi/The Bridgeman Art Library; 68 AA/A Kouprianoff; 69 AA/A Kouprianoff; 71 Riccardo Sala/Photolibrary; 73 Arterra Picture Library/Alamy; 74 Ian Dagnall/Alamy; 75 St. Bavo Cathedral, Ghent, Belgium/Giraudon/The Bridgeman Art Library; 76 AA/D Forss; 81 AA/M Moody; 82 AA/J Smith; 85 AA/J Tims; 90 AA/J Tims; 93 AA/J Tims; 94 AA/N Setchfield; 95 AA/W Voysey; 97 AA/J Tims; 101 AA/K Blackwell; 102 AA/K Blackwell; 104 AA/K Blackwell; 105 AA/K Blackwell; 106 AA/J Tims; 110 AA; 111 AA/J Wyand; 112 AA/D Clapp; 115 AA/D Clapp; 116 AA/P Bennett; 117 AA/D Clapp; 118 AA/T Woodcock; 121 AA/ McBride; 123 AA/J Smith; 126 AA/J Smith; 127 AA/ McBride; 128 AA/ McBride; 129 AA/J Wyand; 130 AA/S McBride; 131 AA/J Wyand; 132 AA/D Forss; 135 AA/J Wyand; 136 F1online digitale Bildagentur GmbH/Alamy; 137 Tibor Bognar/Alamy; 139 AA/D Forss; 144 Morten Svenningsen/Alamy; 148 AA/D Forss; 150 AA/D Forss; 151 The Art Archive/Alamy; 152 Layne Kennedy/Corbis; 154 Photoshot Holdings Ltd/Alamy; 155 AA; 157 Peter Lilja/Photolibrary; 158 PCL; 163 Manfred Gottschalk/Alamy; 164 AA/I Dawson; 168 AA/J Edmanson; 169 AA/J Tims; 170 AA/C Sawyer; 171 AA/R Strange; 173 AA/K Blackwell; 176 AA/K Blackwell; 178 AA/K Blackwell; 179 AA/K Paterson; 180 AA/K Blackwell; 181 AA/M Jourdan; 182 AA/J Tims; 185 K Blackwell; 187 AA/J Wyand; 189 AA/J Wyand; 191 AA/J Wyand; 192 AA/J Wyand; 193 AA/I Morejohn; 197 AA/J Tims; 198 AA/J Tims; 199 AA/J Tims; 201 Jon Arnold Images Ltd/Alamy; 203 AA; 205 AA/B Smith; 206 AA/A Kouprianoff; 211 AA/A Baker; 212 AA/C Sawyer; 213 AA/M Jourdan; 215 AA/A Kouprianoff; 219 Anne-Marie Palmer/Alamy; 222 AA/T Souter; 223 AA/A Kouprianoff; 224 AA/A Baker; 227 AA/A Hemmisen; 229 Bildarchiv Monheim GmbH/Alamy; 233 AA/M Jourdan; 235 AA/C Sawyer; 236 AA/T Souter; 237 Oliver Hoffmann/Alamy; 238 AA/Mockford & Bonetti; 243 AA/Mockford & Bonetti; 246 AA/Mockford & Bonetti; 247 AA/Mockford & Bonetti; 248 AA/Mockford & Bonetti; 251 AA/R Surman; 252 AA/J Smith; 257 AA/J Smith; 260 AA/J Smith; 261 AA/J Smith; 262 AA/J Smith; 263 AA/J Smith; 265 AA/K Paterson; 266 AA/C Hill; 270 AA/C Jones; 271 AA/C Hill; 273 AA/K Blackwell; 276 AA/K Blackwell; 277 AA/K Blackwell; 278 AA/K Blackwell; 279 AA/K Blackwell; 281 AA/K Blackwell; 282 AA/A Mockford & N Bonetti; 287 AA/J Tims; 288 AA/A Mockford & N Bonetti; 289 AA/A Mockford & N Bonetti; 291 AA/C Sawyer; 296 AA/ Mockford & Bonetti; 298 AA/Mockford & Bonetti; 299 AA/Mockford & Bonetti; 300 AA/Mockford & Bonetti; 301 AA/ Mockford & Bonetti; 305 AA/J Tims; 307 AA; 308 AA/M Jourdan; 312 AA/M Jourdan; 313 Jon Arnold Images Ltd/Alamy; 317 AA/A Mockford & N Bonetti; 319 AA/A Mockford & N Bonetti; 320 AA/S McBride; 321 AA/C Sawyer; 322 Jon Arnold Images Ltd/Alamy; 324 David Robertson/Alamy; 327 Travelshots.com/Alamy; 331 blickwinkel/Alamy; 332 Lana Sundman/Alamy; 333 David Robertson/Alamy; 334 AA/A Robinson; 336 AA/A Robinson; 338/39 AA/A Robinson; 339b AA/A Robinson; 341 AA/A Robinson; 345 AA/A Robinson; 346 AA/K Paterson; 347 AA/A Robinson; 348 AA/A Robinson; 349 AA/A Robinson; 351 CW Images/Alamy; 353 David R. Frazier Photolibrary, Inc./Alamy; 354 moodboard/Alamy; 355 AA/K Paterson; 356 Kjell Sandved/Alamy; 360 AA; 361 imagebroker/Alamy; 363 Body Philippe/Photolibrary; 364 Jon Arnold Images Ltd/Alamy; 369 AA/K Naylor; 370 AA/P Wilson; 372 AA/M Wells; 374 AA/M Wells; 375 AA/M Wells; 377 AA/M Wells; 381 AA/M Wells; 383 AA/M Wells; 384 AA/M Wells; 385 AA/T Harris; 388 AA/A Mockford & N Bonetti; 390 AA/A Mockford & N Bonetti; 391 AA/A Kouprianoff; 392 AA/M Bonnet; 396 AA/M Jourdan; 397 Peter Wilson; 399 AA/M Chaplow; 401 AA/M Bonnet; 405 AA/R Strange; 406 AA/M Jourdan; 407 AA/M Jourdan; 408 AA/R Strange; 409 AA/M Chaplow; 412 AA/M Bonnet; 413 AA/M Bonnet; 414 AA/M Jourdan; 415 AA/M Bonnet; 417 AA/T Carter; 418 imagebroker/Alamy; 421 Banana Pancake/Alamy; 422 Banana Pancake/Alamy; 423 Hemis/Alamy; 424 Jon Arnold Images Ltd/Alamy; 427 Jon Arnold Images Ltd/Alamy; 429 AA/C Sawyer; 430 Banana Pancake/Alamy; 432 Banana Pancake/Alamy; 435 AA/K Naylor; 438 AA/K Naylor; 439 Jennifer Broadus/Photolibrary; 440 Chad Ehlers/Photolibrary; 441 Banana Pancake/Alamy; 442 Sweden And Swedish/Alamy; 444 Tibor Bognar/Alamy; 449 imagebroker/Alamy; 450 Hemis/Alamy; 455 Andre Jenny/Alamy; 459 Cosmo Condina Western Europe/Alamy; 460 Prisma Bildagentur AG/Alamy; 494 www.ecb.int; 495 AA/S Montgomery; 495 AA/S Montgomery; 498 www.ecb.int; 499 AA/A Kouprianoff; 499 AA/A Kouprianoff; 503 AA/J Tims; 503 AA/S Montgomery; 507 AA/J Wyand; 507 AA/J Wyand; 511 AA/J W Jorgensen; 511 AA/Y Levy; 515 Ilja Dubovskis/Alamy; 515 Douglas Lander/Alamy; 519 AA/P Bennett; 519 AA/K Blackwell; 523 AA/M Jourdan; 523 AA/M Jourdan; 527 AA/S Day; 527 AA/Mockford & Bonetti; 531 AA/K Paterson; 531 Vlad Breazu/Alamy; 535 AA/S Whitehorne; 535 AA/K Blackwell; 539 AA/Mockford & Bonetti; 539 AA/N Setchfield; 543 Nick Scott/Alamy; 543 AA/A Kouprianoff; 547 AA/A Robinson; 547 AA/A Robinson; 551 David Robertson/Alamy; 551 dk/Alamy; 555 AA/M Wells; 555 AA/A Mockford & N Bonetti; 559 AA/M Bonnet; 559 AA/M Bonnet; 563 Stuwdamdorp/Alamy; 563 Lucky Look/Alamy; 567 Rob Lacey/vividstock.net/Alamy; 567 Rob Lacey/vividstock.net/Alamy.

Central Intelligence Agency – Flags – 494, 498, 502, 506, 510, 514, 518, 522, 526, 530, 534, 538, 542, 546, 550, 554, 558, 562, 566.

MRI Bankers' Guide to Foreign Currency, Houston, USA – Currency – 502, 506, 510, 514, 518, 522, 526, 530, 534, 538, 542, 546, 550, 554, 558, 562, 566.

Every effort has been made to trace the copyright holders, and we apologise in advance for any unintentional omissions or errors. We would be pleased to apply any corrections in a following edition of this publication.